The Social Animal

Books by Elliot Aronson

1. *Handbook of Social Psychology* (with G. Lindzey). 2nd ed. Reading, Mass.: Addison-Wesley, 1968–1969.
2. *Theories of Cognitive Consistency* (with R. Abelson et al.). Chicago: Rand McNally, 1968.
3. *Voices of Modern Psychology.* Reading, Mass.: Addison-Wesley, 1969.
4. *The Social Animal.* New York: W. H. Freeman, 1972, 1976, 1980, 1984, 1988, 1992, 1995.
5. *Readings About The Social Animal.* New York: W. H. Freeman, 1972, 1976, 1980, 1984, 1988, 1992, 1995.
6. *Social Psychology* (with R. Helmreich). New York: Van Nostrand, 1973.
7. *Research Methods in Social Psychology* (with Carlsmith & Ellsworth). Reading, Mass.: Addison-Wesley, 1976.
8. *The Jigsaw Classroom.* Beverly Hills, Calif.: Sage, 1978.
9. *Burnout: From Tedium to Personal Growth* (with A. Pines & D. Kafry). New York: Free Press, 1981.
10. *Energy Use: The Human Dimension* (with P. C. Stern). New York: W. H. Freeman, 1984.
11. *The Handbook of Social Psychology* (with G. Lindzey). 3rd ed. New York: Random House, 1985.
12. *Career Burnout* (with A. Pines). New York: Free Press, 1988.
13. *Methods of Research in Social Psychology* (with Ellsworth, Carlsmith, & Gonzales). New York: Random House, 1990.
14. *Age of Propaganda* (with A. R. Pratkanis). New York: W. H. Freeman, 1992.
15. *Social Psychology: Volumes 1, 2, & 3* (with A . R. Pratkanis), London: Elgar Ltd., 1992.
16. *Social Psychology: The Heart and the Mind* (with T. Wilson & R. Akert). New York: HarperCollins, 1994.

Seventh Edition

The Social Animal

Elliot Aronson

University of California, Santa Cruz

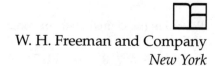

W. H. Freeman and Company
New York

A Series of Books in Psychology

EDITORS: Richard C. Atkinson
Gardner Lindzey
Richard F. Thompson

Cover drawing by Tom Durfee.

Chapter-opening drawings by Saul Steinberg from
The Passport, The Labyrinth, The New World, and *The Catalogue.*
Copyright © 1954, 1960, 1962, 1965 by Saul Steinberg.
Permission granted by Julian Bach Literary Agency, Inc.

Library of Congress Cataloging-in-Publication Data

Aronson, Elliot.
    The social animal / Elliot Aronson. — 7th ed.
        p.   cm. — (A series of books in psychology)
    Includes bibliographical references and index.
    ISBN 0-7167-2613-0. — ISBN 0-7167-2618-1 (pbk.)
    1. Social psychology.   I. Title.   II. Series.
HM251.A79   1994
302—dc20   94-27611
                                                                              CIP

Printed in the United States of America

1 2 3 4 5 6 7 8 9 0   VB   9 9 8 7 6 5 4

to Vera, of course

Contents

Why I Wrote This Book

In 1970–1971, I was invited to spend the year in Stanford, California, at the Center for Advanced Study in the Behavioral Sciences. During that year, I was given all the support, encouragement, and freedom to do whatever I wanted, and I was assured that I was not responsible to anyone for anything. There, on a beautiful hill, roughly thirty miles from San Francisco (my favorite city), with a whole year in which to do anything my heart desired, I chose to write this book. Surrounded as I was by the beauty of the countryside, and close as I was to the excitement of San Francisco, why did I lock myself in a cubicle and write a book? It's not that I'm crazy, and it's not that I needed the money. If there's a single reason why I wrote this book, it's that I once heard myself tell a large class of sophomores that social psychology is a young science — and it made me feel like a coward.

Let me explain: We social psychologists are fond of saying that social psychology is a young science—and it is a young science. Of

course, astute observers have been making interesting pronouncements and proposing exciting hypotheses about social phenomena at
least since the time of Aristotle, but these pronouncements and
hypotheses were not seriously tested until well into the twentieth
century. The first systematic social psychological experiment (to my
knowledge) was conducted by Triplett in 1898 (he measured the
effect of competition on performance), but it was not until the late
1930s that experimental social psychology really took off, primarily
under the inspiration of Kurt Lewin and his talented students. By the
same token it is interesting to note that, although Aristotle first
asserted some of the basic principles of social influence and persuasion around 350 B.C., it was not until the middle of the twentieth
century that those principles were put to the experimental test by
Carl Hovland and his associates.

In another sense, however, to claim that social psychology is a
young science is to be guilty of a gigantic cop-out: It's a way of
pleading with people not to expect too much from us. Specifically, it
can be our way of dodging the responsibility for, and avoiding the
risks inherent in, applying our findings to the problems of the world
we live in. In this sense, protesting that social psychology is a young
science is akin to claiming that we are not yet ready to say anything
important, useful, or (if the reader will forgive me for using an
overused word) relevant.

The purpose of this volume is unashamedly (but with some
trepidation) to spell out the relevance that sociopsychological research might have for some of the problems besetting contemporary
society. Most of the data discussed in this volume are based on
experiments; most of the illustrations and examples, however, are
derived from current social problems—including prejudice, propaganda, war, alienation, aggression, unrest, and political upheaval. This
duality reflects two of my own biases—biases that I cherish. The first
is that the experimental method is the best way to understand
a complex phenomenon. It is a truism of science that the only way
to really know the world is to reconstruct it: That is, in order to
truly understand what causes what, we must do more than simply
observe—rather, we must be responsible for producing the first
"what" so that we can be sure that it really caused the second "what."
My second bias is that the only way to be certain that the causal
relations uncovered in experiments are valid is to bring them out of

the laboratory and into the real world. Thus, as a scientist, I like to work in a laboratory; as a citizen, however, I like to have windows through which I can look out upon the world. Windows, of course, work in both directions: We often derive hypotheses from everyday life. We can best test these hypotheses under the sterile conditions of the laboratory; and in order to try to keep our ideas from becoming sterile, we attempt to take our laboratory findings back out through the window to see if they hold up in the real world.

Implicit in all this is my belief that social psychology is extremely important—that social psychologists can play a vital role in making the world a better place. Indeed, in my more grandiose moments, I nurse the secret belief that social psychologists are in a unique position to have a profound and beneficial impact on our lives by providing an increased understanding of such important phenomena as conformity, persuasion, prejudice, love, and aggression. Now that my secret belief is no longer a secret, I can promise only to try not to force it down the readers' throats on the following pages. Rather, I'll leave it to the readers to decide, after they have finished this volume, whether social psychologists have discovered or can ever discover anything useful, much less anything uniquely important.

Compared to other texts in social psychology, this is a slim volume—and purposely so. It is meant to be a brief introduction to the world of social psychology, not an encyclopedic catalog of research and theory. Because I opted to make it brief, I had to be selective. This means both that there are some traditional topics I chose not to cover and that I have not gone into exhaustive detail with those topics I did choose to cover. Because of my desire to keep the book compact and accessible, it was a difficult book to write. I have had to be more a "news analyst" than a "reporter." For example, there are many controversies that I did not fully describe. Rather, I exercised my own judgment; made an educated (and, I hope, honest) assessment of what is currently the most accurate description of the field, and stated it as clearly as I could.

This decision was made with the student in mind—this book was written for students, not for my colleagues. If I have learned one thing in almost forty years of college teaching, it is that, although a detailed presentation of all positions is useful (and sometimes even fascinating) to one's colleagues, it tends to leave students cold. Students, in effect, ask us what time it is, and we, in effect, present them with a chart showing the various time zones around the world, a history of time-telling from the sundial to the latest computerized creation, and a detailed description of the anatomy of the grandfather clock. By the time we've finished, they've lost interest in the question. Nothing is safer than to state all sides of all issues, but few things are more boring. Although I have discussed controversial issues, I have not hesitated to draw conclusions. In short, I have attempted to be brief without being unfair, and I have tried to present complex material simply and clearly without oversimplifying. Only the reader can determine how successful I have been in accomplishing either of these goals.

When I finished writing the first edition of this book in 1972, I thought I was done with it. How naive. Early in 1975, I decided, with some reluctance, to revise this book for the first time. A lot had happened in three years. Not only had new and exciting things been discovered in the field of social psychology, but even more important, the world had taken a few major turns since the winter of 1972, when I put the final scrawl on my yellow pad for the first edition. To name just a few of the major events: A brutal, draining, and divisive war came to an end; a vice president and a president of the United States were forced to resign in humiliation; and the women's liberation movement was beginning to have a significant impact on the consciousness of the nation. These were sociopsychological events of the greatest significance. The indolent slob who lives inside me was forced to acknowledge (with a long sigh) that any book that purports to be about our lives—yours and mine—must strive to stay abreast of the times.

Needless to say, it didn't end with one revision. As it turned out, the steady march of events has forced me to revise the book every three or four years. Again, not only do societal events change rapidly, but, social psychology, being a vibrant science, continues to produce interesting new concepts and findings. To fail to keep in touch with this research would be a disservice to the serious student. But here an author must be careful. In our zeal to be thoroughly modern, there is a tendency for textbook writers to neglect perfectly respectable research just because it happens to be more than ten years old.

Here's how it happens: We writers want to retain the classics and we want to add the research that has come out since the last edition. But we don't want the book to get much fatter. Something has to go; and so a lot of research gets swept aside, not always because it has been replaced by something better, only by something newer. This creates the illusion that the field lacks continuity—that is, there's the classic research and the modern research with very little in between. This is terribly misleading.

Over the past twenty-five years, I have tried to deal with this problem by steadfastly refusing to replace a fine "middle-aged" study by a newer one in a given area, unless the newer one adds something important to our understanding of the phenomenon being discussed. My hope is that the revisions of *The Social Animal* retain the compact grace of the original and remain up to date without eliminating or shortchanging the fine research of the recent past.

Acknowledgments

I am indicated on the title page as the sole author of this book, and it is certainly true that I wrote down all the words and did most of the thinking that produced them. Accordingly, if there are any stupidities in this book, they are mine, and if anything you read on these pages makes you angry, I'm the person you should yell at. At the same time, I want to confess that I never do anything entirely by myself: Many people contributed their knowledge and ideas to my word factory, and I would like to take this opportunity to thank them for their generous help.

Vera Aronson and Ellen Berscheid were particularly helpful. They painstakingly went over the original manuscript, page by page and line by line, making numerous suggestions and criticisms that had a significant impact on the final form of this book. Moreover, their enthusiasm for the project was infectious and helped me to climb out of frequent bouts of "writer's despair."

Several other people contributed valuable ideas and suggestions. I cannot possibly cite them all, but the most significant contributors were Nancy Aston, Leonard Berkowitz, David Bradford, John Darley, Richard Easterlin, Jonathan Freedman, James Freel, Robert Helmreich, Michael Kahn, John Kaplan, Judson Mills, and Jev Sikes.

Thanks are also due to Judy Hilton and Faye Gibson, who typed and retyped various drafts of the manuscript as if they really enjoyed doing it; and to Lyn Ellisor, who worked patiently on the bibliographical notes; and to William Ickes, who prepared the indexes. Most of this book was written while I was a fellow at the Center for Advanced Study in the Behavioral Sciences at Stanford, California, and I am deeply grateful to the staff of that fine institution for providing me with the necessary leisure and facilities.

Finally, I am pleased to report that my friend and mentor, Leon Festinger, did not have anything to do with this manuscript—directly. He never read it, and to my knowledge, he was not even aware that I was writing it. He is, however, responsible for its existence. Leon was a wonderful teacher and a demanding role model. I could say that he taught me all I know about social psychology, but that would be a gross understatement. He taught me something much more valuable than that: He taught me how to find out the things that neither I nor anybody else knew.

March 1972

This book is now in its seventh edition. One might say that I have grown old revising it. It is a bittersweet feeling to be able to trace the passage of time by watching the face on the back cover of this book (*my* face!) become increasingly wrinkled and grey-bearded. As indicated above, when I first wrote the book, I was moved to acknowledge my indebtedness to my friend and mentor, Leon Festinger. It goes without saying that I still feel gratitude and affection for that good and great man. If anything, these feelings intensified over the years. I loved being his student—and I guess I will never stop being his student. In 1989, Leon died, marking the end of an important era in social psychology. He is sorely missed, not only by those of us who knew and loved him but also by anyone who has been influenced by his research and theories; this would include just about anyone who has ever been a student of social psychology.

In addition, as this book and I have grown older, I have become increasingly aware of my indebtedness to *my own* students. While reworking the original manuscript for each revision, it became necessary to examine and reexamine much of my own research and to reformulate many of my ideas. In the process, I have been struck with the realization that these are not simply my own ideas—rather, they are ideas I have developed in collaboration with one or more of a long line of remarkably talented students with whom it has been my privilege to work. Now that I have grown old revising *The Social Animal,* it is easier to see that my students have taught me a great deal. And I mean all my students, from my very first research assistants when I was just starting out in 1960—Merrill Carlsmith, Tony Greenwald, and John M. Darley—to the gifted young people who are my current collaborators.

For the seventh edition, I have benefited greatly from the sustained efforts of my students, Carrie Fried and Andre Kardush-Podell, and from the sage suggestions of my colleague, Anthony Pratkanis.

There is also a sense in which this book is, in part, a family enterprise. This has been especially true in recent years when I have experienced the unique gratification of being deeply influenced by my grown children—each in his/her own fashion. My youngest son, Joshua Aronson, who is an experimental social psychologist, works hard to keep me on my toes regarding recent methodological and theoretical innovations. My oldest son, Hal Aronson, who is an environmental sociologist, helps to keep my focus broader than the confines of the laboratory. And my middle children, Neal Aronson who is a firefighter for the city of Santa Cruz, and Julie Aronson who is an expert on public policy, are in the trenches of human service on a day-to-day basis, reminding me by their example that, ultimately, social psychology must strive to be useful to people in their daily lives.

Finally, as you may have noticed, the dedication of this book reads, "To Vera, of course." The Vera in question is Vera Aronson, who has been my best friend and favorite consultant for almost forty years and who (to my great good fortune) also happens to be my wife. To anyone who knows us well, the phrase "of course" in the dedication is redundant. And because redundancy is an occupational hazard in the teaching game, I must admit (with a blush) that it is almost certainly not the last redundancy you will need to put up with.

August 1994   Elliot Aronson

The Social Animal

Man is by nature a social animal; an individual who is unsocial
naturally and not accidentally is either beneath our notice or more
than human. Society is something in nature that precedes the
individual. Anyone who either cannot lead the common life or is so
self-sufficient as not to need to, and therefore does not partake of
society, is either a beast or a god.

Aristotle
Politics, c. 328 B.C.

1
What Is Social Psychology?

As far as we know, Aristotle was the first person to formulate some of the basic principles of social influence and persuasion; but, although he did say that man is a social animal, he was probably *not* the first person to make that observation. Moreover, chances are he was not the first person to marvel at the truth of that statement while simultaneously puzzling over its triteness and insubstantiality. Although it is certainly true that people are social animals, so are a host of other creatures, from ants and bees to monkeys and apes. What does it mean to say that humans are "social animals"? Let's look at some concrete examples:

A college student named Sam and four of his acquaintances are watching a presidential candidate make a speech on television. Sam is favorably impressed; he likes him better than the opposing candidate because of his sincerity. After the speech, one of the other students asserts that she was turned off by the candidate—that she considered him to be a complete phony—and that she prefers the opposing candidate. All of the others are quick to agree with her. Sam looks puzzled and a trifle distressed. Finally, he mumbles to his acquaintances, "I guess he didn't come across as sincere as I would have hoped."

A second-grade teacher stands before her class and asks, "What is the sum of six, nine, four, and eleven?" A boy in the third row puzzles over the question for several seconds, hesitates, raises his hand tentatively, and when called on, haltingly answers, "Thirty?" The teacher nods, smiles at him, says, "Nice work, Ted," and pastes a gold star on his forehead. She then asks the class, "What is the sum of seven, four, eight, three, and ten?" Without wasting a moment, Ted leaps to his feet and shouts, "Thirty-two!"

A four-year-old girl is given a toy drum for her birthday. After pounding on it for a few minutes, she casts it aside and studiously ignores it for the next several weeks. One day a friend comes to visit, picks up the drum, and is about to play with it. Suddenly the young "owner" tears the drum from her friend's grasp and proceeds to play with it as if it had always been her favorite toy.

A ten-year-old girl avidly consumes two bowls of Wheaties daily because an Olympic gymnastics champion endorses the product and implies that she owes her athletic prowess, in part, to the consumption of that particular brand of cereal.

A shopkeeper who has lived his entire life in a small town in Montana has never had any contact with real, live black people, but he "knows" they are shiftless, lazy, and oversexed.

Charlie, a high-school senior, has recently moved to a new city. He used to be quite popular, but not anymore. Although the kids at school are civil to him, they have not been particularly friendly. He is feeling lonely, insecure, and unattractive. One day, during lunch period, he finds himself at a table with two of his female classmates. One of them is warm, attractive, brilliant, and vivacious; he has been admiring her and daydreaming about her. For several weeks he has been longing for an opportunity to talk to her. The other young woman is not nearly as appealing. Charlie ignores the vivacious woman of his dreams and begins an earnest conversation with her companion.

Following the 1970 tragedy at Kent State University, in which four students were shot and killed by Ohio National Guardsmen while demonstrating against the war in Southeast Asia, a high-school teacher from Kent, Ohio, asserted that the slain students deserved to die. She made this statement even though she was well aware of the fact that at least two of the victims were not participating in the demonstration but were peacefully walking across campus at the time of the shooting. Indeed, she went on to say, "Anyone who appears on the streets of a city like Kent with long hair, dirty clothes, or barefooted deserves to be shot."[1]

When the Reverend Jim Jones sounded the alert, over nine hundred members of the People's Temple settlement in Guyana gathered before him. He knew that some of the members of a congressional investigation party had been murdered and that the sanctity and isolation of Jonestown would soon be violated. Jones proclaimed that it was time for them to die. Vats of poison were prepared, and amidst only scattered shouts of protest or acts of resistance, mothers and fathers administered the fatal mixture to their infants and children, drank it themselves, and lay down, arm in arm, waiting to die.

Mary has just turned nine. For her birthday, she received a Suzie Homemaker baking and cooking set, complete with "her own little oven." Her parents chose this present because she seems very interested in culinary things and is forever helping mommy set the table, prepare the meals, and clean the house. "Isn't it wonderful," says Mary's father, "how at age nine she is already interested in being a housewife? Little girls must have housewifery built into their genes. Those feminists don't know what they're talking about."

My boyhood friend, George Woods, is an African American. When he and I were growing up together in Massachusetts in the 1940s, he thought of himself as a "colored boy" and felt inferior to his white friends.[2] There were many reasons for this feeling. That George was treated like an inferior by the white community had a direct influence upon him, of course; a number of other forces influenced him less directly. In those days, George could entertain himself by turning on the radio and listening to "Amos 'n Andy," an enormously popular radio show in which black adults were portrayed as naive children, as stupid, lazy, and illiterate, but rather cute—not unlike friendly domesticated animals. The black characters were, of course, played by white actors. In films, George could see the stereotyped "colored man," usually a chauffeur or some other menial. A standard plot would have the "colored man" accompany the white hero into a haunted house, where they would hear a strange and ominous noise: The camera pans in on the "colored man's" face; his eyes grow large with fright; he screams, "Feets, do your stuff!" and dashes through the door, not taking time to open it first. We can only guess what George experienced while viewing these films in the company of his white friends.

Things change. Although discrimination and unfairness are still very much a part of our society, George Woods's children, growing up in the 1970s and 1980s, did not face quite the same prospect as George himself did. The mass media now depict blacks in roles that are not exclusively menial; and a new pride in blackness has emerged, along with an interest in, and enthusiasm about, African American history and culture. The society is influencing George's children in a much different way than it influenced George.

Although things do change, we should not be complacent in the belief that all changes are in a linear, humanistic direction. On August 30, 1936, during the Spanish Civil War, a single plane bombed Madrid. There were several casualties, but no one was killed. The world was profoundly shocked by the idea of a congested city being attacked from the air. Newspaper editorials around the world expressed the general horror and indignation of the citizenry. Only nine years later, U.S. planes dropped nuclear bombs on Hiroshima and Nagasaki. More than one hundred thousand people were killed and countless thousands suffered severe injuries. Shortly thereafter, a poll indicated that only 4.5 percent of the U.S. population felt we should not have used those weapons, and an astonishing 22.7 percent felt we should have used many more of them before Japan had a chance to surrender.[3] Clearly, something had happened during those nine years to influence opinion.

A Definition

What is social psychology? There are almost as many definitions of social psychology as there are social psychologists. Instead of listing some of these definitions, it might be more informative to let the subject matter define the field. The examples presented on the preceding pages are all illustrations of sociopsychological situations. As diverse as these situations may be, they do contain one common factor: social influence. The opinion of Sam's friends on the merits of the presidential candidate influenced Sam's judgment (or at least his public statement regarding that judgment). The rewards emanating from the teacher influenced the speed and vigor of Ted's classroom responses. The four-year-old seemed to find her toy drum more attractive because of the inadvertent influence of her friend's interest. The Olympic athlete's influence on our Wheaties-eating youngster, on the other hand, was far from inadvertent; rather, it was intentionally designed to motivate her to convince her parents to buy Wheaties. The Montana shopkeeper was certainly not born with an unflattering stereotype of black people in his head—somebody, somehow, put it there. That Charlie ignored the woman of his dreams almost certainly has something to do with his fear of rejection, the way he was feeling about himself, and his implicit assumption about the relative likelihood of being rejected by either of the two women. Exactly how the high-school teacher in Kent, Ohio, came to believe that innocent people deserved to die is a fascinating and frightening question; for now, let us simply say that this belief was probably influenced by her own indirect complicity in the tragic events on campus. A still more disturbing question arises from Jonestown: What forces could compel parents to help poison their children? Again, this is a complex question to which I hope to provide some partial answers and insights as this text unfolds. Turning to little Mary and her Suzie Homemaker set, it is conceivable, as Mary's father says, that "housewifery" is genetic, but it is far more likely that, from infancy onward, Mary was rewarded and encouraged every time she expressed an interest in such traditionally "feminine" things as cooking, sewing, and dolls—to a far greater extent than if she expressed an interest in football, boxing, and chemistry. It is also reasonable to assume that, if Mary's kid brother had shown an interest in "housewifery," he would *not* have received a Suzie Homemaker set for *his* birthday. Also, as with young George Woods, who felt inferior to his playmates, Mary's self-image could have been shaped by the mass media, which tend to depict women in roles that the culture encourages them to play: housewife, secretary, nurse, schoolteacher—the mass media rarely depict women as biochemists, college professors, or business executives. If we compare the young George Woods with his children, we will see that the self-images of minority-group members can change, and these changes can influence and be influenced by changes in the mass media and changes in the attitudes of the general population. This, of course, is graphically illustrated by the opinions of Americans about the use of nuclear weapons in 1945.

The key phrase in the preceding paragraph is "social influence." And this becomes our working definition of social psychology: the influences that people have upon the beliefs or behavior of others. Using this as our definition, we will attempt to understand many of the phenomena described in the preceding illustrations. How are people influenced? Why do they accept influence—or, put another way, what's in it for them? What are the variables that increase or decrease the effectiveness of social influence? Does such influence have a permanent effect, or is it merely transitory? What are the variables that increase or decrease the permanence of the effects of social influence? Can the same principles be applied equally to the attitudes of the high-school teacher in Kent, Ohio, and to the toy preferences of young children? How does one person come to like another person? Is it through these same processes that we come to like our new sports car or a box of Wheaties? How does a person develop prejudices against an ethnic or racial group? Is it akin to liking—but in reverse—or does it involve an entirely different set of psychological processes?

Most people are interested in questions of this sort; in a sense, therefore, most people are social psychologists. Because most of us spend a good deal of our time interacting with other people—being influenced by them, influencing them, being delighted, amused, and angered by them—it is natural that most of us develop hypotheses about social behavior. Although most amateur social psychologists test these hypotheses to their own satisfaction, these "tests" lack the rigor and impartiality of careful scientific investigation. Often, the results of scientific research are identical with what most people "know" to be true. This is not surprising; conventional wisdom is usually based upon shrewd observation that has stood the test of time.

In fact, when you are reading the experiments in this volume, you may occasionally find yourself thinking: "That's obvious—why did they spend time and money to find that out?" There are several reasons why we do experiments, even though the findings often seem unsurprising. For one thing, we are all susceptible to the *hindsight effect*, which refers to our tendency to overestimate our powers of prediction once we know the outcome of a given event. For example, research has shown that on the day after an election, when people are asked which candidates they would have picked to win, they almost always believe they would have picked the actual winners—even though the day *before* the election, their predictions wouldn't have been nearly as accurate.[4] Similarly, the outcome of an experiment almost always seems more predictable once we have the results in hand than if we had been asked to predict the results without the benefit of hindsight.

In addition, it is important to conduct research—even if the results seem obvious—because many of the things we "know" to be true turn out to be false when carefully investigated. Although it seems reasonable, for example, to assume that people who are threatened with severe punishment for engaging in a certain behavior might eventually learn to despise that behavior, it turns out that when this question is studied scientifically, just the reverse is true: People who are threatened with mild punishment develop a dislike for the forbidden behavior; people who are severely threatened show, if anything, a slight increase in liking for the forbidden behavior. Likewise, most of us, from our own experience, would guess that, if we overheard someone saying nice things about us (behind our backs), we would tend to like that person—all other things being equal. This turns out to be true. But what is equally true is that we tend to like that person even more if some of the remarks we overhear are anything but nice. More will be said about these phenomena in the following chapters.

In their attempts to understand human social behavior, professional social psychologists have a great advantage over most amateur social psychologists. Although, like the amateur, they usually begin with careful observation, they can go far beyond that. They do not need to wait for things to happen so that they can observe how people respond; they can, in fact, *make* things happen. That is, they can conduct an experiment in which scores of people are subjected to particular conditions (for example, a severe threat or a mild threat; overhearing nice things or overhearing a combination of nice and nasty things). Moreover, they can do this in situations in which everything can be held constant except the particular conditions being investigated. Professional social psychologists can, therefore, draw conclusions based on data far more precise and numerous than those available to the amateur social psychologist, who must depend upon observations of events that occur randomly and under complex circumstances.

Nearly all the data presented in this book are based upon experimental evidence. It is important, for this reason, that the reader (1) understand what constitutes an experiment in social psychology and (2) understand the advantages, disadvantages, ethical problems, excitements, headaches, and heartaches that are associated with this kind of enterprise. Although an understanding of the experimental method is important, it is by no means essential to an understanding of the substantive material presented here. Therefore, the chapter "Social Psychology as a Science" is the final one in this book. As a reader, you can peruse this chapter before reading on (if you prefer to understand the technicalities before delving into the substantive material), or you can read it at any point on your journey through the book—whenever your interest is piqued.

People Who Do Crazy Things Are Not Necessarily Crazy

The social psychologist studies social situations that affect people's behavior. Occasionally, these natural situations become focused into pressures so great they cause people to behave in ways easily classifiable as abnormal. When I say "people," I mean very large numbers of people. To my mind, it does not increase our understanding of human behavior to classify these people as psychotic. It is much more useful to try to understand the nature of the situation and the processes that were operating to produce the behavior. This leads us to Aronson's first law:

> "People who do crazy things are not necessarily crazy."

Let us take, as an illustration, the Ohio schoolteacher who asserted that the four Kent State students deserved to die. I don't think she was alone in this belief—and although all the people who hold this belief *may* be psychotic, I seriously doubt it, and I doubt that so classifying them does much to enhance our understanding of the phenomenon. Similarly, in the aftermath of the Kent slayings, the rumor spread that the slain girls were pregnant anyway—so that it was a blessing they died—and that all four of the students were filthy and so covered with lice that the mortuary attendants became nauseated while examining the bodies. These rumors, of course, were totally false. But, according to James Michener,[5] they spread like wildfire. Were all the people who believed and spread these rumors insane? Later in this book, we will examine the processes that produce this kind of behavior—processes to which most of us are susceptible, under the right sociopsychological conditions.

Ellen Berscheid[6] has observed that people have a tendency to explain unpleasant behavior by attaching a label to the perpetrator ("crazy," "sadistic," or whatever), thereby excluding that person from the rest of "us nice people." In that way, we need not worry about the unpleasant behavior, because it has nothing to do with us nice folks. According to Berscheid, the danger in this kind of thinking is that it tends to make us smug about our own susceptibility to situational pressures producing unpleasant behavior, and it leads to a rather simple-minded approach to the solution of social problems. Specifically, such a simple-minded solution might include the development of a set of diagnostic tests to determine who is a liar, who is a sadist, who is corrupt, who is a maniac; social action might then consist of identifying these people and relegating them to the appropriate institutions. Of course, this is not to say psychosis does not exist or that psychotics should never be institutionalized. Nor am I saying all people are the same and respond exactly as crazily to the same intense social pressures. To repeat, what I am saying is that some situational variables can move a great proportion of us "normal" adults to behave in very unappetizing ways. It is of paramount importance that we attempt to understand these variables and the processes producing unpleasant behavior.

An illustration might be useful. Think of a prison. Consider the guards. What are they like? Chances are that most people would imagine prison guards to be tough, callous, unfeeling people. Some might even consider them to be cruel, tyrannical, and sadistic. People who take this kind of *dispositional* view of the world might suggest that the reason people become guards is to have an opportunity to exercise their cruelty with relative impunity. Picture the prisoners. What are they like? Rebellious? Docile? No matter what specific pictures exist inside our heads, the point is there *are* pictures there—and most of us believe that the prisoners and the guards are quite different from us in character and personality.

This *may* be true, but don't be too sure. In a dramatic piece of research, Philip Zimbardo and his students created a simulated prison in the basement of the Psychology Department at Stanford University. Into this "prison" he brought a group of normal, mature, stable, intelligent young men. By flipping a coin, Zimbardo designated one-half of them prisoners and one-half of them guards, and they lived as such for several days. What happened? Let's allow Zimbardo to tell us in his own words:

At the end of only six days we had to close down our mock prison because what we saw was frightening. It was no longer apparent to us or most of the subjects where they ended and their roles began. The majority had indeed become "prisoners" or "guards," no longer able to clearly differentiate between role-playing and self. There were dramatic changes in virtually every aspect of their behavior, thinking and feeling. In less than a week, the experience of imprisonment undid (temporarily) a lifetime of learning; human values were suspended, self-concepts were challenged, and the ugliest, most base, pathological side of human nature surfaced. We were horrified because we saw some boys ("guards") treat other boys as if they were despicable animals, taking pleasure in cruelty, while other boys ("prisoners") became servile, dehumanized robots who thought only of escape, of their own individual survival, and of their mounting hatred of the guards.[7]

2
Conformity

One consequence of the fact that we are social animals is that we live in a state of tension between values associated with individuality and values associated with conformity. James Thurber has captured the flavor of one kind of conformity in the following description:

> Suddenly somebody began to run. It may be that he had simply remembered, all of a moment, an engagement to meet his wife, for which he was now frightfully late. Whatever it was, he ran east on Broad Street (probably toward the Maramor Restaurant, a favorite place for a man to meet his wife). Somebody else began to run, perhaps a newsboy in high spirits. Another man, a portly gentleman of affairs, broke into a trot. Inside of ten minutes, everybody on High Street, from the Union Depot to the Courthouse was running. A loud mumble gradually crystallized into the dread word "dam." "The dam has broke!" The fear was put into words by a little old lady in an electric car, or by a traffic cop, or by a small boy: nobody knows who,

nor does it now really matter. Two thousand people were abruptly in full flight. "Go east!" was the cry that arose—east away from the river, east to safety. "Go east! Go east!" A tall spare woman with grim eyes and a determined chin ran past me down the middle of the street. I was still uncertain as to what was the matter, in spite of all the shouting. I drew up alongside the woman with some effort, for although she was in her late fifties, she had a beautiful easy running form and seemed to be in excellent condition. "What is it?" I puffed. She gave a quick glance and then looked ahead again, stepping up her pace a trifle. "Don't ask me, ask God!" she said.[1]

This passage from Thurber, although comical, is an apt illustration of people conforming. One or two individuals began running for their own reasons; before long, everyone was running. Why? Because others were running. According to Thurber's story, when the running people realized that the dam hadn't given way after all, they felt pretty foolish. And yet, how much more foolish would they have felt if they hadn't conformed and the dam had, in fact, burst? Is conformity good or bad? In its simplest sense, this is an absurd question. But words do carry evaluative meaning—thus, to be called an individualist or a nonconformist is to be designated, by connotation, as a "good" person. The label evokes an image of Daniel Boone standing on a mountaintop with a rifle slung over his shoulder, the breeze blowing through his hair, as the sun sets in the background. To be called a conformist is somehow to be designated as an "inadequate" person. It evokes an image of a row of Madison Avenue ad men with gray flannel suits, porkpie hats, and attaché cases, looking as though they had been created by a cookie cutter, and all saying simultaneously, "Let's run it up the flagpole and see if anyone salutes."

But we can use synonymous words that convey very different images. For *individualist* or *nonconformist*, we can substitute *deviate*; for *conformist* we can substitute *team player*. Somehow, *deviate* does not evoke Daniel Boone on the mountaintop, and *team player* does not evoke the cookie-cutter-produced Madison Avenue ad man.

When we look a little closer, we see an inconsistency in the way our society seems to feel about conformity (team playing) and nonconformity (deviance). For example, one of the best-sellers of the 1950s was a book by John F. Kennedy called *Profiles in Courage*, wherein the author praised several politicians for their courage in resisting great pressure and refusing to conform. To put it another way, Kennedy was praising people who refused to be good team players, people who refused to vote or act as their parties or constituents expected them to. Although their actions earned Kennedy's praise long after the deeds were done, the immediate reactions of their colleagues were generally far from positive. Nonconformists may be praised by historians or idolized in films or literature long after the fact of their nonconformity, but they are usually not held in high esteem, at the time, by those people to whose demands they refuse to conform. This observation receives strong support from a number of experiments in social psychology. For example, in a classic experiment by Stanley Schachter,[2] several groups of students met for a discussion of the case history of a juvenile delinquent named Johnny Rocco. After reading the case, each group was asked to discuss it and to suggest a treatment for Johnny on a scale that ranged from "very lenient treatment" on one end to "very hard treatment" on the other. A typical group consisted of approximately nine participants, six of whom were real subjects and three of whom were paid confederates of the experimenter. The confederates took turns playing one of three roles that they had carefully rehearsed in advance: the *modal* person, who took a position that conformed to the average position of the real subjects; the *deviate,* who took a position diametrically opposed to the general orientation of the group; and the *slider,* whose initial position was similar to the deviate's but who, in the course of the discussion, gradually "slid" into a modal, conforming position. The results clearly showed that the person who was liked most was the modal person who conformed to the group norm; the deviate was liked least. In a more recent experiment, Arie Kruglanski and Donna Webster[3] found that when the nonconformist voiced a dissenting opinion close to the deadline (when groups were feeling the pinch to come to closure), they were rejected even more than when they voiced their dissenting opinion earlier in the discussion.

Thus, the data indicate that the "establishment" or modal group tends to like conformists better than nonconformists. Clearly, there are situations in which conformity is highly desirable and nonconformity would constitute an unmitigated disaster. Suppose, for example, that I were suddenly to decide that I was fed up with being a conformist. So I hop in my car and start driving down the *left*-hand side of the road—not a very adaptive way of displaying my rugged individualism, and not very fair to you if you happen to be driving toward me (conformist-style) on the same street. Similarly, consider the rebellious teenager who smokes cigarettes, stays out late, or dates a certain boy just because she knows that her parents disapprove. She is not manifesting independence so much as she is displaying *anticonformity*, not thinking for herself but automatically acting contrary to the desires or expectations of others.

On the other hand, I do not intend to suggest that conformity is always adaptive and nonconformity always maladaptive. There are compelling situations in which conformity can be disastrous and tragic. Moreover, even knowledgeable and sophisticated decision makers can fall prey to special kinds of conformity pressures inherent in making group decisions. Consider the following examples: In his memoirs, Albert Speer, one of Adolf Hitler's top advisers, describes the circle around Hitler as one of total conformity—deviation was not permitted. In such an atmosphere, even the most barbarous activities seemed reasonable, because the absence of dissent, which conveyed the illusion of unanimity, prevented any individual from entertaining the possibility that other options might exist.

> In normal circumstances people who turn their backs on reality are soon set straight by the mockery and criticism of those around them. In the Third Reich there were not such correctives. On the contrary, every self-deception was multiplied as in a hall of distorting mirrors, becoming a repeatedly confirmed picture of a fantastical dream world which no longer bore any relationship to the grim outside world. In those mirrors I could see nothing but my own face reproduced many times over.[4]

A more familiar but perhaps less dramatic example concerns some of the men involved with Richard Nixon and his "palace guard" in the Watergate cover-up. Here, men in high government office —many of whom were attorneys—perjured themselves, destroyed evidence, and offered bribes without an apparent second thought. This was due, at least in part, to the closed circle of single-mindedness that surrounded the president in the early 1970s. This single-mindedness made deviation virtually unthinkable—until after the circle had been broken. Once the circle was broken, several people (for example, Jeb Stuart Magruder, Richard Kleindienst, and Patrick

Grey) seemed to view their illegal behavior with astonishment, as if it were performed during some sort of bad dream. John Dean put it this way:

> Anyway, when you picked up the newspaper in the morning and read the new cover story that had replaced yesterday's cover story, you began to believe that today's news was the *truth*. This process created an atmosphere of unreality in the White House that prevailed to the very end. If you said it often enough, it would become true. When the press learned of the wiretaps on newsmen and White House staffers, for example, and flat denials failed, it was claimed that this was a national-security matter. I'm sure many people believed that the taps *were* for national security; they weren't. That was concocted as a justification after the fact. But when they said it, you understand, they really *believed* it.[5]

On January 28, 1986, the space shuttle Challenger exploded seconds after launching. Seven astronauts, including a civilian schoolteacher, perished in a fireball of smoke and flames. The decision had been made to go ahead with the launch, despite a near disaster on an earlier Challenger flight in 1983, and despite more recent strenuous objections and warnings from knowledgeable engineers about the defective O-rings at the joints of the booster rockets. Were key NASA administrators ignorant of the danger or cavalier about the lives of the astronauts? I doubt it.

A more likely explanation involves a number of factors that contributed to flaws in NASA's decision-making process. First, NASA had already conducted two dozen successful launches with essentially the same equipment. With their confidence boosted by previous successes, NASA administrators were oriented toward a "go" decision. Second, NASA officials, like the general public, were caught up in the enthusiasm surrounding the launching of the first civilian (schoolteacher Christa McAuliffe) into space.

Further, according to a recent analysis by Arie Kruglanski,[6] there were additional, practical reasons for NASA administrators to be victimized by their own wishful thinking: Given NASA's need to secure congressional funding by displaying its efficiency and productivity, given the intense public interest in the "teacher in space" program, given NASA's wish to demonstrate its technological capabilities, "liftoff was clearly a more desirable decision than delay. Any mention of possible system failure would have suggested a need to spend more money, a conclusion NASA found distasteful in light of its commitment to cost-effectiveness and economy."

Finally, in this atmosphere of enthusiasm and external pressures, no one at NASA wanted to be reminded that any kind of accident was possible—and they weren't. Unlike NASA administrators, engineers at Morton Thiokol (the company that manufactured the solid rocket boosters) were not concerned about the political, economic, and public relations implications of a decision of whether or not to launch. All they cared about was whether or not the damn thing would work—and given subfreezing temperatures at the launch site, they objected strenuously to the launch.

But the top executives at Morton Thiokol were not so fortunate. For them, more was at stake than a successful launch. As engineers, they were sensitive to the opinions of their fellow engineers. On the other hand, as executives, they were dependent on NASA for a contract worth approximately $400 million per year. Thus, they tended to identify with the same concerns that NASA administrators did. According to his testimony before a presidential investigative commission, Robert Lund, Thiokol's vice president for engineering, at first opposed the launch but changed his position after he was told to "take off his engineering hat and put on one representing management." How did the Morton Thiokol executives such as Lund deal with this conflict? Before their last conference with NASA administrators, they polled Thiokol employees, but *not* the engineers—only other management personnel, who voted to "go" with the launch. Thus, in a conference between NASA officials and Thiokol executives the night before the fateful launch, participants reinforced one another's commitment to proceed.

To return to the above three examples: What do Hitler's inner circle, Nixon's "palace guard," and NASA administrators share in common, aside from the fact that they made tragic decisions? They were relatively cohesive groups isolated from dissenting points of view. When such groups are called upon to make decisions, they often fall prey to what social psychologist Irving Janis calls *groupthink*.[7] According to Janis, groupthink is "the mode of thinking that persons engage in when *concurrence seeking* becomes so dominant in a cohesive ingroup that it tends to override realistic appraisal of alternative courses of action." Groups engaging in this maladaptive decision-making strategy typically perceive themselves as invulnerable—they're blinded by optimism. And this optimism is perpetuated when dissent is discouraged. In the face of conformity pressures, individual group members come to doubt their own reservations and refrain from voicing dissenting opinions. Consensus seeking is so important that certain members of the group sometimes become "mindguards"—people who censor troublesome incoming information, as did the executives at Morton Thiokol.

By citing these examples, I do not mean to suggest that individuals who make foolish, disastrous decisions should not be held accountable. What I *do* intend to suggest is that it is a lot easier to conduct an inquiry and assign blame than it is to understand the psychological processes underlying faulty decision making. But it is only through digging deeper and trying to understand these processes that we can have any hope of improving the way people make decisions, and thus, of reducing the frequency of disastrous decisions in the future.

What Is Conformity?

Conformity can be defined as a change in a person's behavior or opinions as a result of real or imagined pressure from a person or group of people. Most situations are not as extreme as the examples cited above. We will attempt to zero in on the phenomenon of conformity by beginning with a less extreme (and perhaps simpler) illustration. Let's return to our friend Sam, the hypothetical college student we first encountered in chapter 1. Recall that Sam watched a presidential candidate on television and was favorably impressed with his sincerity. However, in the face of the unanimous opinion of his friends that the candidate was insincere, Sam acceded—verbally, at least—to their opinion.

Several questions can be asked about this kind of situation: (1) What causes people to conform to group pressure? Specifically, what was in it for Sam? (2) What was the nature of the group pressure? Specifically, what were Sam's acquaintances doing to induce conformity? (3) Did Sam revise his opinion of the candidate during that brief but horrifying period when he learned that *all* his fellow students disagreed with him? Or was it the case that Sam maintained his original opinion but only modified what he *said* about the candidate? If there was a change in opinion, was it permanent or merely transient?

Unfortunately, we cannot say precisely and definitely what was going on in Sam's mind at the time, because there are many factors in the situation that we don't know about. For example, we don't know how confident Sam was in his initial opinion; we don't know how much he liked the people with whom he watched the candidate; we don't know whether Sam considered himself to be a good judge of sincerity or whether he considered the others to be good judges of sincerity; we don't know whether Sam is generally a strong person or a wishy-washy person; and so on. What we can do is construct an experimental situation that is somewhat like the one in which Sam found himself, and we can control and vary the factors we think might be important. Such a basic situation was devised by Solomon Asch[8] in a classic set of experiments. Put yourself in the following situation: You have volunteered to participate in an experiment on perceptual judgment. You enter a room with four other participants. The experimenter shows all of you a straight line (line X). Simultaneously, he shows you three other lines for comparison (lines A, B, and C). Your job is to judge which of the three lines is closest in length to line X. The judgment strikes you as being a very easy one.

It is perfectly clear to you that line B is the correct answer, and when your turn comes, you will clearly say that B is the one. But it's *not* your turn to respond. The young man whose turn it is looks carefully at the lines and says "Line A." Your mouth drops open and you look at him quizzically. "How can he believe it's A when any fool can see that it's B?" you ask yourself. "He must be either blind or crazy." Now it's the second person's turn to respond. He also chooses line A. You begin to feel like Alice in Wonderland. "How can it be?"

X   A   B   C

you ask yourself. "Are *both* of these people blind or crazy?" But then the next person responds, and he also says, "Line A." You take another look at those lines. "Maybe *I'm* the only one who's crazy," you mutter inaudibly. Now it's the fourth person's turn, and he also judges the correct line to be A. Finally, it's your turn. "Why, it's line A, of course," you declare. "I knew it all the time."

This is the kind of conflict that the college students in Asch's experiment went through. As you might imagine, the individuals who answered first were in the employ of the experimenter and were instructed to agree on an incorrect answer. The perceptual judgment itself was an incredibly easy one. It was so easy that, when individuals were not subjected to group pressure but were allowed to make a series of judgments of various sizes of lines while alone, there was almost a complete absence of errors. Indeed, the task was so easy, and physical reality was so clear-cut, that Asch himself firmly believed that there would be little, if any, yielding to group pressure. But his prediction was wrong. When faced with a majority of their fellow students agreeing on the same incorrect responses in a series of twelve judgments, approximately three-quarters of the subjects conformed at least once by responding incorrectly. When we look at the entire spectrum of judgments, we find that an average of 35 percent of the overall responses conformed to the incorrect judgments rendered by Asch's accomplices.

The situation in the Asch experiment is especially intriguing because, unlike many situations in which we may tend to conform, there were no explicit constraints against individuality. In many situations, the sanctions against nonconformity are clear and unequivocal. For example, I hate to wear a tie, and under most circumstances I can get away with this minor idiosyncrasy. On occasion, however, I can't. I often find myself stopped at the entrance to a restaurant and politely (but firmly) informed that if I refuse to don the tie offered me by the headwaiter, I cannot dine in the restaurant. I can either put on the tie and eat in the restaurant or leave, open-necked and comfortable, but hungry. The negative consequences of nonconformity are made very explicit.

But in Asch's experiment (and in the hypothetical example of Sam watching the candidate on television), the situations were much more subtle. In these situations, there were no explicit rewards for conformity and no explicit punishment for deviance. Why, then, did

Asch's subjects and Sam conform? There seem to be two major possibilities; either they became convinced, in the face of the judgment of the unanimous majority, that their own opinions were wrong, or they "went along with the crowd" (while inwardly knowing that their judgments were right) in order to be accepted by the majority or to avoid being disliked by them for disagreeing.

In short, what I am suggesting is that these individuals had two important goals: the goal of being correct and the goal of staying in the good graces of other people by living up to their expectations. In many circumstances, both of these goals can be satisfied by a simple action. Driving on the right-hand side of the road is the correct thing to do, and it satisfies other people's expectations. So, too, are telephoning your mother on Mother's Day, giving proper directions to a visitor in town, and studying hard to perform well on an exam. Similarly, if others agreed with your judgment of the lengths of the lines, you could satisfy both goals by being true to your own estimate. But, in Asch's experiment, these two goals were placed in conflict. If you were a subject in that experiment, and you initially believed that the correct answer was line B, then saying so might satisfy your desire to be correct—but it might also violate the expectations of your peers, and they might think you a bit odd. On the other hand, choosing line A might win you the acceptance of the others, but, unless you became convinced that they were correct, it would violate your desire to be right.

Apparently, most people believe that *they* are motivated primarily by a desire to be correct, but that *others* are motivated primarily by a desire to stay in the good graces of other people. For example, when people unobtrusively observe an Asch-like conformity experiment, they typically predict that the experimental subjects will conform more than they actually do.[9] Interestingly enough, these same surreptitious observers predict that *they* will conform *less* than people like themselves actually do. That is, we know *other* people conform, but we underestimate the extent to which *we* can be induced to follow the group.

Was Sam convinced by his fellow college students that his preferred presidential candidate was a phony, or did he simply go along with their judgment in order to be accepted, while continuing to believe in the sincerity of the candidate? Because Sam is a hypothetical person, we cannot answer that question definitively. Were the yielders in Asch's experiment convinced that their initial judgment was incorrect and the unanimous judgment of the others was right? We could ask them; indeed, in Asch's experiment, the yielders *were* asked afterward whether they really saw the lines differently or whether they merely said so. A few of the subjects insisted that they really saw it that way. But how can we be certain that the subjects were being truthful? Put yourself in a subject's place. Suppose you bowed to group pressure, even though you remained certain that your initial judgment was correct. This might be embarrassing for you to admit, because it would make you appear weak and wishy-washy. Moreover, you would be admitting that you were not following the experimenter's instruction to present *your own* judgment. Thus, it is quite possible that subjects who said they actually saw it the way the group saw it might have been deceiving the experimenter in order to save face.

How, then, can we determine whether or not group pressure actually affects one's judgment? Let's speculate for a moment. If we could follow Sam into the voting booth and witness which candidate he chooses, we could discover whether he was actually convinced by his acquaintances that his original preference was a phony or if he merely mumbled his agreement with them while still privately trusting the candidate. But we can't follow Sam into the voting booth. Fortunately, we *can* determine whether the public behavior exhibited by subjects in the Asch experiment corresponds with their private acceptance of those judgments. Suppose we were to repeat the experiment, but, although we would allow the real subjects to see the responses of the accomplices as before, we would *not* require them to make their judgments in the presence of the others. If the subjects' private choices were identical with their public ones, then we would see that the responses of the others in the original experiment did actually convince the subjects that their initial judgments were wrong. If, on the other hand, the subjects were going against their own best judgment only in order to mollify the group, then there would be significantly less yielding to the judgments of others in decisions made in private. This proposition has been tested experimentally on several occasions. The results are consistent: Although assurance of total privacy has not been achieved in any of these studies, the greater the privacy, the less the conformity. This finding has held up consistently, whether the subjects were judging lengths of lines,[10] the number of metronome clicks,[11] or the aesthetic value of a piece of modern art.[12] Thus, it appears that pressure to conform to the judgments of others has little (if any) effect on the *private* judgments of experimental subjects.

Variables That Increase or Decrease Conformity

In situations like the one investigated by Asch, one of the crucial factors that determine the likelihood that the subject's opinion will conform to that of the majority is whether or not the majority opinion is unanimous. If a participant is joined by even one ally who gives the correct response, the subject's tendency to conform to the erroneous judgment of the majority drops sharply.[13] In fact, even if unanimity is broken by a non-ally, the power of the group is seriously diminished.[14] That is, if one of the other group members gives an incorrect response that is *different* from the error of the majority (answering that the correct line is C, as the rest of the group responds A), the presence of this fellow dissenter dramatically reduces the pressure to conform, and the subject is likely to give the correct response: line B. A fellow dissenter exerts a powerful freeing effect from the influence of the majority. If there *is* unanimity, however, the actual size of the majority need not be very great in order for it to elicit maximum conformity from a person. In fact, the tendency for someone to conform to group pressure is about as great when the unanimous majority consists of only three other people as it is when the unanimous majority is sixteen.

One way conformity to group pressure can be decreased is by inducing the individual to make some sort of commitment to his or her initial judgment. Picture yourself as an umpire at a major-league baseball game. There is a close play at first base and you call the runner out—in the presence of 50,000 fans. After the game, the three other umpires approach you and each says that he thought the runner was safe. How likely are you to alter your judgment? Compare this with a situation (like the Asch situation) in which each of the three umpires calls the runner safe and *then* it is your turn to make a judgment. Such a comparison was made in an experiment by Morton Deutsch and Harold Gerard,[15] who used the Asch paradigm and found that, where there was no prior commitment (as in the Asch experiment), 24.7 percent of the responses conformed to the erroneous judgment of the majority. But, when the individuals had publicly committed themselves *before* hearing the judgment of the other "umpires," only 5.7 percent of their new responses were conformist.

Two other important factors are the kind of person the individual is and who constitutes the group. Individuals who have a generally low opinion of themselves are far more likely to yield to group pressure than those with high self-esteem. Furthermore, task-specific self-esteem can be influenced within a given situation. Thus, individuals who are allowed to have prior successes with a task like judging the lengths of lines are far less likely to conform than those who walk into the situation cold. By the same token, if individuals believe they have little or no ability for the task at hand, their tendency to conform increases.[16] There are also cultural differences. For example, it has been shown that Norwegians conform to a greater extent than the French, and Japanese students are more willing to take a minority position than U.S. students.[17] In addition, early studies seemed to show sex differences, with women conforming more than men when confronted face-to-face with the unanimous judgment of a group.[18] However, these differences were generally small. Moreover, in more careful studies, women conformed more than men only when the researcher was male or when the group task was male-oriented.[19]

The other side of that issue, of course, has to do with the makeup of the group exerting the pressure. A group is more effective at inducing conformity if (1) it consists of experts, (2) the members (individually or collectively) are important to the individual, or (3) the members (individually or collectively) are comparable to the individual in some way. Thus, to go back to Sam, our hypothetical college student, I would speculate that it is more likely that Sam would conform to the pressure exerted by his acquaintances if he thought they were expert in politics and in making judgments about human relations. Similarly, he would be more likely to yield to those people if they were important potential friends than if they were of no consequence to him. And finally, their being fellow students gives the judgments of Sam's acquaintances more impact on his behavior than, say, the judgment of a group of ten-year-old children, a group of hard-hat workers, or a group of Portuguese biochemists. There is at least one exception to the comparability phenomenon. Research has shown that, if the unanimous majority consists of white children, more conformity is induced in other children—both white *and* black.[20] Apparently, among children, whites are seen as having more power than blacks.[21] Thus, the power granted to whites by our culture is sufficient to overcome the tendency for people to be more influenced by comparable others, though this may be changing as blacks continue to gain power in our society.

The results for the black children may be due in part to feelings of insecurity. For example, to return to our previous illustration, if Sam had felt sure that he was liked and accepted by his acquaintances, he would be more likely to voice disagreement than if he felt insecure in his relationship with them. This assertion receives strong support from an experiment by James Dittes and Harold Kelley[22] in which college students were invited to join an attractive and prestigious group and subsequently were given information about how secure their position was in that group. Specifically, all members of the group were informed that, at any point during the lifetime of the group, the members could remove any member in the interest of efficiency. The group then engaged in a discussion of juvenile delinquency. Periodically, the discussion was interrupted and each member was asked to rate every other member's value to the group. After the discussion, each member was shown how the others rated him; in actuality, the members were given prearranged false feedback. Some members were led to believe they were well accepted, and others were led to believe they were not terribly popular. Each member's conformity was measured by the opinions he subsequently expressed in the discussion of juvenile delinquency and by his vulnerability to group pressure during the performance of a simple perceptual task. The results showed that, for the individuals who valued their membership in the group, those who were led to feel only moderately accepted were more likely to conform to the norms and standards set by the group than were those who were led to feel totally accepted. In other words, it's easier for an individual who is securely ensconced in a group to deviate from that group.

Factors associated with conformity are similar when the source of influence is an individual rather than a group. Thus, we are more likely to conform to the behavior or opinions of an individual who is similar or important to us, or who appears to have expertise or authority in a given situation. For example, research has shown that people are more willing to comply with a demand from a person wearing a uniform, as compared with someone in civilian clothes—even when it comes to relatively trivial matters. In one study,[23] pedestrians were asked to give spare change to a motorist (actually one of the experimenters) who was parked at an expired meter. When approached by a uniformed parking officer, subjects complied with her request far more often than when she was wearing either sloppy clothes or professional, business attire. Thus, the appearance of authority—as potently symbolized by a uniform—can lend legitimacy to a demand, thereby generating high rates of compliance.

Rewards and Punishments Versus Information

As I suggested earlier, there are two possible reasons why people like us might conform. One is that the behavior of others might convince us that our initial judgment was erroneous. The other is that we may wish to avoid punishment (such as rejection or ridicule) or to gain a reward (such as love or acceptance) from the group. The behavior of the individuals in Asch's experiment and in similar other experiments seemed to be largely a matter of attempting to obtain a reward or to avoid punishment. This can be inferred from the fact that there was very little conformity when subjects were allowed to respond privately.

At the same time, there are many situations in which we conform to the behavior of others because their behavior is our only guide to appropriate action. In short, we often rely on other people as a means of determining reality. The quotation from Thurber at the beginning of this chapter gives an example of this type of conformity. According to Leon Festinger,[24] when physical reality becomes increasingly uncertain, people rely more and more on "social reality"—that is, they are more likely to conform to what other people are doing, not because they fear punishment from the group but because the group's behavior supplies them with valuable information about what is expected of them. An example should help clarify this distinction: Suppose that you need to use the toilet in an unfamiliar classroom building. Under the sign "Rest Rooms" there are two doors, but, unfortunately, a vandal has removed the specific designations from the doors—that is, you cannot be certain which is the men's room and which is the women's room. Quite a dilemma—you are afraid to open either door for fear of being embarrassed or embarrassing others. As you stand there in dismay and discomfort, hopping from one foot to the other, the door on your left opens and out strolls a distinguished-looking gentleman. With a sigh of relief, you are now willing to forge ahead, reasonably secure in the knowledge that left is for men and right is for women. Why are you so confident? As we have seen, research has shown that the more faith an individual has in the expertise and trustworthiness of the other person, the greater the tendency to follow his lead and conform to his behavior. Thus, the distinguished-looking gentleman would almost certainly be followed to a greater extent than, say, a seedy-looking fellow with wildly darting eyes.

Indeed, research on jaywalking indicates that people will more often conform to the behavior of a seemingly high-status person than someone who looks less respectable or less well-to-do. Across several studies, researchers have found that, when in the presence of a model who refrains from jaywalking, other pedestrians are more likely to curb the impulse to jaywalk, as compared with control subjects who are not exposed to any model. This conformity effect is much stronger, however, when the person modeling the behavior is neat and well attired rather than disheveled and dressed in shabby clothes.[25]

On Wasting Water and Littering. Let us take this one step further. Institutions frequently request us to perform certain behaviors without making an outright demand. For example, in the men's shower room at my university's field house, there is a sign asking us to practice conservation by turning off the water while soaping up. Since this behavior is slightly inconvenient, I was not surprised when our systematic observation revealed that only 6 percent of the students conformed to this request. Subsequently, Michael O'Leary and I conducted a simple experiment aimed at inducing a greater number of people to conserve water and the energy needed to heat it.[26] We reasoned that people would be more likely to turn off the shower while soaping up if they believed other students took the request seriously. Accordingly, we enlisted the aid of a few male students who simply acted as models for the desired behavior. But we didn't want people to conform out of a fear of disapproval or punishment, so we set up the experiment in the following way: Our model entered the shower room (an open shower room consisting of eight shower nozzles spaced at regular intervals) when it was empty, went to the far end, turned his back to the entrance, and turned on the shower. As soon as he heard someone enter, he turned off the shower, soaped up, turned it back on, briefly rinsed off, and left the room without so much as glancing at the student who had entered. As he left, another student (our observer) entered and surreptitiously noted whether the "subject" turned off the shower while soaping up. We found that 49 percent of the students followed suit! Moreover, when two students simultaneously modeled the appropriate behavior, the percentage of people obeying the sign zoomed to 67. Thus, in an ambiguous situation, other people can induce conformity by simply providing us with information suggestive of what people generally do in a given situation.

Let's look at the cultural norm against littering. Littering doesn't seem like a big deal to most people—and that's part of the problem: Most people think nothing of leaving a little trash around; but the little trash accumulates, polluting our environment and costing taxpayers a great deal of money. In California alone, the cost of cleaning up roadside litter now exceeds $100 million a year. Suppose, as you approach your car in a parking lot of the local library, you notice that someone has stuck one of those annoying flyers under your windshield wiper. So you remove it and, without thinking, crumple it up. The crucial question: Do you throw it on the ground or shove it in your pocket so that you can drop it in a trash can later? The answer: To a large extent, it depends on what other people are doing. In a clever experiment, Robert Cialdini and his associates[27] placed flyers under the windshield wipers of a number of cars and waited to observe what each driver would do when he or she discovered them. Cialdini arranged things so that, for some people, when they first left the library, they saw a person (an accomplice of Cialdini's) walk past them, stoop down, pick up a bag from a fast-food restaurant (that someone had discarded in the street), and place it in a trash can. When they got to their car and noticed the flyers, almost none of these drivers threw the flyer on the ground. In the control condition (with no one modeling responsible behavior), well over one-third of the drivers threw the flyer on the ground.

In a parallel experiment, Cialdini and his colleagues[28] used a more subtle technique of informational influence. They eliminated the human model and, instead, manipulated what the parking lot looked like. Specifically, when the experimenters had previously littered the parking lot with fliers, the majority of the drivers simply followed suit—probably thinking, "after all, if no one cares about the cleanliness of the parking lot, why should I?" Interestingly enough, people were much less likely to litter if there was one piece of litter on the ground nearby than if the parking lot were completely free of litter. The reason is that seeing one piece of litter reminds us of litter—and shows us that the vast majority of people are subscribing to that norm. If the parking lot is free of litter, most people probably do not even think about the norm and, therefore, will be more likely to litter mindlessly.

In the experiments in the shower room and in the parking lot (discussed above), conformity was induced by information rather than by fear. But it is not always easy to distinguish between the two types of conformity. Often the behavior is identical; but the key element that differentiates the two processes is the presence or absence of a punitive agent. Imagine that, in the mythical nation of Freedonia, it is considered gracious for guests to belch after eating as a way of showing the host they enjoyed the meal. Suppose you didn't know this, and you were visiting the home of a Freedonian dignitary in the company of some diplomats from the U.S. State Department. If, after the meal, these diplomats began to belch, chances are you would belch also. They are providing you with valuable information. On the other hand, suppose you were in the same home in the company of some rather rude and brawny young men who were introduced to you as members of the Freedonian Olympic heavy-weight wrestling team. If these behemoths belched after their meal, my guess is that you might not go along with this behavior. That is, you would probably consider this an act of bad manners and would avoid belching. However, if they glared at you for your failure to follow suit, you might indeed belch too—not because of the information they supplied, but because you feared rejection or reprisals for refusing to be a good sport by going along with their boorish behavior.

I would suggest that conformity resulting from the observation of others for the purpose of gaining information about proper behavior tends to have more powerful ramifications than conformity in the interest of being accepted or of avoiding punishment. I would argue that, if we were to find ourselves in an ambiguous situation wherein we must use the behavior of other people as a template for our own behavior, it is likely we will repeat our newly learned behavior, without cue, on subsequent similar occasions. This would be the case unless, of course, we later received clear evidence that our actions were inappropriate or incorrect. Thus, to go back to our example, suppose you are reinvited to the home of the Freedonian dignitary for dinner. But this time you are the only guest. The question is: Do you or don't you belch after the meal? A moment's reflection should make the answer perfectly clear: If you had belched after the first meal at his home because you realized it was the proper thing to do (as would have been the case had you dined in the company of the diplomats), you would be quite likely to belch when dining alone with the dignitary. However, if you had belched the first time out of fear of rejection or punishment (as would have been the case had you dined in the company of the wrestlers), you would almost certainly not belch when you were the lone guest. To go back to Sam and the political candidate on television, you can now readily understand one of the many reasons why it would be so difficult for us to predict how Sam would actually vote in the election. If he had been merely going along with the group to avoid punishment or to gain acceptance, he would be likely, in the privacy of the polling booth, to vote in opposition to the view expressed by his acquaintances. If, on the other hand, Sam had been using the group as a source of information, he would almost certainly vote against the candidate that he had initially preferred.

Social Influence and Emotion.   To repeat: When reality is unclear, other people become a major source of information. The generality of this phenomenon is nicely illustrated by some research performed by Stanley Schachter and Jerome Singer, who demonstrated that people conform to others even in assessing something as personal and idiosyncratic as the quality of their own emotions.[29] Before describing this research, it is useful to clarify what is meant by "emotions." According to William James,[30] an emotion has both a "feeling" content and a cognitive content. His two-part conception of emotions can be likened to the process of playing a song on a jukebox: First you need to activate the machine by inserting the coin; then you select the song you want to hear by pushing the right buttons. An emotion also requires both physiological arousal and a label. Specifically, if we are walking in the forest and bump into a hungry and ferocious bear, we undergo a physiological change. This change produces excitement—physiologically, this is a response of the sympathetic nervous system similar to one that might be produced by coming across a person with whom we are angry. We interpret this response as fear (rather than anger, say, or euphoria) only when we cognitively become aware that we are in the presence of a fear-producing stimulus (a ferocious bear). But what if we experienced physiological arousal in the absence of an appropriate stimulus? For example, what if someone surreptitiously slipped into our drink a chemical that produced the same physiological response? Would we experience fear? William James would probably say that we wouldn't—not unless there was an appropriate stimulus around.

Here is where Schachter and Singer enter the picture. In one experiment, subjects were injected either with epinephrine—a synthetic form of adrenaline, which causes physiological excitation—or with a harmless placebo. All the subjects were told that this chemical was a vitamin supplement called "suproxin." Some of the subjects who received epinephrine were informed there would be side effects, including palpitations of the heart and hand tremors. These, indeed, are some of the effects of epinephrine. Accordingly, when these subjects experienced the epinephrine symptoms, they had an appropriate explanation. In effect, when the symptoms appeared, they would say to themselves, "My heart is pounding and my hands are shaking because of this injection I received and for no other reason." But other subjects were not forewarned about these symptoms. Thus, when their hearts started pounding and their hands started trembling, what were they to make of it? The answer is that they made of it whatever the people around them made of it. Specifically, a stooge was introduced into the situation, and the subjects were informed that he had also received an injection of "suproxin." In one situation, the stooge was programed to behave in a euphoric manner; in another, he was programed to express a great deal of anger. Picture yourself in this situation: You are alone in this room with a person who supposedly has just been injected with the same drug you received. He bounces around energetically and happily wads up paper into balls and begins sinking hook shots into the wastebasket. His euphoria is obvious. Gradually, the chemical you were given begins to take effect, and you begin to feel your heart pounding, your hands trembling, and so on. What emotion do you feel? Most subjects in this situation reported a feeling of euphoria—and behaved happily. On the other hand, imagine that instead of being placed in a room with a euphoric stooge, you were placed in a room with a stooge programed to behave in an angry manner. He complains about a questionnaire you both are filling out, and eventually, in a fit of extreme annoyance, he rips up the questionnaire and angrily hurls it into the wastebasket. Meanwhile, the symptoms of epinephrine are becoming apparent; you feel your own heart pounding, and your hands begin to tremble. How do you feel? In this situation, the vast majority of the subjects felt angry and behaved in an angry fashion.

It should be noted that, if subjects were given a placebo (that is, an injection of a benign solution that produces no symptoms), or if they were forewarned about the symptoms of the drug that they had been given, they were relatively unaffected by the antics of the stooge. To sum up this experiment: When physical reality was clear and explainable, the subjects' emotions were not greatly influenced by the behavior of other people—but when they were experiencing a strong physiological response, the origins of which were not clear, they interpreted their own feelings as either anger or euphoria, depending on the behavior of other people who supposedly were in the same chemical boat.

Social Influence: Life and Death. As we have seen, the influence of other people, whether intentional or not, can have an important effect on a person's behavior. Unless we understand how this process works, these effects can have major unwanted consequences for society as well. An investigation by Craig Haney into the *death quali-fication procedure* provides an interesting and instructive example.[31] Basically, the death qualification procedure refers to the process whereby, in selecting a jury for a murder trial in a state where capital punishment is an option, prospective jurors who are opposed to the death penalty are systematically excluded from sitting on the jury. This procedure takes place in the presence of those people who are eventually selected to serve on the jury. Haney, who is both an attorney and a social psychologist, reasoned that it is possible that when jurors who believe in capital punishment witness others being dismissed because they oppose the death penalty, this may subtly suggest to them that the law disapproves of people who oppose the death penalty. This may increase their tendency to impose the death penalty. To test this notion, Haney performed an experiment in which a random sample of adults were shown a videotape of a convincing jury selection procedure filmed in the moot courtroom of a law school—a highly realistic setting complete with legal accouterments. Experienced trial lawyers served as prosecutor, defense attorney, and judge on the videotape. In one condition the procedure included a segment on death qualification; in the other condition (control), this segment did not appear. Compared to subjects in the control condition, subjects who viewed the death qualification segment were more convinced of the defendant's guilt, they believed it was more likely that he would receive the death penalty, and they also believed that the judge thought he was guilty. They themselves were also more likely to impose the death penalty if the defendant were convicted. Thus, the factors that influence our opinions and behavior can be subtle—and they may be a matter of life and death.

Responses to Social Influence

Thus far, I have been describing two kinds of conformity in more or less commonsensical terms. This distinction was based upon (1) whether the individual was being motivated by rewards and punishments or by a need to know, and (2) the relative permanence of the conforming behavior. Let us move beyond this simple distinction to a more complex and useful classification that applies not only to conformity but to the entire spectrum of social influence. Instead of using the simple term *conformity*, I would like to distinguish among three kinds of responses to social influence: *compliance, identification,* and *internalization.* [32]

Compliance. This term best describes the mode of behavior of a person who is motivated by a desire to gain reward or avoid punishment. Typically, the person's behavior is only as long-lived as the promise of reward or the threat of punishment. Thus, one can induce a rat to run a maze efficiently by making it hungry and placing food at the end of the maze. One can also get most peasants from an underdeveloped country to recite the pledge of allegiance to the U.S. flag by threatening them with pain if they don't comply or by promising to feed and enrich them if they do. On the level of compliance, many experimenters see little difference between humans and other animals, because all organisms respond to rewards and punishments. Thus, remove the food from the goal box and the rat will eventually stop running; remove the food or the threat of punishment and the peasant will cease reciting the pledge of allegiance.

Identification. This is a response to social influence brought about by an individual's desire to be like the influencer. In identification, as in compliance, we do not behave in a particular way because such behavior is intrinsically satisfying; rather, we adopt a particular behavior because it puts us in a satisfying relationship to the person or persons with whom we are identifying. Identification differs from compliance in that we do come to believe in the opinions and values we adopt, although we do not believe in them very strongly. Thus, if we find a person or a group attractive or appealing in some way, we will be inclined to accept influence from that person or group and adopt similar values and attitudes—not in order to obtain a reward or avoid a punishment (as in compliance), but simply to be like that person. I refer to this as the good-old-Uncle-Charlie phenomenon. Suppose you have an uncle named Charlie who happens to be a warm, dynamic, exciting person; and ever since you were a young child you loved him a lot and wanted to grow up to be like him. Uncle Charlie is a corporate executive who has a number of strong opinions, including a deep antipathy to social-welfare legislation—that is, he is convinced that anyone who really tries can earn a decent wage, and that, by handing money to people, the government only succeeds in eliminating their desire to work. As a young child, you heard Uncle Charlie announce this position on several occasions, and it has become part of your system of beliefs—neither because you thought it through and it seemed right to you, nor because Uncle Charlie rewarded you for adopting (or threatened to punish you for not adopting) this position. Rather, it has become part of your system because of your liking for Uncle Charlie, which has produced in you a tendency to incorporate into your life that which is his.

Internalization. The internalization of a value or belief is the most permanent, most deeply rooted response to social influence. The motivation to internalize a particular belief is the desire to be right. Thus, the reward for the belief is intrinsic. If the person who provides the influence is perceived to be trustworthy and of good judgment, we accept the belief he or she advocates and we integrate it into our system of values. Once it is part of our own system, it becomes independent of its source and will become extremely resistant to change.

Let us discuss some of the important distinguishing characteristics of these three responses to social influence. Compliance is the least enduring and has the least effect on the individual, because people comply merely to gain reward or to avoid punishment. The complier understands the force of the circumstance and can easily change his or her behavior when the circumstance no longer prevails. At gunpoint, I could be made to say most anything; but with the threat of death removed, I could quickly shrug off those statements and their implications. If a child is kind and generous to his younger brother in order to obtain a cookie from his mother, he will not necessarily become a generous person because of it. He has not learned that generosity is a good thing in and of itself—what he *has* learned is that generosity is a good way to get cookies. When the cookie supply is exhausted, his generous behavior will eventually cease, unless that behavior is bolstered by some other reward (or punishment). Rewards and punishments are very important means, then, to get people to learn and to perform specific activities but are very limited as techniques of social influence because they must be ever present to be effective—unless the individual discovers some additional reason for continuing the behavior. This last point will be discussed shortly.

Continuous reward or punishment is not necessary for the response to social influence I call identification. The person with whom the individual identifies need not be present at all; what is needed is only the individual's desire to be like that person. For example, if Uncle Charlie moves to a different city, and months (or even years) go by without your seeing him, you will continue to hold beliefs similar to his as long as (1) he remains important to you, (2) he still holds the same beliefs, and (3) these beliefs are not challenged by counteropinions that are more convincing. But, by the same token, these beliefs *can* be changed if Uncle Charlie has a change of heart, or if your love for Uncle Charlie begins to fade. They can also change if a person or group of people who are more important to you than Uncle Charlie profess a different set of beliefs. For example, suppose you are away at college and you find yourself a group of new, exciting friends who, unlike Uncle Charlie, are strongly in favor of social welfare. If you admire them as much as (or more than) your uncle, you may change your beliefs in order to be more like them. Thus, a more important identification may supersede a previous identification.

The effect of social influence through identification can also be dissipated by a person's desire to be right. If you have taken on a belief through identification and you are subsequently presented with a counterargument by an expert and trustworthy person, you will probably change your belief. Internalization is the most permanent response to social influence precisely because your motivation to be right is a powerful and self-sustaining force that does not depend upon constant surveillance in the form of agents of reward or punishment, as does compliance, or on your continued esteem for another person or group, as does identification.

It is important to realize that any specific action may be due to either compliance, identification, or internalization. For example, let us look at a simple piece of behavior: obedience of the laws pertaining to fast driving. Society employs highway patrol officers to enforce these laws, and as we all know, people tend to drive within the speed limit if they are forewarned that a certain stretch of highway is being carefully scrutinized by these officers. This is compliance. It is a clear case of people obeying the law in order to avoid paying a penalty. Suppose you were to remove the highway patrol. As soon as people found out about it, many would increase their speed. But some people might continue to obey the speed limit; a person might continue to obey because Dad (or Uncle Charlie) always obeyed speed limits or always stressed the importance of obeying traffic laws. This, of course, is identification. Finally, people might conform to the speed limit because they are convinced that speed laws are good, that obeying such laws helps to prevent accidents, and that driving at moderate speed is a sane and reasonable form of behavior. This is internalization. And with internalization you would observe more flexibility in the behavior. For example, under certain conditions—at 6:00 A.M., say, on a clear day with perfect visibility and with no traffic for miles around—the individual might exceed the speed limit. The compliant individual, however, might fear a radar trap, and the identifying individual might be identifying with a very rigid model—thus, both would be less responsive to important changes in the environment.

Let us look at the major component in each response to social influence. In compliance, the important component is *power*—the power of the influencer to dole out the reward for compliance and punishment for noncompliance. Parents have the power to praise, give love, provide cookies, scream, give spankings, withhold allowances, and so on; teachers have the power to paste gold stars on our foreheads or flunk us out of college; and employers have the power to praise, promote, humiliate, or discharge us. The U.S. government has the power to increase or withhold economic and military aid from a dependent nation. Thus, our government can use this technique to persuade, say, some country in Latin America to hold a more or less democratic election. Rewards and punishments are effective means for producing this kind of compliance, but we might ask whether or not mere compliance is desirable: To induce a nation to hold a democratic election is easier than to induce the rulers of that nation to think and rule democratically.

In identification, the crucial component is *attractiveness*—the attractiveness of the person with whom we identify. Because we identify with the model, we want to hold the same opinions that the model holds. Suppose a person you admire takes a particular stand on an issue. Unless you have strong feelings or solid information to the contrary, there will be a tendency for you to adopt this position. Incidentally, it is interesting to note that the reverse is also true: If a person or group that you dislike announces a position, there will be a tendency for you to reject that position or adopt the opposite position. Suppose, for example, that you dislike some particular group (say, the Nazi party in the United States), and that group comes out against draft registration. If you know nothing about the issue, your tendency will be to favor draft registration—all other things being equal.

In internalization, the important component is *credibility*—the credibility of the person who supplies the information. For example, if you read a statement by a person who is highly credible—that is, someone who is both expert and trustworthy—you would tend to be influenced by it because of your desire to be correct. Recall our earlier example of the diplomats at the Freedonian dinner party. Your acceptance of their expertise made their behavior (belching after the meal) seem like the right thing to do. Accordingly, my guess is that this behavior (your tendency to belch after a meal at the home of a Freedonian dignitary) would become internalized—you would do it, thereafter, because you believed it to be right.

Recall the experiment on conformity performed by Solomon Asch, in which social pressure induced many subjects to conform to the erroneous statements of a group. Recall further that, when the subjects were allowed to respond in private, the incidence of conformity dropped considerably. Clearly, then, internalization or identification was not involved. It seems obvious that the subjects were *complying* with the unanimous opinion of the group in order to avoid the punishment of ridicule or rejection. If either identification or internalization had been involved, the conforming behavior would have persisted in private.

The trichotomy of compliance, identification, and internalization is a useful one. At the same time, it should be made clear that, like most ways of classifying the world, it is not perfect; there are some places where the categories overlap. Specifically, although it is true that compliance and identification are generally more temporary than internalization, there are circumstances that can increase their permanence. For example, permanence can be increased if an individual makes a firm commitment to continue to interact with the person or group of people that induced the original act of compliance. Thus, in an experiment by Charles Kiesler and his associates,[33] when subjects believed that they were going to continue interaction with an unattractive discussion group, they not only complied publicly, but they also seemed to internalize their conformity— that is, they changed their private opinions as well as their public behavior. This kind of situation will be discussed in greater detail in chapter 5.

Permanence can also result if, while complying, we discover something about our actions, or about the consequences of our actions, that makes it worthwhile to continue the behavior even after the original reason for compliance (the reward or punishment) is no longer forthcoming. For example, when the speed limit was reduced nationally from 70 to 55 miles per hour, the law was strictly enforced and most drivers reduced their speed. Some people found they enjoyed the less hectic pace and the increased safety and gas mileage, so that, even when the enforcement effort decreased and highway speeds picked up, they continued to drive within the speed limit. The generalizability of this phenomenon, called a *secondary gain*, is borne out by some of the research done on that aspect of social learning known as *behavior modification*. Typically, in behavior modification, an attempt is made to eliminate unwanted or maladaptive behavior by systematically punishing that behavior, by rewarding alternative behaviors, or both. For example, various attempts have been made to use this technique as a way of getting people to stop excessive drinking or smoking cigarettes.[34] Individuals might be given a series of painful electric shocks while performing the usual rituals of smoking—that is, while lighting a cigarette, bringing it up to their lips, inhaling, and so on. After several trials, the individual will refuse to smoke. Unfortunately, it is fairly easy for people to notice a difference between the experimental situation and the world outside: They realize they will not be shocked when smoking outside of the experimental situation. Consequently, a person may later experience a little residual anxiety when lighting a cigarette, but because electric shocks are clearly not forthcoming, the anxiety eventually fades. Thus, many people who temporarily cease smoking after this form of behavior modification will eventually return to cigarettes after electric shock is no longer a threat. How about those who stay off cigarettes after behavior modification? Here is the point: Once we have been induced to comply, and therefore do not smoke for several days, it is possible for us to make a discovery. Over the years, we may have come to believe it was inevitable that we awaken every morning with a hacking cough and a hot, dry mouth, but, after refraining from cigarettes for a few days, we may discover how delightful it feels to have a clear throat and a fresh, unparched mouth. This discovery may be enough to keep us from smoking again. Thus, although compliance, in and of itself, usually does not produce long-lasting behavior, it may set the stage for events that will lead to more permanent effects.

Obedience as a Form of Compliance

I indicated that acts of compliance are, in general, ephemeral. This does not mean they are trivial. Impermanent behavior can be extremely important. This fact has been demonstrated dramatically by

Stanley Milgram in his studies of obedience.[35] Picture the scene: Subjects volunteer for an experiment advertised as a study of learning and memory. But this is just the cover story; actually, it is a study of the extent to which people will obey authority. When the volunteer appears at the lab for his appointment, he is paired with another participant, and a somewhat stern experimenter in a technician's coat explains that they will be testing the effects of punishment on learning. The exercise requires one participant, the learner, to memorize a list of word pairs on which the other participant, the teacher, will test him. The subject and his partner draw slips to determine roles; the subject draws the role of teacher. He is led to a "Shock Generator," which has an instrument panel with a row of thirty toggle switches, calibrated from a low point of 15 volts (labeled "Slight Shock") and extending through levels of moderate and severe shocks to a high of 450 volts (labeled "XXX"). By throwing the successive switches, the teacher is to deliver an increasingly intense shock each time the learner fails to answer correctly. Then the teacher follows the experimenter and the other participant into the next room, where the learner is strapped into an electric chair apparatus and is attached by electrodes to the "Shock Generator." In response to the learner's inquiry about his mild heart condition, the experimenter reassures him, "Although the shocks can be extremely painful, they cause no permanent tissue damage."

In actuality, the learner knows that he needn't worry. He is an accomplice of the experimenter, and the drawing to assign roles has been rigged so that he would play the role of the learner and the subject would be the teacher. The learner is not really wired to the electricity. But the teacher, who *is* the real subject, firmly believes that the victim in the next room *is* wired to the "Shock Generator" that he operates. He has even experienced a sample shock (from a 45-volt battery inside the machine), he hears the learner react as if he is really being hurt, and he is convinced the shocks are extremely painful. The subject does not realize that what he is actually hearing is a tape recording, or that the learner is answering according to a prepared script.

As the exercise begins, the learner responds correctly several times but makes mistakes on a few trials. With each error, the subject throws the next switch, supposedly administering a shock of increasing intensity. With the fifth shock, at 75 volts, the victim begins to grunt and moan. At 150 volts, he asks to be let out of the experiment.

At 180 volts, he cries out that he can't stand the pain. As the shock levels approach the point labeled "Danger: Extreme Shock," the subject hears the victim pound the wall and beg to be let out of the room. But this, of course, does not constitute a correct response, so the experimenter instructs the teacher to increase the voltage and deliver the next shock by throwing the next switch.

The participants in this experiment were a random sample of businessmen, professional men, white-collar workers, and blue-collar workers. What percentage of these people continued to administer shocks to the very end of the experiment? How long would you have continued? Every year in my social psychology class, I pose these questions, and every year some 99 percent of the 240 students in the class indicate that they would not continue to administer shocks after the learner began to pound on the wall. The guesses made by my students are consistent with the results of Milgram's survey of forty psychiatrists at a leading medical school. The psychiatrists predicted that most subjects would quit at 150 volts, when the victim first asks to be freed. These psychiatrists also predicted that only about 4 percent of the subjects would continue to shock the victim after he refused to respond (at 300 volts), and that less than 1 percent would administer the highest shock on the generator.

How do subjects respond when they are actually in the situation? Milgram found, in the typical study as described above, that the great majority of his subjects—more than 62 percent—continued to administer shocks to the very end of the experiment, although some of them required a degree of prodding from the experimenter. The obedient subjects did not continue administering shocks because they were particularly sadistic or cruel people. Indeed, when Milgram and Alan Elms compared subjects' scores on a series of standardized personality tests, they discovered no differences between individuals who were fully obedient and those who successfully resisted the pressure to obey.[36] Nor were obedient subjects insensitive to the apparent plight of the victim. Some protested; many subjects were observed to sweat, tremble, stutter, or show other signs of tension; and they occasionally had fits of nervous laughter. But they obeyed.

This behavior is not limited to American men living in Connecticut. Wherever the Milgram procedure has been tried it has produced a significant degree of obedience. For example, replications of the experiment[37] have demonstrated that people in Australia, Jordan,

Spain, and West Germany react in much the same way Milgram's subjects did. Similarly, women have been found to be at least as obedient as men.[38]

Implications: An astonishingly large proportion of people will cause pain to other people in obedience to authority. The research may have important counterparts in the world outside of the experimental laboratory. For example, it is difficult to read these studies without noticing a loose kind of similarity between the behavior of Milgram's subjects and the blind obedience expressed by Adolf Eichmann, who attributed his responsibility for the murder of thousands of innocent civilians to the fact that he was a good bureaucrat merely obeying orders issued by his superiors in the Nazi regime. More recently, in our own nation's history, Lieutenant William Calley, who was convicted of the deliberate and unprovoked murder of Vietnamese women and children at My Lai, freely admitted to these acts but said he felt this was justifiable obedience to the authority of his superior officers. Interestingly, one of Milgram's subjects, obedient throughout the experiment, reported when questioned after the session, "*I* stopped, but he [the experimenter] made me go on."

As provocative as these comparisons are, we should be cautious lest we overinterpret Milgram's results. Given that 62 percent of the subjects in Milgram's experiment complied with the experimenter's command, some commentators have been tempted to suggest that perhaps most people would have behaved as Adolf Eichmann or Lieutenant Calley did if they found themselves in a similar situation. This may be true; but it should be emphasized that there are, in fact, some important factors in the situation encountered by Milgram's subjects that tend to maximize obedience. The subject has consented to participate, and he assumes the victim has also volunteered; he may perceive an obligation on their part to avoid disrupting the experiment. He faces the demands of the experimenter alone; a variation of the study demonstrated that the proportion of fully obedient subjects drops to just 10 percent when they are joined by two fellow teachers who defy the experimenter.[39] Also, in most of Milgram's studies, the authority figure issuing the orders was a scientist in a prestigious laboratory at Yale University, and his cover story credits the experiment as being an investigation of an important scientific question. In our society, we have been conditioned to believe that scientists tend to be responsible, benevolent people of high integrity. This is especially true if the scientist is affiliated with a well-known and highly respected institution like Yale. The subjects might reasonably assume, then, that no scientist would issue orders that would result in the death or injury of a human as a part of his experiment. This was clearly not true in either the Eichmann or the Calley example.

Some evidence in support of this conjecture comes from further research by Milgram. He conducted a separate study[40] comparing the obedience of subjects to the commands of a scientist at Yale University with the obedience of subjects to the commands of a scientist working in a suite of offices in a rather rundown commercial building in the downtown shopping area of the industrial city of Bridgeport, Connecticut. In this study, the Yale scientist achieved an obedience rate of 65 percent, while only 48 percent of the subjects in Bridgeport were obedient. Thus, removing the prestige of Yale University did seem to reduce the degree of obedience somewhat.

Of course, 48 percent is still a high figure. Would even fewer people have obeyed if the person conducting the experiment were not a scientist or other legitimate authority figure? Milgram addressed this question in another version of the study, in which the scientist-experimenter was replaced at the last minute by a nonauthoritative "substitute." Here's how it worked: After making the usual preparations for the learning task, but without designating what shock levels were to be used, the experimenter was called away from the study by a prearranged telephone call. Another subject (actually a confederate) assumed the experimenter's role. The substitute pretended to hit upon the idea of having the teacher raise the shock level every time the learner made a mistake. He also prodded the teacher to proceed with the shocks, just as the scientist-experimenter had done in previous versions of the experiments. Under these conditions, the number of fully obedient subjects plummeted to 20 percent, demonstrating that, for most people, only legitimate authority can command high obedience, not just any person assuming the role of authority.

Another factor that reduces the extent of obedience is the physical absence of the authority figure. Milgram found that, when the experimenter was out of the room and issued his orders by telephone, the number of *fully* obedient subjects dropped to below 25 percent. Moreover, several of the subjects who did continue with the experiment "cheated"; specifically, they administered shocks of lower intensity than they were supposed to—and never bothered to tell the experimenter that they deviated from the proper procedure. This last datum, I feel, represents a touching attempt by some individuals to be responsive to the demands of legitimate authority while, at the same time, minimizing the pain they inflict on others. It is reminiscent of the behavior of Dunbar, a character in Joseph Heller's novel *Catch 22*. During World War II, Dunbar is ordered to bomb some villages in Italy. Unwilling either to rebel openly or to harm innocent civilians, he drops his bombs over empty fields close to the Italian villages designated as his targets.

Dunbar's sensitivity to the potential victims of his bombs is especially poignant, given the distance and anonymity afforded by his position high in the sky above the villagers. Indeed, Milgram found in subsequent studies that the farther subjects were from the learner, the more willing they were to obey the commands of authority. When subjects could actually see the learner, only 40 percent continued to deliver painful shocks as compared to 62 percent who could merely hear the victim's cries of agony. Similarly, when subjects were instructed to physically force the learner's arm down on the shock plate—instead of using the more remote shock generator to deliver shocks—the rate of obedience dropped to 30 percent. Thus, vividly witnessing the suffering of others makes it more difficult to continue inflicting pain upon them. Conversely, the weapons used in modern warfare preclude such close proximity to potential victims, making it easier for those who wield the instruments of death to be indifferent toward the plight of innocent targets.

Some subjects in the Milgram experiments chose to defy the experimenter, and human history is replete with inspiring examples of courage. For example, there are "freedom museums" in Norway, Denmark, and other European countries that celebrate the efforts of a heroic few to resist the occupation of the Nazis. But these acts of mercy and bravery, however encouraging, should not blind us to the pervasiveness of our tendency to obey authority. Many of us tour such museums and admire the displays, certain that we, too, would exhibit such courage. We harbor a myth of our personal invulnerability. When subjects were asked to predict their own performance in the Milgram study, their values and self-conceptions caused all of them to predict that they would discontinue the shocks at the moderate level.[41] But we have seen how the forces of the actual situation can override those values and self-conceptions. One year, when I asked

my social-psychology students whether they might continue delivering shocks until the end of the scale, only one hand slowly rose—
everyone else in the class was confident that he or she would defy the
experimenter's instructions. But the student who raised his hand was
a Vietnam veteran who was in a position to know; he had experienced the impact of similar pressures, and he painfully and tragically
came to recognize his own vulnerability in certain situations. Indeed,
not only do we find it difficult to resist pressures to hurt people, we
often avoid taking action when presented with opportunities to help
other humans.

The "Uninvolved" Bystander as Conformist

In 1964, a young woman named Kitty Genovese was stabbed to
death in New York City. This was a tragic event, but not, in itself, a
particularly novel occurrence. After all, in a major population center,
brutal murders are not uncommon. What is interesting about this
event is that no fewer than thirty-eight of her neighbors came to their
windows at 3:00 A.M. in response to her screams of terror—and
remained at their windows watching in fascination for the thirty
minutes it took her assailant to complete his grisly deed, during
which time he returned for three separate attacks. No one came to
her assistance; no one so much as lifted the phone to call the police,
until too late.[42] Why?

Well, perhaps the onlookers were sleepy or dazed. After all, people are hardly in full control of their mental faculties at three o'clock
in the morning. Perhaps. But it was in broad daylight that Eleanor
Bradley, while shopping on Fifth Avenue in New York, tripped, fell,
and broke her leg. She lay there for forty minutes in a state of shock,
while literally hundreds of passersby paused momentarily to gawk at
her and then kept on walking.

Why did these bystanders fail to help? Are people impervious to
the distress of others? Have they become so accustomed to disaster
that they can be nonchalant in the face of pain and violence? Were
the bystanders in these situations different from you and me in some
way? The answer to all of these questions appears to be no. Interviews
conducted with the bystanders in the Genovese murder revealed that

they were anything but nonchalant—they were horrified. Why, then, didn't they intervene? This is a difficult question to answer.

One possible explanation concerns the existence of different norms for helping in large cities, as opposed to smaller towns. Several experiments[43] have found that the likelihood of receiving help is greater in nonurban than in urban locales. However, these studies examined small requests for help—change for a quarter, the time, and so forth. Whether or not these rural-urban differences occur in serious emergency situations, like those faced by Kitty Genovese and Eleanor Bradley, is unclear.

More convincing explanations have been suggested by a series of ingenious experiments conducted by John Darley, Bibb Latane, and their colleagues.[44] These investigators hypothesized that the very number of people witnessing the tragedies militated against anyone's helping—that is, a victim is less likely to get help if there are a large number of people watching his or her distress. Thus, nonintervention can be viewed as an act of conformity. In this case it appears that, for each individual, the other people were defining the reasonableness and appropriateness of helping or not helping. As we have seen, it is often reasonable to take one's cue from others. Occasionally, however, it can be misleading; and it tends to be particularly misleading in critical situations. In our society, it is considered "uncool" to reveal strong emotions in public. When we are with others, most of us try to appear less fearful, less worried, less anxious, or less sexually aroused than we really are. For example, from the blasé looks on the faces of the patrons of topless nightclubs, one would never guess they were turned on, or even interested. Similarly, the proverbial visitor from Mars would never suspect the anxiety of the patients in a dentist's waiting room by observing the impassive looks on their faces.

With these things in mind, let us consider the case of the woman who fell and broke her leg on Fifth Avenue. Suppose you arrived at the scene ten minutes after she fell. You see a woman lying on the ground in apparent discomfort. What else do you see? You see scores of people walking past the woman, glancing at her, and continuing on their way. How will you define the situation? You may conclude that it's inappropriate for you to intervene. Perhaps it's not serious; perhaps she's intoxicated; perhaps she is playacting; perhaps the whole thing is staged for "Candid Camera," and you will make a fool of yourself on national television if you intervene. "After all," you ask yourself, "if it's so damn important, why are none of these other people doing anything about it?" Thus, the fact that there are a lot of other people around, rather than increasing the likelihood that *someone* will help, actually *decreases* the likelihood that any *one* of them will help.[45]

This is an interesting conjecture, but is it true? To find out, Bibb Latane and Judith Rodin[46] conducted an experiment constructed around a "lady in distress." In this experiment, a female experimenter asked college students to fill out a questionnaire. The experimenter then retired to the next room through an unlocked collapsible curtain, saying she would return when they finished the questionnaire. A few minutes later, she staged an "accident." What the students actually heard was the sound (from a hidden tape recording) of the young woman climbing a chair, followed by a loud scream and a crash, as if the chair had collapsed and she had fallen to the floor. They then heard moaning and crying and the anguished statement, "Oh, my God, my foot I . . . I can't move it. Oh . . . my ankle . . . I can't get this thing off me." The cries continued for about a minute and gradually subsided.

The experimenters were interested in determining whether or not the subjects would come to the young woman's aid. The important variable in the experiment was whether or not the subjects were alone in the room. Of those who were alone, 70 percent offered to help the young woman; of those who were participating in pairs with strangers, only 20 percent offered help. Thus, it is clear that the presence of another bystander tends to inhibit action. When interviewed subsequently, the unhelpful subjects who had been in the room with another subject said they had concluded the accident probably wasn't serious, at least in part because of the inactivity of their partner.

In the Genovese murder, there was probably an additional reason the bystanders did not help. In such a situation, it may be that, if people are aware an event is being witnessed by others, the responsibility felt by any individual is diffused. Each witness to the Genovese slaying who noticed lights flick on and faces watching in several other windows might have felt no personal responsibility to act. Since others were watching, each bystander could have concluded that someone else was calling the police or that it was someone else's duty to do so. To test this idea, Darley and Latane[47] arranged an experimental situation in which subjects were placed in separate rooms but were able to communicate with each other by microphones and earphones. Thus, the subjects could hear one another but couldn't see one another. The investigators then staged a simulated epileptic attack: They played a tape recording that imitated an epileptic seizure on the part of one of the participants. In one experimental condition, each subject was led to believe that he or she was the only one whose intercom was tuned in during the seizure; in other conditions, each subject was led to believe that one or more people were tuned in also. Subjects who thought they were the only listener were far more likely to leave their room and try to help than those who thought others were listening, too. As the number of people listening increased, the likelihood of assistance decreased.

The behavior of the onlookers in the Genovese murder case and the subjects in the Darley-Latane experiments projects a rather grim picture of the human condition. Is it true that people avoid helping each other if at all possible—that is, if someone provides a bad example by not intervening, or if the responsibility for action seems the least bit diffuse? Perhaps not. Perhaps there are situations in which people are inspired to come to the aid of their fellows. An incident in my own experience may shed some light on this issue. I was camping in Yosemite National Park several years ago. It was late at night, and I was just dropping off to sleep when I heard a man's voice cry out. I couldn't be certain whether it was a cry of pain, surprise, or joy. I had no idea whether some people were just horsing around or whether one of my fellow campers was being attacked by a bear. I crawled out of my sleeping bag and looked around, trying to shake the cobwebs out of my head and trying to ascertain the place from which the scream had come, when I noticed a strange phenomenon. From all over the area, a myriad of flickering lights were converging on a single point. These were lanterns and flashlights being carried by dozens of campers running to the aid of the individual who had screamed. It turned out his scream had been one of surprise caused by a relatively harmless flare-up in his gasoline stove. The other campers seemed almost disappointed when they learned no help was needed. They trudged back to their tents and, I assume, dropped off to sleep immediately. Not so with me, however: I tossed and turned, unable to get back to sleep. As a social psychologist with a great deal of faith in scientific data, I spent the night puzzling over the fact that my fellow campers had behaved in a totally different manner from the subjects in the Darley-Latane experiments.

Why had the campers behaved so differently? In what way were the situations different? There were at least two factors operating in the campground that were either not present or were present only to a very small degree in the situations previously discussed. One of these factors is reflected in my use, in the preceding paragraph, of the term "my fellow campers." Specifically, a feeling of "common fate" or mutuality may be engendered among people sharing the same interests, pleasures, hardships, and environmental conditions of a closed environment like a campground, a feeling of mutuality that is stronger than among people who are merely residents of the same country, county, or city. A second, somewhat related factor is that there was no escape from the face-to-face aspect of the situation: The onlookers in the Genovese case could walk away from their windows into the relative protection and isolation of their own homes; the people on Fifth Avenue could walk past the woman lying on the sidewalk and keep on going, right out of her environment; the subjects in the Darley-Latane experiments were not in a face-to-face relationship with the victim, and they knew they could escape from the environment in a very short time. In the campground, the events were occurring in a relatively restricted environment; whatever the campers allowed to happen that night they were going to have to face squarely the next morning. It seems that, under these circumstances, individuals are more willing to take responsibility for each other.

Of course, this is mere speculation. The behavior of the campers at Yosemite—while provocative—is not conclusive, because it was not part of a controlled experiment. One of the major problems with observational data like these is that the observer has no control over who the people in the situation are. Thus, differences between people always loom as a possible explanation for the differences in their behavior. For example, one might argue that individuals who go camping are—by nature or experience—kinder, gentler, more thoughtful, and more humane than New Yorkers. Perhaps they were Boy Scouts and Girl Scouts as children—hence the interest in camping—and, in scouting, they were taught to be helpful to other people. One of the reasons for doing experiments is to control this kind of uncertainty. Indeed, a subsequent experiment lends support to my speculation about my campground experience. This was an experiment performed by Irving Piliavin and his associates[48] in one of the cars of a train in the New York subway system. In this experiment, an accomplice of the experimenters staggered and collapsed in the presence of several individuals riding the subway. The "victim" remained stretched out on the floor of the train, staring at the ceiling. This scene was repeated 103 times under a variety of conditions. The most striking result was that, a large part of the time, people spontaneously rushed to the aid of the "stricken" individual. This was especially true when the victim was made to seem obviously ill; in more than 95 percent of the trials, someone offered help immediately. Even when the "victim" had been given a liquor bottle to carry and was made to reek of alcohol, he received immediate help from someone on 50 percent of the trials. Unlike the behavior of the subjects that Darley and Latane dealt with, the helping behavior of the people on the subway train was not affected by the number of bystanders. People helped just as often and just as speedily on crowded trains (where there could be a diffusion of responsibility) as they did on virtually empty trains. Although the people doing the helping were New Yorkers (as in the Genovese case, the Fifth Avenue case, and the Darley-Latane experiments), they were also in an environment that, although very much unlike Yosemite National Park, did have two things in common with the campground: (1) people riding on the same subway car do have the feeling of sharing a common fate, and (2) they were in a face-to-face situation with the victim from which there was no immediate escape.

How can the tendency to help be increased? Consider the questions that would run through your mind should you confront a possible emergency: "Is the situation really serious? Does it require my personal intervention? Will helping be difficult or costly for me? Will my help benefit the victim? Can I easily leave?" Your response will depend on your answers to each of these questions.

The first prerequisite for helping is to define the situation as an emergency. We have seen that the clues provided by the presence of unresponsive bystanders can discourage other onlookers from concluding that an emergency exists. But the interpretations of bystanders can also influence perceptions in the opposite direction. In an experiment conducted by Leonard Bickman,[49] female students sitting in cubicles and listening over intercoms heard a crash and a victim's scream, followed by the reaction of a witness to the apparent accident. When the subjects heard the witness interpret the event as a certain emergency, they helped more frequently and more quickly than when the interpretation was uncertain or when the event was labeled a nonemergency. The less ambiguous the emergency, the greater the likelihood of helping.

Defining the situation as an emergency is the first step; assuming personal responsibility for intervening is the next. Onlookers are more likely to help when they cannot reduce their sense of responsibility by assuming others will act. I have described an experiment by Darley and Latane demonstrating that people help more when they think they are the only ones aware of an emergency; in Bickman's experiments, though the subjects thought others were *aware* of the situation, some were led to believe that the other participants were unable to respond. Specifically, some of the female students were informed that the other participants they would hear over the intercom were located in nearby cubicles, while others were told that one voice (turning out to be the victim's) was originating from a nearby cubicle but that the other participant was speaking from a different building. Subjects responded significantly more speedily to the emergency in the latter condition, when perceiving that the other bystander was unable to help. In fact, those subjects who could not diffuse their responsibility intervened as quickly as those who thought nobody else heard the accident.

Although an event might be a clear emergency that demands their aid, people help less when the costs of their assistance are high. In a variation of the Piliavins's subway experiments,[50] the victim sometimes bit a capsule of red dye as he collapsed, so he appeared to be bleeding from the mouth. Though the "blood" made the emergency appear more serious, the bleeding victims were helped less frequently than those who collapsed without bleeding. Apparently, potential helpers were scared or repulsed by the blood, reducing their inclination to help. Other kinds of costs also can enter the calculation, including seemingly trivial ones, as John Darley and Daniel Batson[51] cleverly illustrated. They enlisted divinity students at Princeton Theological Seminary, ostensibly for the purpose of recording a speech. Each subject practiced his talk in one room; then he was instructed to walk to another building, where his presentation would be taped. At this point, some of the students were told they were late for their appointments and were hurried out. Others were told they were on time, and the rest that they had time to spare. On their way to the recording session in the other building, subjects encountered a victim slumped in a doorway, with head down and eyes closed, who coughed as the subjects went by. Students in a hurry were more likely to pass by the victim. While over half of the subjects who were early or on time stopped to assist the victim, only 10 percent of the students who thought they were late for their appointment offered help, even when the speech they were to deliver involved the parable of the Good Samaritan!

In addition to assessing the costs of helping, people consider the benefits their assistance will provide. There is a good deal of evidence that people will help one another if they are certain they can do something helpful.[52] For example, in one experiment, Robert Baron[53] showed that, when an individual was in obvious pain—and when the bystander knew his or her response could alleviate the suffering—then, the greater the apparent pain, the more quickly the bystander responded. In the same experiment, it was shown that, when the bystander did not believe he or she could reduce the victim's pain, there was an inverse relationship between pain and speed of responding—that is, the greater the apparent pain, the more slowly the bystander responded. To make sense out of these results, we need to make use of the concept of *empathy:* in this case, our tendency to experience unpleasant physiological responses at the sight of another person in pain. The more the victim's pain, the greater our unpleasant feeling. We can reduce this unpleasant feeling either by helping the victim or by psychologically removing ourselves from the situation. If there is clearly something we can do about it, we act quickly—especially when the victim is in great pain. If we believe there is nothing we can do about it, the greater will be our tendency to turn away from it (in order to reduce our own feelings of unpleasantness), especially if the victim is in *great* pain.

Up to this point, we have been focusing on the considerations surrounding a decision to help a victim. As this discussion of empathy exemplifies, it is clear the bystander also considers the personal benefits and costs of not helping. The discomfort aroused by seeing a victim's plight can be allayed if the witness can redefine the incident as a nonemergency or relinquish the responsibility for intervening. When it is easy to remove oneself from the situation, helping is reduced. Several factors, however, strengthen the connection the bystander feels with the victim and thereby discourage leaving. We have all heard anecdotes of people going to extraordinary lengths—entering burning buildings or stepping in front of moving cars—to save members of their family. We tend to feel more empathy and assume more responsibility when the victim is someone close to us. The connection can be more superficial; for instance, potential helpers render more assistance to those who exhibit attitudes similar to their own. In 1971, as protesters demonstrated in Washington against President Nixon's Vietnam policy, Peter Suedfeld and his colleagues[54] staged an experiment to test the relationship between similarity of attitudes and willingness to help. They trained a young woman to approach individual demonstrators with a request to help her male friend, who was ill. Her ailing friend carried a sign reading either "Dump Nixon" or "Support Nixon." Demonstrators offered more assistance to a fellow protester carrying the anti-Nixon placard than to a seeming supporter of Nixon. Finally, as I mentioned when discussing the Yosemite camping incident and the subway experiments, helping is more likely when people share a sense of common fate. This sense of interdependence is easily disregarded in our society; the predominant explanation given by the thirty-eight onlookers to the Genovese murder was, "I didn't want to get involved."

A Note on the Ethics of Experiments

In their quest for knowledge, experimental social psychologists occasionally subject people to some fairly intense experiences. In this chapter alone I have discussed experiments in which people have been led into conflict between the evidence of their own eyes and the unanimous judgments of other people, in which they have been ordered to deliver intense electric shock to an apparently suffering victim, and in which scores of innocent people riding a subway have been forced to witness the apparent agony of a person in distress.

These procedures raise serious ethical problems. A more complete treatment of ethics is presented in chapter 9; here, let it suffice to make two general points: First, it is the responsibility of all experimenters in this field to protect the experimental subject from all harm. The experimenter must take steps to ensure that subjects leave the experimental situation in a frame of mind that is at least as sound as it was when they entered the experimental situation. This frequently requires postexperimental "debriefing" procedures that require more time and effort than the main body of the experiment.

Given the ethical thin ice that experimenters must skate upon, why bother with these kinds of experiments at all? This brings me to the second point of ethics I want to emphasize at this time: For social psychologists, the ethical issue is not a one-sided affair. In a real sense, they are obligated to use their research skills to advance our knowledge and understanding of human behavior for the ultimate aim of human betterment. In short, social psychologists have an ethical responsibility to the society as a whole; they would be remiss in fulfilling this responsibility if they failed to conduct research to the best of their ability. Social psychologists face a dilemma when their general ethical responsibility to society conflicts with their more specific ethical responsibility to each individual experimental subject; and to compound the situation, the conflict is greatest when investigating such important issues as conformity, obedience, helping, and the like, because, in general, the more important the issue, (1) the greater the potential benefit for society and (2) the more likely it is that an individual subject will experience discomfort, anxiety, or upset. Again, for a more complete treatment of this topic, the reader is directed to chapter 9.

3
Mass Communication, Propaganda, and Persuasion

In 1977, the first "blockbuster" television miniseries was presented. Over 130 million viewers tuned in to watch at least one of the segments of "Roots," the ABC television network's production of Alex Haley's history of several generations of an African American family in the United States. The shows received widespread acclaim for promoting the awareness of black history and for inspiring blacks' pride in their heritage. Six years later, ABC aired "The Day After," a made-for-TV movie that graphically depicted the aftermath of a nuclear attack on the United States. In November 1983, over 40 million U.S. households tuned in—the audience was bigger than anyone's wildest predictions. To say that the movie was controversial would be an understatement. Indeed, well before it was shown, "The Day After" was the subject of numerous cover stories in national news magazines. Movie stars, physicists, and political leaders (including the president) aired their views about the program and its potential impact. Educators and psychologists were concerned about the impact of "The Day After" on children, and even adults were warned: "Watch 'The Day After' . . . But *Don't* Watch It Alone."[1]

"The Day After" clearly did have impact, even on those who had not actually watched the show but had merely heard some of the hype. After the movie aired, watchers and nonwatchers alike thought more about nuclear war, thought nuclear war was more likely, felt that surviving such a war was less likely, and viewed survival as less positive. Moreover, both groups reported that they intended to work toward preventing a nuclear war by supporting a nuclear-weapons freeze and engaging in other antinuclear activities. These effects were generally stronger for those who watched "The Day After." Amazingly, just two hours of prime-time television had a major impact on most Americans, influencing both their attitudes and their intentions to do something positive about the threat of nuclear war.[2]

A simple two hours of television can also have powerfully negative effects, preventing viewers from taking action. Some years ago, CBS aired a film called "Cry Rape." Essentially, the story made it clear that a rape victim who chooses to press charges against her attacker runs the risk of undergoing an ordeal that may be as harrowing as the rape itself. In this case, the rapist, exuding boyish innocence, presented a convincing argument to the effect that he had been seduced by the woman. During the next few weeks, there was a sharp decrease in the number of rapes reported by victims to police— apparently because victims, taking their cue from the television movie, feared the police would not believe them.[3]

It is a truism to say we live in an age of mass communication; indeed, it can even be said that we live in an age characterized by attempts at mass persuasion. Every time we turn on the radio or television set, every time we open a book, magazine, or newspaper, someone is trying to educate us, to convince us to buy a product, to persuade us to vote for a candidate, or to subscribe to some version of what is right, true, or beautiful. This aim is most obvious in advertising: Manufacturers of nearly identical products (aspirins, for example, or toothpastes, or detergents) spend vast amounts of money to persuade us to buy the product in *their* package. Influence through the mass media need not be so blatant—the impact of "Roots" and "The Day After," for instance, extended far beyond their most obvious effects as documentaries or dramatizations. This influence can be very subtle indeed, even unintentional. As the example of the movie about rape aptly illustrates, even when communicators are not making a direct attempt to sell us something, they can succeed in influencing the way we look at the world and the way we respond to important events in our lives.

Let's look at something supposedly objective—like the news. Are the newscasters *trying* to sell us anything? Probably not. But those who produce television news can exert a powerful influence on our opinions simply by determining which events are given exposure— and how much exposure they are given. For example, near the end of his presidency, George Bush sent U.S. troops into Somalia because thousands of people were suffering the ravages of famine while roving bands of armed thugs were roaming the streets and countryside, effectively preventing the distribution of food to the starving masses. In the summer of 1993, Bill Clinton, the newly elected president, upped the ante by sending in additional armed personnel including a division of crack troops to try to disarm the militiamen. Several astute political analysts including the redoubtable Cokey Roberts,[4] while not questioning the humanitarian motives of our presidents, wondered why we were helping in Somalia and not in several other places, like Sudan, where similar tragedies were occurring. Ms. Roberts's conclusion: There were a great many powerful pictures of starving Somalians (but not of starving Sudanese) being aired on American television, leading to massive public support for such a military intervention.

Let us take one additional graphic example. A few years ago, a motorist named Rodney King was stopped for reckless driving. In the course of the arrest, he was savagely beaten by officers of the Los Angeles Police Department. By a fluke of luck, a resident of the neighborhood recorded the event on videotape; during the next several weeks, the tape was shown over and over again on TV screens across the nation. Subsequently, in the spring of 1992, when a jury found the police officers innocent of any wrongdoing, the inner city of Los Angeles erupted in the worst riot in U.S. history. By the time peace was restored, forty-four people had been killed, some two thousand were seriously injured, entire city blocks in south-central Los Angeles were in flames—resulting in over a billion dollars in property damage. Needless to say, there were a great many underlying causes of the riot. But certainly one of the triggers of the riot was the fact that people had seen that beating a great many times and were therefore in a position to be outraged by the verdict.

Given the power of TV newscasts, it is reasonable to ask what factors determine which news items are selected for television newscasts. The answer is not a simple one, but one major factor has to do with the *entertainment* value of the news item. Indeed, it has been said by no less an expert than the director of the British Broadcasting Corporation that television news is a form of *entertainment.* A study of why people watch the news agrees, concluding that most viewers want to be amused and diverted, and being informed is only a secondary motive for watching.[5] Accordingly, when those in charge of news programing make decisions about which news events to cover and which fraction of the miles of daily videotape to present to the public, they make their decisions, at least in part, on the basis of the entertainment value of their material. Film footage of a flooded metropolis has much more entertainment value than footage devoted to a dam built to prevent such a flooding: It is simply not very exciting to see a dam holding back a flood. And yet, the dam may be more important news. Just as such action events as football games are more entertaining on television than such quiet events as chess matches, so it is more likely that riots, bombings, earthquakes, massacres, and other violent acts will get more airtime than stories about people helping each other or people working to prevent violence. Thus, news telecasts tend to focus on the violent behavior of individuals—terrorists, protesters, strikers, or police—because action makes for more exciting viewing than does a portrayal of people behaving in a peaceful, orderly manner. Such coverage does not present a balanced picture of what is happening in the nation, not because the people who run the news media are evil and trying to manipulate us but simply because they are trying to entertain us. And, in trying to entertain us, they may unwittingly influence us to believe people behave far more violently now than ever before. This may cause us to be unhappy and even depressed about the temper of the times or the state of the nation. Ultimately, it might affect our vote, our desire to visit major urban centers, our attitudes about other nations, and so on. As we shall see, it may actually *cause* people to behave violently.

Such biased coverage was dramatically illustrated by the manner in which the media handled the nonriot that occurred in Austin, Texas, during the first week in May 1970. The background of the story was a familiar one on college campuses during the war in Southeast Asia. Tensions were running high between University of Texas students and local police following a confrontation at an impromptu student demonstration against the invasion of Cambodia by U.S. troops. During the demonstration, some six thousand students marched on the state capitol, broke a few windows, and skirmished with police; the students were teargassed, and several police officers and students were injured. But this was a mere preface—a minor event compared to what seemed to be coming. A few days later, students at the University of Texas were outraged at the wanton slaying of four students at Kent State University by members of the Ohio National Guard. To protest this event, the Texas students planned a gigantic march into downtown Austin—twenty thousand students were expected to turn out.

The Austin City Council, fearing trouble, refused to issue a parade permit. In frustration and anger, the students decided to march anyway; their leaders opted to confine the march to the sidewalks, where, technically, it would not be illegal. Rumors spread that hundreds of armed rednecks and hooligans were descending on Austin from all over the state with the intention of assaulting the students. Other rumors abounded to the effect that state troopers and Texas Rangers (not known for their friendliness to students) had been called in and were determined to take strong and violent action against anyone disobeying the law by straying or falling off the sidewalk. In retrospect, it appears these rumors were almost certainly untrue, but the important point is that they were widely believed. Because the probability of keeping a crowd of twenty thousand people from pushing itself off the sidewalk was remote, the situation seemed certain to be a prelude to extreme violence. Sniffing an exciting story, news teams affiliated with the major television networks were alerted. As it turned out, however, the explosive situation was defused at the eleventh hour: A team of university psychologists, law professors, and law students succeeded, at the last moment, in convincing a federal judge to issue a temporary restraining order to prevent the city from enforcing the antiparade ordinance. Moreover, it quickly became known that the testimony of several members of the police force, in favor of allowing the students to march, was instrumental in the judge's decision. This event—especially because of the role played by the police—resulted not only in the total absence of violence but in a genuine explosion of goodwill and solidarity among various diverse elements of the community. Twenty thousand students did march, but they marched in a spirit of harmony. Some of them offered cold drinks to the police officers who were diverting traffic away from the parade route; students and police exchanged friendly greetings, shook hands warmly, and so on. Interestingly enough, the national television networks completely ignored this encouraging turn of events. Because most of us were aware that teams of nationally prominent reporters from a variety of news media had descended on the city during the week, the lack of coverage seemed puzzling indeed. An unsettling explanation was provided by Phillip Mann and Ira Iscoe, who stated: "Since there was no violence, news media teams left town and there was no national publicity, a commentary whose implications are by now sadly self-evident."[6]

It is interesting to note that, in the same city thirteen years later, a great deal of coverage was given to an event of higher drama but of far less importance. On February 19, 1983, some fifty members of the Ku Klux Klan staged a march to the capitol building in Austin. They were greeted by about one thousand hecklers. Some rocks and bottles were thrown, and a few people received minor cuts and bruises. The skirmish was featured in network television news reports, and major stories as well as photographs appeared in newspapers from coast to coast.

Similarly, in October 1982, when seven people in the Chicago area died after taking Tylenol headache capsules laced with cyanide, the tragedy was widely publicized by the national news media. Indeed, for several days it was difficult to turn on the television, the radio, or pick up a newspaper without learning about the Tylenol poisonings. Of course, it was both tragic and bizarre—and therefore *very good* copy. The effects of this prominent coverage were immediate: Similar poisonings were reported in cities across the country, involving contaminations of mouthwash, eyedrops, nasal spray, soda pop, even hot dogs. Dramatically billed as "copycat poisonings," these poisonings, in turn, received widespread media attention. The public reaction took on all the properties of a spiral: Many people panicked, seeking medical aid for burns and poisonings when they suffered from no more than common sore throats and stomachaches. False alarms outnumbered actual cases of product tampering by seven to one.[7] Because these events occurred just prior to Halloween, worried officials in scores of communities banned trick-or-treating, fearing that many individuals might mimic the murders by contaminating children's candy.

The initial Chicago poisonings were almost certainly the work of one person. Subsequent events were caused by the publicity given to the Chicago poisonings. But the belief was spread that the wave of poisoning constituted "an epidemic without a cure," in the words of one news service,[8] and was itself the symptom of a "sick" society, a country going "crazy." Many newspapers found themselves in the ironic position of first sensationalizing the poisoning incidents and then sensationalizing the subsequent critical comments of media experts discussing the disastrous consequences of such publicity.

More recently, in March 1986, four teenagers in New Jersey made a suicide pact and then carried out their plan. Within a week of this multiple suicide, two teenagers in the Midwest were found dead under similar circumstances. Media reports no doubt spotlighted the confusion and grief surrounding teenage suicide. But is it possible that the media's coverage of these tragedies actually inspired copycat suicides? According to sociologist David Phillips, the answer is a qualified "yes."

Phillips and his colleagues studied suicide rates among teenagers following network television news or feature stories about suicide. Their research tracked fluctuations in teenage suicides by comparing suicide rates before the stories with rates after the stories. Within a week of the broadcasts, the increase in teenage suicides was far greater than could be explained by chance alone. Furthermore, the more coverage devoted by major television networks to suicide, the greater the subsequent increase in suicides among teenagers. The increases held even when the researchers took other possible causes into account. Thus, the most likely explanation for the increase in teenage suicides following media publicity is that such publicity actually triggers subsequent copycat suicides.[9]

Copycat suicides are not something peculiar to teenagers. In another study on the effects of highly publicized suicides, Phillips chose to examine fatal car crashes.[10] Some people, trying to save family members from the trauma of a suicide, will choose to kill themselves in car crashes that may look like accidents. These suicides should show up on official records as single-car one-passenger fatal accidents. Phillips reasoned that after a publicized suicide, there should be a dramatic increase in these types of accidents, and that the victims should be similar in some respect to the publicized suicide victim. This is exactly what he found after examining highway-patrol records both before and after highly publicized suicides. There were no changes in multiple-car accidents or single-car accidents with passengers, and the victims in these accidents did not resemble the publicized suicide victims. There was, however, an increase in "suicide-type" accidents, and the victims' ages were highly correlated with the age of the publicized suicide victim. Again, the most likely explanation for these findings is that the publicity of one suicide incited others to take their own lives.

The Tylenol poisonings and copycat suicides were newsworthy. I am not suggesting that the media created these events or that they should not have been reported. Rather, I am underlining the obvious fact that selective emphasis puts the media in the position of determining subsequent events —not simply reporting them.

As I stated earlier, this form of influence is probably unintentional; the news media are not *trying* to foster violence or create the illusion that most people are cruel. But the pervasiveness of electronic media cannot be overstated. In fact, sometimes the role of the media in reporting an event becomes more newsworthy than the event itself. For example, let's look at the Beirut hostage crisis of 1985, in which some forty innocent U.S. passengers on a TWA jet were held captive by Shiite terrorists. Television cameras offered viewers back home around-the-clock coverage of all aspects of the crisis—important and trivial alike. There were press conferences held by the terrorists, press conferences held by the hostages, intimate shots of anguished families, demands, counterdemands, pistol wavings, outrageous statements, luncheon menus, and so on. . . . The television camera crews did everything but follow the hostages into the restrooms!

At one point, it was suggested that the electronic media might be prolonging the ordeal by giving so much free publicity to the Shiite cause. So what did the television networks do? They televised a series of panel discussions by learned pundits about the role of the media in such a situation. The message became the media itself. In its endlessness, it reminded me of a brand of table salt, popular when I was a kid; on the box was a picture of a little girl holding up a box of the table salt on which there was a picture of a little girl holding up a box of the table salt on which there was a picture of a little girl. . . .

Let's turn from these subtle forms of media influence and take a look at a more conscious, direct attempt to persuade people by the judicious selection of material to be presented in the media. Imagine the following hypothetical situation: Two men are running for the Senate. One of the candidates has far less money to spend on his campaign than the other. Accordingly, in order to get maximum free exposure, he consents to numerous interviews and appears frequently at news conferences and on panel-type programs on television. The interviewers on these occasions are seasoned reporters who are not always sympathetic to the candidate. Frequently, they ask him difficult questions—occasionally, they ask him questions that are downright hostile. The candidate finds himself forever on the defensive. Sometimes, the camera catches him at an unflattering angle or in the act of scratching his nose, yawning, or fidgeting. While viewing at home, his mother is surprised at the bags under his eyes and at how tired and old he looks. Sometimes, when faced with a tough or unexpected question, he has difficulty finding the right response; he hems and haws and sounds inarticulate.

His opponent with the well-stocked campaign chest does not need to appear in these kinds of forums. Instead, he spends vast amounts of money videotaping spot commercials. Because he pays the camera crew and the director, his countenance is captured only from the most flattering angles. His personal makeup person works extra hard to cover the bags under his eyes and to make him appear young and dynamic. His mother, watching him at home, never saw him looking so well. The interviewer asks him questions prepared and rehearsed in advance, so that his answers are reasonable, concise, and articulate. If the candidate does happen to stumble over a word or to draw a blank, the cameras are stopped and the scene is shot over and over again until it is letter-perfect.

The situation outlined above is no nightmarish projection into the future. As a matter of fact, it closely approximates what occurred, on a much more important and dramatic scale, during the 1968 *presidential* election. In an extraordinary behind-the-scenes account of Richard Nixon's campaign, journalist Joe McGinness reported on the adeptness with which Nixon's advisors controlled the image of the candidate that was projected to the American people. In reporting these events, McGinness suggests television may be a powerful means of seducing voters to vote for *images* of candidates rather than the candidates themselves. Or, as one Nixon staffer put it: "This is the beginning of a whole new concept. . . . This is the way they'll be elected forevermore. The next guys up will have to be performers."[11] This proved to be prescient indeed—for in 1980, a seasoned movie and television personality was swept into office and was reelected by a landslide in 1984. Moreover, he managed to retain his *personal* popularity, despite the fact that public opinion polls indicated most Americans felt he was not doing a good job.

Back to Nixon. His staffer was referring specifically to a television program that was arranged to look as though candidate Nixon was spontaneously answering questions phoned in by voters. In reality, he was answering questions prepared by his staff and carefully rehearsed. When a voter asked a question on the telephone, Nixon's staff simply reworded it in the form of the prepared question, attributed the question to the voter, and allowed candidate Nixon to recite his prepared answer.

When McGinness's book made its appearance, many people were shocked and appalled at what they considered to be unethical and dishonest behavior. On the other hand, the overwhelming majority of voters either did not care or thought Nixon's deceptiveness was merely an indication that he was a clever, shrewd politician. Richard Nixon's popularity remained high throughout his first term in office, and in 1972 he was reelected in one of the most lopsided landslides in our nation's history, despite the fact that, at the time, it was known that a group of individuals financed by the Committee to Re-elect the President had been caught breaking into the offices of the Democratic National Committee in a building called Watergate.

Nixon's large margin of victory could be interpreted as indicating that such deceptive programing was effective. On the other hand, one astute observer, John Kenneth Galbraith, has commented that Nixon may have won *in spite of* these devices. Unfortunately, there is no way to assess how well this strategy actually worked in these campaigns. No one studied its effectiveness at the time of these elections. What we *can* do is look at this and other issues in a more general way. First, let us look at the broad issue of persuasion through the mass media. Subsequently, we will look at specific techniques of persuasion.

Effectiveness of Media Appeals

The broad question is this: How credible and effective are obvious attempts to package and sell products (toothpaste, aspirin, presidential candidates) through the mass media? The prima facie evidence suggests that they are extremely effective: Why else would corporations spend hundreds of millions of dollars a year trumpeting their products? Moreover, as parents, most of us have seen our children being seduced by toy commercials that artfully depict the most drab toys in an irresistible way. Similarly, a child watching cartoons on any Saturday morning is deluged by fast-paced ads for cereal, carryout food, and candy. The aim is to get kids to demand that their parents buy them the products they have seen in the commercials, and it seems to work. Over 90 percent of preschool-age children asked for toys or food they saw advertised on television, according to a survey of their mothers.[12] In fact, almost two-thirds of the mothers reported hearing their children sing commercial jingles they learned from television, most by the age of *three*.

Most children do catch on after a time; I've seen my own children, after several disappointments, develop a healthy skepticism (alas, even a certain degree of cynicism) about the truthfulness of these commercials. Indeed, a survey[13] found that only 12 percent of sixth graders believed television commercials told the truth all or most of the time; by the tenth grade, only 4 percent felt they were truthful even most of the time. This kind of skepticism is common among adults as well. A public opinion poll showed that the overwhelming majority of the adult respondents believed television commercials contain untruthful arguments. Moreover, the results indicate that the more educated the person, the more skeptical, and that people who are skeptical believe their skepticism makes them immune to persuasion. This might lead us to conclude that the mere fact of knowing a communicator is biased serves to protect us from being influenced by the message. This is not true. Simply because we *think* we are immune to persuasion does not necessarily mean we *are* immune to persuasion. In the case of many consumer products, the public will tend to buy a specific brand for no other reason than the fact that it is heavily advertised.

Let's look at the headache remedy business. Daryl Bem,[14] a social psychologist, provides us with an interesting analysis of our susceptibility to television commercials even when we know they are biased. According to Bem, a well-known brand of aspirin (which we will call "Brand A") advertises itself as 100 percent pure aspirin; the commercial goes on to say government tests have shown that no other pain remedy is stronger or more effective than Brand A. What the maker didn't bother to mention is that the government test actually showed no brand was any weaker or less effective than any of the others. In other words, all tested brands were equal—except in price, that is. For the privilege of gulping down Brand A, consumers must pay approximately three times the price of an equally effective but unadvertised brand. Or perhaps you prefer an aspirin proclaiming it is "unsurpassed in speed—no other brand works faster," buffered so "none is gentler to your stomach." The same government test showed that this buffered brand works no faster than regular aspirin, nor is there any difference between the two in the frequency of stomach upset. This well-known brand sells briskly at five times the price of equally effective products with less familiar brand names.

Another product proclaims it uses the ingredient "that doctors recommend." By reading the label, we discover the "magic" ingredient to be good old, inexpensive aspirin. Several pharmaceutical companies also market "extra strength" varieties of "arthritic pain" formulations. You will pay a premium price for these products, but are they worth it? Actually, their extra strength comes from extra aspirin (or acetaminophen, an aspirin substitute), along with a dose of caffeine. Taking additional aspirin would be less expensive, but it sounds great in the ads: "Not one, but a combination of medically proven ingredients in an extra-strength formula."

Such blatant attempts at mass persuasion seem pitifully obvious. Yet the cash registers ring, and tremendous numbers of consumers apparently set aside their skepticism even though they know the message is an obvious attempt to sell a product. Of course, there may be a basic difference between susceptibility to aspirin commercials and susceptibility to commercials for presidential candidates. When we are dealing with identical or very similar products, mere familiarity may make a huge difference. Robert Zajonc[15] has shown that, all other things being equal, the more familiar an item is, the more attractive it is. Suppose I walk into a grocery store looking for a laundry detergent. I go to the detergent section and I am staggered by the wide array of brand names. Because it doesn't matter too much to me which one I buy, I may simply reach for the most familiar one— and chances are it is familiar because I've heard and seen the name on television commercials over and over again. If this is the case, then sudden increases in television exposure should produce dramatic changes in familiarity and, perhaps, in sales.

Let's look at the data. Several years ago, the Northwest Mutual Life Insurance Company conducted a nationwide poll to find out how well the public recognized its name. It came out thirty-fourth among insurance companies. Two weeks later the company repeated the poll. This time it came out third in name familiarity. What caused this amazing leap from obscurity to fame? Two weeks and $1 million worth of advertising on television.

Of course familiarity does not necessarily mean sales, but the two are frequently linked. Thus, A & W root beer boosted its share of the market from 15 percent to 50 percent after six months of television advertising. By switching the channel on a Saturday morning, a child can watch "Ronald McDonald" in up to a dozen colorful, fast-paced commercials *each hour;* perhaps this is one reason why the chain sells so many billions of hamburgers.

But is voting for a presidential candidate the same kind of decision as choosing a soft drink or a breakfast cereal? The answer is a qualified "yes." After the 1972 U.S. congressional primaries, Joseph Grush and his colleagues[16] examined the amount of money candidates spent on political advertising for the elections and found that a large majority of races were won by big spenders. Four years later,[17] Grush looked at campaign expenditures in the 1976 Democratic presidential primaries and again discovered that candidates who spent the most money typically received the most votes. In both studies, however, those who tended to gain the most from media exposure were candidates who were relatively unknown to the voters prior to their campaigns. As we saw earlier, the more familiar an item, the greater its appeal. Thus, unfamiliar political candidates in primary races may benefit from the effects of mere exposure. But, in presidential elections in which candidates are highly familiar, massive media "blitzes" tend to be less influential.

There are, however, important exceptions to these findings. Recent history suggests that intensive media coverage can, in fact, have a powerful impact on election results when the campaign centers on a highly charged issue that arouses strong emotions in voters. To illustrate, let's consider the 1988 presidential campaign between George Bush and Michael Dukakis, former governor of Massachusetts. In the summer of 1988, Bush trailed far behind Dukakis in the race for the presidency. Many observers were convinced that Dukakis's lead was insurmountable. Within a few short months, however, the lead had all but evaporated, and on election day, Bush won handily. A number of political analysts credit Willie Horton with playing a major role in this turnaround. Indeed, *Time Magazine* went so far as to refer to Willie Horton as "George Bush's most valuable player."[18]

But who was Willie Horton? He was not one of Bush's advisors, nor was he a major financial contributor to the Bush campaign. Indeed, the two men had never met. As some of you may recall, Willie Horton was a convicted felon who had been released from a Massachusetts prison, before the end of his term, as part of a furlough program. While on furlough, Horton escaped to Maryland; there, he raped a woman after wounding and binding her male companion. Michael Dukakis was governor of Massachusetts when Horton's furlough was granted. Claiming that Dukakis was soft on crime, Bush ran a series of television and print ads showing mug shots of a scowling Willie Horton and depicting criminals going in and out of prison through a revolving door. These ads struck a respondent chord in many Americans who have legitimate fears of street crime and who strongly suspect that the criminal justice system favors criminals at the expense of victims. Moreover, the fact that Willie Horton is black, and that his victims were white, was not lost on most viewers.[19]

How did Dukakis fight back? With an abundance of facts and figures: He pointed out that Massachusetts was only one of many states with furlough programs and that even the federal government (of which Bush was a member) furloughed inmates from its prisons. In addition, he noted, furlough programs were generally very effective. For example, in 1987, 53,000 inmates received over 200,000 furloughs and only a small percentage got into trouble.[20] Dukakis also pointed out that, typically, furloughs were granted to convicts who were near the end of their terms, and the furloughs are intended to orient them to the outside world. He insisted that the whole issue was a contrivance—that, if elected, George Bush had no intention of changing the furlough system.

Are you getting bored yet? So were the voters. If Michael Dukakis had a social psychologist on his staff, he would have received better advice; as Anthony Pratkanis and I[21] have pointed out, when people are scared and angry, facts and figures, in and of themselves, are not very convincing. Facts and figures *can* be effective if they are tied to solutions to problems the voters are deeply concerned about.

In the 1992 presidential election, candidate Bill Clinton (apparently having learned a lesson from the Dukakis campaign), kept the attention of the American people focused on one overriding issue—the sorry state of the economy—and did not allow himself to be sidetracked onto issues where there was no real difference between the candidates.[22]

Education or Propaganda?

Aspirin commercials are obvious attempts to sell something at a high price by intentionally misleading the audience. They can be considered propaganda. "Selling" a presidential candidate, however, is much more complicated. Thus, the devices used by Nixon's staff to display him in a favorable manner could conceivably be considered as education—an attempt to educate the public on the policies and virtues of the candidate by allowing him to present his views as clearly, efficiently, and articulately as possible. What is the difference between propaganda and education? *The American Heritage Dictionary of the English Language* defines *propaganda* as "the systematic propagation of a given doctrine" and *education* as "the act of imparting knowledge or skill." Again, we could all agree that aspirin ads are propaganda designed to promote the sale of certain brands. But what about U.S. television, which still tends to depict women, old people, and minorities in stereotyped roles? Or, more subtly, what about the vast majority of high-school textbooks on U.S. history that virtually ignore the contributions of blacks and other minorities to the U.S. scene? Is this merely imparting knowledge?

The problem of distinguishing between education and propaganda can be more subtle still. Let us look at arithmetic as taught in the public schools. What could be more educational? By that I mean, what could be more pure, objective, factual, untainted by doctrine? Watch out. Do you remember the examples used in your elementary-school arithmetic text? Most of the examples dealt with buying, selling, renting, working for wages, and computing interest. As Zimbardo, Ebbesen, and Maslach[23] point out, these examples do more than simply reflect the capitalistic system in which the education is occurring: They systematically endorse the system, legitimize it, and, by implication, suggest it is the natural and normal way. As a way of illustrating multiplication and percentages, the textbook might have Mr. Jones borrowing $8,000 at 14 percent interest from a bank in order to purchase a new car. Would this example be used in a society that felt it was sinful to charge interest, as early Christian societies believed? Would this example be used in a society that believed people shouldn't seek possessions they can't afford? I am not suggesting it is wrong or evil to use these kinds of illustrations in arithmetic books; I am merely pointing out that they are a form of propaganda and it might be useful to recognize them as such.

In practice, whether a person regards a particular course of instruction as educational or propagandistic depends, to a large extent, on his or her values. Reflect, for a moment, on a film about drug abuse my children were required to see in their high school. At one point, the film mentioned that many hard-core narcotics addicts began by sampling marijuana. I'm certain most school officials would probably regard the presentation of this piece of factual knowledge as a case of "imparting knowledge," and most marijuana users would probably regard it as "the systematic propagation of a given doctrine"—that is, the implication that marijuana leads to the use of addictive drugs. By the same token, consider the topic of sex education in the schools as viewed by a member of the Moral Majority, on the one hand, or by the editor of *Playboy* magazine, on the other hand. This is not to say all communications are drastically slanted and one-sided. Rather, when we are dealing with an emotionally charged issue about which people's opinions differ greatly, it is probably impossible to construct a communication that people on both sides of the issue would agree was fair and impartial.

I will present a more detailed discussion of communication as viewed through "the eye of the beholder" in the next chapter. For now, it is important to note that, whether we call it propaganda or education, persuasion is a reality. It won't go away if we ignore it. We should therefore attempt to understand it by analyzing the experimental literature on persuasion.

Two Major Routes to Persuasion

When we are in contact with a persuasive argument, do we think deeply about it—or do we accept it without much thought? This question underlies much of our understanding of persuasion. According to the theorizing of Richard Petty and John Cacioppo,[24] we are inclined to think deeply about it if the issue is one that is relevant and important to us. In these circumstances we will be inclined to give the argument careful scrutiny. But sometimes, even if the issue is important, we might be distracted or busy—or if the communication is slickly presented, we will not give it close scrutiny.

Petty & Cacioppo call their theory *the elaboration likelihood model* because it deals with the circumstances under which it is likely that people will think about or *elaborate* on the basic message they are presented with. Petty & Cacioppo's theory holds that there are two major routes to persuasion: the *central* route and the *peripheral* route. The central route relies on solid arguments based on relevant facts and figures that get people to think about the issues. The peripheral route, rather than attempting to engage a person's thinking, provides cues that stimulate acceptance of the argument without much thinking. For example, in a presidential election debate, if a candidate presented a serious discussion of the economy including a carefully crafted plan for the reduction of unemployment, this would be taking the central route because, whether or not people agree with the plan, it gets people thinking about it. On the other hand, the Willie Horton ad (mentioned above), a candidate's visit to a flag factory or his cruising down a polluted river—while the TV cameras are rolling—would be taking the peripheral route. It should be clear that we are not talking about the importance of the issues. That is, we are certainly not suggesting that crime, patriotism, or pollution are not important issues; we *are* saying that the manner in which any issue is presented can either stimulate thinking or trigger immediate agreement—depending on the route that the communicator is taking.

A good way to understand the difference between the central route and the peripheral route is by comparing computer ads with either soft drink or cigarette ads in the print media. For the most part, computer ads describe the specifics of what the computer can do, the ease of operation, and the price. They rarely are endorsed by rock stars or other cultural icons. This is taking the central route. The manufacturers probably believe that people who are in the market for a computer are more comfortable with the central route—that they want to scrutinize and elaborate on the message. On the other hand, soft drink ads rest heavily on endorsement by the "now" people—like

Madonna, Michael Jordan, and Ray Charles ("You got the right one, baby. Uh huh."); cigarette ads attempt to associate their product with the great outdoors, with springtime, or with "manliness"—as in the Marlboro man commercial. Both are taking the peripheral route.

Let us look at the issue in a bit more detail. What are the key factors that can increase the effectiveness of a communication? Basically, there are three classes of variables that are important: (1) the source of the communication (who says it), (2) the nature of the communication (how he or she says it), and (3) characteristics of the audience (to whom he or she says it). Put most simply: *Who* says *what* to *whom?* We will look at each of these separately.

The Source of the Communication

Credibility. Picture the following scene: Your doorbell rings, and when you answer it, you find a middle-aged man in a rather loud, checkered sports jacket. His tie is loose, his collar is frayed, his pants need ironing, he needs a shave, and his eyes keep looking off to the side and over your head as he talks to you. He is carrying a small can in his hand with a slot on the top, and he's trying to convince you to contribute a few dollars to a charitable organization you've never heard of. Although his actual pitch sounds fairly reasonable, what are the possibilities of his succeeding in prying you loose from your money?

Now let's turn back the clock a few minutes: You open your door in response to the ringing of the doorbell, and standing there is a middle-aged man in a conservative business suit, well tailored and well pressed. He looks you squarely in the eye, introduces himself as a vice president of the City National Bank, and asks you if you would contribute a few dollars to a charitable organization (that you've never heard of), using exactly the same words as the fellow in the loud, checkered jacket. Would you be more likely to contribute some money?

I was struck by this phenomenon several years ago when I saw the poet Allen Ginsberg on one of the late-night talk shows. Ginsberg was among the most popular of the poets of the so-called beat generation; his poem "Howl" had shocked and stimulated the literary establishment in the 1950s. On the talk show, Ginsberg was at it again: Having just finished boasting about his homosexuality, he was talking about the generation gap. The camera panned in. He was fat, bearded, and looked a trifle wild-eyed (was he stoned?); long hair grew in unruly patches from the sides of his otherwise bald head; he was wearing a tie-dyed T-shirt with a hole in it, and a few strands of beads. Although he was talking earnestly—and, in my opinion, very sensibly—about the problems of the young, the studio audience was laughing. They seemed to be treating him like a clown. It dawned on me that, in all probability, the vast majority of the people at home, lying in bed watching the poet from between their feet, could not possibly take him seriously—no matter how sensible his message, and no matter how earnestly he delivered it. His appearance and his reputation were, in all probability, overdetermining the audience's reaction. The scientist in me longed to substitute the conservative-looking banker in the neatly pressed business suit for the wild-eyed poet and have him move his lips while Ginsberg said the same words off camera. My guess is that, under these circumstances, Ginsberg's message would have been well received.

No need. Similar experiments have already been done. Indeed, speculations about the effects of prestige on persuasion are ancient. More than three hundred years before Christ, Aristotle, the world's first published social psychologist, wrote:

> We believe good men more fully and more readily than others: this is true generally whatever the question is, and absolutely true where exact certainty is impossible and opinions are divided. . . . It is not true, as some writers assume in their treatises on rhetoric, that the personal goodness revealed by the speaker contributes nothing to his power of persuasion; on the contrary, his character may almost be called the most effective means of persuasion he possesses.[25]

It required some 2,300 years for Aristotle's observation to be put to a rigorous scientific test. This was accomplished by Carl Hovland and Walter Weiss.[26] What these investigators did was very simple: They presented large numbers of people with a communication that argued a particular point of view—for example, that building atomic-powered submarines was a feasible undertaking (this experiment was performed in 1951, when harnessing atomic energy for such purposes was merely a dream). Some of the people were informed that the argument was made by a person possessing a great deal of credibility; for others, the same argument was attributed to a source with low credibility. Specifically, the argument that atomic-powered submarines could be built in the near future was attributed to J. Robert Oppenheimer, a nationally known and highly respected atomic physicist, or to *Pravda,* the official newspaper of the Communist Party in the Soviet Union—a publication not famous in the United States for its objectivity and truthfulness. Before reading the arguments, the members of the audience were asked to fill out some rating scales that revealed their opinions on the topic. They then read the communication. A large percentage of those people who believed the communication came from J. Robert Oppenheimer changed their opinions—they then believed more strongly in the feasibility of atomic submarines. Very few of those who read the identical communication attributed to *Pravda* shifted their opinions in the direction of the communication.

This same phenomenon has received repeated confirmations by several different investigators using a wide variety of topics and attributing the communications to a wide variety of communicators. Careful experiments have shown that a judge of the juvenile court is better than most people at swaying opinion about juvenile delinquency, that a famous poet and critic can sway opinion about the merits of a poem, and that a medical journal can sway opinion about whether or not antihistamines should be dispensed without a prescription. What do the physicist, the judge, the poet, and the medical journal have that *Pravda* doesn't have? That is, what is the difference that makes the difference in their effectiveness? Aristotle said we believe "good men," by which he meant people of high moral caliber. Hovland and Weiss use the term *credible,* which removes the moral connotations present in the Aristotelian definition. Oppenheimer, a juvenile court judge, and the poet are all credible—that is, they are not necessarily "good," but they are both *expert* and *trustworthy.* It makes sense to allow yourself to be influenced by communicators who are trustworthy and who know what they are talking about. It makes sense for people to be influenced by J. Robert Oppenheimer when he is voicing an opinion about atomic power, and it makes sense for people to be influenced by someone like T. S. Eliot when he is talking about poetry. These are expert, trustworthy people.

But not all people are equally influenced by the same communicator. Indeed, the same communicator may be regarded by some members as possessing high credibility and by others as possessing low credibility. Moreover, certain peripheral attributes of the communicator may loom large for some members of the audience; such attributes can serve to make a given communicator either remarkably effective or remarkably ineffective.

This phenomenon was forcefully demonstrated in an experiment I performed in collaboration with Burton Golden,[27] in which we presented sixth graders with a speech extolling the usefulness and importance of arithmetic. The communicator was introduced either as a prizewinning engineer from a prestigious university or as someone who washed dishes for a living. As one might expect, the engineer was far more effective at influencing the youngsters' opinions than the dishwasher. This finding is consistent with previous research; in and of itself, it is obvious and not very interesting. But, in addition, we varied the race of the communicator: In some of the trials the communicator was white, and in others, black. Several weeks prior to the experiment, the children had filled out a questionnaire designed to measure the degree of their prejudice against black people. The results were striking: Among those children who were most prejudiced against blacks, the black engineer was *less* influential than the white engineer, although both delivered the same speech. Moreover, among those children who were the least prejudiced against blacks, the black engineer was *more* influential than the white engineer. It seems unreasonable that such a peripheral attribute as skin color would affect a person's credibility. It might be argued that, in a purely rational world, a prestigious engineer should be able to influence sixth graders about the importance of arithmetic regardless of the color of his or her skin, but apparently this is not a purely rational world. Depending upon listeners' attitudes toward blacks, they were either *more* influenced or *less* influenced by a black communicator than an otherwise identical white communicator.

This kind of behavior is not very adaptive. If the quality of your life depended on the extent to which you were to allow a communication about arithmetic to influence your opinion, the expertise and trustworthiness of the communicator would seem to be the most reasonable factors to heed. To the extent other factors (such as skin color) decrease or increase your susceptibility to persuasion on an issue irrelevant to such factors, you are behaving in a maladaptive manner. But advertisers bank on this maladaptive behavior and often count on irrelevant factors to increase a spokesperson's credibility. For example, since television was in its infancy, actors who have played the role of doctors in TV dramas seem to show up regularly on commercials peddling aspirin, cold medicine, and advising us of the ill effects of caffeinated coffee. In the old days, Parnell Roberts, who played the lead character in "Trapper John, M.D.," and Robert Young, who played the wise and kindly physician in "Marcus Welby, M.D.," were hired to persuade us about what kinds of health products to buy. More recently, one ad featured an actor who confessed: "I'm not a doctor, but I play one on TV."

Similarly, for some twenty years, Karl Malden starred in a series of commercials in which Americans traveling in a foreign country either lose all their money or have it stolen. The tourists are distraught, humiliated, traumatized, panicky. At the end of the commercial Karl Malden appears and, in an authoritative voice, warns us not to carry money while traveling—and recommends "American Express Traveler's Cheques—don't leave home without 'em." What makes Karl Malden an expert on vacation financing? Nothing, but he is perceived as somewhat of an expert on *crime.* For several television seasons, Malden portrayed Lt. Mike Stone in "The Streets of San Francisco," a popular detective show. Though Mr. Roberts, Mr. Young, and Mr. Malden probably do not know a great deal more about health, crime, traveler's checks, or even aspirin than the average viewer, they almost certainly gained a false credibility and trust merely because they were identified with their particular roles. This is a clear example of the peripheral route to persuasion.

Not only are such peripheral aspects of the communicator often emphasized in commercials, but frequently they are the *only* aspects of the communicator the viewer is able to perceive. Who is an expert on the topic of razor blades or shaving cream? Well, perhaps a barber; maybe a dermatologist or a cosmetologist. Who is it that tells us which blades or lather we should use? Most often it is a professional football player. Throughout the 1950s and 1960s, one of the most persistent peddlers of breakfast food was former Olympic decathlon champion Bob Richards, who was probably far more effective at selling Wheaties than some learned professor of nutrition, no matter *how* expert he or she might have been. In the 1970s, Richards was replaced by another gold-medal decathlon champion, Bruce Jenner. How effective *are* these people? We cannot be sure—but, when Bruce Jenner was finally replaced in the 1980s, the Wheaties people again decided not to use a nutritionist and hired Mary Lou Retton, an Olympic gymnastics gold medalist. When the Minnesota Twins won the World Series in 1987, Wheaties issued a special box with a photograph of the entire team on the front. And there was no real surprise when Wheaties wrote a very large check to feature the amazing Michael Jordan on their box and to induce him to utter those famous words, "You better eat your Wheaties," to millions of television fans in the 1990s. Apparently, whoever is in charge of selling Wheaties to the masses favors athletes as communicators.

With the likes of Michael Jordan and Joe Montana—as well as, of course, Bo Jackson and the "Bo Knows" campaign—the athletic shoe business also makes good use of the famous athlete to sell its products. On the surface, this may seem to make sense; these guys make more money in their sneakers than most of us will ever make in our wing tips or heels. Perhaps they do know a thing or two about cleats, high-tops, and cross-trainers. But is this really the case, or is athletic ability simply another peripheral factor that increases how credible the communicator seems? One specific ad may shed some light on this question. The ad shows a man, always from the waist up, playing racketball, basketball, and several other sports. The ad ends with the camera focusing on the man's face, the shoe logo is superimposed over him, and as the camera pulls back we see that the man is in a wheelchair and has no legs. If advertisers truly believed that viewers see athletes as shoe experts, this ad would never have been produced. No matter how good an athlete this man might be, there's no reason to think he knows much about athletic shoes. Clearly, the advertisers are convinced that athletes are effective spokespersons— regardless of their expertise regarding the particular product being sold.

Is this conviction justified? Will people be influenced by an ad just because a prominent sports personality is involved? Even if we admire the skill such athletes display on the playing field, can we really trust them to be telling us the truth about the products they endorse? After all, we all know that the sports star peddling shaving cream, beer, or breakfast cereal is getting paid handsomely for his or her time. My guess is that most people would be quick to say, "No. Maybe *other people* might be persuaded to run out and buy something because a sports figure tells them to, but *I* certainly wouldn't trust even my favorite player's advice on how to spend my hard-earned cash." But can people really predict their own behavior? Before answering, let's take a closer look at the factor of "trust."

Increasing Trustworthiness.   Clearly, trust is an important factor in determining whether or not a communicator will be effective. It may be that the crucial reason why the relatively more prejudiced sixth graders in the Aronson-Golden experiment were less influenced by the black engineer than by the white engineer was that they simply did not trust blacks. If this is true, then if we could offer the audience clear, independent evidence that a person is trustworthy, that person should be a very effective communicator.

How might communicators make themselves seem clearly trustworthy to us? One way is to argue against their own self-interest. If people have nothing to gain (and perhaps something to lose) by convincing us, we will trust them and they will be more effective. An illustration may be helpful. Suppose a habitual criminal recently convicted as a smuggler and peddler of heroin was delivering a communication on the abuses of the U.S. judicial system. Would he influence you? Probably not. Most people would probably regard him as unattractive and untrustworthy: He seems clearly outside of the Aristotelian definition of a "good man." But suppose he was arguing that criminal justice was too lenient—that criminals almost always beat the rap if they have a smart lawyer, and even if criminals are convicted, the sentences normally meted out are too soft. Would he influence you?

I'm certain he would; in fact, I performed this very experiment in collaboration with Elaine Walster and Darcy Abrahams,[28] and it confirmed our hypothesis. In the actual experiment, we presented our subjects with a newspaper clipping of an interview between a news reporter and Joe "The Shoulder" Napolitano, who was identified in the manner described above. In one experimental condition, Joe "The Shoulder" argued for stricter courts and more severe sentences. In another condition, he argued that courts should be more lenient and sentences less severe. We also ran a parallel set of conditions in which the same statements were attributed to a respected public official. When Joe "The Shoulder" argued for more lenient courts, he was totally ineffective; indeed, he actually caused the subjects' opinions to change slightly in the opposite direction. But when he was arguing for stricter, more powerful courts, he was extremely effective—as effective as the respected public official delivering the same argument. This study demonstrates that Aristotle was not completely correct—a communicator can be an unattractive, immoral person and still be effective, as long as it is clear the person has nothing to gain (and perhaps something to lose) by persuading us.

Why was Joe "The Shoulder" so effective in our experiment? Let's take a closer look. Most people would not be surprised to hear a known convict arguing in favor of a more lenient criminal justice system. Their knowledge of the criminal's background and self-interest would lead them to expect such a message. When they receive the opposite communication, however, these expectations are disconfirmed. To make sense of this contradiction, the members of the audience might conclude the convict had reformed, or they could entertain the notion that the criminal is under some kind of pressure to make the anticrime statements. In the absence of any evidence to substantiate these suppositions, however, another explanation becomes more reasonable: Maybe the truth of the issue is so compelling that, even though it apparently contradicts his background and self-interest, the spokesman sincerely believes in the position he espouses. Think back to the incident of the "nonriot" in Austin, and recall the controversy surrounding the enforcement of the antiparade ordinance. When the police, who were assumed to dislike protests and were expected to oppose the demonstration, testified in favor of permitting the parade, their testimony was very influential.

Further evidence for this phenomenon comes from a more recent experiment. Alice Eagly and her colleagues[29] presented students with a description of a dispute between business interests and environmental groups over a company polluting a river. The students then read a statement about the issue. In some conditions the spokesman was described as having a business background and was said to be speaking to a group of businessmen. In others, his background and audience were varied, thereby altering the subjects' expectations for his message. The results supported the reasoning above; when the message conflicted with their expectations, listeners perceived the communicator as being more sincere, and they were more persuaded by his statement. For example, it's hard to imagine a more convincing spokesperson for an antismoking campaign than someone whose fortune was made off the habits of millions of U.S. smokers. In fact, Patrick Reynolds, who inherited $2.5 million from the R. J. Reynolds

Tobacco Company founded by his grandfather, has taken a strong public stand against smoking and has recently gone so far as to urge victims of smoking-related illnesses to file lawsuits against tobacco companies![30]

Similarly, among the most effective opponents of the nuclear arms race in recent years have been several professionals who have taken stands that seemingly contradict their backgrounds. These communicators—for example, a respected nuclear physicist who cautions against the further development of nuclear technology, and a former naval commander who campaigns for a halt to military growth—have been perceived as highly credible precisely because of the discontinuity between their messages and the apparent interests of their professions. First of all, they are experts. Second, since they have nothing to gain (and perhaps collegial esteem to lose), it seems that only the compelling need for disarmament has led them to speak out. Not only do we tend to take more notice of unexpected events, but we also attribute more credibility to speakers who appear to resist the pressures of their colleagues and who take stands in opposition to their backgrounds.

The trustworthiness of a person can also be increased if the audience is absolutely certain the person is not *trying* to influence them. Suppose a stockbroker calls you up and gives you a hot tip on a particular stock. Will you buy? It's hard to be sure. On the one hand, the broker is probably an expert, and this might influence you to buy. On the other hand, the stockbroker has something to gain by giving you this tip (a commission), and this could lower her effectiveness. But suppose you happened to overhear her telling a friend a particular stock was about to rise. Because she was obviously not *trying* to influence you, you might be more readily influenced.

Indeed, a nonhypothetical brokerage firm, E. F. Hutton, incorporated this very scenario into its television commercials in an attempt to increase its prestige and trustworthiness. A typical commercial opened with a shot of two people engaged in private conversation in a noisy and crowded restaurant. When one person began to pass on some stock advice from E. F. Hutton, a sudden hush fell over the room and everyone—waiters, customers, even busboys—strained toward the speaker to better "overhear" the tip. "When E. F. Hutton talks," said the announcer, "people listen." The implication is clear: Everyone in the restaurant is getting in on advice that wasn't intended for them, and the information is all the more valuable as a result. When communicators are not *trying* to influence us, their potential to do so is increased.

This is exactly what was discovered in an experiment by Elaine Walster and Leon Festinger.[31] In this study, a conversation was staged between two graduate students in which one of them expressed his opinion on an issue. The situation was arranged so that an undergraduate subject was allowed to overhear this conversation. In one experimental condition, it was clear to the subject that the graduate students were aware of his presence in the next room; therefore, the subject knew anything being said could conceivably be directed at him with the intention of influencing his opinion. In the other condition, the situation was arranged so that the subject believed the graduate students were unaware of his presence in the next room. In this condition, the subject's opinion changed significantly more in the direction of the opinion expressed by the graduate students.

This phenomenon may explain the preponderance of "hidden camera" advertisements on television. A good example of such tactics is evident in the recent Folgers coffee campaign, where the Folgers folks visit five-star restaurants and secretly replace the house coffee with Folgers Crystals. Patrons, who are unaware that they are being filmed, are then asked about the quality of their cup of coffee. Of course, all those who are interviewed (or at least all those who wind up in the commercial) lavishly praise the coffee and seem astonished when told it's an instant coffee—something they could have made at home for pennies a cup. Obviously, these people are not coffee experts. So why are they such persuasive communicators? Because they aren't trying to be. If we are convinced a person has been caught unaware, we don't attribute a persuasive intent to the message. Believing the person is acting spontaneously, we are more persuaded by his or her testimony.

Attractiveness. Where do these findings leave our friend the football player holding up his can of shaving cream? Clearly he is *trying* to influence us—the shaving cream company is not paying him all that money *not* to sell shaving cream. Moreover, he seems to be operating in his own self-interest; when we take a good look at the situation, it's clear the only reason he's up there with the shaving cream is to make a buck. We expect him to recommend a certain brand, and we know he expects us to see the commercial. These factors should make him less trustworthy. But does that make him less effective?

Not necessarily. Although most of us might not *trust* football players or other sports stars, that does not necessarily mean we wouldn't buy the products they endorse. Another crucial factor determining the effectiveness of communicators is how attractive or likable they are—regardless of their overall expertise or trustworthiness. Some years ago, Judson Mills and I did a simple laboratory experiment demonstrating that a beautiful woman—simply because she was beautiful—could have a major impact on the opinions of an audience on a topic wholly irrelevant to her beauty, and furthermore, that her impact was greatest when she openly expressed a desire to influence the audience.[32] More recently, Alice Eagly and Shelly Chaiken carried out an experiment that not only replicated the finding that more likable communicators are more persuasive but went on to show that attractive sources are expected to support desirable positions.[33]

It appears we associate the attractiveness of the communicator with the desirability of the message. We seem to be influenced by people we like. Where our liking for a communicator is involved (rather than his or her expertise), we behave as though we were trying to please that source. Accordingly, the more that communicator wants to change our opinions, the more we change them—but *only about trivial issues.* That is, it is true football players can get us to use a particular shaving cream and beautiful women can get us to agree with them on an abstract topic, whether or not we are willing to admit it. At the same time, it is unlikely they could influence us to vote for their presidential candidate or to adopt their position on the morality of abortion.

To summarize this section, we might list these phenomena:

1. Our opinions are influenced by individuals who are both expert and trustworthy.

2. A communicator's trustworthiness (and effectiveness) can be increased if he or she argues a position apparently opposed to his or her self-interest.

3. A communicator's trustworthiness (and effectiveness) can be

increased if he or she does not seem to be trying to influence our opinion.

4. At least where trivial opinions and behaviors are concerned, if we like and can identify with a person, his or her opinions and behaviors will influence our own more than their content would ordinarily warrant.

5. Again, where trivial opinions and behaviors are concerned, if we like a person, we will tend to be influenced even if it is clear he or she is trying to influence us and stands to profit by doing so.

The Nature of the Communication

The manner in which a communication is stated plays an important role in determining its effectiveness. There are several ways in which communications can differ from one another. I have selected five I consider to be among the most important: (1) Is a communication more persuasive if it is designed to appeal to the audience's reasoning ability, or is it more persuasive if it is aimed at arousing the audience's emotions? (2) Are people more swayed by a communication if it is tied to a vivid personal experience or if it is bolstered by a great deal of clear and unimpeachable statistical evidence? (3) Should the communication present only one side of the argument, or should it also include an attempt to refute the opposing view? (4) If two sides are presented, as in a debate, does the order in which they are presented affect the relative impact of either side? (5) What is the relationship between the effectiveness of the communication and the discrepancy between the audience's original opinion and the opinion advocated by the communication?

Logical versus Emotional Appeals. Several years ago, I was living in a community that was about to vote on whether or not to fluoridate the water supply as a means of combating tooth decay. An information campaign that seemed quite logical and reasonable was launched by the proponents of fluoridation. It consisted largely of statements by noted dentists describing the benefits of fluorides and discussing the evidence on the reduction of tooth decay in areas with fluoridated water, as well as statements by physicians and other health authorities to the effect that fluoridation has no harmful effects. The opponents used an appeal much more emotional in flavor. For example, one leaflet consisted of a picture of a rather ugly rat, along with the inscription "Don't let them put rat poison in your drinking water." The referendum to fluoridate the water supply was soundly defeated. Of course, this incident doesn't prove conclusively that emotional appeals are superior, mainly because the incident was not a scientifically controlled study. We have no idea how the people would have voted on fluoridation if no publicity were circulated, nor do we know whether the antifluoridation circular reached more people, whether it was easier to read than the proponents' literature, and so forth. Although the actual research in this area is far from conclusive, there is some evidence favoring an appeal that is *primarily* emotional. In one early study, for example, George W. Hartmann[34] tried to measure the extent to which he could induce people to vote for a particular political candidate as a function of what kind of appeal he used. He demonstrated that individuals who received a *primarily* emotional message voted for the candidate endorsed by the message more often than did people who received a *primarily* logical message.

The word *primarily* is italicized for good reason—it defines the major problem with research in this area. Namely, there are no foolproof, mutually exclusive definitions of "emotional" and "rational." In the fluoridation illustration, for example, most people would probably agree that the antifluoridation pamphlet was designed to arouse fear; yet, it is not entirely illogical, because it is indeed true that the fluoride used in minute concentrations to prevent tooth decay is also used in massive concentrations as a rat poison. On the other side, to present the views of professional people is not entirely free from emotional appeal; it may be comforting (on an emotional level) to know that physicians and dentists endorse the use of fluorides.

Because, in practice, operational distinctions between "logical" and "emotional" are difficult to draw, some researchers have turned to an equally interesting and far more researchable problem: the problem of the effect of various levels of a specific emotion on opinion change. Suppose you wish to arouse fear in the hearts of your audience as a way of inducing opinion change. Would it be more effective to arouse just a little fear, or should you try to scare the hell out of them? For example, if your goal is to convince people to drive more carefully, would you be more effective if you showed them gory technicolor films of the broken and bloody bodies of the victims of highway accidents, or would you be more effective if you soft-pedaled your communication—showing crumpled fenders, discussing increased insurance rates due to careless driving, and pointing out the possibility that people who drive carelessly may have their driver's licenses suspended? Common sense argues on both sides of this street. On the one hand, it suggests that a good scare will motivate people to action; on the other hand, it argues that too much fear can be debilitating—that is, it might interfere with a person's ability to pay attention to the message, to comprehend it, and to act upon it. We've all believed, at one time or another, "it only happens to the other guy—it can't happen to me." Thus, people continue to drive at very high speeds and to insist on driving after they've had a few drinks, even though they should know better. Perhaps this is because the possible negative consequences of these actions are so great we try not to think about them. Thus, it has been argued that, if a communication arouses a great deal of fear, we tend *not* to pay close attention to it.

What does the evidence tell us? The overwhelming weight of experimental data suggests that, all other things being equal, the more frightened a person is by a communication, the more likely he or she is to take positive preventive action. The most prolific researchers in this area have been Howard Leventhal and his associates.[35] In one experiment, they tried to induce people to stop smoking and to take chest X rays. Some subjects were exposed to a low-fear treatment: They were simply presented with a recommendation to stop smoking and get their chests X-rayed. Others were subjected to moderate fear: They were shown a film depicting a young man whose chest X rays revealed he had lung cancer. The people subjected to the high-fear condition saw the same film the "moderate-fear" people saw—and, in addition, they were treated to a rather gory color film of a lung-cancer operation. The results showed that those people who were most frightened were also most eager to stop smoking and most likely to get chest X rays.

Is this true for all people? It is not. There is a reason why common sense leads some people to believe that a great deal of fear leads to inaction: It does—for certain people, under certain conditions. What Leventhal and his colleagues discovered is that people who had a reasonably good opinion of themselves (high self-esteem) were the ones who were most likely to be moved by high degrees of fear arousal. People with low opinions of themselves were the least likely to take immediate action when confronted with a communication arousing a great deal of fear—but (and here is the interesting part) after a delay, they behaved very much like the subjects with high self-esteem. That is, if immediate action were not required but action could be taken later, people with low self-esteem were more likely to take that action if they were exposed to a communication arousing a great deal of fear. People who have a low opinion of themselves may have a great deal of difficulty coping with threats to themselves. A high-fear communication overwhelms them and makes them feel like crawling into bed and pulling the covers up over their heads. Low or moderate fear is something they can more easily deal with at the moment they experience it. But, if given time—that is, if it's not essential they act immediately—they will be more likely to act if the message truly scares the hell out of them.

Subsequent research by Leventhal and his co-workers lends support to this analysis. In one study, subjects were shown films of serious automobile accidents. Some subjects watched the films on a large screen from up close; others watched them from far away on a much smaller screen. Among those subjects with high or moderate self-esteem, those who saw the films on the large screen were much more likely to take subsequent protective action than were those who saw the films on the small screen. Subjects with low self-esteem were more likely to take action when they saw the films on a small screen; those who saw the films on a large screen reported a great deal of fatigue and stated they had great difficulty even thinking of themselves as victims of automobile accidents. Thus, people with low self-esteem are apparently too overwhelmed by fear to take action when an immediate response is required.

It should be relatively easy to make people with high self-esteem behave like people with low self-esteem. We can overwhelm them by making them feel there is nothing they can do to prevent or ameliorate a threatening situation. This will lead most people to bury their heads in the sand—even those who have high self-esteem. Conversely, suppose you wanted to reduce the automobile accident rate or to help people give up smoking, and you were faced with low self-esteem people. How would you proceed? If you were to construct a message containing clear, specific, and optimistic instructions, it might increase the feeling among the members of your audience that they could confront their fears and cope with the danger. These speculations have been confirmed; experiments by Howard Leventhal and his associates show that fear-arousing messages containing specific instructions about how, when, and where to take action are much more effective than recommendations not including such instructions. For example, a campaign conducted on a college campus urging students to take tetanus shots included specific instructions about where and when they were available. The campaign materials included a map showing the location of the student health service and a suggestion that each student set aside a convenient time to stop by. The results showed high-fear appeals to be more effective than low-fear appeals in producing favorable *attitudes* toward tetanus shots among the students, and they also increased the students' stated intentions to take the shots. The highly specific instructions about how to get the shots did not in any way affect these opinions and intentions, but the instructions did have a big effect on the *actual behavior:* Of those subjects who were instructed about how to proceed, 28 percent actually got the tetanus shots; but of those who received no specific instructions, only 3 percent went down to get them. In a control group exposed only to the action instructions—no fear-arousing message—there was no shot taking. Thus, specific instructions alone are not enough to produce action—fear is a necessary component for action in such situations.

Very similar results were uncovered in Leventhal's cigarette experiment. Leventhal found that a high-fear communication produced a much greater *intention* to stop smoking. Unless it was accompanied by recommendations for specific behavior, however, it produced little behavior change. Similarly, specific instructions ("buy a magazine instead of a pack of cigarettes; drink plenty of water when you have the urge to smoke," and so on) without a fear-arousing communication were relatively ineffective. The combination of fear arousal and specific instructions produced the best results; the students in this condition were smoking less four months after they were subjected to the experimental procedure.

So, in some situations, fear-arousing appeals accompanied by specific instructions for appropriate action can and *do* produce recommended behaviors. But as Leventhal and his colleagues[36] have indicated, the impact of fear appeals is context-specific. There are some situations in which fear appeals—even when coupled with specific instructions—will not produce the desired effect. Let's consider one of the most publicized health problems of the past two decades: Acquired Immune Deficiency Syndrome (AIDS). AIDS is widely recognized as the world's most devastating public health problem. It has been described by the mass media as "The Plague of the Eighties,"[37] and it appears to be gaining momentum in the 1990s; current estimates suggest that the death toll will reach forty million by the year 2000. Health officials have worked hard to educate the public about the hazards of unsafe sexual practices and intravenous drug use, and attempts have been made to teach sexually active people about the causes of AIDS and to convince them that the threat to life is real. Such information has been accompanied by specific recommendations for preventive action—such as celibacy, monogamy, or the use of condoms. Although celibacy and monogamy may be worthwhile goals, it has proved to be unrealistic to expect the great majority of teenagers and young adults to exercise these options. Even politically conservative experts like former Surgeon General C. Everett Koop eventually came to believe that for most sexually active young adults, the proper use of condoms may be the most realistic mode of AIDS prevention.[38]

Thus, the goal becomes to persuade sexually active people to use condoms. And what form have these persuasive appeals taken? They have typically involved vivid descriptions of the dangers of unsafe sex and the ravages of the disease. The implicit assumption of policymakers and educators seems to be that arousing a great deal of fear will induce people to change their sexual behavior. Condom manufacturers apparently share that assumption: For example, in one advertisement for condoms, an attractive woman is shown saying, "I love sex, but I'm not willing to die for it."[39] That sounds "catchy." But there is some indication that, in the case of AIDS prevention, such an approach may be ineffective at best, and perhaps even counterproductive. Why? Most individuals, when contemplating having sex, do not want to be thinking about death or disease. If the cognitive association between death and condoms is too powerful, the thought of using condoms may be so noxious as to diminish the pleasure associated with sex. Under these circumstances, a great many individuals will block all thoughts of death, disease, and condoms out of their minds, adopting a posture of denial. But they won't stop having sex. Thus, they will convince themselves that "It can't happen to me," or "I'm not attracted to the kind of person who would have AIDS," or "I can spot a person with AIDS just by looking at him." Others will defend against a fear-arousing message by refusing to believe the data presented in the communication; Akiva Liberman and Shelly Chaiken[40] recently showed that the more relevant the fearful message was for the behavior of any member of the audience (and hence the more threatening it was), the more he or she was convinced that the dangers contained in the message were overstated.

This analysis is supported by a host of recent findings in the AIDS literature. For example, research by Russell Clark[41] indicates that the AIDS epidemic has had little effect upon the general willingness of young adults to have casual sex; Katie Leishman[42] found that "many people at high risk nevertheless dispense with even minimal precautions"; research by Sunyna Williams and her colleagues[43] shows that college students justify their continued engagement in unsafe sex by the false belief that, if they know and like their partner, then he or she could not possibly be HIV positive. Similarly, surveys on college campuses across the country indicate that the majority of sexually active college students are not engaging in safe sex, are not discussing sexually transmitted diseases with their partners, and have never even purchased a condom.[44]

If fear arousal is ineffective because it leads to denial, must we simply sit back and brace ourselves for the onslaught of a major epidemic? Not necessarily. There is no simple solution to this problem. But, if we believe that getting people to use condoms is the most realistic way to stem the spread of AIDS, one possibility is to design the message to overcome whatever it is that sexually active people find unattractive about condoms. For example, in our survey of sexually active college students, we found that the great majority see the putting on of condoms as a "turnoff," as "an antiseptic procedure" that detracts from the romantic sequence of a sexual encounter.[45] Accordingly, one possible approach to this problem might be to find a way to change people's mind-set—perhaps by convincing people that the putting on of the condom could become a mutual event that can be used as an erotic aspect of foreplay—a prelude to lovemaking rather than a burdensome interference.[46] Other strategies aimed at dealing with this important issue will be described in Chapter 5.

Consensual Statistical Evidence versus a Single Personal Example. Suppose you are in the market for a new car and the single most important thing you are looking for is reliability and longevity. That is, you don't care about looks, style, or mileage—what you *do* care about is the frequency of repair. As a reasonable and sensible person, you consult *Consumer Reports* and learn that the car with the best repair record is clearly the Volvo. No other car even comes close. Naturally, you decide to buy a Volvo. But suppose the night before you are to make the purchase you attend a dinner party and announce your intention to one of your friends. He is incredulous: "You can't be serious," he says. "My cousin bought a Volvo last year and has had nothing but trouble ever since. First the fuel injection system broke down; then the transmission fell out; then strange undiagnosable noises started to come from the engine; finally, oil started to drip from some unknown place. My poor cousin is literally afraid to drive the car for fear of what will happen next."

Let's suppose the ranking made by *Consumer Reports* was based on a sample of 1,000 Volvo owners. Your friend's cousin's unfortunate experience has increased the size of the sample to 1,001. It has added one negative case to your statistical bank. Logically, this should not affect your decision. But a large body of research by Richard Nisbett and his associates[47] (from whose work this example was "borrowed") indicates that such occurrences, because of their vividness, assume far more importance than their logical, statistical status would imply. Indeed, such occurrences are frequently decisive. Thus, it would be very difficult for you to rush out and purchase a Volvo with the example of the plight of your friend's cousin firmly fixed in your mind.

In addition, the more vivid the examples are, the greater their persuasive power. A real-life demonstration of this comes from the area of energy conservation. Several years ago my students and I set out to persuade homeowners to make the improvements necessary to have an energy-efficient house.[48] We worked with home auditors from local utility companies and taught them to use vivid examples when recommending home improvements. For example, most auditors, when left to their own devices, simply point to cracks around doors and recommend that the homeowner install weatherstripping. Instead, we trained several auditors to tell homeowners that if all the cracks around all the doors were added up, they would equal a hole the size of a basketball in their living room wall. "And if you had a hole that size in your wall, wouldn't you want to patch it up? That's what weatherstripping does." The results were striking. Auditors trained to use this kind of vivid language increased their effectiveness fourfold; whereas previously only 15 percent of the homeowners had the recommended work done, after the auditors began to use more vivid communication, this increased to 61 percent. Most people are more deeply influenced by one clear, vivid, personal example than by an abundance of statistical data. Thus, your friend's Volvo story, or the thought of a basketball-sized hole in your living room, will probably be extraordinarily powerful.

One-Sided versus Two-Sided Arguments. Suppose you are about to make a speech attempting to persuade your audience that capital punishment is necessary. Would you persuade more people if you simply stated your view and ignored the arguments against capital punishment, or would you be more persuasive if you discussed the opposing arguments and attempted to refute them? Before trying to answer this question, let us try to understand what is involved. If a communicator mentions the opposition's arguments, it might indicate he or she is an objective, fair-minded person; this could enhance the speaker's trustworthiness and thus increase his or her effectiveness. On the other hand, if a communicator so much as mentions the arguments on the other side of the issue, it might suggest to the audience that the issue is a controversial one; this could confuse members of the audience, make them vacillate, and ultimately reduce the persuasiveness of the communication. With these possibilities in mind, it should not come as a surprise to the reader that there is no simple relation between one-sided arguments and the effectiveness of the communication. It depends to some extent upon how well informed the audience is: The more well informed the members of the audience are, the less likely they are to be persuaded by a one-sided argument and the more likely they are to be persuaded by an argument that brings out the important opposing arguments and then proceeds to refute them. This makes sense: A well-informed person is more likely to know some of the counterarguments—when the communicator avoids mentioning these, the knowledgeable members of the audience are likely to conclude the communicator is either unfair or is unable to refute such arguments. On the other hand, an uninformed person is less apt to know of the existence of opposing arguments. If the counterargument is ignored, the less-informed members of the audience are persuaded; if the counterargument is presented, they may get confused.

Another factor playing a vital role is the initial position of the audience. As we might expect, if a member of the audience is already predisposed to believe the communicator's argument, a one-sided presentation has a greater impact on his or her opinion than a two-sided presentation. If, however, a member of the audience is leaning in the opposite direction, then a two-sided refutational argument is more persuasive.[49] Most politicians seem to be well aware of this phenomenon; they tend to present vastly different kinds of speeches, depending upon who constitutes the audience. When talking to the party faithful, they almost invariably deliver a hell-raising set of arguments favoring their own party platform and candidacy. If they do mention the opposition, it is in a derisive, mocking tone. On the other hand, when appearing on network television or when speaking to any audience of mixed loyalties, they tend to take a more diplomatic position, giving the opposing view a reasonably accurate airing before proceeding to demolish it.

The Order of Presentation.   Imagine you are running for the city council. You and your opponent are invited to address a large audience in the civic auditorium. It is a close election—many members of the audience are as yet undecided—and the outcome may hinge on your speech. You have worked hard on writing and rehearsing it. As you take your seat on the stage, the master of ceremonies asks you whether you would prefer to lead off or speak last. You ponder this for a moment. You think, *Speaking first may have an advantage, because first impressions are crucial; if I can get the audience on my side early, then my opponent will not only have to sell himself, he'll also have to unsell the audience on me—he'll be bucking a trend. On the other hand, if I speak last, I may have an advantage, because when the people leave the auditorium, they may remember the last thing they heard. The early statements made by my opponent, no matter how powerful, will be buried by my rhetoric simply because my speech will be more memorable.* You stammer: "I'd like to speak first . . . no, last . . . no, first . . . no, wait a minute." In confusion, you race off the stage, find a telephone booth, and call your friend the social psychologist. Surely, she must know which order has the advantage.

I'm afraid that if you expect a one-word answer, you are in for a disappointment. Moreover, if you wait to hear all of the social psychologist's elaborations and qualifying remarks, you might miss the opportunity of ever delivering your speech at all. Indeed, you might miss the election itself.

Needless to say, the issue is a complex one involving both learning and retention. I'll try to state it as simply as possible. The issues are similar to the commonsense issues that you, as our hypothetical politician, pondered alone. It is true that, all other things being equal, the audience's memory should be better for the speech made last, simply because it is closer in time to the election. On the other hand, the actual learning of the second material will not be as thorough as the learning of the first material, simply because the very existence of the first material disrupts and inhibits the learning process. Thus, from our knowledge of the phenomena of learning, it would appear that, all other things being equal, the first argument will be more effective; we'll call this the *primacy effect.* But from our knowledge of the phenomena of retention, on the other hand, it would appear that, all other things being equal, the last argument will be more effective; we'll call this the *recency effect.*

The fact that these two approaches seemingly make for opposite predictions does not mean it doesn't matter which argument comes first; nor does it mean it is hopeless to attempt to make a definitive prediction. What it does mean is that, by knowing something about the way both inhibition and retention work, we can predict the conditions under which either the primacy effect or the recency effect will prevail. The crucial variable is *time*—that is, the amount of time separating the events in the situation: (1) the amount of time between the first communication and the second communication, and (2) the amount of time between the end of the second communication and the moment when the members of the audience must finally make up their minds. Here are the crucial points: (1) Inhibition (interference) is greatest if very little time elapses between the two communications; here, the first communication produces maximum interference with the learning of the second communication, and a primacy effect will occur—the first speaker will have the advantage. (2) Retention is greatest, and recency effects will therefore prevail, when the audience must make up its mind immediately after hearing the second communication.

Okay. Are you still on the phone? Here's the plan: If you and your opponent are to present your arguments back to back, and if the election is still several days away, you should speak first. The primacy of your speech will interfere with the audience's ability to learn your opponent's arguments; with the election several days away, differential effects due to memory are negligible. But if the election is going to be held immediately after the second speech, and there is to be a prolonged coffee break between the two speeches, you would do well to speak last. Because of the coffee break between speeches, the interference of the first speech with the learning of the second speech will be minimal; because the audience must make up its mind right after the second speech, as the second speaker, you would have retention working for you. Therefore the recency effect would be dominant: All other things being equal, the last speech will be the more persuasive.

These speculations were confirmed in an experiment by Norman Miller and Donald Campbell.[50] In this experiment, a simulated jury trial was arranged in which subjects were presented with a condensed version of the transcript of an actual jury trial of a suit for damages brought against the manufacturers of an allegedly defective vaporizer. The *pro* side of the argument consisted of the testimony of witnesses for the plaintiff, cross-examination of defense witnesses by the plaintiff's lawyer, and the opening and closing speeches of the plaintiff's lawyer. The *con* side of the argument consisted of the testimony of witnesses for the defense, the defense lawyer's cross-examinations, and his opening and closing speeches. The condensed version of this transcript was arranged so that all of the *pro* arguments were placed in one block and all of the *con* arguments were placed in another block. The investigators varied the interval between the reading of the two arguments and between the reading of the last argument and the announcement of the verdict. A recency effect was obtained when there was a large interval between the first and second arguments and a small interval between the second argument and the verdict. A primacy effect was obtained when there was a small interval between the first and second arguments and a large interval between the second argument and the verdict. The topic of this experiment (a jury trial) serves to underscore the immense practical significance these two phenomena may have. Most jurisdictions allow the prosecution to go first (opening statement and presentation of evidence) *and* last (closing arguments), thus giving the state the advantage of both primacy and recency effects. Because the order of presentation may influence a jury's verdict of guilt or innocence, I would recommend that our trial procedures be modified to prevent any possible miscarriages of justice due to primacy or recency effects.

The Size of the Discrepancy. Suppose you are talking to an audience that strongly disagrees with your point of view. Will you be more effective if you present your position in its most extreme form or if you modulate your position by presenting it in such a way that it does not seem terribly different from the audience's position? For example, suppose you believe people should exercise vigorously every day to stay healthy; any physical activity would be helpful, but at least an hour's worth would be preferable. Your audience consists of college professors who seem to believe turning the pages of a book is sufficient exercise for the average person. Would you change their opinion to a greater extent by arguing that people should begin a rigorous daily program of running, swimming, and calisthenics or by suggesting a briefer, less-taxing regimen? In short, what is the most effective level of discrepancy between the opinion of the audience and the recommendation of the communicator? This is a vital issue for any propagandist or educator.

Let us look at this situation from the audience's point of view. As I mentioned in chapter 2, most of us have a strong desire to be correct—to have "the right" opinions and to perform reasonable actions. When someone comes along and disagrees with us, it makes us feel uncomfortable because it suggests our opinions or actions may be wrong or based on misinformation. The greater the disagreement, the greater is our discomfort. How can we reduce this discomfort? Simply by changing our opinions or actions. The greater the disagreement, the greater our opinion change will be. This line of reasoning, then, would suggest that the communicator should argue for the daily program of rigorous exercise; the greater the discrepancy, the more the opinion change. Indeed, several investigators have found that this "linear" relation holds true. A good example of this relation was provided by an experiment by Philip Zimbardo.[51] Each of the college women recruited as subjects for the experiment was asked to bring a close friend with her to the laboratory. Each pair of friends was presented with a case study of juvenile delinquency, and then each of the subjects was asked, separately and in private, to indicate her recommendations on the matter. Each subject was led to believe her close friend disagreed with her—either by a small margin or by an extremely large margin. Zimbardo found that the greater the apparent discrepancy, the more they changed their opinions toward what they supposed were the opinions of their friends.

However, a careful look at the research literature also turns up several experiments disconfirming the line of reasoning presented above. For example, James Whittaker,[52] found a curvilinear relation between discrepancy and opinion change. By "curvilinear" I mean that, as a small discrepancy increased somewhat, so did the degree of opinion change; but as the discrepancy continued to increase, opinion change began to slacken; and finally, as the discrepancy became large, the amount of opinion change became very small. When the discrepancy was very large, almost no opinion change was observed.

Building on Whittaker's finding, Carl Hovland, O. J. Harvey, and Muzafer Sherif [53] argued that, if a particular communication differs considerably from a person's own position, it is, in effect, outside of one's "latitude of acceptance," and the individual will not be much influenced by it. In the experiment by Hovland and his colleagues, the communication was based on a red-hot issue—one the subjects felt strongly about: whether their state should remain "dry" or "go wet"—that is, whether or not to change the law prohibiting the distribution and sale of alcoholic beverages. The voters of the state were virtually equally divided on this issue, and the subjects were a representative sample: Some of the subjects felt strongly that the state should remain dry, others felt strongly it should go wet, and the rest took a moderate position. The subjects were divided into groups of people reflecting all three positions. The members of each group were presented with communications supporting one of the three opinions, so that, in each group, there were subjects who found the communication close to their own position, some who found it moderately discrepant from their own position, and some who found it extremely discrepant from their own position. Specifically, some groups were presented with a "wet" message, which argued for the unlimited and unrestricted sale of liquor; some groups were presented with a "dry" message, which argued for complete prohibition; and some groups, with a moderately "wet" message, which argued to allow some drinking but with certain controls and restrictions. The greatest opinion changes occurred when there was a *moderate* discrepancy between the actual message and the opinions of individual members of the groups.

For a scientist, this is an exciting state of affairs. When there exists a substantial number of research findings pointing in one direction and a similarly substantial number of research findings pointing in a different direction, it doesn't necessarily mean someone has to be wrong; rather, it suggests there is a significant factor that hasn't been accounted for—and this is indeed exciting, for it gives the scientist an opportunity to play detective. I beg the reader's indulgence here, for I would like to dwell on this issue—not only for its substantive value, but also because it provides us with an opportunity to analyze one of the more adventurous aspects of social psychology as a science. Basically, there are two ways of proceeding with this game of detective. We can begin by assembling all the experiments that show one result and all those that show the other result and (imaginary magnifying glass in hand) painstakingly scrutinize them, looking for the one factor common to the experiments in group A and lacking in group B; then we can try to determine, conceptually, why this factor should make a difference. Or, conversely, we can begin by speculating conceptually about what factor or factors might make a difference, then we can glance through the existing literature, with this conceptual lantern in hand, to see if the experiments in group A differ from the experiments in group B on this dimension.

As a scientist, my personal preference is for the second mode. Accordingly, with two of my students—Judith Turner and Merrill Carlsmith—I began to speculate about what factor or factors might make such a difference. We began by accepting the notion discussed above: The greater the discrepancy, the greater the discomfort for the members of the audience. But we reasoned that this does not necessarily mean the members of an audience will change their opinion. There are at least four ways in which the members of an audience can reduce their discomfort: (1) They can change their opinion; (2) they can induce *the communicator* to change his or her opinion; (3) they can seek support for their original opinion by finding other people who share their views, in spite of what the communicator says; or (4) they can derogate the communicator—convince themselves the communicator is stupid or immoral—and thereby invalidate that person's opinion.

In a great many communication situations, including those in these experiments, the message is delivered either as a written statement (as a newspaper or magazine article, for example) or by a communicator who is not approachable by the audience (as on television, on the lecture platform, and so on). Also, the subject is often alone or part of an audience whose members have no opportunity to interact with each other. Thus, under these circumstances, it is virtually impossible for the recipients of the communication either to have immediate impact on the communicator's opinion or to seek immediate social support. This leaves the recipients two major ways of reducing this discomfort—they can change their opinion, or they can derogate the communicator.

Under what circumstances would an individual find it easy or difficult to derogate the communicator? It would be very difficult to derogate a liked and respected personal friend; it would also be difficult to derogate someone who is a highly trustworthy expert on the issue under discussion. But if the communicator's credibility were questionable, it would be difficult *not* to derogate him. Following this line of reasoning, we suggested that, if a communicator's credibility were high, the greater the discrepancy between the communicator's opinions and the audience's opinions, the greater the influence exerted on the opinions of the audience. However, if the communicator's credibility were not very high, he would be, by definition, subject to derogation. This is not to say he couldn't influence the opinions of the audience. He would probably be able to influence people to change their opinions if his opinions were not too different from theirs. But the more discrepant such a communicator's position is from those of his audience, the more the audience might begin to question his wisdom, intelligence, and sanity. The more they question his wisdom, intelligence, and sanity, the less likely they are to be influenced.

Let's return to our example involving physical exercise: Imagine a seventy-three-year-old man, with the body of a man half his age, who had just won the Boston Marathon. If he told me that a good way to stay in condition and live a long healthy life was to exercise vigorously for at least two hours every day, I would believe him. Boy, would I believe him! He would get much more exercise out of me than if he suggested I should exercise for only ten minutes a day. But suppose a person somewhat less credible, such as a high-school track coach, were delivering the communication. If he suggested I exercise ten minutes a day, his suggestion would be within my own latitude of acceptance, and he might influence my opinion and behavior. But if he advised me to embark on a program of vigorous exercise requiring two hours every day, I would be inclined to write him off as a quack, a health freak, a monomaniac—and I could comfortably continue being indolent. Thus, I would agree with Hovland, Harvey, and Sherif: People will consider an extremely discrepant communication to be outside their latitude of acceptance—but only if the communicator is not highly credible.

Armed with these speculations, my students and I scrutinized the existing experiments on this issue, paying special attention to the ways in which the communicator was described. Lo and behold, we discovered that each of the experiments showing a direct linear relation between discrepancy and opinion change happened to describe the source of the communication as more credible than did those whose results showed a curvilinear relation. This confirmed our speculations about the role of credibility. But we didn't stop there: We constructed an experiment in which we systematically investigated the size of the discrepancy and the credibility of the communicator in one research design.[54] In this experiment, college women were asked to read several stanzas from obscure modern poetry and to rank them in terms of how good they were. Then each woman was given an essay to read purporting to be a criticism of modern poetry that specifically mentioned a stanza she had rated as poor. For some subjects, the essayist described this particular stanza in glowing terms— this created a large discrepancy between the opinion of the communicator and the opinion voiced by the students in this experimental condition. For some subjects, the essayist was only mildly favorable in the way he described the stanza—this set up a moderate discrepancy between the essayist and the students in this condition. In a third condition, the essayist was mildly scornful in his treatment of the stanza—which placed the recipients of this communication in a "mild-discrepancy" situation. Finally, to one-half of the women in the experiment, the writer of the essay was identified as the poet T. S. Eliot, a highly credible poetry critic; to the rest of the subjects, the essay writer was identified as a college student. The subjects were subsequently allowed to rank the stanzas once again. When T. S. Eliot was ostensibly the communicator, the essay had the most influence on the students when its evaluation of the stanza was most discrepant from theirs; when a fellow student of medium credibility was identified as the essayist, the essay produced a little opinion change when it was slightly discrepant from the opinion of the students, a great deal of change when it was moderately discrepant, and only a little opinion change when it was extremely discrepant.

To sum up this section, the conflicting results are accounted for: When a communicator has high credibility, the greater the discrepancy between the view he or she advocates and the view of the audience, the more the audience will be persuaded; on the other hand, when a communicator's credibility is doubtful or slim, he or she will produce maximum opinion change at moderate discrepancies.

Characteristics of the Audience

All listeners, readers, or viewers are not alike. Some people are more difficult to persuade. In addition, as we have seen, the kind of communication that appeals to one person may not appeal to another. For example, recall that the level of knowledge audience members possess and their prior opinions will play major roles in determining whether a two-sided communication will be more effective than a one-sided communication.

Self-Esteem. What effect does an individual's personality have on his or her persuasibility? The one personality variable most consistently related to persuasibility is self-esteem. Individuals who feel inadequate are more easily influenced by a persuasive communication than individuals who think highly of themselves.[55] This seems reasonable enough; after all, if people don't like themselves, then it follows they don't place a very high premium on their own ideas. Consequently, if their ideas are challenged, they may be willing to give them up. Recall that people want to be right. If Sam, who has high self-esteem, listens to a communication at variance with his own opinion, he must make up his mind whether he stands a better chance of being right if he changes his opinion or if he stands pat. A person with high self-esteem may experience some conflict when he finds himself in disagreement with a highly credible communicator. He might resolve this conflict by changing his opinion, or he might remain firm. But if Sam had low self-esteem, there would be little or no conflict—because he doesn't think very highly of himself, he probably believes he stands a better chance of being right if he goes along with the communicator.

Prior Experience of the Audience. Another audience-related factor of considerable importance is the frame of mind the audience is in just prior to the communication. An audience can be made receptive to a communication if it has been well fed and is relaxed and happy. Indeed, as Irving Janis and his associates have discovered, people who have been allowed to eat desirable food while reading a persuasive communication are more influenced by what they read than are people in a control (noneating) group.[56]

Conversely, members of an audience can be made less receptive and less persuadable. As I noted, people predict they will be able to resist persuasive communications such as television commercials. One way of decreasing their persuasibility is by forewarning the individuals that an attempt is going to be made to persuade them.[57] This is especially true if the content of the message differs from their own beliefs. I would argue that the phrase "And now, a message from our sponsor" renders that message less persuasive than it would have been if the communicator had simply glided into it without prologue. The forewarning seems to say "Watch out, I'm going to try to persuade you," and people tend to respond by marshaling defenses against the message. This phenomenon was demonstrated in an experiment by Jonathan Freedman and David Sears.[58] Teenagers were told they would be hearing a talk entitled "Why Teenagers Should Not Be Allowed to Drive." Ten minutes later, the speaker presented them with a prepared communication. In a control condition, the same talk was given without the ten-minute forewarning. The subjects in the control condition were more thoroughly convinced by the communication than were those who had been forewarned.

People tend to protect their sense of freedom. According to Jack Brehm's theory of reactance,[59] when our sense of freedom is threatened, we attempt to restore it. For example, I like to receive birthday presents. But if a borderline student (in danger of flunking my course) presented me with an expensive birthday present just as I was about to read term papers, I would feel uncomfortable. My sense of freedom or autonomy would be challenged. Similarly, persuasive communications, if blatant or coercive, can be perceived as intruding upon one's freedom of choice, activating a person's defenses to resist the messages. For example, if an aggressive salesperson tells me I must buy something, my first reaction is to reassert my independence by leaving the store.

In an experiment by Lillian Bensley and Rui Wu,[60] college students watched one of two messages opposed to the drinking of alcoholic beverages. One was a heavy-handed, dogmatic message stating that there was no safe amount of alcohol and all people should abstain all the time. The second message was a milder message that stressed the importance of controlling one's drinking. The second message was far more effective at getting people to reduce their consumption of alcohol. This was especially true for heavy drinkers—who almost certainly experienced the most reactance when confronted with the heavy-handed message.

Reactance can operate in a number of interesting ways. Suppose that, as I walk down the street, I am gently asked to sign a petition. I don't know much about the issue, and as it is being explained to me, another person accosts us and begins to pressure me not to sign. Reactance theory predicts that, to counteract this pressure and reassert my freedom of choice, I would be more likely to sign. This scenario was actually staged by Madeline Heilman,[61] and the results confirmed her prediction that, under most circumstances, the more intense the attempts to prevent subjects from signing, the more likely they were to sign the petitions. Of course, as we have seen in this chapter and the preceding one, people can be and are influenced and do comply with implicit social pressures, as in the Asch experiment. But when those pressures are so blatant that they threaten people's feelings of freedom, they not only resist them but tend to react in the opposite direction.

There is still another aspect of this need for freedom and autonomy that should be mentioned. All other things being equal, when faced with information that runs counter to important beliefs, people have a tendency, whenever feasible, to invent counterarguments on the spot.[62] In this way, they are able to prevent their opinions from being unduly influenced and protect their sense of autonomy. But it is possible to overcome some of this resistance. Leon Festinger and Nathan Maccoby[63] conducted an experiment in which they attempted to prevent members of their audience from inventing arguments to refute the message being presented to them. This was accomplished by simply distracting the audience somewhat while the communication was being presented. Two groups of students who belonged to a college fraternity were required to listen to a tape-recorded argument about the evils of college fraternities. The argument was erudite, powerful, and as you might imagine, widely discrepant from the beliefs of the audience. During the presentation of the communication, one of the groups was distracted. Specifically, they were shown a highly entertaining silent film. Festinger and Maccoby reasoned that, because this group was engaged in two tasks simultaneously—listening to the tape-recorded argument against fraternities and watching an entertaining film—their minds would be so occupied they would have little or no opportunity to think up arguments to refute the tape-recorded message. The members of the control group, on the other hand, were not distracted by a film; therefore, they would be better able to devote some of their thoughts to resisting the communication by thinking up counterarguments. The results of the experiment confirmed this reasoning. The students who were distracted by watching the film underwent substantially more opinion change against fraternities than did the students who were not distracted.

How many of us have been distracted by a movie during an important persuasive appeal? Not many, I bet. But most of us are familiar with another form of distraction—political heckling. Lloyd Sloan, Robert Love, and Thomas Ostrom[64] examined the effect of heckling on the attitudes of an audience toward a political speaker. Specifically, they measured subjects' attitudes toward Senator Edmund Muskie before having the subjects view a videotaped presentation of Muskie's 1970 election-eve broadcast. During the presentation, confederates vocally attacked Muskie and his views. After the broadcast, the subjects' opinions of Muskie were measured again. For those subjects who were initially neutral in their feelings toward Muskie, the presence of hecklers produced opposition to the speaker; for those subjects with initially extreme opinions (either positive or negative), heckling produced a change toward neutrality. Thus, the effects of distraction seem to depend on a person's initial opinion, and contrary to popular belief, heckling may actually cause those who are most persuasible (that is, the undecideds) to evaluate a speaker's message more negatively.

Let us take a closer look at the other side of the issue. How can we help people to resist attempts to influence them? An elaborate method for inducing such resistance has been developed by William McGuire and his associates. This method has been appropriately dubbed the *inoculation effect*. We have already seen that a two-sided (refutational) presentation is more effective for convincing most audiences than a one-sided presentation. Expanding on this phenomenon, McGuire suggested that, if people receive prior exposure to a brief communication that they are then able to refute, they tend to be "immunized" against a subsequent full-blown presentation of the same argument, in much the same way that a small amount of an attenuated virus immunizes people against a full-blown attack by that virus. In an experiment by William McGuire and Dimitri Papageorgis,[65] a group of people stated their opinions; these opinions were then subjected to a mild attack—and the attack was refuted. These people were subsequently subjected to a *powerful* argument against their initial opinions. Members of this group showed a much smaller tendency to change their opinions than did the members of a control group whose opinions had not been previously subjected to the mild attack. In effect, they had been inoculated against opinion change and made relatively immune. Thus, not only is it often more effective as a propaganda technique to use a two-sided refutational presentation, but if it is used skillfully, such a presentation tends to increase the audience's resistance to subsequent counterpropaganda.

In an exciting field experiment, Alfred McAlister and his colleagues[66] inoculated seventh-grade students against existing peer pressures to smoke cigarettes. For example, the students were shown advertisements implying that truly liberated women are smokers— "You've come a long way, baby!" They were then inoculated by being taught that a woman couldn't possibly be liberated if she were hooked on tobacco. Similarly, since teenagers tend to smoke because it seems cool or "tough" (like the Marlboro man), McAlister felt that peer pressure might take the form of being called "chicken" if one didn't smoke. Accordingly, the seventh graders role-played a situation in which they practiced countering that argument by saying something like "I'd be a real chicken if I smoked just to impress you." This inoculation against peer pressure proved to be very effective. By the time the students were in the ninth grade, they were half as likely to smoke as those in a control group from a similar junior high school.

Research[67] has found that, in producing resistance, inoculation is most effective when the belief under attack is a cultural truism. A cultural truism is a belief accepted as unquestionably true by most members of a society, like "The United States is the best country in the world to live in," or "If people are willing to work hard, they can succeed." Cultural truisms are rarely called into question; when they are not, it is relatively easy for us to lose sight of why we hold them. Thus, if subjected to a severe attack, such beliefs may crumble. To motivate us to bolster our beliefs, we must be made aware of their vulnerability, and the best way to do this is to attack those beliefs mildly. Prior exposure, in the form of a watered-down attack on our beliefs, produces resistance to later persuasion because (1) we become motivated to defend our beliefs, and (2) we gain some practice in doing so. We are then better equipped to resist a more serious attack.

This is an important point frequently ignored or misunderstood by policymakers. For example, in the aftermath of the Korean War, when several of our prisoners of war were supposedly brainwashed by the Chinese Communists, a Senate committee recommended that, in order to build resistance among the people to brainwashing and other forms of Communist propaganda, courses on "patriotism and Americanism" should be instituted in our public school system. But William McGuire's results suggest the best way to help our soldiers resist anti-American propaganda would be to challenge their belief in the American way of life, and the best way to build resistance to pro-Communist propaganda would be to teach courses on Communism, presenting both sides of the argument. If such an idea had been proposed in the 1950s, when the Cold War was in full swing and Senator Joseph McCarthy was conducting his witch hunt, this idea would probably have been considered to be part of the Communist conspiracy. It is hoped the day of the ostrich is over; we cannot resist propaganda by burying our heads in the sand. The person who is easiest to brainwash is the person whose beliefs are based on slogans that have never been seriously challenged.

How Well Do the Principles Work?

Suppose you inherited controlling interest in a television network. Here is a golden opportunity to influence people's opinions on important issues. Let's say you are an enthusiastic proponent of national health insurance, and you would like to persuade others to agree with you. Having just finished reading this chapter, you know how to do it, and you are in control of a very powerful medium of communication. How do you set about doing it? That's simple: You choose a time slot following a highly intellectual program (in order to be certain that well-informed people are watching), and accordingly, you present a two-sided argument (because two-sided arguments work best on well-informed people). You arrange your arguments in such a manner that the argument in favor of national health insurance is stronger and appears first (in order to take advantage of the primacy effect). You describe the plight of the poor—how they get sick and die for lack of affordable medical care. You use vivid personal examples of people you know. You discuss these events in a manner that inspires a great deal of fear; at the same time, you offer a specific plan of action, because this combination produces the most opinion change and the most action in the most people. You present some of the arguments against your position and offer strong refutation of these arguments. You arrange for the speaker to be expert, trustworthy, and extremely likable. You make your argument as strongly as you can, in order to maximize the discrepancy between the argument presented and the initial attitude of the audience. And then you sit back, relax, and wait for those opinions to start changing.

It's not that simple. Imagine a typical viewer: Let's say she is a forty-five-year-old middle-class real estate broker who believes the government interferes too much in the private lives of individuals. She feels any form of social legislation undermines the spirit of individuality which is the essence of democracy. She comes across your program while looking for an evening's entertainment. She begins to hear your arguments in favor of free health care. As she listens, she becomes slightly less confident in her original convictions. She is not quite as certain as she had been that the government shouldn't intervene in matters of health. What does she do? If she is anything like the subjects in Lance Canon's[68] experiment, she would reach over, turn the dial on her television set, and begin to watch "Wheel of Fortune." Canon found that, as one's confidence is weakened, a person becomes less prone to listen to arguments against his or her beliefs. Thus, the very people you most want to convince and whose opinions might be the most susceptible to being changed are the ones *least* likely to continue to expose themselves to a communication designed for that purpose.

Must you resign yourself to broadcasting your message to an audience composed of viewers who already support national health insurance? That may be so—if you insist on airing a serious documentary devoted to the issue. After considering your alternatives, however, you might decide to take another approach. You call a meeting of your network executives. The programing director is instructed to commission a couple of scripts dramatizing the plight of families facing financial ruin due to costs associated with serious illness. You order the news department to investigate the success of national health insurance in other countries. Finally, you provide the late-night talk show host with a couple of jokes he might tell about his inept but affluent doctor. While none of these communications would match the documentary in terms of the information provided, their cumulative impact could be more significant. Embedded in dramas or news segments, they would not necessarily come labeled as arguments supporting national health insurance; they seem innocuous, but their message is clear. Not appearing to be explicit attempts at persuasion, they should arouse little resistance, avoiding an inoculation effect and inhibiting the formation of counterarguments by distracting the audience. Most importantly, people will probably *see* them without switching channels.

I do not mean to imply that television executives conspire to disguise persuasive communications within other contexts, but as I stated near the beginning of this chapter, television plays a major role in shaping how we perceive the world. The sheer volume of television Americans see is staggering. The typical household's television set is turned on for over seven hours a day;[69] and the average American watches thirty hours of television a week—that's a little over fifteen hundred hours a year. At that rate, if you are an average viewer, you will see about 37,800 commercials a year, or more than 100 a day.[70] The average high-school graduate has spent much less time in the classroom than in front of the television.[71] Children in particular come to *care* about television to an extent that seems bizarre. Three examples will suffice to illustrate our point. A University of Nebraska survey asked fifteen thousand children which they would want more—a father or a television set. Half of the children said they preferred to have the television. A fifteen-year-old boy recently committed suicide, leaving behind a note that blamed the cancelation of his favorite television series for his death. Another youngster killed himself after his father took his television set away. The thirteen-year-old's suicide note said "I can't stand another day . . . without television. . . . In my heart I will take my TV with me."[72]

The medium has impact, and the view of reality it transmits seldom remains value-free. George Gerbner and his associates[73] have conducted the most extensive analysis of television yet. Since the late 1960s, these researchers have been videotaping and carefully analyzing thousands of prime-time television programs and characters. Their findings, taken as a whole, suggest that television's representation of reality is grossly inaccurate and misleading. In prime-time programing, males outnumber females by 3 to 1, and women are younger than the men they encounter on television. Nonwhites (especially Latinos), young children, and the elderly are underrepresented; and members of minority groups are disproportionally cast in minor roles. Moreover, most prime-time characters are portrayed as professional and managerial workers: Although 67 percent of the work force in the United States is employed in blue-collar or service jobs, only 25 percent of television characters hold such jobs. Finally, crime on television is at least ten times as prevalent as in real life. Over half of television's characters are involved in a violent confrontation each week; in reality, less than 1 percent of people in the nation are victims of criminal violence in any given year, according to FBI statistics. David Rintels, a television writer and former president of the Writers Guild of America, summed it up best when he said, "From 8 to 11 o'clock each night, television is one long lie."[74]

Gerbner and his associates have also compared the attitudes and beliefs of heavy viewers (those who watch more than four hours a day) and light viewers (those who watch less than two hours a day). They found that heavy viewers: (1) express more racially prejudiced attitudes; (2) overestimate the number of people employed as physicians, lawyers, and athletes; (3) perceive women as having more limited abilities and interests than men; (4) hold exaggerated views about the prevalence of violence in society; and (5) believe old people are fewer in number and less healthy today than they were twenty years ago, even though the opposite is true. What's more, heavy viewers tend to see the world as a more sinister place than light viewers; they are likely to agree that most people are just looking out for themselves and would take advantage of you if they had a chance. Gerbner concludes that these attitudes and beliefs reflect the inaccurate portrayals of American life provided to us by television.*

Of course, each of us has had extensive personal contact with many people in a myriad of social contexts; the media are just one source of our knowledge about the sexes and different ethnic or occupational groups. The information and impressions we receive through the media are probably less influential when we can also rely on firsthand experience. Thus, those of us who have been in close contact with several women in jobs outside of the home are probably less susceptible to the stereotypes of women portrayed on television. On the other hand, while each of us has formed conceptions about crime and violence, it is unlikely that many of those opinions developed from our personal experience. Television is virtually our only vivid source of information about crime. A major portion of television programing is comprised of crime shows—the average fifteen-year-old has viewed over thirteen thousand television killings. In a penetrating analysis of "television criminology," Craig Haney and John Manzolati[75] point out that crime shows dispense remarkably consistent images of both the police and criminals. For example, they found that television policemen are amazingly effective, solving almost every crime, and are infallible in one regard: The wrong person was *never* in jail at the end of a show. Television fosters an illusion of certainty in crime fighting. Television criminals generally turn to crime because of psychopathology or insatiable (and unnecessary) greed. Television emphasizes criminals' personal responsibility for their actions and largely ignores situational pressures correlated with crime, such as poverty and unemployment. Haney and Manzolati go

---

* It should be noted that Gerbner's research is *correlational*, not experimental. It is therefore impossible to determine whether heavy viewing actually causes prejudiced attitudes and inaccurate beliefs or whether people already holding such attitudes and beliefs simply tend to watch more television. To bolster their conclusions, Gerbner and his associates sampled viewers from all age, education, income, and ethnic groups. After taking such viewer characteristics into account, they found that the relationship between heavy viewing and inaccurate beliefs still occurred in *every* category.

on to demonstrate that this portrayal has important social consequences. People who watch a lot of television come to adopt this belief system, which affects their expectations and can cause them to take a hard-line stance when serving on juries. Heavy viewers are likely to reverse the presumption of innocence, believing "defendants must be guilty of *something*, otherwise they wouldn't be brought to trial."

It has also been shown that the incidence of larceny (theft) increases when television is introduced into an area.[76] Why should this be the case? The most reasonable explanation is that television promotes the consumption of goods through advertisements; it also depicts upper-class and middle-class lifestyles as the norm. This illusion of widespread wealth and consumption may frustrate and anger deprived viewers who compare their lifestyles with those portrayed on television, thereby motivating them to "share in the American dream" any way they can.

It is nearly impossible to specify the precise extent to which exposure to the media influences public opinion and behavior. Too many other factors are involved. Because the research described above is not *experimental*, it is difficult to separate the effects of mass communications from the impact of personal experiences and contact with family and friends. But experiments can be done. For example, let's suppose that, as the network executive, you went ahead with your original plan to televise the documentary on national health care. In this instance, it would be relatively easy for you to determine whether your message was persuasive. At the most basic level, both before and after the telecast you could poll cross-sections of viewers about their opinions concerning national health insurance. If they changed in a favorable direction, you might conclude your program was effective. If you were interested in maximizing its effectiveness, you might tape several versions of the documentary to test different speakers, arguments, and styles of presentation. If you presented these versions to various test audiences, you could compare the effects of different combinations of factors. Indeed, this scenario approximates the way most of the research described earlier in this chapter was carried out. Communications about a variety of topics were prepared. Certain aspects were manipulated—the credibility of the speakers, for example, or the order of the arguments—and the resulting versions of the message were presented to audiences. By polling audience opinion, the effects of the variables can be measured. This procedure allows great control over the message and is well suited for testing large numbers of subjects. This method is so efficient, in fact, it has been adapted to a computer-controlled procedure for varying certain factors surrounding the messages and presenting them to people seated at computer consoles.[77] With the advent of cable television networks that have the technological capability for home viewers to communicate back to the station, such as the QUBE-TV system, it is now possible to instantaneously sample the responses of thousands of viewers to actual presentations.

Suppose that, instead of deciding to televise the documentary, you opted to broadcast the series of more subtle messages disguised within the regular programs and presented repeatedly. It would be much more difficult to measure and assess the impact of this approach, but it probably is more common. Rarely are we presented with explicit persuasive messages in favor of a given position immediately prior to deciding on an issue, except perhaps during political campaigns. Most of our beliefs develop more gradually, through repeated contacts with people and information over an extended period of time. In general, beliefs people hold important are difficult to change through direct communication. There appears to be a basic difference between an issue like national health insurance, on the one hand, and issues like the feasibility of atomic-powered submarines, whether antihistamines should be sold without a prescription, and the practical importance of arithmetic, on the other. What is the difference? One difference is that the medical-care issue is more important. Who cares about the feasibility of atomic-powered submarines, anyway? It is a trivial issue. But what is the criterion for judging whether an issue is important or trivial?

To provide an answer to this question, we must first examine what we mean by the term *opinion*, which has been used throughout this chapter. On the simplest level, an opinion is what a person believes to be factually true. Thus, it is my opinion that there are fewer than ten thousand students enrolled at the University of California at Santa Cruz, that wearing seat belts reduces traffic fatalities, and that New York City is hot in the summer. Such opinions are primarily cognitive—that is, they take place in the head rather than in the gut. They are also transient—that is, they can be changed by good, clear evidence to the contrary. Thus, if consumer advocate

Ralph Nader (whom I regard as a highly credible source on the traffic issue) presented me with data indicating that seat belts, as they are currently constructed, do not reduce fatalities significantly, I would change my opinion on that issue.

On the other hand, suppose a person holds the opinion that Jews engage in "sharp" business practices, or that Asians are sneaky, or that people under twenty-five have a special wisdom, or that the United States of America is the greatest (or most awful) country in the history of the world, or that New York City is a jungle. How do these opinions differ from the ones stated in the preceding paragraph? They tend to be both emotional and evaluative—that is, they imply likes or dislikes. Believing Asians are sneaky implies that the person doesn't like Asians. The opinion that New York City is a jungle is different from the opinion that New York City is hot in the summer. The opinion that New York City is a jungle is not simply cognitive— it carries with it a negative evaluation and some degree of fear or anxiety. An opinion that includes an evaluative and an emotional component is called an *attitude*. Compared to opinions, attitudes are extremely difficult to change.

Suppose Sam is an ardent and careful consumer who is deeply concerned about matters of health. Over the years, he has come to trust Ralph Nader's research on a great many issues, including unsafe cars, cholesterol in hot dogs, hazardous electrical appliances, air pollution, and so on. But further suppose that Sam happens to be a white supremacist who believes that the white race is intellectually superior to all other races. What if Ralph Nader conducted an exhaustive study indicating that, when given culture-free intelligence tests, racial minorities score as high as whites. Would this information be likely to change Sam's attitude? Probably not. How come? Doesn't Sam regard Nader as a careful researcher? It is my guess that, because the issue is rooted in emotion, Nader's findings about intelligence testing would not influence Sam as easily or as thoroughly as Nader's findings about cars, cholesterol, or pollution. Attitudes are harder to change than simple opinions.

Human thinking is not always logical. Although we humans are capable of accurate and subtle thinking, we are equally capable of distortions and great sloppiness in our thought processes. In order to understand how to *change* attitudes, first it is essential to understand the complexities of human thinking as well as the motives that lead people to resist change. These are interesting and important issues that I will explore in the next two chapters: Chapter 4 is an attempt to understand how people construe and misconstrue social events; chapter 5 is a description of the major motives underlying construal and misconstrual.

4
Social Cognition

In his masterpiece, *Public Opinion*, the distinguished political analyst Walter Lippmann[1] recounts the story of a young girl, brought up in a small mining town, who one day went from cheerfulness into a deep spasm of grief. It seems that a gust of wind had suddenly cracked a kitchen windowpane. The young girl was inconsolable and spoke incomprehensibly for hours. When she was finally able to speak rationally, she explained that a broken pane of glass meant that a close relative had died. She was therefore mourning her father whom she was convinced had just passed away. The young girl remained disconsolate until, days later, a telegram arrived verifying that her father was still very much alive. The girl had constructed a complete fiction

I am indebted to my friend and colleague Anthony R. Pratkanis for drafting this chapter.

based on a simple external fact (a broken window), a superstition (broken window means death), fear, and love for her father.

During the Middle Ages in Europe, it was common practice to empty chamber pots—containers that stored a day's supply of urine and excrement—by throwing the contents out the window and into the street and gutter below. The urine and excrement often remained in the street—breeding pestilence and disease—until a heavy rain washed it away.[2] To our modern mind, the medieval chamber pot seems primitive, barbaric, and downright stupid, especially when one realizes that indoor plumbing was developed centuries before by the Romans. How did the chamber pot come into being? During the Middle Ages, a belief arose that nudity was not only sinful but that an unclothed body was subject to attack by evil spirits that could cause bodily harm. The Roman practice of daily bathing was abandoned and replaced by a once-a-year bath. Gradually, the indoor plumbing of the Romans fell into disrepair and society lost the plumbing skills needed to maintain indoor toilets. The chamber pot was born of necessity. It was centuries later that the "spirit" theory of disease was replaced by our modern theory based on viruses and bacteria.[3]

The point of the story of the young girl and of the medieval chamber pot is not to explore the inner workings of the abnormal mind, nor is it an attempt to show the advances in health and hygiene that have occurred in modern times. Instead, I pose the two stories to raise a fundamental question: "How much are we like the young girl from the mining town and the owner of that medieval chamber pot? To what extent do *our* fictions guide our behavior and actions?" It is the point of this chapter that we are more similar to that young girl and chamber pot owner than we might think.

It would not surprise me if the writer of a social psychology textbook in the twenty-second century would begin her chapter on social cognition, not with a story about chamber pots, but with a tale of pesticide runoff or deaths due to the AIDS virus. The story might go something like this:

> During the twentieth and twenty-first centuries millions died of famine—not from lack of food, but because their food had been poisoned by years of chemical runoff gradually building up in the food chain. A great many knowledgeable people suspected this was

happening, but, unaccountably, little or nothing was done to prevent it. In addition, over a hundred million people died of the AIDS virus because they didn't know how to (or refused to) practice sex safely. The modern reader may be wondering how a culture that could place men and women on the moon and cure many diseases could commit mass suicide. In those days, many believed that talking about the operation of their sexual parts was sinful and weakened the soul, thereby opening up the body to the possibility of pain and suffering. Most people did not fully understand that technology—although able to accomplish great things—also brings with it certain costs. It was not until recently that scientists were able to comprehend the full impact of a given technology on the ecosystem. My point in relating these stories is not, however, to point out how simpleminded most people were in the twentieth and twenty-first centuries, but to ask a more fundamental question: "How much are we like those heedless AIDS victims or those farmers who used pesticides so carelessly?"

How we make sense of our social world makes a difference! And we attempt to make sense of our world hundreds of times a day. Whenever we meet a new person at school or work, we form a first impression. Every time we enter a supermarket, we walk down an aisle full of several brands for each of hundreds of products; we must attempt to discern which are best. Often we are asked questions about ourselves, and we must think back over the bits and pieces of our lives to construct answers. It is a common occurrence that we must "figure out" what caused a particular event or happening. Every day we make decisions—who to vote for, who to have lunch with, who to trust, which movie to see, which social policy to support. The results of these decisions are dependent on how we perceive and construe social events. It behooves us then to look closely at how we construct and make sense of our social world.

How Do We Make Sense of the World?

Human beings have wonderful brains—powerful and efficient. But, as wonderful as our brains are, they are far from perfect. One consequence of this imperfection is that most of us end up "knowing" a lot of things that simply are not true. Let us take a common example: A great many people harbor the belief that relatively infertile couples who adopt a baby are, subsequently, more likely to conceive a child of their own than relatively infertile couples who do not adopt. The reasoning goes something like this: After the adoption, the pressure is off; now that the couple is relaxed, this somehow makes conception easier. But according to Tom Gilovich,[4] this is simply not true; relatively infertile couples who adopt a baby are no more likely to conceive than relatively infertile couples who do not adopt. Why do most people believe it is so? Two reasons: (1) It is such a charming idea that we *want* it to be true; (2) we tend to focus our attention on those few instances when adoptive parents conceived a baby of their own and *not* on those instances when they failed to conceive or when non-adoptive parents conceived a baby. Thus, because of selective attention and selective memory, it sure *seems* to be true. Indeed, as many of you may have noticed, those who know things that simply are not true are very hard to persuade otherwise.

Are we rational animals or not? We sure try to be. One common view of human cognition is that it is fully rational in nature—each individual attempts to do his or her best to be right and to hold correct opinions and beliefs. One of the primary proponents of this view of human thought was the eighteenth-century utilitarian philosopher Jeremy Bentham. According to Bentham, we engage in a *felicific calculus* or happiness calculation to determine what is good and what is bad.[5] Suppose I wanted to purchase a new car. In determining the make and model to buy, I would add up the pleasure each brand would bring—sporty design, comfortable interior, likelihood of turning the heads of my neighbors—and subtract the pain—the monthly payments will mortgage my future, the car is not capable of going past a gas station without a fill-up, my mechanic will be able to send his two kids to an Ivy League college on the profits from repairing my car alone. I then select the car that brings me the most pleasure and the least pain. For Bentham, it was the role of governments and economic systems to insure "the greatest happiness for the greatest number." Others agreed, for Bentham's concept of felicific calculus became a fundamental assumption underlying modern capitalism.

More recently, the social psychologist Harold Kelley has advanced a slightly more complex view of the rationality of human thought: People attempt to function as *naive scientists*.[6] In order to explain a given event or phenomenon, scientists look for covariation in their data—that is, they attempt to find cases where "X came before Y and always varied with Y and only with Y to conclude that X caused Y." Similarly, in explaining why others do things, people look for three pieces of information: the *consistency* of the actor's action (Does he or she always behave in this manner in other situations and at other times?), *consensus* (Do others behave in the same way in the same situation?), and the *distinctiveness* of the action (Is he or she the only one to behave in this manner?).

For example, suppose Beth kissed Scott and someone asked you why. According to Kelley, you would want to know if Beth goes around kissing almost everyone at the drop of a hat. If so, then you would probably conclude that Beth is a very affectionate person. Suppose you found out that almost *everybody* kisses Scott. Then you might argue that Scott is a very attractive person who is well liked by all. Finally, if Beth kisses only Scott and no one else kisses Scott, then you would probably infer that this highly distinctive behavior is due to some special relationship between Beth and Scott—they are in love.

But do humans figure things out as rationally as Bentham and Kelley suggest we do?[7] There is little argument that we *do* on *some* occasions. Benjamin Franklin routinely performed a felicific calculation by writing down the pros and cons for major decisions. There are times when many of us behave in the same way—as when purchasing a new car or deciding which university to attend. The ease with which you could generate the conclusions about Beth and Scott when given the appropriate covariation information indicates that it is at least possible to think like a naive scientist. However, rational thought requires that at least two conditions hold: (1) the thinker has access to accurate, useful information, and (2) the thinker has unlimited resources with which to process life's data. In truth, these conditions rarely hold in everyday life.

We do *not* possess a "God's-eye" view of the world—a perspective that is all-knowing and free from bias. Consider something as simple as my car purchase. I probably do not know all the facts in the case. Perhaps no one has ever calculated the repair rate for this particular model, or if they have, it is buried away in some dusty library where I can't find it without some difficulty. My view of the car is bounded by my own perspective and limitations; I hear about the car only from advertisers and my friends, both of whom exaggerate certain features depending on their circumstances. I have limited experience with the car—a dealer-supervised test drive as opposed to a year's driving to and from work. If something as common as a new car purchase can be fraught with missing and misleading information, imagine the difficulty when it comes to making more unusual decisions such as when to go to war, whom to marry, or how to spend tax money.

I also do not possess the leisure time or the resources to devote to a full-scale analysis of every problem I encounter. Suppose I go ahead and make a felicific calculation on which car to purchase, and it takes about three hours. In the meantime, a dozen other decisions need to be made—What shall I do for lunch? How should I revise my lecture notes? Which job candidate is best to hire? Does my daughter really need those expensive braces on her teeth—what's wrong with an overbite?

Am I to spend two or three hours listing the pros and cons on each one of these decisions while dozens of upcoming decisions are postponed? We live in a message-dense and decision-rich environment. The average American will see over seven million advertisements in his or her lifetime and will need to make countless decisions every day—some important, some trivial, some seemingly trivial but with important consequences. It is impossible to think deeply about each and every piece of information that comes our way and about each and every decision that must be made.

What then do people do? As you might guess, we try to take shortcuts whenever we can. According to the social psychologists Susan Fiske and Shelley Taylor, human beings are *cognitive misers*—that is, we humans are forever trying to conserve our cognitive energy.[8] Given that we have a limited capacity to process information, we attempt to adopt strategies that simplify complex problems. We accomplish this by ignoring some information to reduce our cognitive load; or we "overuse" other information to keep from having to search for more; or we may be willing to accept a less than perfect alternative because it is almost good enough. The strategies of the cognitive miser may be efficient—making fairly good use of our limited cognitive capacity to process a near infinite world of information—but these strategies can also lead to serious errors and biases, especially when we select the wrong simple strategy, or in our rush to move on, we ignore a vital piece of information.

Some readers may be disheartened to find that they are not as rational or as thorough in their thinking as they might have supposed. It is comforting to believe that the human mind has unlimited, even hidden powers—as proclaimed in many pop psychology books. It is comforting to believe that one has a personal pipeline to the absolute. But it is dangerous to fail to realize that one's shortcuts can produce biases and prejudices that are far from the absolute. Unless we recognize our cognitive limitations we cannot take steps to over-come them. For example, if we fail to realize that we often judge others on the basis of stereotypes or that the way information is presented can distort our judgment, we are unable to take steps to correct our errors. And what is worse, by not admitting that we are cognitive misers, we may come to believe that our personal perspec-tive is the only perspective there is, and it is thereby synonymous with Truth. As history demonstrates, it is very easy to commit acts of hatred and cruelty when one knows oneself to be absolutely right.[9]

The fact that we are cognitive misers does not mean that we are doomed to distort. Indeed, once we know some of the limitations and common biases of the human mind, we can begin to think a little better and make smarter decisions. It is my purpose in this chapter not simply to list some of these limitations of our thinking, but rather, by exploring these limitations, it is my hope that we can learn to think a little more clearly.

The Effects of Context on Social Judgment

Let's begin by looking at how the social context—the way things are presented and described—affects our social judgment and cognition. We will take, in turn, four different aspects of the social context: the comparison alternatives, the thoughts primed by a situation, how a decision is framed or posed, and the way information is presented. As we do so, a basic principle of social thinking should emerge: Judg-ment is relative; how we think about a person or thing is dependent on its surrounding context.

Reference Points and Contrast Effects.   Real estate agents implicit-ly understand this one basic principle of social cognition—*judgment is relative.* How we evaluate and perceive an object is highly depend-ent on the nature of the alternatives around it—the point of reference we use to make a comparison. An object can appear to be better or worse depending on the quality of objects it is compared to. Sometimes this effect can be quite subtle yet have powerful consequences.

Let's see what we mean by going on a typical trip with a real estate agent. After determining your needs, the agent drives you to some homes "you might find of interest." The first stop is a tiny two-bedroom house sitting on a smallish lot. The house needs a new coat of paint; the interior is in disarray; the linoleum in the kitchen is buckling; the living room carpet is worn; the master bedroom is so small that an average-sized bedroom suite simply won't fit. When the realtor tells you the asking price, you exclaim, "Holy cow! They want that price for this place? Who'd be dumb enough to pay so much for this shack?" Probably not you and probably not anyone else. But that dilapidated house may influence you to more readily buy another home and to pay a *higher* price than you might have otherwise paid.

How can this come about? This process can be clarified by looking at an experiment conducted by Anthony Pratkanis and his colleagues.[10] In this experiment, students were asked to make decisions such as the following: Which would you select (a or b)?

a. *Nutri-burger:* a tofu burger that is rated very good on nutrition but only average on taste.

b. *Tasti-burger:* a hamburger that is rated very good on taste but only average on nutrition.

For some decisions, a decoy was given as an additional option. A decoy is an alternative that is inferior to other possible selections. For example, which would you prefer (a, b, or c)?

a. *Nutri-burger:* the tofu burger described above.

b. *Tasti-burger:* the hamburger described above.

c. *Bummer-burger:* a hamburger that is rated only *good* on taste and only average on nutrition.

In this case, the decoy is Option C—the hamburger that is only *good* on taste (as opposed to *very* good). No reasonable person would select this inferior burger. If you wanted a lunch that tasted great, you would select Option B—the very good tasting *Tasti-burger.* If you wanted nutrition, you would go for the tofu burger. Indeed, in the experiment the decoy was almost never selected.

But that does not mean it wasn't influential. The Pratkanis experiment investigated decisions about nine common consumer products. They found that including a decoy (like the one in Option C, above) increased the probability of selecting the *Tasti-burger* (the very good hamburger) over the *Nutri-burger* (the tofu burger) by 6.7 percent. Does 6.7 percent seem like a small amount? To put this in perspective, a 1 percent change in market share for a small brand manufactured by a company like Proctor & Gamble or General Motors could mean over a $10 million increase in sales each year.

How did this relatively worthless decoy change students' choices? The answer in a nutshell is: *contrast effects*. To contrast means to make the differences apparent. When an object is contrasted with something similar but not as good, or not as pretty, or not as tall, that particular object is judged to be better, prettier, taller than would normally be the case. If a man of normal height (say 5 feet 11 inches) is in the company of midgets, he seems very tall. If he is a member of a professional basketball team, he seems very short. Some of you may recall a young man who played basketball for the Boston Celtics—"Tiny" Archibald. Would it surprise you to learn that "Tiny" stood at 6 feet 1 inch tall? In Jonathan Swift's classic novel *Gulliver's Travels*, the hero, a man of normal height, was considered a giant when traveling among the residents of Lilliput and a dwarf when traveling among the residents of Brobdingnag.

As just one example of contrast effects, Douglas Kenrick and Sara Gutierres[11] asked male college students to rate the attractiveness of a potential blind date before or after watching the television show "Charlie's Angels." The males rated the woman as *less* attractive after they saw the show than before. Presumably, the gorgeous Angels provided a stringent context for rating attractiveness; the blind date appeared to be far less physically attractive when compared to the Angels than to women in general.

In the Pratkanis experiment on consumer decision making, two contrast effects occurred that made the *Tasti-burger* look more attractive. The presence of a decoy made the very good tasting *Tasti-burger* appear to be even better tasting and the average tasting *Nutri-burger* to be even *poorer* tasting. In other words, the decoy "spread apart" the *Tasti-* and *Nutri-burgers* on the dimension of taste. With this change in the perception of tastiness, the choice became much clearer for our subjects.

Now we can see how that visit to the dilapidated house can influence our purchase. Perhaps the next house you look at is not really ideal. But compared to that last one—what an improvement! The yard and the master bedroom are bigger. The interior is in good shape. We won't need to paint it for at least three years. And the price is only slightly higher than what they were asking for that old shack. What a deal! We'll take it right away—before the owner has a chance to change his mind!

Contrast effects can occur subtly and can have powerful effects. A used-car dealer may place an old clunker on the lot to "improve the appearance" of the other autos. A presidential candidate may select a vice-presidential running mate of lesser stature to enhance the positive perception of his or her own presidential qualities. A presidential policy allowing seven hostages to remain in Beirut doesn't seem so bad compared to one associated with the kidnapping of an entire embassy in Iran.

The lesson to be learned from research on contrast effects is that the selection of comparisons makes a difference. Depending on the context, objects and alternatives can be made to look better or worse. Often we do not pay much attention to the influence of context, much less question the validity of the alternatives presented. This greatly enhances the power of "context makers" such as politicians, advertisers, journalists, and sales agents. The context they set can influence our perceptions and judgments, lulling us into decisions that we would not normally make.

Priming and Construct Accessibility. One of the standard comedic devices on television sitcoms is the *double entendre.* A typical double entendre goes like this: Early in the show the young teenage daughter tells everyone but her father that she made the school's coed softball team as the starting catcher. On the other hand, her father finds out about a big party sponsored by some of the daughter's classmates which promises to have "some wild goings-on" and just happens to be scheduled on the same night as the softball game. The climactic scene involves the father overhearing his "innocent" daughter telling her friend about a pitcher:

> "Boy, I can hardly wait for tonight—I am so excited. I've never played with Tommy before. I love his technique. If he tries, I know he can go all the way. Tommy has wonderful stuff."

The father is outraged and storms out of the house to intercept his young daughter. The audience is "entertained" because they know what is happening; the father thinks his daughter is talking about sex when she is really discussing softball.

The double entendre of the sitcom illustrates a principle of social cognition: How we interpret social events—especially ambiguous ones—often depends on what we are currently thinking about, what beliefs and categories we use to make sense of things. The categories we use to interpret the world can vary with individuals—some people see the world through rose-colored glasses, whereas others see it in hostile or depressive terms. It can also depend on the situation through a procedure known as *priming:* Recently and frequently activated concepts are more likely to readily come to mind and thus be used in interpreting social events.

A study by Tory Higgins, William Rholes, and Carl Jones illustrates the role of priming in the formation of impressions about other people.[12] In this experiment, subjects were asked to participate in two "different" research projects—one on perception and one on reading comprehension. The first experiment served to prime different trait categories; some of the subjects were asked to remember positive trait words (adventurous, self-confident, independent, and persistent), whereas the others were asked to remember negative traits (reckless, conceited, aloof, and stubborn). Five minutes later, as part of the "reading comprehension" study, subjects then read an ambiguous paragraph about a fictitious person named "Donald." The paragraph described a number of behaviors performed by Donald that could be seen as adventurous or reckless (e.g., skydiving), self-confident or conceited (e.g., believes in his abilities), independent or aloof (e.g., doesn't rely on anyone), and persistent or stubborn (e.g., doesn't change his mind often). The subjects then described Donald in their own words and rated how desirable they considered him to be. The results showed that the priming manipulation influenced the subjects' impressions of Donald. When negative trait categories had been primed, they characterized Donald in negative terms and saw him as less desirable than when positive categories had been primed.

The effects of priming on social judgment are not limited to television sitcoms and laboratory demonstrations. Priming can and does have a major impact on the attitudes and behavior of a great many people—even of seasoned professionals in life and death situations in the real world. For example, consider experienced physicians who work with AIDS patients. One might imagine that they would have a clear and solid idea about their own risk of infection. Linda Heath and her colleagues[13] found that this is not necessarily the case. They asked several hundred physicians about their perceived risk of contracting HIV on the job. For one group of physicians, Heath primed their thoughts about the danger by getting them to imagine their being exposed to the virus while doing their work. The assessment of risk of these physicians was deeply affected by the priming. Specifically, those physicians who were instructed to imagine themselves being exposed to HIV on the job subsequently felt that there was a significantly higher risk of their being infected than those who were not primed. This was true regardless of the extent of the physicians' actual experiences with HIV-infected patients.

Let us look at priming in the mass media. Several studies have shown that there is a link between which stories the media covers and what viewers consider to be the most important issues of the day.[14] In other words, the mass media make certain issues and concepts readily accessible and thereby set the public's political and social agenda. To take one example, in a pioneering study of an election in North Carolina, Maxwell McCombs and Donald Shaw[15] found that the issues voters came to consider to be most important in the campaign coincided precisely with the amount of coverage of those issues in the local media. Similarly, the problems of drug abuse, NASA's incompetence, and nuclear energy were catapulted into the nation's consciousness by the coverage of dramatic events such as the drug-related death of basketball star Len Bias, the Challenger explosion, and the events of Three-Mile Island and Chernobyl.

In a set of ingenious experiments, the political psychologists Shanto Iyengar and Donald Kinder demonstrated the importance of priming to account for the relationship between repeated media exposure and issue importance.[16] In their studies, Iyengar and Kinder actually varied the contents of news shows watched by the participants in their experiments. Specifically, Iyengar and Kinder edited the evening news so that participants received a steady dose of news about a specific problem facing the United States. For example, in one of their experiments, some participants watched reports of the weaknesses of the U.S. defense capabilities; others watched shows emphasizing pollution concerns; a third group watched accounts of inflation and economic matters.

The results were clear. After a week of viewing the edited programs, participants emerged from the experiment convinced that the target problem—the one primed by extensive coverage in the shows that they watched—was a more important problem for the country to solve than they did before viewing the shows. What's more, the research participants acted on their newfound perceptions, evaluating the current U.S. president's performance on the basis of how he handled the target problem, and were more positively disposed toward candidates who stated strong positions on those issues. As the political scientist Bernard Cohen observed, the mass media

> may not be successful much of the time in telling people *what to think,* but it is stunningly successful in telling its readers *what to think about.* . . . The world will look different to different people, depending . . . on the map that is drawn for them by the writers, editors, and publishers of the papers they read.[17]

Framing the Decision. Another factor influencing how we construct our social world is decision framing—whether a problem or decision is presented in a such a way that it appears to represent the potential for a loss or for a gain. To illustrate the power of decision framing, let's imagine that you are the president of the United States and the country is bracing itself for the outbreak of an unusual epidemic expected to kill six hundred people. Your top advisors have prepared two alternative programs to combat the disease and have estimated, to the best of their abilities, the likely consequences of each program.

If Program A is adopted, two hundred people will be saved.

If Program B is adopted, there is a one-third probability that six hundred people will be saved and a two-thirds probability that no people will be saved.

Ms. or Mr. President, which program do you favor? Please think about this carefully and answer before you read on.

If you are like most of the subjects in an experiment performed by Daniel Kahneman and Amos Tversky, you would select Program A (72 percent of their subjects selected this option).[18] You might think to yourself, "Program A guarantees that two hundred people will be saved, and Program B gambles the lives of these people for only a 1 in 3 chance that we could save more lives."

But suppose your advisors had asked for your judgment in a different manner. Suppose they presented the problem this way:

If Program A is adopted, four hundred people will die.

If Program B is adopted, there is a one-third probability that nobody will die and a two-thirds probability that six hundred people will die.

Which program would you favor? Please think about this carefully and answer the question before reading more.

The two options are the same. Program A means that two hundred people will live and four hundred will die. Program B results in a one-third chance that no one will die and six hundred people will live and a two-thirds chance that no one will be saved and six hundred people will die. But for most people, their thinking about the epidemic is quite different. "If I go with Program A, four hundred people will surely die. I might as well gamble on B." When asked in this second manner, 78 percent of Kahneman and Tversky's subjects favored *Program B!*

Why did such a simple rewording of the options produce such a drastic switch in answers? Kahneman and Tversky have noted that people dislike losses and seek to avoid them. It is more painful to give up twenty dollars than it is pleasurable to gain twenty dollars. Your advisors framed the first policy decision so that Program B looked like the bigger loss; in the second version your advisors framed it so that Program A looked like a sure loss. How the question is framed is of enormous importance.

But this is just an imaginary event. It is a hypothetical situation. Surely such a simple rewording of a request cannot influence real behavior. Don't bet on it. In a recent experiment I did with Marti Gonzales and Mark Costanzo, we showed that framing can play a major role in determining whether or not people are willing to commit hundreds of dollars to insulate their homes in order to conserve energy.[19] In one condition, after examining each home, energy experts gave each homeowner a detailed individual description of how much money they could *save* each year on heating bills. In the other condition, auditors were trained to frame the description in terms of *loss;* that is, they provided the same information but informed the homeowner that they were losing money every day—that it was akin to throwing money out the window. Homeowners in the "loss" condition were twice as likely to insulate their homes as those in the "save" condition.

Let's look at the prevention of breast cancer. Breast cancer poses a serious health threat for a great many women. Fortunately, early detection and diagnosis of breast cancer can greatly improve a woman's chances of surviving the disease. However, one of the best methods for detecting breast cancer, a monthly breast self-examination, is not performed regularly by the vast majority of women. Beth Meyerowitz and Shelly Chaiken developed and distributed three pamphlets designed to increase routine breast self-examination by women.[20] One pamphlet contained only information concerning the need to perform self-examinations plus how to do it. Another pamphlet contained this information plus arguments emphasizing the positive consequences of self-examination (e.g., women who perform such examinations have an *increased* chance of finding a tumor at the early, treatable stage). A third pamphlet stressed the negative consequences of failing to perform a self-examination (e.g., women who do *not* perform such examinations have a *decreased* chance of finding the tumor at the early, treatable stage). Meyerowitz and Chaiken found that, four months after reading the pamphlet, only those women who received the pamphlet stressing the negative consequences were significantly more likely to perform a breast self-examination. How you frame a decision can make a big difference in a life-and-death situation.

The Ordering of Information. Another factor influencing the way we organize and interpret the social world is the manner in which information is arranged and distributed. Let's look at two characteristics of the way information is presented and their effects on social judgment: (a) what comes first and (b) the amount of information given.

The Primacy Effect and Impression Formation. In the preceding chapter, we discussed the order of presentation for persuasive arguments—that is, in a debate, the conditions under which it is more effective to state one's arguments first *(primacy effect)* or last *(recency effect).* When it comes to forming impressions of other people, how-ever, there is not much of a contest: With few exceptions, the old saw "Put your best foot forward" turns out to be accurate; the things we learn first about a person (*the primacy effect*) have a decisive impact on our judgment of that person. In a pioneering experiment, Solomon Asch demonstrated the power of the primacy effect.[21] In Asch's study, subjects received sentences such as the following and then were asked to rate the person described in each sentence.

a. Steve is intelligent, industrious, impulsive, critical, stubborn, and envious.

b. Steve is envious, stubborn, critical, impulsive, industrious, and intelligent.

Note that the two sentences contain exactly the same information about Steve; however Sentence A puts the positive traits first whereas Sentence B puts them last. Asch found that Steve was rated more positively when he was described by Sentence A compared to B—a primacy effect.

Asch's original finding has been repeated many times in many ways. For example, in experiments by Edward Jones and his col-leagues, research participants observed another individual perform-ing on a series of thirty intelligence-test items.[22] In each case, the person answered fifteen of the thirty questions correctly. However, sometimes the person would start out "hot," that is, answering a lot of questions correctly at the beginning, and then would decline in performance; at other times the person would start out slow, answer-ing few questions correctly at first, and then would finish with a bang, answering most of the final items. Who was perceived as most in-telligent? As one might expect based on what we know about the primacy effect, the individual who started out "hot" was seen as more intelligent than the "late bloomer," despite the fact that both an-swered the same number of items correctly.

An interesting exception to this rule was discovered recently in an experiment by Joshua Aronson and Edward Jones.[23] Aronson and Jones motivated their subjects to try and improve the performance of a target person ("their student") on a set of anagrams. Half of the subjects were instructed simply to try to raise their student's score; the remaining subjects were instructed to try and improve the *ability* of their student to solve anagrams. Within each of these conditions, after training their student, each received information about that person's performance. This performance information was exactly like that in the Jones experiment cited above: That is, some received information that the earlier performance of their student was very good and the later performance was not so good; others received information that the early performance was not so good and the later performance was very good. The sum total was identical—only the order differed.

Those subjects who were motivated to improve the performance of their students rated them as more intelligent when their *early* performance was good. This is the primacy effect: They trained their students to do well and, after the first few trials, concluded their students were intelligent—regardless of their later performance. But those subjects who were trying to improve the *ability* of their students to solve anagrams rated as more intelligent those who started poorly but ended up doing well. In other words, they were more impressed with *increases* in performance than with a fast start. "Ability" is something that develops—thus, we like to see our students improve; it means they have ability.

Although the results of the Aronson and Jones experiment demonstrates the complexity of the phenomenon, it is an interesting exception to the general rule. And with very few exceptions, in forming impressions of people, primacy predominates.

Why does the primacy effect in impression formation occur? Researchers have found evidence for two explanations—either of which can be true depending on the circumstances. According to the *attention decrement* explanation, the latter items in a list receive less attention as the observers tire and their minds start to wander, and thus these items have less impact on judgment. According to the *interpretive set* explanation, the first items serve to create an initial impression that then is used to interpret subsequent information either through the discounting of incongruent facts (i.e., if Steve is intelligent, why should he be envious?) or by subtle changes in the meaning of the words further down the list (i.e., being critical is a positive attribute if Steve is intelligent, but a negative one if he is stubborn). Regardless of the explanation, primacy effects have an important impact on social judgment. Moreover we usually have little control over the order in which we receive information—whether that information is from a television news show or from our everyday observations of friends and neighbors. Therefore, it is important to realize the existence of these effects so that we might try to correct for them.

The Amount of Information. When pondering a difficult decision, a common plea is often heard: "If I only had more information." Although having more information may sometimes be helpful, it can also change how an object is perceived and evaluated through what is called the *dilution effect.* The dilution effect is the tendency for neutral and irrelevant information to weaken a judgment or impression. Consider this example, taken from an experiment by Henry Zukier.[24] Which student has the highest grade point average?

Tim spends about thirty-one hours studying outside class in an average week.

Tom spends about thirty-one hours studying outside class in an average week. Tom O. has one brother and two sisters. He visits his grandparents about once every three months. He once went on a blind date and shoots pool about once every two months.

If you are similar to the students in Zukier's study, you would believe that Tim is smarter than Tom. Zukier found that including irrelevant and nondiagnostic information (such as information on siblings, family visitation, and dating habits) which has nothing to do with the issue at hand can dilute—that is, make less potent—the impact of relevant information (that both Tim and Tom spend a lot of time studying).

The dilution effect has obvious practical value for those interested in managing impressions, such as those in sales or politics. Advertisers know that including weak or irrelevant claims can reduce the impact of a strong sales appeal. A disliked politician can reduce the impact of his negative image by including irrelevant information —a story about his or her childhood or a description of the family house—in campaign advertisements.

But why does the dilution effect occur? After all, it makes little sense to pay attention to nondiagnostic information in making a judgment. Why should information on dating habits make someone appear to be less intelligent or a story about the birthplace of a politician lessen the impact of his or her negative image? One answer is that irrelevant information about a person makes that person seem more similar to others and thus more average and like everyone else. An average person is less likely to have an extremely high grade-point average or to be terribly negative.

Judgment Heuristics

One way that we make sense of the buzzing, booming array of information that comes our way is through the use of *heuristics*. A heuristic is a simple, but often only approximate, rule or strategy for solving a problem.[25] Some examples include: "If a man and a woman are walking down a street, the man walks on the outside." "If a particular food item is found in a 'health food store,' it must be good for you." "If the person is from a rural town in Arkansas, he or she must be intellectually backward." Heuristics require very little thought—just the selection of the rule (which may not be the correct one to use) and a straightforward application to the issue at hand. It can be contrasted with more systematic thinking in which we may look at a problem from a number of angles, array and evaluate as much relevant information as possible, and work out in detail the implications of various solutions. Let's look at two of the most common classes of heuristics—the representative and the attitude heuristics.

The Representative Heuristic. According to Amos Tversky and Daniel Kahneman, who coined the term, the *representative heuristic* uses the similarity or resemblance of an object to another object to infer that the first object acts like the second one. For example, we know that high-quality products often come with expensive price tags. I see two bottles of wine on the shelf; one has a higher price. Which is better? Quite obviously, the one with the higher price, because higher price is a common attribute of quality products. I select the one feature of price (among many others that I *might* have focused on—such as type of grape, vintner, vintage, wine-growing region), and I use that to infer that the high-priced bottle is like other high-priced things—high in quality. As most smart consumers know, high price does not always mean high quality. Let's look in more detail at the implications of the use of the representative heuristic by eavesdropping on a conversation between mother and child in the aisle of a local supermarket.

The story begins when seven-year-old Rachel spots her favorite cereal, Lucky Charms, takes a box off the shelf, and quietly delivers it to the shopping cart. Her mom looks at the box in disgust. It is bright red. A leprechaun is sprinkling shining stars (must be sugar) over pink and purple marshmallow bits. On the back of the box her mom finds a message informing her that an enclosed special pair of glasses are to be used to spot hidden leprechauns.

Mom sternly announces, "Rachel, put that junk back on the shelf. It is loaded with sugar and nothing but empty calories."

Rachel replies, "But Mom, it tastes good. The other stuff tastes yukky."

Being a smart mom, she offers Rachel another choice and a little inducement, "Why not this one? It's called 100% Natural. It is good for you. You'll be a big girl."

Rachel looks at the box. It is small but heavy. The front features a bowl of light brown cereal set against a wood-grain background and a couple of stalks of unprocessed grains. On the back of the box is a lot of small, hard-to-read writing.

Rachel exclaims, "Yukko! I don't want to be a big girl."

How would you resolve the great breakfast cereal standoff? Would you side with the mother and opt for nutrition even though Rachel may not eat it? Or would you feel that Rachel, even at this tender age, should be making her own decisions regardless of the consequences? My recommendation may surprise you because, chances are, you fell into my trap! The fight is for naught. Tell Rachel and her mom to buy the Lucky Charms because, in actuality, it is more nutritional than the "natural" cereal. Let me explain.

In 1981, the magazine *Consumer Reports,* a highly respected source of consumer information, conducted a test of breakfast cereals.[26] Their researchers fed young rats, which have nutritional requirements remarkably similar to humans, an exclusive diet of water and one of thirty-two brands of breakfast cereals for a period of fourteen to eighteen weeks. They found that the rats grew and remained healthy on a diet of Lucky Charms. On the other hand, a diet of Quaker's 100% Natural retarded their growth.

A comparison between Lucky Charms and 100% Natural shows that Lucky Charms is lower in calories and in saturated fats than

100% Natural.[27] While it is also slightly higher in sugar, this difference is negligible and of no dietary importance.

What caused the disagreement between Rachel and her mom? It is clear that they used the cereal *package* (not the cereal) as a representative heuristic. In this case, the problem for Mom was to select a nutritious cereal; for Rachel the problem was to get a cereal that is fun and tasty. The box of Lucky Charms resembles a child's toy—bright colors, cartoon character; there is even a kid's game on the box. We infer that this cereal is "childish," and since children eat junk food if not carefully supervised, this cereal must be junk. On the other hand, the earth tones and pictures of unprocessed grains on the 100% Natural box resembles nature itself (and, of course, the brand name is consistent). Nature is good and wholesome. The cereal must be nutritious. In both cases, the cereal packages were designed so that Rachel and her mom would infer certain attributes about the products—qualities that may or may not be present in the actual products. Armed with these conclusions, people can make the choice of which cereal to purchase and proceed without much additional thought—and they will often make poor choices.

The representative heuristic can be used in places other than the supermarket.[28] An analysis of folk remedies and early Western medicine shows that a common assumption is that the cure should resemble the cause of the disease. For example, in one culture, epilepsy is treated with a drug made from a monkey whose movements appear epileptic. Similarly, in Western culture, newspapers initially ridiculed Walter Reed's suggestion that yellow fever was carried by a mosquito, since there is little resemblance between the cause (mosquitoes) and the result (malaria). The representative heuristic is used to identify psychological causes as well. An old saw contends that a child born with a "veil" (part of the amniotic sac over the face) is marked for eminence. Many believe that political radicalism and nonconformity are based on permissive child-rearing practices. In early psychoanalytic theorizing, an obsessive-compulsive personality is known as anal-retentive and was oversimply viewed as the result of early and severe toilet-training practices.

The representative heuristic is often used to form impressions and to make judgments about other persons. The first information that we pick up about a person—information about gender, race, physical attractiveness, and social status—is usually associated with simple rules that guide thought and behavior. Gender and racial stereotypes tell us "just how men and women differ" and "what a particular member of an ethnic group is like." Much research has demonstrated that most people leap to the conclusion that beautiful people are more successful, sensitive, warmer, and of better character than less attractive people. Persons of high social stature, often inferred by dress and mannerisms, are respected and held in high esteem. Is it any wonder that "get ahead" self-help books often describe how to take advantage of these heuristics by urging their readers to "dress for success," that is, to wear the *right* clothes to create the *right* image or to use the *right* cosmetics to enhance their attractiveness?

The Attitude Heuristic. An attitude is a special type of belief that describes the evaluative properties of an object; an attitude is thus a stored evaluation—good or bad—of an object. For example, chocolate ice cream, pay increases, and my wife are good; snakes, federal deficits, and whining colleagues are bad. According to Anthony Pratkanis and Anthony Greenwald, attitudes can be used as a heuristic to solve problems.[29] Attitudes can be used to assign objects to a favorable class (for which strategies of favoring, approaching, praising, cherishing, and protecting are appropriate) or to an unfavorable category (for which strategies of disfavoring, avoiding, blaming, neglecting, and harming are used). For example, if Sam dislikes former President Ronald Reagan, then, according to Sam, the current federal deficit is the result of Reagan's "charge card" economic policies.

Much research has shown that attitudes can be used to make sense of our social world. For example, a study by Anthony Pratkanis found that a person's attitudes could even affect what he or she knows to be true.[30] In this study, college students were asked to identify which of two possible statements—such as the following—was true:

a. Ronald Reagan maintained an "A" average at Eureka College.

b. Ronald Reagan never achieved above a "C" average at Eureka College.

What did Pratkanis find? It depended on the student's attitude toward Ronald Reagan. Students who liked Ronald Reagan were more likely to believe Statement A—yes, the ex-president did very well in school. On the other hand, students who disliked Reagan were more likely to believe Statement B. What is more, the more extreme the attitude toward Reagan—the more liked and disliked—the more confidence the students had in their judgments. In other words, the students in this study used their attitudes as a heuristic to discern what is true and then believed that what they determined was correct. For those of you who are curious, Statement B is correct. Reagan never achieved above a "C" average in college. This is an actual fact and has nothing to do with my personal attitude toward Mr. Reagan!

The use of an attitude heuristic can influence our logic and ability to reason. For example, in the late 1940s, Donald Thistlewaite asked respondents to state whether syllogisms such as the following were valid:[31]

> *Given:* If production is important, then peaceful industrial relations are desirable. If production is important, then it is a mistake to have Negroes for foremen and leaders over Whites.
>
> *Therefore:* If peaceful industrial relations are desirable, then it is a mistake to have Negroes for foremen and leaders over Whites.

A moment's reflection shows that the syllogism, as stated, is illogical; the conclusion does not logically follow from the premises. But Thistlewaite found that prejudiced individuals (who agree with the conclusion) are far more likely to indicate (incorrectly) that the logic is valid compared to less prejudiced people.

Two other examples of the attitude heuristic have been termed the *halo* and *false-consensus effects.* The halo effect is a general bias in which a favorable or unfavorable impression of a person biases future expectations and inferences about that person. For example, a liked individual—such as a job candidate, a student taking a test, a politician announcing a new policy—is expected to possess positive traits, which act like an angel's halo, and thus any negative performance is discounted and positive performance is overvalued. Similarly, a disliked individual is assumed to possess negative traits with their performance subsequently devalued.

The false-consensus effect refers to the tendency to overestimate the percentage of people who agree with us on any issue—if I believe it, then just about everyone else does too. For example, in one experiment, Lee Ross and his colleagues[32] asked college students if they were willing to wear a sign around campus that said "Eat at Joe's." Those who agreed to wear the sign thought that most other people would too; those who decided against wearing the sign estimated that few other students would wear the sign. In other words, we often make the (not necessarily true) assumption that others like what we like and do what we prefer to do.

When Do We Use Heuristics? Of course, decisions don't have to be based on heuristics. Rachel's mother might have carefully read the ingredients on the cereal box, subscribed to a consumer magazine, or consulted nutrition textbooks. Similarly, we could carefully reason about an issue or study the record and accomplishments of a politician; this would make us less likely to use our attitudes as a simple way to make sense of the world. And, occasionally, most of us *do* go through the decision-making process in a rational manner.

This raises an important question: What conditions are most likely to lead to heuristic use rather than rational decision making? Research has identified at least five such conditions.[33] Heuristics are most likely to be used when we don't have *time* to think carefully about an issue, when we are so *overloaded with information* that it becomes impossible to process the information fully, or when the issues at stake are *not very important*, so that we do not care to think about it. Heuristics are also used when we have *little other knowledge or information* to use in making a decision and when a given heuristic *comes quickly to mind* as we are confronted with a problem.

A moment's thought will reveal that the persuasion landscape faced by Rachel and her mother contains many of the features that lead to heuristic decision making. If she is like most Americans, Rachel's mother is feeling increasingly time-pressed since her leisure time has eroded considerably in the last ten years. As a consumer, she faces a message-dense environment complete with a choice of over three hundred different brands of cereal currently on the market. She probably has had little consumer education or training. At the same time, she has been the recipient of millions of advertisements, each repeating and repeating a brand image, so that this image will quickly come to mind in the aisles of the local supermarket. Given this state of affairs, it is a wonder that *all* decisions aren't made heuristically.

Categorization and Social Stereotypes

Before the Persian Gulf War of 1991, the United States Congress held a series of debates on the positive and negative consequences of going to war. Those who supported the war described Saddam Hussein as "the new Hitler"; they emphasized the parallels between Saddam's gassing of the Kurds and Hitler's gassing of the Jews, Iraq's invasion of Kuwait and Germany's invasion of Poland and the Baltics, and Saddam and Hitler's buildup of armaments. Those who opposed the war saw the situation in Iraq as paralleling that of Vietnam; they saw both incidents as civil wars—a fight between North and South Vietnam and between various Arab factions; they worried about the U.S. military's ability to fight in foreign terrains of swamps and deserts; they characterized the war efforts as a war in support of "big business" and "big oil."

The debate over war with Iraq was really a debate over whose categorization of ambiguous events was "correct." And with good reason! For once it is decided how an event or person should be categorized, it becomes clear what course of action should be taken. If Saddam is truly a "new Hitler," then the policy of economic sanctions (which some considered a form of appeasement) will only bring additional threats to peace and ultimately a much worse war. If Iraq is another Vietnam, then intervention would lead to a long and divisive war, becoming mired in a quagmire with no clear victors and losers.[34]

We make the "debate" over how to categorize persons and events thousands of times a day, and although we often do not go to war over the results, the consequences of how we interpret and define events can be significant. For example, I know a social psychologist whom I consider one of the best researchers of his generation. He is also a thoughtful and considerate human being and a leading contributor to theory X. However, he is rarely described as "a leading light in the field who cares about people" or "a major proponent of theory X." Instead, he is known as a "very talented black psychologist." What are the consequences for this person and for the field of social psychology to constantly refer to this individual as black as opposed to any of a number of other equally applicable attributes? Later in this book, we will look in detail at the nature and consequences of prejudice. For now, let us look at how we categorize events and persons and with what effect.

Stereotypic Knowledge and Expectations.   One of the most important consequences of categorization is that it can invoke a set of specific data or *stereotypes* that then guides our expectations. For example, each of the following words probably invokes some very specific meanings: Yuppie, college professor, party girl, racist, and liberal democrat. Once we categorize a person or an event using one of these terms (as opposed to others), we base our expectations about future interactions on the accompanying stereotypes. Suppose I go into a restaurant and classify it as a "bar" as opposed to a "fine dining establishment." I will probably think of the restaurant in different terms and act in different ways—and probably foolishly if I have mistakenly categorized the restaurant and invoked the wrong script.

An interesting study by John Darley and Paget Gross[35] demonstrates the power of expectations created by a stereotype to influence the way we think and make judgments. In their experiment, they told four different stories about "Hannah"—a fourth-grade schoolchild. After hearing one of the four stories, Princeton college students were asked to estimate Hannah's academic abilities. In the first two stories, subjects merely saw a videotape of Hannah playing in either a high socioeconomic or a low socioeconomic neighborhood, designed to create expectations that Hannah was either from a poor or affluent background. In the second two stories, subjects saw one of these videotapes of Hannah playing and, in addition, viewed a film of Hannah completing twenty-five achievement-test problems. Hannah's performance on these tests was ambiguous—she sometimes answered tough questions and sometimes missed easy ones.

Darley and Gross found that, when subjects saw just one of the two videotapes of Hannah playing, they rated her ability as average; Hannah was just like everyone else in her class. In other words, subjects who saw these films did not use their stereotypes in making their judgments. However, when subjects also watched the film of Hannah solving achievement-test problems, the effects of stereotypes became apparent: Subjects rated Hannah as having *less* ability when she came from the low as opposed to high socioeconomic background; they also interpreted her ambiguous performance as consistent with their judgments—evaluating the test as easier and estimating that fewer problems were solved when Hannah came from a poor background. Two lessons can be learned about stereotypes from this experiment. First, most people seem to have some knowledge of stereotype effects and an ability to control them to some extent. Second, despite this knowledge about stereotypes, they still influence perception and judgments when there is additional information that lends a false sense of rationality to the judgment.

Seeing Relationships Where There Are None: The Illusory Correlation. Still another effect of categorization and stereotyping is called the *illusory correlation*—we see a relationship that we think should be there, but in reality it is not. An experiment by David Hamilton and Terrence Rose illustrates the illusory correlation.[36] In this experiment, subjects read twenty-four statements that described different persons by name, occupation, and two trait adjectives. For example, subjects read statements such as "Tom, the salesman, is talkative and boring," or "Bill, the accountant, is timid and courteous." Sometimes the trait words were stereotypic of the occupation—that is, salesmen are enthusiastic and talkative, and accountants are perfectionist and timid. Subjects overestimated the frequency with which stereotypic words were used to describe each occupation. In other words, even though there was no relationship between an occupation and a trait word, subjects thought there was one if the trait word fit their stereotype of the occupation.

The illusory correlation shows itself quite often in social judgments. Consider these two examples: In informal surveys, people consistently overestimate the extent to which lesbians are likely to contract the AIDS virus.[37] In fact, lesbians have the lowest rate of HIV infection compared to male homosexuals and male and female heterosexuals. However, knowledge that male homosexuals have high rates of HIV infection coupled with the categorization of a woman as homosexual leads to the mistaken judgment that lesbians are likely to have AIDS. In clinical judgments, categorizing an individual into a certain diagnostic category (such as schizophrenic or manic-depressive) can lead to the perception of a relationship (even when none exists) between the individual and behavior consistent with that diagnosis.[38] Regardless of the setting, the illusory correlation does much to confirm our original stereotypes and beliefs; our stereotype leads us to see a relationship that then seems to provide evidence that the original stereotype is true.

In-Group/Out-Group Effects.   One of the most common ways of categorizing people is to divide the world into two groups: those in "my" group and the "out" group. For example, we often divide the world into us versus them, my school versus yours, my sports team versus the opponent, Americans versus foreigners, my ethnic group versus yours, or those who sit at my lunch table versus the rest of you. When we divide the world into two such realities, researchers have found considerable evidence for at least two consequences which can be termed "they-all-look-alike-to-me" effect and in-group favoritism.

In general, we tend to see members of out-groups as more similar to each other than the members of our own group. For example, Bernadette Park and Myron Rothbart asked members of three dif-ferent sororities to indicate how similar members of each sorority were to each other.[39] They found that the women perceived more similarity of members in other sororities compared to their own. In other words, the women in other sororities all looked alike. One explanation for this effect is that when the subjects thought of mem-bers in their own group, they thought of them as individuals, each with a unique personality and lifestyle. On the other hand, when they thought of out-group members, they considered them in terms of the group label and stereotype and thus saw them each as similar to this group identity.

In-group favoritism refers to the tendency to see one's own group as "better" on any number of dimensions and to allocate rewards to one's own group. In-group favoritism has been extensively studied using what has come to be known as the *minimum group paradigm.* In this procedure, first identified by the British social psychologist Henri Tajfel,[40] complete strangers are formed into groups using the most trivial, inconsequential criteria imaginable. For example, in one study, subjects watched a coin toss that randomly assigned them to "Group X" or "Group W." In another study, subjects were first asked to express their opinions about artists that they had never heard of before and were then randomly assigned either to a group that appreciates "Klee" or one that enjoys "Kandinsky" styles, ostensibly due to their picture preferences.

What makes Tajfel's research so curious are that results are often obtained on the basis of very little. That is, despite the fact that subjects were total strangers prior to the study, never interact with each other during the study and probably never will—and despite the fact that their actions are completely anonymous, *they act as if those who share their meaningless label are their good friends or close kin.* Subjects indicate that they like those who share their label. They rate others who share their label as likely to have a more pleasant personality and to have produced better output than out-group members. Most strikingly, subjects allocate more money and rewards to those who share their label. As we will see in chapter 7, these tendencies can form the basis of racial and ethnic prejudice.

(Re)Constructive Memory

What is the role of memory in social cognition? Human memory is primarily reconstructive in nature. By this I mean that we do not record a literal translation of past events—like a tape recorder or a VCR—but instead re-create many of our memories from bits and pieces that we can recall and from our notions and expectations of what should have been. Perhaps you disagree with this assertion about human memory; most people do.[41] If you do happen to disagree, you should expect an argument from Timothy Hennis, a sergeant in the U.S. Army. The research that led to the conclusion that memory is (re)constructive probably saved Sergeant Hennis's life. Let me explain.

On July 4, 1986, Hennis was convicted of the triple murder of Kathryn, Kara, and Erin Eastburn and the rape of Kathryn Eastburn.[42] The crime was a particularly grisly one. Apparently an intruder had broken into the Eastburn home, held a knife to Kathryn Eastburn, raped her, and then slit her throat and stabbed her fifteen times. Three-year-old Erin and five-year-old Kara were each stabbed almost a dozen times. The police followed a quick lead. Earlier in the week Timothy Hennis had answered the Eastburn's newspaper ad requesting someone to adopt their black Labrador retriever. Hennis had taken the dog on a trial basis.

During the trial, two eyewitnesses placed Hennis at the scene of the crime. Chuck Barrett testified he had seen Timothy Hennis walking in the area at 3:30 A.M. on the morning of the murders. Sandra Barnes testified she had seen a man that looked like Hennis using a bank card that police had earlier identified as one stolen from the Eastburn residence. In spite of the fact that Hennis had an airtight alibi for his whereabouts on the night of the murder and there was no physical evidence (fingerprints, clothing fibers, footprints, bloodstains, hair) to link him to the scene, a jury convicted Hennis and sentenced him to death by lethal injection.

Hennis spent 845 days awaiting his execution on death row before a judge from the court of appeals ordered a new trial on the basis of a procedural technicality unrelated to the eyewitness testimony. Hennis's lawyers knew that if Hennis had any chance of overturning his conviction, they would need to attack the eyewitness testimony placing him at the scene of the crime. And it was weak evidence. Chuck Barrett had originally told police two days after the murders that the man he saw had brown hair (Hennis is blond) and was six feet tall (Hennis is much taller), and when asked to identify Hennis in a photo lineup, Barrett was uncertain of his judgment. When Sandra Barnes was first contacted by police a few weeks after the crime, she told them firmly and emphatically that she had not seen anyone at the bank machine that day. Why then at the trial had both of these witnesses so confidently placed Hennis at the scene of the crime? Were they both liars? Probably not; their memories of the events had been leveled and sharpened—constructed and shaped—by over a year of questioning by police and lawyers.

Elizabeth Loftus, a talented cognitive psychologist, served as an expert witness at the second Hennis trial. Loftus had conducted a fascinating program of research on reconstructive memory—investigating how such "suggestive" questioning can influence memory and subsequent eyewitness testimony.[43] In one of her experiments, Loftus showed subjects a film depicting a multiple car accident. After the film, some of the subjects were asked, "About how fast were the cars going when they *smashed* into each other?" Other subjects were asked the same question, but the word *smashed* was replaced by the word *hit*. Subjects who were asked about *smashing* cars, as opposed to *hitting* cars, estimated that the cars were going significantly faster and, a week after seeing the film, were more likely to state that there was broken glass at the accident scene (even though no broken glass was shown in the film).

Leading questions can not only influence the judgment of facts (as in the case above), but also can affect the memory of what has happened as well. In another experiment, Loftus showed subjects a series of slides depicting an auto-pedestrian accident.[44] In a critical slide, a *green* car drove past the accident. Immediately after viewing the slides, half of the subjects were asked, "Did the *blue* car that drove past the accident have a ski rack on the roof?" The remaining subjects were asked this same question but with the word *blue* deleted. The results showed that those subjects who were asked about the "blue" car were more likely to claim incorrectly that they had seen a blue car (even though in reality it was green). A simple question had changed their memory. In subsequent experiments, Loftus[45] has succeeded in planting false memories of childhood experiences in the minds of young adults by simply instructing a close relative to talk about these events as fact. For example, if a young man's older sister says to him, "Remember the time when you were five years old and you got lost for several hours at the University City shopping mall? And you went into a panic—and an oldish man tried to help you? When we discovered you, you were holding the old man's hand and were crying?" Within a few days of hearing such a story, most people will have incorporated that planted memory into their own history, will have embroidered it with details ("oh, yeah, the old man who helped me was wearing a flannel shirt), and will be absolutely certain that it really happened—when, in fact, it didn't.

In her testimony at the Hennis trial, Loftus discussed the nature of reconstructive memory and the way that an interrogation can lead an observer to construct an imaginary scenario and then believe that it really happened. Consider the testimony of Sandra Barnes. At first she could not recall the presence of anyone at the bank teller machine. However, after listening to months of television coverage and reading a year's worth of newspaper stories about the crime, coupled with the pressure stemming from the fact that she was the only one who might have seen the real murderer, Barnes reconstructed a memory of her visit to the bank machine that included someone who looks like Hennis—in a manner similar to the students who recalled a blue rather than a green car in the Loftus experiment. By rehearsing this new construction repeatedly for lawyers and judges, Barnes came to accept it as fact. It is important to note that Sandra Barnes was not intentionally lying. She was simply reconstructing the event. She came to believe what she was saying. A similar story can be told about Chuck Barrett's testimony. Subsequently, the man he saw the morning of the murder was conclusively identified as another man on his way to work—not Hennis.

Fortunately for Hennis, this was not the end of the story. On April 20, 1989, a second jury declared Timothy Hennis to be innocent of the crimes, noting that there was no physical evidence linking Hennis to the scene and that the eyewitness testimony was weak. *Hennis had been a victim of mistaken identification and the lack of realization that memory is often (re)constructive.* The case remains unsolved as of this writing, but police are following two new leads: a second rape and murder in a neighboring town that bears a striking similarity to the Eastburn murders and was performed while Hennis was on death row, and a convincing series of "Thank you" notes sent to Hennis and police, by an unknown person, thanking Hennis for taking the rap for his crime.

It is clear that memory can be reconstructive for quick, snapshot-like events such as a murder or an accident. But what about something more enduring such as the recall of someone's own personal history? A clever experiment by Michael Ross, Cathy McFarland, and Garth Fletcher demonstrates how a change in attitude can also result in a change in how one recalls past, personal events.[46] In their experiment, college students received either a persuasive message arguing that daily toothbrushing is a good thing to do, a message arguing that toothbrushing is bad for you, or a message that was irrelevant to toothbrushing. The toothbrushing messages proved very effective and changed people's attitudes toward toothbrushing in the expected direction. The change of attitude also resulted in a change of memory. Students were later asked, "How many times have you brushed your teeth in the past two weeks?" Those who received the anti-toothbrushing message said they brushed their teeth less frequently, whereas those who received the pro-toothbrushing message said they brushed their teeth more frequently than the students receiving the irrelevant (control) message. The students were using their newly found attitudes to reconstruct their pasts.

How we reconstruct the past depends on our theory of how the past changed to become the present. Consider for a minute the case of Tony, who enrolled in a study skills program at his university. Often these courses are of little value, and indeed, after six months of the program, Tony's grades were the same as before.[47] However, Tony believed that the program had improved his scholastic achievement. Such a state of affairs is quite common—we believe that we have changed or improved in some manner, but in actuality we have not. For example, each year Americans spend over $50 million on subliminal self-help tapes—those audiotapes and videotapes that supposedly have hidden messages designed to improve our self-esteem, memory abilities, or sexual prowess. In surveys, frequent users of these tapes often claim that they work wonders; yet scientific tests of subliminal self-help tapes have been unable to document their effectiveness.[48]

Why then do people often believe they have improved as a result of a pop therapy, a bogus study skills course, or a subliminal tape, when in fact there is little evidence of a change? The social psychologists Michael Conway and Michael Ross were curious about this phenomenon and decided to track people like Tony through a study skills course.[49] In their experiment, students signed up for a study skills improvement course offered at their university. Some of the subjects were randomly placed on a "waiting list" and thus served as a control group for those actually taking the course. The study skills course "taught" such skills as effective note-taking, effective listening, and skim reading. In truth, the study skills course did nothing to improve the student's grades; those students taking the course received grades identical to those on the waiting list. Nevertheless, their expectations—"this course will improve my study habits"—led them to believe that it had! Those students completing the course were more likely to claim greater improvement in study skills and to expect better grades in school. Moreover, the course actually caused these students some harm: Because their grades didn't improve, they eventually came to believe that they were poorer students than they actually were before taking the course. That is, because they believed that the course was a good one, the fact that their grades remained low had to be explained; the easiest explanation was "I am a terrible failure." The Conway and Ross study illustrates once again the reconstructive nature of memory and should give us pause in accepting at face value personal testimonials as to the power and effectiveness of various "pop" therapies and educational fads.

How Conservative Is Human Cognition?

Imagine that you are in a dark room looking at a photographic image so blurred that it is impossible to identify what is depicted. Gradually the picture is brought into focus until it is just slightly blurred. At this point you are asked to guess what it is. If you are like most subjects who have participated in this study,[50] you will be correct about 25 percent of the time. But suppose you started by looking at the slightly blurred picture without the early gradual focusing. Even though you would now have a shorter exposure time, without the gradual focusing you would be correct almost 75 percent of the time—a threefold increase in accuracy. How come? The results of this experiment illustrate what is known as confirmation bias—the tendency to seek to confirm our original hypotheses and beliefs. When the picture is very blurred, most people will generate hypotheses about what it might be—it looks like an ice cream cone; no, a rearing horse; no, the Eiffel Tower. These preliminary guesses later interfere with the ability to interpret the slightly blurred picture.

Much evidence has accrued to indicate that the confirmation bias is a common tendency in human thought. For example, in an experiment by Mark Snyder and William Swann,[51] female college students were told that the person they were about to meet was either an extrovert (outgoing, warm, and friendly) or an introvert (reserved, cool, and aloof). They then prepared a set of questions that they would like to ask this person in order to get to know them. What types of questions did they wish to ask? In general, subjects sought to confirm their original hypotheses. Subjects who thought they would meet an extrovert were more likely to ask questions that confirmed this hypothesis, such as: "What do you do to liven up a party?" and "In what situations are you most talkative?" Those expecting to meet an introvert were likely to ask: "In what situations do you wish you could be more outgoing?" and "What things do you dislike about loud parties?" Notice that, if the question is sincerely answered, the subjects' personality hypothesis is confirmed. That is, a person who is neither extroverted nor introverted will look extroverted when he or she answers the first set of questions and introverted when he or she answers the second set of questions.

Not only do we tend to confirm our hypotheses, but we are often quite confident that they are true. This can be illustrated by what Baruch Fischhoff termed the *hindsight bias,* or the "I-knew-it-all-along" effect.[52] As you may recall from our discussion in chapter 1, once we know the outcome of an event, we have a strong tendency to believe that we could have predicted it in advance. In the Fischhoff experiments, subjects were given a test assessing their knowledge of historical events. The subject's task was to indicate the likelihood that four possible outcomes for the event could have actually occurred. Some of the subjects were told that one of the four possibilities had actually happened but were asked to make the estimates that they would have made had they not first been told the "right" answers. The results showed that subjects could not ignore this information; they substantially overestimated their prior knowledge of correct answers. In other words, even though subjects really didn't know the answers to the test, once they were told an answer, they believed that they knew it all along and that their memories had not changed.

The hindsight bias can serve as an obstacle to education and learning. Suppose a student is told that the answer to a question is A and not B. The student responds, "Oh, A makes so much sense. I knew it all along; I just gave the wrong response." Well, perhaps the student did know it all along. However, in cases when he or she didn't, the student has missed an opportunity to explore why the first answer was wrong and to think about why the new answer is right. Such an exploration could point out other mistaken beliefs and lead to a more complete understanding of the issues at hand.

The confirmation and hindsight biases provide support for the proposition that *human cognition tends to be conservative.* By conservative, I do not mean that the mind adopts a certain political orientation. When applied to social cognition, conservatism refers to the tendency to preserve that which is already established—to maintain our preexisting knowledge, beliefs, attitudes, and hypotheses. Throughout this chapter we have seen numerous examples of cognitive conservatism: The first information received is almost always the most influential; easily accessible categories are overused in forming judgments; representative and attitude heuristics are sometimes misused; stereotypes distort information processing to confirm the usefulness of the stereotype; and memory is reconstructed to fit with current perspectives.

In a provocative article, Anthony Greenwald[53] has argued that cognitive conservatism has at least one benefit—it allows us to perceive the social world as a coherent and stable place. For example, suppose that every time the library received some new books that didn't fit its previous cataloging system, a librarian renumbered and recataloged all the books in the library. The "HM251s" (social psychology books) were changed suddenly to "AP57s" and the "BFs" (psychology) were now divided into the "EAs" and the "DBs." It would probably take that librarian, even for a modest-sized library, years to recatalog the books. When you show up to do your term paper on social cognition, you find it nearly impossible to locate the books and articles you need; the library would be a place of utter confusion. To keep the library operating and coherent, it makes sense to modify *only slightly* the current cataloging system and "fit" the new books into the old system. Similarly, to keep our mind operating and coherent, it makes some sense to practice cognitive conservatism and to modify *only slightly* our cognitive categories.

However, as we have seen throughout this chapter, cognitive conservatism is not without its costs. The misuse of inappropriate categories may cause a person to distort events or to miss important information. The misapplication of a heuristic can lead to poor decision making. The failure to update our conception of the world in the face of new and discrepant information can result in a mistaken picture of reality. The consequences are not just mental but can show their face in social problems that we call racism, sexism, prejudice, and just plain stupid thinking.

What can be done to avoid the negative consequences of cognitive conservatism? Here are four rules of thumb that might help. First, be wary of those who attempt to create your categories and definitions of the situations. There are many ways to define and label a person or event. Ask yourself, "Why is this particular label being suggested?" Second, try to use more than one way to categorize and describe a person or event. By seeing a person or event in a number of different ways, we do not rely on a single category that we then misemploy—bending and twisting the data so that it fits a preconceived notion. Third, try to think of persons and important events as unique—while they are members of a particular salient category (say, a given race or gender), they are also members of many other categories and have their own unique attributes. Individuation can help prevent the overuse of a given stereotype or heuristic. Finally, think that you might be mistaken—that you have fallen victim to one or more of the cognitive biases described in this chapter. In our next chapter, on self-justification, we will continue to explore cognitive conservatism and look at additional ways to protect ourselves from the adverse consequences of distorted thinking.

How Do Attitudes and Beliefs Guide Behavior?

In the last few sections we have looked at how our beliefs influence how we think about the social world. A reasonable question to ask is: What is the relationship between our beliefs and behavior? Can we use our attitudes to predict how we will behave? For example, suppose I like vanilla ice cream, but you dislike it. Would you and I behave differently toward vanilla ice cream? Our intuition says yes. Most people would expect that I would purchase a lot of vanilla ice cream—choosing it over other flavors; you, on the other hand, would rarely indulge in vanilla ice cream. This tends to be true for vanilla ice cream. But we would be making a serious mistake if we assumed it were always the case. A long history of research suggests that in a great many situations our intuitions are wrong.

Let's take a closer look. One of the classic studies of the attitude-behavior relationship was conducted in the early 1930s by Robert LaPiere.[54] At the time, there was considerable overt and blatant prejudice in the United States directed toward people with nonwhite skin. Often, Americans of Asian, Hispanic, or African descent were denied easy access to public rest rooms, the use of water fountains, restaurants, and hotel lodging. In 1933, LaPiere contacted 128 hotel and restaurant proprietors and assessed their attitude toward Chinese people by asking them, "Will you accept members of the Chinese race as guests in your establishment?" Over 90 percent of those contacted said, "No!" However, on a tour of the country with a young Chinese couple, LaPiere found that of these 128 establishments, only one—located in a small town in California—refused service to the Chinese couple. The proprietors' attitudes concerning Chinese people did not predict their actual behavior.

If LaPiere's results were merely an isolated occurrence, then we could maintain our intuition that attitudes and beliefs are excellent predictors of behavior. In 1969, Alan Wicker undertook a scholarly review of over forty studies that had explored the attitude-behavior relationship. These studies investigated a wide range of attitudes and opinions such as job satisfaction, ethnic prejudice, consumer preferences, and political beliefs. Wicker found only weak support for the hypothesis that attitudes predict behavior. As he says, "Taken as a whole, these studies suggest that it is considerably more likely that attitudes will be unrelated or only slightly related to overt behaviors than that attitudes will be closely related to actions" (p. 65).[55]

The Attitude-Behavior Relationship in Our Heads. How can we reconcile this body of research with our intuition that a person's beliefs are strongly related to his or her behavior? One way is to conclude that there is no relationship between attitudes and behavior—it is all in our heads; we just imagine that people act consistently with their beliefs and attitudes. There is some support for this proposition. In the last two chapters we saw the power of the social situation to induce conformity. LaPiere's innkeepers undoubtedly faced strong social pressures to say "no" to an inquiry about admitting Chinese people; at the same time, they faced contrary pressures (to avoid making a scene) to lodge the young Chinese couple once they appeared at the hotel. Perhaps they simply caved in to the most immediate pressures. Perhaps we are nothing more than creatures of our immediate social environment.

In support of the hypothesis that the perception of attitude-behavior consistency is "all in our head" is the common tendency among people to attribute the cause of an individual's behavior to characteristics of the individual such as personality traits and attitudes rather than the power of the situation itself. For example, the inquiry "Why did little Johnny fail on his homework assignment?" is often answered "Because he is stupid or lazy"—ignoring such situational factors as overcrowded schools or a poor academic environment. In other words, when we see something happen to a person, most of us assume that the event is consistent with the kind of person he or she is. We would like to believe that people get what they deserve and deserve what they get.

Edward Jones and his colleagues call this tendency to attribute the cause of a behavior to a corresponding characteristic of a person a *correspondent inference*[56]—that is, the behavior of the person is explained in terms of an attribute or trait that is just like the behavior. Some examples include: "Sam spilled wine on the carpet because he is clumsy (not because of a momentary distraction)," and "Amy spoke sarcastically to Ted because she is a hostile person (not because she momentarily lost her temper)."

An experiment by Edward Jones and Victor Harris demonstrates that such inferences can be pervasive.[57] In this experiment, subjects read essays either favorable or unfavorable to Fidel Castro's regime in Cuba allegedly written by students in a political science course. Half the subjects were told that the essay writers freely chose the position of their essay, whereas the others were told that the writers had been forced to take that position and were instructed to make the best case they could. Subjects then had to guess the essay writer's true attitude toward Castro. What did the results show? When the essay writer could choose a position freely, subjects assumed that the content of their essays reflected their attitudes: those writing pro-Castro essays were believed to be pro-Castro, and those writing anti-Castro essays were assumed to be anti-Castro. This was not surprising. What *was* surprising is that the *same* results occurred when the essay writer had been *forced* to argue an *assigned* position. In other words, essay writers forced to argue for Castro were assumed to be pro-Castro, and those forced to argue against Castro were assumed to be anti-Castro. In making their inferences, subjects discounted the situational pressures to take a position and assumed that the essayist's behavior was a result of a firmly held belief. In this case, the attitude–behavior relationship was located in the head of the observer.

When Do Attitudes Predict Behavior? Just because attitudes don't always predict beliefs does not mean attitudes never predict behavior. The role of scientists is to try to determine the conditions under which an event is more or less likely to occur. Recently, Russell Fazio[58] has identified one major factor that increases the likelihood that we will act on our attitude—accessibility. A highly accessible attitude is one in which the evaluation of the object comes readily, almost immediately, to mind when we encounter the object. For example, if I say "snake," most people will immediately think "bad, dangerous." If I say "Rembrandt painting," most will quickly respond "beautiful." We all know people about whom we immediately think, "Oh no, not that jerk again," or conversely, "Wow! What a wonderful person." These are highly accessible attitudes.

Not all attitudes and beliefs are highly accessible. For example, we may have opinions on Puerto Rican statehood or the value of advertising, but for most of us these opinions do not readily come to mind. Sometimes we have no *real* attitude—that is, no evaluation of the object stored in memory. Nevertheless, we might venture an opinion if asked. For example, survey researchers find that respondents are capable of giving their opinion about "made-up" issues such as a phony piece of legislation or foreign aid to a nonexistent country. In these latter two cases, our less-accessible attitudes and "nonattitudes" are not likely to guide behavior.

How do highly accessible attitudes influence behavior? According to Fazio, attitudes are used to interpret and perceive an object selectively and to make sense of a complex situation. We have seen previously how attitudes can influence cognitive processing; an attitude serves as a heuristic to influence interpretations, explanations, reasoning, and judgment of a situation. But any given attitude is only one of many factors that can be used to make sense of a situation. For example, to make sense of a complex situation, we may use the objective features of the situation, or what other people say about it, or our general attitude about similar situations. When an attitude is highly accessible, it is more likely to be used, relative to other possible means, for defining a situation. We then act, if possible, on our perceptions and interpretations.

There is considerable evidence to support the proposition that highly accessible attitudes guide behavior. One measure of attitude accessibility is the speed with which an individual can provide an evaluative response of an object or issue. In the presidential election of 1984, Russell Fazio and Carol Williams[59] used "speed of response" to predict who would vote for either Ronald Reagan or Walter Mondale. About five months before the election, Fazio and Williams took a small microcomputer to a local shopping mall and asked passersby to give their opinions about various issues including an evaluation of each of the two presidential candidates. The computer recorded the speed with which they evaluated the presidential candidates. This was their measure of accessibility. Later, Fazio and Williams contacted the subjects and asked them about their perceptions of two presidential debates. After the election, they asked for whom they had voted. The results showed that those individuals with highly accessible attitudes (fast responses) five months before the election were more likely to vote for their favored candidate and to perceive the presidential debates in a manner consistent with their attitudes. In subsequent research, Fazio and his colleagues[60] have manipulated the accessibility of an attitude by having subjects repeatedly express their opinions or by giving subjects the opportunity to have direct experience with the attitude object. They consistently find the same results: Highly accessible attitudes are predictive of subsequent behavior—less accessible attitudes are not.

Fazio's concept of attitude accessibility provides us with several ways of interpreting the lack of an attitude-behavior relationship in the LaPiere study of innkeepers. The problem is that we do not know how accessible attitudes toward Chinese people were for each of the innkeepers. Moreover, it may be that different attitudes were activated by the questionnaire and by the actual visit of the Chinese couple. For example, a survey item mentioning only Chinese people may remind an innkeeper of his or her prejudice, whereas the presence of a young Chinese couple in the company of an older white man may invoke any number of thoughts and feelings—such as thoughts about income generated from the business, the reputation of the establishment, what other customers might think, or even the attire of the couple—that then come to control the situation. Finally, even if prejudiced attitudes were highly accessible and subsequently influenced perceptions of the situation, there is no guarantee that the innkeepers would or could act on those perceptions. Perhaps the presence of the white male made the innkeepers fearful of the repercussions of acting on their attitudes. Perhaps the experience was a new one for the proprietors, and they did not know how to act. All such factors limit the extent to which a person will act on his or her beliefs.

Acting on Perceptions.   There is another way that attitudes and beliefs can influence behavior: The belief can come to create the social world in which we live. A recent experiment by Paul Herr illustrates how this can occur.[61] Using a word puzzle game, Herr intentionally increased the accessibility of the concept "hostility" in some of his subjects using the technique of priming which we discussed earlier in the chapter. Specifically, Herr's subjects were required to find hidden names of persons in a matrix of letters. For half the subjects, the hidden names were of persons associated with hostility—Charles Manson, Adolf Hitler, Ayatollah Khomeini, and Dracula. The other subjects sought and found the names of relatively gentle people—Peter Pan, Pope John Paul, Shirley Temple, and Santa Claus. The subjects then read an ambiguous description of a person named "Donald," whose behavior could be seen as either hostile or nonhostile, and rated Donald's level of hostility. Consistent with our earlier discussion, we would expect the different puzzles to influence judgments about Donald. Compared to Hitler and Manson, almost everyone looks *less* hostile, including Donald, whereas compared to the Pope and Santa Claus, almost everyone appears *more* hostile, including Donald. This is exactly what Herr found. Those subjects primed with the extremely hostile persons rated Donald as less hostile compared with those who received the gentle primes.*

But Herr's experiment didn't stop there. Next, the subjects played a bargaining game with a person whom they thought was Donald. In this game, participants were required to choose between one of two strategies—competing or cooperating. Herr found that when subjects expected to play against a hostile Donald, they played in a highly competitive manner; when they expected a gentle Donald, they played with far more cooperation. Interestingly, the subjects who were naively playing the "Donald" role also perceived this competitiveness; they rated their opponent's level of hostility in a manner consistent with the way they played the game. In sum, a subtle context had influenced beliefs and expectations that in turn affected behavior and subsequently affected the next round of perceptions.

---

* The reader should note the crucial difference between this experiment and one by Higgins et al., discussed earlier in this chapter (p. 127). In the Higgins experiment, the researchers were priming a category—"negativity." This influences observers to see subsequent ambiguous stimuli (like Donald) more negatively—because that is what people are primed to look for. In the Herr experiment, the researchers were priming *exemplars* of hostility (like Hitler). Here, a contrast effect occurs: Compared to extremely hostile people, an ambiguous person (like Donald) comes off looking like a teddy bear.

Summary. What then can we conclude from the considerable research on attitudes and behavior? First and foremost, the collective research on attitudes and behavior underscores a principle we will see quite often in this book: Subtle situational variables are often strong determinants of our behavior. Second, most people tend to overlook the importance of the situation in explaining behavior, preferring instead to explain other people's actions in terms of assumptions about their personalities and attitudes. In other words, most of us assume that people's attitudes do indeed forecast their behavior, and then we overapply this belief in interpreting the behavior of others. We see attitude-behavior relationships even when they might not exist in reality.

But, on some occasions, attitudes *do* predict behavior. When an attitude is highly accessible—that is, when it comes readily to mind—then it is very likely to predict our behavior. Readily accessible attitudes color and modify our interpretation of our social world. We then act on our perceptions, and in so doing, our actions come to create the world we previously only perceived.

Three Possible Biases in Social Explanation

Every day of our lives we seek to explain a variety of events and happenings: Why did Saddam Hussein invade Kuwait? Why did that attractive person across the room ignore me? How did it come to pass that I did so poorly and you did so well on the recent essay assignment? Why did my mother not cook my favorite meal while I was home during the Christmas holidays? Our explanations are often rational and accurate. But they are vulnerable to bias and inaccuracy. In studying how we interpret our social world, social psychologists have identified three general biases that often affect our attributions and explanations: the *fundamental attribution error,* the *actor-observer bias,* and the *self-biases.*

The Fundamental Attribution Error. The term "fundamental attribution error" refers to a general human tendency to overestimate the importance of personality or dispositional factors relative to situational or environmental influences when describing and explaining the causes of social behavior.[62] We have already seen one example of this tendency—correspondent inference. That is, when explaining why Sam took a specific political position or performed a specific behavior, we tend to use personality characteristics (he believes strongly in the issue; he is lazy) as opposed to situational factors (he was assigned that position; he was very tired that day). This may lead us to believe that there is more consistency of motive and behavior in the world than actually exists.

Another example of the fundamental attribution error is provided by an experiment conducted by Gunter Bierbrauer.[63] In this experiment, subjects witnessed a faithful reenactment of a person's performance in Stanley Milgram's famous experiment on obedience to authority (described in chapter 2). Recall that in this experiment, Milgram constructed a situation that elicited high rates of obedience—in this case, the behavior involved administering severe electric shocks to a "learner." Like most subjects in the Milgram experiment, the person in the reenactment showed a high level of obedience, administering the maximum level of electric shock. After showing the reenactment, Bierbrauer then asked his subjects to estimate how many of Milgram's subjects in general would be obedient in this situation. The results showed that subjects consistently underestimated the actual degree of obedience. Specifically, Bierbrauer's subjects estimated that only 10 to 20 percent of the people in this setting would give the maximum shock of 450 volts. In actuality, as you will recall, Milgram found that over 65 percent of the subjects administered this level of shock. In other words, Bierbrauer's subjects assumed that the behavior of the particular subject they observed reflected distinguishing personal dispositions (i.e., that he was particularly aggressive or obedient); they failed to attribute the behavior to the power of the situation to produce this behavior in most people.

As observers, we frequently lose sight of the fact that each individual plays many *social roles,* but we might observe only one of them. Thus, the importance of social roles can be easily overlooked in explaining a person's behavior. For example, I know a psychology professor whom I will call Dr. Mensch. The students adore Dr. Mensch. When they describe him on teacher evaluations and informally, they use words such as warm, caring, concerned about students, approachable, charismatic, brilliant, and friendly. However, Dr. Mensch's professional colleagues have a different image of him, especially those who have given professional talks when he was in the audience. Like the students, they see him as brilliant, but they also describe Dr. Mensch as intense, critical, tough, argumentative, and relentless.

Who has the right impression—the students or the psychologists? Is he really a tough critical person who is simply putting on an act in front of students? Or is he really a warm and caring individual who pretends to be tough when confronting other psychologists? These are the wrong questions. The fact is my friend is capable of a wide range of behaviors. Some social roles tend to pull behavior from one part of the spectrum; other social roles tend to pull behavior from a different part of the spectrum. The students see Dr. Mensch in only one role—that of teacher. He is a very good teacher, and the job of a good teacher is to "get the best out of the student"; this usually requires warm and caring behavior. The students have accurately described my friend's behavior within this role. On the other hand, the role of a useful professional colleague sometimes requires adversarial behavior. In order to discover the truth, a good professional often will strongly press an argument to see how far it will go. This frequently results in sharp, intense, and relentless criticism. Thus, Dr. Mensch's professional colleagues also accurately describe the behavior that they see. However, both students and professional colleagues make a fundamental attribution error when they then assume that the behavior they observe is due entirely to some personality characteristic; rather, it is largely based on the way Dr. Mensch perceives the requirements of his social role. This is not to say that personality is irrelevant. Not everyone is capable of the wide array of behaviors manifested by Dr. Mensch. But to assume that he is either "tough" or "warm" is to ignore the power of the social role.

A clever experiment by Lee Ross, Teresa Amabile, and Julia Steinmetz illustrates how the impact of social roles can be underestimated in explaining behavior.[64] In one of their experiments, they set up a "quiz show" format in which they randomly assigned subjects to one of two roles: (a) a questioner whose task it was to prepare difficult questions for (b) a contestant whose task it was to answer them. An observer watched this simulated quiz show and then estimated the questioner's and the contestant's general knowledge. Try to put yourself in the role of the observer. What do you see? Well, unless you are very careful, you will see one very smart, knowledgeable person and one rather stupid person.

But please take a closer look. Notice how these two roles constrain the behavior of the participants. The questioner is likely to come up with some fairly difficult questions based on esoteric knowledge. "In what baseball park did Babe Ruth hit his second to last home run?" "What is the capital city of Lithuania?" and "What is the date of Thomas Jefferson's death?"[65] By simply *asking* these questions, the questioner looks smart. On the other hand, the contestant is faced with answering these difficult questions and is likely to miss a few. This makes him or her look a little stupid. And this is exactly what Ross and his colleagues found. The observers felt that the questioners were far more knowledgeable than the contestants. However, since everyone was randomly assigned to their roles, it is extremely unlikely that questioners were *actually* more knowledgeable than all of the contestants. What is most interesting is that the observers *knew* that the participants had been randomly assigned to these roles. Yet they failed to consider the impact of social roles in making their judgments about the quiz show participants and fell into the trap of attributing what they saw to personal dispositions.

If the fundamental attribution error were limited to judgments about college professors and quiz show participants, it probably would not be much of a cause for concern. However, its implications are far-reaching. Consider a common reaction of most Americans to a person using food stamps at a supermarket: "She is lazy; if she just tried harder, she could get a job." Or consider this characterization of a convicted burglar: "He is a terrible human being; what type of villain could commit such acts?" Both descriptions could be accurate; but what is more likely is that they represent the fundamental attribution error in action. Although this is not the place for a full discussion of the situational determinants of poverty and crime, there can be many factors other than personal characteristics that can explain why a person is poor or commits a crime. These include lack of job opportunities, illiteracy, economic recession, the lack of positive role models in one's neighborhood, and growing up in a dysfunctional family. By focusing on personal rather than situational factors, we will advocate different policies for dealing with social problems such as poverty and crime. For example, the attribution "this criminal is a fiend" will result in a policy of spending more money on bigger and stronger prisons and doling out longer prison sentences. Perceiving the causes of crime as largely due to unemployment, poor role models, and illiteracy will result in policies such as increased spending for better schools and better teachers and tax credits to businesses that invest in high poverty areas. Don't get me wrong. I am not suggesting that dispositional factors such as laziness, clumsiness, or visciousness do not exist. They do. I am merely pointing out that most of us, most of the time, are too prone to invoke a dispositional attribution when the cause of the behavior may well be situational. At the very least, our knowledge of the fundamental attribution error should alert us to the possibility that our dispositional attributions may not always be correct and that we should take seriously the motto of the novelist Samuel Butler: "There, but for the grace of God, go I."

The Actor-Observer Bias. Another common bias in social judgment is known as the *actor-observer bias:* The tendency for actors to attribute their own actions to situational factors whereas observers tend to attribute the same actions to stable personality dispositions of the actors.[66] For example, in my judgment, I go to the beach a lot because the weather is beautiful; but, in my judgment, you go to the beach a lot because you are probably a beach bum. Political leaders often describe wise moves and blunders as largely inescapable under the circumstances, whereas private citizens are likely to see both as a consequence of the leader's personal characteristics. Recall the Kitty Genovese murder discussed in chapter 2. After Ms. Genovese was murdered in view of thirty-eight witnesses in New York City, the eyewitnesses claimed that the situation was ambiguous and it was difficult to know what to do; newspaper reporters called it "bystander apathy." In other words, I give myself the benefit of the doubt—I use situational causes to explain *myself.* But I don't give you the same benefit—when I try to explain *your* behavior, I make the fundamental attribution error.

There is considerable evidence that the actor-observer bias is pervasive. For example, studies have shown that: (a) in explaining success and failure on an intelligence test, college students are likely to explain others' performance in terms of their ability, whereas they explain their own performance in terms of the difficulty of the test items; (b) college students who volunteered to participate in psychological research attributed their participation to the importance of the research, whereas observers viewed their participation as reflecting a personal inclination to participate in any and all research; (c) when observing a peer's behavior, college students leap to the conclusion that this person will continue to act in a similar manner in the future (thus implying an underlying disposition to behave in a particular way), whereas the "actors" indicated that they personally would probably act differently in the future; (d) students described their best friend's choice of girlfriends and a college major in terms of the qualities of their best friend but explained their own choices in terms of the qualities of their girlfriend or major; and (e) people ascribe more personality traits to other people than to themselves.[67]

What is the cause of the actor-observer bias? An experiment by Michael Storms indicates that it is a function of where a person's attention is focused.[68] The actor's attention is usually focused on the environment and on past history; he or she may have special knowledge about the factors that led up to the behavior and how he or she felt about the behavior. On the other hand, the observer's attention is almost always focused on the actor; therefore the observer may be unaware of historical or environmental reasons for why the actor did what he or she did.

In the Storms experiment, two subjects engaged in a conversation while two observers watched; each observer was instructed to monitor one of the conversationalists. After the conversation, the actors and the observers indicated to what extent behaviors such as friendliness, talkativeness, nervousness, and dominance were due either to personal characteristics or to the situation. As you might expect, the actors were more likely to explain their behavior in terms of the situation, whereas observers explained the behavior in terms of the actor's personality dispositions. This was not surprising; it is consistent with what we know about the actor-observer bias. However, the study had an interesting twist. Some subjects viewed a videotape of the conversation that was played back either from the same angle they originally saw it (that is, the actors saw a videotape of the other person, and the observers saw the person they were asked to monitor) or from a reverse angle (that is, the actors saw themselves, and the observers saw the other person). When the camera angle was the same, the actor-observer bias occurred; however, when the camera angle was reversed, so was the actor-observer bias. Actors who saw themselves from the observer's point of view were more likely to explain their own behavior in terms of *dispositional* factors, whereas observers who saw the world from the point of view of actors were more likely to explain behavior in *situational* terms.

Often the actor-observer bias can lead to misunderstanding and conflict. For example, if Sam "shows up late for a date" with Susan, he (the actor) may explain his tardiness by noting that "all the traffic lights happened to be red," whereas Susan (the observer) may conclude that Sam "is losing interest in me." Similarly, when the Soviet Union invaded Afghanistan, they described the act as "a response to local uprisings and the necessity of protecting their southern border," whereas outside observers saw the action as another instance of Soviet aggressiveness. When the United States invaded Panama, it was to "overthrow a drug lord," whereas outside observers considered it as an imperialistic act of aggression. These perceptions and attributions then serve as the basis for subsequent action that might serve to escalate the conflict.

The Storms experiment points to one method for nipping this potential conflict in the bud before it happens: Change the actor's and the observer's perspective. One tactic for doing this is to promote empathy through role-playing the other's point of view. Another tactic, used on the international front, is cultural exchange programs where citizens of one country live in another. Both tactics change both the perspective and the information available for making attributions. In chapter 8 we will look at a very powerful and successful technique called "sensitivity training" which is aimed at increasing interpersonal understanding by providing feedback on how others see and feel about the world.

The Self-Biases. It is now time to turn our attention to what happens to our social cognitions when our most important social cognition—the self—is involved. Psychologically one of our major goals is maintaining and enhancing our view of ourselves. In William James's view, this is especially true for our social and our "spiritual" selves. As James put it:

> The social self . . . ranks higher than the material self. . . . We must care more for our honor, our friends, our human ties, than for a sound skin or wealth. And the spiritual self is so supremely precious that, rather than lose it, a man ought to be willing to give up friends and good fame, and property, and life itself.[69]

As a primary source of motivation, the way in which we conceive of the self greatly influences all of our social cognitions.[70] We will be discussing self-processes in more detail in the next chapter. For now, let us note two general ways that the self influences social cognition—*egocentric thought* and the *self-serving bias.*

Egocentric Thought.   Egocentric thought refers to the tendency to perceive one's self as more central to events than it actually is.[71] The vast majority of humans remember past events as if the self were a leading player, in control and influencing the behavior of others.

There are many examples of egocentric thought. Perhaps one of the most interesting is provided by the research of Robert Jervis, a political scientist.[72] He argues that important world leaders have a strong tendency to believe, unreasonably, that an act of a foreign nation is either made in response to *their* prior decisions or made with the intent of eliciting a response from *them*. In other words, the world leader perceives the world of foreign affairs to be revolving about himself. For example, during World War II, Hitler attributed the fact that the British were not bombing German cities to the British desire to reciprocate German restraint rather than to the fact that the British were short on planes—which was actually the case.

Often world leaders believe that their action thwarts an adversary's evil intent when in fact no evil act was planned or it was aborted for other reasons. Such was the case with officials in the Nixon administration who predicted a massive North Vietnamese offensive during the visit of President Richard Nixon to China and then claimed to have prevented the attacks with massive bombing raids. After the war, it became clear that no such offensive was contemplated. Currently, the decline of the Soviet Union is seen as primarily the result of former President Ronald Reagan's military spending program rather than economic and structural problems of the Soviet Union that had been festering for years. Jervis draws a chilling conclusion about the effects of egocentric thought on heads of state: The (largely mistaken) belief that one has been the cause of the behavior of other nations leads to an enhanced faith in deterrence—the belief that one can prevent future events by punishment and threats of punishment. This is almost always erroneous.

It goes without saying that world leaders aren't the only ones who believe that they control events. It is a common phenomenon among us ordinary folks, as well. Ellen Langer demonstrated the power of the "illusion of control" in a simple experiment.[73] In this study, subjects bought lottery tickets; but here is the important twist—some subjects chose their ticket, whereas others were assigned the ticket by the experimenter. Later, the subjects were given the opportunity to sell the ticket back to the experimenter. Langer found that those who had chosen their ticket demanded up to four times the amount of money for the ticket as those who were assigned the ticket. The subjects in this experiment were under the illusion that their behavior of *choosing* a ticket could influence the outcome; therefore they considered the ticket more valuable because they selected the numbers. Of course, as we all know, the winning ticket is determined by chance alone; no number has a greater chance of winning than any other number—regardless of who chose it. But the illusion of control fostered by egocentric thought is a powerful one. It is small wonder that most state lotteries allow us to select our own numbers.

The belief that "one's self is the center of the universe" helps explain a paradox that occurs every day in U.S. newspapers. Although many Americans are proud of their technological and scientific achievements, fewer than 10 percent of daily newspapers carry a regular column on science. In contrast, over 90 percent of these newspapers carry a daily feature on astrology—a means of attempting to predict the future using the position of the stars at birth. How come? The stock-in-trade of the newspaper horoscope is the so-called "Barnum statement"—named after the showman P. T. Barnum, who once noted "there is a sucker born every minute." A Barnum statement is a personality description that is composed of statements that are true of almost everyone. For example: "You are probably reserved in unfamiliar social situations." "You view life with an average mixture of optimism and pessimism." "You often carry an open mind but can take a firm stand if need be." These descriptions apply to almost everyone. But because of our tendency to think egocentrically, almost everyone believes that the Barnum statement applies mostly to their own selves; most do not stop to think that almost everyone else feels the same way. Thus, the newspaper horoscope is an appealing item for a great many people.

In one experiment designed to test the believability of Barnum statements, Richard Petty and Timothy Brock[74] gave subjects a phony personality test and then administered bogus personality feedback and results. Half the subjects received a positively written Barnum statement describing them as "open-minded" (i.e., you can see many sides of an issue), whereas the other half received a positive-ly written statement describing them as "closed-minded" (i.e., once you make up your mind, you take a firm stand). Although the per-sonality feedback was bogus, almost all the subjects believed it to be a very good description of their personality. What is more, Petty and Brock found that subjects' "new-found personality" influenced their subsequent behavior. Specifically, "open-minded" and "closed-minded" subjects were asked to list their thoughts on two controver-sial issues. Those subjects who randomly received a Barnum state-ment describing them as open-minded listed thoughts on both sides of the issue, whereas those who received a closed-minded personality tended to list arguments on only one side of the issue. This is still another example of how our beliefs and expectations can create social reality.

The tendency for egocentric thought occurs in subtle ways that frequently include our memory for past events and information. One very common finding is that people have superior memory for infor-mation descriptive of the self.[75] Moreover, when working in groups, individuals tend to focus on and recall their own performance at the expense of retaining information about the performance of others. In addition, when a person plays an active role in generating informa-tion, that information is better recalled than when it was passively received. Finally, studies repeatedly show superior memory for infor-mation that is related to the self—that is, when people think about how a term or object applies to themselves, they remember it better than when the same term or object applies to others. The role of egocentric thought in memory does have practical implications for the student: One of the best ways to recall material from this book is to relate it to your personal experiences—to think how it applies to you. This will help you do better on the upcoming quiz.

The Self-Serving Bias. The self-serving bias refers to a tendency for individuals to make dispositional attributions for their successes and situational attributions for their failures. For example, in a bas-ketball game, if Linda sinks a difficult shot, chances are she will attribute it to her great eye and leaping ability. On the other hand, if she misses, she might claim that she was fouled or that there was a soft spot in the floor that led to a mistiming of her jump.

Automobile driving provides many opportunities for motorists to engage in the self-serving bias. For example, the following are actual written reports given by drivers involved in automobile accidents. As can be seen, the self-serving bias is much in evidence.[76]

> The telephone pole was approaching fast; I attempted to swerve out of its way, when it struck the front of my car.

> An invisible car came out of nowhere, struck my vehicle, and vanished.

> My car was legally parked as it backed into the other vehicle.

> As I reached an intersection, a hedge sprang up, obscuring my vision. I did not see the other car.

> A pedestrian hit me and went under my car.

Researchers have gathered a great deal of evidence in support of the informal observation that we take credit for the good and deny the bad. For example: (a) Students who do well on an exam attribute their performance to ability and effort, whereas those who do poorly attribute it to a poor exam or bad luck; (b) gamblers perceive their successes as based on skill and their failures as a fluke; (c) when married persons estimate how much of the housework each routinely did, their combined total of housework performed amounts to more than 100 percent—in other words, each person thinks he or she did more work than their partner thinks he or she did; (d) in general, people rate themselves more positively than others do, believing that they themselves are "better than average"; (e) two-person teams performing a skilled task accept credit for the good scores but assign most of the blame for the poor scores to their partner; and (f) when asked to explain why someone else dislikes them, college students take little responsibility for themselves (i.e., there must be something wrong with this other person), but when told that someone else likes them, the students attributed it to their own personality.[77] As Greenwald and Breckler note, "The presented self is (usually) too good to be true; the (too) good self is often genuinely believed."[78]

An interesting question is: "Why do people engage in the self-serving bias?" One explanation that accounts for some of the data is purely cognitive; individuals are aware of different information as actors compared to when they are observers.[79] Consider the finding that couples' estimation of their contribution to housework totals more than 100 percent. This could easily be an effect due to differential attention and memory. For example, every time I scrub the floor, clean the toilet, or wash the dishes I am much more likely to keep track and recall my contributions than when you do it. It is very likely that I can recall doing the dishes four times last week, taking out the trash, cleaning up the garage, grooming the dog, and mowing the yard. I recall that you cleaned the oven, but I missed (or forgot) the fact that you cooked dinner and washed dishes on three nights, purchased the groceries, vacuumed the rugs, trimmed the hedges, and paid the bills. When I go to estimate the amount of housework each of us does, of course, I think I do more.

But a purely cognitive-informational explanation cannot account for all the examples of the self-serving bias. For example, the amount of information available to successful and unsuccessful test-takers and gamblers is likely to be similar. Another explanation proposed for the self-serving bias is that we are *motivated* to engage in such attributions to protect and maintain our self-concepts and self-esteem. According to this perspective, if I have a positive self-view, it is easy for me to see and accept myself as accomplishing positive things; on the other hand, a threat to this positive self-view must be defended against—perhaps through denial or a good excuse. This is called "ego defensive" behavior.

How can we be certain that some of this behavior is motivated by a desire to maintain high self-esteem? Let us look at the conditions under which we are most likely to engage in ego-defensive attributions. In a series of experiments, Gifford Weary and her colleagues[80] found that the likelihood of giving a self-serving explanation increases when (a) the person is highly involved in the behavior; (b) the person feels responsible for the outcome of his or her action; and (c) the person's behavior is publicly observed by others. Further, people are least likely to offer a self-serving attribution when they feel that they can't get away with it—that is, when the audience makes it clear that an excuse is not appropriate or that an excuse will set up unreasonable expectations about future performance. In other words, self-serving explanations occur most when the self is "on the line"—

when the self is clearly threatened or when the person sees an opportunity to achieve a positive image.

What happens when an individual does not possess a positive self-image to enhance and defend? This is the case with people who are depressed or have low self-esteem. In an ingenious set of experiments, Lauren Alloy and Lyn Abramson found evidence for what can be termed "depressive realism"—the lack of a self-serving bias in people suffering depression.[81] In their experiments, subjects were asked to press a button. If a light went on after the button was pressed, the subject would win money, but if it didn't go on, they would lose money. For some subjects, button pressing actually controlled the light. In the more interesting case, some subjects had only partial control over whether the light would come on when they pressed the button. At the end of the experiment, subjects were asked how much control they believed their button pressing had upon the lights. When the subject had partial control of the light, normal subjects estimated that they were controlling the light when they won money to a greater degree than when they lost money. This is an excellent example of the self-serving bias. However, depressives *accurately* estimated the amount of control they had over the light. In other words, depressives did not fall prey to the self-serving bias. The fact that they were feeling badly about themselves served to dampen their "normal" motivation to see themselves in the best possible light. The depressives were, in the words of Alloy and Abramson, "sadder, but wiser."

Of What Value Are Self-Biases? When we treat mental processes as objects and discover that the overwhelming majority of people engage in such behavior as egocentric thought and the self-serving bias, it would be easy to conclude that (a) humans are pathetic, irrational, silly organisms who blind themselves from seeing things as they are, and (b) self-biases should be eliminated at all cost. Such conclusions would be a gross oversimplification. First, as mentioned earlier, although we humans frequently engage in biased thinking, we are also capable of clear, rational thought. Moreover, the self-biases can serve important purposes. The individual who believes that he or she is the cause of good things will try harder and persist longer at achieving difficult goals. Such efforts can result in new scientific discoveries, great works of art, or political agreements that can be of great benefit to millions of people.

An interesting example of this kind of process emerges from the results of a study of basketball players done by Robert Grove and his colleagues.[82] Grove found that winning teams attributed their success to stable causes, while teams that lost attributed their failures to unstable causes like flukes, bad breaks, and the like. This bias can be beneficial (at least in the short run) because it allows losing teams to avoid being psychologically devastated by setbacks, to hang in there and continue playing in the face of a string of defeats.

There may be even more important temporary benefits to the self-biases as well. Recently, social psychologist Shelley Taylor[83] interviewed hundreds of people who have faced tragic or near-tragic events. Her interviewees included rape victims, cancer patients, and others with a life-threatening illness. She found that, far from destroying these individuals, the tragic event had given most of them a "new lease on life." This was especially true if they held overly *optimistic* perceptions concerning their chances of recovery from disease or believed that they could control the likelihood of future victimization. The belief that one can overcome tragic obstacles—even if this belief was an illusion—led these people to adopt better health practices and to develop coping strategies for dealing with life stress which had a salutary effect on their lives.

Similarly, Martin Seligman[84] has found across a variety of studies that an optimistic style of thinking—believing that a defeat is due to bad luck and can be overcome by effort and ability—leads to more achievement, better health, and an improved mental outlook. In brief, engaging in egocentric thought and self-serving attributions has an array of benefits. At the same time, it is important to bear in mind that these positive consequences are not without their price— and as you have undoubtedly gathered, the major price is a somewhat distorted picture of our self and the world in general.

Ironically, as we have seen, this distorted picture of the world is frequently caused by a motive to justify ourselves and our behavior— to interpret or distort the meaning of our actions so as to bring it in line with what we would regard as consistent with the actions of a morally good and sensible human being. For me, one of the most fascinating aspects of the social animal is our touching need to see ourselves as good and sensible people—and how this need to see ourselves as good and sensible people frequently leads us into performing actions that are neither good nor sensible. The human tendency for self-justification is so important that it deserves a chapter all to itself; it is to this chapter that we now turn.

5
Self-Justification

Picture the following scene: A young man named Sam is being hypnotized. The hypnotist places him under a posthypnotic suggestion and tells him that, when the clock strikes four, he will (1) go to the closet, get his raincoat and galoshes, and put them on; (2) grab an umbrella; (3) walk eight blocks to the supermarket and purchase six bottles of bourbon; and (4) return home. Sam is told that, as soon as he reenters his apartment, he will "snap out of it" and be himself again.

When the clock strikes four, Sam immediately heads for the closet, dons his raincoat and galoshes, grabs his umbrella, and trudges out the door on his quest for bourbon. There are a few strange things about this errand: (1) it is a clear, sunshiny day—there isn't a cloud in the sky; (2) there is a liquor store half a block away that sells bourbon for the same price as the supermarket eight blocks away; and (3) Sam doesn't drink.

Sam arrives home, opens the door, reenters his apartment, snaps out of his "trance," and discovers himself standing there in his rain-coat and galoshes, with his umbrella in one hand and a huge sack of liquor bottles in the other. He looks momentarily confused. His friend, the hypnotist, says,

> "Hey, Sam, where have you been?"
> "Oh, just down to the store."
> "What did you buy?"
> "Um . . . um . . . it seems I bought this bourbon."
> "But you don't drink, do you?"
> "No, but . . . um . . . um . . . I'm going to do a lot of entertaining during the next several weeks, and some of my friends do."
> "How come you're wearing all that rain gear on such a sunny day?"
> "Well . . . actually, the weather is quite changeable this time of year, and I didn't want to take any chances."
> "But there isn't a cloud in the sky."
> "Well, you never can tell."
> "By the way, where did you buy the liquor?"
> "Oh, heh, heh. Well, um . . . down at the supermarket."
> "How come you went that far?"
> "Well, um . . . um . . . it was such a nice day, I thought it might be fun to take a long walk."

Most people are motivated to justify their own actions, beliefs, and feelings. When a person does something, he or she will try, if at all possible, to convince himself or herself (and others) that it was a logical, reasonable thing to do. There *was* a good reason why Sam performed those silly actions—he was hypnotized. But, because Sam didn't know he had been hypnotized, and because it was difficult for him to accept the fact that he was capable of behaving in a nonsensi-cal manner, he went to great lengths to convince himself (and his friend) that there was a method to his madness, that his actions were actually quite sensible.

The experiment by Stanley Schachter and Jerry Singer discussed in chapter 2 (pp. 31–32) can also be understood in these terms. Recall that these investigators injected people with epinephrine. Those who were forewarned about the symptoms caused by this drug (palpita-tions of the heart, sweaty palms, and hand tremors) had a sensible explanation for the symptoms when they appeared. "Oh, yeah, that's just the drug affecting me." Those who were misled about the after-effects of the drug, however, had no such handy, logical explanation for their symptoms. But they couldn't leave the symptoms unjustified—they tried to account for them by convincing themselves they were either deliriously happy or angry, depending on the social stimuli in the environment.

The concept of self-justification can be applied more broadly still. Suppose you are in the midst of a great natural disaster, such as an earthquake. All around you buildings are toppling and people are getting killed and injured. Needless to say, you are frightened. Is there any need to seek justification for this fear? Certainly not, the evidence is all around you; the injured people and the devastated buildings are ample justifications for your fear. But suppose, instead, the earthquake occurred in a neighboring town. You can feel the tremors, and you hear stories of the damage done to the other town. You are terribly frightened, but you are not in the midst of the devastated area; neither you nor the people around you have been hurt, and no buildings in your town have been damaged. Would you need to justify this fear? Yes. Much like the people in the Schachter-Singer experiment experiencing strong physical reactions to epinephrine but not knowing why, and much like our hypnotized friend in the raincoat and galoshes, you would be inclined to justify your own actions or feelings. In this situation, you see nothing to be afraid of in the immediate vicinity, so you would be inclined to seek justifications for the fact that you are scared out of your wits. These disaster situations are not hypothetical examples—they actually occurred in India. In the aftermath of an earthquake, investigators collected and analyzed the rumors being spread. What they discovered was rather startling: Jamuna Prasad,[1] an Indian psychologist, found that when the disaster occurred in a neighboring town such that the residents of the village in question could feel the tremors but were not in impending danger, there was an abundance of rumors forecasting impending doom. Specifically, the residents of this village believed and helped spread rumors to the effect that (1) a flood was rushing toward them; (2) February 26 would be a day of deluge and destruction; (3) there would be another severe earthquake on the day of the lunar eclipse; (4) there would be a cyclone within a few days; and (5) unforeseeable calamities were on the horizon.

Why in the world would people invent, believe, and communicate such stories? Were these people masochists? Were they paranoid? Certainly these rumors would not encourage the people to feel calm and secure. One rather compelling explanation is that the people were terribly frightened, and because there was not ample justification for this fear, they invented their own justification. Thus, they were not compelled to feel foolish. After all, if a cyclone is on the way, isn't it perfectly reasonable that I should be wild-eyed with fear? This explanation is bolstered by Durganand Sinha's study of rumors.[2] Sinha investigated the rumors being spread in an Indian village following a disaster of similar magnitude. The major difference between the situation in Prasad's study and the one in Sinha's study was that the people being investigated by Sinha had actually suffered the destruction and witnessed the damage. They were scared, but they had good reasons to be frightened—they had no need to seek additional justification for their fears. Thus, their rumors contained no prediction of impending disaster and no serious exaggeration. Indeed, if anything, the rumors were comforting. For example, one rumor predicted (falsely) that the water supply would be restored in a very short time.

The kind of process I have been discussing here has been encapsulated into a theory of human cognition and motivation by Leon Festinger.[3] Called the theory of cognitive dissonance, it is, as theories go, remarkably simple; but as we shall see, the range of its application is enormous. First, I will discuss the formal aspects of the theory, and then I will discuss its ramifications. Basically, cognitive dissonance is a state of tension that occurs whenever an individual simultaneously holds two cognitions (ideas, attitudes, beliefs, opinions) that are psychologically inconsistent. Stated differently, two cognitions are dissonant if, considering these two cognitions alone, the opposite of one follows from the other. Because the occurrence of cognitive dissonance is unpleasant, people are motivated to reduce it; this is roughly analogous to the processes involved in the induction and reduction of such drives as hunger or thirst—except that, here, the driving force arises from cognitive discomfort rather than physiological needs. To hold two ideas that contradict each other is to flirt with absurdity, and—as Albert Camus, the existentialist philosopher, has observed—humans are creatures who spend their lives trying to convince themselves their existence is not absurd.

How do we convince ourselves our lives are not absurd—that is, how do we reduce cognitive dissonance? By changing one or both cognitions in such a way as to render them more compatible (more consonant) with each other, or by adding more cognitions that help bridge the gap between the original cognitions.*

Let me cite an example that is, alas, all too familiar to many people. Suppose a person smokes cigarettes and then reads a report of the medical evidence linking cigarette smoking to lung cancer and other respiratory diseases. The smoker experiences dissonance. The cognition "I smoke cigarettes" is dissonant with the cognition "cigarette smoking produces cancer." Clearly, the most efficient way for a person to reduce dissonance in such a situation is to give up smoking. The cognition "cigarette smoking produces cancer" is consonant with the cognition "I do not smoke."

But, for most people, it is not easy to give up smoking. Imagine Sally, a young woman who tried to stop smoking but failed. What does she do to reduce dissonance? In all probability, she will try to work on the other cognition: "Cigarette smoking produces cancer." Sally might attempt to make light of evidence linking cigarette smoking to cancer. For example, she might try to convince herself that the experimental evidence is inconclusive. In addition, she might seek out intelligent people who smoke and, by so doing, convince herself that if Debbie, Nicole, and Larry smoke, it can't be all that dangerous. Sally might switch to a filter-tipped brand and delude herself into believing that the filter traps the cancer-producing materials. Finally, she might add cognitions that are consonant with smoking in an attempt to make the behavior less absurd in spite of its danger. Thus, Sally might enhance the value placed on smoking; that is, she might come to believe smoking is an important and highly enjoyable activity that is essential for relaxation: "I may lead a shorter life, but it will be a more enjoyable one." Similarly, she might actually try to make a virtue out of smoking by developing a romantic devil-may-care self-image, flouting danger by smoking cigarettes. All such behavior reduces dissonance by reducing the absurdity of the notion

---

* In the preceding chapter ("Social Cognition"), we learned that beliefs and attitudes are not always good predictors of a person's behavior—that is to say, that behavior is not always consistent with relevant beliefs and attitudes. Here, we are making the point that most people *feel* that their beliefs and attitudes *should be* consistent with their behavior and, therefore, are motivated to justify their behavior when it is inconsistent with a preexisting attitude.

of going out of one's way to contract cancer. Sally has justified her behavior by cognitively minimizing the danger or by exaggerating the importance of the action. In effect, she has succeeded either in constructing a new attitude or in changing an existing attitude.

Indeed, shortly after the publicity surrounding the original surgeon general's report in 1964, a survey was conducted[4] to assess people's reactions to the new evidence that smoking helps cause cancer. Nonsmokers overwhelmingly believed the health report, only 10 percent of those queried saying the link between smoking and cancer had not been proven to exist; these respondents had no motivation to disbelieve the report. The smokers faced a more difficult quandary. Smoking is a difficult habit to break; only 9 percent of the smokers had been able to quit. To justify continuing the activity, smokers tended to debunk the report. They were more likely to deny the evidence: 40 percent of the heavy smokers said a link had not been proven to exist. They were also more apt to employ rationalizations: Over twice as many smokers as nonsmokers agreed there were many hazards in life and that both smokers and nonsmokers get cancer.

Smokers who are painfully aware of the health hazards associated with smoking may reduce dissonance in yet another way—by minimizing the extent of their habit. One study[5] found that, of 155 smokers who smoked between one and two packs of cigarettes a day, 60 percent considered themselves moderate smokers; the remaining 40 percent considered themselves heavy smokers. How can we explain these different self-perceptions? Not surprisingly, those who labeled themselves as "moderates" were more aware of the pathological, long-term effects of smoking than were those who labeled themselves as heavy smokers. That is, these particular smokers apparently reduced dissonance by convincing themselves that smoking one or two packs a day isn't really all that much. "Moderate" and "heavy" are, after all, subjective terms.

Imagine a teenage girl who has not yet begun to smoke. After reading the surgeon general's report, is she apt to believe it? Like most of the nonsmokers in the survey, she should. The evidence is objectively sound, the source is expert and trustworthy, and there is no reason not to believe the report. And this is the crux of the matter. Earlier in this book, I made the point that people strive to be right and that values and beliefs become internalized when they appear to be correct. It is this striving to be right that motivates people to pay close attention to what other people are doing and to heed the advice of expert, trustworthy communicators. This is extremely rational behavior. There are forces, however, that can work against this rational behavior. The theory of cognitive dissonance does not picture people as rational beings; rather, it pictures them as rationalizing beings. According to the underlying assumptions of the theory, we humans are motivated not so much to be right; rather, we are motivated to believe we are right (and wise, and decent, and good).

Sometimes, our motivation to be right and our motivation to *believe* we are right are working in the same direction. This is what is happening with the young woman who doesn't smoke and therefore finds it easy to accept the notion that smoking causes lung cancer. This would also be true for a smoker who encounters the evidence linking cigarette smoking to lung cancer and *does* succeed in giving up cigarettes. Occasionally, however, the need to reduce dissonance (the need to convince oneself that one *is* right or good) leads to behavior that is maladaptive and therefore irrational. For example, psychologists who have helped people give up smoking often report that people who try to quit smoking and *fail* will come, in time, to develop a less intense attitude toward the dangers of smoking than those who have not yet made a concerted effort to quit. Why might this change of heart occur? If a person makes a serious commitment to a course of action, such as quitting smoking, and then fails to keep that commitment, his or her self-concept as a strong, self-controlled individual is threatened. This, of course, arouses dissonance. One way to reduce this dissonance and regain a healthy sense of self—if not a healthy set of lungs—is to trivialize the commitment by perceiving smoking as less dangerous. A study that tracked the progress of 135 students who made New Year's resolutions supports this observation.[6] Individuals who broke their resolutions—such as to quit smoking or lose weight—not only initially felt bad about themselves for failing, but subsequently played down the importance of the resolution. Ironically, making light of a commitment they failed to keep serves both to restore their self-esteem even as it makes self-defeat a near certainty in the future. In the short run, they are able to feel better about themselves; in the long run, however, they have drastically reduced the chances that they'll ever succeed in quitting smoking or losing weight.

Is this the only way to reduce the dissonance associated with failing to achieve a goal? No. An alternative response—and perhaps a less maladaptive one—would be to lower one's expectations for success. For example, a person who has been unable to give up smoking completely—but who has cut down on the number of cigarettes smoked daily—could interpret this outcome as a partial success, rather than as a complete failure. This course of action would soften the blow to his or her self-esteem for having failed, while still holding out the possibility of achieving success in future efforts to quit smoking altogether.

Let's stay with the topic of cigarette smoking for a moment and consider an extreme example: Suppose you were one of the top executives of a major cigarette company—you are in a situation of maximum commitment to the idea of cigarette smoking. Your job consists of producing, advertising, and selling cigarettes to millions of people. If it is true that cigarette smoking causes cancer, then, in a sense, you are partially responsible for the illness and death of a great many people. This would produce a painful degree of dissonance: Your cognition "I am a decent, kind human being" would be dissonant with your cognition "I am contributing to the early death of a great many people." In order to reduce this dissonance, you must try to convince yourself that cigarette-smoking is not harmful; this would involve a refutation of the mountain of evidence suggesting a causal link between cigarettes and cancer. Moreover, in order to further convince yourself that you are a good, moral person, you might go so far as to demonstrate how much you disbelieve the evidence by smoking a great deal yourself. If your need is great enough, you might even succeed in convincing yourself cigarettes are good for people. Thus, in order to see yourself as wise, good, and right, you take action that is stupid and detrimental to your health.

This analysis is so fantastic that it's almost beyond belief—almost. In 1994, under the chairmanship of Henry Waxman, the U.S. Congress conducted hearings on the dangers of smoking. At these hearings, the top executives of most of the major tobacco companies admitted they were smokers and actually argued that cigarettes are no more harmful or addictive than playing video games or eating twinkies! This kind of public denial is nothing new, of course. Some twenty-five years ago, the following news item was released by the *Washington Post* News Service:

> Jack Landry pulls what must be his 30th Marlboro of the day out of one of the two packs on his desk, lights a match to it and tells how he doesn't believe all those reports about smoking and cancer and em-

physema. He has just begun to market yet another cigarette for Philip Morris U.S.A. and is brimming over with satisfaction over its prospects. But how does he square with his conscience the spending of $10 million in these United States over the next year to lure people into smoking his new brand? "It's not a matter of that," says Landry, Philip Morris' vice president for marketing. "Nearly half the adults in this country smoke. It's a basic commodity for them. I'm serving a need. . . . There are studies by pretty eminent medical and scientific authorities, one on a theory of stress, on how a heck of a lot of people, if they didn't have cigarette smoking to relieve stress, would be one hell of a lot worse off. And there are plenty of valid studies that indicate cigarette smoking and all those diseases are not related." His satisfaction, says Landry, comes from being very good at his job in a very competitive business, and he will point out that Philip Morris and its big-selling Marlboro has just passed American Tobacco as the No. 2 cigarette seller in America (R. J. Reynolds is still No. 1). Why a new cigarette now? Because it is there to be sold, says Landry. And therein lies the inspiration of the marketing of a new American cigarette, which Landry confidently predicts will have a 1 percent share of the American market within 12 months. That 1 percent will equal about five billion cigarettes and a healthy profit for Philip Morris U.S.A.[7]

Do you think any amount of rational evidence or argument could induce Mr. Landry to believe cigarette smoking causes cancer? Near the close of chapter 3, I discussed the fact that information campaigns are relatively ineffective when they attempt to change deep-seated attitudes. We can now see precisely why information campaigns are of limited effectiveness. If people are committed to an attitude, the information the communicator presents arouses dissonance; frequently, the best way to reduce the dissonance is to reject or distort the evidence. The deeper a person's commitment to an attitude, the greater his or her tendency to reject dissonant evidence.

The reader may or may not be convinced by this kind of evidence. For example, it is always possible that Mr. Landry knows that cigarettes are harmful but is simply being cynical. Likewise, it is possible that Landry always believed cigarettes were good for people even before he began to peddle them. Obviously, if either of these possibilities were true, his excitement about the benefits of cigarette smoking could hardly be attributed to dissonance. Much more convincing would be a demonstration of a clear case of attitudinal distortion in a unique event. Such a demonstration was provided back in the 1950s by (of all things) a football game in the Ivy League. An important game between Princeton and Dartmouth, the contest was billed as a grudge match, and this soon became evident on the field: The game is remembered as the roughest and dirtiest in the history of either school. On the Princeton team was an All-American named Dick Kazmaier; as the game progressed, it became increasingly clear the Dartmouth players were out to get him. Whenever he carried the ball, he was gang-tackled, piled on, and mauled. He was finally forced to leave the game with a broken nose. Meanwhile, the Princeton team was not exactly inactive: Soon after Kazmaier's injury, a Dartmouth player was carried off the field with a broken leg. Several fist fights broke out on the field in the course of the game, and many injuries were suffered on both sides.

Sometime after the game, a couple of psychologists—Albert Hastorf of Dartmouth and Hadley Cantril of Princeton[8]—visited both campuses and showed films of the game to a number of students on each campus. The students were instructed to be completely objective and, while watching the film, to take notes of each infraction of the rules, how it started, and who was responsible. As you might imagine, there was a huge difference in the way this game was viewed by the students at each university. There was a strong tendency for the students to see their own fellow students as victims of illegal infractions rather than as perpetrators of such acts of aggression. Moreover, this was no minor distortion: It was found that Princeton students saw fully twice as many violations on the part of the Dartmouth players as the Dartmouth students saw. Again, people are not passive receptacles for the deposition of information. The manner in which they view and interpret information depends on how deeply they are committed to a particular belief or course of action. Individuals will distort the objective world in order to reduce their dissonance. The manner in which they will distort and the intensity of their distortion are highly predictable.

Lenny Bruce, a perceptive comedian and social commentator (who almost certainly never read about cognitive dissonance theory), had the following insight into the 1960 presidential election campaign between Richard Nixon and John Kennedy:

> I would be with a bunch of Kennedy fans watching the debate and their comment would be, "He's really slaughtering Nixon." Then we

would all go to another apartment, and the Nixon fans would say, "How do you like the shellacking he gave Kennedy?" And then I realized that each group loved their candidate so that a guy would have to be this blatant—he would have to look into the camera and say: "I am a thief, a crook, do you hear me, I am the worst choice you could ever make for the Presidency!" And even then his following would say, "Now there's an honest man for you. It takes a big guy to admit that. There's the kind of guy we need for President."[9]

People don't like to see or hear things that conflict with their deeply held beliefs or wishes. An ancient response to such bad news was to kill the messenger—literally. A modern-day figurative version of "killing the messenger" is to blame the media for the presentation of material that produces the pain of dissonance. For example, when Ronald Reagan was running for president in 1980, *Time* published an analysis of his campaign. Subsequent angry letters to the editor vividly illustrated the widely divergent responses of his supporters on the one hand, and his detractors on the other. Consider the following two letters:[10]

> Lawrence Barrett's pre-election piece on Candidate Ronald Reagan [Oct. 20] was a slick hatchet job, and you know it. You ought to be ashamed of yourselves for printing it disguised as an objective look at the man.

> Your story on "The Real Ronald Reagan" did it. Why didn't you just editorially endorse him? Barrett glosses over Reagan's fatal flaws so handily that the "real" Ronald Reagan came across as *the* answer to all our problems.

Dissonance Reduction and Rational Behavior

I have referred to dissonance-reducing behavior as "irrational." By this I mean it is often maladaptive, in that it can prevent people from learning important facts or from finding real solutions to their problems. On the other hand, it does serve a purpose: Dissonance-reducing behavior is ego-defensive behavior; by reducing dissonance, we maintain a positive image of ourselves—an image that depicts us as good, or smart, or worthwhile. Again, although this ego-defensive behavior can be considered useful, it can have disastrous consequen-

ces. In the laboratory, the irrationality of dissonance-reducing behavior has been amply demonstrated by Edward Jones and Rika
Kohler.[11] These investigators selected individuals who were deeply
committed to a position on the issue of racial segregation—some of
the subjects were in favor of segregation, and others were opposed to
it. These individuals were allowed to read a series of arguments on
both sides of the issue. Some of these arguments were extremely
sensible and plausible, and others were so implausible they bordered
on the ridiculous. Jones and Kohler were interested in determining
which of the arguments people would remember best. If people were
purely rational, we would expect them to remember the plausible
arguments best and the implausible arguments the least; why in the
world would people want to keep implausible arguments in their
heads? Accordingly, the rational person would rehearse and remember all the arguments that made sense and would slough off all
ridiculous arguments. What does the theory of cognitive dissonance
predict? It is comforting to have all the wise people on your side and
all the fools on the other side: A silly argument in favor of one's own
position arouses some dissonance, because it raises some doubts
about the wisdom of that position or the intelligence of the people
who agree with it. Likewise, a plausible argument on the other side of
the issue also arouses some dissonance, because it raises the possibility the other side is right. Because these arguments arouse dissonance, one tries not to think about them—that is, one might not
learn them very well, or one might simply forget about them. This is
exactly what Jones and Kohler found. Their subjects did not remember in a rational-functional manner. They tended to remember the
plausible arguments agreeing with their own position and the *implausible* arguments agreeing with the opposing position.

In a conceptually similar experiment, Charles Lord, Lee Ross,
and Mark Lepper[12] showed that we do not process information in an
unbiased manner. Rather, we distort it in a way that fits our preconceived notions. These investigators selected several Stanford University students who opposed capital punishment and several who
favored capital punishment. They showed the students two research
articles that discussed whether or not the death penalty tends to deter
violent crimes. One of the studies confirmed and the other study
disconfirmed the existing beliefs of the students. If these students
were perfectly rational, they might conclude that the issue is a com-

plex one, and accordingly, the two groups of students might move closer to each other in their beliefs about capital punishment. On the other hand, dissonance theory would predict that individuals will distort the articles such that they will clasp the confirming article to their bosoms and hail it as clearly supportive of their belief—while finding methodological or conceptual flaws in the "disconfirming" article, refusing to be influenced by it. This is precisely what happened. Indeed, rather than coming closer in their beliefs after being exposed to this two-sided presentation, the two groups of students were in greater disagreement with one another than they were beforehand. This process probably accounts for the fact that, on issues like politics and religion, people who are deeply committed will almost never come to see things *our* way, no matter how powerful and balanced our arguments are.

Those of us who have worked extensively with the theory of cognitive dissonance do not deny that humans are capable of rational behavior. The theory merely suggests that a good deal of our behavior is not rational—although, from inside, it may seem very sensible indeed. If you ask the hypnotized young man why he wore a raincoat on a sunny day, he'll come up with an answer he feels is sensible; if you ask the vice president of Philip Morris why he smokes, he'll give you a reason that makes sense to him—he'll tell you how good it is for everyone's health; if you ask Jones and Kohler's subjects why they remembered a particular set of arguments rather than others, they'll insist that the arguments they remembered were a fair and representative sample of those they read. Similarly, the students in the experiment on capital punishment will insist that the evidence against their position is flawed. It is important to note that the world is not divided into rational people on the one side and dissonance-reducers on the other. People are not all the same, and some people are able to tolerate dissonance better than others, but we are all capable of rational behavior and we are all capable of dissonance-reducing behavior, depending on the circumstances. Occasionally, the same person can manifest both behaviors in rapid succession.

The rationality and irrationality of human behavior will be illustrated over and over again during the next several pages as we list and discuss some of the wide ramifications of our need for self-justification. These ramifications run virtually the entire gamut of human behavior, but for the sake of conserving time and space, I will sample only a few of these. Let us begin with the decision-making process, a process that shows humans at their most rational and their most irrational in quick succession.

Dissonance as a Consequence of Making a Decision

Suppose you are about to make a decision—about the purchase of a new car, for example. This involves a significant amount of money, so it is, by definition, an important decision. After looking around, you are torn between getting a van and purchasing a compact model. There are various advantages and disadvantages to each: The van would be convenient; you can haul things in it, sleep in it during long trips, and it has plenty of power, but it gets atrocious mileage and is not easy to park. The compact model is less roomy, and you are concerned about its safety, but it is less expensive to buy and operate, it is more fun to drive, and you've heard it has a pretty good repair record. My guess is that, *before* you make the decision, you will seek as much information as you can. Chances are you will read *Consumer Reports* to find out what this expert, unbiased source has to say. Perhaps you'll confer with friends who own a van or a compact car. You'll probably visit the automobile dealers to test-drive the vehicles to see how each one feels. All of this predecision behavior is perfectly rational. Let us assume you make a decision—you buy the compact car. What happens next? Your behavior will begin to change: No longer will you seek objective information about all makes of cars. Chances are you may begin to spend more time talking with the owners of small cars. You will begin to talk about the number of miles to the gallon as though it were the most important thing in the world. My guess is you will not be prone to spend much time thinking about the fact you can't sleep in your compact. Similarly, your mind will skim lightly over the fact that driving your new car can be particularly hazardous in a collision and that the brakes are not very responsive, although your failure to attend to these shortcomings could conceivably cost you your life.

How does this sort of thing come about? Following a decision—especially a difficult one, or one that involves a significant amount of time, effort, or money—people almost always experience dissonance. This is so because the chosen alternative is seldom entirely positive, and the rejected alternatives are seldom entirely negative. In this example, your cognition that you bought a compact is dissonant with your cognition about any deficiencies the car may have. Similarly, all the positive aspects of the other cars that you considered buying but did not purchase are dissonant with your cognition that you did not buy one of them. A good way to reduce such dissonance is to seek out exclusively positive information about the car you chose and avoid negative information about it. One source of safe information is advertisements; it is a safe bet an ad will not run down its own product. Accordingly, one might predict that a person who had recently purchased a new car will begin to read advertisements selectively, reading more ads about his or her car *after the purchase* than people who have *not* recently purchased the same model. Moreover, owners of new cars will tend to steer clear of ads for other makes of cars. This is exactly what Danuta Ehrlich and her colleagues[13] found in a well-known survey of advertising readership. In short, Ehrlich's data suggest that, *after* decisions, people try to gain reassurance that their decisions were wise by seeking information that is certain to be reassuring.

People do not always need help from Madison Avenue to gain reassurance; they can do a pretty good job of reassuring themselves. An experiment by Jack Brehm[14] demonstrates how this can come about. Posing as a marketing researcher, Brehm showed each of several women eight different appliances (a toaster, an electric coffeemaker, a sandwich grill, and the like) and asked that she rate them in terms of how attractive each appliance was to her. As a reward, each woman was told she could have one of the appliances as a gift—and she was given a choice between two of the products she had rated as being equally attractive. After she chose one, it was wrapped up and given to her. Several minutes later, she was asked to rate the products again. It was found that after receiving the appliance of her choice, each woman rated the attractiveness of that appliance somewhat higher and decreased the rating of the appliance she had a chance to own but rejected. Again, making a decision produces dissonance: Cognitions about any negative aspects of the preferred object are dissonant with having chosen it, and cognitions about the positive aspects of the unchosen object are dissonant with *not* having chosen it. To reduce dissonance, people cognitively spread apart the alternatives. That is, *after the decision,* the women in Brehm's study emphasized the positive attributes of the appliance they decided to own, while de-emphasizing its negative attributes; for the appliance they decided *not* to own, they emphasized its negative attributes and deemphasized its positive attributes.

The tendency to justify one's choices is not limited to consumer decisions. In fact, research has demonstrated that similar processes can even affect our romantic relationships and our willingness to consider becoming involved with alternative partners. In a study conducted by Dennis Johnson and Caryl Rusbult,[15] college students were asked to evaluate the probable success of a new computer dating service on campus. Subjects were shown pictures of individuals of the opposite sex, who they believed were applicants to the dating service. Subjects were then asked to rate the attractiveness of these applicants, as well as how much they believed they would enjoy a potential date with him or her—a possibility that was presented in a realistic manner. The results of this study were remarkably similar to Brehm's findings about appliances: The more heavily committed the students were to their current romantic partners, the more negative were their ratings of the attractiveness of alternative partners presented in the study. In a subsequent experiment, Jeffry Simpson and his colleagues[16] also found that those in committed relationships saw opposite sex persons as less physically and sexually attractive than did those who weren't in committed relationships. In addition, Simpson showed that this effect only holds for "available others"; when presented with individuals who were somewhat older or who were of the same sex, people in committed relationships did not derogate their attractiveness. In short, no threat, no dissonance; no dissonance, no derogation.

In sum, whether we are talking about appliances or romantic partners, once a firm commitment has been made, people tend to focus on the positive aspects of their choices and to downplay the attractive qualities of the unchosen alternatives.

Some Historical Examples of the Consequences of Decisions. Although some of the material discussed above is benign enough, it is impossible to overstate the potential dangers posed by our susceptibility to these tendencies. When I mentioned that ignoring potential danger in order to reduce dissonance could conceivably lead to a person's death, I meant that literally. Suppose a madman has taken over your country and has decided to eradicate all members of your religious group. But you don't know that for sure. What you do know is that your country is being occupied, that the leader of the occupation forces does not like your religious group very much, and that, occasionally, members of your faith are forced to move from their homes and are kept in detention camps. What do you do? You could try to flee from your country; you could try to pass as a member of a different religious group; or you could sit tight and hope for the best. Each of these options is extremely dangerous: It is difficult to escape or to pass and go undetected; and if you are caught trying to flee or disguising your identity, the penalty is immediate execution. On the other hand, deciding to sit tight could be a disastrous decision if it turns out your religious group is being systematically annihilated. Let us suppose you decide not to take action. That is, you commit yourself to sit tight—turning your back on opportunities to try either to escape or to pass. Such an important decision naturally produces a great deal of dissonance. In order to reduce dissonance, you convince yourself you made a wise decision—that is, you convince yourself that, although people of your religious sect are made to move and are being treated unfairly, they are not being killed unless they break the law. This is not difficult to maintain because there is no unambiguous evidence to the contrary.

Suppose that, months later, a respected man from your town tells you that while hiding in the forest, he witnessed soldiers butchering all the men, women, and children who had recently been deported from the town. I would predict that you would try to dismiss this information as untrue—that you would attempt to convince yourself that the reporter was lying or hallucinating. If you had listened to the man who tried to warn you, you might have escaped. Instead, you and your family are slaughtered.

Fantastic? Impossible? How could anyone not take the "respected man" seriously? The events described above are an accurate account of what happened in 1944 to the Jews in Sighet, Hungary.[17]

The processes of cognitive distortion and selective exposure to information may have been an important factor in the escalation of the war in Vietnam. In a thought-provoking analysis of the Pentagon Papers, Ralph White suggested that dissonance blinded our leaders to information incompatible with the decisions they had already made. As White put it, "There was a tendency, when actions were out of line with ideas, for decision makers to align their ideas with their actions." To take just one of many examples, the decision to continue to escalate the bombing of North Vietnam was made at the price of ignoring crucial evidence from the CIA and other sources that made it clear that bombing would not break the will of the North Vietnamese people but, quite the contrary, would only strengthen their resolve:

> It is instructive, for instance, to compare McNamara's highly factual evidence-oriented summary of the case against bombing in 1966 (pages 555–63 of the Pentagon Papers) with the Joint Chief's memorandum that disputed his conclusion and called the bombing one of our two trump cards, while it apparently ignored all of the facts that showed the opposite. Yet it was the Joint Chiefs who prevailed.[18]

White surmises the reason they prevailed was that their advice was consonant with decisions already made and with certain key assumptions then operating that later proved to be erroneous.[19]

Escalation is self-perpetuating. Once a small commitment is made, it sets the stage for ever-increasing commitments. The behavior needs to be justified, so attitudes are changed; this change in attitudes influences future decisions and behavior. The flavor of this kind of cognitive escalation is nicely captured in an analysis of the Pentagon Papers by the news magazine *Time:*

> Yet the bureaucracy, the Pentagon Papers indicate, always demanded new options; each option was to apply more force. Each tightening of the screw created a position that must be defended; once committed, the military pressure must be maintained.[20]

The process underlying escalation has been explored, on a more individual level, under controlled experimental conditions. Suppose you would like to enlist someone's aid in a massive undertaking, but you know the job you have in mind for the person is so difficult and will require so much time and effort that the person will surely decline. What should you do? One possibility is to get the person involved in a much smaller aspect of the job, one so easy that he or she wouldn't dream of turning it down. This action serves to commit the individual to "the cause." Once people are thus committed, the likelihood of their complying with the larger request increases. This phenomenon was demonstrated by Jonathan Freedman and Scott Fraser.[21] They attempted to induce several homeowners to put up a huge sign in their front yards reading "Drive Carefully." Because of the ugliness and obtrusiveness of this sign, most residents refused to put it up; only 17 percent complied. A different group of residents, however, were first "softened up" by an experimenter who "put his foot in the door" by getting them to sign a petition favoring safe driving. Because signing a petition is an easy thing to do, virtually all who were asked agreed to sign. A few weeks later, a different experimenter went to each resident with the obtrusive ugly sign reading "Drive Carefully." More than 55 percent of these residents allowed the sign to be put up on their property. Thus, when individuals commit themselves in a small way, the likelihood they will commit themselves further in that direction is increased. This process of using small favors to encourage people to accede to larger requests had been dubbed the foot-in-the-door technique. It is effective because having done the smaller favor sets up pressures toward agreeing to do the larger favor; in effect, it provides justification in advance for complying with the large request.

Similar results were obtained by Patricia Pliner and her associates.[22] These investigators found that 46 percent of their sample were willing to make a small donation to the Cancer Society when they were approached directly. A similar group of people were asked one day earlier to wear a lapel pin publicizing the fund-raising drive. When approached the next day, approximately twice as many of these people were willing to make a contribution.

The Importance of Irrevocability

One of the important characteristics of the examples presented above is the relative irrevocability of the decision. This needs some explaining: Occasionally, we make tentative decisions. For example, if you had indicated you might buy an expensive house near San Francisco, but the decision was not finalized, chances are you would not expend any effort trying to convince yourself of the wisdom of the decision. Once you had put your money down, however, and you knew you couldn't easily get it back, you would probably start minimizing the importance of the dampness in the basement, the cracks in the foundation, or the fact that it happened to be built on the San Andreas fault. Similarly, once a European Jew has decided not to pass and has allowed himself to be identified as a Jew, it is irrevocable—he can't very easily pretend to be a Gentile. By the same token, once Pentagon officials intensified the bombing, they could not undo it. And once a homeowner has signed the petition, commitment to safe driving is established.

Some direct evidence for the importance of irrevocability comes from a clever study of the cognitive gyrations of gamblers at a race track. The race track is an ideal place to scrutinize irrevocability because once you've placed your bet, you can't go back and tell the nice man behind the window you've changed your mind! Robert Knox and James Inkster[23] simply intercepted people who were on their way to place two-dollar bets. They had already decided on their horses and were about to place their bets when the investigators asked them how certain they were their horses would win. Because they were on their way to the two-dollar window, their decisions were not irrevocable. The investigators collared other bettors just as they were leaving the two-dollar window, *after* having placed their bets, and asked them how certain they were their horses would win. Typically, people who had just placed their bets gave their horses a much better chance of winning than did those who were about to place their bets. But, of course, nothing had changed except the finality of the decision. Similar results were obtained in a survey of Canadian voters.[24] Those voters interviewed immediately *after* voting were more certain their candidates would win and liked their candidates more than those voters interviewed immediately *before* they had cast their votes. In short, when a decision is irrevocable, more dissonance is aroused; to reduce this dissonance, people become more certain they are right *after* there is nothing they can do about it.

While the irrevocability of a decision always increases dissonance and the motivation to reduce it, there are circumstances in which irrevocability is unnecessary. Let me explain with an example. Suppose you enter an automobile showroom intent on buying a new car. You've already priced the car you want at several dealers—you know you can purchase it for about $9,300. Lo and behold, the salesman tells you he can sell you one for $8,942. Excited by the bargain, you agree to the deal and write out a check for the downpayment. While the salesman takes your check to the sales manager to consummate the deal, you rub your hands in glee as you imagine yourself driving home in your shiny new car. But alas, ten minutes later, the salesman returns with a forlorn look on his face—it seems he made a calculation error and the sales manager caught it. The price of the car is actually $9,384. You can get it cheaper elsewhere; moreover, the decision to buy is not irrevocable. And yet, far more people in this situation will go ahead with the deal than if the original asking price had been $9,384—even though the reason for purchasing the car from this dealer (the bargain price) no longer exists. Indeed, Robert Cialdini,[25] a social psychologist who temporarily joined the sales force of an automobile dealer, discovered that the strategy described above is a common and successful ploy called lowballing, or "throwing the customer a lowball."

What is going on in this situation? There are at least three important things to notice. First, while the customer's decision to buy is certainly reversible, there *is* a commitment emphasized by the act of signing a check for a downpayment. Second, this commitment triggered the anticipation of a pleasant or interesting experience: driving out with a new car. To have the anticipated event thwarted (by not going ahead with the deal) would have produced dissonance and disappointment. Third, although the final price is substantially higher than the customer thought it would be, it is only slightly higher than the price somewhere else. Under these circumstances, the customer in effect says, "Oh, what the hell. I'm already here; I've already filled out the forms—why wait?"[26] Clearly, such a ploy would not be effective if the consequences were somewhat higher—as in matters of life and death.

The Decision to Behave Immorally. How can an honest person become corrupt? Conversely, how can we get a person to be *more* honest? One way is through the dissonance that results from making a difficult decision. Suppose you are a college student enrolled in a biology course. Your grade will hinge on the final exam you are now taking. The key question on the exam involves some material you know fairly well—but, because of anxiety, you draw a blank. You are sitting there in a nervous sweat. You look up, and lo and behold, you happen to be sitting behind a woman who is the smartest person in the class (who also happens, fortunately, to be the person with the most legible handwriting in the class). You glance down and notice she is just completing her answer to the crucial question. You know you could easily read her answer if you chose to. What do you do? Your conscience tells you it's wrong to cheat—and yet, if you don't cheat, you are certain to get a poor grade. You wrestle with your conscience. Regardless of whether you decide to cheat or not to cheat, you are doomed to experience dissonance. If you cheat, your cognition "I am a decent moral person" is dissonant with your cognition "I have just committed an immoral act." If you decide to resist temptation, your cognition "I want to get a good grade" is dissonant with your cognition "I could have acted in such a way that would have ensured a good grade, but I chose not to."

Suppose that, after a difficult struggle, you decide to cheat. How do you reduce the dissonance? Before you read on, think about it for a moment. One way to reduce dissonance is to minimize the negative aspects of the action you have chosen (and to maximize the positive aspects)—much the same way the women did after choosing an appliance in Jack Brehm's experiment. In this instance, an efficacious path of dissonance reduction would entail a change in your attitude about cheating. In short, you will adopt a more lenient attitude. Your reasoning might go something like this: "Cheating isn't so bad, under some circumstances. As long as nobody gets hurt, it's really not very immoral—anybody would do it—therefore, it's a part of human nature, . . . so how could it be bad? Since it *is* only human, those who get caught cheating should not be severely punished but should be treated with understanding."

Suppose that, after a difficult struggle, you decide *not* to cheat. How would you reduce dissonance? Once again, you could change your attitude about the morality of the act—but in the opposite direction. That is, in order to justify giving up a good grade, you must convince yourself cheating is a heinous sin, that it's one of the lowest things a person can do, and that cheaters should be found out and severely punished.

The interesting and important thing to remember here is that two people acting in the two different ways described above could have started out with almost identical attitudes. Their decisions might have been a hair's breadth apart—one came within an ace of resisting but decided to cheat, while the other came within an ace of cheating but decided to resist. Once they have made their decisions, however, their attitudes toward cheating will diverge sharply as a consequence of their decisions.

These speculations were put to the test by Judson Mills[27] in an experiment with sixth graders. Mills first measured their attitudes toward cheating. He then had them participate in a competitive exam with prizes being offered to the winners. The situation was arranged so it was almost impossible to win without cheating; also, it was easy for the children to cheat, thinking they would not be detected. As one might expect, some of the students cheated and others did not. The next day, the sixth graders were again asked to indicate how they felt about cheating. In general, those children who had cheated became more lenient toward cheating, and those who resisted the temptation to cheat adopted a harsher attitude toward cheating.

The data from Mills's experiment are provocative indeed. One thing they suggest is that the most zealous opponents of a given position are not those who have always been distant from that position. For example, one might hazard a guess that the people who are most angry at the apparent sexual freedom associated with the current generation of young people may *not* be those who have never been tempted to engage in casual sexual activity themselves. Indeed, Mills's data suggest the possibility that the people who have the strongest need to crack down hard on this sort of behavior are those who have been sorely tempted, who came dangerously close to giving in to this temptation, but who finally resisted. People who *almost* decide to live in glass houses are frequently the ones who are most prone to throw stones.

Early in this chapter, I mentioned that the desire for self-justification is an important reason why people who are strongly committed to an attitude on an issue tend to resist any direct attempts to change that attitude. In effect, such people are invulnerable to the propaganda or education in question. We can now see that the same mechanism that enables a person to cling to an attitude can induce that individual to *change* an attitude. It depends on which course of action will serve most to reduce dissonance under the circumstances. A person who understands the theory can set up the proper conditions to induce attitude change in other people by making them vulnerable to certain kinds of beliefs. For example, if a modern

Machiavelli were advising a contemporary ruler, he might suggest the following strategies based on the theory and data on the consequences of decisions:

1. If you want people to form more positive attitudes toward an object, get them to commit themselves to own that object.

2. If you want people to soften their moral attitudes toward some misdeed, tempt them so that they perform that deed; conversely, if you want people to harden their moral attitudes toward a misdeed, tempt them—but not enough to induce them to commit the deed.

The Psychology of Inadequate Justification

Attitude change as a means of reducing dissonance is not, of course, limited to postdecision situations. It can occur in countless other contexts, including every time a person says something he or she doesn't believe or does something stupid or immoral. The effects can be extremely powerful. Let us look at some of them.

In a complex society, we occasionally find ourselves saying or doing things we don't completely believe. Does this *always* lead to attitude change? No. To illustrate, I will choose a simple example. Joe Lawyer enters the office and sees that his law partner, Joyce, has hung a perfectly atrocious painting on the wall of the office they share. He is about to tell her how awful he thinks it is when she says proudly, "How do you like the painting? I did it myself — you know, in the art class I'm taking at night."

"Very nice, Joyce," Joe answers. Theoretically, Joe's cognition "I am a truthful person" is dissonant with the cognition "I said that painting was nice, although it really is disastrous." Whatever dissonance might be aroused by this inconsistency can easily and quickly be reduced by Joe's cognition that it is important not to hurt other people: "I lied so as not to hurt Joyce; why should I tell her it's an ugly painting? It serves no useful purpose." This is an effective way of reducing dissonance, because it completely justifies the action Joe took. In effect, the justification is situation-determined. I will call this *external justification.*

But what happens if there is not ample justification in the situation itself? For example, imagine that Joe Lawyer, who is politically conservative, finds himself at a cocktail party with many people he doesn't know very well. The conversation turns to politics. The people are talking with horror about the fact that the United States seems to be drastically escalating its friendly overtures toward Castro's regime in Cuba. Joe's belief is a complicated one; he has mixed feelings about the topic, but generally he is opposed to our forming an alliance with the Cuban dictatorship because he feels it is an evil regime and we should not compromise with evil. Partly because Joe's companions are sounding so pious, and partly as a lark, he gradually finds himself taking a much more liberal-radical position than the one he really holds. As a matter of fact, Joe even goes so far as to assert that Fidel Castro is an extraordinarily gifted leader and that the Cuban people are better off with communism than they've been in hundreds of years. Somebody counters Joe's argument by talking about the many thousands of people that Castro is alleged to have murdered or imprisoned in order to achieve a unified government. In the heat of the situation, Joe replies that those figures are grossly exaggerated. Quite a performance for a man who does, in fact, believe that Castro killed thousands of innocent people during his rise to power.

When Joe awakens the next morning and thinks back on the previous evening's events, he gasps in horror. "Oh, my God, what have I done?" he says. He is intensely uncomfortable. Put another way, he is experiencing a great deal of dissonance. His cognition "I misled a bunch of people; I told them a lot of things about Cuba that I don't really believe" is dissonant with his cognition "I am a reasonable, decent, and truthful person." What does he do to reduce dissonance? He searches around for *external justifications*. First, it occurs to Joe that he might have been drunk and therefore not responsible for what he said. But he remembers he had only one or two beers—no external justification there. Because Joe cannot find sufficient external justification for his behavior, it is necessary for him to attempt to justify his behavior *internally*, by changing his attitude in the direction of his statements. That is, if Joe can succeed in convincing himself that his statements were not so very far from the truth, then he will have reduced dissonance—that is, his behavior of the preceding night will no longer be absurd in his own view. I do not mean to imply Joe would suddenly become an avowed communist revolutionary. What I do mean is that he might begin to feel a little less harsh about the Cuban regime than he had felt before he made those statements. Most events and issues in our world are neither completely black nor completely white; there are many gray areas. Thus, Joe might begin to take a different look at some of the events that have taken place in Cuba during the past fifty years. He might start looking into Castro's politics and decisions and become more disposed toward seeing wisdom that he hadn't seen before. He might also begin to be more receptive to information that indicates the extent of the corruption, brutality, and ineptitude of the previous government. To repeat: If an individual states a belief that is difficult to justify *externally,* that person will attempt to justify it *internally* by making his or her attitudes more consistent with the statement.

I have mentioned a couple of forms of external justification. One is the idea that it's all right to tell a harmless lie in order to avoid hurting a person's feelings—as in the case of Joe Lawyer and his partner. Another is drunkenness as an excuse for one's actions. Still another form of external justification is reward. Put yourself in Joe's shoes for a moment, and suppose you and I both were at that cocktail party, and that I am an eccentric millionaire. As the conversation turns to Cuba, I pull you aside and say, "Hey, I would like you to come out strongly in favor of Fidel Castro and Cuban communism." What's more, suppose I hand you $5,000 for doing it. After counting the money, you gasp, put the $5,000 in your pocket, return to the discussion, and defend Fidel Castro to the hilt. The next morning when you wake up, would you experience any dissonance? I don't think so. Your cognition "I said some things about Fidel Castro and Cuban communism that I don't believe" is dissonant with the cognition "I am a truthful and decent person." But, at the same time, you have adequate external justification for having made that statement: "I said those favorable things about Cuban communism in order to earn $5,000—and it was worth it." You don't have to soften your attitude toward Castro in order to justify that statement, because you know why you made those statements: You made them not because you think they are true, but in order to get the $5,000. You're left with the knowledge you sold your soul for $5,000—and it was worth it.

This has been called the "saying is believing" paradigm. That is, dissonance theory predicts that we begin to believe our own lies—but only if there is not an abundance of external justification for making the statements that run counter to our original attitudes. Let's now elaborate on our earlier discussion of conformity. Recall in chapter 2 we found that the greater the reward for compliance, the greater the probability a person will comply. Now we can go one step further: When it comes to producing a *lasting* change in attitude, the greater the reward, the *less* likely any attitude change will occur. If all I want you to do is recite a speech favoring Fidel Castro, the Marx brothers, socialized medicine, or anything else, the most efficient thing for me to do would be to give you the largest possible reward. This would increase the probability of your complying by making that speech. But suppose I have a more ambitious goal: Suppose I want to effect a lasting change in your attitudes and beliefs. In that case, just the reverse is true. The smaller the external reward I give to induce you to recite the speech, the more likely it is you will be forced to seek additional justification for delivering it, in the form of convincing yourself that the things you said were actually true. This would result in an actual change in attitude, rather than mere compliance. The importance of this technique cannot be overstated. If we change our attitudes because we have made a public statement for minimal external justification, our attitude change will be relatively permanent; we are not changing our attitudes because of a reward (compliance) or because of the influence of an attractive person (identification). We are changing our attitudes because we have succeeded in *convincing ourselves* that our previous attitudes were incorrect. This is a very powerful form of attitude change.

Thus far, we have been dealing with highly speculative material. These speculations have been investigated scientifically in several experiments. Among these is a classic study by Leon Festinger and J. Merrill Carlsmith.[28] Festinger and Carlsmith asked college students to perform a very boring and repetitive series of tasks—packing spools in a tray, dumping them out, and then refilling the tray over and over, or turning rows and rows of screws a quarter turn and then going back and turning them another quarter turn. The students engaged in these activities for a full hour. The experimenter then induced them to lie about the task; specifically, he employed them to tell a young woman (who was waiting to participate in the experiment) that the task she would be performing was interesting and enjoyable. Some of the students were offered twenty dollars for telling the lie, others were offered only one dollar for telling the lie. After the experiment was over, an interviewer asked the "lie tellers" how much they had enjoyed the tasks they had performed earlier in the experiment. The results were clear-cut: Those students who had been paid twenty dollars for lying—that is, for saying the spool packing and screw turning had been enjoyable—actually rated the activity as dull. This is not surprising—it *was* dull. But what about the students who had been paid only one dollar for telling their fellow student the experiment was enjoyable? They did, indeed, rate the task as an enjoyable one. In other words, people who received an abundance of external justification for lying told the lie but didn't believe it, whereas those who told the lie *in the absence* of a great deal of external justification did, indeed, move in the direction of believing that what they said was true.

Research support for the "saying is believing" phenomenon has extended beyond relatively unimportant attitudes like the dullness of a monotonous task. Attitude change has been shown on such important issues as police brutality and the legalization of marijuana. In one experiment, Arthur R. Cohen[29] induced Yale men to engage in a particularly difficult form of counterattitudinal behavior. Cohen conducted his experiment immediately after a student riot in which the New Haven police had behaved in a rather brutal manner toward the students. The students (who strongly believed the police had behaved badly) were asked to write an essay in support of the actions taken by the police. Students were urged to write the strongest, most forceful defense of the police actions they could muster. Before writing the essay, students were paid for their efforts. There were four conditions: Some students were paid ten dollars; others, five dollars; still others, one dollar; and a fourth group, the paltry sum of fifty cents. After writing his essay, each young man was asked to indicate his own private attitudes about the police actions. The results were perfectly linear: the smaller the reward, the greater the attitude change. Thus, students who wrote in support of the New Haven police for the meager sum of fifty cents developed a more favorable attitude than did those who wrote the essay for one dollar; the students who wrote the essay for one dollar developed a more favorable attitude toward the actions of the police than did those who wrote the essay for ten dollars; and so on. The less the external justification in terms of money, the greater the attitude change.[30]

Of course, as I mentioned a moment ago, external justification can and does come in a variety of forms. People can be persuaded to say things or do things that contradict their beliefs or preferences if they are threatened with punishment or enticed by other rewards besides monetary gain—such as praise or the desire to please. Furthermore, most of us would consider doing something that we otherwise wouldn't do if a good friend asked us to do it as a favor. To take a far-fetched example, suppose a friend asked you to eat an unusual food she or he had recently learned to prepare in an "exotic foods" cooking class. And just to make things interesting, let's say the food in question was a fried grasshopper. Now, imagine the reverse situation—that someone you didn't like very much asked you to sink your teeth into a fried grasshopper.

Okay, are you ready? Assuming you went ahead and ate the grasshopper, under which circumstance do you think you would enjoy the taste of it more—when asked to eat it by a good friend or someone you didn't like? Common sense might suggest that the grasshopper would taste better when recommended by a friend. After all, a friend is someone you can trust and, hence, would be a far more credible source of information than someone you didn't like. But think about it for a moment: Which condition involves less external justification? Common sense notwithstanding, the theory of cognitive dissonance would predict that you would come to like eating grasshoppers more if you ate one at the request of someone you didn't like.

Here's how it works: Your cognition that eating a grasshopper is repulsive would be at odds with the fact that you just ate one. But if it was your *friend* who made the request, you would have a great deal of external justification for having eaten it—you did it as a favor for a good friend. On the other hand, you would not have adequate external justification for munching on a grasshopper if you did it at the request of someone you didn't like. In this case, how could you justify your contradictory behavior to yourself? Simple. The way to reduce dissonance would be to change your attitude toward grasshoppers in the direction of liking them better—"Gee, they're pretty tasty critters after all."

While this may seem a rather bizarre example of dissonance-reducing behavior, it's not as far-fetched as you might think. Indeed,

Philip Zimbardo and his colleagues conducted an analogous experiment in which army reservists were asked to try fried grasshoppers as part of a study allegedly about "survival" foods.[31] For half the subjects, the request was made by a warm, friendly officer; for the other half, it was made by a cold, unfriendly officer. The reservists' attitudes toward eating grasshoppers were measured before and after they ate them. The results were exactly as predicted above: Reservists who ate grasshoppers at the request of the unpleasant officer increased their liking for them far more than those who ate grasshoppers at the request of the pleasant officer. Thus, when sufficient external justification was present—when reservists complied with the friendly officer's request—they experienced little need to change their attitudes toward grasshoppers. They already had a convincing explanation for why they ate them—they did it to help a "nice guy." But reservists who complied with the unfriendly officer's request had little external justification for their actions. As a result, they adopted more positive attitudes toward eating grasshoppers in order to rationalize their discrepant behavior.

What Is Inadequate Justification?   Throughout this section, I have made reference to situations where there is "inadequate" external justification and to those with "an abundance" of external justification. These terms require some additional clarification. In the Festinger-Carlsmith experiment, all of the subjects did, in fact, agree to tell the lie—including all of those paid only one dollar. In a sense, then, one dollar was *adequate*—that is, adequate to induce the subjects to tell the lie; but as it turns out, it wasn't sufficient to keep them from feeling foolish. In order to reduce their feelings of foolishness, they had to reduce the dissonance that resulted from telling a lie for so paltry a sum. This entailed additional bolstering in the form of convincing themselves it wasn't completely a lie and the task wasn't quite as dull as it seemed at first—as a matter of fact, when looked at in a certain way, it was actually quite interesting.

It would be fruitful to compare these results with Judson Mills's data on the effects of cheating among sixth graders.[32] Recall that, in Mills's experiment, the decision about whether or not to cheat was almost certainly a difficult one for most of the children. This is why they experienced dissonance regardless of whether they cheated or resisted temptation. One could speculate about what would happen if the rewards to be gained by cheating were very large. For one thing, it would be more tempting to cheat—therefore, more children would actually cheat. But, more important, if the gains for cheating were astronomical, those who cheated would undergo very little attitude change. Much like the college students who lied in Festinger and Carlsmith's twenty-dollar condition, those children who cheated for a great reward would have less need to reduce dissonance, having been provided with "an abundance" of external justification for their behavior. In fact, Mills did include this refinement in his experiment, and his results are consistent with this reasoning: Those who cheated in order to obtain a small reward tended to soften their attitudes about cheating more than those who cheated in order to obtain a large reward. Moreover, those who refrained from cheating in spite of the temptation of a large reward—a choice that would create a great deal of dissonance—hardened their attitudes about cheating to a greater extent than those who refrained in the face of a small reward—just as one might expect.

Dissonance and the Self-Concept. The analysis of the dissonance phenomenon presented in this section requires a departure from Festinger's original theory. In the experiment by Festinger and Carlsmith, for example, the original statement of dissonance went like this: The cognition "I believe the task is dull" is dissonant with the cognition "I said the task was interesting." Several years ago, I reformulated the theory in a way that focuses more attention on the way people conceive of themselves.[33] Basically, this reformulation suggests that dissonance is most powerful in situations in which the self-concept is threatened. Thus, for me, the important aspect of dissonance in the situation described above is not that the cognition "I said 'X' " is dissonant with the cognition "I believe 'not X.' " Rather, the crucial fact is that I have misled people: The cognition "I have told people something I don't believe " is dissonant with my self-concept; that is, it is dissonant with my cognition that "I am a person of integrity."

This formulation is based on the assumption that most individuals like to think of themselves as decent people who wouldn't ordinarily mislead someone. For example, consider Kathy, who believes marijuana is dangerous and should definitely not be legalized. Suppose she is induced to make a speech advocating the use of marijuana. Let us assume she makes the speech to an audience consisting of individuals whom she knows to be irrevocably opposed to the use of marijuana (for example, the members of a vice squad, the Daughters of the American Revolution, or prohibitionists). In this case, there is little likelihood that she will influence members of the audience because of the firmness of their convictions. According to my view of dissonance theory, Kathy would not change her attitude, because she has not affected anyone's behavior. Similarly, if Kathy were asked to make the same statement to a group of individuals whom she knows to be irrevocably committed to the use of marijuana, there would be no possibility of impacting the audience. On the other hand, if Kathy were induced to make the identical speech to a group of individuals who have no prior information about marijuana, we would expect her to experience much more dissonance than in the other situations. Her cognition that she is a good and decent person is dissonant with her cognition that she has said something she doesn't believe that is likely to have serious *belief* or *behavioral consequences* for her audience. To reduce dissonance, she needs to convince herself the position she advocated is correct. This would allow her to believe that she is a person of integrity. Moreover, in this situation, the smaller the incentive she receives for advocating the position, the greater the attitude change. I tested and confirmed this hypothesis in collaboration with Elizabeth Nel and Robert Helmreich.[34] We found an enormous change in attitudes toward marijuana when subjects were offered a small reward for making a videotape recording of a speech favoring the use of marijuana—but only when they were led to believe the tape would be shown to an audience that was *uncommitted on the issue.* On the other hand, when subjects were told the tape would be played to people who were irrevocably committed on the subject of marijuana (one way or the other), there was relatively little attitude change on the part of the speaker. Thus, lying produces greater attitude change when the liar is undercompensated for lying, especially when the lie is likely to evoke a change in the audience's belief or behavior.*

---

* It should be mentioned that, in this as well as in the other experiments discussed here, each subject was completely debriefed as soon as he or she had finished participating in the experiment. Every attempt was made to avoid causing a permanent change in the attitudes of the subjects. It is always important to debrief subjects after an experiment; it is especially important when the experiment induces a change in an important attitude or has important behavioral consequences.

A great deal of subsequent research[35] supports this reasoning and allows us to state a general principle about dissonance and the self-concept: Dissonance effects are greatest when (1) people feel personally responsible for their actions and (2) their actions have serious consequences. That is, the greater the consequences and the greater our responsibility for it, the greater the dissonance; the greater the dissonance, the greater our own attitude change.

My notion that dissonance is aroused whenever the self-concept is challenged has many interesting ramifications. Let us look at one in some detail. Suppose you are at home and someone knocks at your door, asking you to contribute to a worthy charity. If you didn't want to contribute, you probably wouldn't find it too difficult to come up with reasons for declining—you don't have much money, your contribution probably wouldn't help much anyway, and so on. But suppose that, after delivering a standard plea for a donation, the fund-raiser adds that "even a penny will help." Refusing to donate after hearing this statement would undoubtedly stir up some dissonance by challenging your self-concept. After all, what kind of person is it who is too mean or stingy to come up with a penny? No longer would your previous rationalizations apply. Such a scenario was tested experimentally by Robert Cialdini and David Schroeder.[36] Students acting as fund-raisers went door to door, sometimes just asking for donations and sometimes adding that "even a penny will help." As conjectured, the residents who were approached with the "even-a-penny" request gave contributions more often, donating almost twice as frequently as those getting just the standard plea. Furthermore, on the average, the "even-a-penny" contributors were likely to give as much money as the others; that is, the statement legitimizing the small donation did not reduce the size of the contributions. Why? Apparently, not only does the lack of external justification for refusing to donate encourage people to give money, but after they have decided *whether* to contribute, the desire to avoid appearing stingy affects their decision of *how much* to give. Once people reach into their pockets, emerging with a mere penny is self-demeaning; a larger donation is consistent with their self-perception of being reasonably kind and generous.

Inadequate Rewards as Applied to Education.   A great deal of research has shown that the insufficient-reward phenomenon applies

to all forms of behavior—not simply the making of counterattitudinal statements. Remember, it has been shown that, if people actually
perform a dull task for very little external justification, they rate the
task as more enjoyable than if they had a great deal of external
justification for performing it.[37] This does not mean people would
rather receive low pay than high pay for doing a job. People prefer to
receive high pay—and they often work harder for high pay. But if
they are offered low pay for doing a job and still agree to do it, there
is dissonance between the dullness of the task and the low pay. To
reduce the dissonance, they attribute good qualities to the job and,
hence, come to enjoy the mechanics of the job more if the salary is
low than if it is high. This phenomenon may have far-reaching consequences. For example, let's look at the elementary-school classroom. If you want Johnny to recite a table of multiplication problems,
then you should reward him; gold stars, praise, high grades, presents,
and the like are good external justifications. Will Johnny recite the
equations just for the fun of it, long after the rewards are no longer
forthcoming? In other words, will the high rewards make him enjoy
the task? I doubt it. But if the external rewards are not too high,
Johnny will add his own justification for performing the math drill;
he may even make a game of it. In short, he is more likely to continue
to memorize the multiplication tables long after school is out and the
rewards have been withdrawn.

For certain rote tasks, educators probably do not care whether
Johnny enjoys them or not, as long as he masters them. On the other
hand, if Johnny can learn to enjoy them, he will perform them outside
of the educational situation. Consequently, with such increased practice, he may come to gain greater mastery over the procedure—and
he may retain it indefinitely. Thus, at least under some conditions, it
may be a mistake to dole out extensive rewards as an educational
device. If students are provided with just barely enough incentive to
perform the task, teachers may succeed in allowing them to maximize
their enjoyment of the task. This may serve to improve long-range
retention and performance. I am not suggesting inadequate rewards
are the only way people can be taught to enjoy material that lacks
inherent attractiveness. What I *am* saying is that piling on excessive
external justification inhibits one of the processes that can help set
the stage for increased enjoyment.

Several experiments by Edward Deci[38] and his colleagues make
this point very nicely. Indeed, Deci carries this analysis one step

further by demonstrating that offering rewards to individuals for performing a pleasant activity actually decreases the intrinsic attractiveness of that activity. In one experiment, for example, college students worked individually on an interesting puzzle for an hour. The next day, the students in the experimental condition were paid one dollar for each piece of the puzzle they completed. The students in the control group worked on the puzzle as before, without pay. During a third session, neither group was paid. The question is: How much liking did each group have for the puzzle? Deci measured this during the third session by noting whether or not each student worked on the puzzle during a free break during which they could do whatever they pleased. The results showed a strong tendency for the unrewarded group to spend more free time on the task than the rewarded group. The rewarded group did work harder on the task during the rewarded session, but their interest waned in the final session. The unrewarded group showed an increase in interest during the third session. In a similar vein, Mark Lepper and David Greene found the same kind of relationship with preschool children.[39] Half of the children were induced to work on a set of plastic jigsaw puzzles by the promise of a more rewarding activity later. Others were not promised the more rewarding activity. After playing with the puzzles, all of the children were allowed to engage in the "more rewarding activity" (but recall that only half of them were led to believe this was a reward for having worked on the puzzles). A few weeks later, all the youngsters were turned loose on the puzzles. Those who had worked on the puzzles in order to earn the chance to engage in the more rewarding activity spent less of their free time playing with the puzzles. In short, by offering the children a reward for playing, the experimenters succeeded in turning play into work.

Insufficient Punishment. Thus far, I have been discussing what happens when a person's *rewards* for saying or doing something are meager. The same process works for punishment. In our everyday lives, we are continually faced with situations wherein those who are charged with the duty of maintaining law and order are threatening to punish us if we do not comply with the demands of society. As adults, we know that if we exceed the speed limit and get caught, we will end up paying a substantial fine. If it happens too often, we will lose our licenses. So we learn to obey the speed limit when there are patrol cars in the vicinity. Youngsters in school know that if they cheat on an exam and get caught, they could be humiliated by the teacher and severely punished. So they learn not to cheat while the teacher is in the room watching them. But does harsh punishment teach them not to cheat? I don't think so. I think it teaches them to try to avoid getting caught. In short, the use of threats of harsh punishment as a means of getting someone to refrain from doing something he or she enjoys doing necessitates constant harassment and vigilance. It would be much more efficient and would require much less noxious restraint if, somehow, people could enjoy doing those things that contribute to their own health and welfare—and to the health and welfare of others. If children would enjoy *not* beating up smaller kids or enjoy *not* cheating or *not* stealing from others, then society could relax its vigilance and curtail its punitiveness. It is extremely difficult to persuade people (especially young children) that it's not enjoyable to beat up smaller people. But it is conceivable that, under certain conditions, they will *persuade themselves* such behavior is unenjoyable.

Let's take a closer look. Picture the scene: You are the parent of a five-year-old boy who enjoys beating up on his three-year-old sister. You've tried to reason with him, but to no avail. So, in order to protect the welfare of your daughter, and in order to make a "nicer" person out of your son, you begin to punish him for his aggressiveness. As a parent, you have at your disposal a number of punishments that range from the extremely mild (a stern look) to the extremely severe (a hard spanking, forcing the child to stand in the corner for two hours, and depriving him of television privileges for a month). The more severe the threat, the greater the likelihood the youngster will mend his ways while you are watching him. But he may very well hit his sister again as soon as you turn your back.

Suppose instead you threaten him with a very mild punishment. In either case (under threat of severe punishment or of mild punishment), the child experiences dissonance. He is aware he is not beating up his little sister—and is also aware he would very much like to beat her up. When the child has the urge to hit his sister and doesn't, he asks himself, in effect, "How come I'm not beating up my little sister?" Under severe threat, he has a ready-made answer in the form of sufficient external justification: "I'm not beating her up because, if I do, that giant over there (my father) is going to spank me, stand me in the corner, and keep me from watching TV for a month." The severe threat has provided the child ample external justification for not hitting his sister while he's being watched.

The child in the mild-threat situation experiences dissonance, too. But when he asks himself, "How come I'm not beating up my little sister?" he doesn't have a good answer, because the threat is so mild it does not provide a superabundance of justification. The child is not doing something he wants to do—and while he does have some justification for not doing it, he lacks complete justification. In this situation, he continues to experience dissonance. He is unable to reduce the dissonance by simply blaming his inaction on a severe threat. The child must find a way to justify the fact he is not aggressing against his little sister. The best way is to try to convince himself he really doesn't like to beat his sister up, that he didn't want to do it in the first place, that beating up little kids is not fun. The less severe the threat, the less external justification; the less external justification, the greater the need for internal justification. Allowing people the opportunity to construct their own internal justification can be a large step toward helping them develop a permanent set of values.

To test this idea, I performed an experiment at the Harvard University nursery school in collaboration with J. Merrill Carlsmith.[40] For ethical reasons, we did not try to change basic values like aggression—parents, understandably, might not approve of our changing important values. Instead, we chose a trivial aspect of behavior—toy preference.

We first asked five-year-old children to rate the attractiveness of several toys; then, in each instance, we chose one toy that the children considered quite attractive and told them they couldn't play with it. We threatened half the children with mild punishment for transgression—"I would be a little angry"; we threatened the other half with more severe punishment—"I would be very angry; I would have to take all of the toys and go home and never come back again; I would think you were just a baby." After that, we left the room and allowed the children to play with the other toys—and to resist the temptation of playing with the forbidden one. Each of the children resisted the temptation—none played with the forbidden toy.

On returning to the room, we asked the children again to rate the attractiveness of all the toys. Our results were both striking and exciting. Those children who underwent a mild threat now found the forbidden toy less attractive than before. In short, lacking adequate external justification for refraining from playing with the toy, they succeeded in convincing themselves they hadn't played with it because they didn't really like it. On the other hand, the toy did not become less attractive for those who were severely threatened. These children continued to rate the forbidden toy as highly desirable—indeed, some even found it more desirable than they had before the threat. The children in the severe-threat condition had good external reasons for not playing with the toy—they therefore had no need to find additional reasons—and consequently, they continued to like the toy.

Jonathan Freedman[41] extended our findings and dramatically illustrated the permanence of the phenomenon. He used as his "crucial toy" an extremely attractive battery-powered robot that scurries around hurling objects at a child's enemies. The other toys were sickly by comparison. Naturally, all of the children preferred the robot. He then asked them not to play with that toy, threatening some children with mild punishment and others with severe punishment. And then he left the school and never returned. Several weeks later, a young woman came to the school to administer some paper-and-pencil tests to the children. The children were unaware of the fact she was working for Freedman or that her presence was in any way related to the toys or the threats that had occurred earlier. But it just so happened she was administering her test in the same room Freedman had used for his experiment—the room where the same toys were casually scattered about. After she administered the test to the children, she asked them to hang around while she scored it—and suggested, offhandedly, that they might want to amuse themselves with those toys someone had left in the room.

Freedman's results are highly consistent with our own. The overwhelming majority of the children who had been mildly threatened weeks earlier refused to play with the robot; they played with the other toys instead. On the other hand, the great majority of the children who had been severely threatened did, in fact, play with the robot. In sum, a severe threat was not effective in inhibiting subsequent behavior—but the effect of one mild threat inhibited behavior as much as nine weeks later. Again the power of this phenomenon rests on the fact the children did not come to devalue this behavior (playing with the toy) because some adult told them it was undesirable; they *convinced themselves* that it was undesirable.

My guess is this process may well apply beyond mere toy preference to more basic and important areas, such as the control of
aggression. Partial support for this guess can be derived from some
correlational studies performed in the area of child development indicating that parents who use severe punishment to stop a child's
aggression tend to have children who, while not very aggressive at
home, display a great deal of aggression at school and at play away
from home.[42] This is precisely what we would expect from the compliance model discussed in chapter 2.

The Justification of Effort

Dissonance theory leads to the prediction that, if a person works hard
to attain a goal, that goal will be more attractive to the individual than
it will be to someone who achieves the same goal with little or no
effort. An illustration might be useful: Suppose you are a college
student who decides to join a fraternity. In order to be admitted, you
must pass an initiation; let us assume it is a rather severe one that
involves a great deal of effort, pain, or embarrassment. After successfully completing the ordeal, you are admitted to the fraternity. When
you move into the fraternity house, you find that your new roommate
has some peculiar habits: For example, he plays his stereo loudly after midnight, borrows money without returning it, and occasionally
leaves his dirty laundry on your bed. In short, an objective person
might consider him to be an inconsiderate slob. But you are not an
objective person any longer: Your cognition that you went through
hell and high water to get into the fraternity is dissonant with any
cognitions about your life in the fraternity that are negative, unpleasant, or undesirable. In order to reduce dissonance, you will try to
see your roommate in the most favorable light possible. Again, there
are constraints imposed by reality—no matter how much pain and
effort you went through, there is no way an inconsiderate slob can be
made to look much like Prince Charming—but, with a little ingenuity, you can convince yourself he isn't so bad. What some people
might call sloppy, for example, you might consider casual. Thus, his
playing the stereo loudly at night and his leaving his dirty laundry
around only serves to demonstrate what an easygoing fellow he is—

and because he's so nice and casual about material things, it's certainly understandable he would forget about the money he owes you.

A Prince Charming he isn't, but he's certainly tolerable. Contrast this viewpoint with what your attitude would have been had you made no investment of effort: Suppose you had moved into a regular campus dormitory and encountered the same roommate. Because there was no investment of effort in obtaining this room, there is no dissonance; because there is no dissonance, there is no need for you to see your roommate in the best possible light. My guess is you would quickly write him off as an inconsiderate slob and try to make arrangements to move to a different location.

These speculations were tested in an experiment I performed more than three decades ago in collaboration with my friend Judson Mills.[43] In this study, college women volunteered to join a group that would be meeting regularly to discuss various aspects of the psychology of sex. The women were told that, if they wanted to join, they would first have to go through a screening test designed to ensure that all people admitted to the group could discuss sex freely and openly. This instruction served to set the stage for the initiation procedure. One-third of the women were assigned to a severe initiation procedure, which required them to recite aloud a list of obscene words. One-third of the students underwent a mild procedure, in which they recited a list of words that were sexual but not obscene. The final one-third of the subjects were admitted to the group without undergoing an initiation. Each subject was then allowed to listen in on a discussion being conducted by the members of the group she had just joined. Although the women were led to believe the discussion was a "live," ongoing one, what they actually heard was a prerecorded tape. The taped discussion was arranged so it was as dull and as bombastic as possible. After it was over, each subject was asked to rate the discussion in terms of how much she liked it, how interesting it was, how intelligent the participants were, and so forth.

The results supported the predictions: Those subjects who underwent little or no effort to get into the group did not enjoy the discussion very much. They were able to see it as it was—a dull and boring waste of time. Those subjects who went through a severe initiation, however, succeeded in convincing themselves that the same discussion was interesting and worthwhile.

The same pattern of results has been shown by other investigators using different kinds of unpleasant initiations. For example, Harold

Gerard and Grover Mathewson[44] conducted an experiment similar in concept to the Aronson-Mills study, except the subjects in the severe-initiation condition were given painful electric shocks instead of a list of obscene words to read aloud. The results paralleled those of Aronson and Mills: Subjects who underwent a series of severe electric shocks in order to become members of a group liked that group better than subjects who underwent a series of mild electric shocks.

It should be clear I am not asserting that people enjoy painful experiences—they do not; nor am I asserting that people enjoy things because they are associated with painful experiences. What I am stating is that, if a person goes through a difficult or a painful experience in order to attain some goal or object, that goal or object becomes more attractive. Thus, if on your way to a discussion group you got hit on the head by a brick, you would not like that group any better; but, if you volunteered to get hit on the head by a brick in order to join the discussion group, you would definitely like the group better. The importance of volunteering to go through the unpleasant experience was nicely demonstrated in an experiment by Joel Cooper.[45] The subjects in this experiment were people who had serious snake phobias. The extent of their fear of snakes was first measured unobtrusively by seeing how closely they would approach a six-foot boa constrictor that was housed in a glass tank. Subjects then were put through either a highly stressful or a highly effortful set of experiences that they were informed might have some therapeutic value in helping reduce their fear of snakes. But—and this is the crucial part—half of the subjects were simply told about the procedure and then put through it. The others were induced to volunteer; they were told that they were not obliged to go through the procedure and were free to leave whenever they wished. After going through the "therapeutic" procedure, each subject was then brought back into the presence of the boa constrictor and asked to approach it as closely as they could. Only those who had been induced to volunteer for the unpleasant therapeutic procedure showed improvement—they were able to come much closer to the boa constrictor than they had before. Those who were simply put through the unpleasant therapeutic procedures (without actually volunteering) showed very little improvement.

In most dissonant situations, there is more than one way to reduce dissonance. In the initiation experiment, for example, we found that people who go through a great deal of effort to get into a dull group convince themselves the group is more interesting. Is this the only way they could have reduced dissonance? No. Another way of making sense of the effort we've expended is to revise our memories of the past—that is, to misremember what things were like before we suffered or worked hard. Recall the experiment by Michael Conway and Michael Ross[46] discussed in the previous chapter. In that experiment, one group of students participated in a study-skills course that promised more than it actually delivered; another group of students signed up but did not participate. Whether or not they took the course, all students were asked to evaluate their study skills. After three weeks of "useless" training, students who participated overestimated their improvement by underestimating the skills they had before they completed the course. Students who signed up but did not participate, showed no such self-justifying behavior; their recollections of earlier self-evaluations were accurate. These results may explain why people who spend time and money to get in shape may feel satisfied, even if they don't fully succeed. They may not be able to convince themselves that they actually reached their goals, but they may be able to overestimate the amount of progress they did make by distorting their memories of how out of shape they were before they went into training. As Conway and Ross pointed out, one way for people to get what they want is to revise what they had.*

Still another way people can reduce dissonance, in this kind of situation, is by convincing themselves that their efforts weren't so great. Indeed, they can use more than one strategy simultaneously. This presents a practical problem: To the extent that all of a person's energies are not aimed in one direction, the potency of any one particular effect is diminished. Thus, suppose you are a basketball coach and you want your team to have a great deal of team spirit,

---

* The astute reader may have noticed a connection between this study and one discussed earlier in this chapter, in which people who broke their New Year's resolutions felt bad about themselves for failing and later played down the importance of the resolution. I suggested that an alternative method of reducing the dissonance associated with failure might involve making one's definition of success less stringent—such as settling for "partial" success. The study by Conway and Ross suggests yet another alternative: If, for example, an individual trying to give up smoking has not succeeded in either cutting down or quitting completely, the dissonance aroused by failure can still be reduced if the person "misremembers" how much he or she smoked prior to the effort to quit.

cohesiveness, and camaraderie. You might put each player through a rugged initiation in order to join the team. Naturally, you would want all of the dissonance produced by the initiation to be reduced by each player's deciding he likes his teammates more. If a player chooses, instead, to convince himself that, "Ah, it wasn't such a tough initiation," he reduces dissonance without increasing his esteem for his teammates. As a coach, you might succeed in channeling the dissonance-reducing energy in the direction of intragroup cohesiveness by making the initiation so severe that a person would be unable to consider it a lark. You might bolster this "channeling" by orally emphasizing how severe the initiation is, in order to make it even more difficult for a player to think of it as easy.

The Justification of Cruelty

Over and over again I have made the point that we have a need to convince ourselves we are decent, reasonable people. We have seen how this can cause us to change our attitudes on issues important to us. We have seen, for example, that if a person makes a counterattitudinal speech favoring the use and legalization of marijuana for little external justification, and learns that the videotape of the speech will be shown to a group of persuadable youngsters, the individual tends to convince him or herself marijuana isn't so bad—as a means of feeling less like an evil person. In this section, I will discuss a variation of this theme: Suppose you performed an action that caused a great deal of harm to an innocent young man. Let us further suppose the harm was real and unambiguous. Your cognition "I am a decent, fair, and reasonable person" would be dissonant with your cognition "I have hurt another person." If the harm is clear, then you cannot reduce the dissonance by changing your opinion on the issue, thus convincing yourself you've done no harm, as the people in the marijuana experiment did. In this situation, the most effective way to reduce dissonance would be to maximize the culpability of the victim of your action—to convince yourself the victim deserved what he got, either because he did something to bring it on himself or because he was a bad, evil, dirty, reprehensible person.

This mechanism might even operate if you did not directly cause the harm that befell the victim, but if you only disliked him (prior to his victimization) and were hoping that harm would befall him. For example, after four students at Kent State University were shot and killed by members of the Ohio National Guard, several rumors quickly spread to the effect that (1) both of the women who were slain were pregnant (and therefore, by implication, were oversexed and wanton); (2) the bodies of all four students were crawling with lice; and (3) the victims were so ridden with syphilis they would have been dead in two weeks anyway.[47] These rumors were totally untrue. The slain students were all clean, decent, bright people. Indeed, two of them were not even involved in the demonstrations that resulted in the tragedy but were peacefully walking across campus when they were gunned down. Why were the townspeople so eager to believe and spread these rumors? It is impossible to know for sure, but my guess is that it was for reasons similar to the reasons rumors were spread among the people in India studied by Prasad and Sinha (see pp. 177–178)—that is, because the rumors were comforting. Picture the situation: Kent is a conservative small town in Ohio. Many of the townspeople were infuriated at the radical behavior of some of the students. Some were probably hoping the students would get their comeuppance; but death was more than they deserved. In such circumstances, any information putting the victims in a bad light helped to reduce dissonance by implying that it was, in fact, a good thing that they died. In addition, this eagerness to believe that the victims were sinful and deserved their fate was expressed in ways that were more direct: Several members of the Ohio National Guard stoutly maintained that the victims deserved to die, and a Kent high-school teacher, whom James Michener interviewed, even went so far as to state "anyone who appears on the streets of a city like Kent with long hair, dirty clothes or barefooted deserves to be shot." She went on to say this dictum applied even to her own children.[48]

It is tempting simply to write such people off as crazy—but we should not make such judgments lightly. Although it's certainly true all people are not as extreme as the high-school teacher, it is also true just about everyone can be influenced in this direction. To illustrate this point, let's look at the behavior of Nikita Khrushchev, just before he became premier of the Soviet Union. In his memoirs, Khrushchev described himself as a tough and skeptical person who certainly wasn't in the habit of believing everything he was told. He cited several examples of his own skepticism and reluctance to believe scandalous stories about people and compared himself favorably, in this regard, with Stalin. But let's look at Khrushchev's credulity when it suited his own needs. Soon after Stalin's death, the head of the secret police, Lavrenty Beria, was on the verge of assuming leadership. Khrushchev convinced the other members of the presidium that Beria was a dangerous man. Beria was then arrested, imprisoned, and eventually executed. Dissonance theory would lead to the prediction that, because of his central role in Beria's downfall, Khrushchev might be willing to believe negative things about him—no matter how absurd. But let's allow Khrushchev to tell it in his own words:

> After it was all over [Beria's arrest], Malenkov took me aside and said, "Listen to what my chief bodyguard has to say." The man came over to me and said, "I have only just heard that Beria has been arrested. I want to inform you that he raped my stepdaughter, a seventh grader. A year or so ago her grandmother died and my wife had to go the hospital, leaving the girl at home alone. One evening she went out to buy some bread near the building where Beria lives. There she came across an old man who watched her intently. She was frightened. Someone came and took her to Beria's home. Beria had her sit down with him for supper. She drank something, fell asleep, and he raped her. . . ." Later we were given a list of more than a hundred girls and women who had been raped by Beria. He had used the same routine on all of them. He gave them some dinner and offered them wine with a sleeping potion in it.[49]

It seems fantastic that anyone would believe that Beria had actually perpetrated this deed on more than one hundred women. And yet, Khrushchev apparently believed it—perhaps because he had a strong need to believe it.

These examples fit my analysis based on dissonance theory, but they do not offer definitive proof. For example, it might be that the National Guardsmen at Kent State believed that the students deserved to die even *before* they fired at them. Perhaps Khrushchev would have believed those fantastic stories about Beria even *before* he had caused Beria's demise; it might even be true Khrushchev *didn't* believe those stories but merely presented them in order to discredit Beria.

To be more certain the justification of cruelty can occur in such situations, it is essential for the social psychologist to step back from the helter-skelter of the real world (temporarily) and test predictions in the more controlled world of the experimental laboratory. Ideally, if we want to measure attitude change as a result of dissonant cognitions, we should know what the attitudes were *before* the dissonance-arousing event occurred. Such a situation was produced in an experiment performed by Keith Davis and Edward Jones.[50] They persuaded students to volunteer to help with an experiment: Each student's participation consisted of watching another student being interviewed and then, on the basis of this observation, telling the other student he believed him to be a shallow, untrustworthy, and dull person. The major finding in this experiment was that subjects who volunteered for this assignment succeeded in *convincing themselves* they didn't like the victim of their cruelty. In short, *after* saying things certain to hurt the other student, they convinced themselves he deserved it—that is, they found him less attractive than they did *before* they hurt him. This shift occurred *in spite of* the fact the subjects were aware the other student had done nothing to merit their criticism and that their victimizing him was merely in response to the experimenter's instructions.

An experiment by David Glass[51] had a similar result. In this study, when induced to deliver a series of electric shocks to other people, individuals who considered themselves good and decent people derogated their victims as a result of having caused them this pain. This result is clearest among people with high self-esteem. If I consider myself to be a scoundrel, then causing others to suffer does not introduce as much dissonance; therefore, I have less of a need to convince myself they deserved their fate. Consider the irony: It is precisely because I think I am such a nice person that, if I do something that causes you pain, I must convince myself you are a rat. In other words, because nice guys like me don't go around hurting innocent people, you must have deserved every nasty thing I did to you.

There are circumstances that limit the generality of this phenomenon. One of those was mentioned above: Namely, people with low self-esteem have less need to derogate their victims. Another factor limiting the derogation phenomenon is the capacity of the victim to retaliate. If the victim is able and willing to retaliate at some future time, then a harm-doer feels equity will be restored and thus has no need to justify the action by derogating the victim. In an ingenious experiment by Ellen Berscheid and her associates,[52] college students volunteered for an experiment in which each of them delivered a painful electric shock to a fellow student; as expected, each subject derogated the victim as a result of having delivered the shock. But half of the students were told there would be a turnabout—that is, the other students would be given the opportunity to shock *them.* Those who were led to believe their victims would be able to retaliate did *not* derogate them. In short, because the victims were able to retaliate, dissonance was reduced. The harm-doers had no need to belittle their victims in order to convince themselves the victims deserved it.

These results suggest that, during a war, soldiers might have a greater need to derogate civilian victims (because they can't retaliate) than military victims. During the court-martial of Lieutenant William Calley for his role in the slaughter of innocent civilians at My Lai, his psychiatrist reported that the lieutenant came to regard the Vietnamese people as less than human. Perhaps the research reported in this section helps to shed some light on this phenomenon. Social psychologists have learned that people do not perform acts of cruelty and come out unscathed. I do not know for sure how Lieutenant Calley (and thousands of others) came to regard the Vietnamese as subhuman, but it seems reasonable to assume that, when we are engaged in a war in which, through our actions, a great number of innocent people are being killed, we might try to derogate the victims in order to justify our complicity in the outcome. We might poke fun at them, refer to them as "gooks," dehumanize them; but, once we have succeeded in doing that, watch out—because it becomes easier to hurt and kill "subhumans" than to hurt and kill fellow human beings. Thus, reducing dissonance in this way has terrible future consequences—it increases the likelihood the atrocities we are willing to commit will become greater and greater. I will elaborate on this theme in the next chapter. For now, I would like to enlarge on a point I made in chapters 1 and 2: In the final analysis, people are accountable for their own actions. Not everyone behaved as Lieutenant Calley behaved. At the same time, it should be noted that Lieutenant Calley was not alone in his behavior; he stands as a striking example of a rather common phenomenon. With this in mind, it is important to acknowledge that certain situational factors can exert a very powerful impact upon human actions. Accordingly, before we can write off such behavior as merely bizarre, or merely crazy, or merely villainous, it would be wise to examine the situation that sets up the mechanism for this kind of behavior. We can then begin to understand the terrible price we are paying for allowing certain conditions to exist. Perhaps, eventually, we can do something to avoid these conditions. Dissonance theory helps to shed some light on this mechanism.

Of course, this kind of situation is not limited to wars. A great number of violent acts can be perpetrated on innocent victims and can lead to justifications which, in turn, can lead to more violence. Imagine you live in a society that is unfair to minority groups like blacks and Latinos. Just to take a wild example, let us pretend that, for several decades, the white majority was not allowing the blacks and Latinos to attend first-rate public schools but instead was providing them with a second-rate and stultifying education. As a consequence of this "benign neglect," the average black child and the average Latino child are less well-educated and less motivated than the average white child at the same grade level. They demonstrate this by doing poorly on achievement tests. Such a situation provides a golden opportunity for civic leaders to justify their discriminatory behavior, and hence, to reduce dissonance. "You see," they might say, "those people are stupid (because they perform poorly on the achievement test); see how clever we were when we decided against wasting our resources by trying to provide them with a high-quality education. These people are unteachable." This phenomenon is called a *self-fulfilling prophecy*. It provides a perfect justification for cruelty and neglect. So, too, is the attribution of moral inferiority to blacks and Chicanos. We imprison racial minorities in overcrowded ghettos; and we set up a situation in which skin color almost inevitably unleashes forces preventing people from participating in the opportunities for growth and success existing for most white Americans. Through the magic of television, they see people succeeding and living in the luxury of middle-class respectability. They become painfully aware of the opportunities, comforts, and luxuries unavailable to them. If their frustration leads them to violence or if their despair leads them to drugs, it is fairly easy for their white brothers and sisters to sit back complacently, shake their heads knowingly, and attribute this behavior to some kind of moral inferiority. As Edward Jones and Richard Nisbett[53] point out, when some misfortune befalls *us,* we tend to attribute the cause to something in the environment; but when we see the same misfortune befalling *another person,* we tend to attribute the cause to some weakness inherent in that person's personality.

The Psychology of Inevitability

George Bernard Shaw was hard hit by his father's alcoholism, but he tried to make light of it. He once wrote: "If you cannot get rid of the family skeleton, you may as well make it dance."[54] In a sense, dissonance theory describes the ways people have of making their skeletons dance—of trying to live with unpleasant outcomes. This is particularly true when a situation arises that is both negative and inevitable. Here people attempt to make the best of things by cognitively minimizing the unpleasantness of the situation. In one experiment, Jack Brehm[55] got children to volunteer to eat a vegetable they had previously said they disliked a lot. After they had eaten the vegetable, the experimenter led half of the children to believe they could expect to eat much more of that vegetable in the future; the remaining children were not so informed. The children who were led to believe it was inevitable that they would be eating the vegetable in the future succeeded in convincing themselves the particular vegetable was not so very bad. In short, the cognition "I dislike that vegetable" is dissonant with the cognition "I will be eating that vegetable in the future." In order to reduce the dissonance, the children came to believe the vegetable was really not as noxious as they had previously thought. John Darley and Ellen Berscheid[56] showed that the same phenomenon works with people as well as vegetables. In their experiment, college women volunteered to participate in a series of meetings in which each student would be discussing her sexual behavior and sexual standards with another woman whom she didn't know. Before beginning these discussion sessions, each subject was given two folders. Each of the folders contained a personality description of a young woman who had supposedly volunteered for the same experience; the descriptions contained a mixture of pleasant and unpleasant characteristics. Half of the subjects were led to believe they were going to interact with the young woman described in folder A, and the remaining subjects were led to believe they were going to interact with the one described in folder B. Before actually meeting these women, the subjects were asked to evaluate each of them on the basis of the personality descriptions they had read. Those subjects who felt it was inevitable they were going to share their intimate secrets with the young woman described in folder A found her much more appealing as a person than the one described in folder B, whereas those who believed they had to interact with the young woman described in folder B found *her* much more appealing. Just as with vegetables, inevitability makes the heart grow fonder. The knowledge that one is inevitably going to be spending time with another person enhances the positive aspects of that person—or at least deemphasizes his or her negative aspects. In short, people tend to make the best of something they know is bound to happen.

Deemphasizing the negative can be an adaptive strategy when what's in store is a disliked vegetable or a discussion with someone whom we've never met. There are situations, however, when such a strategy can prove disastrous. Consider the case of students at the University of California at Los Angeles (UCLA). Geological studies conducted in the mid 1980s indicated that there was a 90 percent probability of at least one major earthquake in Los Angeles during the next twenty years.

In the face of such an impending disaster, "rational" people would no doubt acknowledge the danger and work to prepare by learning all they can about it and by taking safety precautions. In 1987, two social psychologists at UCLA, Darrin Lehman and Shelley Taylor, conducted interviews with 120 undergraduates at their university and determined that such is not the case.[57] Their findings were unsettling: Only 5 percent had taken any safety precautions (such as locating the nearest fire extinguisher); only one-third knew that the best action to take during a quake is to crawl under a heavy piece of furniture or to stand in a doorway; and not one respondent had taken preparatory measures recommended by experts. It seems that even among well-educated people, a typical response to an inevitable catastrophe is to do very little to prepare for it.

It's noteworthy that coping styles varied as a function of the students' living situation. Those students living in seismically unsafe residence halls were more likely than those living in relatively safe residence halls to "cope" with the impending disaster by refusing to think about the quake or by minimizing the damage expected. That is, those who were most at risk in the event of a quake were the very ones who refused to think about the imminent catastrophe or who underestimated its severity. In short, if I'm pretty sure there's going to be an earthquake, how can I justify continuing to live in an unsafe residence hall? Easy: I deny that there's going to be an earthquake—and refuse to think about it. Self-justifying responses to dangerous and inevitable events can be comforting in the short run. But, when they keep us from taking steps to enhance our safety, such responses can, in the long run, prove deadly.

Needless to say, the geological predictions of the mid-1980s came about: In the winter of 1994, there *was* a major earthquake in the Los Angeles area—resulting in a great deal of property damage and the destruction of freeways which disrupted transportation for several months. Fortunately, because the quake took place at 4:30 in the morning of a holiday, there was relatively little loss of life. While this was a major earthquake, most experts agree that "the big one" is still pending. Do you think that the earthquake of '94 will lead people to be better prepared for the next one?

As you may have noticed, there is a curious difference between the responses of children facing a disliked vegetable or college students facing an inevitable interaction with another person, on the one hand, and the responses of UCLA students to the threat of an impending earthquake, on the other hand. In the former situations, the inevitable is accepted and attitudes stressing the positive aspects of the unavoidable event are embraced. The latter situation, however, involves confronting a highly probable event that is life-threatening and largely uncontrollable. It would be stretching the limits of the human imagination to redefine a major earthquake as desirable—or as anything less than a catastrophe. And we can't prevent earthquakes; the best we can hope for is to respond adaptively to one, with no guarantee that safety measures will really save us. Thus, the nature of our response may very well depend on whether we believe preventive steps will genuinely increase our sense of control over the inevitable. If such steps seem largely futile, then the prospect of expending energy on them will only serve to increase our feelings of dissonance even further. Under such circumstances we are likely to justify not taking safety measures by denying the probability of the potential disaster or vastly underestimating its magnitude.

The Importance of Self-Esteem

Throughout this chapter, we have seen how our commitment to a particular course of action can freeze or change our attitudes, distort our perception, and determine the kind of information we seek out. In addition, we have seen that a person can become committed to a situation in a number of different ways—by making a decision, by working hard in order to attain a goal, by believing something is inevitable, by engaging in any action having serious consequences (such as hurting someone), and so on. As I have mentioned before, the deepest form of commitment takes place in those situations in which a person's self-esteem is at stake. Thus, if I perform a cruel or a stupid action, this threatens my self-esteem, because it turns my mind to the possibility I am a cruel or stupid person. In the hundreds of experiments inspired by the theory of cognitive dissonance, the clearest results were obtained in those situations in which a person's self-esteem was involved. Moreover, as one might expect, we have seen that those individuals with the highest self-esteem experience the most dissonance when they behave in a stupid or cruel manner.

What happens when an individual has low self-esteem? Theoretically, if such a person were to commit a stupid or immoral action, he or she would not experience much dissonance. The cognition "I have done an immoral thing" is *consonant* with the cognition "I am a schlunk." In short, people who believe themselves to be schlunks expect to do schlunky things. In other words, people with low self-esteem will not find it terribly difficult to commit immoral acts—because committing immoral acts is not dissonant with their self-concept. On the other hand, people with high self-esteem are more likely to resist the temptation to commit immoral acts, because to behave immorally would produce a great deal of dissonance.

I tested this proposition in collaboration with David Mettee.[58] We predicted that individuals who had a low opinion of themselves would be more likely to cheat (if given the opportunity) than individuals who had a high opinion of themselves. It should be made clear we were not making the simple prediction that people who believe themselves to be dishonest will cheat more than people who believe themselves to be honest. Our prediction was a little more daring; it was based on the assumption that, if normal people receive a temporary blow to their self-esteem (for example, if they are jilted by their lover or flunk an exam) and thus feel low and worthless, they are more likely to cheat at cards, kick their dog, wear mismatched pajamas, or do any number of things consistent with a low opinion of themselves. As a function of feeling they are low people, individuals will commit low acts.

In our experiment, we temporarily modified the self-esteem of female college students by giving them false information about their personalities. After taking a personality test, one-third of the students were given positive feedback; specifically, they were told the test indicated they were mature, interesting, deep, and so forth. Another one-third of the students were given negative feedback; they were told the test indicated they were relatively immature, uninteresting, rather shallow, and the like. The remaining one-third of the students were not given any information about the results of the test.

Immediately afterward, the students were scheduled to participate in an experiment, conducted by a different psychologist, that had no apparent relation to the personality inventory. As a part of this second experiment, the subjects participated in a game of cards against some of their fellow students. This was a gambling game in which the students were allowed to bet money and were told they could keep whatever money they won. In the course of the game, the subjects were presented with a few opportunities to cheat in a situation where it seemed impossible to be detected. The situation was arranged so that if a student decided *not* to cheat, she would certainly lose, whereas if she decided to cheat, she would be certain to win a sizable sum of money.

The results clearly showed that those students who had previously received information designed to lower their self-esteem cheated to a far greater extent than those who had received the high self-esteem information. The control group—those receiving no information—fell exactly in between. These findings suggest it would be well worth the effort of parents and teachers to alert themselves to the potentially far-reaching consequences of their own behavior as it affects the self-esteem of their children and students. Specifically, if low self-esteem is an important antecedent of criminal or cruel behavior, then we might want to do everything possible to help individuals learn to respect and love themselves.

Physiological and Motivational Effects of Dissonance

How far can the effects of dissonance extend? In the past several years, researchers have shown it can go beyond attitudes; it can modify the way we experience basic physiological drives. Under certain well-specified conditions, dissonance reduction can lead hungry people to experience less hunger, thirsty people to experience less thirst, and people undergoing intensive electric shock to experience less pain. Here's how it works: Imagine that Vic Volunteer is induced to *commit himself* to a situation in which he will be deprived of food or water for a long time, or in which he will experience electric shock. If Vic has *low external justification* for doing this, he will experience dissonance. His cognitions concerning his hunger pangs, his parched throat, or the pain of electrical shock are each dissonant with his cognition that he volunteered to go through these experiences and is not getting very much in return. In order to reduce this dissonance, Vic convinces himself the hunger isn't so intense, or the thirst isn't so bad, or the pain isn't so great. This should not be astonishing. Although hunger, thirst, and pain all have physiological bases, they also have a strong psychological component. For example, through suggestion, meditation, hypnosis, placebo pills, the bedside manner of a skillful physician, or some combination of these, perceived pain can be reduced. Experimental social psychologists have shown that, under conditions of high dissonance arousal, ordinary people, without any special skills in hypnosis or meditation, can accomplish the same ends for themselves.

Thus, Philip Zimbardo and his colleagues[59] have subjected many people to intense electric shocks. Half of these people were in a high-dissonance condition—that is, they were induced to commit themselves to volunteer for the experience and were given very little external justification—and the other half were in a low-dissonance condition—that is, they had no choice in the matter and had a great deal of external justification. The results showed that the people in the high-dissonance condition reported experiencing less pain than the people in the low-dissonance condition. Moreover, this phenomenon extended beyond their subjective reports: There is clear evidence that the physiological response to pain (as measured by the galvanic skin response) was somewhat less intense in the high-dissonance condition. In addition, the pain of subjects in the high-dissonance condition interfered less with the tasks they were performing. Thus, not only was their pain reported as less intense, but it also affected their behavior less intensely.

Similar results have been shown for hunger and thirst. Jack Brehm[60] reported a series of experiments in which people were deprived of either food or water for long periods of time. In addition to experiencing hunger or thirst, these individuals were experiencing either high or low dissonance for much the same reasons Zimbardo's subjects were experiencing high or low dissonance. Specifically, some of the subjects had low external justification for undergoing the hunger or thirst, while others had high external justification. For the subjects experiencing great dissonance, the best available way to reduce it was to minimize the experience of hunger or thirst. In separate experiments on hunger and thirst, Brehm reported that the subjects in the high-dissonance condition said they were less hungry (or thirsty) than low-dissonance subjects who were deprived of food (or water) for the same length of time. Again, this was no mere verbal report—after the experiment, when all of the subjects were allowed to eat (or drink) freely, the high-dissonance subjects actually consumed less food (or water) than the low-dissonance subjects.

A Critical Look at Cognitive Dissonance as a Theory

I'd like to invite the reader backstage again. Recall that, in chapter 3 (pp. 98–102), we went backstage to look at how scientists worked to make sense out of conflicting data about how the size of a discrepancy affects opinion change. This time we will go behind the scenes to look at the evolution and development of a theory. Why do scientists invent theories? A theory is proposed in order to make sense out of an occurrence or a number of apparently unrelated occurrences. In addition, by providing us with a new way of looking at the world, a theory can generate new hypotheses, new research, and new facts. Theories are neither right nor wrong. Rather, theories are judged according to how useful they are; they are more or less useful depending on how well they account for the existing facts and how fruitful they are at generating new information. But no theory provides us with a perfect accounting of the way the world is. Thus, theories are frequently challenged and criticized. These challenges inevitably result in the reformulation of an existing theory or in the invention of an entirely new theory that seems to provide a better fit. When theories are reformulated, they are altered either to increase or decrease their scope. For example, if a theory is too vague or imprecise, an attempt may be made to simplify it, to limit its domain, or to restructure its language in order to increase our certainty about the nature of the prediction being made. With this in mind, let us examine the theory of cognitive dissonance.

The Refinement of Dissonance Theory. As we have seen, dissonance theory has proved to be a useful way of looking at human interaction. But there were some serious conceptual problems with the theory as originally stated. Perhaps the major difficulty stems from the fact that the original statement was conceptually vague. Recall the original theoretical statement: "Cognitive dissonance is a state of tension that occurs whenever an individual simultaneously holds two cognitions that are psychologically inconsistent. Because the occurrence of cognitive dissonance is unpleasant, people are motivated to reduce it." But precisely in what way are cognitions inconsistent? The vagueness stems from the fact that the scope of the theory was not limited to situations inconsistent on logical grounds alone. Rather, the inconsistencies that produce dissonance are psychological inconsistencies. Indeed, this makes the theory exciting and increases its scope. Unfortunately, it also renders the theory less than perfectly precise. It would be relatively easy to make a precise statement about the domain of the theory if its predictions were limited to instances of logical inconsistency because there are strict rules for determining whether conclusions do or do not follow from premises on the basis of formal logic. For example, take the famous syllogism:

> All men are mortal.
> Socrates is a man.
> Therefore, Socrates is mortal.

If someone believed Socrates was not mortal, while accepting the first two premises, this would be a clear case of dissonance. By contrast, let us take the typical dissonance situation:

> I believe that smoking cigarettes causes cancer.
> I smoke cigarettes.

The cognition "I smoke cigarettes" is not inconsistent with the cognition "cigarette smoking causes cancer" on formal logical grounds. It is inconsistent on psychological grounds; that is, the implications of the two statements are dissonant because we know most people do not want to die. But it is sometimes difficult to be certain what will be psychologically inconsistent for any one person. For example, suppose you have great admiration for Franklin Delano Roosevelt; then you learn that, throughout his marriage, he was carrying on a clandestine love affair. Will that cause dissonance? It is difficult to know. If you place a high value on marital fidelity and you also believe great historical figures should not violate this sanction, then you will experience some dissonance. To reduce it you will either change your attitudes about Roosevelt or soften your attitudes about marital infidelity. Because a large number of people probably do not hold these values simultaneously, however, they will not experience dissonance. Moreover, even if a person does hold these two values simultaneously, the cognitions may not be particularly salient—so how do we know whether or not they cause dissonance? This leads us to a major point: Even when the cognitions are undeniably salient, the degree of dissonance is certain to be small compared to what it would be if you had violated your own values—as was true, for example, in Judson Mills's experiment with the youngsters who cheated on their tests.

In recent years, a great deal of the initial vagueness of the conceptual statement has been reduced by several theorists.[61] For example, as discussed earlier in this chapter, my own research[62] has led me to conclude that dissonance effects may be limited to situations in which our behavior violates our own self-concept. This can happen in one of two ways: (1) if we consciously and knowingly do something stupid; (2) if we do something that hurts another person—even if we do it unknowingly. An example of a stupid act might be going through a severe initiation to get into a group that could easily turn out to be very uninteresting, or perhaps volunteering to write a counterattitudinal essay for very little reward. An example of a hurtful, guilt-producing action would be misleading a person by convincing him or her to do something you think might be harmful, saying cruel things to a person who has done you no harm, administering an electric shock to an innocent victim, and so on.

But these changes in the conceptualization of dissonance theory did not materialize out of thin air. They came gradually—partly as a result of external criticism. For example, twenty years ago I believed dissonance could exist between any two cognitions and the predicted results would inevitably follow. Mostly the results did follow because, without our realizing it, we dissonance theorists were designing our experiments in a manner such that a violation of the self-concept was almost always involved. That is, in our experiments, people were either knowingly committing themselves to stupid acts (like writing a counterattitudinal essay) or doing something immoral (like cheating or deceiving another person). Because we didn't realize these factors were involved, we were occasionally surprised when what seemed like a clear prediction did not turn out. For example, Milton Rosenberg[63] once performed an experiment similar to Arthur Cohen's experiment (reported on pp. 202–203) in which subjects were paid either a large reward or a small reward for writing an essay against their own beliefs. Rosenberg's results came out quite differently from Cohen's, with those subjects who were given a large reward showing a greater change in their own beliefs. This produced a great deal of confusion. Then, Darwyn Linder and his colleagues[64] focused attention on what had seemed to be a minor difference between the two experiments. The subjects in Cohen's experiment knowingly committed themselves to write an essay favoring the rather brutal actions of the New Haven police during a student demonstration, but they were informed at the outset they didn't have to do it if they didn't want to. Unlike the participants in Cohen's experiment, Rosenberg's subjects were not given a clear idea of what they were going to do before they agreed to do it. That is, while they were supposedly waiting to participate in one experiment, they were induced to commit themselves to help out another researcher. It wasn't until after they had been committed to the task that they realized they were going to have to write an essay that went against their own beliefs. It was too late to pull out. In this situation, it was easy for the subjects to remove their self-concept from the situation by saying in effect, "How was I supposed to know?"*

---

* Recall the two ways in which dissonance can be aroused through a violation of the self-concept: (1) knowingly doing something stupid, or (2) doing something that hurts another person. In the first situation, there will be little dissonance if it's easy to say, "How was I supposed to know?" In the second situation, the fact that someone gets hurt makes it impossible to avoid dissonance simply by saying, "How was I supposed to know?"

Intrigued by this difference, Linder and his associates then performed an experiment in which they systematically varied the subjects' freedom of choice. They found clear evidence: When the subjects knew what they were letting themselves in for in advance, there was a dissonance effect—those who wrote a counterattitudinal essay for a small reward changed their beliefs in the direction of their essay to a greater extent than those who did it for a large reward. When the subjects did not have this freedom of choice but committed themselves to an unknown task, the results were just the opposite. Thus, Linder's experiment and subsequent research[65] have clarified the limitations of dissonance effects and pointed to a new direction in the evolution of the theory.

Alternative Explanations of Dissonance Effects.   Although the evolution of dissonance theory in terms of the self-concept has clarified the theory and has led to more precise predictions, the theory is still subject to challenge. For example, Daryl Bem[66] was not happy with the theory because it relied too much on the assumption of internal events that are difficult to measure. Bem made an earnest attempt to explain some of the phenomena discovered by dissonance theory in more concrete and readily observable terms. Briefly, his idea was to move away from a conceptual reliance on such internal states as "cognitions" and "psychological discomfort" and to replace such concepts with the more precise "stimulus-response" language of behaviorism. Bem concentrated his efforts on the area of counterattitudinal advocacy. Let's look at the situation through Bem's eyes.

Suppose you see a woman walk into a cafeteria, survey all of the desserts being offered, pick up a wedge of rhubarb pie, and begin to eat it. What would you conclude? Simple: "She must like rhubarb pie." Given the fact she has freedom of choice and a great many options, why else would she have chosen rhubarb pie? So far, so good. Now, suppose you walk into a cafeteria, select a wedge of rhubarb pie, and eat it. What would you conclude from your own actions? Simple: "I must like rhubarb pie—why else would I be eating it?" Bem applied this reasoning to an area the reader is very familiar with by now. Suppose you observe somebody writing an essay favoring the fierce actions of the New Haven police during a student demonstration, and you know he's being paid only fifty cents to do it. Wouldn't you conclude he must really believe that the actions of the New Haven police were right and reasonable? Why else would he say so? Surely not for the fifty cents. Suppose you find yourself writing an essay favoring the fierce actions of the New Haven police for a payment of fifty cents?

In short, Bem's notion is that many of the dissonance effects are nothing more than reasonable inferences people make about their attitudes based upon their perceptions of their own behavior. To test his notion, Bem has designed a method that is as simple as his theory. He merely describes an experimental procedure to his subjects—for example, Cohen's experiment on attitudes about the behavior of the New Haven police outlined above. He then asks his subjects to guess the real attitude of each of the subjects in the experiment he has just described—for example, how much did each of Cohen's essay writers really favor the actions of the New Haven police? Bem's results parallel those of the original experiment: His subjects guessed that the people who wrote essays for fifty cents favoring the actions of the New Haven police must have believed what they said to a greater extent than those who wrote similar essays for five dollars.

Bem's reasoning is elegant in its simplicity; his analysis is certainly more sparse than the traditional analyses of these data in terms of such hypothetical constructs as psychological discomfort, self-concept, and so on. Scientists strive for simplicity and parsimony; if two theories accurately account for a body of data, the simpler one is preferable. But does Bem's conceptualization account for these data as accurately as dissonance theory? It's difficult to be certain, but Bem's research seems to ignore a vital fact: The actor in a situation has more information than the observer. That is, when I write an essay favoring the brutal behavior of the New Haven police, chances are I know what my beliefs were before I wrote it; when you observe me writing an essay favoring the actions of the New Haven police, you don't know what my beliefs were beforehand. Both Russell Jones and his colleagues and Jane Piliavin and her colleagues[67] have demonstrated that, when observers know the prior beliefs of the actor in the situation, their statements no longer parallel those of the subjects in the original experiment—that is, Bem's results are not replicated. Does this mean Bem's analysis is inaccurate? Not necessarily. It is possible that, in many situations, even the actors are uncertain or ambivalent about their own prior beliefs and attitudes and thus utilize their observation of this behavior as a cue for determining what they are. Bem calls this concept a process of "self-reference" or "self-judgment." That is, it is conceivable that, prior to writing an essay favoring the actions of the New Haven police, Cohen's subjects may not have had a clear notion of how they felt about it—their behavior provided them with useful information. In the clearest examples of the operation of dissonance reduction, however, one's prior beliefs are well-defined; for example, subjects in the Festinger-Carlsmith experiment knew, initially, that the task they had performed was boring. It is when their behavior contradicts their beliefs and values—when they tell another person the task is interesting and fun—that dissonance is aroused and they begin striving to reduce it by altering their attitudes. Where the inconsistency between one's attitudes and behavior is significant and clear, recent research[68] supports dissonance theory over self-reference processes to explain and predict the resulting changes.

Dissonance as a State of Arousal.   A crucial part of my restatement of dissonance theory contends that a person's tendency to change his or her attitudes is motivated by an aversive state of arousal caused by the violation of the self-concept. It's difficult for me to believe discomfort does not accompany dissonance. Like almost all investigators who have performed experiments testing hypotheses derived from dissonance theory, I am convinced that a person experiencing dissonance shows signs of being uncomfortable. Phenomenologically, when people encounter a dissonance-producing situation, their behavior does not seem to match the cool, calculated, objective, unemotional induction game Bem describes. But such unsystematic perceptions by researchers, by themselves, do not constitute convincing data. Is there any independent evidence that people experiencing dissonance are in a state of discomfort? An experiment by Michael Pallak and Thane Pittman[69] lends support to the notion that psychological discomfort exists during a state of dissonance. Before describing their experiment, I should first mention a phenomenon discovered through research on the psychology of learning: Suppose you are performing a task that has several possible responses that compete for your attention (as opposed to a task for which there is one clear response). If you are in a state of high arousal (that is, if you are very hungry, very thirsty, very sexy, or whatever), you will perform more poorly than if you are in a state of low arousal. On the other hand, if the task is a clear and simple one, arousal seems to energize a person without causing interference; hence, performance on such a task will be enhanced when people are aroused. Pallak and Pittman simply put some subjects in a highly dissonant situation and others in a situation that produced very little dissonance. The low-dissonance subjects performed better than the high-dissonance subjects on a complex task (one with many competing responses), whereas the high-dissonance subjects performed better than the lows on a simple task (one with few competing responses). Thus, dissonance arousal seems to act like hunger or thirst.

An interesting experiment by Mark Zanna and Joel Cooper[70] provides further evidence that dissonance causes arousal. Participants in their study were given a *placebo*—a sugar pill having no physiological effect whatever. Some were told the pill would arouse them and make them feel tense, while others were told the pill would relax them. Participants in a control condition were told the pill would not affect them. After ingesting a pill, each person voluntarily wrote a counterattitudinal essay (sound familiar?), thus creating dissonance. Zanna and Cooper found that participants in the control condition underwent considerable attitude change, as would be expected. Participants in the "aroused" condition, however, did not change their attitudes—they apparently attributed their discomfort to the pill, not the counterattitudinal essay. But the most exciting results occurred in the "relaxed" condition. These people changed their attitudes even *more* than control participants did. How come? There is only one reasonable explanation: They inferred that writing the counterattitudinal essay was *very* tension-producing, *very* inconsistent with their perception of themselves as "decent, good, and reasonable" because they experienced tension (due to the dissonance manipulation) even after taking a "relaxation" pill. Thus, their attitudes changed even more. Furthermore, in a recent experiment, Charles Bond[71] gave students a description of the Zanna-Cooper study; he then asked them to predict which groups would undergo the most and the least attitude change. Contrary to Bem's theory, these predictions were dissimilar to the actual behavior of Zanna and Cooper's subjects.

Taken together, these data indicate the presence of something akin to physiological discomfort during dissonance arousal. Accordingly, although Bem's explanation of dissonance phenomena is simple, straightforward, and useful, the analysis in terms of "discomfort produced by a violation of the self-concept" strikes me as being a richer and more accurate reflection of dissonance phenomena.

Practical Applications of Dissonance Theory

One of the reasons the theory of cognitive dissonance has attracted such great interest and inspired so much research is its ability to explain and predict phenomena not readily explainable in common-sense terms. Furthermore, as the reader has seen, dissonance theory has been applied to account for a great many phenomena ranging from how rumors are spread to major changes in important attitudes and behaviors—from practicing safer sex to preserving vital planetary resources.

Understanding Responses to Disaster. It is exciting to use the theory as a way of understanding a number of events in contemporary society that otherwise might be puzzling indeed. For example, consider the Three Mile Island crisis in 1979, when an accident at the nuclear power plant caused an unstable condition in the reactor that lasted for several days, posing the threat of a meltdown that would result in catastrophic contamination of the surrounding area and endanger hundreds of thousands of people living in the vicinity. Common sense would suggest that the people living closest to the power plant would be the most frightened and, therefore, the most likely to take action. Dissonance theory makes a different prediction. Suppose you were living within a few miles of the plant at the time of the incident. Since radioactive steam escaped from the reactor during the initial stages of the accident, it is possible you and your loved ones have already been contaminated. How will you respond? You can evacuate the area, but leaving your job and finding temporary lodging would be costly and fraught with hardship. Besides, even if you *do* evacuate, there is that likelihood you have already been exposed to the radiation. Many contradictory reports are circulating about the extent of the danger. Some of your neighbors have decided to leave; others are belittling the magnitude of the threat. After a time, the authorities from the Nuclear Regulatory Commission (NRC) arrive on the scene, issuing reassuring statements that the danger of leakage of radiation was minor and the probability of a serious disaster is minimal. How likely are you to believe these statements?

My guess at the time was that people living closest to the power plant would be the most likely to latch on to these pronouncements and believe them, grasping at whatever reassurances they could find. If you were living near Three Mile Island, your cognition that you chose to live close enough to the nuclear power plant to absorb harmful radiation in case of an accident would be dissonant with your self-concept as smart, reasonable, prudent, and caring for your family. Therefore, regardless of whether or not you have evacuated, you would be eager to believe these reassurances. Even when the authorities changed their stance a couple of days later, advising that pregnant women should evacuate, the tendency of those living near the plant would be to trust the NRC spokesman when he said they are merely being cautious and the danger still is minimal. Contrast this with the reaction of those living just outside the immediate danger zone. These people are also worried and scared, though they are threatened less directly and have not already been contaminated. Since they are not as deeply committed as those living in the immediate danger zone, they should be more able to express their skepticism and anger—indeed, it would be in their self-interest to do so, because they would be imperiled if the situation in the nuclear power plant deteriorated or if the crisis was more serious than what was being publicized. My speculations, that residents nearest the Three Mile Island reactor would attribute more credibility to the pronouncements of the Nuclear Regulatory Commission than would those living farther away, were confirmed by an extensive survey conducted shortly after the incident.[72] The data reveal that respondents closest to the plant were significantly more likely to say that the information conveyed by the NRC was extremely useful; those living further than fifteen miles away were more inclined to say that the information was totally useless.*

---

* It should be noted, however, that these findings are open to alternative explanations. Those who lived closest to the nuclear power plant at Three Mile Island may differ in important ways from those who lived farther away. For example, the very fact that they *chose* to live close to the nuclear plant could conceivably reflect a more positive attitude about the nuclear power industry. Thus, even before the accident, those living closest to the plant might have perceived the NRC as more credible than those living farther away.

Anecdotal evidence also supports this conclusion: It was reported that the most dire rumors about the crisis came from as far away as California, and while the national media were filled with reports of the NRC's incompetence and inadequacy, the populace near Three Mile Island was said to have greeted the NRC "like cavalry riding to a nick-of-time rescue."[73]

Reducing Weight by Reducing Dissonance. Beyond its power to help us understand and predict a variety of phenomena, a theory is of particular value if it can be practically applied in ways that benefit people. Earlier in this chapter, I pointed out cognitive dissonance theory's relevance for educators wishing to instill intrinsic motivation for learning in their students, or for parents looking for a more effective means than severe punishment for helping their children learn moral and humane values. Institutions like the marine corps and college fraternities have long employed a severe initiation to increase their members' commitment to the group. An experiment by Danny Axsom and Joel Cooper[74] provides a particularly compelling example of how dissonance theory can be used to help solve a difficult personal problem—obesity. Hypothesizing that expending a great deal of effort to reach an objective would increase a person's commitment to that goal, they induced a number of overweight women to volunteer for a weight-control program and engaged them in intellectual activities requiring either a large or a small amount of effort but that were unrelated to losing weight. Over the four weeks of the program, only slight weight losses were observed in either group. But six months and a year later, when the experimenters contacted the women again, they discovered major differences: The women who had expended a great amount of effort had lost an average of eight pounds, while those who had performed tasks requiring little effort in the program had not lost any weight. Changing one's attitudes in order to justify one's behavior not only can have powerful effects but can initiate processes that are remarkably persistent over long periods of time.

Dissonance and AIDS Prevention. As you know, dissonance makes people uncomfortable. Thus, not only do we strive to reduce dissonance whenever we experience it, but in addition, we try to defend ourselves against experiencing dissonance in the first place. One way of remaining oblivious to dissonance is by steadfastly refusing to pay close attention to what we are doing. A good example of this "mindless" behavior can be found in the sexual behavior of millions of young adults in the face of the AIDS epidemic. You will recall that I discussed this issue briefly in chapter 3. Bear with me as I expand on it here. As you know, hundreds of millions of dollars have been spent on AIDS information and prevention campaigns in the mass media. While these campaigns have been reasonably effective at conveying information, they have not been nearly as successful at preventing people from engaging in risky sexual behavior. For example, although sexually active college students are aware of AIDS as a serious problem, only a surprisingly small percentage use condoms regularly. The reason for this seems to be that condoms are inconvenient and "unromantic," and remind them of disease—something they do not want to be reminded of when getting ready to make love. Rather, as researchers have consistently discovered, there is a strong tendency for people to go into denial—in this case, to come to the belief that, while AIDS is a problem for other people, they themselves are not at risk. If the mass media have been ineffective, is there anything that can be done?

Recently, my students and I have had considerable success at convincing people to use condoms by employing a variation of the "saying is believing" paradigm discussed earlier in this chapter. As you will recall, in the typical "saying is believing" experiment, individuals are asked to make a speech advocating a point of view that runs counter to their own opinion. This arouses dissonance; dissonance is then reduced by changing their attitudes to bring it more into line with the position they advocated. How can this paradigm be applied to the AIDS epidemic?

As researchers, here is the problem we faced: When it comes to practicing safe sex, almost everybody believes in the message—that is, almost everybody believes that AIDS is a danger and that, if people are going to be sexually active, using condoms is a good idea—it's just that very few of these people who profess these beliefs actually use condoms regularly. So how do you get a person to experience dissonance by making an argument favoring the use of condoms, when they already believe that using condoms is a good idea? It's a dilemma. Our solution was actually quite simple: Because people were insulating themselves from dissonance via the mechanism of denial, we attempted to cut through this denial by confronting people with their own hypocrisy.

In our experiments,[75] we began by asking college students to compose a speech describing the dangers of AIDS and advocating the use of condoms "every single time you have sex." Every student was more than willing to do it—because every one of them believed it was a good idea for sexually active people to use condoms. In one condition, the students merely composed the arguments. In another condition, after composing the arguments, the students recited them in front of a video camera after being informed that the resulting videotape would be played to an audience of high-school students as part of a sex-education class. In addition, prior to making the speech, half the students in each condition were made mindful of their own failures to use condoms by making a list of the circumstances in their own lives when they found it particularly difficult, awkward, or "impossible" to use condoms.

Essentially then, the participants in one condition—those who made a video for high-school students *after* having been made mindful of their own failures to use condoms—were in a state of high dissonance. This was caused by being made aware of their own hypocrisy; that is, they were fully aware of the fact that they were preaching behavior to high school students that they themselves were not practicing. In order to remove the hypocrisy and maintain their self-esteem, they would need to start practicing what they were preaching. And that is exactly what we found. At the close of the experiment, students in the hypocrisy condition were far more likely to purchase condoms (on display on a table outside the experimental room) than in any of the other conditions. Furthermore, several months later, a large proportion of students in this condition reported that they were using condoms regularly.

Dissonance and Water Conservation.   A few years ago, while central California was suffering through one of its chronic water shortages, water was being rationed in the city of Santa Cruz—where my university is located. On my campus, the administration was trying desperately to find ways to induce students to conserve water by taking shorter showers. Direct appeals to the students' values regarding conservation had an effect—but a small one. As mentioned in chapter 2, several years earlier, we had obtained a somewhat larger effect by inducing students to conform to the behavior of appropriate role models. In order to have a still greater impact on water conservation, we set about to induce feelings of dissonance, by utilizing the hypocrisy model—in much the same way as we did in the condom experiment discussed above.

In the shower experiment,[76] my research assistant intercepted students on their way to take a shower at the university field house. As in the condom experiment, we varied both *commitment* and *mindfulness*. In the commitment conditions, each student was asked if she would be willing to sign a poster encouraging people to conserve water. The flyer read: "Take shorter showers. If I can do it, so can you!" In the mindful conditions we also asked the students to respond to a water conservation "survey," which consisted of items designed to make them aware of their proconservation attitudes and the fact that their showering behavior was sometimes wasteful.

The students then proceeded to the shower room, where a second research assistant was unobtrusively waiting (with hidden waterproof stopwatch) to time their showers. Exactly as in the condom experiment, we had a major impact on the students' behavior only in the high dissonance condition—that is, where the students were induced to advocate short showers and also were made mindful of their own past behavior. In this condition, students became aware that they were not practicing what they were preaching. In this condition, the length of the average shower was just over three and a half minutes (that's short!) and was far shorter than in the control conditions.

Shedding Light on the Power of Cult Leaders. Finally, dissonance theory has been used as a way of increasing our understanding of events that totally confound our imagination—like the enormous power certain cult leaders like Jim Jones (the massacre at Jonestown) and David Koresh (the conflagration at Waco, Texas) have had over the hearts and minds of their followers. Let us focus on the Jonestown massacre, because more information is available on that one. It goes without saying that the event was tragic in the extreme. It seems beyond comprehension that a single individual could have such power that, at his command, hundreds of people would kill their own children and themselves. How could this happen? The tragedy at Jonestown is far too complex to be understood fully by a simple and sovereign analysis. But one clue does emanate from the *foot in the door* phenomenon discussed earlier in this chapter. Jim Jones extracted great trust from his followers one step at a time. Indeed, close scrutiny reveals a chain of ever-increasing commitment on the part of his followers. While it is almost impossible to comprehend fully the final event, it becomes slightly more comprehensible if we look at it as part of a series. As I mentioned earlier in this chapter, once a small commitment is made, the stage is set for ever-increasing commitments.

Let us start at the beginning. It is easy to understand how a charismatic leader like Jones might extract money from the members of his church. Once they have committed themselves to donating a small amount of money in response to his message of peace and universal brotherhood, he is able to request and receive a great deal more. Next, he induces people to sell their homes and turn over the money to the church. Soon, at his request, several of his followers pull up stakes, leaving their families and friends, to start life anew in the strange and difficult environment of Guyana. There, not only do they work hard (thus increasing their commitment), but they also are cut off from potential dissenting opinion, inasmuch as they are surrounded by true believers. The chain of events continues. Jones takes sexual liberties with several married women among his followers, who acquiesce, if reluctantly; Jones claims to be the father of their children. Finally, as a prelude to the climactic event, Jones induces his followers to perform a series of mock ritual suicides as a test of their loyalty and obedience. Thus, in a step-by-step fashion, the commitment to Jim Jones increases. Each step *in and of itself* is not a huge and ludicrous leap from the one preceding it.

Again, this is an admittedly oversimplified analysis. A great many events occurred among Jones's followers in addition to the gradual increases in commitment I have described. These contributed to the tragic outcome. At the same time, viewing the final outcome in the context of increasing commitment brought about by preceding events *does* shed a ray of light on a phenomenon that at first seems totally unfathomable.

"Man" Cannot Live by Consonance Alone

Near the beginning of this chapter, I made the point that people are capable of rational, adaptive behavior as well as dissonance-reducing behavior. Let's return to that issue. If individuals spend all of their time protecting their egos, they will never grow. In order to grow, we must learn from our mistakes. But if we are intent on reducing dissonance, we will not admit to our mistakes. Instead, we will sweep them under the rug, or worse still, we will turn them into virtues. The memoirs of former presidents are full of the kind of self-serving, self-justifying statements that are best summarized in the words of former President Lyndon Johnson: "If I had it all to do over again, I would not change a thing."[77] Similarly, in former President Ronald Reagan's autobiography he insists on denying the unsavory facts of his administration's involvement in the Iran-Contra affair—despite all evidence to the contrary. Rather, he argues: "To this day, I still believe that the Iran initiative was *not* an effort to swap arms for hostages. . . . We never had any contact with the kidnappers."[78]

On the other hand, people do frequently grow—people do frequently learn from their mistakes. How? Under what conditions? Ideally, when I make a mistake, it would be useful for me to be able to bring myself to say, in effect, "OK, I blew it. What can I learn from the experience so I will not end up in this position again?" This can come about in several ways:

1. Through an understanding of my own defensiveness and dissonance-reducing tendencies.

2. Through the realization that performing stupid or immoral actions does not necessarily mean I am an irrevocably stupid or immoral person.

3. Through the development of enough ego strength to tolerate errors in myself.

4. Through increasing my ability to recognize the benefits of admitting our errors in terms of my own growth and learning.

Of course, it is far easier to list these procedures than it is to accomplish them. How does a person get in touch with his or her defensiveness and dissonance-reducing tendencies? How can we come to realize that bright, moral people like ourselves can occasionally perform a stupid or immoral action? It is not enough to know it abstractly or superficially; in order to fully utilize this knowledge, a person must consciously practice it. Methods of fostering this kind of self-knowledge will be explored in chapter 8, where we will take up the issue of authenticity and nondefensive communication in our relationships with others.

6
Human Aggression

Several years ago, at the height of the Vietnam war, I was watching Walter Cronkite broadcast the news on television. In the course of his newscast, he reported an incident in which U.S. planes dropped napalm on a village in South Vietnam believed to be a Vietcong stronghold. My oldest son, who was about ten at the time, asked brightly, "Hey, Dad, what's napalm?"

"Oh," I answered casually, "as I understand it, it's a chemical that burns people; it also sticks so that if it gets on your skin, you can't remove it." And I continued to watch the news.

A few minutes later, I happened to glance at my son and saw tears streaming down his face. Struck by my son's pain and grief, I grew dismayed as I began to wonder what had happened to me. Had I become so brutalized that I could answer my son's question so matter-of-factly—as if he had asked me how a baseball is made or how a leaf functions? Had I become so accustomed to human brutality that I could be casual in its presence?

In a sense it is not surprising. We are living in an age of unspeakable horrors. During the past three decades, we have witnessed countless examples of "man's inhumanity to man." In addition to the near-random destruction of noncombatants in Vietnam, we have seen brutal civil wars in Central America, the mass execution of hundreds of thousands of innocent civilians in Cambodia, the bloodbath in Bosnia and Rwanda, the induced suicide of over nine hundred people in Jonestown, the conflagration in Waco, Texas, and on and on and on. And yet, as tragic as these events are, occurrences of this kind are not peculiar to the present era. Many years ago, a friend showed me a very thin book—only ten or fifteen pages long—that purported to be a capsule history of the world. It was a chronological listing of the important events in recorded history. Can you guess how it read? Of course—one war after another, interrupted every now and then by a few nonviolent events, such as the birth of Jesus and the invention of the printing press. What kind of species are we if the most important events in the brief history of humankind are situations in which people kill one another en masse?

Moreover, we Americans display a chilling acceptance of violence that at times seems utterly absurd and mindless. Let me give you one rather poignant example. In 1986, U.S. warplanes bombed Libya in retaliation for an upsurge in that country's acts of terrorism. When our citizens were later asked whether they approved of this military action, a whopping 71 percent responded "yes," even though only 31 percent believed the raid would actually be effective in curbing future terrorism.[1] What else can we conclude but that a substantial number of U.S. citizens find acts of pure vengeance an acceptable part of U.S. foreign policy?

We humans have shown ourselves to be an aggressive species. With the exception of certain rodents, no other vertebrates so consistently and wantonly kill members of their own kind. I have defined social psychology as the study of social influence—that is, one person's (or group's) influence on another. The most extreme form of aggression (physical destruction) can be considered to be the ultimate degree of social influence. Is aggression inborn—is it part of our very nature as human beings? Can it be modified? What are the social and situational factors that increase or decrease aggression?

Aggression Defined

It is difficult to present a clear definition of *aggression* because, in the popular vernacular, the term is used in so many different ways. Clearly, the Boston Strangler, who made a hobby of strangling women in their apartments, was performing acts of aggression. But a football player making a tackle is also considered aggressive. A tennis player who charges the net is called aggressive. So, too, is a successful insurance salesperson who is "a real go-getter." The young girl who staunchly defends her own possessions against the encroachment of other children and the young girl who goes out of her way to clobber her brother are both considered aggressive. On a more subtle level, if a neglected husband sulks in the corner during a party, this may be an act of "passive aggression." Also, a child who wets the bed, a jilted boyfriend who threatens suicide, or a student who doggedly attempts to master a difficult mathematical problem could conceivably be labeled as illustrations of an aggressive tendency in human beings. And what of the violence exerted by the state in its attempt to maintain law and order—and the less direct forms of aggression through which people of one race or religion humiliate and degrade people of different races or religions? If all these behaviors are to come under the blanket term *aggression,* the situation is indeed confused. As a way of increasing our understanding of aggression, we must cut through this morass and separate the "assertive" aspects of the popular definition from the destructive aspects. That is, a distinction can be made between behavior that harms others and behavior that does not harm others. Accordingly, the go-getting salesperson or the student doggedly sticking to the mathematical problem would not be considered aggressive, but the behavior of the Boston Strangler, the clobbering child, the suicidal boyfriend, and even the sulking, neglected husband would all be defined as aggressive.

But this distinction is not altogether satisfactory because, by concentrating on an outcome alone, it ignores the intention of the person perpetrating the act, and this is the crucial aspect of the definition of *aggression*. I would define an act of aggression as a behavior aimed at causing harm or pain. Thus, by definition, the football player is *not* considered to be performing an act of aggression if his aim is simply to bring down his opponent as efficiently as possible—but he *is* behaving aggressively if his aim is to cause pain or injury, whether or not he succeeds in doing so. To illustrate, suppose a three-year-old boy slaps at his father in anger. The slap may be totally ineffectual—it may even cause his father to laugh. But it is, nonetheless, an aggressive act. Similarly, the same child may, in total innocence, thrust a sharp elbow into his father's eye, causing severe pain and colorful contusions. Because its painful consequences were unintentional, this would not be defined as an act of aggression.

It might be useful to make one additional distinction within the category of intentional aggression, namely, a distinction between aggression that is an end in itself and aggression that is instrumental in achieving some goal. The first I will call hostile aggression; the second I will call instrumental aggression. Thus, a football player might intentionally inflict an injury on the opposing quarterback in order to put him out of the game and thus increase his own team's probability of winning. This would be instrumental aggression. On the other hand, he might perform this action on the last play of the last game of the season to "pay back" the quarterback for some real or imagined insult or humiliation; this is hostile aggression since the aggressive act is an end in itself. Similarly, dropping a bomb on a ball-bearing factory in Munich in World War II can be considered an act of instrumental aggression, while shooting down defenseless women and children in a Vietnamese village can be considered an act of hostile aggression. The "hit man" working for the Mafia who guns down a designated victim is probably behaving instrumentally; thrill killers, such as members of the Manson family, probably are not.

Is Aggression Instinctive?

Psychologists, physiologists, ethologists, and philosophers are in disagreement over whether aggression is an innate, instinctive phenomenon or whether such behavior has to be learned. This is not a new controversy; it has been raging for centuries. For example, Jean-

Jacques Rousseau's concept of the noble savage[2] (first published in 1762) suggested that we humans, in our natural state, are benign, happy, and good creatures and that a restrictive society forces aggression and depravity upon us. Others have taken the view that we humans, in our natural state, are brutes and that only by enforcing the law and order of society can we curb or sublimate our natural instincts toward aggression. Sigmund Freud[3] is a good example of a proponent of this general position. Besides suggesting that humans are born with an instinct toward life, which he called *Eros*, Freud postulated that humans are also born with a death instinct, *Thanatos*. When turned inward, the death instinct manifests itself in self-punishment, which in the extreme case, becomes suicide; when turned outward, this instinct manifests itself in hostility, destructiveness, and murder. "It is at work in every living being and is striving to bring it to ruin and to reduce life to its original condition of inanimate matter."[4] Freud believed this aggressive energy must come out somehow, lest it continue to build up and produce illness. This notion can be described as a "hydraulic" theory—that is, the analogy is one of water pressure building up in a container: Unless aggression is allowed to drain off, it will produce some sort of explosion. According to Freud, society performs an essential function in regulating this instinct and in helping people to sublimate it—that is, in helping people to turn the destructive energy into acceptable or useful behavior.

Taking the notion of innate aggression one step further, some scholars believe humans in their natural state not only are killers but that their wanton destructiveness is unique among animals. Consequently, these scholars suggest that to call human behavior "brutal" is to libel nonhuman species. This point of view has been expressed eloquently by Anthony Storr:

> We generally describe the most repulsive examples of man's cruelty as brutal or bestial, implying by these adjectives that such behavior is characteristic of less highly developed animals than ourselves. In truth, however, the extremes of "brutal" behavior are confined to man; and there is no parallel in nature to our savage treatment of each other. The sombre fact is that we are the most cruel and most ruthless species that has ever walked the earth; and that although we may recoil in horror when we read in the newspaper or history book of the

atrocities committed by man upon man, we know in our hearts that each one of us harbours within himself those same savage impulses which lead to murder, to torture, and to war.[5]

There is a lack of definitive or even clear evidence on the subject of whether or not aggression is instinctive in humans. I suppose that is why the controversy still rages. Much of the evidence, such as it is, stems from observation of, and experimentation with, species other than humans. In one such study, for example, Zing Yang Kuo[6] attempted to explode the myth that cats will instinctively stalk and kill rats. His experiment was a very simple one. He raised a kitten in the same cage with a rat. Not only did the cat refrain from attacking the rat, but the two became close companions. Moreover, the cat refused either to chase or to kill other rats. It should be noted, however, that this experiment does not prove that aggressive behavior is not instinctive; it merely demonstrates that aggressive behavior can be inhibited by early experience. Thus, in an experiment reported by Irenaus Eibl-Eibesfeldt,[7] it was shown that rats raised in isolation (that is, without any experience in fighting other rats) will attack a fellow rat when one is introduced into the cage; moreover, the isolated rat uses the same pattern of threat and attack experienced rats use. Thus, although aggressive behavior can be modified by experience (as shown by Kuo's experiment), Eibl-Eibesfeldt showed that aggression apparently does not need to be learned. On the other hand, one should not conclude from this study that aggression is necessarily instinctive, for, as John Paul Scott[8] has pointed out, in order to draw this conclusion, there must be physiological evidence of a spontaneous stimulation for fighting that arises from within the body alone. The stimulus in the above experiment came from the outside—that is, the sight of a new rat stimulated the isolated rat to fight. Scott concluded from his survey of the evidence that there is no inborn need for fighting: If an organism can arrange its life so there is no outside stimulation to fight, then it will not experience any physiological or mental damage as a result of not expressing aggression. This view contradicts Freud's contention and, in effect, asserts there is no instinct of aggression.

The argument goes back and forth. Scott's conclusion has been called into question by the distinguished ethologist Konrad Lorenz.[9]

Lorenz observed the behavior of certain cichlids, which are highly aggressive tropical fish. Male cichlids will attack other males of the same species apparently as an aspect of territorial behavior—that is, to defend their territory. In its natural environment, the male cichlid does not attack female cichlids, nor does he attack males of a different species—he only attacks males of his own species. What happens if all other male cichlids are removed from an aquarium, leaving only one male alone with no appropriate sparring partner? According to the hydraulic theory of instinct, the need to aggress will build up to the point where the cichlid will attack a fish that doesn't usually serve as an appropriate stimulus for attack; and that is exactly what happens. In the absence of his fellow male cichlids, he attacks males of other species—males he previously ignored. Moreover, if *all* males are removed, the male cichlid will eventually attack and kill females.

And the controversy continues. Leonard Berkowitz,[10] one of the world's leading experts on human aggression, believes humans are essentially different from nonhumans in that learning plays a more important role in their aggressive behavior. In humans, aggression is a function of a complex interplay between innate propensities and learned responses. Thus, although it is true that many animals, from insects to apes, will attack an animal that invades their territory, it is a gross oversimplification to imply, as some popular writers have, that humans are likewise programed to protect their territory and behave aggressively in response to specific stimuli. There is much evidence to support Berkowitz's contention that, among humans, innate patterns of behavior are infinitely modifiable and flexible. Human cultures vary dramatically on this dimension. For example, there are a great many primitive tribes like the Lepchas of Sikkim, the Pygmies of Central Africa, and the Arapesh of New Guinea who manage to live in cooperative friendliness, both within their own tribe and in their relations with others. Among these people, acts of aggression are extremely rare. Meanwhile, in a more "civilized" society like our own we are economically crippled by an astronomical "peacetime" military budget and drive-by shootings have become a commonplace fact of urban life.

Even more striking is the observation that, within a given culture, changing social conditions can lead to changes in aggressive behavior. For example, the Iroquois Indians lived in peace for hundreds of years as a hunting nation. But in the seventeenth century, a growing trade with the newly arrived Europeans brought the Iroquois into direct competition with the neighboring Hurons over furs (to trade for manufactured goods). A series of wars developed—and the Iroquois became ferocious and successful warriors, not because of uncontrollable aggressive instincts, but because a *social* change produced increases in competition.[11]

There is even a good deal of evidence for such flexibility among nonhumans. For example, by electrically stimulating a certain area of a monkey's brain, one can evoke an aggressive response in the monkey. This area can be considered to be the neural center of aggression; but that does not mean that when this area is stimulated the monkey will always attack. If a male monkey is in the presence of other monkeys who are less dominant than he in their social hierarchy, he will indeed attack them when the appropriate area of his brain is stimulated; but if the same area is stimulated while he is in the presence of monkeys who are *more* dominant than he, he will *not* attack; rather, he will tend to flee the scene. Thus, the same physiological stimulation can produce widely different responses, depending upon learning. This appears to be true for humans. We can conclude after reviewing these data that, although aggression may have an instinctual component in humans, the important point for the social psychologist is that it *is* modifiable by situational factors. How can it be modified? How much can it be modified? Should it be modified? Before getting to these questions, we must first understand what the situational factors are and how they operate.

Is Aggression Necessary?

The Survival of the Fittest. We know that animals can be bred for aggression. For example, Kirsti Lagerspetz[12] observed the behavior of a group of normal mice. She then took those that were behaving most aggressively and allowed them to mate with one another. Similarly, she allowed the least aggressive to mate with one another. She then repeated this procedure for twenty-six generations, ending up with one group of extremely fierce mice and another group of extremely docile ones. Moreover, some investigators have suggested that certain kinds of aggression are useful and perhaps even essential. Konrad Lorenz,[13] for example, has argued that aggression is "an essential part of the life-preserving organization of instincts." Basing his argument on his observation of nonhumans, he sees aggression as being of prime evolutionary importance, allowing the young animals to have the strongest and wisest mothers and fathers and enabling the group to be led by the best possible leaders. From their study of Old World monkeys, anthropologist Sherwood Washburn and psychiatrist David Hamburg concur.[14] They find that aggression within the same group of monkeys plays an important role in feeding, reproduction, and determining dominance patterns. The strongest and most aggressive male in a colony will assume a dominant position through an initial display of aggressive behavior. This serves to reduce subsequent serious fighting within the colony (the other males know who's boss). Furthermore, because the dominant male dominates reproduction, the colony increases its chances of survival as the strong male passes on his vigor to subsequent generations.

A similar pattern is reported among elephant seals by Burney LeBoeuf.[15] Each year before mating season, pairs of males square off against each other and engage in ferocious blood battles for dominance. The strongest, most aggressive, and shrewdest male is not only number one in the dominance hierarchy among his fellows, but he becomes number-one lovemaker in the group. For example, in one observation, the number-one or "alpha" male in a particular rookery of 185 females and 120 males was responsible for half of the observed copulations. In smaller rookeries of 40 or fewer females, the alpha male is typically responsible for 100 percent of the copulations.

With these data in mind, many observers urge caution in attempting to control aggression in humans, suggesting that, as in lower animals, aggression is necessary for survival. This reasoning is based in part on the assumption that the same mechanism that drives one man to kill his neighbor drives another to "conquer" outer space, "sink his teeth" into a difficult mathematical equation, "attack" a logical problem, or "master" the universe.

But, as I argued earlier, this reasoning is based on an exaggerated definition of aggression. To equate high achievement and advancement with hostility and aggression is to confuse the issue. A problem or skill can be mastered without harming other people or even without attempting to conquer them. This is a difficult distinction for us to grasp, because the Western mind—and perhaps the American mind in particular—has been trained to equate success with victory, to equate doing well with beating someone. M. F. Ashley Montagu[16] feels that an oversimplification and misinterpretation of Darwin's theory has provided the average person with the mistaken idea that conflict is necessarily the law of life. Ashley Montagu states that it was convenient, during the industrial revolution, for the wealthy industrialists, who were exploiting the workers, to justify their exploitation by talking about life being a struggle and it being natural for the fittest (and only the fittest) to survive. The danger is that this kind of reasoning becomes a self-fulfilling prophecy and can cause us to ignore or play down the survival value of nonaggressive and noncompetitive behavior. For example, Peter Kropotkin[17] concluded in 1902 that cooperative behavior and mutual aid have great survival value for many forms of life. There is ample evidence to support this conclusion. The cooperative behavior of certain social insects, such as termites, ants, and bees, is well known. Perhaps not so well known is a form of behavior in the chimpanzee that can only be described as altruistic. It goes something like this: Two chimpanzees are in adjoining cages. One chimp has food and the other doesn't. The foodless chimpanzee begins to beg. Reluctantly, the "wealthy" chimp hands over some of his food. In a sense, the very reluctance with which he does so makes the gift all the more significant. It indicates he likes the food and would dearly enjoy keeping it for himself. Accordingly, it suggests the urge to share may have deep roots, indeed.[18] But Kropotkin's work has not been given much attention—in fact, it has been largely ignored, perhaps because it did not fit the temper of the times or the needs of those who were profiting from the industrial revolution.

Let us look at our own society. As a culture, we Americans seem to thrive on competition; we reward winners and turn away from losers. For two centuries, our educational system has been based on competitiveness and the laws of survival. With very few exceptions, we do not teach our kids to love learning—we teach them to strive for high grades. When sportswriter Grantland Rice said that what's important is not whether you win or lose but how you play the game, he was not *describing* the dominant theme in U.S. life; he was *prescribing* a cure for our preoccupation with winning. From the Little League ball player who bursts into tears after his team is defeated to the college students in the football stadium chanting "We're number one!"; from presidents like Lyndon Johnson, whose judgment during the Vietnam conflict was almost certainly distorted by his oft-stated desire not to be the first U.S. president to lose a war, and George Bush, who, while president, struggled "manfully" to overcome his "wimp" image, to the thirdgrader who despises his classmate for a superior performance on an arithmetic test, we manifest a staggering cultural obsession with victory. Vince Lombardi, a very successful professional football coach, may have summed it all up with the simple statement "Winning isn't the most important thing, it's the *only* thing." What is frightening about the acceptance of this philosophy is that it implies that the goal of victory justifies whatever means we use to win, even if it's only a football game—which, after all, was first conceived of as a recreational activity. An interesting and appalling footnote to Lombardi's statement involves the manner in which the residents of Green Bay, Wisconsin, treated his successor, Dan Devine, when he had the misfortune to lead that team to a losing season. As a result, he was the target of physical threats, his family was insulted, his dog was shot in front of his house, people made obscene phone calls in the middle of the night, and false rumors spread that his daughters were the town sluts and his wife was an alcoholic.[19]

It may be true that, in the early history of human evolution, highly competitive and aggressive behaviors were adaptive. Some writers have traced human aggression to the time when our ancestors were hunters and gatherers who had to kill animals and forage widely to survive. On the other hand, more recent archaeological evidence unearthed by Richard Leakey and his associates[20] indicates that this assumption may be invalid, that human aggression grew much later, as people began to cultivate the land and became concerned with ownership and property. But in either case, as we look about and see a world full of strife, of international and interracial hatred and distrust, of senseless slaughter and political assassination, we feel justified in questioning the current survival value of this behavior. With the major powers in possession of enough nuclear warheads to destroy the world's population twenty-five times over, I wonder whether building still more warheads might not be carrying things a bit too far. Anthropologist Loren Eiseley paid tribute to our ancient ancestors but warned against imitating them when he wrote: "The need is now for a gentler, a more tolerant people than those who won for us against the ice, the tiger, and the bear."[21]

Catharsis. There is another sense in which it sometimes has been argued that aggression serves a useful and perhaps a necessary function. I refer here to the psychoanalytic position. Specifically, as mentioned earlier, Sigmund Freud believed that unless people were allowed to express themselves aggressively, the aggressive energy would be dammed up, pressure would build, and the energy would seek an outlet, either exploding into acts of extreme violence or manifesting itself as symptoms of mental illness. Is there any evidence to support this contention? The evidence, such as it is, suggests that *conflict about aggression* can lead to a state of high emotional tension in humans. This has led some investigators to the faulty conclusion that the inhibition of an aggressive response in humans produces either serious symptoms or intensely aggressive behavior. But there is no direct evidence for this conclusion.

"But still," one might ask, "can the expression of aggression be beneficial?" It is tempting to think so. Most of us, when frustrated or angry, have experienced something akin to a release of tension when we have "blown off steam" by yelling or cursing someone or perhaps even hitting someone. But does an act of aggression reduce the need for further aggression? Consider some of the ways in which aggressive energy can be discharged: (1) by expending it in the form of a socially acceptable aggressive, physical activity like football or hockey; (2) by engaging in a nondestructive form of fantasy aggression—like dreaming about hitting someone, or writing a violent story; and (3) by engaging in direct aggression—lashing out at someone, hurting him, getting him into trouble, saying nasty things about him, and the like.

Let us take the first one—engaging in socially acceptable aggressive behavior. There is widespread belief this procedure works, and it is amply promoted by psychoanalytically oriented therapists. For example, the distinguished psychiatrist William Menninger has asserted that "competitive games provide an unusually satisfactory out-let for the instinctive aggressive drive."[22] It would seem reasonable to ask if there is any evidence that competitive games reduce aggressive behavior. In his careful analysis of the existing data, Berkowitz[23] could find no simple, unequivocal findings to support the contention that intense physical activity reduces aggression. In fact, a field study by Arthur Patterson[24] leads to quite the opposite conclusion. He measured the hostility of high-school football players, rating them both one week before and one week after the football season. If it is true that the intense physical activity and aggressive behavior that are part of playing football serve to reduce the tension caused by pent-up aggression, we would expect the players to exhibit a decline in hostility over the course of the season. Instead, the results of the measures showed a significant *increase*. Similarly, in an exhaustive study of college athletes, Warren Johnson[25] found no consistent evidence to support the notion of catharsis. He concluded that not only is it absurd to argue that wars have been won on the playing fields of Eton, but it is even more absurd to hope we can prevent them there. This is not to say that people do not get pleasure out of these games. They do. But engaging in these games does not decrease aggression.

Even though engaging in competitive and aggressive games does not result in less aggression, perhaps *watching* these kinds of games does. Gordon Russell,[26] a Canadian sports psychologist, measured the hostility of spectators at an especially violent ice hockey match. As the game progressed, the spectators became increasingly belligerent—their level of hostility did not return to the pregame level until after the game was over. Thus, *watching* a competitive activity not only fails to decrease aggressive behavior—it temporarily increases it.

Let us examine the second form of aggression—fantasy. If fantasy works to reduce subsequent aggression, attacking another person in fantasy would be a particularly beneficial way of relieving aggressive tensions; remember that, with fantasy aggression, no one actually gets hurt. There is some evidence that engaging in fantasy aggression can make people feel better and can even result in a temporary reduction in aggression. In an interesting experiment by Seymour Feshbach,[27] students were insulted by their instructor; then, half of the students were given the opportunity to write imaginative stories about aggression, while the other half were not given this opportunity. There was also a control group who were not insulted. Feshbach's results showed that, immediately afterward, the people who had been given the opportunity to write stories about aggression were slightly less aggressive than were those who were not given this opportunity. It should be pointed out that both of these groups of insulted students were considerably more aggressive than a group of students who were not insulted at all. Thus, the utility of fantasy was limited: It did not reduce a great deal of aggressive energy. Indeed, an experiment by Jack Hokanson and Meredith Burgess[28] demonstrated that, when subjects were provoked by an experimenter, engaging in fantasy aggression against him reduced their arousal to a far lesser extent than did acts of direct aggression against their tormentor.

Let us now take a closer look at research on such acts of direct aggression: Do they reduce the need for further aggression? Although the evidence is not unequivocal, the overwhelming majority of experiments on the topic have failed to find such effects.[29] In fact, by far the most common finding resembles the research on watching violence cited above; namely, when people commit acts of aggression, such acts increase the tendency toward future aggression. For example, in an experiment by Russell Geen and his associates,[30] each subject was paired with another student, who was actually a confederate of the experimenters. First, the subject was angered by the confederate; during this phase, which involved the exchanging of opinions on various issues, the subject was given electric shocks when his partner disagreed with his opinion. Next, during a study of "the effects of punishment on learning" the subject acted as a teacher while the confederate served as learner. On the first learning task, some of the subjects were required to shock the confederate each time he made a mistake; other subjects merely recorded his errors. On the next task, all the subjects were given the opportunity to deliver shocks. If a cathartic effect were operating, we would expect the subjects who had previously shocked the confederate to administer fewer and less intense shocks the second time. This didn't happen; in fact, the subjects who had previously shocked the confederate expressed *more* aggression when given the subsequent opportunity to attack him. This phenomenon is not limited to the laboratory; the same tendency has also been observed systematically in naturally occurring events in the real world, where verbal acts of aggression served to facilitate further attacks. In this "natural experiment," several technicians who had recently been laid off were provided with a chance to verbalize their hostility against their ex-bosses; later, when asked to describe that person, these technicians were much *more* punitive in their descriptions than those technicians who had not previously voiced their feelings.[31]

In summary, the weight of the evidence does not support the catharsis hypothesis. It appears to be a reasonable idea, in a limited way. That is, when somebody angers us, venting our hostility against that person does indeed seem to make us feel better. However, it does not reduce our hostility. What could be going on to contradict these predictions? With humans, aggression is not merely dependent on tensions—what one feels—but also on what a person *thinks*. Put yourself in the place of a subject in the previous experiments: After once shocking another person or expressing hostility against your old boss, it becomes easier to do so a second time. Aggressing the first time can reduce your inhibitions against committing other such actions; the aggression is legitimized, and it becomes easier to carry out such assaults. Furthermore, the main thrust of the research on this issue indicates that committing an overt act of aggression against a person changes one's feelings about that person, increasing one's negative feelings toward the target and therefore increasing the probability of future aggression against that person.

Why? As we have seen in the preceding chapter, when a person does harm to another person, it sets cognitive processes in motion aimed at justifying that act of cruelty. Specifically, when we hurt another person, we experience cognitive dissonance. The cognition "I have hurt Sam" is dissonant with the cognition "I am a decent, reasonable, good person." A good way for me to reduce dissonance is somehow to convince myself that hurting Sam was not an indecent, unreasonable, bad thing to do. I can accomplish this by blinding myself to Sam's virtues and by emphasizing his faults, by convincing myself that Sam is a terrible human being who deserved to be hurt. This would especially hold if the target is an *innocent* victim of my aggression. Thus, in experiments by David Glass and by Keith E. Davis and Edward E. Jones[32] (discussed in the preceding chapter), the subject inflicted either psychological or physical harm on an innocent person who had done the subject no prior harm. The subjects then proceeded to derogate the victim, convincing themselves he was not a very nice person and therefore deserved what he got. This reduces dissonance all right, and it also sets the stage for further aggression—once you have derogated a person, it makes it easier for you to hurt that person in the future.

But what happens if the victim isn't so innocent? What happens if he or she has done something to make you angry and therefore does indeed deserve retaliation? Here the situation becomes more complex and more interesting. One of several experiments performed to test this issue was a brilliantly conceived doctoral dissertation by Michael Kahn.[33] In Kahn's experiment, a medical technician, taking some physiological measurements from college students, made some derogatory remarks about these students. In one experimental condition, the subjects were allowed to vent their hostility by expressing their feelings about the technician to his employer—an action that looked as though it would get the technician into serious trouble, perhaps even cost him his job. In another condition, they were not provided with the opportunity to express any aggression against the person who had aroused their anger. What would psychoanalytic theory predict would occur? That's easy: The inhibited group would experience tension, a good deal of anger, and hostile feelings against the technician, while the group that expressed their feelings would feel relieved, relaxed, and not as hostile toward the technician. In short, according to psychoanalytic theory, expressing hostility would purge the insulted subjects of their hostile feelings. Being a good Freudian, Kahn expected these results. He was surprised and (to his credit) excited to find evidence to the contrary. Specifically, those who were allowed to express their aggression subsequently felt greater dislike and hostility for the technician than did those who were inhibited from expressing their aggression. In other words, expressing aggression did not inhibit the tendency to aggress, it tended to increase it—even when the target was not simply an innocent victim.

What Kahn's experiment illustrates is that, when people are made angry, they frequently engage in overkill. In this case, costing the technician his job is a serious overkill compared to the harm the technician perpetrated. The overkill produces dissonance in much the same way hurting an innocent person produces dissonance. That is, there is a discrepancy between what the person did to you and the force of the retaliation. That discrepancy must be justified—and just as in the "innocent victim" experiments—the justification takes the form of derogating the object of your wrath *after* you have hurt that person.

But what happens if you can arrange it so that retaliation is not allowed to run roughshod over the target? That is, what if the degree of retaliation is reasonably controlled so it is not significantly more intense than the action that precipitated it? In such a circumstance, I would predict there would be little or no dissonance. "Sam has insulted me; I've paid him back; we're even. I have no need to retaliate further." This is what was found in an experiment by Anthony Doob and Larraine Wood.[34] As in Kahn's experiment, Doob and Wood arranged things so their subjects were humiliated and annoyed by an accomplice. In one condition, they were given the opportunity to retaliate by administering a series of electric shocks to their tormentor. In this situation, once the score was evened, they had no further need to punish their tormentor. But those subjects who had not been given the opportunity to retaliate *did* subsequently choose to punish their tormentor. Thus, we have seen that retaliation can reduce the need for further aggression if something akin to equity has been restored. There is a major point here that must be underscored: Most situations in the real world are not as neat as the Doob and Wood situation, where retaliation can be made functionally similar to the original act. In my opinion, the world is usually closer to the situation in Michael Kahn's experiment: Retaliation typically outstrips the original act by a great deal. For example, whatever the students at Kent State University might have been doing to the members of the Ohio National Guard (shouting obscenities, teasing, taunting), it hardly merited being shot and killed. Moreover, most victims of massive aggression are totally innocent. In all these situations, the opposite of catharsis takes place. Thus, once I have shot dissenting students at Kent State, I will convince myself they *really* deserved it, and I will hate dissenting students even more than I did before I shot them; once I have slaughtered women and children at My Lai, I will be even more convinced Asians aren't really human than I was before I slaughtered them; once I have denied black people a decent education, I will become even more convinced they are stupid and couldn't have profited from a good education to begin with. In most situations, violence does *not* reduce the tendency toward violence: Violence breeds more violence.

If violence breeds more violence, then what are we to do with our angry feelings? There is an important difference between being angry and expressing that anger in a violent and destructive manner. To experience anger in appropriate circumstances is normal and harmless. Indeed, there is very little one can do to avoid anger. It is certainly possible to express that anger in a nonviolent manner, for example, by a forceful and simple statement: "I am very angry at you because of what you did." Indeed, such a statement in and of itself is a vehicle for self-assertion and probably serves to relieve tension and to make the angered person feel better. At the same time, because the target does not get hurt, such a response does not set in motion those cognitive processes that would lead the angered person to justify his or her behavior by ridiculing or derogating the target person. More will be said on this issue in chapter 8.

Catharsis, Public Policy, and the Mass Media

What does all of this tell us about public policy? Consider the most extreme example of human aggression: war. In addition to hypothesizing that the death instinct worked on a personal level, Freud theorized that it operated on a societal level as well, manifesting itself in battles between nations.[35] But do wars have cathartic effects, helping to provide an outlet for a society's aggressive tendencies? If so, we would expect that, in the years following a nation's involvement in a war, there would be a decrease in violent crime among its citizens. Dane Archer and Rosemary Gartner[36] compared the crime rates for roughly 110 countries since 1900. They found that wars actually *encourage* domestic violence. Compared with similar nations that remained at peace, countries that fought wars exhibited substantial postwar increases in their homicide rates. Rather than reducing the tendency toward aggression, wars increase aggressive behavior by legitimizing it.

In spite of the mounting evidence against the catharsis hypothesis, it still seems to be widely believed by most people, including people who make important decisions that affect all of us. Thus, it is frequently argued that playing football[37] or watching people getting murdered on television[38] serves a valuable function in draining off aggressive energy. We have seen already that playing football fails to reduce general hostility and may even increase it. Furthermore, in a classic series of experiments, Albert Bandura and his associates[39] demonstrated that watching violence on television also failed to yield cathartic effects. Quite the contrary; simply seeing another person behave aggressively can *increase* the aggressive behavior of young children. The basic procedure in these studies was to have an adult knock around a plastic, air-filled "Bobo" doll (the kind that bounces back after it's been knocked down). Sometimes, the adult would accompany her physical aggression with verbal abuse against the doll. The kids were then allowed to play with the doll. In these experiments, not only did the children imitate the aggressive models, they also engaged in other forms of aggressive behavior after having witnessed the aggressive behavior of the adult. In short, the children did more than copy the behavior of an adult; seeing a person behave aggressively served as an impetus for them to engage in innovative aggressive behavior.

This evidence suggests that violence on television is potentially dangerous, in that it serves as a model for behavior—especially for children. And what do we see on television? For over twenty-five years, George Gerbner and his associates have been conducting analyses of prime-time and Saturday morning television programing. They have found that violence prevails in eight out of every ten programs. Moreover, an average of five to six violent incidents occurs each hour. And what about cartoons, the favorite television fare of most young children? They contain the most violence—roughly eighteen acts of aggression every hour.[40] The most recent estimate suggests that by the time he or she is twelve years old the average child will have witnessed 100,000 acts of violence on TV.

For decades, spokespersons for the major television networks have attempted to shrug off the Bandura experiments because they do not involve aggression against people. After all, who cares about what a kid does to a "Bobo" doll? More recent experimental evidence demonstrates, however, that the effects of watching violence are *not* limited to walloping a "Bobo" doll: It induces kids to wallop each other as well. In one study, Liebert and Baron[41] exposed a group of children to an episode of a popular, violent cops-and-robbers type of program. In a control condition, a similar group of children were exposed to a video of an exciting sporting event for the same length of time. The children were then allowed to play in another room with a group of other children. Those who had watched the violent television program showed far more aggression against the other children than those who had watched the sporting event.

Ross Parke and his colleagues[42] have extended these findings to a more natural setting. They showed movies to boys living in juvenile detention facilities in the United States and Belgium, showing aggressive films to the boys living in some cottages within the facilities and showing nonviolent movies to those boys living in the other cottages. Both during and after the week of films, the boys who viewed the aggressive movies displayed more physical and verbal aggression against the other children. Further studies demonstrated that the effects could arise from seeing just *one* movie, and that the increase in aggressive behavior was most pronounced in those boys who were initially *lower* in aggression. In a longitudinal study, Leonard Eron and Rowell Huesmann[43] found a high correlation between watching violence on television and aggressive behavior among eight-year-old boys. They then restudied 211 of these boys some eleven years later. Those nineteen-year-olds who had watched a great deal of TV violence at age eight were more aggressive than those who had not. Moreover, it was reasonably clear that TV viewing caused aggressive behavior (rather than vice versa) because the aggressive nineteen-year-olds who had watched a lot of violent TV at age eight did not necessarily watch violent TV at age nineteen. In short, watching violence on television at age eight predicted subsequent aggression; being aggressive at age eight did not predict subsequent violence-watching. And more recent longitudinal studies have revealed that this relationship holds both in the United States and Finland.[44] Results of laboratory and field studies have led Eron and Huesmann[45] to conclude that the relationship between viewing TV violence and subsequent aggression is indisputable. Of course, results from nonexperimental field studies are open to interpretation—cause-effect relationships can't be "proved." But results of such studies of naturally occurring behaviors lend support to conclusions based on laboratory experiments: Viewing television violence fosters aggressive behavior.

More recently, William Josephson[46] demonstrated that watching violence on TV has the greatest impact on those youngsters who are most aggressive to begin with. In this experiment, youngsters were exposed to either a film depicting a great deal of police violence or an exciting, nonviolent film about bike racing. They then played a game of floor hockey. Watching the violent film had the effect of increasing the number of aggressive acts committed during the hockey game— primarily by those youngsters who had previously been rated as highly aggressive by their teachers. During the hockey game, it was these kids who were the most prone to hit others with their sticks and throw elbows.

Viewing television violence not only increases aggressive acts on the part of the viewer, it also can serve to numb the reactions of people when they are faced with aggression in their day-to-day lives. Margaret Hanratty Thomas and her colleagues[47] had children watch either a violent police drama or an exciting (but nonviolent) volleyball game. After a short break, the children observed a verbally and physically aggressive interaction between two youngsters. Those children who had watched the police show responded less emotionally than did those who had watched the volleyball game. That is, viewing the initial violence *desensitized* the children to further acts of violence— they were not upset by an incident that, by all rights, should have upset them. While such a reaction may psychologically protect us from the debilitating effects of repeated violence, it also hardens us to the feelings of those who are the targets of aggression.

Thus far, we have focused much of our attention on children. But it is not only children who are inclined to model themselves after things they see on TV or in films. For example, in the autumn of 1993, a movie called *The Program* depicted a college student, as a demonstration of his courage, lying down on the center line of a highway as trucks whizzed by. Within two weeks of the film's release, a young man in New Jersey and another in Pennsylvania tried the same stunt. But they were not so lucky; they were struck and killed by unsuspecting motorists. And a few years ago, a man drove his truck through the window of a crowded cafeteria in Killeen, Texas, emerged from the cab, and began shooting people at random. By the time police arrived, he had killed twenty-two people, making this the most destructive shooting spree in U.S. history. He then turned the gun on himself. In his pocket, police found a ticket stub to the film *Fisher King*. In this film, a deranged man fires a shotgun into a crowded bar, killing several people.

And these are not isolated incidents. Far from it. Several years ago, a national magazine reported the following occurrences:

> In San Francisco, three teenage girls lured two younger girls down a lonely path and sexually molested them. In Chicago, two boys attempted to extort $500 from a firm by means of a bomb threat. In Boston, a youthful gang set a woman on fire with gasoline. In all three cases police officials concluded that the crimes had been directly inspired by shows the adolescents had recently watched on prime-time television.[48]

These events lend a macabre twist to Alfred Hitchcock's tongue-in-cheek statement, "One of television's great contributions is that it brought murder back into the home where it belongs." Indeed, it appears that Oscar Wilde was correct in his observation that life often imitates art.

I am certainly not suggesting that watching violence on television or movie videos is the major antecedent of violence. That would be far too facile. We have a society where a great many people (especially those living in our inner cities) are suffering from the effects of hopelessness, grinding poverty, teenage gangs, the easy availability of drugs and guns—all of which are important factors in the occurrence of violence. Nevertheless, it would be naive to deny that violence in the media is an important contributing factor to violence in the streets and in the home. This, after all, is the society in which the major TV networks tripped all over themselves in their zeal to be the first on the air with a dramatization of *The Amy Fisher Story*. Who is Amy Fisher? A disturbed teenager, who, in the midst of an affair with an automobile mechanic twice her age, knocked on the door of his house and shot his wife. And this is the society where youngsters in elementary school are saying, "*Hasta la vista*, baby," in faithful imitation of Arnold Schwarznegger's feelingless farewell to his victim as he casually blows him away. Even the term "blows him away" is a graphic example of the casualness with which the media depict murder to our youngsters.

Systematic research by David Phillips[49] suggests that the incidents of life imitating art described earlier might be just the tip of the iceberg—particularly dramatic illustrations of a general trend. We have already encountered some of Phillips's research in chapter 3, during our discussion of so-called copycat suicides. Phillips has used similar techniques to look at homicides and other acts of violence. This research, because it examines real events, serves as a valuable addition to laboratory experiments on the antecedents of aggression. For example, in one study[50] Phillips investigated the effects of a special kind of media violence — publicized prizefights — on violent behavior. He chose prizefights in particular because this kind of violence is real, exciting, and for the most part accepted and rewarded. Furthermore, the participants in these sporting events are portrayed as intending to injure their victims.

The results of Phillips's study are sobering. In the days following publicized heavyweight championship prizefights, there was a significant increase in homicides in the United States. Moreover, the more publicity surrounding the fight, the greater the subsequent increase in homicides. What is more surprising is that the race of prizefight "losers" was related to the race of victims of murders after the fights. After white boxers lost fights, there was a corresponding increase in murders of white men, but not black men; conversely, after black boxers lost fights, there was an increase in murders of black men, but not white men.

Even a cursory look at the evidence suggests that it would be prudent for those in the entertainment industry to place some limits on the amount of violence (real or fictional) shown on television. Surely those individuals who produce, package, and distribute violence on television and in films are aware of a problem. What are they doing about it? Very little. Typically, they view themselves as merely responding to the needs and tastes of the public. For example, Samuel Arkoff, as board chairman of American International Pictures (one of our leading manufacturers of violent films), said: "Maybe the need to view violence will someday be reduced by watching pro football."[51] Unfortunately, the data indicate this need is being increased, not satiated by people like Mr. Arkoff. How responsible are these people? "The effects on society?" asks Joe Wizan, another producer of violent films. "I don't give it a thought. Psychiatrists don't have the answers, so why should I?"[52] And still more recently, after attending a conference on violence in the media in the summer of 1993, Ted Harbert, the president of the entertainment division of the American Broadcasting Company, said, "I have not seen any evidence that proves a causal link between TV violence and violence in society."[53]

In the face of the evidence, such attitudes would appear cynical in the extreme. It is reasonably clear that film producers believe that violent films bring people into the theaters and network executives believe that violence sells products. But, ironically, this may not be true. Edward Diener and Darlene DeFour[54] conducted an experiment in which college students were shown a televised adventure program ("Police Woman") and then asked how much they liked it. Some students saw an uncut (violent) version and others saw an edited (nonviolent) version. Both groups equally liked the program they watched—that is, the inclusion of violence did nothing to enhance the program's popularity. While this one experiment is hardly conclusive, it does suggest the possibility that film and television producers might be premature in leaping to the conclusion that Americans prefer violence to nonviolence.

The Media, Pornography, and Violence against Women.   A particularly troubling aspect of aggression in this country is the apparent increase in violence expressed by some men against women—especially in the form of rape. In 1990 approximately 103,000 women are known to have been raped in the United States. This is more than one rape every five minutes. According to the FBI, the number of reported rapes has quadrupled since the mid-1960s.[55] And the actual occurrences are almost certainly much higher since a great many rapes go unreported, particularly those involving "date rape," in which the victim is acquainted with the assailant.

Coincidental with the increase in rape during the past few decades is an increase in the availability of the depiction of vivid explicit sexual behavior in magazines and on film and videocassettes. For better or worse, in recent years, our society has become increasingly freer and more tolerant of pornography. If, as we've seen, the viewing of violence in films and on television contributes to violence, shouldn't it follow that viewing pornographic material would increase the incidence of rape? While this has been argued from both pulpit and lectern, it is much too simplistic an assumption. It should be understood that rape is primarily an act of violence, not of sensuousness. And, indeed, after studying the available evidence, the Commission on Obscenity and Pornography concluded that explicit sexual material, in and of itself, did not contribute to sexual crimes, violence against women, or other antisocial acts.

The key phrase in the preceding sentence is "in and of itself." One might ask if there are undesirable effects of materials that combine sex with violence. During the past several years, Neil Malamuth, Edward Donnerstein and their colleagues have conducted careful studies to determine the effects, if any, of violent pornography. Taken together, these studies indicate that exposure to violent pornography promotes greater acceptance of sexual violence toward women and is one factor associated with actual aggressive behavior toward women in naturalistic and laboratory settings.[56] In one experiment,[57] Donnerstein showed men one of three films—an aggressive-erotic one involving rape, a purely erotic one without aggression, or a neutral film that was neither aggressive nor erotic. After viewing one of these films, the men took part in a supposedly unrelated study that involved teaching either a male or female confederate some nonsense syllables. The men were instructed to administer electric shocks to the confederate when he or she gave incorrect answers; they were also allowed to choose whatever level of shock they wished to use. (Unbeknownst to the subjects, no shocks were actually delivered.) Those men who had earlier seen the rape film subsequently administered the most intense shocks—but only to the *female* confederate.

Similarly, Malamuth conducted an experiment[58] in which male college students viewed one of two erotic films. One version portrayed two mutually consenting adults engaged in lovemaking; the other version portrayed a rape incident. After viewing the film, the men were asked to engage in sexual fantasy. Those men who had watched the rape version of the film created more violent sexual fantasies than those who had watched the mutual-consent version. In another experiment,[59] Malamuth arranged for college students to watch either a violent-sexual feature-length film or a film with no violent or sexual acts. Several days later, the students filled out a

Sexual Attitude Survey. For the male students, exposure to the violent-sexual film increased their acceptance of interpersonal violence against women. In addition, these males came to believe certain myths about rape—for example, that women provoke rape and actually enjoy being raped. For the female students, there was a tendency for those who were exposed to the violent-sexual film to be less accepting of violence against women and less accepting of myths about rape.

I should elaborate on this myth. Pamela Foa, a philosopher and feminist, gives us a clue as to how this might have developed.

> Every American girl . . . is well acquainted with the slippery-slope argument by the time she is ten. She is told that if she permits herself to become involved in anything more than a peck on the cheek, anything but the most innocent type of sexual behavior, she will inevitably become involved in behavior that will result in intercourse and pregnancy. And such behavior is wrong. That is, she is told that if she acquiesces to any degree to her feelings, then she will be doing something immoral. Meanwhile, every American boy is instructed, whether explicitly or not, that the girls have been given this argument (as a weapon) and that therefore, since everything that a girl says will be a reflection of this argument (and not of her feelings), they are to ignore everything that she says.[60]

There is a sense in which all of us have been victimized by a society that has ambivalent and even hypocritical attitudes toward adolescent sexuality. Foa is writing of the present situation. Her analysis is highly consistent with the experiences of my own adolescence. When I was a teenager (in the late 1940s and early 1950s), adolescent women were socialized to pretend that they were not interested in sex and that they didn't enjoy sex. The notion fostered by the adult world was that "nice girls" shouldn't enjoy sex until after they were safely married. Adolescent men were forever trying to "take liberties," and adolescent women were forever trying to push their hands away. But, over the course of time, say by the fourth date, as acquaintance and intimacy increased, the norms of "respectability" would allow for a limited degree of sexual behavior. The fact is, for a combination of biological and cultural reasons, young women in our society were—and still are—forced into the role of "line-drawers" and "limit-setters." That is, it is the woman who is at risk of becoming pregnant, and it is the woman whose reputation might be damaged if she is considered promiscuous. But if a woman did become interested in a specific young man, she would allow greater intimacy over time. This sequence of increasing intimacy might have led some adolescent males to form the erroneous general belief that when women said "no," they often meant "maybe" or "later." Hollywood contributed to this belief and, in my opinion, magnified and generalized it. I wish I had a dollar for every film I've seen where the romantic hero takes the heroine in his arms and begins to kiss her. She fights him off—her hands push him away. But gradually she begins to succumb; the hands that were pushing him away begin to clasp him around the neck and slide sensuously through his hair. Her resistance yields to excitement, her excitement simmers into passion—all in the space of fifteen seconds! Such flimflam might create the illusion that women are conflicted about sexuality and *want* to be taken forcefully.

It would be a tragic mistake to construe this analysis as a justification for either persistent sexual advances on the part of men in our society or for the erroneous belief that, deep down, women want to be taken forcefully. Such a construal would constitute a crass example of blaming the victim. While such behavior and beliefs are unjustifiable, the analysis does help us to gain some much-needed insight into their sources. I should also point out that the belief in the rape myth is not limited to men. In a survey of university women, Malamuth and his colleagues found that, while not a single woman felt that she, personally, would derive any pleasure from being overpowered sexually, a substantial percentage believed that some other women might.[61] Again, exposure to aggressive pornography tends to increase the tendency of men to believe the rape myth. There is some evidence indicating that this myth is not necessarily part of a deep-seated belief system. For example, in one study, when college men were shown a pornographically aggressive film, their belief in the rape myth increased as predicted. But after the film, when they were provided with an explanation of the experimental procedure, they became *less* accepting of the rape myth than a control group that neither viewed the film nor received the explanation.[62]

This finding should not lull us into complacency, however, for research also suggests that a steady diet of violent pornography can lead to emotional desensitization and calloused attitudes regarding violence against women. Moreover, there is reason to believe that repeated exposure to R-rated "slasher" movies—which are extremely violent but less sexually explicit than pornographic films—may have more damaging effects than nonviolent X-rated movies. In a recent study,[63] Daniel Linz and his co-researchers found desensitization effects after exposing male subjects to as few as two "slasher" films, spaced two days apart. That is, when their reactions to the first and second films were compared, the men showed reduced emotional response to the violent content of the film and found the treatment of the women in the film less degrading. In addition, the researchers compared the effects of R-rated "slasher" movies, X-rated "soft porn" movies, and teen-sex movies on men's attitudes toward rape victims. Two days after watching the films, subjects participated in a sup- posedly unrelated study in which they viewed a reenactment of a rape trial and were asked to make judgments about the victim and defen- dant. Once again, the "slasher" films had a powerful and damaging impact on the attitudes of male viewers. Compared to subjects who watched the nonviolent pornography or teen-sex films, men exposed to the "slasher" films expressed less sympathy for the rape victim in the trial, as well as less empathy for rape victims in general. These findings suggest that our society's rating systems for movies are off- target and misleading: Sexually explicit but nonviolent films are given more restrictive "X" ratings, while the graphically violent "slasher" movies earn only an "R" rating—and thus are more widely seen— despite evidence of their negative impact.

To sum up, the combination of sex and violence—whether in pornographic films or R-rated "slasher" films—has effects remark- ably similar to those associated with other violence in the media: The level of aggression is increased, and in many instances, attitudes con- doning violence are strengthened. Viewing violence (pornographic or otherwise) does *not* serve a cathartic function but seems, rather, to stimulate aggressive behavior. These data raise complex policy issues involving censorship and First Amendment rights that extend be- yond the scope of this book. While I personally am opposed to the imposition of censorship, I would think that an impartial reading of the research would lead those decision makers within the media to exercise some prudent self-restraint.

Aggression to Attract Public Attention. After the 1992 riots in south central Los Angeles, the president of the United States indicated that he was deeply concerned and that he would provide federal aid and create jobs for the unemployed. Do you think he would have placed such a high priority on the jobless in that area if there had been no riot? In a complex and apathetic society like ours, aggressive behavior might be the most dramatic way for an oppressed minority to attract the attention of the powerful majority. No one can deny that, over the years, the effects of riots in Watts, Detroit, and south central Los Angeles served to alert a large number of decent but apathetic people to the plight of ethnic and racial minorities in the United States. No one can doubt that the bloodshed at the state prison at Attica, New York, has led to increased attempts at prison reform. Are such outcomes worth the dreadful price in human lives? I cannot answer that question. But, as a social psychologist, what I can say (again and again) is that violence almost never ends simply with a rectification of the conditions that brought it about. Violence breeds violence—not only in the simple sense of the victim striking back against his or her enemy, but also in the infinitely more complex and insidious sense of the attackers seeking to justify their violence by exaggerating the evil they see in their enemies and thereby increasing the probability they will attack again (and again, and again . . .).

There will never be a war to end all wars—quite the contrary: Bellicose behaviors strengthen bellicose attitudes, which increase the probability of bellicose behaviors. We must search for alternative solutions. A less aggressive form of instrumental behavior might serve to redress social ills without producing an irreconcilable cycle of conflict. Consider Gandhi's success against the British in India during the 1930s. Strikes, boycotts, and other forms of civil disobedience eventually led to the end of British rule, without fostering a rapid escalation of hatred between citizens of the two countries. Such nonviolent strategies as sit-ins and boycotts also have been used effectively by Martin Luther King, Cesar Chavez, and others to awaken our own nation to real grievances. Accordingly, I would echo Loren Eiseley's call for a gentler people, but I would add to that; I would also call for a people more tolerant of differences between one another—but not a people tolerant of injustice: a people who will love and trust one another, but who will yell, scream, strike, boycott, march, sit-in (and even vote!) to eliminate injustice and cruelty. Again, as we have seen in countless experiments, violence cannot be turned on and off like a faucet. Research has shown over and over again that the only solution is to find ways of reducing violence as we continue to reduce the injustice that produces the frustrations that frequently erupt in violent aggression.

Frustration and Aggression

Aggression can be prompted by any unpleasant or aversive situation, such as anger, pain, boredom, and the like. Of these aversive situations, the major instigator of aggression is *frustration*. Imagine the following situation: You must drive across town for an important job interview. On your way to the parking lot you realize you are a bit late for your appointment, so you break into a fast trot. When you find your car you notice, to your dismay, that you have a flat tire. "Okay, I'll be twenty minutes late—that's not too bad," you say as you take the jack and lug wrench out of the trunk. After much tugging and hauling, you remove the old tire, put on the spare tire, tighten the lugs—and, lo and behold, the spare tire also is flat! Seething with frustration, you trudge back to your dorm and enter your room. Your roommate sees you standing there, resume in hand, sweaty, dirty, and rumpled. Immediately sizing up the situation, he asks humorously, "How did the interview go?" Shouldn't he be prepared to duck?

If an individual is thwarted on the way to a goal, the resulting frustration will increase the probability of an aggressive response. This does not mean frustration *always* leads to aggression or that frustration is the *only* cause of aggression. There are other factors that will determine whether or not a frustrated individual will aggress—and there are other causes of aggression.

A clear picture of the relation between frustration and aggression emerges from a classic experiment by Roger Barker, Tamara Dembo, and Kurt Lewin.[64] These psychologists frustrated young children by showing them a roomful of very attractive toys, which were then kept out of reach. The children stood outside a wire screen looking at the toys, hoping to play with them—even expecting to play with them—but were unable to reach them. After a painfully long wait, the children were finally allowed to play with the toys. In this experiment, a separate group of children were allowed to play with the toys directly without first being frustrated. This second group of children played joyfully with the toys. But the frustrated group, when finally given access to the toys, were extremely destructive. They tended to smash the toys, throw them against the wall, step on them, and so forth. Thus, frustration can lead to aggression.

Several factors can accentuate this frustration. Suppose you were about to bite into a thick, juicy hamburger, and somebody snatched it away. This would be more likely to frustrate you—and lead to an aggressive response—than if someone stopped you on your way to McDonald's. An analogue of this was demonstrated in a field study by Mary Harris.[65] She had students cut in front of people waiting in line for tickets, outside of restaurants, or to check out of a grocery store; sometimes they cut in front of the second person in line, other times in front of the twelfth person. As we would expect, the responses of the people standing behind the intruder were much more aggressive when the student cut into the second place in line. Frustration is increased when a goal is near and your progress toward it is interrupted. When the interruption is unexpected or when it seems illegitimate, the frustration is increased still further, as an experiment by James Kulik and Roger Brown points out.[66] Subjects were told they could earn money by telephoning for donations to charity and obtaining pledges. Some of them were led to expect a high rate of contributions, being informed that previous calls had been successful almost two-thirds of the time; others were led to expect far less success. When the potential donor refused to contribute, as all of them did (the subjects were actually calling confederates of the experimenters), the callers with the high expectations exhibited more aggression, speaking more harshly and slamming down the phone with more force. The experimenters also varied the reasons the confederates gave for refusing to contribute, sometimes making them sound legitimate ("I can't afford to contribute") and sometimes having them sound arbitrary and illegitimate ("Charities are a waste of time and a rip-off"). The subjects who heard refusals that seemed unjustified displayed more aggression. As these experiments demonstrate, frustration is most pronounced when the goal is becoming palpable and drawing within reach, when expectations are high, and when it is blocked unjustifiably.

These factors help to point out the important distinction between frustration and deprivation. Children who simply don't have toys do not necessarily aggress. Rather, the earlier experiment indicates it was those children who had every reason to expect to play with the toys who experienced frustration when that expectancy was thwarted; this thwarting was what caused the children to behave destructively. In accord with this distinction, the psychiatrist Jerome Frank has pointed out that, in the 1960s, two of the most serious riots by U.S. blacks in history did not take place in the geographical areas of greatest poverty; rather, they took place in Watts and Detroit, where things were not nearly so bad for blacks as they were in some other sections of the country. The point is, things were bad, relative to what "Whitey" had. Revolutions usually are not started by people whose faces are in the mud. They are most frequently started by people who have recently lifted their faces out of the mud, looked around, and noticed that other people are doing better than they are and that the system is treating them unfairly. Thus, frustration is not simply the result of deprivation; it is the result of *relative* deprivation. Suppose, after graduating from high school, I choose not to pursue a higher education and you choose to be educated; ten years later, if you have a better job than I do, I may be unhappy with my job, but I will not experience frustration; I made a free choice and these are the reasonable consequences of my choice. But if we've both been educated, and you have a white-collar job and I (because I'm black, or a Chicano, or a woman) am handed a broom, I will feel frustrated; or, if you find it easy to get an education, but because I grew up in an impoverished ghetto, an education is denied me, I will also feel frustrated. This frustration will be exacerbated every time I turn on the television and see all those beautiful houses white people live in, and all those lovely appliances for sale to other people, and all that gracious living and leisure I cannot share. When you consider all the economic and social frustrations faced by minority groups in this affluent society, it is surprising there are so few riots. As Alexis de Tocqueville wrote more than 150 years ago, "Evils which are patiently endured when they seem inevitable, become intolerable once the idea of escape from them is suggested."[67] As long as there is hope that is unsatisfied, there will be frustrations that can result in aggression. Aggression can be reduced by satisfying that hope, or it can be minimized by eliminating it.

Hopeless people are apathetic people. The Ugandans, when they were under the tyrannical, repressive, and wantonly violent dictatorship of Idi Amin, dared not dream of improving conditions or rebelling against Amin's rule. The South African blacks, and to some extent, the blacks in the United States, did not revolt as long as they were prevented from hoping for anything better. Clearly, eliminating people's hope would be an undesirable means for reducing aggression. The saving grace of our nation is that—theoretically, at least—this is a land of promise. We teach our children, explicitly and implicitly, to hope, to expect, and to work to improve their lives. But unless this hope stands a reasonable chance of being fulfilled, turmoil will be inevitable.

Social Learning and Aggression

Although frustration and pain can be considered the major causes of aggression, there are many factors that can intervene either to induce aggressive behavior in a person who is suffering very little pain or frustration, or to inhibit an aggressive response in a person who is frustrated. These factors are the result of social learning. We have already seen how social learning can inhibit an aggressive response. Recall that, when the area of a monkey's brain that characteristically produces aggressive behavior is stimulated, the monkey will not aggress while in the presence of a monkey whom it has learned to fear.

Another qualification based upon social learning is the intention attributed to an agent of pain or frustration. One aspect of behavior that seems to distinguish human beings from other animals is our ability to take the intentions of others into account. Consider the following situations: (1) a considerate person accidentally steps on your toe; (2) a thoughtless person that you know doesn't care about you steps on your toe. Let us assume the amount of pressure and pain is exactly the same in both cases. My guess is the latter situation would evoke an aggressive response, but the former would produce little or no aggression. Thus, I am suggesting that frustration and pain do not inexorably produce aggression.

Indeed, the response can be modified—and one of the primary things that can modify aggression is the intention attributed to the frustrator. This phenomenon was demonstrated in an experiment by

Shabaz Mallick and Boyd McCandless[68] in which they frustrated third-grade schoolchildren by having another child's clumsiness prevent them from achieving a goal that would have resulted in a cash prize. Some of these children were subsequently provided with a reasonable and "unspiteful" explanation for the behavior of the child who fouled them up. Specifically, they were told he had been "sleepy and upset." The children in this condition directed much less aggression against the "thwarting" child than did children who were not given this explanation. Moreover, later research[69] using adult subjects indicates that we are less apt to retaliate against someone who has provoked our anger when we hear a good excuse for their behavior *before* it occurs, rather than after the fact.

On the other side of the coin, certain stimuli can evoke aggressive behavior on the part of individuals who do not appear to be frustrated. In the "Bobo" doll experiments, Bandura and his associates showed that seeing another person behave aggressively increased the children's tendency to act aggressively. It is important to note, however, that the children did not confine their behavior to mere imitation but invented new and creative forms of aggression. This indicates that the effect of a model generalizes—it is not simply a matter of the children doing exactly what adults are doing—which means children can be stimulated to perform a range of aggressive actions. Bandura and his co-workers also demonstrated that the outcome was important. If the aggressive models were rewarded for their aggressive behavior, the children who witnessed it were subsequently more aggressive than those who witnessed these models being punished for aggressing.

The tendency for frustration to provoke aggression will be strengthened when the experience of frustration is combined with exposure to violent stimuli. This was demonstrated in an experiment by Wendy Josephson.[70] In this study, boys in the second and third grades watched either a violent film involving S.W.A.T. killings or a high-action movie featuring motocross bicycle racing. After watching one of these shows, the children were put in a frustrating situation: Much to their disappointment, they learned that due to an equipment problem they would be unable to watch an exciting cartoon show they had been expecting to see. Finally, the now-frustrated children were organized into teams and played a game of floor hockey. Those children who had watched the violent show committed more aggressive acts than children who had been exposed to the nonviolent film.

Carrying this one step further, Leonard Berkowitz and his colleagues have shown that, if an individual is angered or frustrated, the mere mention of a word or name associated with the provocation will increase that person's level of aggression. In one experiment,[71] subjects were paired with another student (actually an accomplice of the experimenter) who was introduced either as a "college boxer" or as a "speech major." This accomplice provoked the subjects by shocking them; then, half of the angered subjects viewed a violent prizefighting scene from a movie while the others watched an exciting but nonaggressive film clip. When subsequently given the chance to shock the confederate, the subject who had seen the violent movie segment administered more and longer shocks, as we would expect from the preceding discussion. Interestingly, however, among the subjects who had seen the prizefighting film, those paired with "the boxer" delivered more shocks to that target than those paired with "the speech major." In a similar experiment,[72] the accomplice was introduced to some subjects as "*Kirk* Anderson" and to others as "*Bob* Anderson." Again, the subjects watched one of the two film segments, and those watching the boxing sequence delivered greater shocks. But among those watching the fight scene, which was taken from the then-popular movie *The Champion*, which starred actor Kirk Douglas, those subjects who had been introduced to "*Kirk* Anderson" administered more shocks than those paired with "*Bob* Anderson." Apparently, the description or the name of a person can act as a cue to increase the aggression directed against that target, even if it has nothing to do with what that person actually *did*.

Similarly, the mere presence of an object associated with aggression can also act as an aggressive cue. In another study,[73] college students were made angry: Some of them were made angry in a room in which a gun was left lying around (ostensibly from a previous experiment), and others in a room in which a neutral object (a badminton racket) was substituted for the gun. Subjects were then given the opportunity to administer some electric shocks to a fellow college student. Those individuals who had been made angry in the presence of the aggressive stimulus administered more electric shocks than did those made angry in the presence of the badminton racket. Again, certain cues associated with aggression act to increase a person's tendency to aggress. These studies point to an opposite conclusion from the slogan often seen on bumper stickers—"Guns don't kill people, people do." As Berkowitz puts it, "An angry person can pull the trigger of his gun if he wants to commit violence; but the trigger can also pull the finger or otherwise elicit aggressive reactions from him, if he is ready to aggress and does not have strong inhibitions against such behavior."[74]

One aspect of social learning that tends to *inhibit* aggression is the tendency most people feel toward taking responsibility for their actions. But what happens if this sense of responsibility is weakened? Philip Zimbardo[75] has demonstrated that persons who are anonymous and unidentifiable tend to act more aggressively than persons who are not anonymous. In Zimbardo's experiment, female students were required to shock another student (actually a confederate) as part of a "study of empathy." Some students were made "anonymous"; they were seated in a dimly lit room, dressed in loose-fitting robes and large hoods, and never referred to by name. Others were easily identifiable; their room was brightly lit, no robes or hoods were used, and each woman wore a name tag. As expected, those students who were anonymous administered longer and more severe shocks. Zimbardo suggests that anonymity induces "deindividuation," a state of lessened self-awareness, reduced concern over social evaluation, and weakened restraints against prohibited forms of behavior.

Because it was part of a controlled laboratory experiment, the kind of aggression displayed by subjects in Zimbardo's research pales in comparison with the wild, impulsive acts of violence typically associated with riots, gang rapes, and vigilante justice. Nevertheless, there is reason to believe that the same kind of deindividuation takes place outside the laboratory. Brian Mullen[76] analyzed newspaper reports of sixty lynchings perpetrated between 1899 and 1946 and found a powerful relationship between mob size and violence—the larger the mob, the more heinous the atrocities committed. Mullen's research suggests that when people are part of a crowd, they are "faceless," less self-aware, and less mindful of prohibitions against aggressive, destructive actions. They are therefore less likely to take responsibility for aggressive acts.

Toward the Reduction of Violence

So far, we have focused our discussion primarily on factors that serve to increase aggressive behavior. If we believe, however, the reduction of our propensity toward aggression is a worthwhile goal, how should we proceed? It is tempting to search for simple solutions. In the early 1970s, no less an expert than a former president of the American Psychological Association suggested that we develop an anticruelty drug to be fed to people (especially national leaders) as a way of reducing violence on a universal scale.[77] The quest for such a solution is understandable and even somewhat touching; but it is extremely unlikely that a drug could be developed that would reduce cruelty without completely tranquilizing the motivational systems of its users. Chemicals cannot make the fine distinction that psychological processes can. Gentle, peace-loving people (like Albert Einstein) who are also creative, courageous, and resourceful are produced by a subtle combination of physiological and psychological forces, of inherited capacities and learned values. It is difficult to conceive of a chemical that could perform as subtly. Moreover, chemical control of human behavior has the quality of an Orwellian nightmare. Whom could we trust to use such methods?

There are probably no simple and foolproof solutions. But let's speculate about some complex and less foolproof possibilities based upon what we've learned so far.

Pure Reason. I am certain we could construct a logical, reasonable set of arguments depicting the dangers of aggression and the misery produced (not only in victims but in aggressors) by aggressive acts. I'm even fairly certain we could convince most people that the arguments were sound; clearly, most people would agree war is hell and violence in the streets is undesirable. But such arguments probably would not significantly curtail aggressive behavior, no matter how sound, no matter how convincing. Even if convinced that aggression, in general, is undesirable, individuals will behave aggressively unless they firmly believe aggression is undesirable *for them.* As Aristotle observed more than two thousand years ago, many people cannot be persuaded by rational behavior: "For argument based on knowledge implies instruction, and there are people whom one cannot instruct."[78] Moreover, because the problem of the control of aggression is one that first occurs in early childhood—that is, at a time when the individual is too young to be reasoned with—logical arguments are of little value. For these reasons, social psychologists have searched for alternative techniques of persuasion. Many of these have been developed with young children in mind but are adaptable to adults as well.

Punishment.   To the average citizen, an obvious way of reducing aggression is to punish it. If one man robs, batters, or kills another, the simple solution is to put him in prison or, in extreme cases, to kill him. If a young girl aggresses against her parents, siblings, or peers, we can spank her, scream at her, remove her privileges, or make her feel guilty. The assumption here is that this punishment "will teach them a lesson," that they will "think twice" before they perform that activity again, and that the more severe the punishment, the better. But it is not that simple. Severe punishment has been shown to be effective temporarily, but unless used with extreme caution, it can have the opposite effect in the long run. Observations of parents and children in the real world have demonstrated time and again that parents who use severe punishment tend to produce children who are extremely aggressive or children who, as adults, favor violent means of obtaining personal and political ends.[79] This aggression usually takes place outside the home, where the child is distant from the punishing agent. But these naturalistic studies are inconclusive. They don't necessarily prove that punishment for aggression, in and of itself, produces aggressive children. Parents who resort to harsh punishment probably do a lot of other things as well—that is, they are probably harsh and aggressive people. Accordingly, it may be that the children are simply copying the aggressive behavior of their parents. Indeed, it has been shown that, if children are physically punished by an adult who has previously treated them in a warm and nurturant manner, they tend to comply with the adult's wishes when the adult is absent from the scene. On the other hand, children who are physically punished by an impersonal, cold adult are far less likely to comply with the adult's wishes once the adult has left the room. Thus, there is some reason to believe punishment can be useful if it is applied judiciously in the context of a warm relationship.

One other factor of great significance to the efficacy of punishment is its severity or restrictiveness. A severe or restrictive punishment can be extremely frustrating; because frustration is one of the primary causes of aggression, it would seem wise to avoid using frustrating tactics when trying to curb aggression. This point was demonstrated very nicely in a study by Robert Hamblin and his colleagues.[80] In this study, hyperactive boys were punished by their teacher by having privileges taken away from them. Specifically, the boys had earned some tokens exchangeable for a wide variety of fun things; but each time a boy aggressed, he was deprived of some of the tokens. During and after the application of this technique, the frequency of aggressive actions among these boys practically doubled. This was probably the result of an increase in frustration.

What about the prisons in our own country—institutions of punishment that are quite severe and restrictive? Though it may seem intuitively correct to think that putting a criminal in such a harsh environment would deter that person from committing crimes in the future, there is precious little evidence to support such an assumption.[81] In fact, as this analysis would predict, imprisonment may have the opposite effect. Determining its specific consequences is difficult, however; in most instances, it is impossible to isolate the effects of being incarcerated because too many other factors influence the person in that situation. Do former inmates wind up returning to prison simply because they are criminal types? In other words, are repeat offenders a select group of "hardened" criminals who would devote themselves to a life of crime no matter how severe the punishment? Are prisons oppressive and violent because prisoners are antisocial and immoral, and because guards are authoritarian and sadistic? While these possibilities usually are hard to test in the real world, two studies in particular provide evidence that prisons fail to deter crime among the inmates who are released and that their violent and dehumanizing nature is not merely due to the personalities of the prisoners and the guards. A Supreme Court decision provided the opportunity for the first study,[82] isolating the effects of imprisonment on recidivism. In 1963, after the *Gideon v. Wainwright* ruling that people could not be convicted of a felony without being provided with a lawyer, a number of the inmates in the Florida prisons were released before the end of their sentences. The only systematic difference between these prisoners and those remaining in jail was that the released prisoners had not previously been represented by counsel. Thus, researchers could compare two groups of convicts that were nearly identical—some had been prematurely released, and others had been punished and "rehabilitated" to the full extent of their sentences. In terms of recidivism, a startling difference emerged between the two groups: The prisoners who served their complete term were twice as likely to return to prison as those who were released early. Does this mean that harsh punishment does not reduce crime? Not necessarily. While this study does offer persuasive evidence that lengthy prison terms do not deter the future criminal behavior of released inmates, it does not completely rule out the possibility that the mere prospect of harsh punishment might curb the criminal tendencies of those who have never been convicted. It is certainly possible that the threat of punishment deters many would-be criminals from ever breaking the law in the first place.

Turning to the second question, are the problems of prisons due to the kind of *people* in prison, or are they caused by the nature of the *environment?* The Stanford Prison Experiment,[83] the dramatic and frightening effects of which are quoted at the end of chapter 1, points to the second conclusion. Philip Zimbardo and his associates created a simulated prison environment and filled it with *the most normal people they could select,* students who completed a battery of psychological tests and who were randomly assigned to the positions of prisoners and guards. Even with this careful selection process, placing these students in an authoritarian, oppressive *environment* resulted in the cruelty and dehumanization that Zimbardo described, causing the two-week experiment to be curtailed after just six days.

Further evidence along these lines indicates that, while severe punishment frequently results in compliance, it rarely produces internalization. In order to establish long-term nonaggressive behavior patterns, it is important to induce people, when they are still children, to internalize a set of values that denigrates aggressive behavior. In two separate experiments discussed more fully in chapter 5, both Merrill Carlsmith and I and Jonathan Freedman[84] demonstrated that, with young children, threats of mild punishment are far more effective than threats of severe punishment. Although these highly controlled experiments dealt only with toy preference in children, they strongly suggest that threats of mild (rather than severe) punishment would curb aggression in the same way.

Here's how it works. Suppose a mother threatens to punish her young son in order to induce him to refrain, momentarily, from aggressing against his little sister. If she is successful, her son will experience dissonance. The cognition "I like to wallop my little sister" is dissonant with the cognition "I am refraining from walloping my little sister." If he were severely threatened, he would have an abundantly good reason for refraining—he would be able to reduce dissonance by saying "The reason I'm not hitting my sister is that I'd get the daylights beaten out of me if I did—but I sure would like to." However, suppose his mother threatens to use a punishment that is mild rather than severe—a punishment just barely strong enough to get the child to stop his aggression. In this instance, when he asks himself why he's not hitting his infinitely hittable little sister at the moment, he can't use the threat as a way of reducing dissonance—that is, he can't easily convince himself he would be walloped if he hit his sister, simply because it's not true—yet he must justify the fact he's not hitting his sister. In other words, his external justification (in terms of the severity of the threat) is minimal; therefore, he must add his own justification in order to justify his restraint. He might, for example, convince himself that he no longer enjoys hitting his little sister. This would not only explain, justify, and make sensible his momentarily peaceful behavior, but more important, *it would decrease the probability of his hitting his little sister in the future.* In short, a counteraggressive value would have been internalized. He would have convinced *himself* that, for *him*, hitting someone is neither desirable nor fun.

Recently, this general notion has been applied with some success in the real world of the schoolyard. David Olweus,[85] working in the Norwegian school system, was able to sharply curtail the prevalence of bullying behavior by as much as 50 percent by training teachers and administrators to be vigilant to the problem and to take swift but moderate punitive action. Taken as a whole, this research indicates that children, who have not yet formed their values, are more apt to develop a distaste for aggression if the punishment for aggressive actions is both timely and not terribly severe.

Punishment of Aggressive Models.

A variation on the theme of punishment involves punishing someone else. Specifically, it has been argued that it might be possible to reduce aggression by presenting the child with the sight of an aggressive model who comes to a bad end. The implicit theory here is that individuals who are exposed to this sight will in effect be vicariously punished for their own aggression and accordingly will become less aggressive. It is probable that, in our nation's past, public hangings and floggings were arranged by people who held this theory. Does it work? Gross data from the real world do not support the theory. For example, according to the President's Commission on Law Enforcement,[86] the existence and use of the death penalty does not decrease the homicide rate. Moreover, on the level of casual data, the mass media frequently depict aggressive people as highly attractive even though they are eventually punished. This tends to induce individuals to identify with these violent characters.

The evidence from controlled experiments presents a more precise picture. Typically, in these experiments, children watch a film of an aggressive person who subsequently is either rewarded or punished for acting aggressively. Later, the children are given an opportunity to be aggressive under circumstances similar to the ones shown in the film. The consistent finding is that the children who watched the film in which the aggressive person was punished display significantly less aggressive behavior than the children who watched the film of the person being rewarded.[87] As mentioned previously, there is also some evidence to indicate that the kids who watched the aggressive film character being punished displayed less aggressive behavior than did children who watched an aggressive film character who was neither rewarded nor punished. On the other hand—and this is most crucial to our discussion—seeing a model being punished for aggression did not decrease the general level of aggression below that of a group of children who were never exposed to an aggressive model. In other words, the major thrust of the research seems to indicate that seeing an aggressor rewarded will increase aggressive behavior in a child and that seeing an aggressor punished will *not* increase the child's aggressive behavior, but it's not clear that seeing an aggressor punished will *decrease* the child's aggressive behavior. It might be just as effective not to expose the child to aggressive models at all. The implications of this research for the portrayal of violence in the mass media have already been discussed.

Rewarding Alternative Behavior Patterns. Another possibility that has been investigated is to ignore a child when he or she behaves aggressively and to reward the child for nonaggressive behavior. This strategy is based in part on the assumption that young children (and perhaps adults as well) frequently behave aggressively as a way of attracting attention. For them, being punished is preferable to being ignored. Paradoxically, then, punishing aggressive behavior may actually be interpreted as a reward—"Hey, look, gang! Mommy pays attention to me every time I slug my little brother. I think I'll do it again." This idea was tested in an experiment conducted at a nursery school by Paul Brown and Rogers Elliot.[88] The nursery-school teachers were instructed to ignore all aggressive behavior on the part of the kids. At the same time, the teachers were asked to be very attentive to the children and especially to give them a lot of attention when they were doing things incompatible with aggression—such as playing in a friendly manner, sharing toys, and cooperating with others. After a few weeks, there was a noticeable decline in aggressive behavior. In a more elaborate experiment, Joel Davitz[89] demonstrated that frustration need not necessarily result in aggression—rather, it *can* lead to constructive behavior, if such behavior has been made attractive and appealing by prior training. In this study, children were allowed to play in groups of four. Some of these groups were rewarded for constructive behavior, while others were rewarded for aggressive or competitive behavior. Then the kids were deliberately frustrated. This was accomplished by building up the expectation they would be shown a series of entertaining movies and be allowed to have fun. Indeed, the experimenters went so far as to begin to show a movie and to hand out candy bars to be eaten later. But then the frustration was administered. The experimenter abruptly terminated the movie at the point of highest interest and took the candy bars away. The children were then allowed to play freely. As you have learned, this is a setup for the occurrence of aggressive behavior. But those children who had been trained for constructive behavior displayed far more constructive activity and far less aggressive activity than those in the other group.

This research is encouraging indeed. Here I find it necessary to state my firm belief that it would be naive to expect many children in our society to spontaneously choose constructive rather than aggressive solutions to interpersonal conflicts and frustrating circumstances. The society at large presents us with all kinds of evidence to the effect that violent solutions to conflict and frustration are not only predominant but also valued. The John Wayne/Clint Eastwood/ Sylvester Stallone/Arnold Schwarznegger type hero has become a cultural icon. Explicitly or implicitly, whether in the guise of the avenging cowboy, the urban cop (Dirty Harry), the prizefighter (Rocky), Rambo, or the Terminator, these movie heroes demonstrate to young kids what is valued by society and what might be expected of them.

Needless to say, our exposure to violent solutions to problems is not confined to films and videos—these events dominate the nightly news as well. For example, as I am writing this chapter, the air waves are still reverberating in the aftermath of four of this decade's most famous jury trials as media events. One involved the brothers Menendez, who, claiming sexual abuse by their father, simply gunned down *both* their parents while the latter were peacefully watching television. Another involved a couple of out-of-control police officers who (under the watchful gaze of a videocamera) savagely beat a young man named Rodney King after apprehending him following a traffic violation. In still another videotaped incident, two young men who, feeling angry and frustrated by the initial acquittal of the police officers mentioned above, pulled an innocent truck driver (Reginald Denny) from the cab of his truck and smashed his head in with a brick. Finally, we have a young housewife, Lorena Bobbitt, who, alleging that her husband had been sexually abusive, solved her problem by simply cutting off his penis one night as he slept. Blessedly, this deed was not videotaped, but her trial was watched with fascination by a huge television audience.

Given the prevalence and widespread telecast of events like these, it should come as no surprise that children learn that adults often solve their conflicts by resorting to violence. Moreover, many children are not even aware that alternative solutions are feasible or appropriate. Accordingly, if we would prefer our children to grow up favoring nonviolent strategies, it would be a good idea to offer them specific training in these techniques as well as encouragement for engaging in them. There is no reason why such specific training cannot be accomplished both in the home and in school.

The Presence of Nonaggressive Models.   An important curb to aggressive behavior is the clear indication that such behavior is inappropriate. And the most effective indicator is *social*—that is, the presence of other people in the same circumstances who are restrained and relatively unaggressive. For example, in a study by Robert Baron and Richard Kepner,[90] subjects were insulted by an individual and then observed that individual receiving electric shocks at the hands of a third person. The third person delivered either intense electric shocks or very mild electric shocks. There also was a control group in which subjects did not observe a model administering shocks. Subjects were then given the opportunity to shock their tormentor. Those who had witnessed a person delivering intense shocks delivered more intense shocks than those in the control condition; those who had witnessed a person delivering mild shocks delivered milder shocks than those in the control condition. Does this paradigm seem familiar? The reader can readily see that the expression of aggressive behavior, like the expression of *any* behavior, can be viewed as an act of conformity. Specifically, in an ambiguous situation, people look to other people for a definition of what is appropriate. Recall that in chapter 2, I described the conditions under which you might belch at the dinner table of a Freedonian dignitary. Here I am suggesting that, if you and your friends are frustrated or made angry, and all around you people in your group are throwing snowballs at your tormentors, it will increase the probability you will throw snowballs; if they are merely talking forcefully, it will increase the probability you will talk forcefully; and, alas, if the people in your group are swinging clubs at the heads of their tormentors, it will increase the probability you will pick up a club and start swinging.

Building Empathy toward Others.   Picture the following scene: There is a long line of cars stopped at a traffic light at a busy intersection. The light turns green. The lead car hesitates for fifteen seconds. What happens? Of course, there is an eruption of horn-honking. Not simply a little toot designed to supply the lead car with the information that the light has changed, but prolonged and persistent blasting indicative of a frustrated group of people venting their annoyance on the hesitating driver. Indeed, in a controlled experiment, it was found that approximately 90 percent of the drivers of the second car tooted their horns in an aggressive manner. As part of the same experiment, a pedestrian crossed the street between the first and the second car *while the light was still red* and was out of the intersection by the time the light turned green. Still, almost 90 percent of the second cars tooted their horns when the light turned green. But suppose the pedestrian were on crutches? Apparently, seeing a person on crutches evoked an empathic response; the feeling of empathy overwhelmed the desire to be aggressive—the percentage of people honking their horns decreased dramatically.[91]

Empathy is an important phenomenon. Seymour Feshbach[92] notes that most people find it difficult to inflict pain purposely on another human being unless they can find some way of dehumanizing their victim. Thus, when our nation was fighting wars against Asians (Japan in the 1940s, Koreans in the 1950s, Vietnamese in the 1960s, our military personnel frequently referred to them as "gooks." We see this as a dehumanizing rationalization for acts of cruelty. It is easier to commit violent acts against a "gook" than it is to commit violent acts against a fellow human being. As I have noted time and again in this book, the rationalization Feshbach points out not only makes it possible for us to aggress against another person, but it also guarantees we will continue to aggress against that person. Recall the example of the schoolteacher living in Kent, Ohio, who, after the killing of four Kent State students by Ohio National Guardsmen, told author James Michener[93] that anyone who walks on the street barefoot deserves to die. This kind of statement is bizarre on the face of it; we begin to understand it only when we realize it was made by someone who had already succeeded in dehumanizing the victims of this tragedy.

We can deplore the process of dehumanization, but at the same time, an understanding of the process can help us to reverse it. Specifically, if it is true most individuals must dehumanize their victims in order to commit an extreme act of aggression, then, by building empathy among people, aggressive acts will become more difficult to commit. Indeed, Norma and Seymour Feshbach[94] have demonstrated a negative correlation between empathy and aggression in children: the more empathy a person has, the less he or she resorts to aggressive actions. More recently, Norma Feshbach developed a method of teaching empathy and successfully tested its effects on aggression.[95] Briefly, she taught primary-school children how to take the perspective of another. The children were trained to identify different emotions in people, they played the role of other people in various emotionally laden situations, and they explored (in a group) their own feelings. These "empathy training activities" led to significant decreases in aggressive behavior. Similarly, in a more recent experiment, Georgina Hammock and Deborah Richardson[96] demonstrated that empathy is an important buffer against committing acts of extreme aggression. Briefly, when they placed college students in a situation where they were instructed to deliver electric shocks to a fellow student, those who had learned to experience empathic concern for the feelings of others actually delivered less severe shocks than those who were less empathic.

There are a great many ways to foster empathy among people; some of these can be learned in elementary-school classrooms—without being specifically taught—but I am not quite ready to discuss them just yet. Before we get to that point, we must first take a look at the other side of the question—dehumanization, the kind of dehumanization that occurs in prejudice, the kind of dehumanization that not only hurts the victim but hurts the oppressor as well. Read the first paragraph of the next chapter and you'll see what I mean.

7
Prejudice

A white policeman yelled, "Hey boy! Come here!" Somewhat bothered, I retorted: "I'm no boy!" He then rushed at me, inflamed, and
stood towering over me, snorting, "What d'ja say, boy?" Quickly he
frisked me and demanded, "What's your name, boy?" Frightened, I
replied, "Dr. Poussaint, I'm a physician." He angrily chuckled and
hissed, "What's your first name, boy?" When I hesitated he assumed
a threatening stance and clenched his fists. As my heart palpitated, I
muttered in profound humiliation, "Alvin." He continued his psychological brutality, bellowing, "Alvin, the next time I call you, you
come right away, you hear? You hear?" I hesitated. "You hear me,
boy?"[1]

Hollywood would have had the hero lash out at his oppressor and
emerge victorious. But in the real world, Dr. Poussaint simply slunk
away, humiliated—or, in his own words, "psychologically castrated."
The feeling of helplessness and powerlessness that is the harvest of

the oppressed almost inevitably leads to a diminution of self-esteem that begins even in early childhood. Many years ago, Kenneth and Mamie Clark[2] demonstrated that black children, some of whom were only three years old, were already convinced being black was not a good thing—they rejected black dolls, feeling that white dolls were prettier and generally superior. This experiment suggests that educational facilities that are "separate but equal" are never equal because the separation itself implies to the minority children that they are being segregated because there is something wrong with them. Indeed, this experiment was specifically cited in the landmark Supreme Court decision (*Brown* v. *Board of Education*, 1954) that declared segregated schools to be unconstitutional.

This diminution of self-esteem is not limited to blacks; it affects other oppressed groups as well. In a study similar to the Clark and Clark experiment, Philip Goldberg[3] demonstrated that women have been taught to consider themselves the intellectual inferiors of men. In his experiment, Goldberg asked a number of female college students to read scholarly articles and to evaluate them in terms of their competence, style, and so on. For some students, specific articles were signed by male authors (for example, John T. McKay); and for others, the same articles were signed by female authors (for example, Joan T. McKay). The female students rated the articles much higher if they were "written" by a male author than if they were "written" by a female author. In other words, these women had "learned their place"—they regarded the output of other women as necessarily inferior to that of men, just as the black youngsters learned to regard black dolls as inferior to white dolls. This is the legacy of a prejudiced society.

In the Goldberg study, subjects' prejudice against members of their own gender led them to perceive the intellectual work of other women as inferior. The impact of prejudice on the oppressed group can, however, be far more insidious: It can move beyond the realm of perceptions into the domain of actual performance. Research suggests that the experience of prejudice can be so powerful that individuals who are merely *assigned* to a low-status, minority position on a temporary basis can suffer deficits in achievement on tasks requiring skill and concentration. In a study by John Jemmott and Elida Gonzalez,[4] for example, fourth graders were placed in groups of four, and each child was assigned to either a high-status or low-status position. The high-status children got to wear a big, fancy button emblazoned with the word *BOSS* and lots of flashy stars, while the low-status children wore small, unimpressive buttons with the word *Helper* written in tiny print. The composition of each four-person group was then arranged so that the child was either in a minority or majority position relative to others in their group. That is, in the minority-status conditions, the child was either a "Boss" in a group with three "Helpers," or was a "Helper" in a group of three "Bosses." Similarly, in the majority-status conditions, the child was either a "Boss" in a group with two other "Bosses" and one "Helper," or was a "Helper" in a group with two other "Helpers" and one "Boss." After engaging in a brief group activity, the children were given a series of ten anagrams, or scrambled-word problems, to solve on their own. Jemmott and Gonzalez found that children given the high-status "Boss" label outperformed children labeled as "Helpers." Moreover, the children assigned to the low-status, minority condition—that is, children who occupied the position of the lone "Helper" in a group of "Bosses"—performed, by a very wide margin, the poorest of all. These findings are especially illuminating, given that the manipulation of status and minority/majority position had no direct connection to the task at hand. The simple fact of being singled out and labeled as an "inferior" was, in and of itself, sufficiently damaging to impair the child's performance. It is also important to recall that the labeling process and its negative effects, were the product of transitory conditions generated in the experimental laboratory. As a result, these findings merely hint at the profound impact of prejudice on individuals who have endured a lifetime of negative labeling and other forms of unfair treatment.

The Clark and Clark experiment was conducted in the 1940s; the Goldberg experiment was conducted in the 1960s. Important changes have taken place in our society since then; indeed, more recent research has indicated that self-esteem among blacks and women may be on the rise.[5]

Such progress is encouraging. But this is not meant to imply that prejudice has ceased to be a serious problem. Prejudice still exists in countless ways. For the most part, it has gone underground and become less overt.[6] But occasionally, it is flagrant enough to capture national headlines. To take one example, in 1987, over twenty thousand marchers—including Coretta Scott King, widow of the late Rev.

Martin Luther King, Jr.—gathered in a small town in Forsyth County, Georgia.[7] They chose the nineteenth anniversary of King's assassination to protest a resurgence of racism there and elsewhere in the United States. The marchers, escorted by Georgia State Troopers and National Guardsmen, were met by an angry crowd of one thousand local residents, some of whom were white-robed Klansmen shouting, "Go home, niggers!" The march was marked by chanting, shouting, and rock throwing.

Several years later, the excessive force employed by several members of the Los Angeles Police Department against Rodney King, complete with its racist overtones, was documented on videotape and in the audiotape of the police report itself. Although these were particularly vivid incidents, they are not rare. Similar, albeit less dramatic, events occur frequently, and in all regions of our nation.

Yet, despite such incidents, few would deny that the situation *is* improving, however painfully and however slowly. Social psychologists have contributed greatly to our understanding of the psychological processes underlying prejudice and discrimination, and have even demonstrated some possible solutions, as we shall see.

Stereotypes and Prejudice

Social scientists have defined prejudice in a variety of ways. Technically, there are positive and negative prejudices; I can be prejudiced against modern artists or prejudiced in favor of modern artists. This means that, before I am introduced to Sam Smear (who I've been told is a modern artist), I will be inclined to like or dislike him—and I will be inclined to expect to see certain characteristics in him. Thus, if I associate the concept "modern artist" with effeminate behavior, I would be filled with shock and disbelief if Sam Smear were to swagger through the door looking for all the world like the middle linebacker for the Chicago Bears. If I associate the concept of "modern artist" with the radical end of the political spectrum, I would be astonished if Sam Smear were wearing a Ronald Reagan political button.

In this chapter, I will not be discussing situations that concern prejudice "in favor" of people; accordingly, my working definition of prejudice will be limited to negative attitudes. I will define prejudice as a hostile or negative attitude toward a distinguishable group based on generalizations derived from faulty or incomplete information. For example, when we say an individual is prejudiced against blacks, we mean he or she is oriented toward behaving with hostility toward blacks; the person feels that, with perhaps one or two exceptions, all blacks are pretty much the same. The characteristics he or she assigns to blacks are either totally inaccurate or, at best, based on a germ of truth the person zealously applies to the group as a whole.

In his classic book *The Nature of Prejudice,* Gordon Allport reported the following dialogue:

> Mr. X: The trouble with the Jews is that they only take care of their own group.
>
> Mr. Y: But the record of the Community Chest campaign shows that they gave more generously, in proportion to their numbers, to the general charities of the community, than did non-Jews.
>
> Mr. X: That shows they are always trying to buy favor and intrude into Christian affairs. They think of nothing but money; that is why there are so many Jewish bankers.
>
> Mr. Y: But a recent study shows that the percentage of Jews in the banking business is negligible, far smaller than the percentage of non-Jews.
>
> Mr. X: That's just it; they don't go in for respectable business; they are only in the movie business or run night clubs.[8]

This dialogue illustrates the insidious nature of prejudice far better than could a mountain of definitions. In effect, the prejudiced Mr. X is saying, "Don't trouble me with facts; my mind is made up." He makes no attempt to dispute the data as presented by Mr. Y. He either proceeds to distort the facts in order to make them support his hatred of Jews, or he bounces off them, undaunted, to a new area of attack. A deeply prejudiced person is virtually immune to information at variance with his or her cherished stereotypes. As famed jurist Oliver Wendell Holmes Junior once said, "Trying to educate a bigot is like shining light into the pupil of an eye—it constricts."

It is reasonably safe to assume that all of us have some degree of prejudice—whether it is against an ethnic, national, or racial group, against people with different sexual preferences, against specific geographical areas as places to live, or against certain kinds of food. Let's take food as an example: In this culture, most people do not eat insects. Suppose someone (like Mr. Y) were to tell you that caterpillars or earwigs were a great source of protein and, when carefully prepared, extremely tasty. Would you rush right home and fry up a batch? Probably not. Like Mr. X, you would probably find some other reason for your prejudice, such as the fact that most insects are ugly. After all, in this culture, we eat only aesthetically beautiful creatures—like lobsters!

Gordon Allport wrote his book in 1954; the dialogue between Mr. X and Mr. Y might seem somewhat dated to the modern reader. Do people really think that way? Is there anyone so simpleminded as to believe that old, inaccurate stereotype about Jewish bankers? Perhaps not. But some twenty years after Allport's dialogue, a similar statement was made—not by an ordinary citizen—but by the single most powerful military officer in the United States. General George S. Brown, chairman of the Joint Chiefs of Staff, in a public speech referring to "Jewish influence in Congress," said, ". . . it is so strong you wouldn't believe, now. . . . They own, you know, the banks in this country, the newspapers. Just look at where the Jewish money is."[9]

The kind of generalization of characteristics or motives to a group of people expressed by General Brown is called stereotyping. To stereotype is to assign identical characteristics to any person in a group, regardless of the actual variation among members of that group. Thus, to believe blacks have a natural sense of rhythm, or Jews are materialistic, is to assume that virtually all blacks are rhythmic, or that virtually all Jews go around collecting possessions. We learn to assign identical characteristics at a very young age. In one study,[10] fifth-grade and sixth-grade children were asked to rate their classmates in terms of a number of characteristics: popularity, leadership, fairness, and the like. The children of upper-class families were rated more positively than the children of lower-class families on every desirable quality. It seems the youngsters were unable to judge their classmates on an individual basis; instead, they had stereotyped them according to their social class.

As we have seen in chapter 4, stereotyping is not necessarily an intentional act of abuse; it is frequently merely a way we humans have of simplifying our view of the world, and we all do it. Most of us have a specific picture in mind when we hear the words "New York cab driver" or "Italian barber" or "high-school cheerleader." To the extent the stereotype is based on experience and is at all accurate, it can be an adaptive, shorthand way of dealing with complex events. On the other hand, if the stereotype blinds us to individual differences within a class of people, it is maladaptive and potentially dangerous.

For example, because of distortion in the media, most white people in our society associate black people with violent behavior. How might this stereotype lead to inequitable and oppressive actions against blacks? Charles Bond and his colleagues addressed this issue in a study comparing the treatment of black versus white patients in a psychiatric hospital run by an all-white staff.[11] In their research, they looked at the two most common methods staff members used to handle incidents of violent behavior by patients: secluding the individual in a "time-out" room, or restraining the individual in a straitjacket, followed by the administration of a sedative drug. An examination of hospital records over an eighty-five-day period revealed that the harsher method—physical restraint and sedation—was used against black patients nearly four times as often as against white patients, despite the fact that there was virtually no difference in the number of violent incidents committed by blacks and whites. Moreover, this discriminatory treatment occurred even though the black patients, on average, had been diagnosed as less violent than the white patients when they were first admitted to the hospital. Over time, however, the staff came to treat black and white patients equally, with the use of restraint against blacks declining dramatically after the first month of residence in the hospital. Evidently, prejudice against blacks as a group was in operation when black patients were relative newcomers to the hospital; then, as familiarity between white staff members and a particular black patient increased, prejudiced behavior against that individual diminished. Thus, this study suggests that the familiarity that comes with prolonged interracial contact can potentially reduce unfair stereotyping and pave the way for recognition of individual characteristics. But, as we shall see later in this chapter, contact between the races, in and of itself, is usually insufficient to break down well-entrenched stereotypes and bigotry.

To illustrate further the insidious effects of racial or ethnic stereotypes, consider the case of minority-group members who are convicted of crimes and sent to prison. When they come up for parole, will their racial or ethnic status outweigh other information—such as life circumstances or "good behavior" while in prison—used to make a parole decision? Research indicates that such a cognitive bias exists. Galen Bodenhausen and Robert Wyer[12] asked college students to read fictionalized files on prisoners who were up for parole, and to use information contained in the files to make a parole decision. Sometimes the crimes "fit" the offenders—for example, when a Latino, Carlos Ramirez, committed assault and battery, or when an upper-class Anglo-Saxon, Ashley Chamberlaine, committed embezzlement. In other instances, the crimes were inconsistent with the stereotypes. When prisoners' crimes were consistent with subjects' stereotypes, the students tended to ignore other relevant information—such as "good behavior" in prison—and were harsher in their recommendations for parole. Thus, when a person behaves in a way that conforms to our stereotypes, we tend to blind ourselves to information that would provide clues about why they *really* behaved as they did. Instead, we assume that it must be something about *them*, not their life circumstances, that caused their behaviors.*

How many of Bodenhausen and Wyer's subjects had ever been assaulted by a Latino, or lost money to an Anglo-Saxon embezzler? More than likely, not very many, for most stereotypes are not based upon valid experience, but are based on hearsay or images concocted by the mass media or are generated within our heads as ways of justifying our own prejudices and cruelty. Like the self-fulfilling prophecy discussed earlier in this book, it is helpful to think of blacks or Latinos as stupid or dangerous if it justifies depriving them of an education or denying them parole, and it is helpful to think of women as being biologically predisposed toward domestic drudgery if a male-dominated society wants to keep them tied to a vacuum cleaner. Likewise, it is useful to perceive individuals from the lower classes as being unambitious, less intelligent, and prone to criminal behavior if we want to pay them as little as possible for doing menial work or

---

* I hasten to add that these data are derived from college students in a hypothetical situation; accordingly, taken by themselves, they do not demonstrate that parole officers behave in the same way. It is likely that parole officers are more experienced and more sophisticated than the subjects in this experiment. What the experiment *does* demonstrate is a cognitive bias that exists even in intelligent and well-meaning people—and, unless we are vigilant, any of us might make the same kind of error.

keep them out of our neighborhoods. In such cases, stereotyping is, indeed, abusive. In recent years, President Clinton's attempt to remove the restrictions against homosexuals serving in the military was met with sturdy opposition. Ancient stereotypes were invoked as some military leaders and politicians predicted dire consequences and a lowering of morale if these citizens were allowed in uniform. The cosmic joke, of course, is that, over the years, thousands of gays and lesbians have been quietly and skillfully performing their patriotic duty in the armed forces without causing trouble.

The quality of the stereotype is not always insulting per se. But it should be clear that stereotyping is harmful to the target, even if the stereotype would seem to be neutral or even positive. For example, it is not necessarily negative to attribute "ambitiousness" to Jews, "a natural sense of rhythm" to blacks, or an "artistic temperament" to homosexuals.[13] But these generalizations are abusive, if only because they rob the person of the right to be perceived and treated as an individual with his or her own individual traits, be they positive or negative.

Moreover, in most cases, stereotyping is not benign—but is directly insulting and can have a debilitating effect on the members of the targeted group. Let us highlight one striking example: Claude Steele[14] notes a disturbing crisis in the educational welfare of African American students. Put simply, among college students, there is an academic performance gap between blacks and whites; moreover, the drop-out rate for blacks is nearly twice that of whites. While there are a great many possible historical and societal explanations for this phenomenon, Steele feels that these explanations fall short; they cannot account for the fact that the gap in school achievement between blacks and whites is as great for students with high preparation (as measured by earlier grades) as it is for those with low preparation. In other words, something seems to be happening that keeps even very bright and well-prepared black students from performing as well as white students with the same level of ability and preparation.

In researching this problem, Claude Steele and Joshua Aronson[15] reasoned that a major contributing factor might involve apprehensiveness among black students (in highly evaluative educational contexts) about confirming the existing negative stereotype of "intellectual inferiority." This extra burden of apprehensiveness, in turn, might actually interfere with their ability to perform on evaluative tasks like tests. In a remarkable experiment, Steele and Aronson administered a difficult verbal test (the GRE) individually to black and white Stanford University students. Half the students were led to believe that the investigator was interested in measuring their intellectual ability; the other half were led to believe that the investigator was merely testing the test—and that it had nothing to do with their actual ability.

The results were clear: White students performed equally well regardless of whether or not they believed the test was being used as a diagnostic tool. Black students who believed the test was nondiagnostic of their abilities performed as well as white students; in contrast, those who were led to believe that the test was measuring their abilities performed more poorly than white students. Such is the power of stereotypes.

Stereotypes and Attributions

Stereotyping is a special case of the phenomenon of attribution. As we saw in chapter 4, when an event occurs, there is a tendency among individuals to try to attribute a cause to that event. Specifically, if a person performs an action, observers will make inferences about what caused that behavior. For example, if the tight end on your favorite football team drops an easy pass, there are many possible explanations: Perhaps the sun got in his eyes; maybe he was distracted by worry over the ill health of his child; maybe he dropped the ball on purpose because he bet on the other team; maybe he "heard footsteps" and got scared; or perhaps he just happens to be an untalented player. Note that each of the above attributions about the cause of the tight end's bobble has a very different set of ramifications. You would feel differently about the athlete if he were worried about his child's illness than if he had bet on the other team.

As you know, this need to find a cause for another person's behavior is part of a human tendency to go beyond the information given. It is often functional. For example, suppose you have just moved into a strange town where you have no friends and you are feeling very lonely. There is a knock on the door—it is Joe, a neighbor, who shakes your hand and welcomes you to the neighborhood. You invite him in. He stays for about twenty minutes, during which time you and he have an interesting conversation. You feel really good about the possibility of having discovered a new friend. As he gets up to leave, he says, "Oh, by the way, if you ever need some insurance, I happen to be in the business and I'd be happy to discuss it with you," and he leaves his card. Is he your friend who happens to be selling insurance, or is he an insurance salesman who is pretending to be your friend in order to sell you insurance? It is important to know, because you must decide whether or not to pursue a relationship with him. To repeat, in making attributions, the individual must go beyond the information given. We do not know the reason why the tight end dropped the pass; we do not know Joe's motivation for friendly behavior. We are guessing. Thus, the attributor's causal interpretations may be accurate or erroneous, functional or dysfunctional.

In an ambiguous situation, people tend to make attributions consistent with their beliefs or prejudices. Thomas Pettigrew has dubbed this "the ultimate attribution error."[16] If Mr. Bigot sees a well-dressed, white Anglo-Saxon Protestant sitting on a park bench sunning himself at three o'clock on a Wednesday afternoon, he thinks nothing of it. If he sees a well-dressed black man doing the same thing, he is liable to leap to the conclusion the man is unemployed—and he becomes infuriated, because he assumes his own hard-earned money is being taxed to pay that shiftless, good-for-nothing enough in welfare subsidies to keep him in fancy clothes. If Mr. Bigot passes Mr. Anglo's house and notices a trash can is overturned and some garbage is strewn about, he is apt to conclude a stray dog has been searching for food. If he passes Mr. Garcia's house and notices the same thing, he is inclined to become annoyed and to assert that "those people live like pigs." Not only does prejudice influence his attributions and conclusions, his erroneous conclusions justify and intensify his negative feelings. Thus, the entire attribution process can spiral. Prejudice causes particular kinds of negative attributions or stereotypes that can, in turn, intensify the prejudice.[17]

Attributions and Gender Roles. This aspect of the attribution process has been demonstrated most clearly in research on gender roles. For example, let's look at a well-controlled experiment by Shirley Feldman-Summers and Sara Kiesler.[18] When confronted with the phenomenon of a highly successful female physician, male undergraduates perceived her as being less competent and having had an easier path toward success than a successful male physician. Female undergraduates saw things a little differently. They did not see either the male physician or the female physician as being less competent, but they saw the male as having had an easier time of it. Both males and females attributed higher motivation to the female physician. It should be noted that attributing a high degree of motivation to a woman can be one way of implying she has less actual skill than her male counterpart. This possibility comes into focus when we examine a similar study by Kay Deaux and Tim Emsweiler[19] in which they showed that, if the sexual stereotype is strong enough, even members of the stereotyped group tend to buy it. Specifically, male and female students were confronted with a highly successful performance on a complex task by a fellow student and were asked to account for it. When it was a man who succeeded, both male and female students attributed his achievement almost entirely to his ability; when it was a woman who succeeded, students of both genders thought luck played a larger role in her achievement than in the man's achievement.

Interestingly enough, the tendency for women to downplay the ability factor in a woman's success even applies to *self-attributions*. John Nicholls[20] found that, while fourth-grade boys attributed their own successful outcomes on a difficult intellectual task to their ability, girls tended to derogate their own successful performance. Moreover, he found that, while boys had learned to protect their egos by attributing their own failures to bad luck, girls took more of the blame for failures on themselves.

This phenomenon of self-attribution may have some interesting ramifications. Suppose a male tennis player loses the first set in a best-of-three-sets match by the score of 6 to 2. What does he conclude? Probably that he didn't try hard enough or that he was unlucky—after all, his opponent did have that incredible string of lucky shots. Now suppose a female tennis player loses the first set. What does she conclude? Given Nicholls's data, she might think she is not as skilled a player as her opponent—after all, she did lose 6 to 2. Here comes the interesting part: The attributions players make about their failure in the first set may, in part, determine their success in subsequent sets. That is, men may try harder to "come from behind" and win the next two sets and the match. However, women may "give up," thus losing the second set and the match. This is, in fact, what seems to happen. In a recent study,[21] the outcomes of 19,300 tennis matches were examined. In those matches where a player lost the first set, men were more likely than women to come back and win the second and third sets. Women were more likely to lose a match in straight sets. This phenomenon occurs even among professional tennis players—players who surely regard themselves as talented and able.

Marlene Turner and Anthony Pratkanis[22] carried the notion of self-attributions a step further by demonstrating that negative self-attributions generated by the manner in which women are selected for a job, can impede their actual performance on the job. Specifically, Turner and Pratkanis were interested in investigating some possible unfortunate side effects of affirmative-action programs. As you know, affirmative-action programs have been generally beneficial inasmuch as they create employment opportunities for talented women who had been previously overlooked when applying for these positions. Unfortunately, there can be a downside as well: Some of these programs have unintentionally stigmatized talented women by creating the illusion that they were selected primarily because of their gender rather than their talent. What effect does this have on the women involved? In a well-controlled experiment, Turner and Pratkanis led some women to believe that they were selected for a job because of their gender, while others were given a difficult test and were then told they were selected for that job on the basis of their meritorious performance on that test. Those women who were told they were selected because of their gender (and not their merit) derogated their own abilities. In addition, they tended to engage in self-handicapping behaviors; specifically, when the task required a great deal of effort, the women who believed they were preferentially selected simply did not try as hard as the women who believed they were selected on the basis of merit.

It should be clear that gender-related attributions—whether they are self-attributions or attributions made by others—can be harmful. Research by Kay Deaux and Janet Taynor[23] demonstrates that these attributions often serve as a double-edged sword; one that produces bias that can cut both ways: Men are expected to succeed, but if they fail, they are treated more harshly than women who fail. In their experiment, Deaux and Taynor had subjects listen to a taped interview with a college student who was a candidate for a prestigious scholarship. If the candidate did well in the interview and was male, he was rated as more competent than a female who had done just as well. However, if the male candidate did poorly in the interview, he was seen as far more incompetent than a female candidate who had done as poorly.

Putting all this research together, it appears that men are expected to succeed in our society and are treated harshly when they do not. Women are *not* expected to succeed—when they do succeed, they are seen by others (*and by themselves*) either as the rare person with an extraordinarily high degree of motivation or as simply lucky. When they fail, they are treated more leniently. Preferential treatment on the basis of gender or minority-group status may succeed in leveling the playing field, but unless it is done properly, it may have unwanted consequences inasmuch as it might lead the recipient of this treatment to unwittingly engage in self-handicapping strategies.

Blaming the Victim

It is not always easy for people who have never experienced prejudice to fully understand what it is like to be a target of prejudice. For relatively secure members of the dominant majority, empathy does not come easily. They may *sympathize* and wish that it weren't so, but frequently a hint of self-righteousness may nevertheless creep into their attitudes, producing a tendency to lay the blame on the victim. This may take the form of the "well-deserved reputation." It goes something like this: "If the Jews have been victimized throughout their history, they must have been doing *something* wrong." Or, "If she got raped, she *must* have been doing something provocative." Or, "If those people (African Americans, Latinos, Native Americans, homosexuals) don't *want* to get into trouble, why don't they just . . ." (stay out of the headlines, keep their mouths shut, don't go where they're not wanted, or whatever). Such a suggestion constitutes a demand that the outgroup conform to demands more stringent than those set for the majority.

Ironically, this tendency to blame victims for their victimization, attributing their predicaments to their own personalities and disabilities, is often motivated by a desire to see the world as a just place. As Melvin Lerner and his colleagues have shown,[24] people tend to assign personal responsibility for any inequitable outcome that is otherwise difficult to explain. For example, if two people work equally hard on the same task and, by a flip of a coin, one receives a sizable reward and the other receives nothing, observers show a strong tendency to rate the unlucky person as having worked less hard. Similarly, negative attitudes toward the poor—including blaming them for their own plight—are more prevalent among individuals who display a comparatively strong belief in a just world.[25] Apparently, we find it frightening to think about living in a world where people, through no fault of their own, can be deprived of what they deserve or need, be it equal pay for equal work or the basic necessities of life. By the same token, if six million Jews are exterminated for no apparent reason, it is somehow comforting to believe they might have done something to warrant such treatment.*

Further understanding of the phenomenon of victim-blaming comes from Baruch Fischhoff's work on the *hindsight bias*,[26] a phenomenon we discussed in chapters 1 and 4. As you may recall, research reveals that most of us are terrific Monday-morning quarterbacks: After we know the outcome of an event, the complex circumstances surrounding its occurrence suddenly seem crystal clear; it seems as if we knew it all along, and if asked to predict the outcome, we could have done so without difficulty. But this is an illusion.

In an interesting set of experiments, Ronnie Janoff-Bulman and her co-workers demonstrated the power of the hindsight bias in increasing subjects' beliefs that rape victims were responsible for their own victimization.[27] They had their subjects read accounts of a date between a man and a woman who had met earlier in a college class. The accounts were identical except for the concluding sentence, which for half the subjects read, "The next thing I knew, he raped me," but for the other half read, "The next thing I knew, he took me home." After being advised to disregard their knowledge of the *actual* outcome of the date, subjects were then asked to predict the like-

---

* The astute reader may have noticed that this is a milder form of our tendency to derogate a person *we* have victimized. In chapters 5 and 6, we saw that, when one person hurts another, the aggressor tends to derogate the target, turn the victim into a nonperson, and hurt that other person again. Now we see that, if one person notices another person has gotten the short end of the stick, he or she somehow feels the victim must have done something to deserve it.

lihood of several possible outcomes, including the one they had read. Even though the events leading up to the outcome were exactly the same in both versions of the story, subjects who read the rape outcome were more likely to predict that the rape would occur than those who read the "take home" outcome. What's more, subjects exposed to the rape scenario tended to blame the woman's behavior—such as letting the man kiss her—for the negative outcome of the date. The implications of these findings are unsettling. To understand and empathize with a victim's plight we must be able to reconstruct events leading up to the victimization from the *victim's* point of view. But as we have seen, it is all too easy to forget that —unlike us—victims did not have the benefit of hindsight to guide their behavior.

Prejudice and Science

Scientists are supposedly an objective, fair-minded lot. But even they can be influenced by the prevailing atmosphere. Louis Agassiz, one of the great U.S. biologists of the nineteenth century, argued that God had created blacks and whites as separate species.[28] In a similar vein, in 1925, Karl Pearson, a distinguished British scientist and mathematician, concluded his study of ethnic differences by stating: "Taken on the average and regarding both sexes, this alien Jewish population is somewhat inferior physically and mentally to the native [British] population."[29] On the basis of his findings, Pearson argued against allowing the immigration of East European Jews into Great Britain. Most contemporary scientists are now sophisticated enough to demand more valid arguments than those put forward by Agassiz and Pearson. For example, we are sophisticated enough to view most standard IQ tests as prejudiced instruments that unintentionally discriminate in favor of white, middle-class suburbanites by stating examples in terms and phrases more familiar to children reared in the suburbs than to children reared in the ghetto or on the farm. Thus, before we conclude that it was stupidity that caused a black person, a Latino, or the resident of a rural community to do poorly on an IQ test, we demand to know whether or not the IQ test was culture-free.

But such sophistication does not guarantee immunity. The traps that well-intentioned people can fall into in a prejudiced society can be very subtle. Let me offer a personal example involving sexism. In the first edition of this book, while discussing individual differences in persuasibility, I made the point that women seem to be more persuasible than men. This statement was based on a well-known experiment conducted in the late 1950s by Irving Janis and Peter Field.[30] A close inspection of this experiment, however, suggests it was weighted unintentionally against women in much the same way IQ tests are weighted against rural and ghetto residents. The topics of the persuasive arguments included civil defense, cancer research, von Hindenberg, and so on—topics the culture has trained men and boys to take a greater interest in than women and girls, even more so in the 1950s than today. Thus, the results may simply indicate that people are more persuasible on topics they don't care about or don't know about. Indeed, these speculations were confirmed by a more recent series of experiments by Frank Sistrunk and John McDavid.[31] In their studies, they used a variety of topics, some of typically greater interest to men and others applying more to the traditional interests and expertise of women. Their results were clear: While women were more persuasible on the masculine-oriented topics, men were more persuasible on the topics that traditionally have appealed to women. Of course, the mere fact women and men are raised not to be interested in certain topics is in and of itself an unfortunate consequence of sex discrimination.

In 1970, when I was writing the first edition of this book, I was unaware of the possible weakness in the experiment by Janis and Field until it was called to my attention (gently but firmly) by a friend who happens to be both a feminist and a social psychologist. The lesson to be gained from this example is a clear one: When we are reared in a prejudiced society, we often accept those prejudices uncritically. It is easy to believe women are gullible because that is the stereotype held by the society. Thus, we tend not to look at supporting scientific data critically, and without realizing it, we use the data as scientific support for our own prejudice.

Some Subtle Effects of Prejudice

The fact that we live in a society with racist and sexist overtones can have subtle but important effects on the behavior of the dominant majority, as well as the behavior of women and minority-group members. A good deal of this behavior occurs without awareness. In an important set of experiments, Carl Word and his associates[32] first trained white Princeton students to interview applicants for a job. Their observations revealed huge differences in the way interviewers interacted with black and white applicants: When the applicant was black, the interviewer unwittingly sat slightly farther away, made more speech errors, and terminated the interview 25 percent sooner than when the applicant was white. Do you suppose this had an effect on the performance of the job applicants? In a second experiment, Word and his colleagues trained their interviewers to treat white students in the same manner that the interviewers had treated either the white applicants or the black applicants in the previous experiment. The experimenters videotaped the students being interviewed. Independent judges rated those who had been treated like the black applicants as being more nervous and less effective than those treated like the white applicants. The results of this experiment lead us to suspect strongly that when women or minority-group members are being interviewed by a white Anglo-Saxon male, their performance may suffer, not because there is anything wrong with them but because, without necessarily intending it, the interviewer is likely to behave in a way that makes them uncomfortable.

Even if we never find ourselves in the position of the interviewers in the study above, we interact with people every day—men, women, young people, old people, blacks, whites, Asians, Latinos, homosexuals, and so on. And our preconceptions about what they're like often influence our behaviors in such a way as to elicit from them the very characteristics and behaviors we expected in the first place. I have referred to the phenomenon elsewhere as the self-fulfilling prophecy. For example, imagine that you and I had never met, but a mutual acquaintance had warned me that you were a cold, aloof, reserved person. When we finally meet, I would likely keep my distance and remain cool and aloof. Suppose that, in reality, you are generally warm and outgoing. My behavior would not afford you the opportunity to show me what a warm, outgoing person you really are. In response to my behavior, you would probably keep your distance from me, and my expectations that you're less than a warm, friendly person would have been confirmed.

This is but one of many situations in which "belief creates reality."[33] When we hold erroneous beliefs or stereotypes about other people, our responses to them often cause them to behave in ways that validate these erroneous beliefs. As sociologist Robert Merton wrote, this self-fulfilling prophecy generates and perpetuates a "reign of error."[34] If people hold stereotypes of women as passive and dependent, or of blacks as lazy and stupid, they may treat them as such and inadvertently create the very behaviors or characteristics associated with these stereotypes. "See," they say to themselves, "I was right all along about those people."

Of course, not all of us hold rigid stereotypes about members of other groups. We often embrace social beliefs only tentatively and work to determine whether or not they are accurate. Frequently we use social interactions to test our hypotheses about what other people are like. But there are pitfalls inherent in our hypothesis-testing strategies. That is, the strategies we use to test our hypotheses about other people can produce confirming evidence, even when the hypotheses themselves are incorrect. Recall (from chapter 4) the experiments by Mark Snyder and William Swann. In one of those experiments, when individuals were asked to test the hypothesis that a person might fit the profile of an extrovert, they chose "extroverted" questions (e.g., "What would you do if you wanted to liven things up at a party?"). When they were asked to test the hypothesis that the person might fit the profile of an introvert, they chose "introverted" questions (e.g., "What factors make it hard for you to really open up to people?"). As you know, Snyder and Swann[35] found that the nature of the question helps determine the response. That is, people who were neither particularly extroverted nor introverted will look extroverted when they answer the first type of question and will look introverted when they answer the second type of question.

Taken together, results of the above studies make it easy to understand why stereotypes are resistant to change. When we hold beliefs about others, the self-fulfilling prophecy ensures that we create a social reality in line with our expectations. And even when we're open-minded enough to test the accuracy of our beliefs, we often unknowingly use "testing" strategies that confirm those beliefs—even when the beliefs are erroneous.

Despite their best efforts to be open-minded, many otherwise decent people are still capable of subtle acts of prejudice. Indeed, many investigators[36] believe that indirect—and perhaps more insidious—forms of prejudice have largely replaced the blatant kinds of racial bigotry expressed by many white Americans in the past. Today, most people probably think of themselves as unprejudiced, even though they may continue to discriminate against minority-group members in less obvious ways.

The kind of subtle racism I'm describing is exactly what David Frey and Samuel Gaertner discovered when they looked at the helping behavior of whites toward a black individual. In their study,[37] they found that white subjects were just as willing to help a black student as a white student, but only when the person needing help had demonstrated sufficient effort. But, when led to believe that the student had not worked hard enough at the task, subjects were more likely to refuse a black student's request for help than a white student's. These findings suggest that subtle racism tends to emerge when it can be easily rationalized: It would be hard to justify refusing to help a minority person whose need for help stemmed from circumstances beyond his or her control—without feeling and looking like a bigot. But, when withholding help seems more reasonable —like when the person asking for help is "lazy"—people can continue to act in prejudiced ways while protecting an image of themselves as unprejudiced.

In a related experiment, Patricia Devine[38] demonstrated that all of us are aware of the commonly held stereotypes associated with minorities. When prejudiced people encounter a minority person, the common stereotypes enter their mind and, on some level, impacts the way they relate to that person. Devine found that, under ordinary circumstances, those of us who are relatively unprejudiced can exert conscious vigilance that serves to prevent these stereotypes from popping into our minds and affecting our beliefs and behavior. But she also found that, under extraordinary circumstances (situations in which conscious control is minimized), even those of us who are relatively unprejudiced slip into automatic and end up thinking or behaving in accord with the common stereotype.

Subtle Sexism and Gender–Role Socialization. Subtle forms of prejudice are also directed toward women. Daryl and Sandra Bem[39] suggest that prejudice against women in our society is an example of a nonconscious ideology—that is, a set of beliefs we accept implicitly but of which we are unaware because we cannot even conceive of alternative conceptions of the world. In this culture, for example, we are socialized in such a way that it becomes difficult for us to imagine a woman going out to work as a truck driver or a custodian while her husband stays home taking care of the kids, mending socks, and cleaning house. If we were to hear of such a situation, many of us would leap to the conclusion that something was wrong with that couple. Why? Because such an arrangement is not held to be a real option in our society. Much as a fish is unaware its environment is wet, we don't even notice the existence of this ideology because it is so totally prevalent.

Recall the example in chapter 1 in which little Mary received a Suzie Homemaker set ("complete with her own little oven") for her ninth birthday. By the time she reached nine, she had been conditioned to know that her place was in the kitchen. This conditioning was so thorough that her father was convinced that "housewifery" was genetic in origin. This is no mere fantasy. Even the first picture books very young children read tend to transmit these role stereotypes.[40] Indeed, studies by Ruth Hartley[41] indicate that, by age five, children have already developed clearly defined notions of what constitutes appropriate behavior for women and men. This nonconscious ideology can have important consequences for society. For example, Jean Lipman-Blumen[42] reports that the vast majority of women who, in early childhood, acquired a traditional view of their gender role (that is, "a woman's place is in the home") opted not to seek advanced education; on the other hand, those women who had acquired a more egalitarian view of gender roles showed a much stronger tendency to aspire to advanced education.

Current trends in the direction of raising women's consciousness are proving to be beneficial to women. Extrapolating from Lipman-Blumen's findings, my guess is that, as traditional gender-role stereotypes continue to crumble, there will be an increase in the number of women who seek advanced education. In fact, this is already beginning to happen: For the first time, women undergraduates outnumbered men on the nation's college campuses during the 1979–80 academic year. The elevation of women's consciousness also is proving beneficial to men. As women widen their interests and enter new occupations, the role prescriptions for men are becoming less restrictive. On a more personal level, the earlier example of my own unconscious chauvinism is instructive. To the extent my friends are able to help me see my own blind spots, they help me to become a better scientist and a less biased person.

Let us broaden this example. In recent years, our society has become increasingly aware of the discrimination and stereotyping that occurs as a result of differential gender roles. The notion of gender roles, or roles appropriate to one's biological sexual identity, is useful in understanding the pressures society places on both men and women. Generally, males are expected to be the breadwinners, the initiators, and the aggressors, all the while hiding their softer emotions and their vulnerabilities. Traditionally, femininity has consistently been correlated with high anxiety, low self-esteem, and low social acceptance.[43] Women are seen as warmer and more expressive but less competent and decisive.[44] The female role has been centered around the home, children, and marriage, with limited access to higher status or more differentiated jobs.

This gender-role stereotyping has serious consequences. In an interesting experiment, Natalie Porter and Florence Geis[45] showed that, compared to their male counterparts, even female graduate students were not given much credit for intellectual leadership. College students were shown a picture of either a group of men or a group of women sitting around a table. The picture was described as a group of graduate students working on a research project. They were asked to guess which member contributed most to the group. Their strong tendency was to choose the person sitting at the head of the table. In another condition, college students were shown a picture of a mixed-gender group (two men and three women) sitting around a table. When a man was at the head of the table, the subjects overwhelmingly named him as the greatest contributor. When a woman was pictured at the head of the table, she was hardly chosen at all. Indeed, each of the men in the picture received more "votes" than all three of the women combined. The results of this experiment provide an excellent example of what is meant by a nonconscious ideology inasmuch as the results were similar for male and female subjects; moreover, the women were severely underchosen by feminists as well as nonfeminists.

The experiment by Porter and Geis indicates that the perpetrators of discriminatory behavior against women are not always men; it is far more common among women than we realize. Moreover, in a recent experiment, Robert S. Baron, Mary Burgess, and C.F. Kao[46] showed that such displays of sexism by women against women often go undetected. In their experiment, male and female subjects read a series of twelve vignettes that described a person behaving in a sexist manner against women. When the person taking the sexist actions was female, both male and female subjects were less likely to label the actions as sexist, and they saw the behavior as less extreme and less intense than if the perpetrator was male.

The gender-role socialization process has led many people to regard the roles of females and males as characteristically rigid and limiting. Researchers in this domain find such traditional labeling antithetical to a rich and full growth process. For example, Sandra Bem advocates that people reduce this gender-role stereotyping by becoming more "androgynous": According to Bem, both men and women "should be encouraged to be both instrumental and expressive, both assertive and yielding, both masculine and feminine—depending upon the situational appropriateness of these various behaviors."[47] To illustrate, when asking for a pay raise, assertiveness is an adaptive, desirable action—for men and women alike. Behaving in a coy, passive, or timid manner probably will not get you your raise. When reconciling after an argument, however, yielding is an adaptive, desirable action—for men and women. Assertiveness may serve to increase the tension.

But the road to androgynous behavior is not an easy one. Women, like the members of many minorities, are often rewarded for actions tending to support the prevailing cultural stereotype—that they are inferior, passive, and dependent. Consequently, the self-fulfilling prophecy is in effect: If a woman were to attempt to view herself as different from the socially accepted norm, she would probably experience some discomfort because her behavior would be discrepant from the self-concept she had been developing since childhood. For example, as mentioned earlier, if a male truck driver and a housewife were to change roles, much dissonance would be aroused, especially when interacting with their peers. In this manner, a socially conditioned stereotype tends to be perpetuated. If a woman attempts to deviate too much from her rigid gender role by being assertive or by seeking an unconventional job, she is risking the loss of friendships and may be evoking even more prejudiced feelings in others. Accordingly, if individuals need to compare themselves to similar others, stepping out of an accepted role is less likely to occur.

There is, however, good reason to believe that popular conceptions of appropriate behavior for men and women are becoming more flexible. Linda Jackson and Thomas Cash[48] found that men and women described as androgynous were actually perceived as *more* likable and better adjusted than those who acted only in ways consistent with traditional gender roles. But here's the catch: When women behaved in a stereotypically masculine manner—to the exclusion of traditionally feminine behavior—they were liked least of all. Similarly, when men behaved only in stereotypically feminine ways, they were considered less well-adjusted than women who engaged in exactly the same behaviors. The lesson here seems to be that it may be acceptable for individuals to engage in cross-gender behavior as long as they are careful to balance it with behaviors considered appropriate for their own sex. To return to our example, the idea of a woman being a truck driver would probably raise fewer eyebrows if she were also a superb cook, seamstress, or ballet dancer. Likewise, a man who chooses to stay home and care for the children might meet with greater social approval if he were also an ace fisherman or handy with a wrench.

Gender-role socialization has many consequences. In a series of experiments in the late 1960s and early 1970s, Matina Horner[49] found that women actually *fear* success, especially when it seems inappropriate to the expectations of their role. In her studies, when female undergraduates were asked to write a story about "Anne, who finds herself at the top of her medical school class," the women were likely to describe Anne's future as an unhappy one, with the character either trying to minimize her own achievement or suffering negative consequences as a result of her success. Interestingly enough, more recent experiments[50] have demonstrated that the same thing happens to men if they experience success in a nontraditional setting. Specifically, men who were told that "John" was at the top of his *nursing* school class anticipated more negative consequences than did women who were told that "Anne" was at the top of her nursing school class. Thus, the "fear-of-success" phenomenon is similar to the "persuasibility" phenomenon; both men and women exhibit behaviors symptomatic of this effect—when and how depends on the situation.

I think two important lessons can be learned here. First, although there may be some differences between the behavior of men and women, many of these differences can be traced to the different situations in which men and women find themselves. That is, women initially may seem more persuasible or afraid of success because they are being evaluated according to the rules of a man's game. Lo and behold, when men are evaluated according to women's rules, they seem more persuasible, afraid of success, or whatever. Moreover, even when men and women behave identically, they are very often judged by different standards. For example, as we saw earlier, when a woman succeeds, her success is usually attributed to hard work or luck, while a man's success is attributed to ability. Likewise, when men fail they are judged more harshly than women, even when their behavior is exactly the same. Thus, before we conclude that one sex is inferior to the other, we must carefully examine the context within which the behavior occurs and whether a double standard is being imposed when the behaviors of men and women are evaluated. Remember Aronson's first law: People who do crazy things are not necessarily crazy. Likewise, people who do "inferior" things are not necessarily inferior.

The second lesson has to do with the realization that all of us—men, women, boys, girls, blacks, Latinos, Asians, whites, rich, poor, homosexuals, heterosexuals—all of us are the victims of confining stereotyped roles. It would be naive to miss the obvious fact that some roles are more restricting and debilitating than others. However, it would also be foolish to fail to realize that one group's effort to free itself from the chains of prejudice indirectly benefits all of us. As we learn to accept another person's out-of-role behavior, so too will our own out-of-role behavior become increasingly accepted—and we will become freer to fulfill our potential as human beings.

Prejudice and the Media

The media play an important institutional role in sustaining prejudice. Not too long ago, newspapers tended to identify the race of a nonwhite criminal or suspect but never bothered to mention the wrongdoer's race if he or she happened to be white. This undoubtedly contributed to a distorted picture of the amount of crime committed by nonwhites. And, until the early 1970s, it was rare to see a black face on television in a nonstereotypic role or in a commercial. When African Americans were limited to roles like the characters in "Amos 'n Andy" or the song-and-dance man on a variety show, the stereotype that blacks are stupid, shiftless, lazy, and have a natural sense of rhythm was potently reinforced.

During the past twenty years, this situation has changed—but how much? Given the tremendous popularity enjoyed by the ground-breaking *Bill Cosby Show* in the 1980s, and the ubiquitous, graceful presence of former basketball-great Michael Jordan endorsing a variety of products from sneakers to soft drinks, it is tempting to assume that the changes have been dramatic. But, although African Americans *have* appeared with greater frequency in the media in recent years, blacks tend to be concentrated in virtually all-black shows or are featured as "token" characters in otherwise all-white shows. Let's look at prime-time dramas—the bellwether of American television fare. As I mentioned in chapter 3, George Gerbner,[51] a distinguished scholar, conducts a yearly exhaustive survey of the media. According to Gerbner, during the past ten years the percentage of African Americans appearing in prime-time dramas has fluctuated between 6 percent and 16 percent, with no clear upward trend during that period.

The situation is even more extreme in other forms of communication and entertainment. Let's look at something simple and common—like the humorous cartoon. A few years ago, one of my students, Ruth Thibodeau,[52] performed a thorough analysis of all of the cartoons appearing in *The New Yorker* magazine between 1946 and 1987. She found that the appearance of African American characters was extremely rare. Moreover, in the early years of her study (the 1940s and 1950s), every time an African American appeared in a cartoon, he or she was presented in a highly stereotypical role. Accordingly, the frequency of African American characters actually *decreased* over the years as it became less acceptable to depict racial minorities in a stereotypical manner. Thibodeau was startled to find that, in the entire forty-two-year period, only a single African American appeared as a central character in a cartoon in which race was completely irrelevant. That's once in 35,874 cartoons! Thibodeau concluded that, in cartoons, a black person is simply not depicted as a representative of an ordinary citizen.

Going back to prime-time television, the overall picture for other recognizable minorities is even bleaker. Gerbner found that, in 1992, slightly more than 1 percent of the characters in prime-time dramas were Latino and less than 1 percent were were either Asian or Native

American. The presence of gays and lesbians is extremely rare—and when they do appear, it is most frequently in stereotypic roles. This is not inconsequential; for most of us, television provides an important source of information about the world. Accordingly, the infrequent and unrealistic portrayal of racial or sexual minorities is misleading and almost certainly harmful because it promotes the illusion that these are inconsequential members of our society—people who don't experience real adventures, ordinary problems, or human emotions. Moreover, the dearth of positive role models in the media undoubtedly fosters feelings of inferiority and estrangement among minority-group members—especially children.

Similar problems affect the portrayal of women. When the media displays women in prime-time television dramas, advertisements, or children's books, they are rarely portrayed as authority figures, intellectuals, or adventurous people. Instead, they are typically viewed as attractive but simpleminded "girls" who worry excessively about which laundry detergent to use and who depend on men for guidance on important issues. According to George Gerbner's analysis, in prime-time dramas, male characters outnumber women by about two to one, and women are more often than men portrayed as victims of violent crime. Similarly, a content analysis of award-winning children's picture books found that, although the number of female pictures and characters had increased in recent years, the portrayals and characterizations of women had not improved over that same time span. Female characters were overwhelmingly depicted as dependent and passive, as working in the home or not working at all, and as preferring indoor activities.[53] Newspaper comic strips also perpetuate gender stereotypes. An analysis of fourteen widely syndicated comic strips—such as "Peanuts," "Spiderman," and "The Wizard of Id"—published over a thirty-day period revealed that women were represented as main characters only 15 percent of the time.[54] In addition, only 4 percent of female characters were shown in working roles, even though roughly 69 percent of women in the United States are actually employed outside of the home.

What are the implications of widespread stereotyping of women in the media? On a subtle level, we tend to believe or accept things we see with great frequency—unless there are powerful reasons against doing so. Moreover, it is very difficult for us to account for what is *not* represented. Thus, if we hardly ever see women in powerful roles, it is easy to conclude that they are incapable of using power effectively or that they prefer the laundry room to the boardroom.

Let's take this a step further. When internalized, such stereotypes may have debilitating effects on women's perceptions of their own life possibilities. Florence Geis and her colleagues suggest that traditional portrayals of women in television commercials provide implicit "scripts" for women's behavior that may inhibit their achievement aspirations. In one study,[55] these researchers showed some subjects stereotyped commercials with women portrayed as sex objects or subservient homemakers catering to the needs of men. Other subjects saw commercials in which the roles were reversed: with, for example, a husband proudly serving a delicious meal to his wife who has just come home after a hard day's work. When asked to imagine their lives "ten years from now," female subjects who saw commercials depicting women as subservient homemakers and sex objects were more likely to de-emphasize careers and other achievement themes. Viewing stereotyped commercials did not simply depress women's aspirations temporarily during the experiment. On the contrary, female control subjects who saw no commercials at all expressed the same low level of achievement aspiration as women exposed to the traditional commercials. Women who saw role-reversed commercials, however, aspired to the same high level of achievement as male subjects. Interestingly enough, the aspirations of male subjects were unaffected by either traditional or nontraditional commercials. These findings suggest that sex-stereotyped commercials reflect a cultural image of women as second-class citizens and that a steady diet of such commercials serves to restrict women's conceptions of goals available to them. Moreover, repeated exposure to nonsexist alternatives would presumably enhance women's expectations for achievement and career success.

Causes of Prejudice

As we have seen, one determinant of prejudice in a person is a need for self-justification. In the last two chapters, for example, we have seen that, if we have done something cruel to a person or a group of people, we derogate that person or group in order to justify our cruelty. If we can convince ourselves that a group is unworthy, subhuman, stupid, or immoral, it helps us to keep from feeling immoral if we enslave members of that group, deprive them of a decent education, or murder them. We can then continue to go to church and to feel like good Christians, because it isn't a fellow human we've hurt. Indeed, if we're skillful enough, we can even convince ourselves that the barbaric slaying of old men, women, and children is a Christian virtue—as the crusaders did when, on the way to the holy land, they butchered European Jews in the name of the Prince of Peace. Again, as we have seen, this form of self-justification serves to intensify subsequent brutality.

Of course, there are other human needs in addition to self-justification. For example, there are status and power needs. Thus, an individual who is low on the socioeconomic hierarchy may need the presence of a downtrodden minority group in order to be able to feel superior to somebody. Several studies indicate that a good predictor of prejudice is whether or not a person's social status is low or declining. For example, Jennifer Crocker and her colleagues[56] found that college women who belonged to low-status sororities expressed more prejudice and disparagement of other sororities than members of higher-status sororities did. Similarly, when researchers have investigated the prejudice of whites against blacks[57] or of Gentiles against Jews,[58] they have found that those whose social status is low or declining are apt to be more prejudiced than those whose social status is high or rising. Moreover, it has been found that white people who are at or near the bottom in terms of education, income, and occupation not only are the highest in their dislike of blacks but also were most likely to resort to violence in order to prevent the desegregation of schools.[59]

These findings raise some interesting questions. Are people of low socioeconomic and educational status more prejudiced because (1) they need someone to feel superior to, (2) they most keenly feel competition for jobs from minority-group members, (3) they are more frustrated than most people and therefore more aggressive, or (4) their lack of education increases the probability of their taking a simplistic stereotypical view of the world? It is difficult to disentangle these variables, but it appears that each of these phenomena contributes to prejudice. Indeed, there is no single cause of prejudice. Prejudice is determined by a great many factors. Let's look at some of these major determinants.

In this chapter, we will look at four basic causes of prejudice: (1) economic and political competition or conflict, (2) displaced aggression, (3) personality needs, and (4) conformity to existing social norms. These four causes are not mutually exclusive—indeed, they may all operate at once—but it would be helpful to determine how important each cause is, because any action we are apt to recommend in an attempt to reduce prejudice will depend on what we believe to be the major cause of prejudice. Thus, for example, if I believe bigotry is deeply ingrained in the human personality, I might throw my hands up in despair and conclude that, in the absence of deep psychotherapy, the majority of prejudiced people will always be prejudiced. This would lead me to scoff at attempts to reduce prejudice by reducing competitiveness or by attempting to counteract the pressures of conformity.

Economic and Political Competition.   Prejudice can be considered to be the result of economic and political forces. According to this view, given that resources are limited, the dominant group might attempt to exploit or derogate a minority group in order to gain some material advantage. Prejudiced attitudes tend to increase when times are tense and there is conflict over mutually exclusive goals. This is true whether the goals are economic, political, or ideological. Thus, prejudice has existed between Anglo and Mexican American migrant workers as a function of a limited number of jobs, between Arabs and Israelis over disputed territory, and between Northerners and Southerners over the abolition of slavery. The economic advantages of discrimination are all too clear when one looks at the success certain craft unions have had, over the years, in denying membership to women and members of ethnic minorities, thus keeping them out of the relatively high-paying occupations the unions control. For example, the decade between the mid-1950s and the mid-1960s was one of great political and legal advancement for the civil rights movement. Yet in 1966 only 2.7 percent of union-controlled apprenticeships were filled with black workers—an increase of only 1 percent over the preceding ten years. Moreover, in the mid-1960s, the U.S. Department of Labor surveyed four major cities in search of minority-group members serving as apprentices among union plumbers, steamfitters, sheetmetal workers, stone masons, lathers, painters, glaziers, and operating engineers. In the four cities, they failed to find a single African American thus employed. Clearly, prejudice pays off for some people.[60] While the 1970s and 1980s have produced significant changes in many of these statistics, they also show that the situation remains far from equitable for minority groups.

Discrimination, prejudice, and negative stereotyping increase sharply as competition for scarce jobs increases. In one of his classic early studies of prejudice in a small industrial town, John Dollard documented the fact that, although there was initially no discernible prejudice against Germans in the town, it came about as jobs became scarce:

> Local whites largely drawn from the surrounding farms manifested considerable direct aggression toward the newcomers. Scornful and derogatory opinions were expressed about these Germans, and the native whites had a satisfying sense of superiority toward them. . . . The chief element in the permission to be aggressive against the Germans was rivalry for jobs and status in the local woodenware plants. The native whites felt definitely crowded for their jobs by the entering German groups and in case of bad times had a chance to blame the Germans who by their presence provided more competitors for the scarcer jobs. There seemed to be no traditional pattern of prejudice against Germans unless the skeletal suspicion against all outgroupers (always present) can be invoked in its place.[61]

Similarly, the prejudice, violence, and negative stereotyping directed against Chinese immigrants in the United States fluctuated wildly throughout the nineteenth century—spurred largely by changes in economic competition. For example, when the Chinese were attempting to mine gold in California, they were described as "depraved and vicious . . . gross gluttons . . . bloodthirsty and inhuman."[62] However, just a decade later, when they were willing to accept dangerous and arduous work building the transcontinental railroad—work that Caucasian Americans were unwilling to undertake—they were generally regarded as sober, industrious, and law-abiding. Indeed, Charles Crocker, one of the western railroad tycoons, wrote: "They are equal to the best white men. . . . They are very trusty, very intelligent and they live up to their contracts."[63] After the completion of the railroad, however, jobs became more scarce; moreover, when the Civil War ended, there was an influx of former soldiers into an already tight job market. This was immediately followed by a dramatic increase in negative attitudes toward the Chinese: The stereotype changed to "criminal," "conniving," "crafty," and "stupid."

These data suggest that competition and conflict breed prejudice. Moreover, this phenomenon transcends mere historical significance—it seems to have enduring psychological effects as well. In a survey conducted in the 1970s, most antiblack prejudice was found in groups that were just one rung above the blacks socioeconomically. And as we might expect, this tendency was most pronounced in situations in which whites and blacks were in close competition for jobs.[64] At the same time, there is some ambiguity in interpreting the data, because in some instances the variables of competition are intertwined with such variables as educational level and family background.

In order to determine whether competition causes prejudice in and of itself, an experiment is needed. But how can we proceed? Well, if conflict and competition lead to prejudice, it should be possible to produce prejudice in the laboratory. This can be done by the simple device of (1) randomly assigning people of differing backgrounds to one of two groups, (2) making those two groups distinguishable in some arbitrary way, (3) putting those groups into a situation in which they are in competition with each other, and (4) looking for evidence of prejudice. Such an experiment was conducted by Muzafer Sherif and his colleagues[65] in the natural environment of a Boy Scout camp. The subjects were normal, well-adjusted, twelve-year-old boys who were randomly assigned to one of two groups, the *Eagles* and the *Rattlers.* Within each group, the youngsters were taught to cooperate. This was largely done through arranging activities that made each group highly intradependent. For example, within each group, individuals cooperated in building a diving board for the swimming facility, preparing group meals, building a rope bridge, and so on.

After a strong feeling of cohesiveness developed within each group, the stage was set for conflict. The researchers arranged this by setting up a series of competitive activities in which the two groups were pitted against each other in such games as football, baseball, and tug-of-war. In order to increase the tension, prizes were awarded to the winning team. This resulted in some hostility and ill will during the games. In addition, the investigators devised rather diabolical devices for putting the groups into situations specifically designed to promote conflict. In one such situation, a camp party was arranged. The investigators set it up so that the *Eagles* were allowed to arrive a good deal earlier than the *Rattlers*. In addition, the refreshments consisted of two vastly different kinds of food: About half the food was fresh, appealing, and appetizing; the other half was squashed, ugly, and unappetizing. Perhaps because of the general competitiveness that already existed, the early arrivers confiscated most of the appealing refreshments, leaving only the less interesting, less appetizing, squashed, and damaged food for their adversaries. When the *Rattlers* finally arrived and saw how they had been taken advantage of, they were understandably annoyed—so annoyed they began to call the exploitive group rather uncomplimentary names. Because the *Eagles* believed they deserved what they got (first come, first served), they resented this treatment and responded in kind. Name calling escalated into food throwing, and within a very short time a full-scale riot was in progress.

Following this incident, competitive games were eliminated and a great deal of social contact was initiated. Once hostility had been aroused, however, simply eliminating the competition did not eliminate the hostility. Indeed, hostility continued to escalate, even when the two groups were engaged in such benign activities as sitting around watching movies. Eventually, the investigators succeeded in reducing the hostility. Exactly how this was accomplished will be discussed later in this chapter.

The "Scapegoat" Theory of Prejudice. In the preceding chapter, I made the point that aggression is caused, in part, by frustration and such other unpleasant or aversive situations as pain or boredom. In that chapter, we saw there is a strong tendency for a frustrated individual to lash out at the cause of his or her frustration. Frequently, however, the cause of a person's frustration is either too big or too vague for direct retaliation. For example, if a six-year-old boy is humiliated by his teacher, how can he fight back? The teacher has too much power. But this frustration may increase the probability of his aggressing against a less-powerful bystander—even if the bystander had nothing to do with his pain. By the same token, if there is mass unemployment, who is the frustrated, unemployed worker going to strike out against—the economic system? The system is much too big and much too vague. It would be more convenient if the unemployed worker could find something or someone less vague and more concrete to blame. The president? He's concrete, all right, but also much too powerful to strike at with impunity.

The ancient Hebrews had a custom that is noteworthy in this context. During the days of atonement, a priest placed his hands on the head of a goat while reciting the sins of the people. This symbolically transferred the sin and evil from the people to the goat. The goat was then allowed to escape into the wilderness, thus cleansing the community of sin. The animal was called a scapegoat. In modern times the term *scapegoat* has been used to describe a relatively powerless innocent who is made to take the blame for something that is not his or her fault. Unfortunately, the individual is not allowed to escape into the wilderness but is usually subjected to cruelty or even death. Thus, if people are unemployed, or if inflation has depleted their savings, they can't very easily beat up on the economic system—but they can find a scapegoat. In Nazi Germany, it was the Jews; in nineteenth-century California, it was Chinese immigrants; in the rural South, it was black people. Some years ago, Carl Hovland and Robert Sears[66] found that, in the period between 1882 and 1930, they could predict the number of lynchings in the South in a given year from a knowledge of the price of cotton during that year. As the price of cotton dropped, the number of lynchings increased. In short, as people experienced an economic depression, they probably experienced a great many frustrations. The frustrations apparently resulted in an increase in lynchings and other crimes of violence.

Otto Klineberg,[67] a social psychologist with a special interest in the cross-cultural aspects of prejudice, describes a unique scapegoating situation in Japan. The Burakumin are a group of two million outcasts, scattered throughout Japan. Although there are no inherited racial or physical differences between the Burakumin and other Japanese, they are considered unclean and fit only for certain undesirable occupations. As you might imagine, the Burakumin usually live in poor, slum areas. Their IQ scores were, on average, some sixteen points lower than that of other Japanese. Burakumin children were absent from school more often and their delinquency rate was three times higher than other Japanese children. According to Klineberg, it was considered taboo for a member of the Burakumin to marry outside of his or her group. They are an invisible race—an outgroup defined more by social class than by any physical characteristics. They can only be identified because of their distinctive speech pattern (which has developed from years of nonassociation with other Japanese) and their identity papers. Although their historical origins are unclear, they probably occupied the lower rungs of the socioeconomic ladder until an economic depression led to their complete expulsion from Japanese society. Now the Japanese consider the Burakumin to be "innately inferior," thus justifying further scapegoating and discrimination.

It is difficult to understand how the lynching of blacks or the mistreatment of the Burakumin could be due only to economic competition. There is a great deal of emotion in these actions that suggests the presence of deeper psychological factors in addition to economics. Similarly, the zeal with which Nazis carried out their attempt to erase all members of the Jewish ethnic group (regardless of economic status) strongly suggests that the phenomenon was not exclusively economic or political, but was (at least in part) psychological.[68] Firmer evidence for the existence of psychological processes comes from a well-controlled experiment by Neal Miller and Richard Bugelski.[69] Individuals were asked to state their feelings about various minority groups. Some of the subjects were then frustrated by being deprived of an opportunity to attend a film and were given an arduous and difficult series of tests instead. They were then asked to restate their feelings about the minority groups. These subjects showed some evidence of increased prejudicial responses following the frustrating experience. A control group that did not go through the frustrating experience did not undergo any change in prejudice.

Additional research has helped to pin down the phenomenon even more precisely. In one experiment,[70] white students were instructed to administer a series of electric shocks to another student as part of a learning experiment. The subjects had the prerogative to adjust the intensity of the shocks. In actuality, the learner was an accomplice of the experimenter and (of course) was not really connected to the apparatus. There were four conditions: The accomplice was either black or white; he was trained to be either friendly or insulting to the subject. When he was friendly, the subjects administered slightly less intense shocks to the black student; when he insulted them, they administered far more intense shocks to the black student than to the white student. In another experiment,[71] college students were subjected to a great deal of frustration. Some of these students were highly anti-Semitic; others were not. The subjects were then asked to write stories based on pictures they were shown. For some subjects, the characters in these pictures were assigned Jewish names; for others, they were not. There were two major findings: (1) After being frustrated, anti-Semitic subjects wrote stories that directed more aggression toward the Jewish characters than did people who were not anti-Semitic; and (2) there was no difference between the anti-Semitic students and the others when the characters they were writing about were not identified as Jewish. In short, frustration or anger leads to a specific aggression—aggression against an outgroup member.

The laboratory experiments help to clarify factors that seem to exist in the real world. The general picture of scapegoating that emerges is that individuals tend to displace aggression onto groups that are disliked, that are visible, and that are relatively powerless. Moreover, the form the aggression takes depends on what is allowed or approved by the ingroup in question: In society, lynchings of blacks and pogroms against Jews were not frequent occurrences, unless they were deemed appropriate by the dominant culture or subculture.

I used the past tense in the preceding sentence because it is comforting to believe that extreme forms of scapegoating are a thing of the past. But, in the present decade, events have taken place that have caused many of us a great deal of consternation. For example, when the Soviet Union fell apart, we were momentarily encouraged as all of Eastern Europe gained its freedom. Unfortunately, in much of the region, this new freedom was accompanied by increased feelings of nationalism, which have, in turn, produced additional prejudice and hostility against outgroups. Thus, in the Balkans, for example, intense nationalism led to eruptions of hostility between Serbs and the Croats, between Azerbaijanis and Uzbekistanis, and between Christians and Muslims in Bosnia. In addition, economic hardship and frustrated expectations throughout Eastern Europe produced a sharp rise in anti-Semitism.

The Prejudiced Personality.   As we have seen, the displacement of aggression onto scapegoats may be a human tendency, but not all people do it to a like degree. We have already identified socioeconomic status as a cause of prejudice. Also, we have seen that people who dislike members of a particular outgroup are more apt to displace aggression onto them than are people who do not dislike members of that outgroup. We can now carry this one step further. There is some evidence to support the notion of individual differences in a general tendency to hate. In other words, there are people who are predisposed toward being prejudiced, not solely because of immediate external influences, but because of the kind of people they are. Theodor Adorno and his associates[72] refer to these individuals as "authoritarian personalities." Basically, authoritarian personalities have the following characteristics: They tend to be rigid in their beliefs; they tend to possess "conventional" values; they are intolerant of weakness (in themselves as well as in others); they tend to be highly punitive; they are suspicious; and they are respectful of authority to an unusual degree. The instrument developed to determine authoritarianism (called the F scale) measures the extent to which each person agrees or disagrees with such items as these:

> Sex crimes such as rape and attacks on children deserve more than mere imprisonment; such criminals ought to be publicly whipped, or worse.

> Most people don't realize how much our lives are controlled by plots hatched in secret places.

> Obedience and respect for authority are the most important virtues children should learn.

A high degree of agreement with such items indicates authoritarianism. The major finding is that people who are high on authoritarianism do not simply dislike Jews or dislike blacks, but rather, they show a consistently high degree of prejudice against *all* minority groups.

Through an intensive clinical interview of people high and low on the F scale, Adorno and his colleagues have traced the development of this cluster of attitudes and values to early childhood experiences in families characterized by harsh and threatening parental discipline. Moreover, people high on the F scale tend to have parents who use love and its withdrawal as their major way of producing obedience. In general, authoritarian personalities, as children, tend to be very insecure and highly dependent on their parents; they fear their parents and feel unconscious hostility toward them. This combination sets the stage for the emergence of an adult with a high degree of anger, which, because of fear and insecurity, takes the form of displaced aggression against powerless groups, while the individual maintains an outward respect for authority.

It is instructive to note that, in a recent study of authoritarianism in the former Soviet Union, Sam McFarland and his colleagues[73] found that people high on the F scale tend to be in favor of overthrowing their newly acquired democracy and restoring the former communist regime. Ideologically, this is quite different from U.S. authoritarians who tend to be anticommunist. The common linkage, of course, is not a specific ideological belief but, rather, a kind of conventionalism and respect for authority. In other words, both U.S. and Russian authoritarians are linked by a common need to conform to the traditional values of their culture and a tendency to be suspicious of new ideas and of people who are different from themselves.

Although research on the authoritarian personality has added to our understanding of the possible dynamics of prejudice, it should be noted that the bulk of the data are correlational. That is, we know only that two variables are related—we cannot be certain what causes what. Consider, for example, the correlation between a person's score on the F scale and the specific socialization practices he or she was subjected to as a child. Although it is true that adults who are authoritarian and highly prejudiced had parents who tended to be harsh and to use "conditional love" as a socialization technique, it is not necessarily true that this is what caused them to develop into prejudiced people. It turns out that the parents of these people tend, themselves, to be highly prejudiced against minority groups. Accordingly, it may be that the development of prejudice in some people is due to conformity through the process of identification, as described in chapter 2. That is, a child might consciously pick up beliefs about minorities from his or her parents because the child identifies with them. This is quite different from, and much simpler than, the explanation offered by Adorno and his colleagues, which is based on the child's unconscious hostility and repressed fear of his or her parents.

This is not to imply that, for some people, prejudice is not rooted in unconscious childhood conflicts. Rather, it is to suggest that many people may have learned a wide array of prejudices on Mommy's or

Daddy's knee. Moreover, some people may conform to prejudices that are limited and highly specific, depending upon the norms of their subculture. Let's take a closer look at the phenomenon of prejudice as an act of conformity.

Prejudice through Conformity. It is frequently observed that there is more prejudice against blacks in the South than in the North. This often manifests itself in stronger attitudes against racial integration. For example, in 1942, only 4 percent of all southerners were in favor of the desegregation of transportation facilities, while 56 percent of all northerners were in favor of it.[74] Why? Was it because of economic competition? Probably not; there is more prejudice against blacks in those southern communities in which economic competition is low than in northern communities in which economic competition is great. Are there relatively more authoritarian personalities in the South than in the North? No. Thomas Pettigrew[75] administered the F scale widely in the North and in the South and found the scores about equal for northerners and southerners. In addition, although there is more prejudice against blacks in the South, there is less prejudice against Jews in the South than there is in the nation as a whole; the prejudiced personality should be prejudiced against everybody—the southerner isn't.

How then do we account for the animosity toward blacks that exists in the South? It could be due to historical causes: The blacks were slaves, the Civil War was fought over the issue of slavery, and so on. This could have created the climate for greater prejudice. But what sustains this climate? One possible clue comes from the observation of some rather strange patterns of racial segregation in the South. One example, a group of coal miners in a small mining town in West Virginia, should suffice. The black miners and the white miners developed a pattern of living that consisted of total and complete integration while they were under the ground, and total and complete segregation while they were above the ground. How can we account for this inconsistency? If you truly hate someone, you want to keep away from him—why associate with him below the ground and not above the ground?

Pettigrew has suggested that the explanation for these phenomena is conformity. In this case, the white miners are simply conforming to the norms that exist in their society (above the ground!). The historical events of the South set the stage for greater prejudice against blacks, but it is conformity that keeps it going. Indeed, Pettigrew believes that, although economic competition, frustration, and personality needs account for some prejudice, the greatest proportion of prejudiced behavior is a function of slavish conformity to social norms.

How can we be certain conformity is responsible? One way is to determine the relation between a person's prejudice and that person's general pattern of conformity. For example, a study of interracial tension in South Africa[76] showed that those individuals who were most likely to conform to a great variety of social norms also showed a higher degree of prejudice against blacks. In other words, if conformists are more prejudiced, the suggestion is that prejudice may be just another thing to conform to. Another way to determine the role of conformity is to see what happens to people's prejudice when they move to a different area of the country. If conformity is a factor in prejudice, we would expect individuals to show dramatic increases in their prejudice when they move into areas in which the norm is more prejudicial, and to show dramatic decreases when they are affected by a less prejudicial norm. And that is what happens. In one study, Jeanne Watson[77] found that individuals who had recently moved to New York City and had come into direct contact with anti-Semitic people became more anti-Semitic themselves. In another study, Pettigrew found that, as southerners entered the army and came into contact with a less discriminatory set of social norms, they became less prejudiced against blacks.

The pressure to conform can be relatively overt, as in the Asch experiment. On the other hand, conformity to a prejudicial norm might simply be due to the unavailability of accurate evidence and a preponderance of misleading information. This can lead people to adopt negative attitudes on the basis of hearsay. Examples of this kind of stereotyping behavior abound in the literature. For example, consider Christopher Marlowe's *The Jew of Malta* or William Shakespeare's *The Merchant of Venice*. Both of these works depict the Jew as a conniving, money-hungry, cringing coward. We might be tempted to conclude that Marlowe and Shakespeare had had some unfortunate experiences with unsavory Jews, which resulted in these bitter and unflattering portraits—except for one thing: The Jews had been expelled from England some three hundred years before these works were written. Thus, it would seem that the only thing with which Marlowe and Shakespeare came into contact was a lingering stereotype. Tragically, their works not only reflected the stereotype but undoubtedly contributed to it as well.

Even casual exposure to bigotry can affect our attitudes and behavior toward a group that is the victim of prejudice. For example, research has demonstrated that merely overhearing someone use a derogatory label—such as a racial or ethnic epithet—toward a given group can increase our likelihood of viewing someone from that group, or someone merely associated with that group, in a negative light. In one experiment,[78] Shari Kirkland and her co-researchers asked subjects to read a transcript of a criminal trial in which a white defendant was represented by a black attorney, whose picture was attached to the trial transcript. While reading the transcript, the subject "overhears" a brief exchange between two experimental confederates, who are posing as subjects. Some subjects hear the first confederate call the black lawyer a "nigger," while other subjects hear the confederate call him a "shyster." In both conditions, the second confederate expresses agreement with the first confederate's derogatory opinion of the black lawyer. With this conformity dynamic in place, the experimenters then asked the subject to evaluate the attorney and the defendant. An analysis of these ratings revealed that subjects who overheard the racial slur rated the black lawyer more negatively than those who overheard a derisive comment that was not related to the lawyer's race. Moreover, the white defendant received particularly harsh verdicts and highly negative evaluations from subjects who heard the racial slur against the black attorney. This latter finding indicates that conformity to the prejudiced norms can have damaging effects that extend beyond the initial target of racism.

Bigoted attitudes can also be fostered intentionally by a bigoted society that institutionally supports these attitudes. For example, a society that supports the notion of segregation through law and custom is supporting the notion that one group is inferior to another. A more direct example: One investigator[79] interviewed white South Africans in an attempt to find reasons for their negative attitudes toward blacks. He found that the typical white South African was convinced that the great majority of crimes were committed by blacks. This was erroneous. How did such a misconception develop? The individuals reported they saw a great many black convicts working in public places—they never saw any white convicts. Doesn't this prove blacks are convicted of more crimes than whites? No. In fact, the rules forbade white convicts from working in public places! In short, a society can *create* prejudiced beliefs by its very institutions. In our own society, forcing blacks to ride in the back of the bus, keeping women out of certain clubs, preventing Jews from staying at exclusive hotels are all part of our recent history—and create the illusion of inferiority or unacceptability.

Stateways Can *Change Folkways*

In 1954, the United States Supreme Court declared that separate but equal schools were, by definition, unequal. In the words of Chief Justice Earl Warren, when black children are separated from white children on the basis of race alone, it "generates a feeling of inferiority as to their status in the community that may affect their hearts and minds in a way unlikely ever to be undone." Without our quite realizing it, this decision launched our nation into one of the most exciting, large-scale social experiments ever conducted.

In the aftermath of this historic decision, many people were opposed to integrating the schools on "humanitarian" grounds. They predicted a holocaust if the races were forced to mingle in schools. They argued that laws cannot force people to like and respect each other. This echoed the sentiments of the distinguished sociologist William Graham Sumner, who, years earlier, had stated "stateways don't change folkways." What Sumner meant, of course, is that you can't legislate morality; you can force people to desegregate, but you can't force them to like one another. A great many people urged that desegregation be delayed until attitudes could be changed.

Social psychologists at that time, of course, believed the way to change behavior is to change attitudes. Thus, if you can get bigoted adults to become less prejudiced against blacks, then they will not hesitate to allow their children to attend school with blacks. Although they should have known better, many social scientists were relatively confident they could change bigoted attitudes by launching information campaigns. They took a "sixteen-millimeter" approach to the reduction of prejudice: If prejudiced people believe blacks are shiftless and lazy, then all you have to do is show them a movie depicting that blacks are industrious, decent people. The idea is that you can combat misinformation with information. If Shakespeare believes Jews are conniving bloodsuckers because he has been exposed to misinformation about Jews, expose him to a more accurate range of information about Jews, and his prejudice will fade away. If most South Africans believe blacks commit virtually all the crimes, show them the white convicts, and they'll change their beliefs. Unfortunately, it is not quite that simple. Whether prejudice is largely a function of economic conflict, conformity to social norms, or deeply rooted personality needs, it is not easily changed by an information campaign. Over the years, most people become deeply committed to their prejudicial behavior. To develop an open, accepting attitude toward minorities when all of your friends and associates are still prejudiced is no easy task. A mere movie cannot undo a way of thinking and a way of behaving that has persisted over the years.

As the reader of this book has learned, where important issues are involved, information campaigns fail, because people are inclined not to sit still and take in information that is dissonant with their beliefs. Paul Lazarsfeld,[80] for example, described a series of radio broadcasts in the early 1940s designed to reduce ethnic prejudice by presenting information about various ethnic groups in a warm and sympathetic manner. One program was devoted to a description of Polish Americans, another to Italian Americans, and so forth. Who was listening? The major part of the audience for the program about Polish Americans consisted of Polish Americans. And guess who made up the major part of the audience for the program on Italian Americans? Right. Moreover, as we have seen, if people are compelled to listen to information uncongenial to their deep-seated attitudes, they will reject it, distort it, or ignore it—in much the same way Mr. X maintained his negative attitude against Jews despite Mr. Y's information campaign, and in much the same way the Dartmouth and Princeton students distorted the film of the football game they watched. For most people, prejudice is too deeply rooted in their own belief systems, is too consistent with their day-to-day behavior, and receives too much support and encouragement from the people around them to be reduced by a book, a film, or a radio broadcast.

The Effects of Equal-Status Contact. Although changes in attitude might induce changes in behavior, as we have seen, it is often difficult to change attitudes through education. What social psychologists have long known, but have only recently begun to understand, is that changes in behavior can affect changes in attitudes. On the simplest level, it has been argued that, if blacks and whites could be brought into direct contact, prejudiced individuals would come into contact with the reality of their own experience, not simply a stereotype; eventually, this would lead to greater understanding. Of course, the contact must take place in a situation in which blacks and whites have equal status; throughout history many whites have always had a great deal of contact with blacks, but typically in situations in which the blacks played such menial roles as slaves, porters, dishwashers, shoe-shine boys, washroom attendants, and domestics. This kind of contact only serves to increase stereotyping by whites and thus adds fuel to their prejudice against blacks. It also serves to increase the resentment and anger of blacks. Until recently, equal-status contact has been rare, both because of educational and occupational inequities in our society and because of residential segregation. The 1954 Supreme Court decision was the beginning of a gradual change in the frequency of equal-status contact.

Occasionally, even before 1954, isolated instances of equal-status integration had taken place. The effects tended to support the notion that behavior change will produce attitude change. In a pioneering study, Morton Deutsch and Mary Ellen Collins[81] examined the attitudes of whites toward blacks in public housing projects. Specifically, in one housing project, black and white families were assigned to buildings in a segregated manner—that is, they were assigned to separate buildings in the same project. In another project, the assignment was integrated—black and white families were assigned to the same building. Residents in the integrated project reported a greater positive change in their attitudes toward blacks subsequent to moving into the project than did residents of the segregated project. From these findings, it would appear that stateways *can* change folkways, that you can legislate morality—not directly, of course, but through the medium of equal-status contact. If diverse racial groups can be brought together under conditions of equal status, they stand a chance of getting to know each other better. This can increase understanding and decrease tension, *all other things being equal.* It should be noted that the study alluded to in this paragraph took place in public housing projects rather than in private residential areas. This is a crucial factor that will be discussed in a moment.

The Vicarious Effects of Desegregation. It wasn't until much later that social psychologists began to entertain the notion that desegregation can affect the values of people who do not even have the opportunity to have direct contact with minority groups. This can occur through the mechanisms we have referred to in chapter 5 as the *psychology of inevitability.* Specifically, if I know that you and I will inevitably be in close contact, and I don't like you, I will experience dissonance. In order to reduce dissonance, I will try to convince myself you are not as bad as I had previously thought. I will set about looking for your positive characteristics and will try to ignore, or minimize the importance of, your negative characteristics. Accordingly, the mere fact that I know I must at some point be in *close contact* with you will force me to change my prejudiced attitudes about you, all other things being equal. As we saw earlier, laboratory experiments have confirmed this prediction: For example, children who believed they must inevitably eat a previously disliked vegetable began to convince themselves the vegetable wasn't as bad as they had previously thought.[82] Similarly, college women who knew they were going to spend several weeks working intimately with a woman who had several positive and negative qualities developed a great fondness for that woman before they even met her; this did not occur when they were *not* led to anticipate working with her in the future.[83]

Admittedly, it's a far cry from a bowl of vegetables to relations between blacks, Latinos, and whites. Few social psychologists are so naive as to believe that deep-seated racial intolerance can be eliminated if people reduce their dissonance simply through coming to terms with what they believe to be inevitable events. I would suggest that, under ideal conditions, such events can begin to unfreeze prejudiced attitudes and produce a *diminution* of hostile feelings in most individuals. I will discuss what I mean by "ideal conditions" in a moment; but first, let us put a little more meat on those theoretical bones. How might the process of dissonance reduction take place?

Turn the clock back to the late 1950s. Imagine a forty-five-year-old white male whose sixteen-year-old daughter attends a segregated school. Let us assume he has a negative attitude toward blacks, based in part on his belief that blacks are shiftless and lazy and that all black males are oversexed and potential rapists. Suddenly, the edict is handed down by the Justice Department: The following autumn, his fair-haired, young daughter must go to an integrated school. State and local officials, while perhaps not liking the idea, clearly convey the fact that there's nothing that can be done to prevent it—it's the law of the land and it must be obeyed. The father might, of course, refuse to allow his child to obtain an education, or he could send her to an expensive private school. But such measures are either terribly drastic or terribly costly. So he decides he must send her to an integrated school. His cognition that his fair-haired young daughter must inevitably attend the same school with blacks is dissonant with his cognition that blacks are shiftless rapists. What does he do? My guess is he will begin to reexamine his beliefs about blacks. Are they *really* all that shiftless? Do they *really* go around raping people? He may take another look—this time, with a strong inclination to look for the good qualities in blacks rather than to concoct and exaggerate bad, unacceptable qualities. I would guess that, by the time September rolls around, his attitude toward blacks would have become unfrozen and would have shifted in a positive direction. If this shift can be bolstered by positive events *after* desegregation—for example, if his daughter has pleasant and peaceful interactions with her black schoolmates—a major change in the father's attitudes is likely to result. Again, this analysis is admittedly oversimplified. But the basic process holds. And look at the advantages this process has over an information campaign. A mechanism has been triggered that *motivated* the father to alter his negative stereotype of blacks.

My analysis strongly suggests that a particular kind of public policy would be most potentially beneficial to society—a policy exactly opposite of what has been generally recommended. As mentioned previously, following the 1954 Supreme Court decision, there was a general feeling that integration must proceed slowly. Most public officials and many social scientists believed that, in order to achieve harmonious racial relations, integration should be delayed until people could be reeducated to become less prejudiced. In short, the general belief in 1954 was that the behavior (integration) must *follow* a cognitive change. My analysis suggests that the best way to produce eventual interracial harmony would be to launch into behavioral change. Moreover, *and most important,* the sooner the individuals realize integration is inevitable, the sooner their prejudiced attitudes will begin to change. On the other hand, this process can be (and has been) sabotaged by public officials through fostering the belief that integration can be circumvented or delayed. This serves to create the illusion that the event is not inevitable. In such circumstances, there will be no attitude change; the result will be an increase in turmoil and disharmony. Let's go back to our previous example: If the father of the fair-haired daughter is led (by the statements and tactics of a governor, a mayor, a school-board chairman, or a local sheriff) to believe there's a way out of integration, he will feel no need to re-examine his negative beliefs about blacks. The result is apt to be violent opposition to integration.

Consistent with this reasoning is the fact that, as desegregation has spread, favorable attitudes toward desegregation have increased. In 1942, only 30 percent of the whites in this country favored desegregated schools; by 1956, the figure rose to 49 percent; in 1970, 75 percent. Finally, in 1980, as it became increasingly clear that school desegregation was inevitable, the figure approached 90 percent.[84] The change in the South (taken by itself) is even more dramatic. In 1942, only 2 percent of the whites in the South favored integrated schools; in 1956, while most southerners still believed the ruling could be circumvented, only 14 percent favored desegregation; but by 1970, as desegregation continued, just under 50 percent favored desegregation—and the figures continued to climb in the 1980s. Of course, such statistical data do not constitute absolute proof that the reason people are changing their attitudes toward school desegregation is that they are coming to terms with what is inevitable—but the data are highly suggestive.

In a careful analysis of the process and effects of school desegregation, Thomas Pettigrew raised the question of why, in the early years of desegregation, violence occurred in some communities, such as Little Rock and Clinton, and not in others, such as Norfolk and Winston-Salem. His conclusion, which lends further support to my reasoning, was that "violence has generally resulted in localities where at least some of the authorities give prior hints that they would gladly return to segregation if disturbances occurred; peaceful integration has generally followed firm and forceful leadership."[85] In other words, if people were not given the opportunity to reduce dissonance, there was violence. As early as 1953, Kenneth B. Clark[86] observed the same phenomenon during the desegregation in some of the border states. He discovered that immediate desegregation was far more effective than gradual desegregation. Moreover, violence occurred in those places where ambiguous or inconsistent policies were employed or where community leaders tended to vacillate. The same kind of thing happened when military units began to desegregate during World War II: Trouble was greatest where policies were ambiguous.[87]

But All Other Things Are Not Always Equal.   In the preceding section, I presented an admittedly oversimplified view of a very complex phenomenon. I did this intentionally as a way of indicating how things can proceed theoretically under ideal conditions. But conditions are seldom ideal. There are almost always some complicating circumstances. Let us now look at some of the complications and then proceed to discuss how these complications might be eliminated or reduced.

When I discussed the fact that prejudice was reduced in an integrated housing project, I made special note of the fact it was a *public* housing project. Some complications are introduced if it involves privately owned houses. Primarily, there is a strong belief among whites that, when blacks move into a neighborhood, real-estate values decrease. This belief introduces economic conflict and competition, which militate against the reduction of prejudiced attitudes. Indeed, systematic investigations in integrated *private* housing show an increase in prejudiced attitudes among the white residents.[88]

Moreover, as I mentioned, the experiments on the psychology of inevitability were done in the laboratory, where the dislikes involved in the studies were almost certainly not as intense or as deep-seated as racial prejudice is in the real world. Although it is encouraging to note that these findings were paralleled by the data from actual desegregation efforts, it would be naive and misleading to conclude that the way to desegregation will always be smooth as long as individuals are given the opportunity to come to terms with inevitability. Frequently, trouble begins once desegregation starts. This is often due, in part, to the fact that the contact between white and minority-group children (especially if it is not begun until high school) is usually not equal-status contact. Picture the scene: A tenth-grade boy from a poor black or Latino family, after being subjected to a second-rate education, is suddenly dropped into a learning situation in a predominately white middle-class school taught by white middle-class teachers, where he finds he must compete with white middle-class students who have been reared to hold white middle-class values. In effect, he is thrust into a highly competitive situation for which he is unprepared, a situation in which the rules are not his rules and pay-offs are made for abilities he has not yet developed. He is competing in a situation that, psychologically, is far removed from his home turf. Ironically enough, these factors tend to produce a diminution of his self-esteem—the very factor that influenced the Supreme Court decision in the first place.[89] In his careful analysis of the research on desegregation, Walter Stephan[90] found no studies indicating significant increases in self-esteem among black children, while 25 percent of the studies he researched showed a significant drop in their self-esteem following desegregation. In addition, prejudice was not substantially reduced. Stephan found that it increased in almost as many cases as it decreased.

With these data in mind, it is not surprising to learn that a newly integrated high school is typically a tense place. It is natural for minority-group students to attempt to raise their self-esteem. One way of raising self-esteem is to stick together, lash out at whites, assert their individuality, reject white values and white leadership, and so on.[91]

Let me sum up the discussion thus far: (1) Equal-status contact under the ideal conditions of no economic conflict can and does produce increased understanding and a diminution of prejudice.[92] (2) The psychology of inevitability can and does set up pressures to reduce prejudiced attitudes, and it can set the stage for smooth, non-violent school desegregation, under ideal conditions. (3) Where economic conflict is present (as in integrated neighborhoods of private domiciles) there is often an increase in prejudiced attitudes. (4) Where school desegregation results in a competitive situation, especially if there are serious inequities for the minority groups, there is often an increase in hostility of blacks or Latinos toward whites that is at least partially due to an attempt to regain some lost self-esteem.

Interdependence—A Possible Solution

School desegregation can open the door to increased understanding among students, but, by itself, it is not the ultimate solution. The issue is not simply getting youngsters of various races and ethnic backgrounds into the same school—it's what happens after they get there that is crucial. As we have seen, if the atmosphere is a highly competitive one, whatever tensions exist initially might actually be increased as a result of contact. The tension that is frequently the initial result of school desegregation reminds me somewhat of the behavior of the young boys in the summer camp experiment by Muzafer Sherif and his colleagues.[93] Recall that hostility was produced between two groups by placing them in situations of conflict and competition. Once the hostility was established, it could no longer be reduced simply by removing the conflicts and the competition. As a matter of fact, once distrust was firmly established, bringing the groups together in equal-status, noncompetitive situations served to *increase* the hostility and distrust. For example, the children in these groups had trouble with each other even when they were simply sitting near each other watching a movie.

How did Sherif eventually succeed in reducing the hostility? By placing the two groups of boys in situations in which they were mutually interdependent—situations in which they had to cooperate with each other in order to accomplish their goal. For example, the investigators set up an emergency situation by damaging the water-supply system. The only way the system could be repaired was if all the children cooperated immediately. On another occasion, the camp truck broke down while the boys were on a camping trip. In order to get the truck going again, it was necessary to pull it up a rather steep hill. This could be accomplished only if all the youngsters pulled together—regardless of whether they were *Eagles* or *Rattlers*. Eventually, there was a diminution of hostile feelings and negative stereotyping. The boys made friends across groups, began to get along better, and began to cooperate spontaneously.

 The key factor seems to be *mutual interdependence*—a situation wherein individuals need one another and are needed by one another in order to accomplish their goal. Several researchers have demonstrated the benefits of cooperation in well-controlled laboratory experiments. Morton Deutsch,[94] for example, has shown that problem-solving groups are both friendlier and more attentive when a cooperative atmosphere is introduced than when a competitive atmosphere prevails. Similarly, research by Patricia Keenan and Peter Carnevale has shown that cooperation within groups can also foster cooperation between groups.[95] That is, cooperative relations that are established in one group often carry over when that group is later called upon to interact with a different group. In their study, groups that engaged in a cooperative task were more cooperative in a subsequent negotiation with another group, as compared to groups who had initially worked in a competitive fashion.

Unfortunately, cooperation and interdependence are not characteristic of the process that exists in most school classrooms, even at the elementary level. We have already alluded to the competitive nature of the process; let us take a closer look at it. First, let's define "process." Whenever people interact, two things exist simultaneously. One of these things is the content and the other is the process. By content, I simply mean the substance of their encounter; by process, I mean the dynamics of the encounter. In a classroom, for example, the content could be arithmetic, geography, social studies, or music; the process is the manner in which these lessons are taught. It goes without saying that the content is of great importance. However, the importance of the process is frequently underestimated. But it is through the process that pupils learn a great deal about the world they live in. Indeed, I would even go so far as to say that, in some respects, the process is a more important source of learning than the content itself.

I was provided with a golden opportunity to observe classroom process some years ago when I was called in as a consultant to the Austin, Texas, school system. Desegregation had just taken place; this was followed by a great deal of turmoil and a number of unpleasant incidents. My colleagues and I entered the system, not to smooth over the unpleasantness but, rather, to see if there was anything we might do to help desegregation achieve some of the positive goals envisioned for it. The first thing my colleagues and I did was systematically observe the process. We tried to do this with fresh eyes —as if we were visitors from another planet—and the most typical process we observed was this: The teacher stands in front of the class, asks a question, and waits for the children to indicate that they know the answer. Most frequently, six to ten youngsters strain in their seats and wave their hands to attract the teacher's attention. They seem eager to be called on. Several other students sit quietly with their eyes averted, as if trying to make themselves invisible. When the teacher calls on one of the students, there are looks of disappointment, dismay, and unhappiness on the faces of those students who were eagerly raising their hands but were not called on. If the student who is called on comes up with the right answer, the teacher smiles, nods approvingly, and goes on to the next question. This is a great reward for the child who happens to be called on. At the same time the fortunate student is coming up with the right answer and being smiled upon by the teacher, an audible groan can be heard coming from the children who were striving to be called on but were ignored. It is obvious they are disappointed because they missed an opportunity to show the teacher how smart and quick they are.

Through this process, students learn several things. First, they learn there is one and only one expert in the classroom: the teacher. They also learn there is one and only one correct answer to any question the teacher asks—namely, the answer the teacher has in mind. The students' task is to figure out which answer the teacher expects. The students also learn that the payoff comes from pleasing the teacher by actively displaying how quick, smart, neat, clean, and well behaved they are. If they do this successfully, they will gain the respect and love of this powerful person. This powerful person will then be kind to them and will tell their parents what wonderful children they are. There is no payoff for them in consulting with their peers. Indeed, their peers are their enemies—to be beaten. Moreover, collaboration is frowned upon by most teachers; if it occurs during class time, it is seen as disruptive, and if it takes place during an exam, it is called "cheating."

The game is very competitive and the stakes are very high—in an elementary-school classroom, the youngsters are competing for the respect and approval of one of the two or three most important people in their world (important for most students, anyway). If you are a student who knows the correct answer and the teacher calls on one of your peers, it is likely you will sit there hoping and praying he or she will come up with the wrong answer so you will have a chance to show the teacher how smart you are. Those who fail when called on, or those who do not even raise their hands and compete, have a tendency to resent those who succeed. Frequently, the "losers" become envious and jealous of the successful students, perhaps they tease them or ridicule them by referring to them as "teacher's pets." They might even use physical aggression against them in the school yard. The successful students, for their part, often hold the unsuccessful students in contempt; they consider them to be dumb and uninteresting. The upshot of this process—which takes place, to a greater or lesser extent, in most classrooms—is that friendliness and understanding are not promoted among *any* of the children in the same classroom. Quite the reverse. The process tends to create enmity, even among children of the same racial group. When ethnic or racial unfamiliarity is added, or when tension brought about by forced busing flavors the stew of an already unhappy process, the situation can become extremely difficult and unpleasant.

Although competitiveness in the classroom is typical, it is not inevitable. In my research, I found that many classroom teachers were eager to try more cooperative techniques. Accordingly, my colleagues and I developed a simple method wherein children were put into interdependent learning groups; we systematically compared their performance, satisfaction, and liking for one another with that of children in more traditional, competitive classroom situations.[96] We called our method the *jigsaw* technique because it works very much like a jigsaw puzzle.

An example will clarify: In our initial experiment, we entered a fifth-grade classroom of a newly desegregated school. In this class-room, the children were studying biographies of famous Americans. The upcoming lesson happened to be a biography of Joseph Pulitzer, the famous journalist. First, we constructed a biography of Joseph Pulitzer consisting of six paragraphs. Paragraph one was about Jo-seph Pulitzer's ancestors and how they came to this country; para-graph two was about Joseph Pulitzer as a little boy and how he grew up; paragraph three was about Joseph Pulitzer as a young man, his education, and his early employment; paragraph four was about his middle-age and how he founded his newspaper; and so forth. Each major aspect of Joseph Pulitzer's life was contained in a separate paragraph. We mimeographed our biography of Joseph Pulitzer, cut each copy of the biography into six one-paragraph sections, and gave every child in each of the six-person learning groups one paragraph about Joseph Pulitzer's life. Thus, each learning group had within it the entire biography of Joseph Pulitzer, but each individual child had no more than one-sixth of the story. Like a jigsaw puzzle, each child had one piece of the puzzle, and each child was dependent on the other children in the group for the completion of the big picture. In order to learn about Joseph Pulitzer, each child had to master a paragraph and teach it to the others. Students took their paragraphs and went off by themselves where they could learn them. In learning the paragraph, the children were free to consult with their counter-parts in one of the other learning groups. That is, if Johnnie had been dealt Joseph Pulitzer as a young man, he might have consulted with Christina, who was in a different learning group and had also been dealt Pulitzer as a young man. They could use each other to rehearse and clarify for themselves the important aspects of that phase of Joseph Pulitzer's life. A short time later, the students came back into session with their six-person groups. They were informed that they had a certain amount of time to communicate their knowledge to one another. They were also informed that, at the end of the time (or soon thereafter), they were going to be tested on their knowledge.

When thrown on their own resources, the children eventually learned to teach and to listen to one another. The children gradually learned that none of them could do well without the aid of each person in the group—and that each member had a unique and essential contribution to make. Suppose you and I are children in the same group. You've been dealt Joseph Pulitzer as a young man; I've been dealt Pulitzer as an old man. The only way I can learn about Joseph Pulitzer as a young man is to pay close attention to what you are saying. You are a very important resource for me. The teacher is no longer the sole resource—he or she isn't even an important resource; indeed, the teacher isn't even in the group. Instead, every kid in the circle becomes important to me. I do well if I pay attention to other kids; I do poorly if I don't. I no longer get rewarded for trying to please the teacher at your expense. It's a whole new ball game.

But cooperative behavior doesn't happen all at once. Typically, it requires several days before children use this technique effectively. Old habits are difficult to break. The students in our experimental group had grown accustomed to competing during all of their years in school. For the first few days, most of the youngsters tried to compete—even though competitiveness was dysfunctional. Let me illustrate with an actual example, typical of the way the children stumbled toward the learning of the cooperative process. In one of our groups there was a Mexican American boy, whom we will call Carlos. Carlos was not very articulate in English, his second language. He had learned over the years how to keep quiet in class because frequently, when he had spoken up in the past, he was ridiculed. In this instance, he had a great deal of trouble communicating his paragraph to the other children; he was very uncomfortable about it. He liked the traditional way better. This is not surprising, because, in the system we introduced, Carlos was forced to speak, whereas before he could always deindividuate himself and keep a low profile in the classroom. But the situation was even more complex than that—it might even be said that the teacher and Carlos had entered into a conspiracy, that they were in collusion. Carlos was perfectly willing to be quiet. In the past, the teacher called on him occasionally; he would stumble, stammer, and fall into an embarrassed silence. Several of his peers would make fun of him. The teacher had learned not to call on him anymore. The decision probably came from the purest of intentions—the teacher simply did not want to humiliate him. But, by ignoring him, she had written him off. The implication was that he was not worth bothering with—at least the other kids in the classroom got that message. They believed there was one good reason why the teacher wasn't calling on Carlos—he was stupid. Indeed, even Carlos began to draw this conclusion. This is part of the dynamic of how desegregation, when coupled with a competitive process, can produce unequal-status contact and can result in even greater enmity between ethnic groups and a loss of self-esteem for members of disadvantaged ethnic minorities.[97]

Let us go back to our six-person group. Carlos, who had to report on Joseph Pulitzer's young manhood, was having a very hard time. He stammered, hesitated, and fidgeted. The other kids in the circle were not very helpful. They had grown accustomed to a competitive process and responded out of this old, overlearned habit. They knew what to do when a kid stumbles—especially a kid whom they believed to be stupid. They ridiculed him, put him down, and teased him. During our experiment, it was Mary who was observed to say: "Aw, you don't know it; you're dumb, you're stupid. You don't know what you're doing." In our initial experiment, the groups were being loosely monitored by a research assistant who was floating from group to group. When this incident occurred, our assistant made one brief intervention: "OK, you can do that if you want to. It might be fun for you, but it's *not* going to help you learn about Joseph Pulitzer's young manhood. The exam will take place in an hour." Notice how the reinforcement contingencies have shifted. No longer does Mary gain much from putting Carlos down—in fact, she now stands to lose a great deal. After a few days and several similar experiences, it began to dawn on the students in Carlos's group that the *only* way they could learn about Joseph Pulitzer's young manhood was by paying attention to what Carlos had to say. Gradually, they began to develop into pretty good interviewers. Instead of ignoring or ridiculing Carlos when he was having a little trouble communicating what he knew, they began asking probing questions—the kind of questions that made it easier for Carlos to communicate what was in his head.

Carlos began to respond to this treatment by becoming more relaxed; with increased relaxation came an improvement in his ability to communicate. After a couple of weeks, the other children concluded Carlos was a lot smarter than they had thought he was. They began to see things in him they had never seen before. They began to like him. Carlos began to enjoy school more and began to see the Anglo students in his group not as tormentors but as helpful and responsible people. Moreover, as he began to feel increasingly comfortable in class and started to gain more confidence in himself, his academic performance began to improve. The vicious cycle had been reversed; the elements that had been causing a downward spiral were changed —the spiral now began to move upward.

Within a few years, my students and I replicated this experiment in scores of classrooms across the country. The results are clear-cut and consistent. Children in the interdependent, jigsaw classrooms grow to like each other better, develop a greater liking for school, and develop greater self-esteem than children in traditional classrooms. The increase in liking among children in the jigsaw classroom crosses ethnic and racial boundaries.[98] The exam performance of members of ethnic minorities is higher in the jigsaw classroom than in the traditional classrooms. For example, in one study,[99] my colleagues and I found that, within two weeks of participating in the jigsaw groups, minority-group children increased their performance almost an entire letter grade, without any cost to the performance of the other children. Finally, teachers enjoyed using the technique and found it to be effective. Most of the teachers who agreed to use the jigsaw method as part of our experiment continued to use it *after* the experiment was over.

Several recent experiments indicate that the jigsaw method's effectiveness at reducing prejudice is not limited to young children. In one such experiment, Donna Desforges and her colleagues[100] had college students interact with a confederate who was portrayed as a former mental patient. The students were led to expect the "former mental patient" to behave in a rather weird manner. The interactions were part of a structured learning situation, with some of the students interacting with the "former mental patient" in a jigsaw group while others interacted with him in a more traditional learning climate. The results are striking: Those in the jigsaw group were quickly able to let go of their stereotypical expectations; they liked him better and enjoyed interacting with him more than did those who encountered him in a more traditional learning situation. Moreover, people who went through the jigsaw session described mental patients, in general, far more positively.

Underlying Mechanisms. Why does the jigsaw strategy produce such positive results? A recent experiment by Samuel Gaertner and his colleagues[101] demonstrates that what seems to happen is that the process of cooperation lowers barriers between groups by changing the cognitive categories people use. In other words, cooperation changes our tendency to categorize the outgroup from "those people" to "us people." In addition, the jigsaw technique encourages the development of empathy. Recall that, in the preceding chapter, I mentioned that increasing a person's empathy—the ability to put oneself in another's position—is beneficial to human relations, enhancing helping behavior and decreasing aggression. In the classroom, the best way to maximize learning—especially in the jigsaw situation—is to pay close attention to the child who is speaking. For example, if I am in a jigsaw group with Carlos and want to learn what he knows, not only must I listen attentively to him, but I must also put myself in his shoes in order to ask him questions in a clear and nonthreatening manner. In the process, I learn a lot not only about the subject, and not only about Carlos, but about the process of seeing the world through another person's eyes.

This was beautifully demonstrated in an experiment by one of my students, Diane Bridgeman.[102] Bridgeman administered a sequence of cartoons to ten-year-old children, half of whom had spent eight weeks participating in jigsaw classes. The cartoons are aimed at measuring a child's ability to empathize. In one cartoon, for example, a little boy looks sad as he says good-bye to his father at the airport. In the next frame, a letter carrier delivers a package to the child. When the boy opens it, he finds a toy airplane—and promptly bursts into tears. When Bridgeman asked the children why the little boy cried, almost all of the children told her the reason: The airplane reminded the child of being separated from his father, which made him sad. So far so good. Now for the crucial part. Bridgeman asked the children what the letter carrier who delivered the package was thinking. Most children that age make a consistent error, based on the egocentric assumption that their own knowledge is universal; specifically, they erroneously assume *the letter carrier* would know the boy was sad because the gift reminded him of his father leaving. The responses of the children who had participated in the jigsaw classes followed a different pattern, however. Because of their jigsaw experience, they were better able to take the letter carrier's perspective; they knew he was not privy to the same information they were and that he wasn't aware of the scene at the airport. Accordingly, the jigsaw children realized the letter carrier would experience *confusion* at the sight of a little boy crying over receiving a nice present. In sum, participation in jigsaw groups has a general impact on a child's ability to see the world through another person's eyes; this seems to be a major cause of the beneficial effects described above.

One of the most encouraging ramifications of this increase in empathy is that the usual tendency people have of giving themselves the benefit of the doubt can now be extended to other people, including people who aren't members of their own ethnic or racial group. Let me explain. You will recall that in making attributions about the cause of failure, people tend to give themselves the benefit of the doubt, but rarely extend that benefit to others. Thus, if I do poorly on an exam, I tend to conclude that I was sleepy or that the questions were unfair; but if *you* do poorly on an exam, I would tend to conclude that you were stupid or lazy. In a series of experiments,[103] my colleagues and I corroborated this finding: We found that, in a competitive situation, not only do children attribute their rivals' failures to lack of ability, they also attribute their rivals' successes to luck. But here is the interesting part: We also found that, in a *cooperative* situation (like jigsaw), children are as generous with their partners as they are with themselves; they attribute their partner's success to skill, and failure to an unlucky break. This is exciting because, when we can begin to think of members of other races and ethnic groups with the same generosity we extend to ourselves, the ultimate attribution error breaks down and prejudice is being reduced at a deep level.

The jigsaw technique was invented in 1971. In recent years, several similar cooperative techniques have been developed by others.[104] The striking results described in this chapter have been successfully replicated in thousands of classrooms in all regions of the country and abroad. The cooperative movement in education has grown by leaps and bounds and, in a relatively brief span of time, has achieved something of a minor revolution within the field of public education. Educational commentator Alfie Kohn[105] estimates that over twenty-five thousand teachers are now using some form of cooperative learning in the United States alone—and hundreds more are adopting it every year. John McConahay,[106] a leading expert on race relations, has called the cooperative learning revolution the single most effective practice for improving race relations in desegregated schools.

Although cooperative learning is clearly a promising strategy, it is not a perfect solution. For example, while jigsaw and other cooperative strategies do produce beneficial effects with high-school students,[107] they work *best* with young children, before prejudiced attitudes have an opportunity to become deeply ingrained. Moreover, prejudice is a complex phenomenon; no one solution can claim to be *the* solution. As we have seen, many aspects of our society are changing simultaneously—more equitable exposure of ethnic minorities via the mass media, greater educational opportunities, and so on. It is a slow process, and equity is still a long distance away. Yet prejudice does seem to be on the wane, and this is encouraging. Recall that, not so long ago, it was argued that desegregation would be impossible without prior attitude change. More generally, just a few decades ago, the conventional wisdom held that prejudice was largely the result of a deeply rooted personality disorder that must be cured before desegregation could proceed. The evidence indicates that, for the vast majority of prejudiced individuals, this is not the case. The first wedge in the diminution of prejudice is desegregation. In the words of Thomas Pettigrew, one of our most tireless investigators in this area:

> Some cynics have argued that successful racial desegregation in the South will require an importation of tens of thousands of psychotherapists, and therapy for millions of bigoted southerners. Fortunately for desegregation, psychotherapists, and southerners, this will not be necessary; a thorough repatterning of southern interracial behavior will be sufficient therapy in itself.[108]

Although Pettigrew may have been overly optimistic, it cannot be denied that, in recent years, social psychologists have made great progress in our quest to find more effective ways to reduce prejudice. It is a quest that continues, both in the laboratory and in the classroom even as I write these words.

In the next chapter, we will attempt to look beyond race and ethnicity and take a broader look at the positive or negative feelings any person might have for any other—and why. That is, we will try to shed some light on what it is that determines whether two strangers will come to like each other, come to hate each other, or remain indifferent to each other.

8
Liking, Loving, and Interpersonal Sensitivity

Early in this book I described several situations, in the laboratory and in the real world, in which people turned their backs on the needs of their fellow human beings. I mentioned incidents in which people watched someone being killed without attempting to help; in which people walked casually by, around, and over a woman with a broken leg lying on a Fifth Avenue sidewalk; in which people, hearing a woman in the next room apparently fall off a stepladder and injure herself, did not so much as ask if she needed assistance. I also described a situation in which people went a step further by apparently causing a person to suffer severe pain: A large number of individuals, in blind obedience to the commands of an authority figure, continued to administer severe electric shocks to another human being even after the person screamed in pain, pounded on the door, begged to be released, and then fell into ominous silence. Finally, we saw how people, through fear, hate, and prejudice, can deprive one another of their civil rights, rob one another of their freedom, and even destroy one another.

With all of these events in mind, I asked if there is any way to diminish aggression and to encourage people to take responsibility for the welfare of their fellow human beings. In this chapter, I will ask this question in a more formal manner: What do we know about the factors that cause one person to like or love another?

The question is almost certainly an ancient one. The first amateur social psychologist, who probably lived in a cave, undoubtedly wondered what he could do to make the fellow in a neighboring cave like him more or dislike him less—or, at least, to make him refrain from clubbing him on the head. Perhaps he bared his teeth as a means of showing he was fierce enough to bite a chunk out of his neighbor's leg if the fellow continued to behave aggressively. According to naturalist Charles Darwin,[1] this simple gesture was successful during the course of our evolution, and the baring of teeth, now called a smile, gradually evolved into a social convention—a way of inducing people not to hurt us, and perhaps even to like us.*

After several thousand years, people are still speculating about the antecedents of attraction—how to behave so the person at the next desk, in the next house, or in the next country likes us more, or at least refrains from insulting us or trying to destroy us. What do we know about the causes of attraction? When I ask my friends why they like some of their acquaintances better than others, I get a wide variety of responses. The most typical responses are that people like most (1) those whose beliefs and interests are similar to their own; (2) those who have some skills, abilities, or competencies; (3) those with some pleasant or "admirable" qualities, such as loyalty, reasonableness, honesty, and kindness; and (4) those who like them in return.

These reasons make good sense. They are also consistent with the advice given by Dale Carnegie in a book with the chillingly manipulative title *How to Win Friends and Influence People.*[2] Manipula-

---

* Contemporary ethologists are not all in agreement with Darwin's view of the origins of the smile. Some believe that the smile began, not as a sign of aggression, but rather as a sign of *submission* to prevent or terminate aggression from dominant, powerful others.

tive title notwithstanding, this recipe book for interpersonal relations seems to have been exactly what people were looking for—it proved to be one of the best sellers of all time. That's not surprising. Americans seem to be deeply concerned with being liked and making a good impression. A series of polls conducted among high-school students during the 1940s and 1950s[3] indicated that their most important concern was the way others reacted to them—and their overwhelming desire was for people to like them more. There is no reason to believe that this concern has changed in recent decades. Such concerns may be greatest during adolescence, when the peer group assumes enormous importance, but the desire to be liked is certainly not limited to U.S. adolescents. The search for a simple formula to attract others seems universal. After all, Dale Carnegie's book was translated into thirty-five languages and was avidly read around the globe.

Carnegie's advice is deceptively simple: If you want people to like you, be pleasant, pretend you like them, feign an interest in things they're interested in, "dole out praise lavishly," and be agreeable. Is it true? Are these tactics effective? To a limited extent they *are* effective, at least in the early stages of the acquaintance process. Data from well-controlled laboratory experiments indicate we like people with pleasant characteristics more than those with unpleasant characteristics;[4] we like people who agree with us more than people who disagree with us; we like people who like us more than people who dislike us; we like people who cooperate with us more than people who compete with us; we like people who praise us more than people who criticize us; and so on. These aspects of interpersonal attraction can be gathered under one sweeping generalization: We like people whose behavior provides us with maximum reward at minimum cost.[5]

A general reward theory of attraction covers a great deal of ground. It allows us to explain why we like people who are physically appealing more than people who are homely—because good-looking people bring us "aesthetic" rewards.[6] At the same time, it allows us to predict we will like people with opinions similar to ours[7] because, when we run into such people, they reward us by providing us with consensual validation for our beliefs—that is, by helping us to believe our opinions are "correct." Moreover, as we learned in the preceding chapter, one way prejudice and hostility can be reduced is by changing the environment in such a way that individuals cooperate with each other rather than compete. Another way of stating this relation is that cooperation leads to attraction. Thus, whether the environment is a summer camp, as in Muzafer Sherif's experiments,[8] or a classroom situation, as in the experiments I performed with my colleagues,[9] there is an increase in mutual attraction if people spend some time cooperating with each other. Cooperative behavior is clearly rewarding by definition—a person who cooperates with us is giving us aid, listening to our ideas, making suggestions, and sharing our load.

A general reward-cost theory can explain a great deal of human attraction, but not all of it—the world is not that simple. For example, a reward-cost theory would lead us to suspect that, all other things being equal, we would like people who live in close proximity to us, because we can get the same reward at less cost by traveling a short distance than we can by traveling a great distance. Indeed, it does tend to be true that people have more friends who live close by than friends who live far away; but this does not necessarily mean it is their physical proximity that makes them attractive. Their physical proximity may simply make it easier to get to know them, and once we get to know them, we tend to like them. Moreover, as I pointed out earlier in this book, individuals also like things or people for which or for whom they have suffered. For example, recall the experiment I did in collaboration with Judson Mills[10] in which we found that people who went through an unpleasant initiation in order to become members of a group liked that group better than did those who became members by paying a smaller price in terms of time and effort. Where is the reward? The reduction of suffering? The reduction of dissonance? How does the reward become attached to the group? It is not clear.

Moreover, simply knowing that something is rewarding does not necessarily help us to predict or understand a person's behavior. For example, recall that in chapters 2, 3, and 5, I analyzed why people conform and why they change their attitudes, and I discussed several reasons: out of a desire to win praise, to be liked, to avoid ridicule; out of a desire to identify with someone whom they respect or admire; out of a desire to be right; or out of a desire to justify their own behavior. In some way, all of these behaviors make sense, or feel good, or both, and therefore can be considered rewards. But simply to label them as rewards tends to obscure the important differences between them. Although both the desire to be right and the desire to avoid ridicule produce a state of satisfaction when gratified, the behaviors a person must employ to gratify these needs are frequently opposite in kind. For example, in judging the size of a line, a person might conform to group pressure out of a desire to avoid ridicule, but that same person might deviate from the unanimous opinion of the other group members out of a desire to be right. Little understanding is gained by covering both behaviors with the blanket term *reward.* For the social psychologist, a far more important task is to determine the conditions under which one or the other course of action will be taken. This point will become clearer as we address some of the research on interpersonal attraction.

The Effects of Praise and Favors

Recall that Dale Carnegie advised us to "dole out praise lavishly." This seems like good old-fashioned common sense: Surely we can "win friends" by praising our teachers' ideas or our employees' efforts. Indeed, several experiments have shown, in general, that we like people who positively evaluate us far more than those who negatively evaluate us.[11] But does it always work? Let's take a closer look. Common sense also suggests there are situations in which criticism might be more useful than praise. For example, suppose you are a brand-new college instructor lecturing to a class full of graduate students and presenting a theory you are developing. In the rear of the classroom are two students. One of these people is nodding and smiling and looks as though he is in rapture. At the close of your presentation, he comes up and tells you that you are a genius and your ideas are the most brilliant he's ever heard. It feels good to hear that, of course. In contrast, the other student shakes her head and scowls occasionally during your presentation, and afterward, she comes up and tells you there are several aspects of your theory that don't make sense. Moreover, she points these out in some detail and with a note of disdain in her voice. That evening, while ruminating on what was said, you realize that the remarks made by the second student, although somewhat extreme and not completely accurate, did contain some valid points and forced you to rethink a few of your assumptions. This eventually leads you to a significant modification of your theory. Which of these two people will you like better? I don't know. Although praise is clearly rewarding, disagreement that leads to improvement may carry its own rewards. Because I am, at this point, unable to predict which of these behaviors is more rewarding, it is impossible to be sure which of the two students you will like better.

The relative impact of praise and criticism is even more complicated—and more interesting. Some research shows that, all other things being equal, a negative evaluation generally increases the admiration we feel for the evaluator—so long as he or she is not evaluating *us!* In one experiment, Theresa Amabile[12] asked college students to read excerpts from two reviews of novels that had appeared in the *New York Times* Book Review section. Both reviews were similar in style and quality of writing—but one was extremely favorable, and the other, extremely unfavorable. Students considered the negative reviewer to be considerably more intelligent, competent, and expert than the positive reviewer—but less likable!

Let us take a different example, one involving the attribution of ulterior motives to the praiser. Suppose Nancy is an engineer and she produces an excellent set of blueprints. Her boss says, "Nice work, Nancy." That phrase will almost certainly function as a reward, and Nancy's liking for her boss will probably increase. But suppose Nancy is having an off day and produces a sloppy set of blueprints—and knows it. The boss comes along and emits the same phrase in exactly the same tone of voice. Will that phrase function as a reward in this situation? I am not sure. Nancy *may* interpret the statement as her boss's attempt to be encouraging and nice, even in the face of a poor performance; because of the boss's display of thoughtfulness, Nancy may come to like him even more than she would have had she, in fact, done a good job. On the other hand, Nancy may attribute all kinds of characteristics or ulterior motives to her boss: She may conclude her boss is being sarcastic, manipulative, dishonest, nondiscriminating, patronizing, seductive, or stupid—any one of which could reduce Nancy's liking for him. A general reward-cost theory loses a good deal of its value if our definition of what constitutes a reward is not

clear. As situations become complex, we find that such general notions decrease in value, because a slight change in the social context
in which the reward is provided can change a "reward" into a punishment.

Research in this area indicates that, although people like to be
praised and tend to like the praiser,[13] they also dislike being manipulated. If the praise is too lavish, if it seems unwarranted, or (most
important) if the praiser is in a position to benefit from the ingratiat-
ing behavior, then he or she is not liked very much. Edward E. Jones
and his students[14] have carried out a great deal of research on this
problem. In a typical experiment, an accomplice watched a young
woman being interviewed and then proceeded to evaluate her. The
evaluations were prearranged so some women heard a positive evaluation, some heard a negative evaluation, and some heard a neutral
evaluation. In one experimental condition, the evaluator was ascribed
an ulterior motive. In this condition, subjects were informed in advance that the evaluator was a graduate student who needed subjects
for her own experiment and would be asking her (the subject) to
volunteer. The results showed that the students liked the evaluators
who praised them better than those who provided them with a negative evaluation—but there was a sharp drop in how much they liked
the praiser with the ulterior motive. Thus the old adage "flattery will
get you nowhere" is clearly wrong. As Jones puts it, "flattery will get
you *somewhere*"—but not everywhere.

By the same token, we like people who do us favors. Favors can
be considered rewards, and we do tend to like people who provide us
with this kind of reward. For example, in a classic study of inmates in
a women's reformatory, Helen Hall Jennings [15] found that the most
popular women were those who initiated new and interesting activities and helped others become a part of those activities. Our liking
for people who do us favors extends even to situations in which these
favors are not intentional. This was demonstrated by Bernice and
Albert Lott[16] in an experiment with young children. The researchers
organized children into groups of three for the purpose of playing a
game that consisted of choosing various pathways on a board. Those
who were lucky enough to choose the safe pathways won the game;
making the wrong choice led to disaster. The children were, in effect,
walking single file in an imaginary mine field, whose mines remained

active even after they exploded. If the child at the front of the line chose the wrong path, that player was "blown up" (out of the game), and the child next in line would, of course, choose a different path. Leaders who happened to choose correctly led the others to a successful completion of the game. The results indicated that those children who were rewarded (by arriving safely at the goal) showed a greater liking for their teammates (who, of course, had been instrumental in helping them achieve the reward) than did those children who did not reach the final goal. In short, we like people who contribute to our victory more than those who do not—even if they had no intention of doing us a favor.

But, as with those who praise us, we do not always like people who do favors for us; specifically, we do not like people whose favors seem as though they may have some strings attached to them. Such strings constitute a threat to the freedom of the receiver. People do not like to receive gifts if a gift is expected in return; moreover, people do not like to receive favors from individuals who are in a position to benefit from that favor. Recall the example I mentioned in a previous chapter: If you were a teacher, you might enjoy receiving gifts from your students. On the other hand, you might be made pretty uncomfortable if a borderline student presented you with an expensive gift just before you were about to grade his or her term paper. Strong support for this reasoning comes from an experiment by Jack Brehm and Ann Cole.[17] In this experiment, college students were asked to participate in a study (which the experimenters characterized as important) in which they would be giving their first impressions of another person. As each subject was waiting for the experiment to begin, the "other person" (actually a stooge) asked permission to leave the room for a few moments. In one condition, he simply returned after a while and resumed his seat. In the other condition, he returned carrying a soft drink, which he immediately gave to the subject. Subsequently, each subject was asked to help the stooge perform a dull task. Interestingly enough, those students who had *not* been given the drink by the stooge were more likely to help him than those who *had* been given the drink.

The upshot of this research is that favors and praise are not universal rewards. For a starving rat or a starving person, a bowl of dry cereal is a reward—it is a reward during the day or during the night, in winter or in summer, if offered by a man or by a woman, and so on. Similarly, for a drowning person, a rescue launch is a reward under all circumstances. That is, such rewards are "transsituational." But praise, favors, and the like are not transsituational—whether or not they function as rewards depends on minor situational variations, some of which can be extremely subtle. Indeed, as we have seen, praise and favors can even function to make praisers or favor-doers less attractive than they would have been had they kept their mouths shut or their hands in their pockets. Thus, Dale Carnegie's advice is not always sound. If you want someone to like you, doing a favor as a technique of ingratiation is indeed risky.

Getting someone to do *you* a favor is a more certain way of using favors to increase your attractiveness. Recall that, in chapter 5, I described a phenomenon called "the justification of cruelty." Briefly, I pointed out that, if individuals cause harm to a person, they will attempt to justify their behavior by derogating the victim. I also analyzed how the justification process could work in the opposite direction: The "foot-in-the-door" technique can be used to make people more likely to do large favors by first getting them to do a small favor. Not only can this increase people's tendency to help; if we do someone a favor, we can also justify this action by convincing ourselves that the recipient of this favor is an attractive, likable, deserving person. In effect, we will say to ourselves, "Why in the world did I go to all of this effort (or spend all of this money, or whatever) for Sam? Because Sam is a wonderful person, that's why!"

This notion is not new—indeed, it seems to be a part of folk wisdom. One of the world's greatest novelists, Leo Tolstoy[18] in 1869 wrote: "We do not love people so much for the good they have done us, as for the good we have done them." Similarly, in 1736, Benjamin Franklin utilized this bit of folk wisdom as a political strategy—with apparent success. Franklin, disturbed by the political opposition and apparent animosity of a member of the Pennsylvania state legislature, set out to win him over:

> I did not . . . aim at gaining his favour by paying any servile respect to him but, after some time, took this other method. Having heard that he had in his library a certain very scarce and curious book I wrote a note to him expressing my desire of perusing that book and request-

ing he would do me the favour of lending it to me for a few days. He sent it immediately and I returned it in about a week with another note expressing strongly my sense of the favour. When we next met in the House he spoke to me (which he had never done before), and with great civility; and he ever after manifested a readiness to serve me on all occasions, so that we became great friends and our friendship continued to his death. This is another instance of the truth of an old maxim I had learned, which says, "He that has once done you a kindness will be more ready to do you another than he whom you yourself have obliged."[19]

While Benjamin Franklin was clearly pleased with the success of his maneuver, as a scientist I am not totally convinced. It is not entirely clear whether Franklin's success was due to this strategy or to any one of many charming aspects of his personality. In order to be certain, a well-controlled experiment is necessary. Just such an experiment was conducted by Jon Jecker and David Landy,[20] over 230 years after Benjamin Franklin's more casual experiment. In this experiment, students participated in a concept-formation task that enabled them to win a rather substantial sum of money. After the experiment was over, one-third of the subjects were approached by the experimenter, who explained that he was using his own funds for the experiment and was running short—which would mean he might be forced to stop the experiment. He asked, "As a special favor to me, would you mind returning the money you won?" Another one-third of the subjects were approached, *not* by the experimenter, but by the departmental secretary, who asked them if they would return the money as a special favor to the psychology department's research fund, which was running low. The remaining subjects were not asked to return their winnings. Finally, all of the subjects were asked to fill out a questionnaire, which included an opportunity to state their feelings about the experimenter. Those subjects who had been cajoled into doing a special favor for the experimenter liked him best; that is, because they did him a favor, they succeeded in convincing themselves he was a decent, deserving fellow.

Similar results were obtained in an experiment by Melvin Lerner and Carolyn Simmons,[21] in which groups of subjects were allowed to observe a student who appeared to be receiving a series of electric shocks as part of an experiment in learning. After watching for a while, some groups of subjects were allowed to vote (by private ballot) on whether or not the "victim" should continue to receive electric shocks. Other groups of subjects were not allowed to vote on this procedure. All subjects who were allowed to vote did, indeed, vote for the termination of the shocks; but some groups of voting subjects were successful in effecting a termination of the shocks, while others were not. Those people who were successful at terminating the shocks came to like the victim the most.

Personal Attributes

As I have already mentioned, there are several personal character-istics that play an important role in determining the extent to which a person will be liked.[22] Thus, people tend to like others who are sincere, competent, intelligent, energetic, and so on. Most of these studies were done in the manner of a public opinion poll—that is, people were simply asked to describe the attributes of people they like and those of people they dislike. In studies of this sort, it is difficult to establish the direction of causality: Do we like people who have pleasant attributes, or do we tend to convince ourselves that our friends tend to have these pleasant attributes? Chances are that caus-ality flows in both directions. In order to be *sure* people with certain positive personal attributes are liked better than others, however, it is necessary to examine this relation under more controlled conditions than exists in the opinion poll. In this section, we will closely examine two of the most important personal attributes: competence and phys-ical attractiveness.

Competence. It would seem obvious that, all other things being equal, the more competent an individual is, the more we will like that person. This is probably because people have a need to be right; we stand a better chance of being right if we surround ourselves with highly able, highly competent people. But, as we continue to learn in this chapter, factors that determine interpersonal attraction are often complex; they cannot always be spelled out in simple terms. As for competence, there is a great deal of apparently paradoxical evidence in the research literature demonstrating that, in problem-solving groups, the participants who are considered the most competent and to have the best ideas tend *not* to be the ones who are best liked.[23] How can we explain this apparent paradox? One possibility is that, although we like to be around competent people, a person who has a great deal of ability may make us uncomfortable. That person may seem unapproachable, distant, superhuman. If this were true, we might like the person more were he or she to show some evidence of fallibility. For example, if Sam were a brilliant mathematician as well as a great basketball player and a fastidious dresser, I might like him better if, every once in a while, he misadded a column of numbers, blew an easy layup, or appeared in public with a gravy stain on his tie.

Over thirty years ago, I was speculating about this phenomenon when I chanced upon some startling data from a Gallup poll: When John Kennedy was president, his personal popularity actually increased immediately after his abortive attempt to invade Cuba at the Bay of Pigs in 1961. This was startling in view of the fact that this attempted invasion was such a phenomenal blunder, it was immediately dubbed (and is still commonly known as) "the Bay of Pigs fiasco." What can we make of it? This was a situation in which a president committed one of our country's greatest blunders (up until that time, that is), and miraculously, people came to like him more for it. Why? One possibility is that John Kennedy may have been "too perfect." What does that mean? How can a person be too perfect?

In 1961, John Kennedy stood very high in personal popularity. He was a character of almost storybook proportions. Indeed, his regime was referred to as Camelot. Kennedy was young, handsome, bright, witty, charming, and athletic; he was a voracious reader, the author of a best seller, a master political strategist, a war hero, and an uncomplaining endurer of physical pain; he was married to a talented and beautiful woman (who spoke several foreign languages), had two cute kids (one boy and one girl), and was part of a commendable, close-knit family. Some evidence of fallibility (like being responsible for a major blunder) could have served to make him more human in the public eye and, hence, more likable.

Alas, this is only one of several possible explanations, and (as the reader knows all too well by now) the real world is no place to test such a hypothesis. In the real world, there are too many things happening simultaneously, any one of which could have increased Kennedy's popularity. For example, after the fiasco occurred, President Kennedy did not try to make excuses or to pass the buck; rather, he bravely accepted full responsibility for the blunder. This selfless action could have done much to make him more attractive in the eyes of the populace. In order to test the proposition that evidence of fallibility in a highly competent person may make that person better liked, an experiment was needed. One of the great advantages of an experiment is that it eliminates or controls extraneous variables (such as the selfless assumption of responsibility) and allows us, therefore, to assess more accurately the effect of one variable on another.

I performed such an experiment in collaboration with Ben Willerman and Joanne Floyd.[24] The subjects were college men at the University of Minnesota. Each subject listened to a simple audiotape recording featuring one of four stimulus persons: (1) a nearly perfect person, (2) a nearly perfect person who commits a blunder, (3) a mediocre person, and (4) a mediocre person who commits a blunder. In preparation, each subject was told he would be listening to a person who was a candidate for the then-popular *College Bowl* quiz show, and that he would be asked to rate one of the candidates by the kind of impression he made, by how likable he seemed, and so forth. Each tape consisted of an interview between a young man (stimulus person) and an interviewer, and contained a set of extremely difficult questions posed by the interviewer; the questions were like those generally asked on *College Bowl*. On one tape, the stimulus person showed a high degree of competence—indeed, he seemed to be virtually perfect, answering 92 percent of the questions correctly—and in the body of the interview, when asked about his activities in high school, he modestly admitted he had been an honor student, the editor of the yearbook, and a member of the track team. On another tape, the stimulus person (actually the same actor using the same tone of voice) was presented as a person of average ability: He answered only 30 percent of the questions correctly, and during the interview he admitted he had received average grades in high school, had been a proofreader on the yearbook staff, and had tried out for the track team but had failed to make it. On the other two recordings (one of the "superior" young man and one of the "average" young man), the stimulus person committed an embarrassing blunder. Near the end of the interview, he clumsily spilled a cup of coffee all over himself. This "pratfall" was created by making a tape recording that included sounds of commotion and clatter, the scraping of a chair, and the anguished voice of the stimulus person saying, "Oh my goodness, I've spilled coffee all over my new suit." To achieve maximum control, the tape of the incident was reproduced, and one copy was spliced onto a copy of the tape of the superior person, while the other copy was spliced onto a tape of the average person. This gave us four experimental conditions: (1) a person of superior ability who blundered, and (2) one who did not; and (3) a person of average ability who blundered, and (4) one who did not.

The superior person who committed a blunder was rated most attractive; the average person who committed the same blunder was rated least attractive. The perfect person (no blunder) was second in attractiveness, and the mediocre person (no blunder) finished third. Clearly, there was nothing inherently attractive about the simple act of spilling a cup of coffee. Although it did serve to add an endearing dimension to the perfect person, making him more attractive, the same action served to make the mediocre person appear that much more mediocre and, hence, less attractive. This experiment presents stronger evidence to support our contention that, although a high degree of competence does make us appear more attractive, some evidence of fallibility increases our attractiveness still further. This phenomenon has been dubbed "the pratfall effect."

More complex experiments have since produced some interesting refinements of this general finding. Basically, the pratfall effect holds most clearly when, within the head of the observer, there is some implicit threat of competition with the stimulus person. Thus, an experiment by Kay Deaux[25] demonstrates that the pratfall effect applies most strongly to males. She found that, although most males in her study preferred the highly competent man who committed a blunder, women showed a tendency to prefer the highly competent nonblunderer, regardless of whether the stimulus person was male or female. Similarly, my colleagues and I found that males with a moderate degree of self-esteem are most likely to prefer the highly competent person who commits a blunder, while males with low self-esteem (who apparently feel little competitiveness with the stimulus person) prefer the highly competent person who *doesn't* blunder.[26]

It should be emphasized that no sizable proportion of people—regardless of their own level of self-esteem—preferred the mediocre person. I want to take special pains to make this point because of a bizarre political event. In the early 1970s, when former president Richard Nixon was at the height of his popularity, he tried, in vain, to appoint to the Supreme Court two strikingly mediocre lower-court judges. In defending these nominees, Senator Roman Hruska argued (seriously, I'm afraid) that while it was true these men were mediocre, the mediocre citizens of the country needed someone on the Supreme Court to represent them, too! Again, our data do not support that argument.

Physical Attractiveness. Imagine you are on a blind date. It is near the end of the evening, and you are wondering whether or not you want to go out with this person again. Which of your partner's characteristics will weigh most heavily: Warmth? Sensitivity? Intelligence? Compassion? *How about good looks?* You guessed it!

Most of us tend to be both incredulous and appalled by such a suggestion. We don't want this to be true. We would like to believe that beauty is only skin deep and, therefore, a trivial determinant of liking. Also, it seems so unfair; why should something like physical attractiveness—which is largely beyond a person's control—play an important role? Indeed, when asked what they looked for in a potential date, most college students put "physical attractiveness" at the very bottom of the list.[27] But I'm afraid this reflects only what students think they *ought* to believe—for, in study after study of their actual behavior, college students (as well as the population at large) are overwhelmingly influenced by another person's physical attractiveness.[28] In one study, for example, Elaine Walster (Hatfield) and her associates[29] randomly matched incoming students at the University of Minnesota for a blind date. The students previously had been given a battery of personality tests. Which of their many characteristics determined whether or not they liked each other? It was not their intelligence, masculinity, femininity, dominance, submission, dependence, independence, sensitivity, sincerity, or the like. The *one* determinant of whether or not a couple liked each other and actually repeated their date was their physical attractiveness. If a handsome man was paired with a beautiful woman, they were most likely to desire to see each other again.

This general phenomenon is not limited to a blind date. Gregory White[30] studied relatively long-term relationships among young couples at UCLA. Like Walster (Hatfield) and her colleagues, White found that physical attractiveness was a very important factor; but in this situation it was the *similarity* of the attractiveness of the members of the couple that was crucial in determining whether or not a relationship had staying power. Specifically, some nine months after the couples started dating, those pairs who were well matched in terms of rated physical attractiveness were more deeply involved with each other than when the members differed from each other in physical attractiveness.

What is clear from these studies of dating couples is that, in one way or another, physical attractiveness plays an important role in determining who likes whom in both the short run and the long run. Moreover, these studies indicate that there are clear cultural standards for physical attractiveness—at least in the United States, where most of this research has been done. Raters had no difficulty judging people on physical attractiveness. And the raters agreed with one another—that is, the ratings were highly *reliable.* Moreover, all other things being equal, people's physical attractiveness not only helps us predict whether or not others will want to date them, but also influences a wide range of attributions. For example, in one study, Karen Dion and her colleagues[31] showed college students photographs of three college-age people. The photos were especially selected for differing degrees of attractiveness: One was attractive, one average, and one unattractive. The subjects were asked to rate each of the people depicted in these photographs on twenty-seven different personality traits and were asked to predict their future happiness. The physically attractive people were assigned by far the most desirable traits and the greatest prognosis for happiness. This was true whether there were men rating men, men rating women, women rating men, or women rating women.

Does it surprise you to learn that most people seem to agree on both the physical characteristics and the concomitant personality traits of so-called beautiful people? Perhaps it shouldn't. From early childhood experiences we learn that a specific definition of beauty is associated with goodness. Walt Disney's movies and the illustrators of children's books have taught us that gentle and charming heroines like Snow White, Cinderella, and Sleeping Beauty—as well as the princes who woo and win them—all look alike. They all have regular features, small pert noses, big eyes, shapely lips, blemish-free complexions, and slim athletic bodies. They all look like Barbie and Ken dolls. Indeed, so do Barbie and Ken dolls! And how are the wicked stepmothers, stepsisters, giants, trolls, and queens depicted?

In addition, television sustains these cultural standards; actors who fit the U.S. stereotype of beauty are carefully selected to play the heroines and heroes of popular TV soap operas and prime-time sitcoms. And then there are the commercials. Anyone who watches a fair amount of television is subjected to a continuous flow of propaganda aimed at selling the idea of beauty in a bottle. Shampoo, skin lotion, deodorant, toothpaste—all are peddled by promoting the conviction that these products will make us beautiful, desirable, and ultimately successful. And exposure to this kind of thing *does* have an impact. For example, in one experiment,[32] young women between the ages of sixteen and eighteen were systematically exposed to some fifteen TV commercials extolling the virtues of beauty preparations. A control group of teenagers was shown fifteen commercials unrelated to "beauty" products. Some time later all of the young women were asked to rank the relative importance of ten attributes—for example, sex appeal, intelligence, a pretty face, industriousness, and so on. The young women who had been shown the beauty ads were more likely than the control group to consider beauty-oriented attributes more important than other qualities.

One of the implications of our discussion is that cultural standards of beauty are learned early. If we learn about beauty by looking at the pictures in storybooks, or from Walt Disney movies, or from watching television, then it should follow that even young children are influenced by these norms. And so they are. In a striking study, Karen Dion and Ellen Berscheid[33] found that, even as early as nursery school, children are responsive to the physical attractiveness of their peers. In their study, Dion and Berscheid first had several independent judges (graduate students) rate the physical attractiveness of the nursery-school children. Then they determined who liked whom among the children themselves. They found that physical attractiveness was very important. The clearest results were obtained for the males: The physically attractive boys were liked better than the physically unattractive boys. Moreover, unattractive boys were considered to be more aggressive than their attractive counterparts, and when the children were asked to name the classmates that "scared them," they tended to nominate the unattractive children. Of course, it might have been the case that the less attractive children actually *behaved* more aggressively. The researchers did not observe the actual behavior of the children in the nursery school, so they could not test that possibility. But there is independent evidence that people do tend to attribute less blame to physically attractive children, regardless of the facts. This finding emerges from another study by Karen Dion.[34] Women were asked to examine reports of rather severe classroom disturbances, apparently written by a teacher. Attached to each report was a photo of the child who was said to have initiated the disturbance. In some instances, the photo was that of a physically attractive boy or girl; in others, the photo was that of a less attractive boy or girl. The women tended to place more blame on the less attractive children and to infer that this was typical of their everyday behavior. When the child was pictured as physically attractive, however, these women tended to excuse the disruptive behavior. As one of the women put it, "She plays well with everyone, but like anyone else, a bad day can occur. Her cruelty . . . need not be taken seriously." When a physically *un*attractive girl was pictured as the culprit in exactly the same situation described in exactly the same way, a typical respondent said, "I think the child would be quite bratty and would probably be a problem to teachers. She would probably try to pick a fight with other children her own age. . . . All in all, she would be a real problem." Thus, it seems that attractive children are given the benefit of the doubt. Their misbehaviors are seen as forgivable aberrations caused by the effects of the situation, other people, or an unfortunate accident. Less attractive children, on the other hand, are not let off the hook so easily; their misdeeds are attributed *internally*—to stable dispositions.

Physical attractiveness seems to have important consequences in the business world as well. Irene Frieze[35] and her associates rated the attractiveness of over seven hundred young adults and tracked their employment histories—starting just after they attained masters degrees in business administration, and continuing for a ten-year period. The results are clear. For men, being physically attractive resulted in a higher starting salary. Moreover, this effect did not fade over time as employers got to know them as whole people—attractive men continued to out-earn their not-so-attractive counterparts over the entire ten-year period. For women, being attractive did not affect starting salaries, but attractiveness began to influence salaries after they had been on the job a while and continued to the conclusion of the study. Attractiveness was rated on a five-point scale. The researchers were able to calculate that each point on the scale was worth about $2,150; thus, theoretically, if you underwent plastic surgery and it improved your looks from a rating of "2" to a rating of "4," that would be worth exactly $4,300 per year!

Physical attractiveness is not always a one-way street. Harold Sigall and I[36] demonstrated that attractive women have more impact on men than less attractive women—for better or for worse. In this experiment, a woman was made to appear either physically attractive or unattractive. This was accomplished by taking a naturally beautiful woman and, in the unattractive condition, providing her with loose, baggy, unflattering clothing, fitting her with a frizzy blond wig that did not quite match her skin coloring, and making her complexion look oily and unhealthy. Then, posing as a graduate student in clinical psychology, she interviewed several college men. At the close of the interview, she gave each student her own personal, clinical evaluation of him. Half of the students received highly favorable evaluations, and half received unfavorable evaluations. We found that, when the evaluator was made to look unattractive, the men didn't seem to care much whether they received a good evaluation or a poor evaluation from her—in both situations, they liked her a fair amount. When she was beautiful, however, they liked her a great deal when she gave them a favorable evaluation, but when she gave them an unfavorable evaluation, they disliked her more than in any of the other conditions. Interestingly enough, although the men who were evaluated negatively by the attractive woman said they didn't like her, they did express a great desire to return in order to interact with her in a future experiment. It seems the negative evaluations from the beautiful woman were so important to the subjects that they wanted the opportunity to return so as to induce her to change her evaluations of them.

Similarly, Harold Sigall and Nancy Ostrove[37] showed that people tend to favor a beautiful woman unless they suspect her of misusing her beauty. Both male and female college students were allowed to read an account of a criminal case in which the defendant was clearly guilty of a crime. Each subject then "sentenced" the defendant to a prison term he or she considered appropriate. The results showed that, when the crime was unrelated to attractiveness (burglary), the sentences were much more lenient when the defendant was physically attractive. When the crime was related to her attractiveness (a swindle in which the defendant induced a middle-aged bachelor to invest some money in a nonexistent corporation), the sentences were much harsher for the physically attractive defendant. It should be noted that this phenomenon is not limited to the judgments people make in hypothetical situations. Chris Downs and Phillip Lyons[38] investigated the fines and bails set by real judges in actual court cases involving 915 female and 1,320 male defendants being charged with either misdemeanors or felonies. These researchers found that, where felonies were involved, the physical attractiveness of the defendant made no difference. But for misdemeanors, the judges were much more lenient with attractive individuals, assessing both lower bail and lower fines than they did for relatively unattractive defendants.

The effects of a person's physical attractiveness go beyond how we evaluate or how much we are influenced by *that* person; it can also change our perceptions about the people with whom he or she is associated. An experiment by Harold Sigall and David Landy[39] demonstrated that, when seen in the company of a beautiful woman, a man is perceived differently from when he is seen with an unattractive woman. In their study, subjects who met a man seated next to an extremely attractive woman tended to like him more and to rate him as friendlier and more self-confident than did subjects who met the same man when he was seated beside an unattractive woman.

Taking all of this research into consideration, it is clear that beauty is more than skin deep. We are affected by physically attractive people, and unless we are specifically abused by them, we tend to like them better and we reward them more than less attractive people. Moreover, in ambiguous situations involving trouble and turmoil, beautiful people tend to be given the benefit of the doubt—they receive more favorable treatment than less attractive people. This begins at a very young age. The disconcerting aspect of these data is the strong possibility that such preferential treatment contains the seeds of a self-fulfilling prophecy: We know the way people are treated affects the way they come to think of themselves. Some evidence for this phenomenon comes from an ingenious experiment conducted by Mark Snyder, Elizabeth Decker Tanke, and Ellen Berscheid.[40] Put yourself in the place of a typical male undergraduate in their experiment: You have volunteered to participate in an investigation of "how people become acquainted with each other," and you have been paired with a female student who is located in another room, ostensibly because the two of you are assigned to the "no nonverbal communication" condition of the study. Though you haven't seen your partner, you have been given a packet of information, which contains a Polaroid snapshot. When you proceed to have a conversation with this woman over an intercom, do you think the physical attractiveness of the woman in the photo will influence your impressions of her? Snyder, Tanke, and Berscheid found it did.

As the reader might suspect, the snapshot viewed by the male subject did not depict his actual partner. For half of the subjects, it pictured a very attractive woman; for the others, it pictured a relatively unattractive woman. But the snapshot did have an effect. The subjects who thought they were talking with an attractive partner rated her as more poised, humorous, and socially adept than did those who thought they were talking with a less attractive woman. This is not very surprising. But what *was* startling was this: When independent observers were allowed to listen to a tape recording of only the woman's half of the conversation (without looking at a photograph), they were far more impressed by the woman whose male partner thought she was physically attractive. In short, since the male partner thought he was talking to an attractive woman, he spoke to her in a way that brought out her best and most sparkling qualities. When these independent observers listened to her conversation, they rated her as more attractive, more confident, more animated, and warmer than the woman whose partner thought her to be less beautiful. Thus, physically attractive people may come to think of themselves as "good" or lovable because they are continually treated that way. Conversely, homely people may begin to think of themselves as "bad" or unlovable because they are continually treated that way—even as children. Ultimately, people may begin to behave in a way consistent with this self-concept—a way that is consistent with how they were treated to begin with.

Please note that, for the most part, our discussion of beauty has focused on "visual" beauty. But there are other kinds of beauty. Our visual perceptual mechanisms exercise a terribly conservative influence on our feelings and behavior. We are wedded to our eyes—especially as a means of determining physical attractiveness. And, as we have seen, once we have categorized a person as good-looking or homely, we tend to attribute other qualities to that person—for example, good-looking people are likely to strike us as being more warm, sexy, exciting, and delightful than homely people. Later in this chapter, I will briefly discuss sensitivity-training groups. Some of these groups allow people to engage in nonvisual sensory experiences. For example, one such experience enables people to "turn off their eyes" and become acquainted with each other solely through the sense of touch. After participating in one of these exercises, group members typically report a dramatic diminution of their prior stereotypes. Basically, individuals find there is little "homeliness" in a nonvisual situation. Moreover, participants are frequently astonished to learn that, for example, the incredibly warm, gentle, and sensitive person they had been having a nonvisual encounter with is, "in reality," the funny-looking guy with the pimples. I doubt that, after even one such nonvisual encounter with him, a person would ever relate to him again as merely a funny-looking guy with pimples. To the extent such experiences can enable people to become aware of the nonvisual aspects of beauty, some of the unfairness due to the inequitable distribution of physical beauty may be reduced.

Similarity and Attraction

Lynne goes to a cocktail party and is introduced to Suzanne. While they chat for only a few moments, it turns out they agree completely on several issues, including the inequity of the income-tax structure, the status of Douglas MacArthur in world history, and the importance of a liberal arts education. Upon returning home, Lynne tells her husband she likes Suzanne a great deal and considers her a wonderful and intelligent person. Literally dozens of tightly controlled experiments by Donn Byrne and his associates[41] have shown over and over again that, if all you know about a person are his or her opinions on several issues, the more similar those opinions are to yours, the more you like the person.

Why is agreement important? There are at least two possibilities. First, people who share our opinion on an issue provide us with a kind of social validation for our beliefs—that is, they provide us with the feeling we are right. This is rewarding; hence, we like those who agree with us. In addition, the other side of the coin may be even more important. Specifically, as Milton Rosenbaum has argued, our desire to avoid people who disagree with us is stronger than our need to associate with those whose attitudes are similar to our own.[42] This is the case because, if a person disagrees with us, the possibility we may be wrong is introduced. This possibility is punishing; hence, we don't like people who disagree with us. Second, it is likely we make certain negative inferences about the character of a person who disagrees with us on a substantive issue, not simply because such disagreement suggests that we might be wrong, but rather, because we suspect the individual's opinion on that issue is indicative of the kind of person we have found in the past to be unpleasant, immoral, or stupid. For example, suppose you believe that the penalties for using drugs are too severe. You then meet a woman who tells you drug users should be put in prison for several years. I then come along, ask you if you liked that woman, and you say, "No." Am I to conclude (1) you didn't like her because hearing her state her belief suggested to you that your belief might be wrong, or (2) you didn't like her because, in your experience, people who favor harsh punishments for drug users tend to be unpleasant, immoral, inhuman, bigoted, harsh, cruel, conventional, punitive, and stupid?

Both of these factors undoubtedly play a role. There is some evidence to suggest the second factor may be of lesser importance. This stems from Harold Sigall's brilliant investigation of the psychological effects of conversion.[43] Sigall showed that, if people are highly involved with an issue, they prefer a "disagreer" to an "agreer" if they can succeed in converting that person to their way of thinking. In short, Sigall demonstrated that people like converts better than loyal members of the flock. Apparently, the competence people feel when they induce someone to convert overcomes any tendency they might have to actively dislike the other person for being the sort who would hold an "awful" opinion to begin with.

One additional factor must be mentioned here: We humans are so certain of the relationship between attitude similarity and liking that if we like someone, we will assume that his or her attitudes must be similar to ours. Thus, causality works in both directions: All other things being equal, we like people whose attitudes are similar to ours, *and* if we like someone, we attribute attitudes to him or her that are similar to ours.[44]

Liking, Being Liked, and Self-Esteem

There is still another reason why we tend to like people who hold opinions similar to ours. Research has shown that when we learn that someone shares our opinions, we are likely to believe he or she will really like us, if and when that person gets to know us.[45] This can be very important because, as it turns out, the single most powerful determinant of whether one person will like another is whether the other likes that person. Several investigators have demonstrated this point: When other people like us, we tend to like them, too.[46]

What's more, merely believing someone likes you can initiate a spiraling series of events that promote increasingly positive feelings between you and the other person. How does this work? To illustrate, imagine that you and I engaged in a brief, rather uneventful conversation at a party after a mutual friend introduced us to each other. A few days later, you run into our friend on campus, and he informs you that, following the party, I had some very complimentary things to say about you. How do you suppose you might act the next time you and I happened to meet? My hunch is that your knowledge that I liked you would probably lead you to like me and to act in ways that let me know that you liked me, too. You'd probably smile more, disclose more about yourself, and generally behave in a more likable manner than if you hadn't already learned that I liked you. And what effect do you think your actions would have on my behavior? Faced with your warm and likable behavior, my fondness for you would undoubtedly grow, and I, in turn, would convey my liking for you in ways that made me even more likable to you . . . and on and on.

But, consider this: What if our mutual friend hadn't exactly been telling the truth? What if he had figured that you and I really would like each other a great deal once we got to know each other, and—to get the ball rolling—had told you that I liked you, even though I hadn't ever expressed such feelings? What are the chances that his well-intentioned (if sneaky) plan would work? Well, if you and I were like the subjects in a recent experiment by Rebecca Curtis and Kim Miller,[47] his scheme would have worked like a charm! These researchers led some subjects to believe that another subject liked them and led others to believe that the other subject disliked them. In a subsequent interaction, those individuals who thought they were liked behaved in more likable ways; they disclosed more about themselves, disagreed less, and generally behaved in a warmer, more pleasant manner toward the other subject than those individuals who thought they were disliked. Moreover, subjects who believed they were liked were, in fact, liked by the other subject, while those who believed they were disliked were not liked by the other subject. Interestingly enough, the behaviors of subjects who thought they were either liked or disliked led to reciprocal behaviors from their partners who—remember—had never actually expressed a liking or disliking for the other subjects. Partners tended to mirror the behaviors of the subject with whom they were paired: When they interacted with "liked" subjects, they—in turn—acted in more likable ways than those who interacted with "disliked" subjects. Once again, these findings demonstrate the pervasiveness of the "self-fulfilling prophecy" discussed earlier: Our beliefs—be they right or wrong—play a potent role in shaping reality.

As we have seen, being liked indeed does make the heart grow fonder. Furthermore, the greater our insecurity and self-doubt, the fonder we will grow of the person who likes us. In a fascinating experiment by Elaine Walster (Hatfield),[48] female college students, while waiting to receive the results of personality tests they had taken previously, were approached by a rather smooth, good-looking, well-dressed young man who was, in fact, an accomplice in the employ of the experimenter. The smooth young man struck up a conversation with the subject, indicated he liked her, and proceeded to make a date. At this point, the experimenter entered and led the young woman into an office to inform her of the results of her tests. In the course of this procedure, the young woman was allowed to read an evaluation of her own personality. Half of the young women received highly positive descriptions, designed expressly to temporarily raise their self-esteem. The other women received somewhat negative descriptions, designed to temporarily lower their self-esteem. Finally, as part of the experiment, the women were asked to rate how much they liked a wide variety of people—a teacher, a friend, ". . . and since we have one space left, why don't you rate that fellow you were waiting with?" Those women who received unfavorable information about themselves (from the personality test) showed far more liking for their male admirer than did those who received favorable information about themselves. In short, we like to be liked—and the more insecure we feel, the more we like someone who likes us.

One of the implications of this experiment is that people who are secure about themselves are less "needy"—that is, they are less likely to accept overtures from just any person who comes along. Just as a starving person will accept almost any kind of food and a well-fed person can be more selective, so too will an insecure person accept almost anyone who expresses interest, while a secure person will be more selective. Moreover, a person who feels insecure may even seek out a less-attractive person in order to diminish the possibility of being rejected. This implication was tested in an interesting experiment by Sara Kiesler and Roberta Baral,[49] who led male college students to believe they had done either very well or very poorly on a test of intellectual achievement. They then took a break and the experimenter joined the student for a cup of coffee. As they entered the coffee shop, the experimenter "recognized" a female student seated alone at a table, joined her, and introduced the male subject to her. Of course, the female student was a confederate, intentionally planted there. Half of the time the confederate was made up to look attractive; the other half of the time she was made to look somewhat less attractive. The investigators observed the degree of romantic interest displayed by the male subjects—whether they asked to see her again, offered to pay for her coffee, asked for her phone number, tried to get her to stay longer, and so on. Interestingly enough, those induced to feel secure about themselves (that is, led to believe they had performed well on the test) showed more romantic interest toward the "attractive" woman; those induced to feel insecure showed more romantic interest toward the "unattractive" woman.

In a related vein, Joel Grube and his colleagues[50] found that males with low self-esteem are attracted more to a "traditional" woman, but that males with high self-esteem tend to be attracted more to a "nontraditional" woman—that is, a woman who expresses feminist values. Grube suggests that male prejudice against feminists and other nontraditional women may stem, in part, from a man's attempt to bolster his self-esteem in the face of perceived threat. That is, a nontraditional woman is usually seen as more assertive and independent than her more traditional counterpart. These traits may threaten the feelings of control and autonomy of a man with low self-esteem; thus, he derogates the nontraditional woman in order to protect his own self-image. A man with high self-esteem, by definition, is more secure and less easily threatened. Thus, he has no need to derogate an assertive, independent woman.

There are a great many factors that can influence a person's self-esteem and therefore can have an important effect on his or her selectivity in the interpersonal marketplace. As the reader knows, one of these factors is physical attractiveness—people who are physically attractive tend to be treated better by others, and this is almost certain to raise self-esteem. How does physical attractiveness affect selectivity? In a study reported by Zick Rubin,[51] a number of women were asked to complete a questionnaire about their dating preferences; the young women were also surreptitiously rated on the dimension of physical attractiveness. When rating their dating preferences, all of the women found men in the high-status occupations (physicians and lawyers, for example) to be acceptable dates, and they rejected those in low-status jobs (janitors, bartenders). However, when it came to judging the acceptability of those men more toward the middle of the status hierarchy (electricians, bookkeepers, plumbers), differences emerged according to the attractiveness of the women— the more attractive women were more selective, finding such men to be unacceptable dates, while the less attractive women reported they would go out with men in these occupations.

The Relation between Similarity and Being Liked. If we like people who hold opinions similar to ours, and if we like people who like us, shouldn't it follow that we will like a person particularly well if we learn he or she is *both* similar *and* he or she likes us? While this seems like common sense, the answer is no; the evidence suggests that these two factors are not additive. In an experiment I performed in collaboration with Edward Jones and Linda Bell,[52] we showed that, although it is nice to be liked by someone who shares our values and opinions, it is far *more* exciting to be liked by someone who doesn't. Each of the college women in this experiment had a brief conversation with another woman in which she discovered they either agreed or disagreed on a number of issues. After the conversation, the subject was allowed to eavesdrop on a conversation the other woman (actually a stooge) was having with a third person. During this conversation, the other woman discussed her feelings about the subject. In one condition, she indicated she liked her; in another condition, she indicated she disliked her. How did this affect the subject's feelings about the stooge? The subjects expressed the greatest liking for people with *dissimilar* attitudes who *liked* them. Thus, although we generally like people who have attitudes similar to our own, if we encounter someone who likes us *in spite* of the fact that our opinions differ, we are inclined to infer there must be something special and unique about us that she finds attractive. In short, people tend to suspect that, where opinions differ, "That person likes me for myself, not for my opinions." Because this realization is especially gratifying, we tend to like that individual more.

The Gain and Loss of Esteem

We have seen that our being liked by a person increases the likelihood we will like him or her. Let us take a closer look at this relation. Imagine that, at a cocktail party, you meet a young woman for the first time and have an animated conversation with her. After a while, you excuse yourself to refill your glass. You return and find her back to you, deep in conversation with another person—and she's talking about you. So, naturally, you pause to listen. Clearly, the things she says about you will have an impact on how you feel about her. It is obvious she has no ulterior motives; indeed, she doesn't even know you are eavesdropping. Thus, if she tells her partner that she was impressed by you, that she liked you, that she found you bright, witty, charming, gracious, honest, and exciting, my guess is this disclosure would have a positive effect on your liking for her. On the other hand, if she indicates that she was unimpressed, that she disliked you, that she found you dull, boring, dishonest, stupid, and vulgar, my guess is this revelation would have a negative effect on your liking for her.

So far so good. But I'm sure that's not very interesting to you; you've always known that the more good things we hear about ourselves, the better we like the speaker (unless that speaker is trying to con us), and the more bad things we hear about ourselves, the more we dislike the person who says them. Everybody knows that—*but it happens to be untrue.* Imagine this: You have attended seven consecutive cocktail parties, and miracle of miracles, the same general event has occurred each time. You chat with a person for several minutes, you leave, and when you come back you overhear her talking about you. It's the same person each time. Her responses might remain constant throughout her seven encounters with you, or they might vary. There are four possibilities that are particularly interesting to me: (1) You overhear the person saying exclusively positive things about you on all seven occasions; (2) you overhear her saying exclusively negative things about you on all seven occasions; (3) her first couple of evaluations are negative, but they gradually become increasingly positive until they equal her statements in the exclusively positive situation, and then level off; and (4) her first couple of evaluations are positive, but they gradually become more negative until they equal her statements in the exclusively negative situation, and then level off. Which situation would render the person most attractive to you?

According to a simple reward-cost idea of liking, you should like the person most in the first situation, in which she says exclusively positive things, and you should like her least (or dislike her most) in the second situation, in which she says exclusively negative things. This seems obvious. Because positive statements are rewarding, the more the better; because negative statements are punishing, the more the worse.

A few years ago, I developed a theory of interpersonal attraction, called the gain-loss theory, that makes a rather different prediction.[53] My theory is a very simple one. It suggests that *increases* in positive, rewarding behavior from another person have more impact on an individual than constant, invariant reward from that person. Thus, if we take being liked as a reward, a person whose liking for us increases over time will be liked better than one who has always liked us. This would be true even if the *number* of rewards was greater from the latter person. Similarly, *losses* in rewarding behavior have more impact than constant punitive behavior from another person. Thus, a person whose esteem for us decreases over time will be disliked more than someone who has always disliked us—even if the number of punishments were greater from the latter person. To return to the cocktail party for a moment, I would predict you would like the individual most in the *gain* situation (where she begins by disliking you and gradually increases her liking), and you would like her least in the *loss* condition (where she begins by liking you and gradually decreases her liking for you).

In order to test my theory, I needed an experimental analogue of the cocktail-party situation—but for reasons of control, I felt it would be essential to collapse the several events into a single long session. In such an experiment, it is important that the subject be absolutely certain the evaluator is totally unaware that she (the evaluator) is being overheard. This eliminates the possibility of the subject's suspecting the evaluator of intentionally flattering him when she says positive things. This situation presents a difficult challenge for the experimentalist. The central problem in devising a way to perform the experiment was one of credibility: How can I provide a believable situation in which, in a relatively brief period of time, the subject (1) interacts with a preprogramed confederate, (2) eavesdrops while the preprogramed confederate evaluates him or her to a third party, (3) engages in another conversation with the confederate, (4) eavesdrops again, (5) converses again, (6) eavesdrops again, and so on, through several pairs of trials. To provide any kind of a cover story would indeed be difficult; to provide a sensible cover story that would prevent subjects from becoming suspicious would seem impossible. But, in collaboration with Darwyn Linder, I did devise such a situation.[54] The devices we used to solve these problems are intricate, and they provide a unique opportunity to look behind the scenes of an unusually fascinating sociopsychological procedure. Accordingly, I would like to describe this experiment in some detail, in the hope it will provide the reader with an understanding of some of the difficulties and excitements involved in conducting experiments in social psychology.

When the subject (a female college student) arrived, the experimenter greeted her and led her to an observation room connected to the main experimental room by a one-way window and an audio-amplification system. The experimenter told the subject that two women were scheduled for that hour: One would be the subject and the other would help perform the experiment—and because she had arrived first, she would be the helper. The experimenter asked her to wait while he left the room to see if the other woman had arrived. A few minutes later, through the one-way window, the subject was able to see the experimenter enter the experimental room with another female student (a paid confederate). The experimenter told the confederate to be seated for a moment and he would return shortly to explain the experiment to her. He then reentered the observation room and began the instructions to the real subject (who believed herself to be the confederate). The experimenter told her she was going to assist him in performing a verbal conditioning experiment on the other student; that is, he was going to reward the other student for certain words she used in conversation. He told the subject these rewards would increase the frequency with which the other woman would use these words. He went on to say that his particular interest was "not simply in increasing the output of those words that I reward; that's already been done. In this experiment, we want to see if the use of rewarded words generalizes to a new situation from the person giving the reward when the person is talking to a different person who does not reward those specific words." Specifically, the experimenter explained he would try to condition the other woman to increase her output of plural nouns by subtly rewarding her with an "mmmm hmmm" every time she said a plural noun. "The important question is: Will she continue to use an abundance of plural nouns when she talks to you, even though you will not be rewarding her?" The real subject was then told her tasks were: (1) to listen in and record the number of plural nouns used by the woman while the latter was talking to the experimenter, and (2) to engage her in a series of conversations (in which the use of plural nouns would not be rewarded) so the experimenter could listen and determine whether generalization occurred. The experimenter then told the subject they would alternate in talking to the woman (first the subject, then the experimenter, then the subject) until each had spent seven sessions with her.

The experimenter made it clear to the subject that the other woman must not know the purpose of the experiment, lest the results be contaminated. He explained that, in order to accomplish this, some deception must be used. The experimenter said that, as much as he regretted the use of deception, it would be necessary for him to tell the "subject" that the experiment was about interpersonal attraction. ("Don't laugh, some psychologists are actually interested in that stuff.") He said the woman would be told she was to carry on a series of seven short conversations with the subject and that, between each of these conversations, both she and the subject would be interviewed—the woman by the experimenter and the subject by an assistant in another room—to find out what impressions they had formed. The experimenter told the subject this "cover story" would enable the experimenter and the subject to perform their experiment on verbal behavior, because it provided the woman with a credible explanation for the procedure they would follow.

The major variable was introduced during the seven meetings the experimenter had with the confederate. During their meetings, the subject was in the observation room, listening to the conversation and dutifully counting the number of plural nouns used by the confederate. Because she had been led to believe the confederate thought the experiment involved impressions of people, it was quite natural for the experimenter to ask the confederate to express her feelings about the subject. Thus, the subject heard herself being evaluated by a fellow student on seven successive occasions.

Note how, by using a cover story that *contains* a cover story involving "interpersonal attraction," we were able to accomplish our aim without arousing suspicion—only four of eighty-four subjects were suspicious of this procedure.

There were four major experimental conditions: (1) positive—the successive evaluations of the subject made by the confederate were all highly positive; (2) negative—the successive evaluations were all highly negative; (3) gain—the first few evaluations were negative, but they gradually became more positive, reaching a level equal to the level of the positive evaluations in the positive condition; and (4) loss—the first few evaluations were positive, but they gradually became negative, leveling off at a point equal to the negative evaluations in the negative condition.

The results confirmed our predictions: The subjects in the gain condition liked the confederate significantly better than the subjects in the positive condition. By the same token, the subjects in the loss condition had a tendency to dislike the confederate more than the subjects in the negative condition. Recall that a general reward-cost theory would lead us to a simple algebraic summation of rewards and punishments and, accordingly, would have led to somewhat different predictions. The results are in line with our general theoretical position: A gain has more impact on liking than a set of events that are all positive, and a loss tends to have more impact than a set of events that are all negative. The philosopher Baruch de Spinoza may have had something like this in mind when, about three hundred years ago, he observed:

> Hatred which is completely vanquished by love passes into love, and love is thereupon greater than if hatred had not preceded it. For he who begins to love a thing which he was wont to hate or regard with pain, from the very fact of loving, feels pleasure. To this pleasure involved in love is added the pleasure arising from aid given to the endeavor to remove the pain involved in hatred accompanied by the idea of the former object of hatred as cause.[55]

Two important conditions are necessary for the gain-loss effect to be operative. First, it is not just any sequence of positive or negative statements that constitute a gain or loss; there must be an integrated sequence implying a change of heart. In other words, if you indicate that you think I'm stupid and insincere, and later you indicate that you think I'm generous and athletic, this does not constitute a gain according to my definition—or Spinoza's. On the other hand, if you indicate I'm stupid or insincere and subsequently indicate you've changed your mind—that you now believe me to be smart and sincere—this is a true gain because it indicates a reversal, a replacement of a negative attitude with its opposite. David Mettee and his colleagues[56] performed an experiment that demonstrated this distinction. A gain effect occurred only when a change of heart was made explicit. Second, the change in attitude must be gradual. The reason for this should be clear: An abrupt about-face is viewed by the stimulus person with confusion and suspicion—especially if it occurs on the basis of very little evidence. If Mary thinks Sam is stupid after three encounters, but brilliant after the fourth encounter, such a dramatic shift is bound to arouse suspicion on Sam's part. A gradual change, on the other hand, makes sense; it does not produce suspicion and hence produces an intensification of the person's liking for his or her evaluator.[57]

Love and Intimacy

Until now, our discussion has focused primarily on factors that influence our initial feelings of like or dislike for someone, early in the process of becoming acquainted. Since first impressions are often lasting ones, they play an important role in whether we go on to develop a closer, more enduring relationship with someone we have recently met. As relationships deepen over time, however, other social-psychological processes come into play, in addition to those we have already examined. We now turn to the topic of close relationships, paying special attention to the experience of love. Later, we will explore how sensitive communication can deepen satisfaction and intimacy in close relationships.

Opposites Do Attract—Sometimes. As we saw earlier, the old adage seems to be true: Birds of a feather do tend to flock together. That is, people who share similar opinions tend to like each other. As we have also learned, however, it is far more complicated than that: If someone already likes us, we may like that individual better if he or she is *different* from us. These data are consistent with some of the findings of investigators who have studied relationships more enduring than those produced in the social-psychological laboratory. Robert Winch,[58] for example, who has done exhaustive studies of the personality characteristics of several engaged and married couples, finds that, under certain limited conditions, opposites attract—that is, people tend to choose people who have needs and characteristics that complement (rather than coincide with) their own needs and characteristics.

The reader will note I used the term "under certain limited conditions," because it turns out there are contradictory data in this research area. Some investigators find that married couples tend to have complementary need systems; others find that married couples tend to have similar need systems. My guess is that whether birds of a feather flock together or whether opposites attract depends on which personality characteristics are under consideration. Imagine a person who values neatness and tidiness. Such a person would be disinclined to marry someone who was casual to the point of slovenliness. Similarly, the slob would not be too happy with an overly neat person. It seems reasonable that neat birds would flock with other neat birds and slobs would flock with slobs. By the same token, a person who was extroverted might not get along too well with an introverted person whose idea of a good time was to sit home watching television. It is also true that people who are similar in wealth, intelligence, religious preference, attractiveness, education, and height do tend to flock together—especially in enduring relationships.[59] On the other hand, if we look at a different set of characteristics—say, nurturance and dependency—then a different picture emerges. A man who is very nurturant might be miserable if he found himself in a relationship with a highly independent woman—and vice versa. By the same token, what could be better for a dependent man than to live out his life on the bosom of someone who really enjoyed being nurturant? The same holds true for masculinity-femininity, assertiveness-passivity, and dominance-submissiveness. And, in a somewhat more facetious vein, what union could be happier than that of a sadist and a masochist?

In a long-term relationship, sociological factors also combine with need complementarity to play a sizable role in determining the extent to which two people will be attracted to each other and stay together. Society sets forth certain "role norms" for married couples. For example, in most of the world, society expects husbands to be relatively dominant and wives to be relatively submissive. If the complementarity of the needs of a couple coincide with the role norms set forth by society, the chances of marital happiness are increased. It should also be noted that, although the notion of need complementarity and the notion of opinion similarity frequently lead to opposite predictions about attraction, this is not necessarily true. People with certain complementary personality needs can be in complete agreement in their opinions about a given issue. To use an example just mentioned, it seems likely a dominant male and a submissive female will share the same opinions concerning sex roles in marriage—that a man should be dominant and a woman submissive. Obviously, these role norms can and do change. My own guess (and hope) is that, as men and women come to place more value on androgyny, the nineteenth-century role norms of the dominant husband and submissive wife will continue to change.

Defining Love. What is love? Is it, for example, simply a more intense version of liking? Or is it something entirely different? Are there many types of love? Or is all love basically the same? Although poets and philosophers throughout the ages—and more recently, social psychologists—have posed these and similar questions regarding love, they have yet to be answered in a fashion that all can agree on. The difficulty in defining love seems to lie, at least in part, in the fact that love is not a unitary, one-dimensional state but, rather, is a complex, multifaceted phenomenon experienced in a broad variety of relationships. Indeed, we use the word *love* to describe such diverse relationships as those between romantic lovers, married couples, parents and children, and close friends.

Given this complexity, social psychologists have developed various approaches to categorizing and describing love in its many forms. Zick Rubin, for example, views loving as conceptually distinct from liking and has developed questionnaires to measure each state.[60] Thus, loving is not simply a greater quantity of liking but typically involves a qualitatively different set of feelings and concerns regarding the loved one. Liking, in this view, is marked by admiration and friendly affection, reflected in such items as: "_____ is the sort of person I would like to be." Loving, in contrast, generally includes feelings of strong attachment, intimacy, and a deep concern for the beloved's welfare. Examples from Rubin's Loving Scale are: "If I could never be with _____, I would be miserable" (attachment), and "I feel that I can confide in _____ about virtually everything" (intimacy).

Rubin administered his loving and liking scales to college students who were dating steadily but not engaged, instructing them first to answer the items with respect to their partner and then in regard to a friend of the same gender. On average, male and female dating partners loved each other equally, but their scores on the liking scale were less strongly related. Rubin also found that the higher the couple's scores on the love scale, the more likely they were to believe they would get married some day. In addition, although men and women reported about the same level of liking for their same-sex friends, women expressed greater love for their friends than men did. In another study, Rubin brought dating couples into the laboratory and, through one-way mirrors, observed how long they maintained simultaneous eye contact with each other. Couples with high scores on the love scale gazed into each other's eyes more often than couples who scored low on the love scale.[61]

While Rubin's research suggests that loving may be a decidedly different experience from liking someone, other researchers have called attention to variations within the experience of love itself. Elaine Walster (Hatfield) and Bill Walster[62] have distinguished between two basic types of love: passionate and companionate. Passionate, or romantic, love is characterized by strong emotions, sexual desire, and intense preoccupation with the beloved. Its onset is often rapid rather than gradual, and almost inevitably, the fiery intensity of passionate love cools down over time. In some relationships, passionate love may be a prelude to the eventual development of companionate love—a milder, more stable experience marked by feelings of mutual trust, dependability, and warmth. Compared to the typically short-lived intensity of romantic passion, companionate love generally lasts longer and deepens over time.

While the distinction between passionate and companionate love is a useful one, it is equally important to realize that these two forms of love are not mutually exclusive. As Sharon Brehm has observed,[63] passionate and companionate love are best viewed as representing endpoints on a continuum. Seen in this light, different relationships—as well as a single relationship as it changes over time—can be understood as reflecting different proportions of each type of love. Thus, in the course of a long-term relationship, such as a successful marriage, companionate love may take on greater significance, even though elements of passionate love may also endure.

The Quest for Communal Relationships. Suppose you are sharing an apartment with an acquaintance named Sam. Sam almost never washes the dishes, empties the trash, or straightens up the living room. If you want a tidy house, you almost always need to do these things yourself. My guess is that, after a while, you might become upset and feel ripped off. But suppose Sam was a very close friend or lover. Would you still feel ripped off?

Margaret Clark and Judson Mills[64] make an important distinction between exchange relationships and communal relationships. In exchange relationships the people involved are concerned about making sure that some sort of equity is achieved—that there is fairness in the distribution of the rewards and costs to each of the partners. In this kind of relationship, if there is a major imbalance, both people become unhappy; the person on the short end usually feels angry or depressed, the person on the long end usually feels guilty.[65] In contrast, a communal relationship is one in which neither one of the partners is keeping score. Rather, a person will be inclined to give of herself or himself in response to the other's need and will readily receive when he or she is feeling needy. While the partners in a communal relationship are not totally unconcerned about achieving a rough kind of equity, they are relaxed about it and have faith that, over the long haul, some semblance of equity will fall into place. The closer and more intimate the relationship, the more communal it becomes. Clark and Mills suggest that prenuptial agreements, in which people about to be married specify precisely what they expect from their partner, are more likely to undermine than enhance their love for each other.

Needless to say, these issues are difficult to study scientifically. Nevertheless, Margaret Clark, Judson Mills, and their colleagues have done some clever experiments that succeed in capturing the essence of this important distinction. In one experiment, for example,[66] each subject was paired with either a very close friend or a stranger. The partner was then taken to another room to work on a complex task. Half the subjects were told that, if their partner needed help, that person would signal by flicking a switch that changed the pattern of some of the lights in the subject's room; the other subjects were told that the signal meant only that their partner was doing well, didn't need any help, and would soon complete the task for a reward which they would both share. The experimenters then observed how frequently the subjects looked at the lights to see if their partner was signaling them. If the partner was a stranger (exchange relationship), they spent far more time looking at the lights when they were told that it meant they might be getting a reward; if the partner was a close friend (communal relationship), they spent far more time looking at the lights when they thought it meant their partner might need help. In short, even in this rather sterile scientific setting, the investigators were able to show that people in communal relationships are eager to be responsive to the needs of their partners.

Gain–Loss Theory: Implications for Close Relationships. Alas, in love, things are never quite that simple. As Steve Duck[67] has recently pointed out, in addition to enormous benefits, there is also a dark side to being in a long-term close, communal relationship. In order to explore one of these less attractive "dark sides," let us first take another look at the distinction between passionate love and companionate love discussed earlier. Compared with the ups and downs of a passionate love affair, the steadier, predictable rhythm of a companionate relationship offers its own special rewards. The benefits of a thriving, long-term relationship include emotional security and the priceless comfort of being accepted by someone who knows your shortcomings as well as your strengths.

What seems to be inherent in the nature of close relationships, however, is a fundamental irony, aptly expressed in the words of the well-known ballad, "You Always Hurt the One You Love." Why might this be so? Recall from our earlier discussion of gain-loss theory the rather surprising fact that we find it more rewarding when someone's initially negative feelings toward us gradually become positive than if that person's feelings for us were entirely positive all along. Conversely, we tend to find it more noxious when a person who once evaluated us positively slowly comes to view us in a negative light than if he or she expressed uniformly negative feelings toward us. What are the implications of these findings for long-term relationships?

One possibility is that, once we have grown certain of the rewarding behavior of a person, that person may become less powerful as a source of reward than a stranger. That is, a gain in liking is a more potent reward than a constant level of liking; accordingly, a close friend (or a mother, a brother, or a mate) probably is behaving near ceiling level and, therefore, cannot provide us with a gain. To put it another way, once we have learned to expect love, favors, and praise from a friend, such behavior is not likely to represent a gain in that friend's esteem for us. By the same token, a loved one has great potential as a punisher. The closer the relationship and the greater the past history of invariant esteem and reward, the more devastating is the withdrawal of that person's esteem. In effect, then, the long-term friend has power to hurt the one he or she loves—but very little power to offer an important reward.

An example may help to clarify this point. After twenty years of marriage, a doting husband and his wife are getting dressed to attend a formal dinner party. He compliments her on her appearance: "Gee, honey, you look great." She hears his words, but they may not fill her with delight. She already knows her husband thinks she's attractive; chances are she will not turn cartwheels at hearing about it for the thousandth time. On the other hand, if the doting husband (who in the past was always full of compliments) were to tell his wife he had decided she was losing her looks and he found her quite unattractive, this would cause her a great deal of pain, because it represents a loss of esteem.

Is she doomed to experience either boredom or pain? No, because there are other people in the world. Suppose Mr. and Mrs. Doting arrive at a party and a total stranger engages Mrs. Doting in conversation. After a while, he says, with great sincerity, that he finds her very attractive. My guess is she would not find this at all boring. It represents a distinct gain for her—it makes her feel good about herself—and because of this it increases her liking for the stranger as well.

This reasoning is consistent with earlier findings. O. J. Harvey[68] found a tendency for subjects to react more positively to strangers than to friends when each was designated as the source of relatively positive evaluations of the subjects. Moreover, subjects tended to react more negatively to friends than to strangers when each was designated as the source of negative evaluations of the subjects. Similarly, several experiments have shown that strangers have more impact on the behavior of young children than either parents or other familiar adults.[69] Most children are accustomed to receiving approval from parents and other adults with whom they are familiar. Therefore, additional approval from them does not represent much of a gain. However, approval from a stranger *is* a gain and, according to gain-loss theory, should result in more positive behavior.

These results and speculations suggest a rather bleak picture of the human condition—we seem to be forever seeking favor in the eyes of strangers while, at the same time, we are being hurt by friends and other familiar people. Before we jump to this conclusion, however, let us take a few steps backward and look at the impact that gain or loss of esteem has on how individuals respond to close friends or strangers. One study is highly pertinent in this respect. Joanne Floyd[70] divided a group of young children into pairs, so each child was either with a close friend or with a stranger. One child in each pair was then allowed to play a game in which he or she earned several trinkets. The child was then instructed to share these with the assigned partner. The perceived stinginess of the sharer was manipulated by the experimenter. Some children were led to believe that the friend (or stranger) was treating them generously, and others were led to believe that the friend (or stranger) was treating them in a stingy manner. Each "receiving" child was then allowed to earn several trinkets and was instructed to share them with his or her partner. As expected, the children showed the most generosity in the gain and loss conditions—that is, they gave more trinkets to generous strangers and stingy friends. In short, they were relatively stingy to stingy strangers (and why not? The strangers behaved as they might have been expected to behave) and to generous friends ("Ho-hum, my friend likes me—so what else is new?"). But when it looked as though they might be gaining a friend (the generous stranger), they reacted with generosity; likewise, when it looked as though they might be *losing* one (the stingy friend), they also responded with generosity. Although it appears true that "you always hurt the one you love," the hurt person appears to be inspired to react kindly—rather than "in kind"—in an attempt to reestablish the positive intensity of the relationship. This suggests the comforting possibility that individuals are inclined to behave in a way that will preserve stability in their relations with others.

Along these lines, as far back as the year 46 B.C., and as recently as 1990, commentators from Cicero[71] to John Harvey and his colleagues[72] have suggested that, in a communal relationship, hurt feelings and conflict can produce healthy and exciting new understandings.

How might these understandings come about? A clue comes from taking another look at the Dotings. Although Mr. Doting has great power to hurt his wife by criticizing her, because of the importance of the relationship, Mrs. Doting is apt to listen closely and be responsive to such criticism and will be inclined to make some changes in order to regain his interest. The reverse is also true: If Mrs. Doting were to suddenly change her high opinion of Mr. Doting, he would be likely to pay close attention and eventually take action to regain her approval. A relationship becomes truly creative and continues to grow when both partners resolve conflicts—not by papering them over, but by striving to grow and change in creative ways—and in all of this, "authenticity" assumes great importance.

Carrying this reasoning a step further, I would suggest that, the more honest and authentic a relationship, the less the possibility of reaching the kind of dull and deadening plateau on which the Dotings appear to be stuck. What I am suggesting is that a close relationship in which the partners do not provide each other with gains in esteem is almost certain to be a relationship in which the partners are not open and honest with each other. In a closed relationship, people tend to suppress their annoyances and to keep their negative feelings to themselves. This results in a fragile plateau that appears stable and positive but that can be devastated by a sudden shift in sentiment. Unfortunately, this may be a common kind of relationship in this country.

In an open, honest, authentic relationship, one in which people are able to share their true feelings and impressions (even their negative ones), no such plateau is reached. Rather, there is a continuous zigzagging of sentiment around a point of relatively high esteem. Indeed, research[73] has shown that marriage partners who use an intimate, nonaggressive, yet *confrontational* method of conflict resolution report higher levels of marital satisfaction. In a relationship of this sort, the partners are reasonably close to the gain condition of the gain-loss experiment. Similarly, a great deal of research on self-disclosure has shown that an exchange of intimate and important aspects of *oneself*—both positive and negative—is necessary for the development of close relationships. Moreover, it has been found that, all other things being equal, we like a person better after *we* have disclosed something important about ourselves—even if it is un-savory. We also tend to like other people better when they honor us by revealing something intimate and negative about themselves; this is especially true when the person is ordinarily reserved, and there-fore, the behavior implies that there is something special about us that made him or her feel like opening up.[74]

To summarize, as a relationship ripens toward greater intimacy, what becomes increasingly important is authenticity—our ability to give up trying to make a good impression and begin to reveal things about ourselves that are honest even if unsavory. In addition, we must be willing to communicate a wide range of feelings to our loved ones and friends under appropriate circumstances and in ways that reflect our caring. Thus, to return again to the Dotings, if two people are genuinely fond of each other, they will have a more satisfying and exciting relationship over a longer period of time if they are able to express both positive and negative feelings than if they are completely "nice" to each other at all times.

Intimacy, Authenticity, and Communication

Honest communication with loved ones—including the sharing of negative as well as positive feelings—is no easy matter. Imagine, if you will, the following scenario:

Phil and Alice Henshaw are washing the dishes. They have had some friends over for dinner, the friends have left, and Phil and Alice are cleaning up. During the evening Alice was her usual charming, witty, vivacious self. But Phil, who is usually delighted by her charm, is feeling hurt and a little angry. It seems that, during a political discussion, Alice had disagreed with his position and sided with Tom. Moreover, she seemed to express a great deal of warmth toward Tom in the course of the evening. In fact, her behavior could be considered mildly flirtatious.

Phil is thinking: "I love her so much. I wish she wouldn't do things like that. Maybe she's losing interest in me. God, if she ever left me, I don't know what I'd do. Is she really attracted to Tom?" Phil actually says: "You sure were throwing yourself at Tom tonight. Everybody noticed it. You really made a fool of yourself."

Alice cares a great deal about Phil. She felt that she had said some very bright things—especially during the political discussion—and felt that Phil didn't acknowledge her intellectual contribution. "He thinks I'm just a housewife."

> Alice: "I don't know what you're talking about. You're just mad because I happened to disagree with you about the president's tax proposal. Tom saw it my way. I think I was right."
>
> Phil: "He saw it *your* way! Are you kidding? What else could he do? You were practically sitting in his lap. The other guests were embarrassed."
>
> Alice (teasing): "Why, Phil, I do believe you're jealous!"
>
> Phil: "I'm *not* jealous! I really don't give a damn. . . . If you want to act like a slut, that's your business."
>
> Alice (angrily): "Boy, are you old-fashioned. You're talking like some Victorian, for God's sake! You're always doing that!"
>
> Phil (coldly): "That just shows how little you know about me. Other people find me up-to-date—even dashing."
>
> Alice (sarcastically): "Yes, I'm sure you cut quite a figure with all the secretaries at your office!"
>
> Phil: "Now, what's *that* supposed to mean?"

Alice falls into a stony silence. Phil makes several attempts to get a response from her, fails, then storms out of the room, slamming the door. What is going on? Here are two people who care about each other. How did they get into such a vicious, hurtful, spiteful argument?

One of the major characteristics of humans that separates us from other organisms is our unique ability to communicate complex information through the use of a highly sophisticated language. The subtlety of communication that is possible among humans as compared to that among other animals is truly awesome. And yet, misunderstandings among people are frequent. Moreover, misunderstandings typify even those relationships that are close and caring. Though hypothetical, the argument between the Henshaws is not at all unrealistic; rather, it is typical of hundreds of such conversations I have heard as a consultant trying to help straighten out dyadic communications that are garbled, indirect, and misleading.

It would be relatively easy to analyze the argument between Phil and Alice. Each had a major concern that was being threatened. Neither was able or willing to state in a clear, straightforward way what that concern was. For Alice, the major concern seemed to be her intellectual competence. She was afraid Phil thought she was dumb; her major *implicit* complaint in this argument was that Phil didn't acknowledge the cogency of her statements during the political discussion, and he seemed to be implying that the only reason Tom paid attention to her or seemed to be interested in her statements was because of lust or sexual flirtation. This hurt her, threatened her self-esteem, and made her angry. She didn't express the hurt. She expressed the anger, but not simply by revealing it; rather, she took the offensive and attacked Phil by implying that he is stodgy and uninteresting.

Phil's major concerns seemed to stem from a feeling of insecurity. While he enjoys Alice's vivacity, he appears to be afraid of the possibility that, with increasing age, he may be losing his own attractiveness as a man. Thus, he assumed that Alice's agreeing with Tom is akin to her siding with Tom against him—and he attached sexual connotations to it because of his own insecurities. When Alice called him "old-fashioned," he seemed mostly to hear the "old"—and he quickly defended his masculinity and sex appeal, which Alice, driven by her *own* anger, promptly ridiculed.

This kind of argument is a familiar one among people living in close relationships. Important feelings and concerns are present. But instead of being discussed openly and honestly, the feelings are allowed to escalate into hostility, which only exacerbates the hurt and insecurity that initiated the discussion in the first place. As the divorce rate continues to soar in the United States, it seems reasonable to ask seriously why this happens. It would be silly to proclaim that all anger, disagreement, hurt, and hostility between people who supposedly care about each other is a function of poor or inadequate communication. Often there are conflicts between the needs, values, desires, and goals of people in close relationships. These produce stresses and tensions, which must either be lived with or resolved by compromise, yielding, or the dissolution of the relationship.

But frequently, the problem *is* largely one of communication. How might Phil have communicated differently? Pretend for the moment you are Phil. And Alice, a person you care about, approaches you and makes the following statement in a tone of voice that was nonblaming and nonjudgmental:

> I'm feeling insecure about my intelligence—or at least the way people view me on that dimension. Since you are the most important person in my world, it would be particularly gratifying to me if you would acknowledge statements of mine that you think are intelligent or worthwhile. When we disagree on a substantive issue and you speak harshly or become impatient with me, it tends to increase my feelings of insecurity. Earlier this evening, during our political discussion, I would have been delighted if you had complimented me on some of my ideas and insights.

Imagine, now, that you are Alice, and Phil had opened the after-dinner discussion in the following way:

> This is difficult to talk about, but I'd like to try. I don't know what it is with me lately, but I was feeling some jealousy tonight. This isn't easy to say . . . but here goes: You and Tom seemed kind of close—both intellectually and physically—and I was feeling hurt and lonely. I've been worried lately about middle age. This may seem silly, but I've been slowing down, feeling tired, developing a paunch. I need some reassurance; do you still find me attractive? I would love it if you'd look at me the way you seemed to be looking at Tom this evening.

My guess is most people would be receptive and responsive to that kind of *straight talk*, by which I mean a person's clear statement of his or her feelings and concerns without accusing, blaming, judging, or ridiculing the other person. Straight talk is effective, precisely because it enables the recipient to listen nondefensively.

Straight talk seems so simple, and it obviously is effective. Why don't people use it as a matter of course? The main reason is that it is not as easy as it appears. In the course of growing up in a competitive society, most of us have learned how to protect ourselves by making ourselves relatively invulnerable. Thus, when we are hurt, we have learned not to show it. Rather, we have learned either to avoid the person who hurt us or to lash out at him or her with anger or ridicule. As we have seen, this will usually result in either a defensive response or a counterattack, and the argument escalates.

In short, the general lesson of our society is never to reveal your vulnerabilities. This strategy may be useful and in some situations even essential, but in many circumstances it is inappropriate, dysfunctional, and counterproductive. It is probably wise not to reveal your vulnerability to someone who is your sworn enemy. But it is almost certainly unwise to conceal your vulnerability from someone who is your friend and cares about you. Thus, if Alice and Phil had known about the other's insecurity, they each could have acted in ways that would have made the other feel more secure. Because each of them had overlearned the societal lesson of "attack rather than reveal," they inadvertently placed themselves on a collision course.

Often, the problem is even more complicated than the one described in this example. Alice and Phil seem to have some idea of what their concerns are and what their feelings are. They got into serious conflict primarily because they had difficulty communicating their insecurity and hurt feelings with each other. But, in many situations, people are not fully aware of their own needs, wants, and feelings. Instead, there may be a vague feeling of discomfort or unhappiness that the person can't easily pinpoint. Often there is misattribution; that is, Phil may feel uncomfortable, and he could attribute the discomfort to embarrassment over Alice's alleged flirtatious behavior rather than to his own underlying insecurities about advancing middle age. Thus, if we are not in touch with our own feelings and cannot articulate them clearly to ourselves, we cannot communicate them to another person. The key issue is sensitivity. Can we learn to be more sensitive to our own feelings? Can we learn to be sensitive to others so that when people *do* make themselves vulnerable, we treat that vulnerability with care and respect?

These skills *can* be learned, and they are best learned through experience rather than simply reading about them in a book like this. This experiential learning is most effective if it takes place in a relatively safe, protected social environment where people can practice straight talk without fear that others will take advantage of their vulnerability. Some fifty years ago, responding to the need for such a safe social environment, social psychologists invented the *T-group*, also referred to as a sensitivity-training group or encounter group.

The first T-group was an accident. But, like most *productive* accidents, it occurred in the presence of a brilliant and creative person who was quick to appreciate the importance and potential utility of what he had stumbled upon. In 1946, Kurt Lewin, perhaps the greatest innovator and theorist in the brief history of social psychology, was asked to conduct a workshop to explore the use of small group discussions as a way of addressing some of the social problems of the day. The participants were educators, public officials, and social scientists. They met during the day in small groups. The small groups were observed by several of Lewin's graduate students, who met in the evenings to discuss their interpretation of the dynamics of the group discussions they had observed during the day.

One evening, a few of the participants asked if they could sit in and listen while the graduate students discussed their observations. Lewin was a little embarrassed by the request, but much to the surprise of his graduate students, he allowed the visitors to sit in. As it happened, one of the educators joined the group just as the observers were discussing and interpreting an episode that she had participated in the preceding morning. As she listened she became increasingly more agitated. Finally, she interrupted and said that the observers' interpretation was all wrong. She then proceeded to give her version of the episode. The discussion proved very exciting. The next night, all fifty of the participants showed up and gleefully joined the discussion, frequently disagreeing with the observations and interpretations of the trained observers. The session was both lively and illuminating.

Lewin and his students were quick to grasp the significance of that event: A group engaged in a problem-solving discussion can benefit enormously by taking time out to discuss its own dynamics or "group process" without special training as observers. Indeed, the participants themselves are much better observers of their own process because each is privy to his or her own intentions—something not easily available to outside observers—no matter how astute and well trained they are. After a time, what evolved was the agendaless group: The group could meet with maximum benefit if it had no formal agenda and no problems to discuss other than its own dynamics.

From their beginnings in 1946, interest in T-groups grew rapidly. They have been conducted in all sections of the country, with members hailing from all walks of life. Interest in T-groups reached its peak in the 1960s and 1970s, when they received wide (and often sensational) publicity. They were often treated with an uncritical, cultish, almost religious zeal by some of their proponents; and they were castigated by the right wing as an instrument of the devil, as a subversive form of brainwashing that was eating away at the moral fabric and soul of the nation.

As it turned out, T-groups were neither the panacea nor the menace they frequently were made out to be. Although their heyday has passed, the practices and principles of communication that evolved from T-groups have filtered into the larger culture, where their influence is felt in a variety of institutions, including large corporations and public education. Similarly, numerous support groups and other self-help organizations have emerged in recent years, many of which incorporate some elements of the T-group experience. Thus, while interest in T-groups, per se, seems to have dwindled, the need for authenticity and "straight talk" certainly has not. As a leader of T-groups for several years, I continue to believe that such groups provide a safe environment for the learning of skills that increase self-awareness and enrich human relations. I also believe, however, that while formal T-groups are no longer as readily available as they were in the 1960s and 1970s, the opportunity for open communication and the safety provided in a T-group can be approximated in any close and caring relationship between individuals who are committed to becoming more intimate and enhancing the quality of their interactions. As a by-product, such communication patterns enhance individual self-awareness and self-knowledge.

Communication Goals. To begin with, let's consider some of the major goals of effective communication in T-groups. These goals also apply to relationships in general, especially intimate ones. They include:

1. Developing ways of communicating that are clear, straight, nonattributional, nonjudgmental, and nonpunitive.

2. Developing a spirit of inquiry and a willingness to examine

one's own behavior and to experiment with one's role in the world.

3. Developing the ability to resolve conflicts and disputes through problem solving rather than through coercion or manipulation.

In addition, an implicit assumption underlying my approach to this topic is that very little can be gained if someone tells us how we are *supposed* to feel, how we are *supposed* to behave, or what we are *supposed* to do with our lives. A parallel assumption is that a great deal can be gained if we understand *what* we're feeling, if we understand the kinds of interpersonal events that trigger various kinds of feelings, if we understand how our behavior is read and understood by other people, and if we understand the wide variety of options available to us. Thus, in a T-group, the role of the leader is not to present us with answers but simply to help establish an atmosphere of trust and intensive inquiry in which we are willing to look closely at our own self-protective behavior. We are then in a position to learn how our self-protective behavior affects others and to begin to experiment with behaving in a more authentic, less defensive manner.

The Problem of Miscommunication.   As we saw in our example involving Phil and Alice, communication between humans can easily become distorted. Occasionally, in our everyday lives, when we think we are communicating something to a person, that person is hearing something entirely different. Suppose, for example, that Fred has warm feelings for Jack, but out of shyness or out of fear of being rejected, he finds it difficult to express these feelings directly. As is common among males in our culture, Fred may choose to communicate those warm feelings by engaging in a teasing, sarcastic kind of banter. Jack may not understand this as warmth, however; indeed, the sarcasm might hurt him. As I indicated earlier, in our culture, it is difficult to communicate hurt feelings, because it indicates weakness and vulnerability. So Jack keeps quiet. Thus, Fred, oblivious to the fact that his behavior is disturbing to Jack, continues to express his warmth via sarcastic jocularity—continuing to hurt the person he likes—until he succeeds in driving Jack away. Not only does Fred lose out on what could have been a warm friendship, but he may also fail

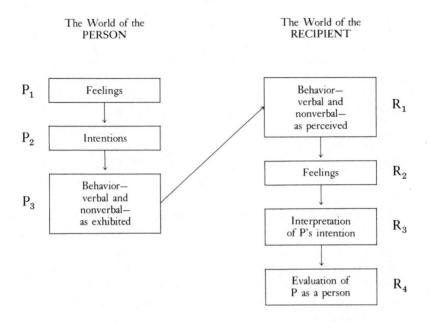

to learn from this experience and may continue to go through life alienating the very people toward whom he feels most warmly.

It may be useful to view the interaction between two people as a chain of events, as illustrated in the figure on this page. The Person (P) has some feelings about the Recipient (R). He intends to communicate a particular feeling. This manifests itself in some kind of behavior—some words, a gesture, a smile, a look, or whatever. The Recipient perceives this behavior in his own way, based on his own needs, feelings, past history, opinions about P, and so on. This perception of P's behavior evokes a feeling in R (warmth, anger, annoyance, love, fear, or whatever). This feeling is quickly translated into an interpretation of what P's intentions were, which in turn flows into an evaluation of what kind of person P is.

There are possibilities for error or distortion along any point in the links of this chain. Thus, to return to our example, Fred has some warm feelings (P_1) toward Jack. He intends to communicate these (P_2), but he does it in an oblique, noncommittal, self-protective way: He teases Jack, makes fun of his clothes, is jocular and sarcastic (P_3). Jack perceives this sarcasm and teasing (R_1); it causes him pain (R_2); and he decides that Fred was trying to put him down (R_3). He concludes, therefore, that Fred is a cruel, aggressive, unfriendly person (R_4).

Error can occur in a different part of the chain. Imagine a totally new situation in which Fred is completely direct and honest, but Jack is suspicious. Suppose Fred expresses his warmth directly—by putting his arm around Jack's shoulder, by telling Jack how much he likes him, and so on. But in this case, such behavior may be too fast for Jack. Accordingly, Jack may feel uncomfortable, and instead of simply admitting his discomfort, he may interpret Fred's behavior as manipulative in its intent. He may evaluate Fred as an insincere, political, manipulative person.

The process described above may be familiar to readers of this book. It has been discussed in chapter 7 under the term *attribution*. If we see a person behaving in a particular way, we have a strong tendency to attribute some motive or personality disposition to the person on the basis of that behavior. If this process can be explored and examined, there is a great deal of potential learning in the encounter for both Fred and Jack. Is Fred too scared to display his warm feelings openly? Is Jack too suspicious to accept genuine warmth without vilifying Fred? These are important questions whose answers can produce a lot of insight, but this can occur only if Fred and Jack openly communicate their feelings with one another.

Characteristics of Effective Communication

The Importance of Immediacy.   For communication to be effective in a close relationship, feelings must be expressed directly and openly. When this strategy is followed, we are able to receive immediate feedback on how our words and behavior are interpreted. With immediate feedback, we are better able to gain insight into the impact of our actions and statements and to consider our options for meeting our own needs as well as our partner's. To illustrate, suppose I perform an act that angers my best friend (who also happens to be my wife). If she doesn't express this anger, I may never become aware of the fact that the action I've performed makes her angry. On the other hand, suppose she gives me immediate feedback; suppose she tells me how these actions on my part make her feel angry. Then, I have at least two options: I can continue to behave in that way, or I can stop behaving in that way—the choice is mine. The behavior may be so important that I don't want to give it up. Conversely, my wife's feelings may be so important that I choose to give up the behavior. In the absence of any knowledge of how my behavior makes her feel, I don't have a choice. Moreover, knowing exactly how she feels about a particular set of actions may allow me to explore a *different* set of actions that may satisfy my needs as well as her needs.

The value of immediate feedback is not limited to the recipient. Frequently, in providing feedback, people discover something about themselves and their own needs. If Sharon feels, for example, that it's always destructive to express anger, she may block out her awareness of this feeling. When the expression of such feelings is legitimized, she has a chance to bring them out in the open, to look at them, and to become aware that her expression of anger has not caused the world to come to an end. Moreover, the direct expression of a feeling keeps the encounter on the up-and-up and thus helps to prevent the escalation of negative feelings. For example, if my wife has learned to express her anger directly, it keeps our discussion on the issue at hand. If she suppresses the anger, but it leaks out in other ways—at different times and in different situations—I do not know where her hostility is coming from and I become confused, hurt, or angry.

For example, suppose we are at a party and I begin to tell a "hilarious" story. When I am midway through my story, my wife says, "Oh, come on, now—I'm sure no one is interested in that tired old joke you keep telling," and she abruptly changes the subject. I am stunned, because I have no idea that her need to put me down is a result of some anger she felt toward me for something I had done two weeks earlier—some anger she was unwilling or unable to express at the time. Indeed, by this time, she herself may be unaware of what caused her to interrupt my "hilarious" story. My response to the put-down might be to become self-righteous about being abused for no apparent reason. This makes me angry, and the conflict escalates.

Feelings versus Judgment. People are often unaware of how to provide constructive feedback. We frequently do it in a way that angers or upsets the recipient, thereby causing more problems than we solve. This point is better illustrated than described in the abstract. I will do this by providing an example of dysfunctional feedback and of how people can be taught to modify their method of providing feedback (without modifying its quality) in order to maximize communication and understanding. This example is an actual event that occurred in a T-group I was leading several years ago.

In the course of the group meeting, one of the members (Sam) looked squarely at another member (Harry) and said, "Harry, I've been listening to you and watching you for a day and a half, and I think you're a phony." Now that's quite an accusation. How can Harry respond? He has several options: He can (1) agree with Sam; (2) deny the accusation and say he's not a phony; (3) say, "Gee, Sam, I'm sorry you feel that way"; (4) get angry and call Sam some names; or (5) feel sorry for himself and go into a sulk. Taken by themselves, none of these responses is particularly productive. In the "real world" it is unlikely that Sam would have come out with this statement; if he had come out with it, there almost certainly would have been trouble. But doesn't Sam have the right to express this judgment? After all, he's only being open.

This sounds like a dilemma: Effective communication requires openness; but openness can hurt people. The solution to this apparent dilemma is rather simple: It is possible to be open and, at the same time, to express oneself in a manner that causes a minimum of pain. The key rests in the term *feeling;* Sam was not expressing a feeling, he was expressing a judgment. To avoid being destructive, our use of open communication must involve the direct expression of feelings rather than judgments. The term *feeling* has several meanings. In this context I don't mean "hunch" or "hypothesis." By *feelings* I mean, specifically, anger or joy, sadness or happiness, annoyance, fear, discomfort, warmth, hurt, envy, excitement, and the like.

How was this encounter handled in the T-group? In this situation, the group leader intervened by asking Sam if he had any feelings about Harry. Sam thought for a moment and then said, "Well, I feel that Harry is a phony." Of course, this is not a feeling, as defined above. This is an opinion or a judgment expressed in the terminology of feelings. A judgment is nothing more or less than a feeling that is inadequately understood or inadequately expressed. Accordingly, the leader probed further by asking Sam what his feelings were. Sam still insisted he felt Harry was a phony. "And what does that do to you?" asked the leader. "It annoys the hell out of me," answered Sam. Here, another member of the group intervened and asked for data: "What kinds of things has Harry done that annoyed you, Sam?" After a few minutes of probing by various members of the group, Sam admitted he got annoyed whenever Harry showed affection to some of the women in the group. On further probing, it turned out Sam perceived Harry as being very attractive to women. What eventually emerged was that Sam owned up to feelings of envy: Sam wished he had Harry's charm and popularity with women. Note that Sam had initially masked this feeling of envy; instead, he had discharged his feelings by expressing disdain, by saying Harry was a phony. This kind of expression is ego-protecting: Because we live in a competitive society, Sam had learned over the years that, if he had admitted to feeling envious, it might have put him "one down" and put Harry "one up." This would have made Sam vulnerable—that is, it would have made him feel weak in relation to Harry. By expressing disdain, however, Sam succeeded in putting himself "one up."

Although his behavior was successful as an ego-protecting device, it didn't contribute to Sam's understanding of his own feelings and of the kinds of events that caused those feelings; and it certainly didn't contribute to Sam's understanding of Harry or to Harry's understanding of Sam (or, for that matter, to Harry's understanding of himself). In short, Sam was communicating ineffectively. As an ego-defensive measure, his behavior was adaptive; as a form of communication, it was extremely maladaptive. Thus, although it made Sam vulnerable to admit he envied Harry, it opened the door to communication; eventually, it helped them to understand each other. Moreover, a few other men also admitted they felt some envy and jealousy about Harry's behavior with women. This was useful information for Harry, in that it enabled him to understand the effects his behavior had on other men.

As we know, Harry has several options: He can continue to behave as he always has and let other people continue to be jealous and perhaps express their jealousy in terms of hostility, or he can modify his behavior in any one of a number of ways in order to cause other people (and ultimately himself) less difficulty. *The decision is his.* Should he decide that his "enviable" behavior is too important to give up, he has still gained a great deal from learning how his behavior affected Sam. Specifically, if a similar situation occurs in the future, Harry, who now knows the effect his behavior may have on other men, will not be surprised by their responses, will be more understanding, will be less likely to overreact, and so forth.

Of course, the preceding example was a relatively easy one to deal with. It ended up with Sam feeling envy for Harry—which is, in fact, a form of admiration. But what if Sam hates Harry—should he express his hatred? What if Sam believes that Harry is an evil person—should he express that belief? Here again, we can see the difference between a feeling and a judgment or evaluation. It would be useful if Sam would express the feelings underlying his judgments and evaluations. Did Harry do something that hurt Sam and made him angry? Is this why Sam hates Harry and thinks he's an evil person? Sam will not get very far by discussing Harry's evilness. *Sam:* "I hate you, Harry; you are evil." *Harry:* "No, I'm not." *Sam:* "Well, that is the way I see it; I'm just giving you feedback like we're supposed to do in here." *Harry:* "That's your problem—besides, you're not so great yourself." By calling Harry names, Sam sets up the situation in a way that invites Harry to defend himself and to counterattack rather than to listen. But if Sam were to lead with his own feelings ("I am hurt and angry"), it would invite Harry into a discussion about what he (Harry) might have done to hurt and anger Sam. This is not to say that it is pleasant to hear someone say he is angry at us or hurt by us—it's not. But it helps us to pay attention and to try to deal with the problem at hand.

Why is it tempting for Sam to call Harry evil rather than to talk about his own hurt? The reasons for this behavior should be clear by now. Being hurt puts us "one down"—it makes us vulnerable. In this society, we tend to glide through life protecting ourselves; in effect, each of us wears a suit of behavioral armor so that other people can't hurt us. This results in a lot of inauthentic behavior—that is, we mask our true feelings from other people. This is often accomplished through the process of short-circuiting. Sometimes, we are so successful at it that we mask our feelings from ourselves as well.

In summary, then, feedback expressed in terms of feelings is a lot easier for the recipient to listen to and deal with than feedback in the form of judgments and evaluations. This is true for two major reasons: First, a person's opinions and judgments about another person are purely a matter of conjecture. Thus, Sam's opinions about Harry being a phony and about Harry being an evil person may reflect reality, or just as likely, they may not—they are merely Sam's theories about Harry. Only Harry knows for sure whether he's being a phony: Sam is only guessing. But Sam's statement that he is feeling envious or angry is not a guess or a theory—it is an absolute fact. Sam is not guessing about his feelings—he knows them; indeed, he is the only person in the world who knows them for sure. Harry may or may not care about Sam's intellectual theories or pontifical judgments, but if he is desirous of interacting with Sam, he is probably very interested in knowing about Sam's feelings and what role he (Harry) plays in triggering those feelings.

The second major reason why feedback expressed in terms of feelings is preferable to feedback expressed in terms of judgments is that, when Sam states an opinion or a judgment about Harry, he is saying something about Harry only, but when he states a *feeling* evoked by Harry's behavior, he is revealing something about himself as well. Indeed, in this instance, Sam's primary statement *is* about himself. Thus, the statement of feeling is a gift. Metaphorically, it is Sam opening the door to his home and letting Harry in. When Sam states a judgment about Harry, however, he is storming Harry's barricades and making attributions about Harry's motives or personality. Harry has good reason to resist this, because Sam has no right to be in his home without an invitation. Harry can let him in by telling him what his feelings are; likewise, Sam can let Harry in by telling him what *his* feelings are.[75]

Feelings and Intentions.   Frequently, in our everyday life, one person will say or do something that hurts another. If the recipient (R) *does* get to the point of expressing his hurt, the person (P) may insist that hurting wasn't her intention. It is useful for P to express her intention, but it is important to move further. If P says, "Oh, I'm sorry, I didn't mean to hurt you—I really like you," and R answers by saying, "Oh, that's fine; I feel better about it now," that may smooth things over and make things tolerable. Much of the time, all we want are interpersonal relations that are tolerable. But, ultimately, we can strive for more—we can learn something about ourselves and the other person. We can accomplish this by moving beyond our tendency to cover over events such as this—by moving toward an exploration of the process: "Why is it I hurt people when I don't intend to?" or "Why am I so easily hurt?"

But even in a simple situation like this one, there is plenty of room for a garbled, ineffective interaction. If P does not *intend* to hurt R, there is often a tendency for her to deny the legitimacy of R's hurt, saying, in effect, "What right do you have to be hurt, now that you know I didn't intend to hurt you?" Again, this kind of attitude neither increases P's learning nor helps R feel cared for. The point of straight communication, however, is not to decide who is right or wrong, but to help us understand ourselves, each other, and the nature of our relationship. In order to accomplish this, it is extremely helpful (even essential) that we each assume responsibility for our own behavior and its effects on others, as well as acknowledge how others' behavior affects us.

Communication in Everyday Life.   As we develop our capacity to communicate openly and honestly in our close relationships, we gradually let ourselves become more vulnerable and learn how not to take advantage of one another's vulnerability. Outside of our most cherished relationships, however, we cannot always expect others to express the kinds of feelings that would make them vulnerable, nor can we be certain that others will not take advantage of our vulnerability. Still, with practice, our everyday interactions with people outside our circle of family and close friends can also benefit (to varying degrees, depending on the individuals and situations involved) from our knowledge of effective communication.

Let me illustrate: When two or more people are engaged in some sort of relationship, they usually have some feelings about each other. If these feelings are not understood, they can get in the way of the task at hand. For example, suppose you and I are members of a six-member committee to raise funds for underprivileged children. Suppose you are intelligent, creative, athletic, wealthy, and personable. I'm feeling competitive with you; I want the other committee members to like and admire me more than they like and admire you. Because of those feelings, if you propose an idea for raising funds, I might be prone to find fault with it, to ridicule it, to argue it down, even if it's a good idea—especially if it's a good idea.

But suppose I have a solid understanding of my own feelings, an understanding learned through engaging in straight talk in a close relationship or a T-group experience. How does that help me? Would I immediately stand up, cross over to where you are sitting, put my hand on your shoulder and say, "I'm feeling envious and competitive, but you have great ideas and are a terrific person—I want to support your ideas"? I doubt it. First of all, I'd be frightened to do that. You may not be inclined to interact according to the norm of openness. You might take advantage of the vulnerable position that my confession has left me in and proceed to put me down.

Furthermore, in the absence of a close relationship with you, I have no business using my openness as a subtle means of coercing you to make yourself vulnerable to me. I have no right to pressure you into being more open than you feel like being. But if I cannot express my feelings directly or make myself vulnerable to you, how can my communication skills be of any value in this situation? To answer by way of illustration, let us go back to the committee meeting: When you propose a good idea, I feel awful. I also feel a compulsion to find fault with your idea. But, if I had learned to confront and understand my feelings of envy and competitiveness, I may stop and think about whether your idea was *really* a bad one, or whether I'm just being competitive again. If I can be aware of my envy and my need to compete, I have a good chance of being able to curb them and thereby become a more productive committee member. Subsequently, if I get to know you better and begin to trust you, I may decide to share with you (in private) my prior feelings of competitiveness. Perhaps I can do it in a way that will serve to invite you into a closer, more honest relationship, without attempting to force you into one. My own personal goal is to develop such relationships with more and more acquaintances, so that my social environment does become increasingly safer, more open, more relaxed, more exciting, and more conducive to learning, understanding, and growth. It isn't easy. And because it isn't easy, it is tempting to retreat to a posture of winning rather than vulnerability, of looking good and "right" rather than communicating clearly and with openness. It is vital that we understand that, if we succumb to this temptation, the divorce rate will continue to rise and the number and depth of truly satisfying interpersonal relations will continue to dwindle.

9

Social Psychology as a Science

The scientific method—regardless of whether it is being applied in physics, chemistry, biology, or social psychology—is the best way we humans have of satisfying our hunger for knowledge and understanding. More specifically, we use the scientific method in an attempt to uncover lawful relationships among things—whether the things are chemicals, planets, or the antecedents of human prejudice or love. The first step in the scientific process is observation. In physics, a simple observation might go something like this: If there is a rubber ball in my child's wagon and she pulls the wagon forward, the ball seems to roll to the back of the wagon. (It doesn't actually roll backward; it only seems that way.) When she stops the wagon abruptly, the ball rushes to the front of the wagon. In social psychology, a simple observation might go something like this: When I am waiting on tables, if I happen to be in a good mood and smile a lot at my customers, my tips seem to be a bit larger than when I am in a foul mood and smile less frequently.

The next step is to make a guess as to why that happens—this guess is our taking a stab at uncovering the "lawful relationship" we mentioned above. The third step is to frame that guess into a testable hypothesis. The final step is to design an experiment (or a series of experiments) that will either confirm or disconfirm the hypothesis. If a series of well-designed, well-executed experiments fails to confirm that guess, we give it up. As my favorite physicist, Richard Feynman,[1] once put it: "It doesn't matter how beautiful the guess is or how smart the guesser is, or how famous the guesser is; if the experiment disagrees with the guess, then the guess is wrong. That's all there is to it!" In my own opinion, this is both the essence of science and its beauty. There are no sacred truths in science.

Science and Art

This sounds very strict. Is there no room for art in our science? Isn't art, like science, a way we humans have of satisfying our hunger for understanding? I believe that the two processes are different but related. Pavel Semonov, a distinguished Russian psychologist did a pretty good job of defining the difference. According to Semonov,[2] as scientists, we look closely at our environment and try to organize the unknown in a sensible and meaningful way. As artists, we reorganize the known environment in order to create something entirely new. To this astute observation, I would add that the requirements of a good experiment frequently necessitate a combination of skills from both of these domains. In a very real sense, as experimenters, we use artistry to enrich our science. I believe this to be particularly true of experiments in social psychology.

Why is this blending of art and science especially true of social psychology? The full answer to this question will emerge as this chapter unfolds. For now, let me simply state that, in social psychology, we are not studying the behavior of chemicals in a beaker or rubber balls in wagons; we are investigating the behavior of intelligent, curious, sophisticated adults who have been living in a social world for their entire lives. It goes without saying that, like the experimenters who are studying them, our experimental subjects have developed their own ideas and theories about what causes their feelings and behavior as well as the feelings and behavior of the people around them. This is not the case when you are performing experiments with chemicals, with laboratory animals, or even with humans in nonsocial situations.

The fact that we are dealing with socially sophisticated human beings is part of what makes social psychology so fascinating as a topic of experimental investigation. At the same time, this situation also demands a great deal of "art" if the experimenter stands a chance of generating valid and reliable findings. In this chapter, I will try to communicate exactly how this happens.

From Speculation to Experimentation

You may recall that, in chapter 2, I described an incident at Yosemite National Park. Briefly, what happened was this: When awakened by sounds of distress, a great many campers rushed to the aid of the person who needed help. Because the behavior of these campers was decidedly different from the behavior of witnesses to the Genovese murder (thirty-eight people watched a woman being stabbed to death without attempting to help in any way), I speculated about what may have caused this difference in behavior in the two situations. But no matter how clever and adroit my speculations might have been, I could not be certain that these speculations were correct. There are literally dozens of differences between the Yosemite campground situation and the Genovese murder case. How can we be sure that the factor I mentioned constitutes a crucial difference—the difference that made the difference?

Speculations are a dime a dozen. Because we humans are all amateur social psychologists, we all speculate about social psychological issues and events—almost all the time. Let me give you a very recent example—one that, at this writing, is only a few hours old. A few minutes ago, while in the midst of revising this chapter, I took time out to glance at the entertainment section of the *New York Times*. I stumbled upon a fascinating article by the critic Neal Gabler about Michael Jackson, arguably the world's most famous entertainer. At the time, Jackson was in the midst of one of the great scandals of the 1990s; he had been accused of sexually molesting children. In this article, Gabler[3] was speculating about the precipitous decline in Michael Jackson's popularity as a result of this, as yet, unsubstantiated accusation. It was Gabler's thesis that the major reason for this decline rests on the fact that the accusation represented a transgression against the image Jackson had projected—as "strange but harmless, the eternal child, the fragile savant, the asexual naif."[4] Gabler went on to contrast Jackson's image with that of Madonna and argued that, because Madonna had established an image of being wild and wanton, she might be able to get away with *anything!* According to Gabler, nothing Madonna might do "would seem to violate her persona, not even if she were suddenly to reverse field and declare herself a born-again Christian."[5]

Well, maybe. Gabler has certainly provided us with a fascinating set of speculations about person perception, images, expectations, and the effect of their violation on a person's popularity. This is exciting social psychological material. But is he on target? Perhaps, the very notion of child molestation is so noxious to most people that they would have turned away from any entertainer tainted with the hint of this scandal—regardless of his or her prior image.

How would you find out? You might simply ask Michael Jackson's disaffected fans why they lost interest in him. But over the years we have learned that people are not always aware of why they do things; so, in a complex situation, simply asking people to explain their behavior will usually not yield reliable results.[6] This is precisely why social psychologists perform experiments. But how can we conduct an experiment on Michael Jackson? We probably can't. In a case like this, we would try to conduct an experiment on the underlying phenomenon, not on the specific instantiation of that phenomenon.

Let me illustrate what I mean by that rather fancy statement. You may recall that, in chapter 8, I discussed a similar kind of speculation. In the early 1960s, we stumbled on an amazing phenomenon: While John F. Kennedy was president, his personal popularity increased immediately after he committed a stupendously costly blunder. Specifically, after Kennedy's tragic miscalculation—known as the Bay of Pigs fiasco—a Gallup poll showed that people liked him better than they had prior to that incident. As a scientist, I speculated about what could have caused that shift toward greater popularity. My guess was that, because Kennedy was such a nearly perfect person, committing a blunder might have made him seem more human, thus allowing ordinary people to feel closer to him. But because there were many things happening at the time of the Bay of Pigs fiasco, it was impossible to be sure that my speculation was accurate. Besides, we were less interested in the fact of Kennedy's popularity than in the phenomenon itself: Does committing a blunder increase the popularity of a nearly perfect person?

In order to answer this more general question, it was necessary to go beyond the event that led to our speculations. My colleagues and I had to design an experiment[7] that allowed us to control for extraneous variables and test the effects of a blunder on attraction in a less complex situation—one in which we could control the exact nature of the blunder as well as the kind of person who committed it. And in that simple situation we found, as predicted, that "nearly perfect" people become more attractive after they commit a blunder, while "rather ordinary" people become *less* attractive after committing the identical blunder. (I have described the details of this experiment in chapter 8.)

Designing an Experiment. As suggested above, in striving for control, the experimenter must bring his or her ideas out of the helter-skelter of the real world and into the rather sterile confines of the laboratory. This typically entails concocting a situation bearing little resemblance to the real-world situation from whence the idea originated. In fact, a frequent criticism is that laboratory experiments are unrealistic and contrived imitations of human interaction that don't reflect the "real world" at all. How accurate is this criticism?

Perhaps the best way to answer this question is to examine one laboratory experiment in great detail, considering its advantages and disadvantages, as well as an alternative, more realistic approach that might have been used to study the same issue. The initiation experiment I performed in collaboration with Judson Mills[8] suits our purpose admirably—because it contains a great many of the advantages and disadvantages of the laboratory. The reader may recall that Mills and I speculated that people might come to like things for which they have suffered. We then designed and conducted a laboratory experiment in which we showed that people who expended great effort (by undergoing a severe initiation) to gain membership into a group liked the group more than did people who became members with little or no effort. Here's how the experiment was performed:

Sixty-three college women who initially volunteered to participate in several discussions on the psychology of sex were subjects of the study. Each student was tested individually. At the beginning of the study, I explained that I was studying the "dynamics of the group-discussion process." I said the actual topic of the discussion was not important to me, but because most people are interested in sex, I selected that topic in order to be certain of having plenty of participants. I also explained I had encountered a major drawback in choosing sex as the topic: Specifically, because of shyness, many people found it difficult to discuss sex in a group setting. Because any impediment to the flow of the discussion could seriously invalidate the results, I needed to know if the subjects felt any hesitancy to enter a discussion about sex. When the subjects heard this, each and every one indicated she would have no difficulty. These elaborate instructions were used to set the stage for the important event to follow. The reader should note how the experimenter's statements tend to make the following material believable.

Up to this point, the instructions had been the same for each subject. Now it was time to give each of the people in the various experimental conditions a different experience—an experience the experimenters believed would make a difference.

Subjects were randomly assigned in advance to one of three conditions:(1) One-third of them would go through a severe initiation, (2) one-third of them would go through a mild initiation, and (3) one-third would not go through any initiation at all. For the no-initiation condition, subjects were simply told they could now join the discussion group. For the severe and mild-initiation conditions, however, I told each subject that, because it was necessary to be positive that she could discuss sex openly, I had developed a screening device, a test for embarrassment, which I then asked her to take. This test constituted the initiation. For the severe-initiation condition, the test was highly embarrassing. It required the subject to recite a list of twelve obscene words and two detailed descriptions of sexual activity taken from contemporary novels. The mild-initiation subjects had to recite only a list of words related to sex that were not obscene.

The three conditions to which subjects were assigned constituted the *independent variable* in this study. Briefly, the investigator's goal in designing and conducting an experiment is to determine if what happens to subjects has an effect on how they respond. *Our* goal was to determine if severity of initiation—the independent variable—*caused* systematic differences in subjects' behaviors. Would subjects who experienced a severe initiation act differently than those who experienced a mild initiation or no initiation at all?

But act differently in what way? After the initiation, each subject was allowed to eavesdrop on a group discussion being conducted by members of the group she had just joined. In order to control the content of this material, a tape recording was used; but the subjects were led to believe it was a live discussion. Thus, all subjects—regardless of whether they had gone through a severe initiation, a mild initiation, or no initiation—listened to the same group discussion. The group discussion was about as dull and as boring as possible; it involved a halting, inarticulate analysis of the secondary sex characteristics of lower animals—changes in plumage among birds, intricacies of the mating dance of certain spiders, and the like. The tape contained long pauses, a great deal of hemming and hawing, interruptions, incomplete sentences, and so on, all designed to make it boring.

At the end of the discussion, I returned with a set of rating scales and asked the subject to rate how interesting and worthwhile the discussion had been. This is called the *dependent variable* because, quite literally, the response is assumed to be "dependent" on the particular experimental conditions the subject had been assigned to. The dependent variable is what the experimenter measures to assess the effects of the independent variable. In short, if the independent variable is the *cause,* then the dependent variable is the *effect.*

The results supported the hypothesis: Women who went through a mild initiation, or no initiation at all, saw the group discussion as relatively dull. But those who suffered in order to be admitted to the group thought it was really an exciting discussion. Remember, all the students were rating *exactly the same discussion.*

Designing and conducting this experiment was a laborious process. Mills and I spent hundreds of hours planning the experiment, creating a credible situation, writing a script for the tape recording of the group discussion, rehearsing the actors who played the roles of group members, constructing the initiation procedures and the measuring instruments, recruiting volunteers to serve as subjects, pilot-testing the procedure, running the subjects through the experiment, and explaining the true purpose of the experiment to each subject (the reason for the deception, what it all meant, and so forth). What we found was that, people who go through a severe initiation in order to gain entry into a group, like that group a great deal more than people who go through a mild initiation (or no initiation at all).

Surely there must be a simpler way! There is. The reader may have noticed a vague resemblance between the procedure used by Mills and me and other initiations, such as those used by primitive tribes and those used by some college fraternities and other exclusive clubs or organizations. Why, then, didn't we take advantage of the real-life situation, which is not only easier to study but also far more dramatic and realistic? Let's look at the advantages: Real-life initiations would be more severe (that is, they would have more impact on the members); we would not have had to go to such lengths to design a group setting the participants would find convincing; the social interactions would involve real people, rather than mere voices from a tape recording; we would have eliminated the ethical problem created by the use of deception and the use of a difficult and un-pleasant experience in the name of science; and, finally, it could all have been accomplished in a fraction of the time the experiment consumed.

Thus, when we take a superficial look at the advantages of a natural situation, it appears Mills and I would have had a much simpler job if we had studied existing fraternities. Here is how we might have done it: We could have rated each group's initiation for severity and later interviewed the members to determine how much they liked their group. If the members who had undergone a severe initiation liked their fraternities more than the mild- or no-initiation fraternity members, the hypothesis would be supported. Or would it? Let's take a closer look at why people bother to do experiments.

If people were asked to name the most important characteristic of a laboratory experiment, the great majority would say "control." And this *is* a major advantage. Experiments have the advantage of control-ling the environment and the variables so the effects of each variable can be precisely studied. By taking our hypothesis to the laboratory, Mills and I eliminated a lot of the extraneous variation that exists in the real world. The severe initiations were all equal in intensity; this condition would have been difficult to match if we had used several "severe-initiation" fraternities. Further, the group discussion was identical for all subjects; in the real world, however, fraternity members would have been rating fraternities that were, in fact, different from each other. Assuming we had been able to find a difference between the "severe-initiation" fraternities and the "mild-initiation" fraternities, how would we have known whether this was a function of the initiation rather than of the differential likableness that already existed in the fraternity members themselves? In the experiment, the *only* difference was the severity of the initiation, so we know that any difference was due to that procedure.

The Importance of Random Assignment

Control *is* a very important aspect of the laboratory experiment, but it is not the major advantage of this procedure. A still more important advantage is that subjects can be randomly assigned to the different experimental conditions. This means each subject has an equal chance to be in any condition in the study. Indeed, the random assignment of subjects to conditions is the crucial difference between the experimental method and nonexperimental approaches. And the great advantage of the random assignment of people to conditions is this: Any variables not thoroughly controlled are, in theory, distributed randomly across the conditions. This means it is extremely unlikely such variables would affect results in a systematic fashion.

An example might help to clarify this point: Suppose you are a scientist and you have the hypothesis that marrying intelligent women makes men happy. How do you test this hypothesis? Let us say you proceed to find a thousand men who are married to intelligent women and a thousand men who are married to not-so-intelligent women, and you give them all a "happiness" questionnaire. Lo and behold, the men married to intelligent women *are* happier than the men married to less intelligent women. Does this mean that being married to an intelligent woman makes men happy? No. Perhaps happy men are sweeter, more good-humored, and easier to get along with, and that, consequently, intelligent women seek out these men and marry them. So it may be that being happy *causes* men to marry intelligent women. The problem doesn't end there. It is also possible there is some third factor that causes *both* happiness *and* being married to an intelligent woman. One such factor could be money: It is conceivable that being rich helps make men happy and that their being rich is what attracts the intelligent women. So it is possible that neither causal sequence is true—it is possible that happiness does not cause men to marry intelligent women and that intelligent women do not cause men to be happy.

The problem is even more complicated. It is more complicated because we usually have no idea what these third factors might be. In the case of the happiness study, it could be wealth; it could also be that a mature personality causes men to be happy and also attracts intelligent women; it could be social grace, athletic ability, power, popularity, using the right toothpaste, being a snappy dresser, or any of a thousand qualities the poor researcher does not know about and could not possibly account for. But if the researcher performs an experiment, he or she can randomly assign subjects to various experimental conditions. Although this procedure does not eliminate differences due to any of these variables (money, social grace, athletic ability, and the like), it neutralizes them by distributing these characteristics randomly across various experimental conditions. That is, if subjects are randomly assigned to experimental conditions, there will be approximately as many rich men in one condition as in the others, as many socially adept men in one condition as in the others, and as many athletes in one condition as in the others. Thus, if we do find a difference between conditions, it is unlikely this would be due to individual differences in any single characteristic, because all of these characteristics had equal (or nearly equal) distribution across all of the conditions.

Admittedly, the particular example of intelligent women and their happy husbands does not easily lend itself to the confines of the experimental laboratory. But let us fantasize about how we would do it if we could. Ideally, we would take fifty men and randomly assign twenty-five to intelligent wives and twenty-five to less intelligent wives. A few months later, we could come back and administer the happiness questionnaire. If the men assigned to the intelligent wives are happier than the men assigned to the less intelligent wives, we would know what caused their happiness—we did! In short, their happiness couldn't easily be attributed to social grace, or handsomeness, or money, or power—these were randomly distributed among the experimental conditions. It almost certainly was caused by their wives' characteristics.

To repeat, this example is pure fantasy—even social psychologists must stop short of arranging marriages for scientific purposes. But this does *not* mean we cannot test important, meaningful, relevant events under controlled laboratory conditions. This book is loaded with such examples. Let's look at one of these examples as a way of clarifying the advantages of the experimental method. In chapter 6, I reported a correlation between the amount of time children spend watching violence on television and their tendency to choose aggressive solutions to their problems.

Does this mean watching aggression on television causes youngsters to become aggressive? Not necessarily. It might. But it might also mean aggressive youngsters simply like to watch aggression, and they would be just as aggressive if they watched *Sesame Street* all day long. But then, as we saw, some experimenters came along and proved that watching violence increases violence.[9] How? By randomly assigning some children to a situation in which they watched a video of an episode of a violent TV series—an episode in which people beat, kill, rape, bite, and slug each other for twenty-five minutes. As a control, the experimenters randomly assigned some other children to a situation in which they watched an athletic event for the same length of time. The crucial point: Each child stood *an equal chance* of being selected to watch the violent video as the nonviolent video; therefore, any differences in character structure among the children in this experiment were neutralized across the two experimental conditions. Thus, the finding that youngsters who watched the violent video showed more aggression afterward than those who watched the athletic event suggests quite strongly that watching violence can lead to violence.

Let us return to the initiation experiment. If we conducted a survey and found that members of severe-initiation fraternities find each other more attractive than do members of mild-initiation fraternities, then we would have evidence that severity of initiation and liking for other members of the fraternity are *positively correlated*. This means that the more severe the initiation, the more a member will like his fraternity brothers. No matter how highly correlated the two variables are, however, we cannot conclude, from our survey data alone, that severe initiations *cause* liking for the group. All we can conclude from such a survey is that these two factors are associated with each other.

It is possible the positive correlation between severe initiation and liking for other members of a fraternity exists not because severe initiations cause members to like their groups more, but for just the opposite reason. It could be that high attractiveness for the group causes severe initiations. If group members see themselves as highly desirable, they may try to keep the situation that way by maintaining an elite group. Thus, they might require a severe initiation in order to discourage people from joining, unless those people have a high desire to do so. From our survey data alone, we cannot conclude that this explanation is false and severe initiations really do lead to liking. The data give us no basis for making this choice, because they tell us nothing about cause and effect. Moreover, as we have seen in our previous example, there could be a third variable that causes both severe initiations and liking. Who would like to give and receive a severe initiation? Why, people with strong sadomasochistic tendencies, of course. Such people may like each other not because of the initiation but because "birds of a feather" tend to like each other. Although this may sound like an outlandish explanation, it is certainly possible. What is more distressing for the researcher are the countless other explanations he or she can't even think of. The experimental method, based as it is on the technique of random assignment to experimental conditions, eliminates all of these in one fell swoop. The sadomasochists in the experiment have just as much chance of being assigned to the no-initiation condition as to the severe-initiation condition. In the real-world study, alas, most of them would most certainly assign themselves to the severe-initiation condition, thus making the results uninterpretable.

The Challenge of Experimentation in Social Psychology

Control versus Impact. All is not so sunny in the world of experimentation. There are some very real problems connected with doing experiments. I mentioned that control is one of the major advantages of the experiment; yet it is impossible to exercise complete control over the environment of human subjects. One of the reasons why many psychologists work with rats, rather than people, is that researchers are able to control almost everything that happens to their subjects from the time of their birth until the experiment ends—climate, diet, exercise, degree of exposure to playmates, absence of traumatic experiences, and so on. Social psychologists do not keep human subjects in cages in order to control their experiences. Although this makes for a happier world for the subjects, it also makes for a slightly sloppy science.

Control is further limited by the fact that individuals differ from one another in countless subtle ways. Social psychologists try to make statements about what *people* do. By this we mean, of course, what most people do most of the time under a given set of conditions. To the extent that unmeasured individual differences are present in our results, our conclusions may not be precise for all people. Differences in attitudes, values, abilities, personality characteristics, and recent past experiences can affect the way people respond in an experiment. Thus, even with our ability to control the experimental situation itself, the same situation may not affect each person in exactly the same way.

Furthermore, when we do succeed in controlling the experimental setting so it is exactly the same for every person, we run the real risk of making the situation so sterile the subject is inclined not to take it seriously. The word *sterile* has at least two meanings: (1) germ-free, and (2) ineffective or barren. The experimenter should strive to make the experimental situation as "germ-free" as possible without making it barren or "unlifelike" for the subject. If subjects do not find the events of an experiment interesting and absorbing, chances are their reactions will not be spontaneous, and therefore, our results will have little meaning. Thus, in addition to control, an experiment must have an impact on the subjects. They must take the experiment seriously and become involved in it, lest it not affect their behavior in a meaningful way. The difficulty for social psychologists is that these two crucial factors, impact and control, often work in opposite ways: As one increases, the other tends to decrease. The dilemma facing experimenters is how to maximize impact on the subjects without sacrificing control over the situation. Resolving this dilemma requires considerable creativity and ingenuity in the design and construction of experimental situations. This leads us to the problem of realism.

Realism. Early in this chapter, I mentioned that a frequent criticism of laboratory experiments is that they are artificial and contrived imitations of the world, that they aren't "real." What do we mean by *real?* Several years ago, in writing a treatise about the experimental method, Merrill Carlsmith and I tried to pinpoint the definition of *real.*[10] We reasoned that an experiment can be realistic in two separate ways: If an experiment has an impact on the subjects, forces them to take the matter seriously, and involves them in the procedures, we can say it has achieved *experimental realism.* Quite apart from this is the question of how similar the laboratory experiment is to the events that frequently happen to people in the outside world. This can be termed *mundane realism.* Often, a confusion between experimental realism and mundane realism is responsible for the criticism that experiments are artificial and worthless because they don't reflect the real world.

Perhaps the difference between the two realisms can be illustrated by an example of a study high in experimental realism but low in mundane realism. Recall the experiment by Stanley Milgram,[11] discussed in chapter 2, in which each subject was asked to deliver a series of shocks, of increasing intensity, to another person who was supposedly wired to an electrical apparatus in an adjoining room. Now, honestly, how many times in our everyday life are we asked to deliver electric shocks to people? It's unrealistic—but unrealistic only in the mundane sense. Did the procedure have experimental realism—that is, were the subjects wrapped up in it, did they take it seriously, did it have an impact on them, was it part of their *real* world at that moment? Or were they merely playacting, not taking it seriously, going through the motions, ho-humming it? Milgram reports that his subjects experienced a great deal of tension and discomfort. But I'll let Milgram describe, in his own words, what a typical subject looked like:

> I observed a mature and initially poised businessman enter the laboratory smiling and confident. Within 20 minutes he was reduced to a twitching, stuttering wreck, who was rapidly approaching a point of nervous collapse. He constantly pulled on his earlobe, and twisted

his hands. At one point he pushed his fist onto his forehead and muttered: "Oh God, let's stop it." And yet he continued to respond to every word of the experimenter, and obeyed to the end.[12]

This hardly seems like the behavior of a person in an unrealistic situation. The things happening to Milgram's subjects were *real*— even though they didn't happen to them in their everyday experience. Accordingly, it would seem safe to conclude that the results of this experiment are a reasonably accurate indication of the way people would react if a similar set of events *did* occur in the real world.

Deception. The importance of experimental realism can hardly be overemphasized. The best way to achieve this essential quality is to design a setting that will be absorbing and interesting to the subjects. At the same time, it is frequently necessary to disguise the true purpose of the study. Why the need for disguise?

Early in this chapter, I mentioned that just about everybody is an amateur social psychologist in the sense that we all live in a social world and are constantly forming hypotheses about things that happen to us in our social world. This includes the individuals who serve as subjects in our experiments. Because they are always trying to figure things out, if they knew what we were trying to get at, they might be apt to behave in a manner consistent with their own hypotheses—instead of behaving in a way that is natural and usual for them. For this reason, we try to conceal the true nature of the experiment from the subjects. Because we are almost always dealing with very intelligent adults, this is not an easy task; but it is an absolute requirement, in most experiments, if we are to stand a chance of obtaining valid and reliable data.

This requirement puts the social psychologist in the position of a film director who's setting the stage for action but not telling the actor what the play is all about. Such settings are called *cover stories* and are designed to increase experimental realism by producing a situation in which the subject can act naturally, without being inhibited by knowing just which aspect of behavior is being studied. For example, in the Aronson-Mills initiation study, subjects were told they were taking a test for embarrassment in order to screen them for membership in a group that would be discussing the psychology of sex—this was the cover story. It was pure deception. In reality, they were being subjected to an initiation to see what effect, if any, this would have on their liking for the group. If the subjects had been aware of the true purpose of the study before their participation, the results would have been totally meaningless. Researchers who have studied this issue have shown that, if subjects know the true purpose of an experiment, they do *not* behave naturally but either try to perform in a way that puts themselves in a good light, or try to "help out" the experimenter by behaving in a way that would make the experiment come out as the subject thinks it ought to. Both of these outcomes are disastrous for the experimenter. The experimenter can usually succeed in curbing the subject's desire to be "helpful," but the desire to "look good" is more difficult to curb. Most people do not want to be thought of as weak, abnormal, a conformist, unattractive, stupid, or crazy. Thus, if given a chance to figure out what the experimenter is looking for, most people will try to make themselves look good or "normal." For example, in an experiment designed specifically to elucidate this phenomenon,[13] when we told subjects that a particular outcome indicated they possessed a "good" personality trait, they exhibited the behavior necessary to produce that outcome far more often than when we told them it reflected a negative trait. Although this behavior is understandable, it does interfere with meaningful results. For this reason, experimenters find it necessary to deceive subjects about the true nature of the experiment.

To illustrate, let's look again at Solomon Asch's classic experiment on conformity.[14] Recall that, in this study, a student was assigned the task of judging the relative size of a few lines. It was a simple task. But a few other students (who were actually accomplices of the experimenter) purposely stated an incorrect judgment. When faced with this situation, a sizable number of the subjects yielded to the implicit group pressure and stated an incorrect judgment. This was, of course, a highly deceptive experiment. The subjects thought they were participating in an experiment on perception, but, actually, their conformity was being studied. Was this deception necessary? I think so. Let's play it back without the deception: Imagine yourself a subject in an experiment in which the experimenter said, "I am interested in studying whether or not you will conform in the face of group pressure," and then he told you what was going to happen. My guess is you wouldn't conform. My guess is almost *no one* would conform, because conformity is considered a weak and unattractive behavior. What could the experimenter have concluded from this? That people tend to be nonconformists? Such a conclusion would be erroneous and misleading. Such an experiment would be meaningless.

Recall Milgram's experiments on obedience. He found that 62 percent of the average citizens in his experiment were willing to administer intense shocks to another person in obedience to the experimenter's command. Yet, each year, when I describe the experimental situation to the students in my class and ask them if *they* would obey such a command, only 1 percent indicate they would. Does this mean my students are nicer people than Milgram's subjects? I don't think so. I think it means that people, if given half a chance, will try to look good. Thus, unless Milgram had used deception, he would have come out with results that simply do not reflect the way people behave when they are led to believe they are in real situations. If we were to give people the opportunity to sit back, relax, and make a guess as to how they would behave if . . . , we would get a picture of how people would like to be rather than a picture of how people are.

Ethical Problems

Using deception may be the best (and perhaps the *only*) way to get useful information about the way people behave in most complex and important situations, but it *does* present the experimenter with a serious ethical problem. Basically, there are three problems:

1. It is simply unethical to tell lies to people. This takes on even greater significance in the post-Watergate era, when it has been revealed that government agencies have bugged citizens illegally, that presidents tell outright lies to the people who elected them, and that all manner of dirty tricks, fake letters, forged documents, and so on have been used by people directly employed by the president. Can social scientists justify adding to the pollution of deception that currently exists?

2. Such deception frequently leads to an invasion of privacy. When people serving as subjects do not know what the experimenter is really studying, they are in no position to give their

informed consent. For example, in Asch's experiment, it is conceivable some students might not have agreed to participate had they known in advance Asch was interested in examining their tendency toward conformity rather than their perceptual judgment.

3. Experimental procedures often entail some unpleasant experiences, such as pain, boredom, anxiety, and the like.

I hasten to add that ethical problems arise even when deception is not used and when experimental procedures are not "extreme." Sometimes even the most seemingly benign procedure can profoundly affect a few subjects in ways that could not easily have been anticipated—even by the most sensitive and caring of experimenters. Consider a series of experiments conducted by Robyn Dawes, Jeanne McTavish, and Harriet Shaklee.[15] Typically, in their investigations of "social dilemmas," subjects are faced with the decision to cooperate or to "defect." If everyone cooperates, everyone benefits financially; but if one or more participants choose to defect, they receive a high payoff, and those who choose to cooperate are at a financial disadvantage. Responses are anonymous and remain so throughout the course of the study. The rules of the game are fully explained to all subjects at the beginning of the experiment. And no deception is involved. This scenario seems innocuous enough.

But twenty-four hours after one experimental session, an elderly man telephoned the experimenter. He had been the only defector in his group and had won nineteen dollars. He wanted to return his winnings to be divided among the other participants (who had cooperated and only won one dollar each). During the conversation, he revealed that he felt miserable about his greedy behavior, that he hadn't slept all night, and so on. After a similar experiment, a woman who cooperated while others defected reported that she felt gullible and had learned that people were not as trustworthy as she had earlier believed.

Despite careful planning by the investigators, the experiments had a powerful impact on subjects *that could not have been easily anticipated.* I intentionally chose the experiments by Dawes, McTavish, and Shaklee because they involved no deception and were well within the bounds of ethical codes. My point is simple but important. No code of ethics can anticipate all problems, especially those created when subjects discover something unpleasant about themselves or others in the course of their participation.

Social psychologists who conduct experiments are deeply concerned about ethical issues, precisely because their work is constructed on an ethical dilemma. Let me explain. This dilemma is based on two conflicting values to which most social psychologists subscribe. On the one hand, they believe in the value of free scientific inquiry. On the other hand, they believe in the dignity of humans and their right to privacy. This dilemma is a real one and cannot be dismissed either by piously defending the importance of preserving human dignity, or by glibly pledging allegiance to the cause of science. And social psychologists must face this problem squarely, not just once, but each and every time they design and conduct an experiment—for there is no concrete and universal set of rules or guidelines capable of governing *every* experiment.

Obviously, some experimental techniques present more problems than others. In general, experiments that employ deception are cause for concern, because the act of lying is, *in and of itself,* objectionable—even if the deception is at the service of uncovering the "truth." And procedures that cause pain, embarrassment, guilt, or other intense feelings present obvious ethical problems.

More subtle but no less important ethical problems result when subjects confront some aspect of themselves that is not pleasant or positive. Recall the experiences of the subjects in the relatively "mild" experiments by Dawes, McTavish, and Shaklee. And many of Solomon Asch's[16] subjects learned that they would conform in the face of group pressure; many subjects in our own experiment (Aronson and Mettee)[17] learned that they were capable of cheating at a game of cards; many of Milgram's[18] subjects learned that they would obey an authority, even if such obedience (apparently) involved harming another person. Finally, recall from chapter 1 that subjects in the Stanford Prison Study[19] engaged in acts of cruelty in the absence of direct, explicit commands to do so.

It could be argued that such "self-discovery" is of therapeutic or educational benefit to subjects—indeed, many subjects, themselves, have made this point. But this does not, in and of itself, justify these procedures. After all, how could an experimenter know in advance that it would be therapeutic? Moreover, it is arrogant of any scientist to decide that he or she has the right or the skill to provide people with a therapeutic experience without their prior permission to do so.

Given these problems, do the ends of social psychological research justify the means? This is a debatable point. Some argue that, no matter what the goals of this science are and no matter what the accomplishments, they are not worth it if people are deceived or put through some discomfort. On the opposite end of the spectrum, others insist social psychologists are finding things out that may have profound benefits for humankind, and accordingly, almost any price is worth paying for the results.

My own position is somewhere in between. I believe the science of social psychology is important, and I also believe experimental subjects should be protected at all times. When deciding whether a particular experimental procedure is ethical or not, I believe a cost-benefit analysis is appropriate. That is, how much "good" will derive from doing the experiment and how much "bad" will happen to the experimental subjects should be considered. Put another way, the benefits to society are compared with the costs to the subjects, and this ratio is entered into the decision calculus. Unfortunately, such a comparison often is difficult to make because, typically, neither the benefit to society nor the harm to subjects is known or calculable. Furthermore, even the anticipated result of an experiment may alter our evaluation of its ethicality. Would we question the ethics of the Milgram procedure if none of the subjects had administered shocks beyond the "Moderate Shock" level? Apparently not. A recent study[20] found that individuals' ratings of the "harmfulness" of the Milgram procedure varied according to the type of outcome they believed to have happened. That is, individuals who were told that a high proportion of the subjects were obedient rated the procedure as more harmful than individuals who were told that a low proportion were obedient. On a more general note, the ethics of *any* experiment may be less open to question when the results tell us something pleasant or flattering about human nature, and more open to question when they tell us something we'd rather not know.

In sum, my decision to do an experiment depends on the particular costs and benefits associated with the research at hand. There are, however, five guidelines I subscribe to at all times:

1. Procedures that cause intense pain or intense discomfort should be avoided. If experimenters exercise a great deal of in-

genuity and caution, they can usually succeed in testing their hypotheses without using extreme methods. Although a less intense procedure usually produces less clear results, experimenters should choose to sacrifice some clarity in the interests of protecting their subjects.

2. Experimenters should be ever alert to alternative procedures to deception. If some other viable procedure can be found, it should be used.

3. Experimenters should provide their subjects with the real option of quitting the experiment if their discomfort becomes too intense.

4. Experimenters should spend considerable time with each subject at the close of the experimental session, carefully explaining the experiment, its true purpose, the reasons for the deception, and so on. They should go out of their way to protect the dignity of subjects, to avoid making them feel stupid or gullible about having "fallen for" the deception. They should make certain that subjects leave the scene in good spirits—feeling good about themselves and their role in the experiment. This can be accomplished by any earnest experimenter who is willing to take the time and effort to repay each subject (with information and consideration) for the very important role that subject has played in the scientific enterprise.

5. Finally, experimenters should not undertake an experiment that entails deception or discomfort "just for the hell of it." Before entering the laboratory, experimenters should be certain their experiment is sound and important—that they are seeking the answer to an interesting question and seeking it in a careful and well-organized manner.

Experimenters in social psychology try hard to be as sensitive as possible to the needs of their subjects. Although many experiments entail procedures that cause some degree of discomfort, the vast majority of these procedures contain many safeguards for the protection of subjects. For example, from the point of view of subject discomfort, most readers would agree that Stanley Milgram's experiment on obedience is one of the most difficult studies reported in this book. There has been considerable debate as to whether or not the experiment should have been conducted. Yet it is evident that Milgram worked hard after the experiment to turn the overall experience into a useful and exciting one for his subjects. It is also clear his efforts achieved a high degree of success: Several weeks after the experiment, 84 percent of the participants reported they were glad to have taken part in the study; 15 percent reported neutral feelings; and only 1 percent stated they were sorry they had participated. (We should view these findings with caution, however. The discussion of cognitive dissonance in chapter 5 has taught us that people sometimes justify their behavior by changing their previously held attitudes.) More convincing evidence comes from a follow-up study: One year after the experimental program was completed, a university psychiatrist interviewed a random sample of the subjects and found no evidence of injurious effects—rather, the typical response was that their participation was instructive and enriching.[21]

The Post-Experimental Session.   The post-experimental session, sometimes called debriefing, is an extremely important part of the experiment. Not only is it of great value as a means of undoing some of the discomfort and deceptions that occurred during the experimental session, but it also provides the experimenter with an opportunity to provide additional information about the topic so the experiment can become an educational experience for the participants. In addition, the experimenter can determine the extent to which the procedure worked—and find out from the one person who knows best (the subject) how the procedure might be improved. In short, the prudent experimenter regards subjects as colleagues, not as objects. For those of you who have never had a firsthand experience with a debriefing session, a description of exactly what is involved and how subjects are treated may provide a more complete understanding of the experimental technique.

At first, the experimenter encourages the subject to give his overall reaction to the experiment and to ask any questions to clear up any existing confusion. She then tries to determine why the subject responded as he did and whether he interpreted the procedures the way they were intended. If deception occurred, was the subject suspicious of the cover story? If the subject was suspicious, the experimenter must decide whether his suspicions were great enough to have affected his behavior. If so, then the subject's responses cannot be included in the data of the experiment. Because the experimenter is interested in how subjects spontaneously behave, any responses motivated by suspicions cannot be spontaneous and are most likely invalid. If more than a few subjects must be discarded for reasons of suspiciousness, the entire experiment must be scrapped.

Throughout this first part of the debriefing, the experimenter probes to try to learn as precisely as possible what the subject's reactions were, and whether they were suspicious. She then informs him of the deception. The pace should be gradual and the manner gentle, so the subject is not suddenly confronted with the information. I can picture Lucy (in the "Peanuts" comic strip) as the world's worst experimenter. How might she break the news to Charlie Brown? "You've been fooled; we've been lying to you, and you fell for it—ha! ha!" Clearly, this kind of approach must be avoided.

Every experimenter has his or her own technique for debriefing. I will discuss my own procedure in some detail. I begin by asking subjects whether the experiment was perfectly clear—if they have any questions about either the purpose or the procedure. I usually ask some open-ended questions—for example, I might simply ask them to tell me frankly how the experiment struck them. Because people do react differently, it helps me to know their feelings. I then begin zeroing in by asking the subject if any part of the procedure seemed odd, confusing, or disturbing. If there are any suspicions, they will probably be revealed by this procedure, or at least I will see signs that indicate the need for further probing; but if not, I continue toward greater specificity and ask if he or she thinks there may be more to the experiment than meets the eye. This is a giveaway. It tells the subject, in effect, there *was* more than meets the eye. Many subjects will indicate they do think so. This does not necessarily mean they had strong and definite suspicions; it means, rather, that some people know deception is frequently a part of certain psychology experiments, and they are vaguely suspicious this experiment may have been one of those. My own questioning may have helped confirm these suspicions. It is important to overtly recognize the subject's lack of gullibility. It is also important to communicate that being fooled by the procedure is not a matter of stupidity or gullibility but that it is a function of the procedure—because if it's a good experiment, *virtually everyone* gets fooled. This is crucial: Being "taken in" hurts only if it leads us to conclude we are extraordinarily stupid or gullible. But this is not true with these experiments. If the experiment is a good one, *everyone* will be "taken in." Accordingly, it is imperative that the experimenter take the time and trouble to make this clear to the subject. This one factor is frequently the crucial determinant of whether the subject goes home feeling good or feeling like a fool. Any experimenter who does not take special care with this part of the experiment has no business in a psychological laboratory.

Any subjects who voice specific suspicions are invited to specify how these might have affected their behavior. The answer to this question is crucial. If the subject does have some clear suspicions (right or wrong), and if these might have affected his or her behavior, I will discard the data for that subject. Obviously, this decision is made in ignorance of whether or not the data from this subject supported the hypothesis! If the subjects' suspicions are not on target, I will tell them it was reasonable to be suspicious, that there *is* more to the experiment, and I will then proceed to describe what I am studying and the reasons for using deception. I try to level with subjects by sharing my own discomfort about using deception. I also try hard to explain why I think the results of the experiment might be important.

If an occasional subject is feeling uncomfortable, or angry, or disdainful, I want to know so I can be of assistance. But most subjects are polite. To help subjects build up the courage to tell me off (if they feel like it), I try to share my own questions and criticisms about the procedure and its impact, in the hope of removing any resistance they may feel in talking about their skepticism, their feeling that the whole experiment seemed trivial and meaningless, their annoyance, their discomfort, or the fact that the procedure had *more* of an impact on them than I had intended. Subjects are usually eager to help me improve the experiment and frequently have provided me with many valuable suggestions.

To close the session, I ask that subjects try to keep their laboratory experiences secret. If future subjects know the study's purpose in advance, their reactions will be invalid and could lead to incorrect conclusions about the results. To avoid this waste of time, experimenters need to secure the help of each person participating in the study. I have been successful at maintaining secrecy by emphasizing the great harm that would be done to the scientific community if sophisticated subjects provided me with results that falsely supported my hypothesis.[22]

In this chapter, I have discussed the advantages of the experimental method and have shown how complex and challenging it is to design a laboratory experiment in social psychology. In addition, I have shared some of the excitement I feel in overcoming difficulties and explored the ways I attempt to insure the well-being, as well as the learning, of my subjects. Experimental subjects have contributed a great deal to our understanding; we are in their debt. The knowledge, information, and insights described in the first eight chapters of this book are based on the techniques and procedures discussed in this chapter, as well as on the cooperation of our experimental subjects. Ultimately, our understanding of human beings in all their complexity rests on our ingenuity in developing techniques for studying behavior that are well controlled and impactful without violating the essential dignity of those individuals who contribute to our understanding by serving as experimental subjects.

The Morality of Discovering Unpleasant Things

There is one additional ethical consideration—a rather knotty one: the moral responsibility of the scientist for what he or she discovers. Throughout this book, I have been dealing with some extremely powerful antecedents of persuasion. This was particularly true in chapter 5, in which I discussed techniques of self-persuasion, and in some of the subsequent chapters, in which I discussed applications of these techniques. Self-persuasion is a very powerful force because, in a very real sense, the persuaded never know what hit them. They come to believe that a particular thing is true, not because J. Robert Oppenheimer or T. S. Eliot or Joe "The Shoulder" convinced them it is true, but because they have convinced *themselves* the thing is true. What's more, they frequently do not know why or how they came to believe it. This renders the phenomenon not only powerful but frightening as well. As long as I know why I came to believe X, I am relatively free to change my mind; but if all I know is that X is true—and that's all there is to it—I am far more likely to cling to that belief, even in the face of a barrage of disconfirming evidence.

The mechanisms I described can be used to get people to floss their teeth, to stop bullying smaller people, to reduce pain, or to love their neighbors. Many people might consider these good outcomes; but they are manipulative just the same. Moreover, the same mechanisms can also be used to get people to buy particular brands of toothpaste and perhaps to vote for particular political candidates. Isn't it immoral to discover ways of manipulating people?

As the reader of this volume must know by this time, as a real person living in the real world, I have a great many values and have made no effort to conceal them; they stick out all over the place. For example, I would like to eliminate bigotry and cruelty. If I had the power, I would employ the most humane and effective methods at my disposal in order to achieve those ends. I am equally aware that, once these methods are developed, others might use them to achieve ends I might not agree with. This causes me great concern. I am also aware you may not share my values—therefore, if you believe these techniques are powerful, *you* should be concerned.

At the same time, I should hasten to point out that the phenomena I have been describing are not new. It was not a social psychologist who got Mr. Landry hooked on Marlboros, and it was not a social psychologist who induced Lieutenant Calley to wantonly kill Vietnamese civilians. They did what they did on their own. Social psychologists are attempting to understand these phenomena and scores of others that take place in the world every day, phenomena that have been occurring since the first two people on earth began interacting. By understanding these phenomena, the social psychologist may be able to help people refrain from a particular kind of behavior when they themselves decide it is maladaptive.

But the mere fact that we, as working social psychologists, know that the phenomena we deal with are not of our own creation does not free us from moral responsibility. Our research often crystallizes these phenomena into highly structured, easily applicable techniques. There is always the possibility some individuals may develop these techniques and use them for their own ends. In the hands of a demagogue, these techniques could conceivably turn our society into an Orwellian nightmare. It is not my intention to preach about the responsibilities of social psychologists. What I am most cognizant of are what I believe to be *my own* responsibilities. Briefly, they are to educate the public about how these techniques might be used and to remain vigilant against their abuse as I continue to do research aimed at furthering our understanding of us social animals—of how we think and how we behave. Frankly, I can think of no endeavor more interesting or more important.

Notes

Chapter 1. What Is Social Psychology?

1. Michener, J. (1971). *Kent State: What happened and why.* New York: Random House.

2. Clark, K., & Clark, M. (1947). Racial identification and preference in Negro children. In T. M. Newcomb & E. L. Hartley (Eds.), *Readings in social psychology* (pp. 169–178). New York: Holt.

3. Harris, J. (1970). *Hiroshima: A study in science, politics, and the ethics of war.* Menlo Park, CA: Addison-Wesley.

4. Powell, J. L. (1988). A test of the knew-it-all-along effect in the 1984 presidental and statewide elections. *Journal of Applied Social Psychology, 18,* 760–773.

5. Michener, *Kent State.*

6. Ellen Berscheid; personal communication.

7. Zimbardo, P. (1971, October 25). *The psychological power and pathology of imprisonment* (p. 3). Statement prepared for the U.S. House of Representatives Committee on the Judiciary; Subcommittee No. 3: Hearings on Prison Reform, San Francisco, CA.

Chapter 2.   Conformity

1. Copyright © 1933, 1961 by James Thurber. From "The day the dam broke," in *My life and hard times* (New York: Harper, 1933), pp. 41, 47. (Originally printed in the *New Yorker.*)

2. Schachter, S. (1951). Deviation, rejection, and communication. *Journal of Abnormal and Social Psychology, 46,* 190–207.

3. Kruglanski, A. W., & Webster, D. W. (1991). Group member's reaction opinion deviates and conformists at varying degrees of proximity to decision deadline and of environmental noise. *Journal of Personality and Social Psychology, 61,* 212–225.

4. Speer, A. (1970). *Inside the Third Reich: Memoirs.* (R. Winston & C. Winston, Trans.). New York: MacMillan.

5. Playboy, January 1975, p. 78.

6. Kruglanski, A. W. (1986, August). Freeze-think and the Challenger. *Psychology Today,* pp. 48–49.

7. Janis, I. L. (1971, November). Groupthink. *Psychology Today,* pp. 43–46. Janis, I. L. (1984). Counteracting the adverse effects of concurrence-seeking in policy-planning groups. In H. Brandstatter, J. H. Davis, & G. Stocker-Kreichgauer (Eds.), *Group decision making.* New York: Academic Press.

8. Asch, S. (1951). Effects of group pressure upon the modification and distortion of judgement. In M. H. Guetzkow (Ed.), *Groups, leadership and men* (pp. 117–190). Pittsburgh: Carnegie. Asch, S. (1956). Studies of independence and conformity: A minority of one against a unanimous majority. *Psychological Monographs, 70* (9, Whole No. 416).

9. Wolosin, R., Sherman, S., & Cann, A. (1975). Predictions of own and other's conformity. *Journal of Personality, 43,* 357–378.

10. Deutsch, M., & Gerard, H. (1955). A study of normative and informational social influence upon individual judgment. *Journal of Abnormal and Social Psychology, 51,* 629–636.

11. Moulton, J., Blake, R., & Olmstead, J. (1956). The relationship between frequency of yielding and the disclosure of personal identity. *Journal of Personality, 24,* 339–347.

12. Argyle, M. (1957). Social pressure in public and private situations. *Journal of Abnormal and Social Psychology, 54,* 172–175.

13. Asch, S. (1955). Opinions and social pressure. *Scientific American,* 193 (5), 31–35. Morris, W., & Miller, R. (1975). The effects of consensus-breaking and consensus-preempting partners on reduction of conformity. *Journal of Experimental Social Psychology, 11,* 215–223. Boya-nowsky, E., Allen, V., Bragg, B., & Lepinski, J. (1981). Generalization of independence created by social support. *Psychological Record, 31,* 475–488.

14. Allen, V., & Levine, J. (1971). Social support and conformity: The role of independent assessment of reality. *Journal of Experimental Social Psychology, 7,* 48–58.

15. Deutsch & Gerard, Normative and informational social influence.

16. Mausner, B. (1954). The effects of prior reinforcement of the interaction of observer pairs. *Journal of Abnormal and Social Psychology, 49,* 65–68. Mausner, B. (1954). The effect on one's partner's success in a relevant task on the interaction of observed pairs. *Journal of Abnormal and Social Psychology, 49,* 557–560. Goldberg, S., & Lubin, A. (1958). Influence as a function of perceived judgment error. *Human Relations, 11,* 275–281. Wiesenthal, D., Endler, N., Coward, T., & Edwards, J. (1976). Reversibility of relative competence as a determinant of conformity across different perceptual tasks. *Representative Research in Social Psychology, 7,* 35–43.

17. Milgram, S. (1961). Nationality and conformity. *Scientific American, 205 (5),* 45–51. Frager, R. (1970). Conformity and anticonformity in Japan. *Journal of Personality and Social Psychology, 15,* 203–210.

18. Maccoby, E., & Jacklin, C. (1974). *The psychology of sex differences* (pp. 268–272). Stanford, CA: Stanford University Press. Cooper, H. (1979). Statistically combining independent studies: A meta-analysis of sex differences in conformity research. *Journal of Personality and Social Psychology, 37,* 131–146.

19. Eagly, A., & Carli, L. (1981). Sex of researchers and sex-typed communications as determinants of sex differences in influenceability: A meta-analysis of social influence studies. *Psychological Bulletin, 90,* 1–20. Javornisky, G. (1979). Task content and sex differences in conformity. *Journal of Social Psychology, 108,* 213–220. Feldman-Summers, S., Montano, D., Kasprzyk, D., & Wagner, B. (1980). Influence attempts

when competing views are gender-related: Sex as credibility. *Psychology of Women Quarterly, 5,* 311–320.

20. Schneider, F. (1970). Conforming behavior of black and white children. *Journal of Personality and Social Psychology, 16,* 466–471.

21. Allport, G. (1954). *The nature of prejudice* (pp. 13–14). Cambridge, MA: Addison-Wesley.

22. Dittes, J., & Kelley, H. (1956). Effects of different conditions of acceptance upon conformity to group norms. *Journal of Abnormal and Social Psychology, 53,* 100–107.

23. Bushman, B. J. (1988). The effects of apparel on compliance: A field experiment with a female authority figure. *Personality and Social Psychology Bulletin, 14,* 459–467.

24. Festinger, L. (1954). A theory of social comparison processes. *Human Relations, 7,* 117–140.

25. Mullen, B., Cooper, C., & Driskell, J. E. (1990). Jaywalking as a function of model behavior. *Personality and Social Psychology Bulletin, 16* (2), 320–330.

26. Aronson, E., & O'Leary, M. (1982–83). The relative effectiveness of models and prompts on energy conservation: A field experiment in a shower room. *Journal of Environmental Systems, 12,* 219–224.

27. Cialdini, R. B., Reno, R. R., & Kallgren, C. A. (1990). A focus theory of normative conduct: Recycling the concept of norms to reduce littering in public places. *Journal of Personality and Social Psycholgy, 58,* 1015–1029.

28. Ibid.

29. Schachter, S., & Singer, J. (1962). Cognitive, social, and physiological determinants of emotional state. *Psychological Review, 69,* 379–399.

30. James, W. (1890). *Principles of psychology.* New York: Smith.

31. Haney, C. (1984). Examining death qualification: Further analysis of the process effect. *Law and Human Behavior, 8,* 133–151.

32. Kelman, H. (1961). Processes of opinion change. *Public Opinion Quarterly, 25,* 57–78.

33. Kiesler, C., Zanna, M., & De Salvo, J. (1966). Deviation and conformity: Opinion change as a function of commitment, attraction, and

presence of a deviate. *Journal of Personality and Social Psychology, 3,* 458–467.

34. Vogler, R., Weissbach, T., Compton, J., & Martin, G. (1977). Integrated behavior change techniques for problem drinkers in the community. *Journal of Consulting and Clinical Psychology, 45,* 267–279. Kuetner, C., Lichtenstein, E., and Mees, H. (1968). Modification of smoking behavior: A review. *Psychological Bulletin, 70,* 520–533.

35. Milgram, S. (1963). Behavioral study of obedience. *Journal of Abnormal and Social Psychology, 67,* 371–378. Milgram, S. (1965). Some conditions of obedience and disobedience to authority. *Human Relations, 18,* 57–76. Milgram, S. (1974). *Obedience to authority.* New York: Harper & Row.

36. Elms, A. C., & Milgram, S. (1966). Personality characteristics associated with obedience and defiance toward authoritative command. *Journal of Experimental Research in Personality, 1,* 282–289.

37. Kilham, W., & Mann, L. (1974). Level of destructive obedience as a function of transmitter and executant roles in the Milgram obedience paradigm. *Journal of Personality and Social Psychology, 29,* 696–702. Shanab, M., & Yahya, K. (1977). A behavioral study of obedience in children. *Journal of Personality and Social Psychology, 35,* 530–536. Miranda, F. B., Caballero, R. B., Gomez, M. G., & Zamorano, M. M. (1981). Obedience to authority. *Psiquis: Revista de Psiquiatria, Psicologia y Psicosomatica, 2,* 212–221. Mantell, D. (1971). The potential for violence in Germany. *Journal of Social Issues, 27,* 101–112.

38. Milgram, S. (1974). *Obedience to authority.* New York: Harper & Row. Sheridan, C., & King, R. (1972, August). Obedience to authority with an authentic victim. Paper presented at the convention of the American Psychological Association.

39. Milgram, S. (1965). Liberating effects of group pressure. *Journal of Personality and Social Psychology, 1,* 127–134.

40. Milgram, S. (1965). Some conditions of obedience and disobedience to authority. *Human Relations, 18,* 57–76.

41. Milgram, S. (1965). Liberating effects of group pressure. *Journal of Personality and Social Psychology, 1,* 127–134.

42. Rosenthal, A. M. (1964). *Thirty-eight witnesses.* New York: McGraw-Hill.

43. Korte, C., & Kerr, N. (1975). Response to altruistic opportunities in

urban and nonurban settings. *Journal of Social Psychology, 95,* 183–184. Rushton, J. P. (1978). Urban density and altruism: Helping strangers in a Canadian city, suburb, and small town. *Psychological Reports, 43,* 987–990.

44. Darley, J., & Latane, B. (1968). Bystander intervention in emergencies: Diffusion of responsibility. *Journal of Personality and Social Psychology, 8,* 377–383. Latane, B., & Darley, J. (1968). Group inhibition of bystander intervention in emergencies. *Journal of Personality and Social Psychology, 10,* 215–221. Latane, B., & Rodin, J. (1969). A lady in distress: Inhibiting effects of friends and strangers on bystander intervention. *Journal of Experimental Social Psychology, 5,* 189–202.

45. Latane, B., & Nida, S. (1981). Ten years of research on group size and helping. *Psychological Bulletin, 89,* 308–324.

46. Latane & Rodin, Lady in distress.

47. Darley & Latane, Bystander intervention.

48. Piliavin, I., Rodin, J., & Piliavin, J. (1969). Good samaritanism: An underground phenomenon? *Journal of Personality and Social Psychology, 13,* 289–299.

49. Bickman, L. (1971). The effect of another bystander's ability to help on bystander intervention in an emergency. *Journal of Experimental Social Psychology, 7,* 367–379. Bickman, L. (1972). Social influence and diffusion of responsibility in an emergency. *Journal of Experimental Social Psychology, 8,* 438–445.

50. Piliavin, J., & Piliavin, E. (1972). The effect of blood on reactions to a victim. *Journal of Personality and Social Psychology, 23,* 353–361.

51. Darley, J., & Batson, D. (1973). "From Jerusalem to Jericho": A study of situational and dispositional variables in helping behavior. *Journal of Personality and Social Psychology, 27,* 100–108.

52. Clark III, R., & Word, L. (1972). Why don't bystanders help? Because of ambiguity? *Journal of Personality and Social Psychology, 24,* 392–400. Solomon, L., Solomon, H., & Stone, R. (1978). Helping as a function of number of bystanders and ambiguity of emergency. *Personality and Social Psychology Bulletin, 4,* 318–321.

53. Baron, R. A. (1970). Magnitude of model's apparent pain and ability to aid the model as determinants of observer reaction time. *Psychonomic Science, 21,* 196–197.

54. Suedfeld, P., Bochner, S., & Wnek, D. (1972). Helper-sufferer similarity and a specific request for help: Bystander intervention during a peace demonstration. *Journal of Applied Social Psychology, 2,* 17–23.

Chapter 3.   Mass Communication, Propaganda, and Persuasion

1. ABC to air major nuclear war film. (1983, September). *Report from Ground Zero, 3*(1), 1–2.

2. Schofield, J. W., & Pavelchak, M. A. (1989). Fallout from "The Day After": The impact of a TV film on attitudes related to nuclear war. *Journal of Applied Social Psychology, 19,* 433–448.

3. *Newsweek,* June 2, 1974, p. 79. O'Connor, J. J. (1974, March 10). They sell all kinds of drugs on television. *The New York Times,* p. D15.

4. Roberts, C. (1993). Special Report, National Public Radio, Morning Edition, September 3, 1993.

5. Mark Levy, quoted in *Time,* October 1, 1979, p. 83.

6. Mann, P., & Iscoe, I. (1971). Mass behavior and community organization: Reflections on a peaceful demonstration. *American Psychologist, 26,* 108–113.

7. *St. Petersburg* (Florida) *Times,* October 21, 1982. *The* (Nashville) *Tennesseean,* October 31, 1982.

8. *Newsbank,* October 1982, Vol. 19, p. 1.

9. Phillips, D. P., & Carstensen, L. L. (1986). Clustering of teenage suicides after television news stories about suicide. *New England Journal of Medicine, 315,* 685–689.

10. Phillips, D. P. (1979). Suicide, motor vehicle fatalities, and the mass media: Evidence toward a theory of suggestion. *American Journal of Sociology, 84,* 1150–1174.

11. McGinness, J. (1970). *The selling of the president: 1968* (p. 160). New York: Pocket Books.

12. Lyle J., & Hoffman, H. (1971). Explorations in patterns of television viewing by preschool-age children. In J. P. Murray, E. A. Robinson, &

G. A. Comstock (Eds.), *Television and social behavior* (Vol. 4, pp. 257–344). Rockville, MD: National Institutes of Health.

13. Lyle J., & Hoffman, H. (1971). Children's use of television and other media. In J. P. Murray, E. A. Robinson, and G. A. Comstock (Eds.), *Television and social behavior* (Vol. 4, pp. 129–256). Rockville, MD: National Institutes of Health.

14. Bem, D. (1970). *Beliefs, attitudes, and human affairs.* Belmont, CA: Brooks/Cole.

15. Zajonc, R. (1968). The attitudinal effects of mere exposure. *Journal of Personality and Social Psychology, Monograph Supplement, 9,* 1–27.

16. Grush, J., McKeough, K., & Ahlering, R. (1978). Extrapolating laboratory exposure research to actual political elections. *Journal of Personality and Social Psychology, 36,* 257–270.

17. Grush, J. E. (1980). Impact of candidate expenditures, regionality, and prior outcomes on the 1976 presidential primaries. *Journal of Personality and Social Psychology, 38,* 337–347.

18. White, J. E. (1988, November 14). Bush's most valuable player. *Time,* pp. 20–21.

19. Rosenthal, A. (1988, October 24). Foes accuse Bush campaign of inflaming racial tension. *The New York Times,* pp. A1, B5. Pandora's box (1988, October). *The New Republic,* pp. 4, 45.

20. Tolchin, M. (1988, October 12). Study says 53,000 get prison furloughs in '87, and few did harm. *The New York Times,* p. A23.

21. Pratkanis, A. R., & Aronson, E. (1992). *The age of propaganda: The everyday use and abuse of persuasion.* New York: W. H. Freeman.

22. Pratkanis, A. R. (1993). Propaganda and persuasion in the 1992 U.S. presidential election: What are the implications for a democracy? *Current World Leaders, 36,* 341–361.

23. Zimbardo, P., Ebbesen, E., & Maslach, C. (1977). *Influencing attitudes and changing behavior* (2nd ed.). Reading, MA: Addison-Wesley.

24. Petty, R. E., & Cacioppo, J. T. (1986). The elaboration likelihood model of persuasion. In L. Berkowitz (Ed.), *Advances in Experimental Social Psychology* (pp. 123–205). Hillsdale, NJ: Erlbaum.

25. Aristotle. (1954). Rhetoric. In W. Roberts (Trans.), *Aristotle, rhetoric and poetics* (p. 25). New York: Modern Library.

26. Hovland, C., & Weiss, W. (1951). The influence of source credibility on communication effectiveness. *Public Opinion Quarterly, 15,* 635–650.

27. Aronson, E., & Golden, B. (1962). The effect of relevant and irrelevant aspects of communicator credibility on opinion change. *Journal of Personality, 30,* 135–146.

28. Walster (Hatfield), E., Aronson, E., & Abrahams, D. (1966). On increasing the persuasiveness of a low prestige communicator. *Journal of Experimental Social Psychology, 2,* 325–342.

29. Eagly, A., Wood, W., & Chaiken, S. (1978). Causal inferences about communicators and their effect on opinion change. *Journal of Personality and Social Psychology, 36,* 424–435.

30. *Santa Cruz Sentinel,* January 13, 1987, p. A8.

31. Walster (Hatfield), E., & Festinger, L. (1962). The effectiveness of "overheard" persuasive communications. *Journal of Abnormal and Social Psychology, 65,* 395–302.

32. Mills, J., & Aronson, E. (1965). Opinion change as a function of communicator's attractiveness and desire to influence. *Journal of Personality and Social Psychology, 1,* 173–177.

33. Eagly, A., & Chaiken, S. (1975). An attribution analysis of the effect of communicator characteristics on opinion change: The case of communicator attractiveness. *Journal of Personality and Social Psychology, 32,* 136–144.

34. Hartmann, G. (1936). A field experience on the comparative effectiveness of "emotional" and "rational" political leaflets in determining election results. *Journal of Abnormal and Social Psychology, 31,* 336–352.

35. Leventhal, H. (1970). Findings and theory in the study of fear communications. In L. Berkowitz (Ed.), *Advances in experimental social psychology* (Vol. 5, pp. 119–186). New York: Academic Press.

36. Leventhal, H., Meyer, D., & Nerenz, D. (1980). The common sense representation of illness danger. In S. Rachman (Ed.), *Contributions to medical psychology* (Vol. 2). New York: Pergammon Press.

37. *Time,* February 16, 1987, pp. 50–53.

38. San Francisco Chronicle, June 19, 1987, p. 9.

39. Leishman, K. (1987, February). Heterosexuals and AIDS. *The Atlantic Monthly,* pp. 39–58.

40. Liberman, A., & Chaiken, S. (1992). Defensive processing of personally relevant health messages. *Personality and Social Psychology, 18,* 669–679.

41. Clark III, R. D. (1990). The impact of AIDS on gender differences in willingness to engage in casual sex. *Journal of Applied Social Psychology, 20,* 771–782.

42. Leishman, K. (1987, February) *The Atlantic Monthly.* Heterosexuals and AIDS, p. 44.

43. Williams, S. S., Kimble, D. L., Cowell, N. H., Weiss L. H., Newton, K. J., Fisher, J. D., & Fisher, W. A. (1992). College students use implicit personality theory instead of safe sex. *Journal of Applied Social Psychology, 22,* 921–933.

44. Hirschorn, M. (1987, April 29). AIDS not seen as a major threat by heterosexuals on campuses. *Chronicle of Higher Education.*

45. Aronson, E. (1989). Excuses, excuses, excuses: Why sexually active college students do not use condoms. Invited address, meeting of the Western Psychological Association, 1989.

46. Aronson, E. (1991). How to persuade sexually active college students to use condoms. Invited address, meeting of the American Psychological Association, San Francisco, California.

47. Nisbett, R., Borgida, E., Crandall, R., & Reed, H. (1976). Popular induction: Information is not always informative. In J. S. Carroll and J. W. Payne (Eds.), *Cognition and social behavior* (pp. 227–236). Hillsdale, NJ: Erlbaum. Nisbett, R., & Ross, L. (1980). *Human inference: Strategies and shortcomings of social judgment.* Englewood Cliffs, NJ: Prentice-Hall. Hamill, R., DeCamp Wilson, T., & Nisbett, R. (1980). Insensitivity to sample bias: Generalizing from atypical cases. *Journal of Personality and Social Psychology, 39,* 578–589. Shelley Taylor, a cognitive social psychologist, argues that the "vividness" effect is not supported by a majority of the experimental findings. For a discussion of this issue, see Taylor, S., & Thompson, S. (1982). Stalking the elusive "vividness" effect. *Psychological Review, 89,* 155–181.

48. Gonzales, M. H., Aronson, E., & Costanzo, M. (1988). Increasing the effectiveness of energy auditors: A field experiment. *Journal of Applied Social Psychology, 18,* 1049–1066.

49. Hovland, C., Lumsdain, A., & Sheffield, F. (1949). *Experiments on mass communications.* Princeton: Princeton University Press.

50. Miller, N., & Campbell, D. (1959). Recency and primacy in persuasion as a function of the timing of speeches and measurements. *Journal of Abnormal and Social Psychology, 59,* 1–9.

51. Zimbardo, P. (1960). Involvement and communication discrepancy as determinants of opinion conformity. *Journal of Abnormal and Social Psychology, 60,* 86–94.

52. Whittaker, J. O. (1963). Opinion change as a function of communication-attitude discrepancy. *Psychological Reports, 13,* 763–772.

53. Hovland, C., Harvey, O. J., & Sherif, M. (1957). Assimilation and contrast effects in reaction to communication and attitude change. *Journal of Abnormal and Social Psychology, 55,* 244–252.

54. Aronson, E., Turner, J., & Carlsmith, J. M. (1963). Communication credibility and communication discrepancy as determinants of opinion change. *Journal of Abnormal and Social Psychology, 67,* 31–36.

55. Zellner, M. (1970). Self-esteem, reception, and influenceability. *Journal of Personality and Social Psychology, 15,* 87–93.

56. Janis, I. J., Kaye, D., & Kirschner, P. (1965). Facilitating effects of "eating-while-reading" on responsiveness to persuasive communication. *Journal of Personality and Social Psychology, 1,* 181–186.

57. Hass, R. G., & Grady, K. (1975). Temporal delay, type of forewarning, and resistance to influence. *Journal of Experimental Social Psychology, 11,* 459–469.

58. Freedman, J., & Sears, D. (1965). Warning, distraction, and resistance to influence. *Journal of Personality and Social Psychology, 1,* 262–266.

59. Brehm, J. (1966). *Explorations in cognitive reactance.* New York: Academic Press.

60. Bensley, L. S., & Wu, R. (1991). The role of psychological reactance in drinking following alcohol prevention messages. *Journal of Applied Social Psychology, 21,* 1111-1124.

61. Heilman, M. (1976). Oppositional behavior as a function of influence attempt intensity and retaliation threat. *Journal of Personality and Social Psychology, 33,* 574–578.

62. Petty, R., & Cacioppo, J. (1977). Forewarning, cognitive responding, and resistance to persuasion. *Journal of Personality and Social Psychology, 35,* 645–655.

63. Festinger, L., & Maccoby, N. (1964). On resistance to persuasive communications. *Journal of Abnormal and Social Psychology, 68,* 359–366.

64. Sloan, L., Love, R., & Ostrom, T. (1974). Political heckling: Who really loses? *Journal of Personality and Social Psychology, 30,* 518–525.

65. McGuire, W., & Papageorgis, D. (1961). The relative efficacy of various types of prior belief-defense in producing immunity against persuasion. *Journal of Abnormal and Social Psychology, 62,* 327–337.

66. McAlister, A., Perry, C., Killen, J., Slinkard, L. A., & Maccoby, N. (1980). Pilot study of smoking, alcohol and drug abuse prevention. *American Journal of Public Health, 70,* 719–721.

67. Pryor, B., & Steinfatt, W. (1978). The effects of initial belief level on inoculation theory and its proposed mechanisms. *Human Communications Research, 4,* 217–230.

68. Canon, L. (1964). Self-confidence and selective exposure to information. In L. Festinger (Ed.), *Conflict, decision, and dissonance* (pp. 83–96). Stanford, CA: Stanford University Press.

69. TV violence for a new generation (1987). *TV Monitor* (p. 2). San Francisco: The Children's Television Resource and Education Center.

70. Statistics cited in Pratkanis, A. R., & Aronson, E. (1992). *Age of propaganda: The everyday use and abuse of persuasion.* New York: W. H. Freeman.

71. Liebert, R. (1975, July 16). Testimony before the Subcommittee on Communications of the House Committee on Interstate and Foreign Commerce.

72. *San Francisco Chronicle,* August 25, 1979, p. 15. *San Francisco Sunday Examiner and Chronicle,* August 26, 1979, p. 2. *San Jose Mercury-News,* February 11, 1982, p. A2.

73. Gerbner, G., Gross, L., Morgan, M., & Signorielli, N. (1986). Living with television: The dynamics of the cultivation process. In J. Bryant & D. Zillman (Eds.), *Perspectives on media effects* (pp. 17–40). Hillsdale, NJ: Erlbaum.

74. Quoted in *Newsweek,* December 6, 1982, p. 140.

75. Haney, C., & Manzolati, J. (1981). Television criminology: Network illusions of criminal justice realities. In *Readings about the social animal* (6th ed., pp. 120–131). San Francisco: W. H. Freeman.

76. Hennigan, K., Heath, L., Wharton, J. D., DelRosario, M., Cook, T., & Calder, B. (1982). Impact of the introduction of television on crime in the United States: Empirical findings and theoretical implications. *Journal of Personality and Social Psychology, 42,* 461–477.

77. Ronis, D., Baumgardner, M., Leippe, M., Cacioppo, J., & Greenwald, A. (1977). In search of reliable persuasion. *Journal of Personality and Social Psychology, 35,* 548–569.

Chapter 4.   Social Cognition

1. Lippmann, W. (1922). *Public opinion.* New York: Harcourt, Brace, & Co.

2. It is during this time that the custom of a man walking between the street and a woman began. In medieval times the custom made some sense; a man's boots were easier to clean, if splashed, than a woman's dress.

3. Panati, C. (1987). *Extraordinary origins of everyday things.* New York: Harper & Row.

4. Gilovich, T. (1991). *How we know what isn't so.* New York: Free Press.

5. Bentham, J. (1876/1948). *A fragment on government and an introduction to the principles of morals and legislation.* Oxford: Blackwell. For a modern version of the felicific calculation, see Fishbein, M., & Ajzen, I. (1975). *Belief, attitude, intention, and behavior: An introduction to theory and research.* Reading, MA: Addison-Wesley.

6. Kelley, H. H. (1967). Attribution theory in social psychology. In D. Levine (Ed.), *Nebraska symposium on motivation* (Vol. 15, pp. 192–241). Lincoln: University of Nebraska Press. Kelley, H. H. (1973). The process of causal attribution. *American Psychologist, 28,* 107–128.

7. Interestingly, it has been argued that even scientists do not always think like scientists and instead fall prey to some of the biases described in this chapter. See Greenwald, A. G., Pratkanis, A. R., Leippe, M. R., & Baumgardner, M. H. (1986). Under what conditions does theory obstruct research progress? *Psychological Review, 93,* 216–229.

8. Fiske, S. T., & Taylor, S. E. (1991). *Social cognition.* New York: McGraw-Hill.

9. Bronowski, J. (1973). *The ascent of man.* Boston: Little, Brown, Co.

Pratkanis, A. R., & Aronson, E. (1991). *The age of propaganda: The everyday use and abuse of persuasion.* New York: W. H. Freeman.

10. Pratkanis, A. R., Farquhar, P. H., Silbert, S., & Hearst, J. (1989). Decoys produce contrast effects and alter choice probabilities. University of California, Santa Cruz.

11. Kenrick, D. T., & Gutierres, S. E. (1980). Contrast effects in judgments of attractiveness: When beauty becomes a social problem. *Journal of Personality and Social Psychology, 38,* 131–140.

12. Higgins, E. T., Rholes, W. S., & Jones, C. R. (1977). Category accessibility and impression formation. *Journal of Experimental Social Psychology, 13,* 141–154.

13. Heath, L. Acklin, M., & Wiley, K. (1991). Cognitive heuristics and AIDS risk assessment among physicians. *Personality and Social Psychology Bulletin, 21,* 1859–1867.

14. Rogers, E. M., & Dearing, J. W. (1988). Agenda-setting research: Where has it been, Where is it going? In J. A. Anderson (Ed.), *Communication Yearbook 11* (pp. 555–594). Beverly Hills, CA: Sage Publications.

15. McCombs, M. E., & Shaw, D. L. (1972). The agenda-setting function of mass media. *Public Opinion Quarterly, 36,* 176–187.

16. Iyengar, S., & Kinder, D. R. (1987). *News that matters.* Chicago, IL: University of Chicago Press.

17. Cited in Rogers and Dearing, Agenda-setting research.

18. Kahneman, D., & Tversky, A. (1984). Choices, values, and frames. *American Psychologist, 39,* 341–350.

19. Gonzales, M. H., Aronson, E., & Costanzo, M. (1988). Increasing the effectiveness of energy auditors: A field experiment. *Journal of Applied Social Psychology, 18,* 1046–1066.

20. Meyerowitz, B. E., & Chaiken, S. (1987). The effect of message framing on breast self-examination attitudes, intentions, and behavior. *Journal of Personality and Social Psychology, 52,* 500–510.

21. Asch, S. (1946). Forming impressions of personality. *Journal of Abnormal and Social Psychology, 41,* 258–290.

22. Jones, E. E., Rock, L., Shaver, K. G., Goethals, G. R., & Ward, L. M.

(1968). Pattern of performance and ability attribution: An unexpected primacy effect. *Journal of Personality and Social Psychology, 10,* 317–340.

23. Aronson, J. M., & Jones, E. E. (1992). Inferring abilities after influencing performances. *Journal of Experimental Social Psychology, 28,* 277–299.

24. Zukier, H. (1982). The dilution effect: The role of the correlation and the dispersion of predictor variables in the use of nondiagnostic information. *Journal of Personality and Social Psychology, 43,* 1163–1174.

25. Nisbett, R., & Ross, L. (1980). *Human inference: Strategies and shortcomings of social judgment.* Englewood Cliffs, NJ: Prentice-Hall. Sherman, S. J., & Corty, E. (1984). Cognitive heuristics. In R. S. Wyer & T. K. Srull (Eds.), *Handbook of Social Cognition* (Vol. 1, pp. 189–286). Hillsdale, NJ: Erlbaum. Tversky, A., & Kahneman, D. (1974). Judgment under uncertainty: Heuristics and biases. *Science, 185,* 1124–1131.

26. "Which cereal for breakfast?" *Consumer Reports,* February 1981, pp. 68–75.

27. Comparison based on "Eating to lower your high blood cholesterol." U.S. Department of Health and Human Services, NIH Publication No. 87-2920, September 1987. Saturated fats such as animal fat and some vegetable fats such as coconut oil, cocoa butter, palm oil, and hydrogenated oils have been shown to raise cholesterol levels. Cereal manufacturers sometimes use such fats, especially coconut, palm, and hydrogenated oils in their products. Many manufacturers are in the process of reformulating their cereals to remove such oils, so check the label before making a final decision.

28. Nisbett & Ross (1980); Shweder, R. (1977). Likeness and likelihood in everyday thought: Magical thinking in judgments about personality. *Current Anthropology, 18,* 637–658.

29. Pratkanis, A. R. (1989). The cognitive representation of attitudes. In A. R. Pratkanis, S. J. Breckler, & A. G. Greenwald (Eds.), *Attitude structure and function* (pp. 71–98). Hillsdale, NJ: Erlbaum. Pratkanis, A. R., & Greenwald, A. G. (1989). A socio-cognitive model of attitude structure and function. In L. Berkowitz (Ed.), *Advances in experimental social psychology* (Vol. 22, pp. 245–285). New York: Academic Press.

30. Pratkanis, A. R. (1988). The attitude heuristic and selective fact identification. *British Journal of Social Psychology, 27,* 257–263.

31. Thistlewaite, D. (1950). Attitude and structure as factors in the distortion of reasoning. *Journal of Abnormal and Social Psychology, 45,* 442–458.

32. Ross, L., Greene, D., & House, P. (1977). The "false-consensus effect": An egocentric bias in social perception and attribution process. *Journal of Experimental Social Psychology, 13,* 279–301.

33. Pratkanis, Cognitive representation.

34. See for a laboratory demonstration, Gilovich, T. (1981). Seeing the past in the present: The effect of associations to familiar judgments and decisions. *Journal of Personality and Social Psychology, 40,* 797–808.

35. Darley, J. M., & Gross, P. H. (1983). A hypothesis-confirming bias in labeling effects. *Journal of Personality and Social Psychology, 44,* 20–33.

36. Hamilton, D. L., & Rose, T. L. (1980). Illusory correlation and the maintenance of stereotypic beliefs. *Journal of Personality and Social Psychology, 39,* 832–845.

37. Pratkanis, A. R., personal communication.

38. Chapman, L. J. (1967). Illusory correlation in observational report. *Journal of Verbal Learning and Verbal Behavior, 6,* 151–155. Chapman, L. J., & Chapman, J. P. (1967). Genesis of popular but erroneous psychodiagnostic observations. *Journal of Abnormal Psychology, 72,* 193–204. Chapman, L. J., & Chapman, J. P. (1969). Illusory correlation as an obstacle to the use of valid psychodiagnostic signs. *Journal of Abnormal Psychology, 74,* 271–280.

39. Park, B., & Rothbart, M. (1982). Perception of out-group homogeneity and levels of social categorization: Memory for the subordinate attributes of in-group and out-group members. *Journal of Personality and Social Psychology, 42,* 1051–1068.

40. For reviews and discussion, see Tajfel, H. (1981). *Human groups and social categories.* Cambridge: Cambridge University Press. Turner, J. C. (1987). *Rediscovering the social group.* New York: Basil Blackwell.

41. Loftus, E. F., & Loftus, G. R. (1980). On the permanence of stored information in the human brain. *American Psychologist, 35,* 409–420.

42. Loftus, E. F., & Ketchum, K. (1991). *Witness for the defense.* New York: St. Martin's Press.

43. Loftus, E. F., & Palmer, J. C. (1974). Reconstruction of automobile

destruction: An example of the interaction between language and memory. *Journal of Verbal Learning and Verbal Behavior, 13,* 585–589.

44. Loftus, E. F. (1977). Shifting human color memory. *Memory and Cognition, 5,* 696–699.

45. Loftus, E. F. (1993). The reality of repressed memories. *American Psychologist, 48,* 518–537.

46. Ross, M., McFarland, C., & Fletcher, G. O. J. (1981). The effect of attitude on the recall of personal history. *Journal of Personality and Social Psychology, 40,* 627–634.

47. Gibbs, G. (1981). *Teaching students to learn.* Milton Keynes, England: Open University Press.

48. Pratkanis, A. R., Eskenazi, J., & Greenwald, A. G. (1990). What you expect is what you believe (but not necessarily what you get): On the effectiveness of subliminal self-help audiotapes. Unpublished manuscript. University of California, Santa Cruz. Greenwald, A. G., Spangenberg, E. R., Pratkanis, A. R., & Eskenazi, J. (1991). Double-blind tests of subliminal self-help audiotapes. *Psychological Science, 2,* 119–122.

49. Conway, M., & Ross, M. (1984). Getting what you want by revising what you had. *Journal of Personality and Social Psychology, 47,* 738–748.

50. Wyatt, D. F., & Campbell, D. T. (1951). On the liability of stereotype or hypothesis. *Journal of Abnormal and Social Psychology, 46,* 496–500. Bruner, J. S., & Potter, M. C. (1964). *Science, 144,* 424–425.

51. Snyder, M., & Swann, W. B. (1978). Hypothesis-testing processes in social interaction. *Journal of Personality and Social Psychology, 36,* 1202–1212.

52. Fischhoff, B. (1975). Hindsight ≠ foresight: The effect of outcome knowledge on judgment under uncertainty. *Journal of Experimental Psychology: Human Perception and Performance, 1,* 288–299. Fischhoff, B. (1977). Perceived informativeness of facts. *Journal of Experimental Psychology: Human Perception and Performance, 3,* 349–358.

53. Greenwald, A. G. (1980). The totalitarian ego: Fabrication and revision of personal history. *American Psychologist, 35,* 603–618.

54. LaPiere, R. (1934). Attitudes versus actions. *Social Forces, 13,* 230–237.

55. Wicker, A. W. (1969). Attitudes versus actions: The relationship of

verbal and overt behavioral responses to attitude objects. *Journal of Social Issues, 25* (4), 41–78.

56. Jones, E. E. (1990). *Interpersonal perception.* New York: W. H. Freeman. Jones, E. E., & Davis, K. E. (1965). From acts to dispositions: The attribution process in person perception. In L. Berkowitz (Ed.), *Advances in Experimental Social Psychology* (Vol. 2, pp. 219–266). New York: Academic Press.

57. Jones, E. E., & Harris, V. A. (1967). The attribution of attitudes. *Journal of Experimental Social Psychology, 3,* 1–24.

58. Fazio, R. H. (1986). How do attitudes guide behavior? In R. M. Sorrentino & E. T. Higgins (Eds.), *Handbook of motivation and cognition* (pp. 204–242). New York: Guilford Press. Fazio, R. H. (1989). On the power and functionality of attitudes: The role of attitude accessibility. In A. R. Pratkanis, S. J. Breckler, & A. G. Greenwald (Eds.), *Attitude structure and function* (pp. 153–179). Hillsdale, NJ: Erlbaum.

59. Fazio, R. H., & Williams, C. J. (1986). Attitude accessibility as a moderator of the attitude-perception and attitude-behavior relations: An investigation of the 1984 presidential election. *Journal of Personality and Social Psychology, 51,* 505–514.

60. Fazio, R. H., Chen, J., McDonel, E. C., & Sherman, S. J. (1982). Attitude accessibility, attitude-behavior consistency, and the strength of the object-evaluation association. *Journal of Experimental Social Psychology, 50,* 339–357. Fazio, R. H., Powell, M. C., & Herr, P. M. (1983). Toward a process model of attitude-behavior relation: Accessing one's attitude upon mere observation of the attitude object. *Journal of Personality and Social Psychology, 44,* 723–735. Fazio, R. H., & Zanna, M. P. (1981). Direct experience and attitude-behavior consistency. In L. Berkowitz (Ed.), *Advances in Experimental Social Psychology* (Vol. 14, pp. 162–202). New York: Academic Press. Regan, D. T., & Fazio, R. H. (1977). On the consistency between attitudes and behavior: Look to the method of attitude formation. *Journal of Experimental Social Psychology, 13,* 38–45.

61. Herr, P. M. (1986). Consequences of priming: Judgment and behavior. *Journal of Personality and Social Psychology, 51,* 1106–1115.

62. Ross, L. (1977). The intuitive psychologist and his shortcomings: Distortions in the attribution process. In L. Berkowitz (Ed.), *Advances in Experimental Social Psychology* (Vol. 10, pp. 173–220). New York: Academic Press.

63. Bierbrauer, G. (1973). Effect of set, perspective, and temporal factors in attribution. Unpublished Ph.D. dissertation, Stanford University, as described in Ross (1977).

64. Ross, L., Amabile, T. M., & Steinmetz, J. L. (1977). Social roles, social control, and biases in social-perception processes. *Journal of Personality and Social Psychology, 35,* 485–494.

65. Answers: Forbes field in Pittsburgh, Vilnius, and July 4, 1826.

66. Jones, E. E., & Nisbett, R. E. (1971). The actor and the observer: Divergent preceptions of the causes of behavior. In E. E. Jones, D. E. Kanouse, H. H. Kelley, R. E. Nisbett, S. Valins, & B. Weiner (Eds.), *Attribution: Perceiving the causes of behavior* (pp. 79–94). Morristown, NJ: General Learning Press.

67. See Jones, E. E., Rock, L., Shaver, K. G., Goethals, G. R., & Ward, L. M. (1968). Pattern of performance and ability attribution: An unexpected primacy effect. *Journal of Personality and Social Psychology, 10,* 317–349. McArthur, L. (1972). The how and what of why: Some determinants and consequences of causal attribution. *Journal of Personality and Social Psychology, 22,* 171–193. Nisbett, R. E., Caputo, C., Legant, P., & Marecek, J. (1973). Behavior as seen by the actor and as seen by the observer. *Journal of Personality and Social Psychology, 27,* 154–164.

68. Storms, M. D. (1973). Videotape and the attribution process: Reversing the perspective of actors and observers. *Journal of Personality and Social Psychology, 27,* 165–175.

69. James, W. (1890/1950). *The principles of psychology* (pp. 314–315). New York: Dover.

70. Greenwald, A. G. (1980). The totalitarian ego: Fabrication and revision of personal history. *American Psychologist, 35,* 603–618. Greenwald, A. G., & Pratkanis, A. R. (1984). The self. In R. S. Wyer & T. K. Srull (Eds.), *Handbook of Social Cognition* (Vol. 3, pp. 129–178). Hillsdale, NJ: Erlbaum.

71. Greenwald, Totalitarian ego.

72. Jervis, R. (1976). *Perception and misperception in international politics.* Princeton, NJ: Princeton University.

73. Langer, E. J. (1975). The illusion of control. *Journal of Personality and Social Psychology, 32,* 311–329. Langer, E. J. (1977). The psychology of chance. *Journal for the Theory of Social Behavior, 7,* 185–208.

74. Petty, R. E., & Brock, T. C. (1979). Effects of "Barnum" personality assessments on cognitive behavior. *Journal of Consulting and Clinical Psychology, 47,* 201–203.

75. Markus, H. (1977). Self-schemata and processing information about the self. *Journal of Personality and Social Psychology, 35,* 63–78. Breckler, S. J., Pratkanis, A. R., & McCann, D. (1991). The representation of self in multidimensional cognitive space. *British Journal of Social Psychology, 30,* 97–112. Brenner, M. (1973). The next-in-line effect. *Journal of Verbal Learning and Verbal Behavior, 12,* 320–323. Slamecka, N. J., & Graf, P. The generation effect: Delineation of a phenomenon. *Journal of Experimental Psychology: Human Learning and Memory, 4,* 592–604. Rogers, T. B., Kuiper, N. A., & Kirker, W. S. (1977). Self-reference and the encoding of personal information. *Journal of Personality and Social Psychology, 35,* 677–688. Klein, S. B., & Loftus, J. (1988). The nature of self-referent encoding: The contributions of elaborative and organizational processes. *Journal of Personality and Social Psychology, 55,* 5–11.

76. *San Francisco Sunday Examiner and Chronicle,* April 22, 1979, p. 35.

77. Greenberg, J., Pyszczynski, T., & Solomon, S. (1982). The self-serving attributional bias: Beyond self-presentation. *Journal of Experimental Social Psychology, 18,* 56–67. Arkin, R. M., & Maruyama, G. M. (1979). Attribution, affect, and college exam performance. *Journal of Educational Psychology, 71,* 85–93. Gilovich, T. (1983). Biased evaluation and persistence in gambling. *Journal of Personality and Social Psychology, 44,* 1110–1126. Ross, M., & Sicoly, F. (1979). Egocentric biases in availability and attribution. *Journal of Personality and Social Psychology, 37,* 322–336. Breckler, S. J., Pratkanis, A. R., & McCann, D. (1991). The representation of self in multidimensional cognitive space. *British Journal of Social Psychology, 30,* 97-112. Johnston, W. A. (1967). Individual performance and self-evaluation in a simulated team. *Organization Behavior and Human Performance, 2,* 309–328. Cunningham, J. D., Starr, P. A., & Kanouse, D. E. (1979). Self as actor, active observer, and passive observer: Implications for causal attribution. *Journal of Personality and Social Psychology, 37,* 1146–1152.

78. Greenwald, A. G., & Breckler, S. J. (1985). To whom is the self presented? In B. R. Schlenker (Ed.), *The self and social life* (pp. 126–145). New York: McGraw-Hill.

79. Miller, D. T., & Ross, M. (1975). Self-serving biases in the attribution of causality: Fact or fiction? *Psychological Bulletin, 82,* 213–225.

80. Weary (Bradley), G. (1978). Self-serving biases in the attribution process: A reexamination of the fact or fiction question. *Journal of Personality and Social Psychology, 36,* 56–71. Weary, G. (1980). Examination of affect and egotism as mediators of bias in causal attributions. *Journal of Personality and Social Psychology, 38,* 348–357. Weary, G., Harvey, J. H., Schwieger, P., Olson, C. T., Perloff, R., & Pritchard, S. (1982). Self-presentation and the moderation of self-serving attributional biases. *Social Cognition, 1,* 140–159.

81. Alloy, L. B., & Abramson, L. Y. (1979). Judgment of contingency in depressed and nondepressed students: Sadder but wiser. *Journal of Experimental Psychology: General, 108,* 441–485.

82. Grove, J. R., Hanrahan, S. J., & McInman, A. (1991). Success/failure bias in attributions across involvement categories in sport. *Personality and Social Psychology Bulletin, 17,* 93–97.

83. Taylor, S. E. (1989). *Positive illusions: Creative self-deception and the healthy mind.* New York: Basic Books.

84. Seligman, M. E. P. (1991). *Learned optimism.* New York: Knopf.

Chapter 5.   Self-Justification

1. Prasad, J. (1950). A comparative study of rumors and reports in earthquakes. *British Journal of Psychology, 41,* 129–144.

2. Sinha, D. (1952). Behavior in a catastrophic situation: A psychological study of reports and rumours. *British Journal of Psychology, 43,* 200–209.

3. Festinger, L. (1957). *A theory of cognitive dissonance.* Stanford: Stanford University Press.

4. Kassarjian, H., & Cohen, J. (1965). Cognitive dissonance and consumer behavior. *California Management Review, 8,* 55–64.

5. Tagliacozzo, R. (1979). Smokers' self-categorization and the reduction of cognitive dissonance. *Addictive Behaviors, 4,* 393–399.

6. Goleman, D. (1982, January). Make-or-break resolutions. *Psychology Today,* p. 19.

7. *Austin American,* November 18, 1971, p. 69.

8. Hastorf, A., & Cantril, H. (1954). They saw a game: A case study. *Journal of Abnormal and Social Psychology, 49,* 129–134.

9. Bruce, L. (1966). *How to talk dirty and influence people* (pp. 232–233). Chicago: Playboy Press, and New York: Pocket Books.

10. *Time,* November 24, 1980, p. 11.

11. Jones, E., & Kohler, R. (1959). The effects of plausibility on the learning of controversial statements. *Journal of Abnormal and Social Psychology, 57,* 315–320.

12. Lord, C., Ross, L., & Lepper, M. (1979). Biased assimilation and attitude polarization: The effects of prior theories on subsequently considered evidence. *Journal of Personality and Social Psychology, 37,* 2098–2109.

13. Ehrlich, D., Guttman, I., Schonbach, P., & Mills, J. (1957). Postdecision exposure to relevant information. *Journal of Abnormal and Social Psychology, 57,* 98–102.

14. Brehm, J. (1956). Postdecision changes in the desirability of alternatives. *Journal of Abnormal and Social Psychology, 52,* 384–389.

15. Johnson, D. J., & Rusbult, C. E. (1989). Resisting temptation: Devaluation of alternative partners as a means of maintaining commitment in close relationships. *Journal of Personality and Social Psychology, 57,* 967–980.

16. Simpson, J. A., Gangestad, S. W., & Lerma, M. (1990). Perception of physical attractiveness: Mechanisms involved in the maintenance of romantic relationships. *Journal of Personality and Social Psychology, 59,* 1192–1201.

17. Wiesel, E. (1969). *Night.* New York: Avon.

18. White, R. (1971, November). Selective inattention. *Psychology Today,* pp. 47–50, 78–84.

19. For a penetrating analysis of the process involved in a number of disastrous political decisions, see Janis, I. (1972). *Victims of groupthink.* Boston: Houghton Mifflin.

20. Pentagon papers: The secret war. (1971, June 28). *Time,* p. 12.

21. Freedman, J., & Fraser, S. (1966). Compliance without pressure: The foot-in-the-door technique. *Journal of Personality and Social Psychology, 4,* 195–202.

22. Pliner, P., Hart, H., Kohl, J., & Saari, D. (1974). Compliance without pressure: Some further data on the foot-in-the-door technique. *Journal of Experimental Social Psychology, 10,* 17–22.

23. Knox, R., & Inkster, J. (1968). Postdecision dissonance at post time. *Journal of Personality and Social Psychology, 8,* 319–323.

24. Frenkel, O. J., & Doob, A. (1976). Post-decision dissonance at the polling booth. *Canadian Journal of Behavioural Science, 8,* 347–350.

25. Cialdini, R., Cacioppo, J., Bassett, R., & Miller, J. (1978). Low-ball procedure for producing compliance: Commitment then cost. *Journal of Personality and Social Psychology, 36,* 463–476.

26. Ibid.

27. Mills, J. (1958). Changes in moral attitudes following temptation. *Journal of Personality, 26,* 517–531.

28. Festinger, L., & Carlsmith, J. M. (1959). Cognitive consequences of forced compliance. *Journal of Abnormal and Social Psychology, 58,* 203–210.

29. Cohen, A. R. (1962). An experiment on small rewards for discrepant compliance and attitude change. In J. W. Brehm & A. R. Cohen, *Explorations in cognitive dissonance* (pp. 73–78). New York: Wiley.

30. It should be mentioned, in passing, that the "saying-is-believing" phenomenon has produced some controversial data. The weight of the evidence tends to support the analysis presented in this text. For a more detailed discussion of this issue, read Aronson, E. (1965). The theory of cognitive dissonance: A current perspective. In L. Berkowitz (Ed.), *Advances in experimental social psychology* (Vol. 4, pp. 1–34). New York: Academic Press.

31. Zimbardo, P., Weisenberg, M., Firestone, I., & Levy, B. (1965). Communicator effectiveness in producing public conformity and private attitude change. *Journal of Personality, 33,* 233–255.

32. Mills, Changes in moral attitudes.

33. Aronson, E. (1968). Dissonance theory: Progress and problems. In R. P. Abelson, E. Aronson, W. J. McGuire, T. M. Newcomb, M. J. Rosenberg, and P. H. Tannenbaum (Eds.), *Theories of cognitive consistency: A sourcebook* (pp. 5–27). Chicago: Rand McNally. Aronson, E. (1969). The theory of cognitive dissonance: A current perspective. In

L. Berkowitz (Ed.), *Advances in experimental social psychology* (Vol. 4, pp. 1–34). New York: Academic Press.

34. Nel, E., Helmreich, R., & Aronson, E. (1969). Opinion change in the advocate as a function of the persuasibility of his audience: A clarification of the meaning of dissonance. *Journal of Personality and Social Psychology, 12,* 117–124.

35. Hoyt, M., Henley, M., & Collins, B. (1972). Studies in forced compliance: Confluence of choice and consequence on attitude change. *Journal of Personality and Social Psychology, 23,* 204–210. Schlenker, B., & Schlenker, P. (1975). Reactions following counterattitudinal behavior which produces positive consequences. *Journal of Personality and Social Psychology, 31,* 962–971. Riess, M., & Schlenker, B. (1977). Attitude change and responsibility avoidance as modes of dilemma resolution in forced-compliance situations. *Journal of Personality and Social Psychology, 35,* 21–30.

36. Cialdini, R., & Schroeder, D. (1976). Increasing compliance by legitimizing paltry contributions: When even a penny helps. *Journal of Personality and Social Psychology, 34,* 599–604.

37. Freedman, J. (1963). Attitudinal effects of inadequate justification. *Journal of Personality, 31,* 371–385.

38. Deci E., (1975). Intrinsic motivation. New York: Plenum. Deci, E. (1971). Effects of externally mediated rewards on intrinsic motivation. *Journal of Personality and Social Psychology, 18,* 105–115. Deci, E., Nezlek, J., & Sheinman, L. (1981). Characteristics of the rewarder and intrinsic motivation of the rewardee. *Journal of Personality and Social Psychology, 40,* 1–10.

39. Lepper, M. R., & Greene, D. (1975). Turning play into work: Effects of adult surveillance and extrinsic rewards on children's intrinsic motivation. *Journal of Personality and Social Psychology, 31,* 479–486.

40. Aronson, E., & Carlsmith, J. M. (1963). Effect of the severity of threat on the devaluation of forbidden behavior. *Journal of Abnormal and Social Psychology, 66,* 584–588.

41. Freedman, J. (1965). Long-term behavioral effects of cognitive dissonance. *Journal of Experimental Social Psychology, 1,* 145–155.

42. Sears, R., Whiting, J., Nowlis, V., & Sears, P. (1953). Some child-rearing antecedents of aggression and dependency in young children. *Genetic Psychology Monographs, 47,* 135–234.

43. Aronson, E., & Mills, J. (1959). The effect of severity of initiation on liking for a group. *Journal of Abnormal and Social Psychology, 59,* 177–181.

44. Gerard, H., & Mathewson, G. (1966). The effects of severity on initiation on liking for a group: A replication. *Journal of Experimental Social Psychology, 2,* 278–287.

45. Cooper, J. (1980). Reducing fears and increasing assertiveness: The role of dissonance reduction. *Journal of Experimental Social Psychology, 16,* 199–213.

46. Conway, M., & Ross, M. (1984). Getting what you want by revising what you had. *Journal of Personality and Social Psychology, 47,* 738–748.

47. Michener, J. (1971). *Kent State: What happened and why.* New York: Random House.

48. Ibid.

49. Khrushchev, N. (1970). In S. Talbot (Ed. and Trans.), *Khrushchev remembers.* Boston: Little, Brown.

50. Davis, K., & Jones, E. E. (1960). Changes in interpersonal perception as a means of reducing cognitive dissonance. *Journal of Abnormal and Social Psychology, 61,* 402–410.

51. Glass, D. (1964). Changes in liking as a means of reducing cognitive discrepancies between self-esteem and aggression. *Journal of Personality, 32,* 531–549.

52. Berscheid, E., Boyce, D., & Walster (Hatfield), E. (1968). Retaliation as a means of restoring equity. *Journal of Personality and Social Psychology, 10,* 370–376.

53. Jones, E., & Nisbett, R. (1971). *The actor and the observer: Divergent perceptions of the causes of behavior.* New York: General Learning Press.

54. Shaw, G. B. (1952). In D. Russel (Ed.), *Selected Prose.* New York: Dodd, Mead.

55. Brehm, J. (1959). Increasing cognitive dissonance by a *fait-accompli. Journal of Abnormal and Social Psychology, 58,* 379–382.

56. Darley, J., & Berscheid, E. (1967). Increased liking as a result of the anticipation of personal contact. *Human Relations, 20,* 29–40.

57. Lehman, D., & Taylor, S. E. (1987). Date with an earthquake: Coping

with a probable, unpredictable disaster. *Personality and Social Psychology Bulletin, 13,* 546–555.

58. Aronson, E., & Mettee, D., (1968). Dishonest behavior as a function of different levels of self-esteem. *Journal of Personality and Social Psychology, 9,* 121–127.

59. Zimbardo, P. (1969). *The cognitive control of motivation.* Glencoe, IL: Scott, Foresman.

60. Brehm, J. (1962). Motivational effects of cognitive dissonance. In *Nebraska Symposium on Motivation, 1962* (pp. 51–77). Lincoln: University of Nebraska Press.

61. Brehm, J., & Cohen, A. (1962). *Explorations in cognitive dissonance.* New York: Wiley.

62. Aronson, E. (1960). The cognitive and behavioral consequences of the confirmation and disconfirmation of expectancies. Unpublished manuscript, Harvard University. Aronson, E., & Carlsmith, J. M. (1962). Performance expectancy as a determinant of actual performance. *Journal of Abnormal and Social Psychology, 65,* 178–182. Aronson, E., & Mettee, D. R. (1968). Dishonest behavior as a function of differential levels of induced self-esteem. *Journal of Personality and Social Psychology, 9,* 121–127. Nel, E., Helmreich, R., & Aronson, E. (1969). Opinion change in the advocate as a function of the persuasibility of his audience: A clarification of the meaning of dissonance. *Journal of Personality and Social Psychology, 12,* 117–124. Aronson, E., Chase, T., Helmreich, R., & Ruhnke, R. (1974). A two-factor theory of dissonance reduction: The effect of feeling stupid or feeling "awful" on opinion change. *International Journal for Research and Communication, 3,* 59–74.

63. Rosenberg, M. J. (1965). When dissonance fails: On eliminating evaluation apprehension from attitude measurement. *Journal of Personality and Social Psychology, 1,* 28–42.

64. Linder, D. L., Cooper, J., & Jones, E. E. (1967). Decision freedom as a determinant of the role of incentive magnitude in attitude change. *Journal of Personality and Social Psychology, 6,* 245–254.

65. Goethals, G., Cooper, J., & Anahita, N. (1979). Role of foreseen, foreseeable, and unforeseeable behavioral consequences in the arousal of cognitive dissonance. *Journal of Personality and Social Psychology, 37,* 1179–1185.

66. Bem, D. J. (1967). Self-perception: An alternative interpretation of cognitive dissonance phenomena. *Psychological Review, 74,* 183–200.

67. Jones, R. A., Linder, D. E., Kiesler, C. A., Zanna, M., & Brehm, J. W. (1968). Internal states or external stimuli: Observers' attitude judgments and the dissonance theory—self-persuasion controversy. *Journal of Experimental Social Psychology, 4,* 247–269. Piliavin, J. A., Piliavin, I. M., Loewenton, E. P., McCauley, C., & Hammond, P. (1969). On observers' reproduction of dissonance effects: The right answers for the wrong reasons? *Journal of Personality and Social Psychology, 13,* 98–106.

68. Fazio, R., Zanna, M., & Cooper, J. (1977). Dissonance and self-perception: An integrative view of each theory's proper domain of application. *Journal of Experimental Social Psychology, 13,* 464–479. Ronis, D., & Greenwald, A. (1979). Dissonance theory revised again: Comment on the paper by Fazio, Zanna, and Cooper. *Journal of Experimental Social Psychology, 15,* 62–69. Fazio, R., Zanna, M., & Cooper, J. (1979). On the relationship of data to theory: A Reply to Ronis and Greenwald. *Journal of Experimental Social Psychology, 15,* 70–76.

69. Pallak, M. S., & Pittman, T. S. (1972). General motivational effects of dissonance arousal. *Journal of Personality and Social Psychology, 21,* 349–358.

70. Zanna, M., & Cooper, J. (1974). Dissonance and the pill: An attribution approach to studying the arousal properties of dissonance. *Journal of Personality and Social Psychology, 29,* 703–709.

71. Bond, C. (1981). Dissonance and the pill: An interpersonal simulation. *Personality and Social Psychology Bulletin, 7,* 398–403.

72. Mountain West Research, Inc. (1979). Three Mile Island telephone survey. Preliminary report on procedures and findings, report submitted to the U.S. Nuclear Regulatory Commission (NUREG CR-1093).

73. *Newsweek,* April 16, 1979, pp. 93, 35. CBS News–New York Times Poll, *The New York Times,* April 10, 1979, pp. 1, 16.

74. Axsom, D., & Cooper, J. (1981). Reducing weight by reducing dissonance: The role of effort justification in inducing weight loss. In E. Aronson (Ed.), *Readings about the social animal* (pp. 181–196). San Francisco: W. H. Freeman.

75. Stone, J., Aronson, E., Crain, A. L., Winslow, M. P., & Fried, C. B. (1994). Inducing hypocrisy as a means of encouraging young adults to use condoms. *Personality and Social Psychology Bulletin, 20,* 116–128.

76. Dickerson, C. A., Thibodeau, R., Aronson, E., & Miller, D. (1992). Using cognitive dissonance to encourage water conservation. *Journal of Applied Social Psychology, 22,* 841–854.

77. Johnson, L. B. (1971). *The vantage point: Perspectives of the presidency 1963–69.* New York: Holt, Rinehart and Winston.

78. Reagan, R. (1990). *An American life* (p. 405). New York: Simon & Schuster.

Chapter 6.   Human Aggression

1. *Newsweek,* April 28, 1986, p. 22.

2. Rousseau, J.-J. (1930). *The social contract and discourses.* New York: Dutton.

3. Freud, S. (1948). *Beyond the pleasure principle.* London: Hogarth Press and Institute of Psycho-Analysis.

4. Freud, S. (1959). Why war? (letter to Albert Einstein, 1932). In E. Jones (Ed.), *Collected papers* (Vol. 5., p. 282). New York: Basic Books.

5. Storr, A. (1970). *Human aggression.* New York: Bantam.

6. Kuo, Z. Y. (1961). Genesis of the cat's response to the rat. In *Instinct* (p. 24). Princeton, NJ: Van Nostrand.

7. Eibl-Eibesfeldt, I. (1963). Aggressive behavior and ritualized fighting in animals. In J. H. Masserman (Ed.), *Science and psychoanalysis, Vol. VI. Violence and war.* New York: Grune and Stratton.

8. Scott, J. P. (1958). *Aggression.* Chicago: University of Chicago Press.

9. Lorenz, K. (1966). *On aggression* (M. Wilson, trans.). New York: Harcourt, Brace and World.

10. Berkowitz, L. (1989). Frustration-aggression hypothesis: Examination and reformulation. *Psychological Bulletin, 106,* 59–73.

11. Hunt, G. T. (1940). *The wars of the Iroquois.* Madison: The University of Wisconsin Press.

12. Lagerspetz, K. (1979). Modification of aggressiveness in mice. In S. Feshbach and A. Fraczek (Eds.), *Aggression in behavior change.* New York: Praeger.

13. Lorenz, *On aggression.*

14. Washburn, S., & Hamburg, D. (1965). The implications of primate research. In I. DeVore (Ed.), *Primate behavior: Field studies of monkeys and apes* (pp. 607–622). New York: Holt, Rinehart and Winston.

15. LeBoeuf, B. (1974). Male-male competition and reproductive success in elephant seals. *American Zoologist, 14,* 163–176.

16. Montagu, A. (1950). *On being human.* New York: Hawthorne Books.

17. Kropotkin, P. (1902). *Mutual aid.* New York: Doubleday.

18. Nissen, H., & Crawford, M. P. (1936). Preliminary study of food-sharing behavior in young chimpanzees. *Journal of Comparative Psychology, 22,* 383–419.

19. *Time,* October 7, 1974.

20. Leakey, R., & Lewin, R. (1978). *People of the lake.* New York: Anchor Press/Doubleday.

21. Eiseley, L. (1946). *The immense journey* (p. 140). New York: Random House.

22. Menninger, W. (1948). Recreation and mental health. *Recreation, 42,* 340–346.

23. Berkowitz, L. (1993). *Aggression.* New York: McGraw-Hill.

24. Patterson, A. (1974, September). *Hostility catharsis: A naturalistic quasi-experiment.* Paper presented at the annual convention of the American Psychological Association, New Orleans.

25. Johnson, W. (1970, October). Guilt-free aggression for the troubled jock. *Psychology Today,* pp. 70–73.

26. Russell, G. (1981). Spectator moods at an aggressive sports event. *Journal of Social Psychology, 3,* 217–227.

27. Feshbach, S. (1955). The drive-reducing function of fantasy behavior. *Journal of Abnormal and Social Psychology, 50,* 3–11.

28. Hokanson, J., & Burgess, M. (1962). The effects of three types of aggression on vascular process. *Journal of Abnormal and Social Psychology, 64,* 446–449.

29. Geen, R., & Quanty, M. (1977). The catharsis of aggression: An evaluation of an hypothesis. In L. Berkowitz (Ed.), *Advances in experimental social psychology* (Vol. 10, pp. 1–36). New York: Academic Press.

30. Geen, R., Stonner, D., & Shope, G. (1975). The facilitation of aggression by aggression: A study in response inhibition and disinhibition. *Journal of Personality and Social Psychology, 31,* 721–726.

31. Ebbesen, E., Duncan, B., & Konecni, V. (1975). Effects of content on verbal aggression: A field experiment. *Journal of Experimental and Social Psychology, 11,* 192–204.

32. Glass, D. (1964). Changes in liking as a means of reducing cognitive discrepancies between self-esteem and aggression. *Journal of Personality, 32,* 531–549. Davis, K. E., & Jones, E. E. (1960). Changes in interpersonal perception as a means of reducing cognitive dissonance. *Journal of Abnormal and Social Psychology, 61,* 402–410. See also Buss, A. H. (1963). Physical aggression in relation to different frustrations. *Journal of Abnormal and Social Psychology, 67,* 1–7.

33. Kahn, M. (1966). The physiology of catharsis. *Journal of Personality and Social Psychology, 3,* 278–298. See also: Berkowitz, L., Green, J., & Macauley, J. (1962). Hostility catharsis as the reduction of emotional tension. *Psychiatry, 25,* 23–31; and DeCharms, R., & Wilkins, E. J. (1963). Some effects of verbal expression of hostility. *Journal of Abnormal and Social Psychology, 66,* 462–470.

34. Doob, A. N., & Wood, L. (1972). Catharsis and aggression: The effects of annoyance and retaliation on aggressive behavior. *Journal of Personality and Social Psychology, 22,* 156–162.

35. Freud, Why war?, p. 282.

36. Archer, D., & Gartner, R. (1976). Violent acts and violent times: A comparative approach to postwar homicide rates. *American Sociological Review, 41,* 937–963.

37. Lorenz, *On aggression.* Menninger, Recreation and mental health.

38. Klapper, J. (1960). *The effects of mass communication.* Glencoe, IL: Free Press.

39. Bandura, A., Ross, D., & Ross, S. (1961). Transmission of aggression through imitation of aggressive models. *Journal of Abnormal and Social Psychology, 63,* 575–582. Bandura, A., Ross, D., & Ross, S. (1963). A comparative test of the status envy, social power, and secondary reinforcement theories of identificatory learning. *Journal of Abnormal and Social Psychology, 67,* 527–534. Bandura, A., Ross, D., & Ross, S. (1963). Vicarious reinforcement and initiative learning. *Journal of Abnormal and Social Psychology, 67,* 601–607.

40. Gerbner, G., Gross, L., Signorielli, N., & Morgan, M. (1980). Television violence, victimization, and power. *American Behavioral Scientist, 23,* 705–716. Gerbner, G., Gross, L., Morgan, M., & Signorielli, N. (1986). Living with television: The dynamics of the cultivation process. In J. Bryant and D. Zillman (Eds.), *Perspectives on media effects* (pp. 17–40). Hillsdale, NJ: Erlbaum.

41. Liebert, R., & Baron, R. (1972). Some immediate effects of televised violence on children's behavior. *Developmental Psychology, 6,* 469–475.

42. Parke, R., Berkowitz, L., Leyens, J., West, S., & Sebastian, R. (1977). Some effects of violent and nonviolent movies on the behavior of juvenile delinquents. In L. Berkowitz (Ed.), *Advances in experimental social psychology* (pp. 135–172). New York: Academic Press.

43. Eron, L. R., & Huesmann, R. (1980). Adolescent aggression and television. *Annals of the New York Academy of Sciences, 347,* 319–331.

44. Huesmann, L. R., Lagerspetz, K., & Eron, L. (1984). Intervening variables in the TV violence-aggression relation: Evidence from two countries. *Developmental Psychology, 20,* 746–775.

45. Eron, L., & Huesmann, L. R. (1986). The role of television in the development of prosocial and antisocial behavior. In D. Olweus, J. Block, and M. Radke-Yarrow (Eds.), *Development of antisocial and prosocial behavior: Research, theories, and issues* (pp. 285–314). Orlando, FL: Academic Press.

46. Josephson, W. D. (1987). Television violence and children's aggression: Testing the priming, social script, and disinhibition prediction. *Journal of Personality and Social Psychology, 53,* 882–890.

47. Thomas, M. H., Horton, R., Lippincott, E., & Drabman, R. (1977). Desensitization to portrayals of real-life aggression as a function of exposure to television violence. *Journal of Personality and Social Psychology, 35,* 450–458.

48. For a recent review of this body of research, see Phillips, D. P. (1986). Natural experiments on the effects of mass media violence on fatal aggression: Strengths and weaknesses of a new approach. In L. Berkowitz (Ed.), *Advances in experimental social psychology* (Vol. 19, pp. 207–250). Orlando, FL: Academic Press.

49. Phillips, D. P. (1983). The impact of mass media violence on U.S. homicides. *American Sociological Review, 48,* 560–568.

50. Phillips, D. P. (1986). Natural experiments on the effects of mass

media violence on fatal aggression: Strengths and weaknesses of a new approach. In L. Berkowitz (Ed.), *Advances in experimental social psychology* (Vol. 19, pp. 207–250). Orlando, FL: Academic Press.

51. The violence bag. (1971, December 13). *Newsweek*, p. 110.

52. Drop that gun, Captain Video. (1975, March 10). *Newsweek*, pp. 81–82.

53. Harbut, T. (1993). Interview with Charlie Rose, PBS.

54. Diener, E., & DeFour, D. (1978). Does television violence enhance program popularity? *Journal of Personality and Social Psychology, 36,* 333–341.

55. Federal Bureau of Investigation. (1990). *Uniform Crime Reports for the United States.* Washington, D.C.: U.S. Government Printing Office.

56. Malamuth, N. M. (1983). Factors associated with rape as predictors of laboratory aggression against women. *Journal of Personality and Social Psychology, 45,* 432–442. Malamuth, N. M. (1986). Predictors of naturalistic sexual aggression. *Journal of Personality and Social Psychology, 50,* 953–962.

57. Donnerstein, E. (1980). Aggressive erotica and violence against women. *Journal of Personality and Social Psychology, 39,* 269–277.

58. Malamuth, N. (1981). Rape fantasies as a function of exposure to violent sexual stimuli. *Archives of Sexual Behavior, 10,* 33–47.

59. Malamuth, N., & Check, J. (1981). The effects of mass media exposure on acceptance of violence against women: A field experiment. *Journal of Research in Personality, 15,* 436–446.

60. Foa, P. (1978). What's wrong with rape. In M. Vetterling-Broggin, F. Elliston, and J. English (Eds.), *Feminism and philosophy* (p. 355). Totowa, NJ: Littlefield Adams.

61. Malamuth, N., Haber, S., & Feshbach, S. (1980). Testing hypotheses regarding rape: Exposure to sexual violence, sex differences, and the "normality" of rapists. *Journal of Research in Personality, 14,* 121–137.

62. Check, J., & Malamuth, N. (1983). Can there be positive effects of participation in pornography experiments? *Journal of Sex Research, 20,* 14–31.

63. Linz, D., Donnerstein, E., & Penrod, S. (1988). Effects of long-term

exposure to violent and sexually degrading depictions of women. *Journal of Personality and Social Psychology, 55,* 758–768.

64. Barker, R., Dembo, T., & Lewin, K. (1941). Frustration and aggression: An experiment with young children. *University of Iowa Studies in Child Welfare, 18,* 1–314.

65. Harris, M. (1974). Mediators between frustration and aggression in a field experiment. *Journal of Experimental and Social Psychology, 10,* 561–571.

66. Kulik, J., & Brown, R. (1979). Frustration, attribution of blame, and aggression. *Journal of Experimental and Social Psychology, 15,* 183–194.

67. Tocqueville, A. de. (1981). *Democracy in America.* Westminster, MD: Random House.

68. Mallick, S., & McCandless, B. (1966). A study of catharsis of aggression. *Journal of Personality and Social Psychology, 4,* 591–596.

69. Johnson, T. E., & Rule, B. G. (1986). Mitigating circumstances information, censure, and aggression. *Journal of Personality and Social Psychology, 50,* 537–542.

70. Josephson, W. L. (1987). Television violence and children's aggression: Testing the priming, social script, and disinhibition predictions. *Journal of Personality and Social Psychology, 53,* 882–890.

71. Berkowitz, L. (1965). Some aspects of observed aggression. *Journal of Personality and Social Psychology, 2,* 359–369.

72. Berkowitz, L., & Geen, R. (1966). Film violence and the cue properties of available targets. *Journal of Personality and Social Psychology, 3,* 525–530.

73. Berkowitz, L., & LePage, A. (1967). Weapons as aggression-eliciting stimuli. *Journal of Personality and Social Psychology, 7,* 202–207.

74. Berkowitz, L. (1971). *Control of aggression* (p. 68). Unpublished.

75. Zimbardo, P. (1969). The human choice: Individuation, reason, and order versus deindividuation, impulse, and chaos. In W. Arnold and D. Levine (Eds.), *Nebraska Symposium on Motivation, 17,* 237–307.

76. Mullen, B. (1986). Atrocity as a function of lynch mob composition: A self-attention perspective. *Personality and Social Psychology Bulletin, 12,* 187–197.

77. Clark, K. (1971). The pathos of power: A psychological perspective. *American Psychologist, 26,* 1047–1057.

78. Aristotle (1954). Rhetoric. In W. R. Roberts (Trans.) *Aristotle, rhetoric and poetics* (p. 22). New York: Modern Library.

79. Sears, R., Maccoby, E., & Levin, H. (1957). *Patterns of child rearing.* Evanston, IL: Row, Peterson. Baumrind, D. (1966). Effects of author-itative parental control on child behavior. *Child Development, 37,* 887–907. Becker, W. (1964). Consequences of different kinds of parental discipline. In M. L. Hoffman and L. W. Hoffman (Eds.), *Review of Child Development Research* (Vol. 1). New York: Russell Sage. Owens, D., & Straus, M. (1975). The social structure of violence in childhood and approval of violence as an adult. *Aggressive Behavior, 1,* 193–211.

80. Hamblin, R., Buckholt, D., Bushell, D., Ellis, D., & Ferritor, D. (1969, January). Changing the game from "get the teacher" to "learn." *Trans-Action,* pp. 20–31.

81. Haney, C. (1979). A psychologist looks at the criminal justice system. In A. Calvin (Ed.), *Challenges and alternatives to the American criminal justice system* (pp. 77–85). Ann Arbor: University International Press.

82. Eichmann, C. (1966). *The impact of the Gideon decision on crime and sentencing in Florida.* Tallahassee, FL: Division of Corrections Publica-tions.

83. Haney, C., Banks, C., & Zimbardo, P. (1973). Interpersonal dynamics in a simulated prison. *International Journal of Criminology and Penology, 1,* 69–97.

84. Aronson, E., & Carlsmith, J. M. (1963). The effect of severity of threat on the devaluation of forbidden behavior. *Journal of Abnormal and Social Psychology, 66,* 584–588. Freedman, J. (1965). Long-term behav-ioral effects of cognitive dissonance. *Journal of Experimental and Social Psychology, 1,* 145–155.

85. Olweus, D. (1991). Bully/victim problems among schoolchildren: Basic facts and effects of a school-based intervention program. In D. Pepler & K. Rubin (Eds.), *The development and treatment of childhood aggression* (pp. 411–448). Hillsdale, NJ: Erlbaum.

86. U.S. President's Commission on Law Enforcement and Administra-tion of Justice. (1967). *The challenge of crime in a free society: A report.* Washington, D.C.: U.S. Government Printing Office.

87. Bandura, A., Ross, D., & Ross, S. (1963). Imitation of film-mediated

aggressive models. *Journal of Abnormal and Social Psychology, 66,* 3–11. Bandura, A., Ross, D., & Ross, S. (1963). Vicarious reinforcement and imitative learning. *Journal of Abnormal and Social Psychology, 67,* 601–607.

88. Brown, P., & Elliot, R. (1965). Control of aggression in a nursery school class. *Journal of Experimental Child Psychology, 2,* 103–107.

89. Davitz, J. (1952). The effects of previous training on postfrustration behavior. *Journal of Abnormal and Social Psychology, 47,* 309–315.

90. Baron, R. A., & Kepner, C. R. (1970). Model's behavior and attraction toward the model as determinants of adult aggressive behavior. *Journal of Personality and Social Psychology, 14,* 335–344.

91. Baron, R. A. (1976). The reduction of human aggression: A field study of the influence of incompatible reactions. *Journal of Applied Social Psychology, 6,* 260–274.

92. Feshbach, S. (1971). Dynamics and morality of violence and aggression: Some psychological considerations. *American Psychologist, 26,* 281–292.

93. Michener, J. (1971). *Kent State: What happened and why.* New York: Random House.

94. Feshbach, N. & Feshbach, S. (1969). The relationship between empathy and aggression in two age groups. *Developmental Psychology, 1,* 102–107.

95. Feshbach, N. (1978, March). Empathy training: A field study in affective education. Paper presented at the American Educational Research Association, Toronto, Ontario, Canada. Feshbach, N., & Feshbach, S. (1981, April). Empathy training and the regulation of aggression: Potentialities and limitations. Paper presented at the convention of the Western Psychological Association.

96. Hammock, G. S., & Richardson, D. R. (1992). Aggression as one response to conflict. *Journal of Applied Social Psychology, 22,* 298–311.

Chapter 7. Prejudice

1. Poussaint, A. (1971). A Negro psychiatrist explains the Negro psyche, in *Confrontation* (pp. 183–184). New York: Random House.

2. Clark, K., & Clark, M. (1947). Racial identification and preference in Negro children. In T. M. Newcomb and E. L. Hartley (Eds.), *Readings in social psychology* (pp. 169–178). New York: Holt.

3. Goldberg, P. (1968, April). Are women prejudiced against women? *Trans-Action*, pp. 28–30.

4. Jemmott, J. B., & Gonzalez, E. (1989). Social status, the status distribution, and performance in small groups. *Journal of Applied Social Psychology, 19*, 584–598.

5. Hraba, J., & Grant, G. (1970). Black is beautiful: A reexamination of racial preference and identification. *Journal of Personality and Social Psychology, 16*, 398–402. Banks, C. (1976). White preference in blacks: A paradigm in search of a phenomenon. *Psychological Bulletin, 83*, 1179–1186. Ward, C. (1979). Differential evaluation of male and female expertise: Prejudice against women? *British Journal of Social and Clinical Psychology, 18*, 65–69. Ward, C. (1981). Prejudice against women: Who, when, and why? *Sex Roles, 7*, 163–171.

6. Pettigrew, T. F. (1989). The nature of modern racism in the United States. *Revue Internationale de Psychologie Sociale, 2*, 291–303.

7. *Time*, February 2, 1987, pp. 18–21.

8. Allport, G. (1954, 1980). *The nature of prejudice* (p. 13). Reading, MA: Addison-Wesley.

9. *Newsweek*, November 25, 1974, p. 39.

10. Neugarten, B. (1946). Social class and friendship among schoolchildren. *American Journal of Sociology, 51*, 305–313.

11. Bond, C. F., Jr., DiCandia, C. G., & MacKinnon, J. R. (1988). Response to violence in a psychiatric setting: The role of the patient's race. *Personality and Social Psychology Bulletin, 14*, 448–458.

12. Bodenhausen, G., & Wyer, R. (1985). Effects of stereotypes on decision making and information-processing strategies. *Journal of Personality and Social Psychology, 48*, 267–282.

13. Shaffer, D. R., & Wallace, A. (1990). Belief congruence and evaluator homophobia as determinants of the attractiveness of competent homosexual and heterosexual males. *Journal of Psychology & Human Sexuality, 3*, 67–87.

14. Steele, C. (1992, April). Race and the schooling of black Americans. *The Atlantic Monthly*, pp. 68–78.

15. Steele, C., & Aronson, J. (1994). Stereotype vulnerability: A psychological approach to underachievement among black Americans. Paper presented at the meeting of the Western Psychological Association, Kona, Hawaii, April, 1994.

16. Pettigrew, T. F. (1979). The ultimate attribution error: Extending Allport's cognitive analysis of prejudice. *Personality and Social Psychology Bulletin, 5,* 461–476.

17. Ibid.

18. Feldman-Summers, S., & Kiesler, S. B. (1974). Those who are number two try harder: The effect of sex on attributions of causality. *Journal of Personality and Social Psychology, 30,* 80–85.

19. Deaux, K., & Emsweiler, T. (1974). Explanations of successful performance on sex-linked tasks: What is skill for male is luck for the female. *Journal of Personality and Social Psychology, 29,* 80–85.

20. Nicholls, J. G. (1975). Causal attributions and other achievement-related cognitions: Effects of task outcome, attainment value, and sex. *Journal of Personality and Social Psychology, 31,* 379–389.

21. Weinberg, R. S., Richardson, P. A., & Jackson, A. (1983). Effect of situation criticality on tennis performance of males and females. *Newsletter of the Society for the Advancement of Social Psychology, 9,* 8–9.

22. Turner, M. & Pratkanis, A. (1993). Effects of preferential and meritorious selection on performance: An examination of intuitive and self-handicapping perspectives. *Personality and Social Psychology Bulletin, 19,* 47–58.

23. Deaux, K., & Taynor, J. (1973). Evaluation of male and female ability: Bias works two ways. *Psychological Reports, 32,* 261–262.

24. Lerner, M. (1965). Evaluation of performance as a function of performer's reward and attractiveness. *Journal of Personality and Social Psychology, 1,* 355–360. Lerner, M. (1980). *The justice motive.* New York: Plenum.

25. Furnham, A., & Gunter, B. (1984). Just world beliefs and attitudes toward the poor. *British Journal of Social Psychology, 23,* 265–269.

26. Fischhoff, B., & Beyth, R. (1975). "I knew it would happen": Remembered probabilities on once-future things. *Organizational Behavior and Human Performance, 13,* 1–16.

27. Janoff-Bulman, R., Timko, C., & Carli, L. L. (1985). Cognitive biases

in blaming the victim. *Journal of Experimental Social Psychology, 21,* 161–177.

28. Gould, S. (1977). *Ever since Darwin: Reflections on natural history* (p. 243). New York: W. W. Norton.

29. Pearson, K., & Moul, M. (1925). The problem of alien immigration into Great Britain, illustrated by an example of Russian and Polish Jewish children. *Annals of Eugenics, 1,* 5–127.

30. Janis, I., & Field, P. (1959). Sex difference and personality factors related to persuasibility. In C. I. Hovland and I. L. Janis (Eds.), *Personality and persuasibility* (pp. 55–68). New Haven: Yale University Press.

31. Sistrunk, F., & McDavid, J. (1971). Sex variable in conforming behavior. *Journal of Personality and Social Psychology, 17,* 200–207.

32. Word, C., Zanna, M., & Cooper, J. (1974). The nonverbal mediation of self-fulfilling prophecies in interracial interaction. *Journal of Experimental Social Psychology, 10,* 109–120.

33. Snyder, M. (1984). When belief creates reality. In L. Berkowitz (Ed.), *Advances in experimental social psychology* (Vol. 18, pp. 247–305). Orlando, FL: Academic Press.

34. Merton, R. F. (1968). The self-fulfilling prophecy. *Antioch Review, 8,* 193–210.

35. Snyder, M., & Swann, W. B., Jr. (1978). Hypothesis-testing processes in social interactions. *Journal of Personality and Social Psychology, 36,* 1202–1212.

36. For a review, see Pettigrew, T. F. (1985). New black-white patterns: How best to conceptualize them? *Annual Review of Sociology, 11,* 329–346.

37. Frey, D. L., & Gaertner, S. I. (1986). Helping and the avoidance of inappropriate interracial behavior: A strategy that perpetuates a non-prejudiced self-image. *Journal of Personality and Social Psychology, 50,* 1083–1090.

38. Devine, P. G. (1989). Stereotypes and prejudice: Their automatic and controlled components. *Journal of Personality and Social Psychology, 56,* 5–18.

39. Bem, D., & Bem, S. (1970, November). We're all nonconscious sexists. *Psychology Today,* pp. 22–26, 115–116.

40. Weitzman, L., Eifler, D., Hokada, E., & Ross, C. (1972). Sex-role socialization in picture books for preschool children. *American Journal of Sociology, 77,* 1125–1150. Kolbe, R., & LaVoie, J. (1981). Sex-role stereotyping in preschool children's picture books. *Social Psychology Quarterly, 44,* 369–374.

41. Hartley, R. (1960). Children's concepts of male and female roles. *Merrill-Palmer Quarterly, 6,* 83–91.

42. Lipman-Blumen, J. (1972). How ideology shapes women's lives. *Scientific American, 226*(1), 34–42.

43. Gray, S. W. (1975). Masculinity-femininity in relation to anxiety and social acceptance. *Child Development, 28,* 203–214.

44. Broverman, I. K., Vogel, S., Broverman, D., Clarkson, F., & Rosencrantz, P. (1972). Sex-role stereotypes: A current appraisal. *Journal of Social Issues, 28,* 59–78.

45. Porter, N., & Geis, F. (1981). Women and nonverbal leadership cues: When seeing is not believing. In C. Mayo and N. Henley (Eds.), *Gender and nonverbal behavior.* New York: Springer-Verlag.

46. Baron, R. S., Burgess, M. L., & Kao, C. F. (1991). Detecting and labeling prejudice: Do female perpetrators go undetected? *Personality and Social Psychology Bulletin, 17,* 115–117.

47. Bem, S. L. (1975). Sex-role adaptability: One consequence of psychological androgyny. *Journal of Personality and Social Psychology, 31,* 634–643. Chesler, P. (1972). *Women and Madness.* New York: Avon Books.

48. Jackson, L. A., & Cash, T. F. (1985). Components of gender stereotypes: Their implications for inferences on stereotypic and nonstereotypic dimensions. *Personality and Social Psychology Bulletin, 11,* 326–344.

49. Horner, M. S. (1970). Femininity and successful achievement: A basic inconsistency. In J. M. Bardwick et al. (Eds.), *Feminine personality and conflict.* Monterey, CA: Brooks/Cole. Horner, M. S. (1972). Toward an understanding of achievement-related conflicts in women. *Journal of Social Issues, 28,* 157–175.

50. Cherry, F., & Deaux, K. (1975). Fear of success versus fear of gender-inconsistent behavior: A sex similarity. Paper presented at the Midwestern Psychological Association Convention.

51. Gerbner, G. (1993). Women and Minorities on Television. Unpub-

lished paper, the Annenberg School for Communication, University of Pennsylvania. Gerbner, G., Gross, L., Morgan, M., & Signorielli, N. (1993). Growing up with television: The cultivation perspective. In J. Bryant and D. Zillman (Eds.), *Media Effects: Advances in theory and research.* Hillsdale, NJ: Erlbaum.

52. Thibodeau, R. (1989). From racism to tokenism: The changing face of blacks in New Yorker cartoons. *Public Opinion Quarterly, 53,* 482–494.

53. Kolbe, R., & LaVoie, J. (1981). Sex-role stereotyping in preschool children's picture books. *Social Psychology Quarterly, 44,* 369–374.

54. Chavez, D. (1985). Perpetuation of gender inequality: A context analysis of comic strips. *Sex Roles, 13,* 93–102.

55. Geis, F., Brown, V., Jennings (Walstedt), J., & Porter, N. (1984). TV commercials as achievement scripts for women. *Sex Roles, 10,* 513–525.

56. Crocker, J., Thompson, L. L., McGraw, K. M., & Ingerman, C. (1987). Downward comparison, prejudice, and evaluations of others: Effects of self-esteem and threat. *Journal of Personality and Social Psychology, 52,* 907–916.

57. Dollard, J. (1987). *Class and caste in a southern town.* New Haven: Yale University Press.

58. Bettelheim, B., & Janowitz, M. (1964). *Social change and prejudice, including dynamics of prejudice.* New York: Free Press.

59. Tumin, M., Barton, P., & Burrus, B. (1958). Education, prejudice, and discrimination: A study in readiness for desegregation. *American Sociological Review, 23,* 41–49.

60. Levitas, M. (1969). *America in crisis.* New York: Holt, Rinehart and Winston.

61. Dollard, J. (1938). Hostility and fear in social life. *Social Forces, 17,* 15–26.

62. Roberts, E., quoted by P. Jacobs and S. Landau (1971). *To serve the devil* (Vol. 2, p. 71). New York: Vintage Books.

63. Crocker, C., quoted by P. Jacobs & S. Landau (1971). *To serve the devil* (Vol. 2, p. 81). New York: Vintage Books.

64. Greeley, A., & Sheatsley, P. (1971). The acceptance of desegregation continues to advance. *Scientific American, 225*(6), 13–19. See also

Vanneman, R. D., & Pettigrew, T. F. (1972). Race and relative deprivation in the urban United States. *Race, 13,* 461–486.

65. Sherif, M., Harvey, O. J., White, B. J., Hood, W., & Sherif, C. (1961).
     Intergroup conflict and cooperation: The Robbers Cave experiment. Nor-
     man: University of Oklahoma Institute of Intergroup Relations.

66. Hovland, C., & Sears, R. (1940). Minor studies of aggression: Corre-
     lation of lynchings with economic indices. *Journal of Psychology, 9,*
     301–310.

67. Klineberg, O. (1971). Black and white in international perspective.
     American Psychologist, 26, 119–128.

68. Speer, A. (1970). *Inside the Third Reich: Memoirs* (R. Winston and C.
     Winston, Trans.). New York: Macmillan.

69. Miller, N., & Bugelski, R. (1948). Minor studies in aggression: The
     influence of frustrations imposed by the in-group on attitudes ex-
     pressed by the out-group. *Journal of Psychology, 25,* 437–442.

70. Rogers, R., & Prentice-Dunn, S. (1981). Deindividuation and anger-
     mediated interracial aggression: Unmasking regressive racism. *Journal
     of Personality and Social Psychology, 41,* 63–73.

71. Weatherly, D. (1961). Anti-semitism and the expression of fantasy
     aggression. *Journal of Abnormal and Social Psychology, 62,* 454–457.

72. Adorno, T., Frenkel-Brunswick, E., Levinson, D., & Sanford, R. N.
     (1950). *The authoritarian personality.* New York: Harper.

73. McFarland, S. M., Ageyev V. S., & Abalakina-Paap, M. A. (1992).
     Authoritarianism in the former Soviet Union. *Journal of Personality and
     Social Psychology, 63,* 1004–1010.

74. Greeley & Sheatsley, Acceptance of desegregation.

75. Pettigrew, T. F. (1959). Regional differences in anti-Negro prejudice.
     Journal of Abnormal and Social Psychology, 59, 28–36.

76. Pettigrew, T. F. (1958). Personality and sociocultural factors and inter-
     group attitudes: A cross-national comparison. *Journal of Conflict Reso-
     lution, 2,* 29–42.

77. Watson, J. (1950). Some social and psychological situations related to
     change in attitude. *Human Relations, 3,* 15–56.

78. Kirkland, S. L., Greenberg, J., & Pyszczynski, T. (1987). Further
     evidence of the deleterious effects of overheard derogatory ethnic

labels: Derogation beyond the target. *Personality and Social Psychology Bulletin, 13,* 216–227.

79. MacCrone, I. (1937). Race attitudes in South Africa. London: Oxford University Press.

80. Lazarsfeld, P. (1940). *Radio and the printed page.* New York: Duell, Sloan & Pearce.

81. Deutsch, M., & Collins, M. E. (1951). *Interracial housing: A psychological evaluation of a social experiment.* Minneapolis: University of Minnesota Press. See also Wilner, D., Walkley, R., & Cook, S. (1955). *Human relations in interracial housing.* Minneapolis: University of Minnesota Press.

82. Brehm, J. (1959). Increasing cognitive dissonance by a fait-accompli. *Journal of Abnormal and Social Psychology, 58,* 379–382.

83. Darley, D., & Berscheid, E. (1967). Increased liking as a result of the anticipation of personal contact. *Human Relations, 20,* 29–40.

84. National Opinion Research Center (1980). *General social surveys, 1972–1980: Cumulative codebook.* Storrs, CT: Roper Public Opinion Research Center, University of Connecticut.

85. Pettigrew, T. F. (1961). Social psychology and desegregation research. *American Psychologist, 16,* 105–112.

86. Clark, K. B. (1953). Desegregation: An appraisal of the evidence. *Journal of Social Issues, 9,* No. 4.

87. Stouffer, S., Suchman, E., DeVinney, L., Star, S., & Williams, R., Jr. (1949). The American soldier: Adjustment during army life. In *Studies in social psychology in WW II* (Vol. 1). Princeton: Princeton University Press.

88. Kramer, B. (1951). Residential contact as a determinant of attitudes toward Negroes. Unpublished Ph.D. dissertation, Harvard University. Winder, A. (1952). White attitudes towards Negro-white interaction in an area of changing racial composition. *American Psychologist, 7,* 330–331.

89. Asher, S., & Allen, V. (1969). Racial preference and social comparison processes. *Journal of Social Issues, 25,* 157–166. Stephan, W., & Kennedy, J. (1975). An experimental study of inter-ethnic competition in segregated schools. *Journal of School Psychology, 13,* 234–247. Gerard, H., & Miller, N. (1976). *School desegregation.* New York: Plenum.

90. Stephan, W. G. (1978). School desegregation: An evaluation of predictions made in *Brown v. The Board of Education. Psychological Bulletin, 85,* 217–238.

91. Lester, J. (1971). Beep! Beep! Bang! Umgawa! Black Power! In R. Kytle (Ed.), *Confrontation: Issues of the 70's* (pp. 162–181). New York: Random House.

92. Deutsch & Collins, *Interracial housing.*

93. Sherif, M., & Sherif, C. (1956). *An outline of social psychology.* New York: Harper & Bros. Sherif, Harvey, White, Hood, & Sherif, Intergroup conflict and cooperation.

94. Deutsch, M. (1949). A theory of cooperation and competition. *Human Relations, 2,* 129–152. Deutsch, M. (1949). An experimental study of the effects of cooperation and competition upon group process. *Human Relations, 2,* 199–232.

95. Keenan, P., & Carnevale, P. (1989). Positive effects of within-group competition on between-group negotiation. *Journal of Applied Social Psychology, 19,* 977–992.

96. Aronson, E., Stephan, C., Sikes, J., Blaney, N., & Snapp, M. (1978). *The jigsaw classroom.* Beverly Hills, CA: Sage Publications. Aronson, E., & Osherow, N. (1980). Cooperation, prosocial behavior, and academic performance: Experiments in the desegregated classroom. In L. Bickman (Ed.), *Applied Social Psychology Annual* (Vol. 1, pp. 163–196). Beverly Hills, CA: Sage Publications.

97. Stephan, W. (1975). An experimental study of inter-ethnic competition in segregated schools. *Journal of School Psychology, 13,* 234–247.

98. Geffner, R. (1978). The effects of interdependent learning on self-esteem, inter-ethnic relations, and intra-ethnic attitudes of elementary school children: A field experiment. Unpublished Ph.D. dissertation, University of California, Santa Cruz. Gonzalez, A. (1979). Classroom cooperation and ethnic balance. Unpublished Ph.D. dissertation, University of California, Santa Cruz.

99. Lucker, W., Rosenfield, D., Sikes, J., & Aronson, E. (1977). Performance in the interdependent classroom: A field study. *American Educational Research Journal, 13,* 115–123.

100. Desforges, D. M., Lord, C. G., Ramsey, S. L., Mason, J. A., Van Leeuwen, M. D., West, S. C., & Lepper, M. R. (1991). Effects of Structured Cooperative Contact on changing negative attitudes to-

wards stigmatized social groups. *Journal of Personality and Social Psychology, 60,* 531–544.

101. Gaertner, S. L., Mann, J. A., Dovidio, J. F., Murrell, A. J., & Pomare, M. (1990). How does cooperation reduce intergroup bias? *Journal of Personality and Social Psychology, 59,* 692–704.

102. Bridgeman, D. (1981). Enhanced role-taking through cooperative interdependence: A field study. *Child Development, 52,* 1231–1238.

103. Stephan, C., Kennedy, J., & Aronson, E. (1977). Attribution of luck or skill as a function of cooperating or competing with a friend or acquaintance. *Sociometry, 40,* 107–111. Presser, N., Stephan, C., Kennedy, J., & Aronson, E. (1978). Attributions to success and failure in cooperative, competitive, and interdependent interaction. *European Journal of Social Psychology, 8,* 269–274. Stephan, S., Burnham, M., & Aronson, E. (1979). Attributions for success and failure after cooperation, competition, or team competition. *European Journal of Social Psychology, 9,* 109–114.

104. Slavin, R. (1990). Research on cooperative learning: Consensus and controversy. *Educational Leadership,* 52–54.

105. Kohn, A. (1986). *No Contest.* Boston: Houghton Mifflin.

106. McConahay, J. B. (1981). Reducing racial prejudice in desegregated schools. In W. D. Hawley (Ed.), *Effective school desegregation.* Beverly Hills, CA: Sage.

107. Gonzalez, A. (1979). Classroom cooperation and ethnic balance. Unpublished Ph.D. dissertation, University of California, Santa Cruz. Aronson, E., & Gonzalez, A. (1988). Desegregation, jigsaw and the Mexican-American experience. In P. Katz and D. Taylor, *Eliminating Racism.* New York: Plenum.

108. Pettigrew, T. F. (1961). Social psychology and desegregation research. *American Psychologist, 15,* 61–71.

Chapter 8.   Liking, Loving, and Interpersonal Sensitivity

1.   Darwin, C. (1910). *The expression of emotions in man and animals.* New York: Appleton.

2. Carnegie, D. (1937). *How to win friends and influence people.* New York: Simon & Schuster.

3. Remmers, H. H., & Radler, D. H. (1958). Teenage attitudes. *Scientific American, 198*(6), 25–29.

4. Lemann, T., & Solomon, R. (1952). Group characteristics as revealed in sociometric patterns and personality ratings. *Sociometry, 15,* 7–90.

5. Homans, G. (1961). *Social behavior: Its elementary forms.* New York: Harcourt, Brace and World.

6. Walster (Hatfield), E., Aronson, V., Abrahams, D., & Rottman, L. (1966). Importance of physical attractiveness in dating behavior. *Journal of Personality and Social Psychology, 5,* 508–516.

7. Byrne, D. (1969). Attitudes and attraction. In L. Berkowitz (Ed.), *Advances in experimental social psychology* (Vol. 4). New York: Academic Press.

8. Sherif, M. (1956). Experiments in group conflict. *Scientific American, 195,* 53–58.

9. Aronson, E., Stephan, C., Sikes, J., Blaney, N., & Snapp, M. (1978). *The jigsaw classroom.* Beverly Hills, CA: Sage Publications. Aronson, E., & Osherow, N. (1980). Cooperation, prosocial behavior, and academic performance: Experiments in the desegregated classroom. In L. Bickman (Ed.), *Applied social psychology annual* (Vol. 1, pp. 163–196). Beverly Hills, CA: Sage Publications.

10. Aronson, E., & Mills, J. (1959). The effect of severity of initiation on liking for a group. *Journal of Abnormal and Social Psychology, 59,* 177–181.

11. Aronson, E., & Darwyn, L. (1965). Gain and loss of esteem as determinants of interpersonal attractiveness. *Journal of Experimental Social Psychology, 1,* 156–171. Aronson, E., & Worchel, P. (1966). Similarity versus liking as determinants of interpersonal attractiveness. *Psychonomic Science, 5,* 157–158. Sigall, H., & Aronson, E. (1969). Liking for an evaluator as a function of her physical attractiveness and nature of the evaluations. *Journal of Experimental Social Psychology, 5,* 93–100.

12. Amabile, T. (1983). Brilliant but cruel: Perceptions of negative evaluators. *Journal of Experimental Social Psychology, 19,* 146–156.

13. Deutsch, M., & Solomon, L. (1959). Reactions to evaluations by others as influenced by self-evaluations. *Sociometry, 22,* 93–112.

14. Jones, E. E. (1964). *Ingratiation.* New York: Appleton-Century-Crofts.

15. Jennings, H. H. (1959). *Leadership and isolation* (2nd ed). New York: Longman, Green.

16. Lott, B., & Lott, A. (1960). The formation of positive attitudes toward group members. *Journal of Abnormal and Social Psychology, 61,* 297–300.

17. Brehm, J., & Cole, A. (1966). Effect of a favor which reduces freedom. *Journal of Personality and Social Psychology, 3,* 420–426.

18. Tolstoy, L. (1942). *War and peace.* New York: Simon & Schuster.

19. Bigelow, J. (Ed.). (1916). *The autobiography of Benjamin Franklin* (pp. 216–217). New York: G. P. Putnam's Sons.

20. Jecker, J., & Landy, D. (1969). Liking a person as a function of doing him a favor. *Human Relations, 22,* 371–378.

21. Lerner, M., & Simmons, C. (1966). Observer's reaction to the "innocent victim": Compassion or rejection? *Journal of Personality and Social Psychology, 4,* 203–210.

22. Lott, A. J., Lott, B. E., Reed, T., & Crow, T. (1960). Personality-trait descriptions of differentially liked persons. *Journal of Personality and Social Psychology, 16,* 284–290.

23. Bales, R. (1958). Task roles and social roles in problem solving groups. In E. E. Maccoby, T. M. Newcomb, and E. L. Hartley (Eds.), *Readings in social psychology* (3rd ed., pp. 437–447). New York: Holt. Bales, R., & Slater, P. (1955). Role differentiation in small decision-making groups. In T. Parsons and R. F. Bales (Eds.), *The family, socialization, and interaction process.* Glencoe, IL: Free Press.

24. Aronson, E., Willerman, B., & Floyd, J. (1966). The effect of a pratfall on increasing interpersonal attractiveness. *Psychonomic Science, 4,* 227–228.

25. Deaux, K. (1972). To err is humanizing: But sex makes a difference. *Representative Research in Social Psychology, 3,* 20–28.

26. Aronson, E., Helmreich, R., & LeFan, J. (1970). To err is humanizing—sometimes: Effects of self-esteem, competence, and a pratfall on interpersonal attraction. *Journal of Personality and Social Psychology, 16,* 259–264.

27. Tesser, A., & Brodie, M. (1971). A note on the evaluation of a "computer date." *Psychonomic Science, 23,* 300.

28. Feingold, A. (1990). Gender differences in effects of physical attractiveness on romantic attraction: A comparison across five research paradigms. *Journal of Personality and Social Psychology, 59,* 981-993.

29. Walster, Aronson, Abrahams, & Rottman, Importance of physical attractiveness.

30. White, G. (1980). Physical attractiveness and courtship progress. *Journal of Personality and Social Psychology, 39,* 660–668.

31. Dion, K., Berscheid, E., & Walster (Hatfield), E. (1972). What is beautiful is good. *Journal of Personality and Social Psychology, 24,* 285–290.

32. Tan, A. S. (1979). TV beauty ads and role expectations of adolescent female viewers. *Journalism Quarterly, 56,* 283–288.

33. Dion, K., & Berscheid, E. (1971). Physical attractiveness and sociometric choice in nursery school children. Mimeographed research report.

34. Dion, K. (1972). Physical attractiveness and evaluations of children's transgressions. *Journal of Personality and Social Psychology, 24,* 207–213. Similar findings reported in Berkowitz, L., & Frodi, A. (1979). Reactions to a child's mistakes as affected by her/his looks and speech. *Social Psychology Quarterly, 42,* 420–425.

35. Frieze, I. H., Olson, J. E., & Russell, J. (1991). Attractiveness and income for men and women in management, *Journal of Applied Social Psychology, 21,* 1039–1957.

36. Sigall, H., & Aronson, E. (1969). Liking for an evaluator as a function of her physical attractiveness and nature of the evaluations. *Journal of Experimental and Social Psychology, 5,* 93–100.

37. Sigall, H., & Ostrove, N. (1975). Beautiful but dangerous: Effects of offender attractiveness and nature of the crime on juridic judgment. *Journal of Personality and Social Psychology, 31,* 410–414.

38. Downs, C. A., & Lyons, P. M. (1991). Natural observations of the links between attractiveness and initial legal judgments. *Personality and Social Psychology Bulletin, 17,* 541–547.

39. Sigall, H., & Landy, D. (1973). Radiating beauty: Effects of having a

physically attractive partner on person perception. *Journal of Personality and Social Psychology, 28,* 218–224.

40. Snyder, M., Tanke, E. D., & Berscheid, E. (1977). Social perception and interpersonal behavior: On the self-fulfilling nature of social stereotypes. *Journal of Personality and Social Psychology, 35,* 656–666.

41. Byrne, Attitudes and attraction.

42. Rosenbaum, M. E. (1986). The repulsion hypothesis: On the nondevelopment of relationships. *Journal of Personality and Social Psychology, 51,* 1156–1166.

43. Sigall, H. (1970). The effects of competence and consensual validation on a communicator's liking for the audience. *Journal of Personality and Social Psychology, 16,* 251–258.

44. Marks, G., Miller, N., & Maruyama, M. (1981). Effect of targets' physical attractiveness on assumptions of similarity. *Journal of Personality and Social Psychology, 41,* 198–206. Granberg, D., & King, M. (1980). Cross-lagged panel analysis of the relation between attraction and perceived similarity. *Journal of Experimental Social Psychology, 16,* 573–581.

45. Aronson, E., & Worchel, S. (1966). Similarity versus liking as determinants of interpersonal attractiveness. *Psychometric Science, 5,* 157–158. Condon, J. W., & Crano, W. D. (1988). Inferred evaluation and the relationship between attitude similarity and interpersonal attraction. *Journal of Personality and Social Psychology, 54,* 789–797.

46. Secord, P., & Backman, C. (1964). Interpersonal congruency, perceived similarity, and friendship. *Sociometry, 27,* 115–127.

47. Curtis, R. C., & Miller, K. (1986). Believing another likes or dislikes you: Behaviors making the beliefs come true. *Journal of Personality and Social Psychology, 51,* 284–290.

48. Walster (Hatfield), E. (1965). The effect of self-esteem on romantic liking. *Journal of Experimental and Social Psychology, 1,* 184–197.

49. Kiesler, S. B., & Baral, R. L. (1970). The search for a romantic partner: The effects of self-esteem and physical attractiveness on romantic behavior. In K. J. Gergen and D. Marlowe (Eds.), *Personality and social behavior.* Reading, MA: Addison-Wesley.

50. Grube, J., Kleinhesselink, R., & Kearney, K. (1982). Male self-accep-

tance and attraction toward women. *Personality and Social Psychology Bulletin, 8,* 107–112.

51. Van Gorp, G., Stempfle, J., & Olson, D. (1973). Dating attitudes, expectations, and physical attractiveness. Unpublished paper, reported in Z. Rubin, *Liking and loving: An invitation to social psychology* (p. 68). New York: Holt, Rinehart and Winston.

52. Jones, E. E., Bell, L., & Aronson, E. (1971). The reciprocation of attraction from similar and dissimilar others: A study in person perception and evaluation. In *Experimental social psychology* (pp. 142–183). New York: Holt, Rinehart and Winston.

53. Aronson, E., & Linder, D. (1965). Gain and loss of esteem as determinants of interpersonal attractiveness. *Journal of Experimental and Social Psychology, 1,* 156–171. See also, Gerard, H., & Greenbaum, C. W. (1962). Attitudes toward an agent of uncertainty reduction. *Journal of Personality, 30,* 485–495. Mettee, D., Taylor, S. E., & Friedman, H. (1973). Affect conversion and the gain-loss like effect. *Sociometry, 36,* 505–519. Aronson, E., & Mettee, D. (1974). Affective reactions to appraisal from others. In *Foundations of interpersonal attraction.* New York: Academic Press. Clore, G. L., Wiggins, N. H. & Itkin, S. (1975). Gain and loss in attraction: Attributions from nonverbal behavior. *Journal of Personality and Social Psychology, 31,* 706–712.

54. Ibid.

55. Spinoza, B. de (1910). The ethics. In A. Boyle (Trans.), *Spinoza's ethics and "De Intellectus Emendatione."* New York: Dutton.

56. Mettee, D. R., Taylor, S. E., & Friedman, H. (1973). Affect conversion and the gain-loss like effect. *Sociometry, 36,* 505–519.

57. Mettee, D. R., & Aronson, E. (1974). Affective reactions to appraisal from others. *Foundations of interpersonal attraction.* New York: Academic Press.

58. Winch, R. (1958). *Mate selection: A study of complementary needs.* New York: Harper & Row.

59. Berscheid, E. (1985). Interpersonal attraction. In G. Lindzey and E. Aronson (Eds.), *Handbook of social psychology* (3rd ed., pp. 413–484). Reading, MA: Addison-Wesley. Berscheid, E., & Walster (Hatfield), E. (1978). Interpersonal attraction. Reading, MA: Addison-Wesley. Kendel, D. (1978). Similarity in real-life adolescent friendship pairs. *Journal of Personality and Social Psychology, 36,* 306–312. Nias, D. K. B.

(1979). Marital choice: Matching or complementation? In M. Cook and G. Wilson (Eds.), *Love and attraction*. Oxford: Pergamon. Fishbein, D., & Thelen, M. H. (1981). Husband-wife similarity and marital satisfaction: A different approach. Paper presented at the convention of Midwestern Psychological Association.

60. Rubin, Z. (1970). Measurement of romantic love. *Journal of Personality and Social Psychology, 16*, 265–273.

61. Rubin, Z. (1973). *Liking and loving: An invitation to social psychology.* New York: Holt, Rinehart and Winston.

62. Walster (Hatfield), E., & Walster, G. W. (1978). *A new look at love.* Reading, MA: Addison-Wesley.

63. Brehm, S. (1985). *Intimate relationships.* New York: Random House.

64. Clark, M. S., & Mills, J. (1979). Interpersonal attraction in exchange and communal relationships. *Journal of Personality and Social Psychology, 37*, 12–24. Mills, J., & Clark, M. S. (1982). Exchange and communal relationships. In L. Wheeler (Ed.) *Review of personality and social psychology* (Vol. III). Beverly Hills, Calif.: Sage. Clark, M. S. (1986). Evidence for the effectiveness of manipulations of desire for communal versus exchange relationships. *Personality and Social Psychology Bulletin, 12*, 425.

65. Walster, E., Walster, G. W., & Traupmann, J. (1979). Equity and premarital sex. In M. Cook and G. Wilson (Eds.), *Love and attraction.* New York: Pergamon Press. Schafer, R. B., & Keith, P. M. (1980). Equity and depression among married couples. *Social Psychology Quarterly, 43*, 430-435.

66. Clark, M. S., Mills, J. R., & Corcoran, D. M. (1989). Keeping track of needs and inputs of friends and strangers. *Personality and Social Psychology Bulletin, 15*, 533–542.

67. Duck, S. (1995). Strategems, spoils and a serpent's tooth: On the delights and dilemmas of personal relationships. In W. R. Cupach and B. H. Spitzberg (Eds.) *The darkside of interpersonal communication.* Hillsdale, NJ: LEA.

68. Harvey, O. J. (1962). Personality factors in resolution of conceptual incongruities. *Sociometry, 25*, 336–352.

69. Stevenson, H., Keen, R., & Knights, J. (1963). Parents and strangers as reinforcing agents for children's performance. *Journal of Abnormal and Social Psychology, 67*, 183–185.

70. Floyd, J. (1964). Effects of amount of reward and friendship status of the other on the frequency of sharing in children. Unpublished Ph.D. dissertation, University of Minnesota.

71. Cicero (46 B.C.). *De amicitia.* Libri Sapientis: Horti Novabaculae, Rome.

72. Harvey, J. H., Weber, A. L., & Orbuch, T. L., (1990). *Interpersonal accounts: A social psychological perspective.* Oxford: Blackwell.

73. Rands, M., Levinger, G., & Mellinger, G. (1981). Patterns of conflict resolution and marital satisfaction. *Journal of Family Issues, 2,* 297–321.

74. Skotko, P. K. (1981). The relation between interpersonal attraction and measures of self-disclosure. *Journal of Social Psychology, 112,* 311–312. Archer, R., & Burleson, J. (1980). The effects of timing of self-disclosure on attraction and reciprocity. *Journal of Personality and Social Psychology, 38,* 120–130. Taylor, D., Gould, R., & Brounstein, P. (1981). Effects of personalistic self-disclosure. *Personality and Social Psychology Bulletin, 7,* 437–492.

75. Kahn, M. (1971). *Sensitivity training at Kresge College.* Unpublished manuscript.

Chapter 9.   Social Psychology as a Science

1. Richard Feynman: The best mind since Einstein. *Nova,* KQED, December 21, 1993.

2. Semonov, P., Personal communication.

3. Gabler, N. (1993). Persona goeth before a fall. *New York Times,* December 12, section 2, p. 1.

4. Ibid, p. 1

5. Ibid, p. 34.

6. Nisbett, R., & Wilson, T. (1977). Telling more than we know: Verbal reports on mental processes. *Psychological Review, 84,* 231–259.

7. Aronson, E., Willerman, B., & Floyd, J. (1966). The effect of a pratfall on increasing interpersonal attractiveness. *Psychonomic Science, 4,* 227–228.

8. Aronson, E., & Mills, J. (1959). The effect of severity of initiation on

liking for a group. *Journal of Abnormal and Social Psychology, 59,* 177–181.

9. Liebert, R., & Baron, R. (1972). Some immediate effects of televised violence on children's behavior. *Developmental Psychology, 6,* 469–475.

10. Aronson, E., & Carlsmith, J. M. (1969). Experimentation in social psychology. In G. Lindzey and E. Aronson (Eds.), *Handbook of Social Psychology,* 2nd Edition, Vol. II. Reading, Mass.: Addison-Wesley, 1–79. See also, Aronson, E., Brewer, M., & Carlsmith, J. M. (1985). Experimentation in social psychology. In G. Lindzey and E. Aronson (Eds.), *Handbook of social psychology* (Vol. 1, pp. 441–486). Reading, MA: Addison-Wesley.

11. Milgram, S. (1963). Behavioral study of obedience. *Journal of Abnormal and Social Psychology, 67,* 371–378.

12. Ibid.

13. Aronson, E., Sigall, H., & Van Hoose, T. (1970). The cooperative subject: Myth or reality? *Journal of Experimental and Social Psychology, 6,* 1–10.

14. Asch, S. (1951). Effects of group pressure upon the modification and distortion of judgment. In M. H. Guetzkow (Ed.), *Groups, leadership, and men* (pp. 177–190). Pittsburgh: Carnegie. Asch, S. (1951). Studies of independence and conformity: A minority of one against a unanimous majority. *Psychological Monographs, 70* (9, Whole No. 416).

15. Dawes, R., McTavish, J., & Shaklee, H. (1977). Behavior, communication, and assumptions about other people's behavior in a common dilemma situation. *Journal of Personality and Social Psychology, 35,* 1–11.

16. Asch, Effects of group pressure.

17. Aronson, E., & Mettee, D. (1968). Dishonest behavior as a function of differential levels of induced self-esteem. *Journal of Personality and Social Psychology, 9,* 121–127.

18. Milgram, S. (1963). Behavioral study of obedience. *Journal of Abnormal and Social Psychology, 67,* 371–378.

19. Zimbardo, P. (1971, October 25). *The psychological power and pathology of imprisonment* (p. 3). Statement prepared for the U.S. House of Representatives Committee on the Judiciary; Subcommittee No. 3: Hearings on Prison Reform, San Francisco, CA.

20. Bickman, L., & Zarantonello, M. (1978). The effects of deception and

level of obedience on subjects' ratings of the Milgram study. *Personality and Social Psychology Bulletin, 4,* 81–85.

21. Milgram, S. (1964). Issues in the study of obedience: A reply to Baumrind. *American Psychologist, 19,* 848–852.

22. Aronson, E. (1966). Avoidance of inter-subject communication. *Psychological Reports, 19,* 238.

Name Index

Subject Index